To Caesar What Is Caesar's

Tribute, Taxes, and Imperial Administration in Early Roman Palestine (63 B.C.E.–70 C.E.)

Fabian E. Udoh

Brown Judaic Studies
Providence, Rhode Island

Library of Congress Cataloging-in-Publication Data

Udoh, Fabian E., 1954-
To Caesar what is Caesar's : tribute, taxes and imperial administration in early Roman Palestine (63 B.C.E.-70 C.E.) / Fabian E. Udoh.
p. cm. — (Brown Judaic studies ; no. 343)
Includes bibliographical references.
ISBN-13: 978-1-930675-25-4 (cloth binding : alk. paper)
ISBN-10: 1-930675-25-9 (cloth binding : alk. paper)
1. Jews—History—168 B.C.-135 A.D. 2. Jews—Taxation—Palestine—History—To 1500. 3. Taxation—Palestine—History—To 1500. 4. Taxation—Rome—History. I. Title. II. Series.

DS122.U36 2006
336.200933'09014—dc22

2005030502

Printed in the United States of America

30150 023665349

To Caesar What Is Caesar's

Program in Judaic Studies
Brown University
Box 1826
Providence, RI 02912

Number 343

TO CAESAR WHAT IS CAESAR'S
Tribute, Taxes, and Imperial Administration
in Early Roman Palestine (63 B.C.E.–70 C.E.)

by
Fabian E. Udoh

Ima, Unyime, and Kufre,
qui attendent

Contents

Preface and Acknowledgments

This book began as a Duke University dissertation, "Tribute and Taxes in Early Roman Palestine (63 BCE-70 CE): The Evidence from Josephus," which I defended in 1996. My dissertation focused on the analysis of the Jewish literary sources on taxation, in particular the writings of Josephus. The scope of the investigation has been expanded. Although I have integrated some of the material from the original (dissertation) study, that material has been entirely recast into parts of the various arguments of the present work, leading sometimes to different conclusions from those that I had originally reached. Furthermore, some of the material in the section "Territorial Grants" in chapter 2 appeared in my article "*Jewish Antiquities* XIV. 205, 207–08 and 'the Great Plain,'" *Palestine Exploration Quarterly* 134 (2002): 130–43.

In the course of writing this book, I have received generous help from many individuals, many more than I can name here, and from various institutions. A National Endowment for the Humanities Fellowship at the W. F. Albright Institute of Archaeological Research, Jerusalem, and travel grants from the Institute for Scholarship in the Liberal Arts, University of Notre Dame, permitted me to spend the year 2001–2002 doing research. The College of Arts and Letters, University of Notre Dame, Dean's Supplemental Research and Teaching funds (2001–2004) enabled me to do research and to hire student assistants. The Program of Liberal Studies, University of Notre Dame, has been very generous to me, particularly in providing undergraduate assistants.

Professor Ed P. Sanders has been, first, my mentor for many years, and now a valued friend and colleague. This study, from its beginnings as a dissertation, is the outcome of our mutual concerns and innumerable conversations. I am profoundly grateful also to Professor Andrew Lintott, Worcester College (Oxford) and Professor Shaye Cohen, Harvard, who read the original manuscript of this book and offered detailed suggestions for revising it.

I wish also to express my gratitude to all the students who have worked with me on various aspects of this book—especially David G.

George, my graduate research assistant, and Donna Bauters, my undergraduate assistant.

The Greek and Latin authors, including the works by Josephus and Philo, are cited according to the Loeb Classical Library (LCL) edition, except where I have provided my own translation. Passages from the Hebrew Bible are quoted from the *Biblia Hebraica,* edited by K. Elliger and W. Rudolph (5th edition, 1997). The text of the Septuagint is given as in the *Septuaginta,* edited by Alfred Rahlfs (1979). I quote the Greek text of the New Testament from *The Greek New Testament,* edited by Kurt Aland (3rd edition, 1983). Unless otherwise noted, passages from the English translation of the Hebrew Bible (and the Apocrypha) and the New Testament are quoted from the New Revised Standard Version. Bibliographical details are provided in the notes for other texts and translations that are quoted in the book.

Fabian E. Udoh
University of Notre Dame
September 2004

Abbreviations

For abbreviations of classical works and other abbreviations not included on this list, see *The SBL Handbook of Style for Ancient Near Eastern, Biblical, and Early Christian Studies*, edited by Patrick H. Alexander et al. (Peabody, Mass.: Hendrickson, 1999).

AB	Anchor Bible
ABD	*Anchor Bible Dictionary*. Edited by D. N. Freedman. 6 vols. New York: Doubleday, 1992
AJP	*American Journal of Philology*
ANRW	*Aufstieg und Niedergang der römischen Welt: Geschichte und Kultur Roms im Spiegel der neueren Forschung*. Edited by H. Temporini and W. Haase. Berlin: Walter de Gruyter, 1972–
AThR	*Anglican Theological Review*
BA	*Biblical Archaeologist*
BAIAS	*Bulletin of the Anglo-Israel Archaeological Society*
BASOR	*Bulletin of the American Schools of Oriental Research*
Bib	*Biblica*
BJS	Brown Judaic Studies
BTB	*Biblical Theology Bulletin*
CAH	*Cambridge Ancient History*
CBQ	*Catholic Biblical Quarterly*
CIL	*Corpus Inscriptionum Latinarum*. Edited by T. Mommsen et al. Berlin, 1863–
CQ	*Classical Quarterly*
CRINT	Compendia rerum iudaicarum ad Novum Testamentum
DJD	Discoveries in the Judaean Desert
EncJud	*Encyclopaedia Judaica*. 16 vols. Jerusalem, 1972–
ER	*The Encyclopedia of Religion*. Edited by M. Eliade. 16 vols. New York: Macmillan, 1987
GRBS	*Greek, Roman and Byzantine Studies*
Hen	*Henoch*
HTR	*Harvard Theological Review*

ICC	International Critical Commentary
IEJ	*Israel Exploration Journal*
IGRR	*Inscriptiones graecae ad res romanas pertinentes.* Edited by R. Cagnat et al. Paris: Ernest Leroux, 1901–27
ILS	*Inscriptiones latinae selectae.* Edited by H. Dessau. 3 vols. Berlin: Weidmann, 1892–1916
INJ	*Israel Numismatic Journal*
JBL	*Journal of Biblical Literature*
JDS	Judean Desert Studies
JESHO	*Journal of the Economic and Social History of the Orient*
JJS	*Journal of Jewish Studies*
JQR	*Jewish Quarterly Review*
JR	*Journal of Religion*
JRAS	*Journal of the Royal Asiatic Society*
JRS	*Journal of Roman Studies*
JSNTSup	Journal for the Study of the New Testament: Supplement Series
LASBF	*Liber annuus studii biblici franciscani*
LCL	Loeb Classical Library
LEC	*Les études classiques*
LSJ	H. Liddell, R. Scott, and H. Jones, *Greek English Lexicon.* Oxford, 1996
NEAEHL	*The New Encyclopedia of Archaeological Excavations in the Holy Land.* Edited by E. Stern. 4 vols. Jerusalem: Israel Exploration Society and Carta, 1993
NewDocs	*New Documents Illustrating Early Christianity.* Edited by G. H. R. Horsley and S. Llewelyn. North Ryde, N.S.W.: Macquarie University Press, 1981–
NTS	*New Testament Studies*
OGIS	*Orientis graeci inscriptiones selectae.* Edited by W. Dittenberger. 4 vols. Leipzig, 1903–5
PBSR	*Papers of the British School at Rome*
PEQ	*Palestine Exploration Quarterly*
RB	*Revue biblique*
RDGE	*Roman Documents from the Greek East: Senatus Consulta and Epistulae to the Age of Augustus.* Edited by R. Sherk. Baltimore: Johns Hopkins University Press, 1969
REJ	*Revue des études juives*
RGE	*Rome and the Greek East to the Death of Augustus.* Edited and translated by R. Sherk. Cambridge: Cambridge University Press, 1984–
RH	*Revue historique*
RSA	*Rivista storica dell'antichità*

SCI	*Scripta classica Israelica*
WD	*Wort und Dienst*
WHJP	The World History of the Jewish People
ZDPV	*Zeitschrift des deutschen Palästina-Vereins*
ZPE	*Zeitschrift für Papyrologie und Epigraphik*

Introduction

Judea (that is, Jewish Palestine) entered, as part of the province of Syria, into Rome's sphere of influence in 63 B.C.E. after the Roman forces led by Pompey the Great together with the Jewish forces loyal to John Hyrcanus II had defeated Aristobulus II. Josephus says that, after reducing and reorganizing the Jewish state, Pompey made it tributary to Rome, which means that Pompey imposed some kind of direct, annual tribute on the Jews. The Senate, it appears, contracted the right to collect the tribute to one of the Roman public companies, the *publicani*. This book is a study of taxation in the Jewish state during the period from the conquest of Palestine by Pompey until the destruction of the temple and the end of the Jewish state in 70 C.E.

The general economic conditions of Judea during this early Roman period received some degree of attention from scholars of Roman imperial administration and from scholars in various other fields between the two World Wars. To these times belong, especially, the works by M. Rostovtzeff and Arnaldo Momigliano, which were preceded by earlier studies particularly by Theodor Mommsen and Joachim Marquardt. In these studies, however, the problem of taxation in Judea often was dealt with in a very general and summary manner. Momigliano was an exception. His study of the Roman administration of Judea included a detailed, yet brief, discussion of taxation. In particular, he provided a comprehensive analysis of Caesar's decrees and the *senatus consulta* in Josephus's *A.J.* 14.190–95, 200–210.[1]

Among students both of Judaism in the late Hellenistic and early Roman periods and of Christianity in the first century C.E., there has been an increasing manifestation of interest in the economic conditions of Judea.[2] F. C. Grant's study of the economic background of the New Testa-

1. Arnaldo Momigliano, *Ricerche sull'organizzazione della Giudea sotto il dominio romano, 63 a. C.-70 d. C.* (Bologna: Annali della R. Scuola Normale Superiore di Pisa, 1934; repr., Amsterdam: Adolf M. Hakkert, 1967), 10–36.

2. See review of literature in Philip A. Harland, "The Economy of First-Century Pales-

ment was one of the earliest by a scholar of early Christianity.[3] This work was normative for more than half a century, and Grant's general perspective and conclusions have continued to influence many New Testament scholars. J. Klausner's essay was equally influential among scholars of Second Temple Judaism.[4] After Klausner, Abraham Schalit included detailed discussions of taxation in his work on Herod the Great.[5] Shimon Applebaum, in his essay on the economy of Palestine in the first century and his subsequent discussions of the economic conditions of Judea in the Second Temple period, relies on the views expressed by these previous authors, particularly Schalit, for the question of taxation in the early Roman period.[6] Apart from Joachim Jeremias's study, in 1933, of Jerusalem in the first century C.E.,[7] comprehensive studies of the economy of Judea in Jesus' time have not been undertaken by New Testament scholars.[8] However, among the New Testament scholars working in the theological perspectives of F. C. Grant, Douglas E. Oakman attempted a detailed discussion of the problem of taxation.[9] From a different perspective, E. P. Sanders also has included insightful discussions of taxation in his studies of Second Temple Judaism.[10]

The purpose of this brief survey of scholarship is to point out that there exists no comprehensive study of taxation in the Jewish state under

---

tine: State of the Scholarly Discussion," in *Handbook of Early Christianity: Social Science Approaches* (ed. Anthony J. Blasi et al.; Walnut Creek, Calif.: Alta Mira Press, 2002), 511–27.

3. Frederick C. Grant, *The Economic Background of the Gospels* (Oxford: Oxford University Press, 1926).

4. J. Klausner, "The Economy of Judea in the Period of the Second Temple," in *World History of the Jewish People*, vol. 7, *Herodian Period* (ed. Michael Avi-Yonah; First Series: Ancient Times; Jerusalem: Massada, 1975 [original, 1930]), 179–205.

5. Abraham Schalit, *König Herodes: Der Mann und sein Werk* (Berlin: Walter de Gruyter, 1969), 262–98, 777–81.

6. Shimon Applebaum, "Economic Life in Palestine," in *The Jewish People in the First Century: Historical Geography, Political History, Social, Cultural and Religious Life and Institutions*, vol. 2 (ed. S. Safrai and M. Stern; CRINT 1; Philadelphia: Fortress Press, 1976), 631–700.

7. See Joachim Jeremias, *Jerusalem in the Time of Jesus: An Investigation Into Economic and Social Conditions during the New Testament Period* (trans. F. H. Cave and C. H. Cave; Philadelphia: Fortress Press, 1969).

8. See the regrets by Seán Freyne, "Herodian Economics in Galilee: Searching for a Suitable Model," in *Modelling Early Christianity: Social Scientific Studies of the New Testament in Its Context* (ed. Philip F. Esler; New York: Routledge, 1995), 24: "The number of serious analytical studies of ancient economies by biblical scholars is few, and in this respect the discipline contrasts unfavourably with that of ancient history generally, where much more attention has been given to the question by historians of Greece and Rome."

9. Douglas E. Oakman, *Jesus and the Economic Questions of His Day* (Lewiston, N.Y.: Edwin Mellen, 1986), 37–91.

10. E. P. Sanders, *Jewish Law from Jesus to the Mishnah: Five Studies* (London: SCM Press, 1990), 43–51; idem, *Judaism: Practice and Belief, 63 BCE-66 CE* (London: SCM Press, 1992), 146–69.

Roman rule. This situation has persisted even in spite of the importance that economic issues have assumed, for both historians of Judaism and New Testament scholars, in the reconstruction of the history of Judea in the early Roman period. From Heinz Kreissig to Applebaum and Martin Goodman; from Grant to Jeremias, Oakman, Richard A. Horsley, and John Dominic Crossan, the burden of taxation, particularly the burden of Herod's taxes, has been considered to be among the root causes of conflicts in Judea.[11] Horsley, expressing a view that is widely shared, writes:

> When the Romans laid greater Judea under tribute, they confirmed the Hasmoneans in their position and sanctioned the continued payment of taxes to the high-priestly government in Jerusalem . . . . Roman imposition of Herod as king then created a third layer of taxes. Herod's rule in Palestine was "efficient," to say the least. Given his ambitious building projects, renowned munificence to imperial figures and Hellenistic cities, and lavish palaces as well as network of fortresses, he had to utilize every possible source of revenue to the maximum without ruining his economic base. While we lack details of his tax system, the general effect on the various districts of his realm is clear.[12]

"The effect," he continues, "on the peasantry in Galilee, as elsewhere, was increasing indebtedness and even alienation of their ancestral lands, as they were unable to support themselves after rendering up percentages of their crops for tribute to Rome, tithes and offerings to priests and Temple, and taxes to Herod."[13] Thus, according to this view, from 63 B.C.E. until the fall of Jerusalem in 70 C.E., Jewish peasants paid three layers of taxes: to the Romans, to the Hasmonean and, later, Herodian aristocracy, and to the priestly aristocracy. Consequently, the Great Revolt of 66 C.E. and the early Christian movement originated in the spiraling conflicts generated by the fiscal pressures brought to bear on the Jewish peasantry as a result of excessive taxation.

Scholars, however, admit, as Horsley does in the passage quoted

---

11. Heinz Kreissig, "Die landwirtschaftliche Situation in Palästina vor dem judäischen Krieg," *Acta Antiqua Academiae Scientiarum Hungaricae* 17 (1969): 223–54; idem, *Die sozialen Zusammenhänge des judäischen Krieges: Klassen und Klassenkampf im Palästina des 1. Jahrhunderts v. u. Z.* (Berlin: Akademie-Verlag, 1970). See, e.g., Shimon Applebaum, "The Zealots: The Case for Revaluation," *JRS* 61 (1971): 155–70. Martin Goodman, *The Ruling Class of Judaea: The Origins of the Jewish Revolt Against Rome, A. D. 66–70* (Cambridge: Cambridge University Press, 1987); idem, "The Origins of the Great Revolt: A Conflict of Status Criteria," in *Greece and Rome in Eretz Israel: Collected Essays* (ed. A. Kasher et al.; Jerusalem: Yad Iẓḥak Ben-Zvi, Israel Exploration Society, 1990), 39–53.

12. Richard A. Horsley, *Galilee: History, Politics, People* (Valley Forge, Pa.: Trinity Press, 1995), 140.

13. Ibid., 60.

above, that they lack details of Herod's tax system and, in fact, also the details of the various systems of taxation that were in operation in Judea during the one hundred years from the conquest by Pompey to the revolts of 66 C.E. In the absence of detailed studies of the systems, scholars have relied on partial analyses of fragments of evidence available in now dated studies by historians of Roman imperial administration; prominent among these is what Glen W. Bowersock aptly calls "[t]he alarmingly indiscriminate collection of sources on the economic life of Roman Syria, compiled by F. Heichelheim for T. Frank's *Economic Survey of Ancient Rome*."[14] In these circumstances, the lucid analysis of the sources is generally abandoned by New Testament scholars. These scholars instead construct models based on economic-anthropological theories about the behavior of preindustrial peasant economies.[15] They often cite theories as if these were historical evidence.

It might be correct that every scholar of the ancient economy must construct a model, especially because ancient economic historians lack the quantitative data upon which to base proper economic explanations.[16] However, my interest in this study is not to construct an overarching theory that explains all the evidence. I have sought, instead, first to bring together the extant sources and, second, to provide a critical and historical analysis of these sources. I have endeavored to understand each piece of evidence and the problem it poses, bearing in mind that the Roman Empire was neither homogeneous nor completely organized. It comes as a corollary of this approach that this work contains extensive arguments based on detailed analyses of the evidence. Moreover, scholars, as I have noted, generally have based their views on taxation in Judea on previous analyses of random pieces of information. This is true especially of New Testament scholars. It has often been necessary, therefore, for me to relate the more recent interpretations of the evidence to their original sources. As a result, there are many more references in this study to older and, in some cases, dated scholarship than would otherwise be expected.

I have found that in Judea, as elsewhere in the ancient world, economic issues cannot be separated completely from political issues. The

---

14. Glen W. Bowersock, "Social and Economic History of Syria under the Roman Empire," in *Archéologie et histoire de la Syrie*, vol. 2, *La Syrie de l'époque achéménide à l'avènement de l'Islam* (ed. Jean-Marie Dentzer and Winfried Orthmann; Saarbrücken: Saarbrücker Druckerei und Verlag, 1989), 63.

15. See, among many others, Freyne, "Herodian Economics," 23–37; for a theoretical exposition of the methodology, see, for instance, John H. Elliott, "Social-Scientific Criticism of the New Testament: More on Methods and Models," *Semeia* 35 (1986): 1–33.

16. See Dominic W. Rathbone, "The Ancient Economy and Graeco-Roman Egypt," in *Egitto e storia antica dell'Ellenismo all'età Araba* (ed. Lucia Criscuolo and Giovanni Geraci; Bologna: Cooperativa Libraria Universitaria Editrice, 1989), 159–60; and Freyne, "Herodian Economics," 23–24.

larger context of this study is, therefore, the Roman provincial administration of the territory during the Roman Republic and early Principate. This is evident in the general organization of the book. Since the problem of taxation in Judea is closely related to the political status of the territory at any given moment in its relationship with Rome, I have divided and studied the subject according to the different historical periods when Palestine underwent significant political changes: under Pompey (63–47 B.C.E.), under Julius Caesar (47–44 B.C.E.), under Cassius and Antony (44–37 B.C.E.), under Herod the Great and his successors (37 B.C.E.-6 C.E.), and under the Roman governors (6–70 C.E.). These divisions correspond to the first five chapters of the book. The sixth chapter deals with tithes in the Second Temple period. Although the dates are merely indicative, the divisions of the work reflect the general view that the fate of the territory, and its tax obligations, depended on its ever-changing relationship to the Roman Empire, which was itself unstable.

In order to speak of a consistent and accumulative tax policy in Judea, scholars have assumed some degree of uniformity between Egypt, Palestine, and other parts of the Roman Empire. Moreover, in Palestine itself a continuum is often established from the Ptolemaic, Seleucid, and Hasmonean periods to the different phases of Roman domination. Both of these assumptions have proven to be largely illusory. The Hasmonean state conquered by Pompey had ceased for a long time to pay tribute to a foreign power. Pompey disrupted the Hasmonean independent system of taxation, about which we know nothing, and began a new era of (initially chaotic) dependence on Rome. Subsequently, the different periods of Roman rule in Judea brought about significant changes in the tax systems to which the Jews were subjected.

Thus, for instance, it is clear from Josephus's narrative and the Roman decrees and *senatus consulta* that he cites, that a turning point came for Judea in 47 B.C.E. after Hyrcanus II and the Jews had demonstrated their bravery and loyalty during Julius Caesar's Alexandrian campaign. Caesar granted the Jews, as an *ethnos*, the legal right to live according to their customs. Together with the decisions that he made regarding direct tribute, Caesar also granted Judea immunity from military service, billeting, and probably from requisitioned transport (*angareia*). Thus, the Jews were exempted from those aspects of Roman imperial administration that constituted by far the most burdensome (indirect) taxes paid by provincial communities to Rome. Caesar also removed the beleaguered tax companies (*publicani*) from Judea.

The system established by Caesar was disrupted after his death by Cassius, who was master of Syria from 43 B.C.E. until the end of civil war in 42 B.C.E. The system was reconfirmed by Antony in 42 B.C.E., but the direct tribute imposed by Caesar was not levied upon the Jews after Herod's appointment as king in 40 B.C.E.

The relationship between the status of Judea in the Roman Empire and the issues of taxation raises two further methodological questions. First, it has been necessary to re-evaluate the status of the Jewish state within the Roman provincial system during the various periods of its subjection to Rome. Following Caesar's grants, for example, Judea remained within the direct control of the provincial governor of Syria and was subject to tribute. With Herod's appointment as king, however, the territory became for the first time a "client kingdom" under Rome's hegemony. The evidence suggests that under the rule of Herod and his successors Judea's relationship with Rome, including taxation, was consonant with Rome's relationship with other client kingdoms within the Empire.

Second, it seems rather obvious that the Roman Empire in the late Republic and early Principate was not an administrative, social, and economic monolith. Rome's relationship with its subject territories varied widely from place to place and from one period to the next. Rome dealt with the Jewish state in much the same ad hoc manner with which it responded to other provincial communities. I have argued that Judea was in various ways like and unlike other provincial territories within the Roman Empire of the late Republic and early Principate. As a result, evidence from an earlier period—for instance, the Seleucid Empire—and from the later Roman period—particularly rabbinic sources—must be used judiciously, if at all. Moreover, I draw parallels with other parts of the Roman Empire only where there is primary evidence for Jewish Palestine. In general, I have rejected the tendency among scholars to describe the conditions in Judea on the basis of what is known about Ptolemaic and Roman Egypt.

Thus, this study of the history of Roman administration of the Jewish state contributes to our understanding of Roman imperial administration. This is not only due to the number of available sources, particularly in the works of Flavius Josephus; it is also because Jewish Palestine, through its similarities and dissimilarities to other provincial communities, serves as an example of Rome's relationship to the subject states under her rule.

Of the traditional Jewish religious dues, only the temple tax and tithes are substantial enough to merit particular attention. I have nothing to add to E. P. Sanders's treatment of the economic implications of the other offerings and sacrifices required by Second Temple Judaism.[17] I have dealt with the temple tax in the context of the efforts made by both Jewish and Roman authorities to protect, from official seizure and from common robbery, the vast sums that the Jews of the Diaspora collected

---

17. See Sanders, *Jewish Law*, 42–57; idem, *Judaism*, 146–69.

and brought to Jerusalem. The detail with which I have treated tithes is proportional to the confusion that persists in scholarly literature about the nature and practice of tithing, on the one hand, and about the relationship of tithes to Roman tribute and other taxes in the early Roman period, on the other hand.

1

Roman Tribute in Jewish Palestine under Pompey (63–47 B.C.E.)

In the summer of 63 B.C.E., the combined Roman and Jewish forces under Pompey defeated the Hasmonean king, Aristobulus II, in Jerusalem. One consequence of this defeat, Josephus says, was that "the country and Jerusalem were laid under tribute."[1] Scholars do not dispute the fact that from then on the Jewish state became tributary to Rome. The problem is that Josephus, apart from simply remarking that the Jewish state became tributary, provides no account of the tribute imposed by Pompey.[2] Therefore, everything is left to speculation.

One such conjecture is that Pompey reimposed upon the Jewish state the same tribute as the Jews had previously paid to the Seleucid kings. Support for this view comes from the generally accepted idea that Rome adopted and modified the tax systems already in existence in the territories she conquered.[3] It would seem that this was what happened in the case of Judea, especially since Pompey left Judea and Syria hastily and there is no evidence that he had either the time or the desire to establish any special tax system for the region. In spite of the arguments in favor of the view that Pompey reimposed on the Jews the existing taxes, it is unlikely that Pompey adopted a Seleucid tax system already in place in Judea. At the time of its conquest, the Jewish state had been independent from the Seleucids and free from Seleucid tribute for about eighty years,

1. Josephus, *B.J.* 1.154: τῇ τε χώρᾳ καὶ τοῖς Ἱεροσολύμοις ἐπιτάσσει φόρον; *A.J.* 14.74: καὶ τὰ μὲν Ἱεροσόμυλα ὑποτελῆ φόρου Ῥωμαίοις ἐποίησεν.

2. Thus, for instance, E. Mary Smallwood, *The Jews under Roman Rule: From Pompey to Diocletian* (2nd ed.; Leiden: Brill, 2001), 28 and n. 25: "The rate and type of taxation are not recorded."

3. See P. A. Brunt, *Roman Imperial Themes* (Oxford: Clarendon, 1990), 237; also A. H. M. Jones, *The Roman Economy: Studies in Ancient Economic and Administrative History* (ed. P. A. Brunt; Oxford: Blackwell, 1974), 161–64; Dominic W. Rathbone, "Egypt, Augustus and Roman Taxation," *Cahiers du centre Gustave Glotz* 4 (1993): 82–86; Andrew Lintott, *Imperium Romanum: Politics and Administration* (London: Routledge, 1993), 70–77; J. S. Richardson, *Roman Provincial Administration, 227 BC to AD 117* (Basingstoke: Macmillan, 1976), 37.

that is, since 142 B.C.E., when Simon the Hasmonean finally delivered the Jews from the Seleucid yoke.[4] During that period, the Jewish kingdom had been a regional power whose successive leaders had seized, destroyed, and imposed tribute on the surrounding city states. If the Jewish state could, therefore, be said to have had a "traditional" tax structure at the time it became tributary to Rome, it was the Hasmonean tax system. There is nothing to support the assumption that the infrastructure for Seleucid taxation continued to exist there after eighty years of independence, unless one assumes—gratuitously—that the Hasmoneans continued to exact the same Seleucid taxes from which they are said to have freed the nation.[5] Hence, Rome cannot be said to have reimposed the "traditional" taxes that hitherto the Jews had paid to the Seleucid Empire.

A second conjecture is that Pompey asked from the Jews the same tribute that he imposed on the rest of the province of Syria. One might point out, in support of this view, that the territory that Pompey left to the Jews was part of the newly constituted province of Syria.[6] The problem here is that there is no information on what Pompey demanded in tribute from the rest of the province.[7] Extrapolations from other Roman provinces fail to address two difficulties: (1) there was no uniformity in the kinds and scale of taxes that Rome levied on her conquered territories;[8] (2) the so-called province of Syria was itself a heterogenous entity on which the Romans had a very tenuous hold.[9] When Pompey and his

---

4. Josephus, *A.J.* 13.113–14; *B.J.* 1.50–53; 1 Macc 13:33–41.

5. Richard A. Horsley (*Archaeology, History, and Society in Galilee: The Social Context of Jesus and the Rabbis* [Valley Forge, Pa.: Trinity Press, 1996], 77–78) shows the *naiveté* with which some New Testament scholars view this problem. He notes, first, that "[o]ne of the functions of the priesthood, then, was to collect the tribute for its imperial sponsors, successively the Persians, Ptolemaic, and Seleucid regimes." "The Hasmonean regime's extension of its control over most of Palestine under John Hyrcanus, Aristobulus, and Alexander Janneus," he continues, "merely extended Hasmonean taxation and (probably) the system of tithes and offerings to priesthood and Temple to the villages and towns of Idumea, Galilee, and other annexed districts." He does not say whether or not "Hasmonean taxation" was the same as the "tribute" that had been collected for the Persian and Hellenistic overlords of Judaea. He, nonetheless, concludes: "When the Romans took control of Palestine they simply adopted the tributary system already in place." For evidence, he cites the decree by Julius Caesar in *A.J.* 14.194–209.

6. See the discussion in chapter 4 below.

7. E. Badian, *Roman Imperialism in the Late Republic* (Ithaca, N.Y.: Cornell University Press, 1968), 75: "We do not know for certain what Pompey did with the taxes of Syria; or, for that matter, with those of Bithynia-Pontus, which he also organised as a province."

8. Cicero makes this point in the well-known passage in *2 Verr.* 3.6.12–15. We shall return to this question in several sections of this work.

9. J.-P. Rey-Coquais, "Syrie romaine, de Pompée à Dioclétien," *JRS* 68 (1978): 48: "Durant le Ier siècle de notre ère, la province romaine de Syrie, qui s'étendait jusqu'aux confins de l'Égypte . . . était une mosaïque de cités, de principautés et de territoires aux statuts divers que Rome entreprit patiemment d'unifier et d'intégrer plus étroitement à l'empire."

lieutenants intervened in the region, Syria was in a state of chaos and anarchy. The Seleucid Empire had disintegrated from decades of internecine wars. Kings and tyrants in the region fought each other and seized territories. The Jews were a case in point: not only did they invade, destroy, and take control of many of the surrounding city-states, but they also engaged in civil wars. From 67 B.C.E. onward, the Hasmonean brothers, Hyrcanus II and Aristobulus II, were in full civil war with each other. Hyrcanus II had invited the Arabs to help instate him on the throne and they were besieging his brother in Jerusalem. These two brothers sent for and invited Pompey to intervene in the affairs of the Jewish state and to help settle their quarrel. The territory thereafter was frequently in revolt. Furthermore, there was always the threat—and indeed the reality—of Parthian invasion. The integration of Syria as a whole into the rest of the Roman Empire was a long, painful process, lasting more than three centuries. It can hardly be expected under these conditions that a general tax code existed that was applicable to all the cities, client kingdoms, and principates of Syria during this early stage of the formation of the province, when Rome hardly had a firm foothold in the region.[10]

Besides, it was not only Syria that was in a state of anarchy. The conquering power, Rome of the late Republic, was also a house divided against itself. As Rey-Coquais correctly observes, Roman annexation, far from bringing peace to Syria, drew the territory into Roman civil wars from which it especially suffered.[11] This state of affairs is of great importance for the discussion of taxation in the province, including Judea. Until the battle of Actium in 31 B.C.E. and the ensuing Augustan peace, leaders of the region performed a political balancing act with the primary focus of aligning themselves with the victorious party in Rome. "Rome" was, in short, an abstraction; in practice what mattered was the individual Roman magistrate who dominated the region at any given time: Pompey and his lieutenants, Caesar, Cassius, or Antony. This meant, as David Kennedy rightly observes, that prior to Octavian's victory, succeeding Roman magistrates in the region systematically extracted and carried off

---

10. See especially Rey-Coquais, "Syrie Romaine," 44–73; Bowersock, "Social and Economic History"; A. N. Sherwin-White, *Roman Foreign Policy in the East, 168 B.C. to A.D. 1* (Norman: University of Oklahoma Press, 1984), 209–12; Richard D. Sullivan, *Near Eastern Royalty and Rome: 100–30 BC* (Toronto: University of Toronto Press, 1990), 203–33; David Kennedy, "Syria," in *CAH,* vol. 10, *The Augustan Empire, 43 B.C.-A.D. 69* (ed. Alan K. Bowman et al.; 2nd ed.; Cambridge: Cambridge University Press, 1996), 708–16, 728–36; in general, Fergus Millar, *The Roman Near East: 31 BC-AD 337* (Cambridge, Mass.: Harvard University Press, 1993). Millar prudently begins his study from 31 E.C.E., after Actium, when Rome began to establish some order in the region.

11. Rey-Coquais, "Syrie Romaine," 45.

the region's movable wealth in forms that included "gifts," advance taxation, war contributions and indemnities, and open robbery.[12]

Consequently, we need to revise the view, common especially among New Testament scholars, that, from 63 B.C.E. onward, Jewish Palestine was filled with Roman *publicani* who extorted Roman tribute from Jewish peasants and shipped it to Rome. The extant evidence suggests that from 63 B.C.E. to 47 C.E. Rome's hold on the Jewish state did not allow for systematic and sustained taxation. Colonial taxes are notoriously difficult to collect even in the best of circumstances. Colonial taxes imposed upon a nation that is frequently in revolt by a power that is itself in civil war are impossible to raise. We cannot conclude, however, that following its annexation by Pompey the Jewish state paid no tribute to the Romans.[13] Those parts of the nation that at some point were not in revolt must have paid tribute. Our sources show, however, that the tribute paid by the Jewish state during this period was largely in the form of what Josephus calls "exactions." By exactions Josephus means arbitrary (that is, not part of a systematic code) impositions, especially the contributions imposed on the authorities in Jerusalem by the Roman governors of Syria in support of their struggle to repel interior and exterior aggression.

Mention is made of Roman tribute in Judea during this period in three brief passages from the works of Cicero, Dio Cassius, and Appian. I shall begin with a detailed discussion of these passages, first because they raise some of the issues that are central to this study, and also because classical, Jewish, and New Testament scholars often cite these sources and exaggerate their significance for the study of the conditions in the Jewish state.

Cicero, Dio Cassius, and Appian

Cicero

Cicero finishes his brief but dramatic defense of Flaccus, governor of Asia in 62 B.C.E., with the invective:

> Even when Jerusalem was standing and the Jews at peace with us, the demands of their religion were incompatible with the majesty of our

12. Kennedy, "Syria," 709.

13. The Crimean Bosporus was restored by Pompey to Pharnaces "without any known financial exactions." Likewise, the kingdom of Armenia and the principality of Nabatene paid indemnities, but without annual tribute. See A. N. Sherwin-White, "Lucullus, Pompey and the East," in *CAH*, vol. 9, *The Last Age of the Roman Republic, 146–43 B.C.* (ed. J. A. Cook et al.; 2nd ed.; Cambridge: Cambridge University Press, 1994), 269.

> Empire, the dignity of our name and the institutions of our ancestors; and now that the Jewish nation has shown by armed rebellion what are its feelings for our rule, they are even more so; how dear it was to the immortal gods has been shown by the fact that it has been conquered, farmed out to tax-collectors and enslaved. (*Flac.* 69)[14]

Flaccus faced, among others, the charge of *auri illa invidia Iudaici*. He was said to have acted improperly in impeding, by an edict, the Jews of Asia from transmitting to the temple in Jerusalem gold that was most likely raised through the temple tax and other offerings.[15]

It is important to note that Judea is not the central issue, even though Cicero's tirade gloats over the recent subjection of the Jewish state to Roman power and the imposition of tribute. Arnaldo Momigliano, however, argues that the Latin word *elocata* in Cicero's speech seems to leave no doubt that, under Pompey, the *publicani* were directly responsible for the collection of tribute in Judea.[16] Whatever meaning one might read into the word *elocata* (*eloco* = "to let or hire out," "to let out to farm"),[17] it is possible that Cicero also had in mind the method of raising the tribute that Pompey and the governors after him imposed on the territory. In the late Roman Republic tribute came either as a percentage of produce (*decumae*) or as a fixed amount (*vectigal*), to be paid annually.[18] During this period Rome ordinarily used "tax-farming" to the *publicani* as the method of collecting tribute in the provinces, except where fixed payments had been introduced. This method minimized losses to the state.[19] If Pompey

14. The last two clauses read in the Latin: nunc vero hoc magis, quod illa gens quid de nostro imperio sentiret ostendit armis; quam cara dis immortalibus esset docuit, quod est victa, quod elocata, quod serva facta.

15. See Cicero, *Flac.* 67–69; Anthony J. Marshall, "Flaccus and the Jews of Asia (Cicero *Pro Flacco* 28.67–69)," *Phoenix* 29 (1975): 139–54.

16. Momigliano, *Ricerche*, 19: "L'espressione di Cicerone (*elocata*) non sembra lasciare dubbio che, al tempo di Pompeo, i pubblicani romani intervenero direttamente a prelevare il tributo . . . ." See Smallwood, *Jews Under Roman Rule*, 28 and n. 25. A. H. M. Jones ("Review and Discussion," review of Arnaldo Momigliano, Ricerche sull' organizzazione della Guidea sotto il domino romano, *JRS* 25 [1935]: 228) is cautious in his assessment of Momigliano's thesis. Momigliano, he writes, "ingeniously deduces that the tribute of Judaea was originally collected by *publicani*, and that Gabinius introduced direct collection." See also David C. Braund, "Gabinius, Caesar, and the *Publicani* of Judaea," *Klio* 65 (1983): 241.

17. See Charlton T. Lewis and Charles Short, *A Latin Dictionary* (rev. and enl. ed.; Oxford: Clarendon, 1984), 639, s.v. *eloco*.

18. See Cicero, *2 Verr.* 3.6.12–13.

19. See W. T. Arnold, *The Roman System of Provincial Administration to the Accession of Constantine the Great* (3rd ed.; rev. E. S. Bouchier; Oxford: Blackwell, 1914), 87–90; Jones, *Roman Economy*, 161–66; E. Badian, *Publicans and Sinners: Private Enterprise in the Service of the Roman Republic* (Ithaca, N.Y.: Cornell University Press, 1972), 11–81; Claude Nicolet, *The*

required a percentage of the annual produce from the Jewish state, the territory would have been farmed out, as would have been the rest of the newly subjected province of Syria, into which Judea was incorporated.[20]

The role of the *publicani* in the Jewish state from 63 B.C.E. is, more directly, the topic of another tirade by Cicero (*Prov. Cons.* 5.10), this time against Gabinius:

> Then, too, there are those unhappy revenue-farmers—and what misery to me were the miseries and troubles of those to whom I owed so much!—he [Gabinius] handed them over as slaves to Jews and Syrians, themselves peoples born to be slaves. From the beginning he made it a rule, in which he persisted, not to hear any suits brought by revenue-farmers; he revoked agreements which had been made in which there was no unfairness; he removed guards; released many from imposts or tribute, forbade a revenue-farmer or any of his slaves to remain in any town where he himself was or was on the point of going. In a word, he would be considered cruel, if he had shown the same feelings towards our enemies as he showed towards Roman citizens, and they too, members of an Order which has always been supported in a way befitting its position by the goodwill of our magistrates.

Gabinius was the fourth governor of Syria (57–55 B.C.E.), and the first who was of consular rank. He was the first governor of Syria to possess the power and the troops necessary to deal with the problems of the new province.[21] This passage from Cicero confirms that tribute in Syria and Judea was farmed out to the *publicani*. Cicero's testimony elsewhere about himself as governor of Cilicia, and about other governors, is evidence that the relationship between the governor and the *publicani* in a province was often complex.[22] There often were conflicts of inter-

---

World of the Citizen in Republican Rome (trans. P. S. Falla; Berkeley: University of California Press, 1980), 171–73; Brunt, *Roman Imperial Themes*, 354–76; Lintott, *Imperium Romanum*, 74–91.

20. We shall see later that Momigliano and many scholars after him do not think that Judaea was a part of the province. This explains the need to demonstrate that the *publicani* were active among the Jews as well.

21. Scaurus, appointed by Pompey, was without adequate powers and troops. He had his hands full keeping the Nabatean Arabs at bay. This was the case also with the next two governors, Marcius Philippus and Lentulus Marcellinus. See Appian, *Syr.* 11.8.51: "Each of these [governors] spent the whole of his two years in warding off the attacks of the neighbouring Arabs. It was on account of these events in Syria that Rome began to appoint for Syria proconsuls, with power to levy troops and engage in war like consuls. The first of these sent out with an army was Gabinius . . . ." See the discussion in Sherwin-White, *Roman Foreign Policy*, 271–79; idem, "Lucullus, Pompey," 271–73.

22. See Cicero, *Att.* 6.1.16: "You ask how I am dealing with the tax-gatherers. I pet them, indulge them, praise and honour them: and take care they trouble no one . . . ." See also his extensive advice to his brother, governor of Asia, on how to deal with the *publicani* in *Quint. fratr.* 1.1.35; Badian, *Publicans and Sinners*, 79–81.

ests.[23] His invective against Gabinius indicates that the *publicani* in Syria came into conflict with the powerful governor. There is no doubt that Gabinius extorted money from the province, with which he enriched himself and financed the many and incessant wars that he fought, some of which were not authorized by the Senate.[24] Momigliano certainly reads too much into Cicero's already dramatic rhetoric, however, when he cites this passage as evidence for the view that Gabinius expelled the *publicani* from Judea and introduced indirect collection of tribute there.[25] Cicero's list of the "anti-*publicani*" measures taken by Gabinius is comprehensive, but it does not include expulsion. Had Gabinius gone that far, Cicero would have crowed, triumphant. Moreover, it is clear from Cicero's text that Gabinius acted against the *publicani* in the whole of his province, in Judea as well as the rest of Syria. There is no evidence for selective expulsion only in Judea. David Braund is therefore correct in rejecting Momigliano's suggestion.[26]

Confusion persists, however, on the topic of Gabinius's so-called tax "reforms" in Syria, generally, and in Judea specifically. A. N. Sherwin-

23. Julius Caesar (*Bell. civ.* 3.3) charges that, at the beginning of the civil war, Pompey "requisitioned a large sum of money from Asia, Syria, and all the kings, potentates, and tetrarchs, and from the free communities of Achaia; and . . . compelled the tax-farming associations of the provinces of which he was himself in control to pay over the large sums." Likewise, he says (*Bell. civ.* 3.31), Scipio "exacted from the tax-farmers of his province the amount owing for two years, and . . . borrowed in advance from the same persons the amount due for the following year . . . ." In *Bell. civ.* 3.103 he charges that "Pompeius gave up his idea of visiting Syria, took the funds belonging to the association of tax-farmers, borrowed money from certain private persons . . . and having armed two thousand men, partly those whom he had selected from the households of the tax-farmers . . . arrived at Pelusium."

24. See Appian, *Syr.* 11.8.51. See below for the evidence in Josephus. According to Cicero (*Prov. Cons.* 4.9), Gabinius engaged in "money bargains with princes, settlements by compounding, robberies, brigandage . . . ." According to Dio (*Hist.* 39.55–56), Gabinius, acquitted of previous charges because of the bribes he gave to Roman magistrates and jurymen, was afterwards convicted (by the *quaestio repetundarum*, engineered by his political enemies) of the charge of having "plundered more than a hundred million [denarii] from the province [of Syria]." In view of this, it is certainly an understatement to say, as Smallwood does (*Jews under Roman Rule*, 33) that Gabinius "possibly . . . made a little on the side out of [his] reform" of the taxation in Judaea.

25. Momigliano, *Ricerche*, 20. Momigliano's reasoning is rather curious. He says that in spite of the rhetorical and generic nature of Cicero's invective, it might be deduced that Gabinius limited the *publicani*'s sphere of action. He then goes on to say that Gabinius must have distanced them from Judaea because, on the one hand, we know ("poichè sappiamo") that the *publicani* had to be excluded from Judaea during those years and, on the other hand, attention must be given to the profound transformation that Gabinius brought about in Judaea. He does not say, however, from where "we know" that the *publicani* had to be excluded.

26. Braund, "Gabinius," 421–22.

White writes that all we know, ("obscurely") on the subject, is from "the ferocious and allusive attack" on Gabinius by Cicero, his political enemy. Sherwin-White goes on to state, however, that "Gabinius hampered or restricted the Roman *publicani* in their activities by rulings at his tribunal and administrative action, including the direct collection of taxation by his own agents in certain cities and principalities."[27] This much may be surmised from Cicero's charges.[28] In Judea, Sherwin-White continues, "Gabinius appears to have established the system of direct payment to the Roman quaestor at Sidon." He finds evidence for this claim in Dio, *Hist.* 39.56.6 (see below), and in the *senatus consultum* of 47 B.C.E. (quoted in Josephus, *A.J.* 14.203), which confirms Julius Caesar's grants to the Jewish state.[29] One may indeed conjecture, as Sherwin-White does (again citing the passage from Cicero), that Pompey and Gabinius introduced the system of *pactiones* into Syria and Judea.[30] This system allowed local authorities to make a *pactio* (agreement) with the *publicani* for a fixed sum, which the authorities then collected from their subjects, instead of the agents of the *publicani* being directly involved with collection from the individual taxpayers.[31] The problem between Gabinius and the *publicani* in Judea, however, does not appear to have been the introduction of such an indirect system of collection.[32] Cicero was delighted by the system of *pactiones* in his own province of Cilicia,[33] and so there is no reason why he

---

27. Sherwin-White, "Lucullus, Pompey," 273.

28. Badian (*Roman Imperialism*, 75) writes that "within a few years the *publicani* were clearly becoming a scourge and Gabinius, at what he must have known was great risk to himself, took strong action against them, in defence of nations born to be slaves."

29. Sherwin-White, "Lucullus, Pompey," 273 and n. 76. Similarly Smallwood, *Jews under Roman Rule*, 33, who speculates that Gabinius's reform would have had the effect of "showing a semblance of respect for the Jewish authorities, and it may have brought some financial relief in its train." On the *senatus consultum* of 47 B.C.E, see chapter 2 below.

30. Sherwin-White, "Lucullus, Pompey," 270 and n. 70; see his discussion in Sherwin-White, *Roman Foreign Policy*, 232–33; also Badian, *Roman Imperialism*, 75.

31. For the system in Cilicia under Cicero, see Cicero, *Att.* 5.14.1: ". . . the following welcome news has reached me, that the Parthians are at peace; secondly that the contracts (*pactiones*) with the tax-farmers have been settled . . . ." Badian, *Publicans and Sinners*, 80; Lintott, *Imperium Romanum*, 75.

32. See T. P. Wiseman, "Caesar, Pompey and Rome, 59–50 B. C," in *CAH*, vol. 9, *The Last Age of the Roman Republic, 146–43 B.C.* (ed. J. A. Crook et al.; 2nd ed.; Cambridge: Cambridge University Press, 1994), 380, 395. Wiseman's statements illustrate well how befuddled scholars are about Gabinius's purposes in Judaea. Wiseman (p. 380) first points out that Gabinius's financial position was such that "Gabinius had to have a rich province to avoid bankruptcy." He then concedes (p. 395) that the details of Gabinius's financial dealings in Syria "are irretrievable behind the slanderous screen of Cicero's invective." He nonetheless concludes that "in the end the main purpose of all his [Gabinius's] activity was surely to maximize Syria's contribution to the public income of the Roman treasury."

33. Cicero, *Att.* 5.13.1: "Still the tax-collectors thrust themselves on my notice as though I had come with an army behind me, and the Greeks as if I were governor of Asia. . . . I hope I shall employ the training I have learned from you and satisfy everybody, the more easily because in my province the contracts (*pactiones*) have been settled."

should have vilified Gabinius for introducing the same system into Syria. Cicero's point seems rather to be that Gabinius canceled such *pactiones*, where they existed, and prevented the *publicani* from fulfilling their contracts.

Dio Cassius

Dio writes about Gabinius:

> He himself then reached Palestine, arrested Aristobulus, who had escaped from Rome and was causing some disturbance, sent him to Pompey, imposed tribute upon the Jews, and after this invaded Egypt.[34]

Momigliano observes that Dio is wrong in saying that Gabinius imposed tribute on Judea after he quelled in 56 B.C.E. the revolt led by Aristobulus II, since tribute had already been imposed, according to Josephus, by Pompey. This error would not have occurred, he argues, if Gabinius had not in some way modified the tribute of the Jewish state. He concludes that this modification must have been the creation of a system of indirect collection of tribute, that is, bypassing the *publicani*.[35]

If Josephus is right about the time when tribute was imposed on the Jewish state, Dio must be wrong. That much is clear. But in what does Dio's error consist? Momigliano fails to remark that Dio, in his earlier account of Pompey's defeat of Aristobulus in 63 B.C.E., says nothing about Pompey having then made the Jewish state tributary (Dio, *Hist.* 37.15–16). Instead, again flatly contradicting what is known from Josephus, Dio says that "all the wealth [of the temple] was plundered" after Pompey had captured the temple (*Hist.* 37.16.4).[36] A plausible conclusion is that Dio mistakenly thinks that, whereas Pompey was content with plundering the treasures of the temple, it was Gabinius who imposed tribute on the Jewish state. Even if one rejected this explanation, however, the creation of a new tax system in Judea, as Momigliano theorizes, would still not be the only or most plausible interpretation of Dio's text. Actually, Gabinius could have levied a war indemnity on the Jewish state for the revolt. Or, as Braund argues, Dio could very well have called "tribute (φόρος)" the

34. Dio, *Hist.* 39.56.6: αὐτὸς δὲ ἐς τὴν Παλαιστίνην ἐλθὼν τόν τε Ἀριστόβουλον (διαδρὰς γὰρ ἐκ τῆς Ῥώμης ὑπετάραττέ τι) συνέλαβε καὶ τῷ Πομπηίῳ ἔπεμψε, καὶ φόρον τοῖς Ἰουδαίοις ἐπέταξε, καὶ μετὰ τοῦτο καὶ ἐς τὴν Αἴγυπτον ἐνέβαλε.

35. Momigliano, *Ricerche*, 20.

36. Josephus, *A.J.* 14.72: "But though the golden table was there and the sacred lampstand and the libation vessels and a great quantity of spices, and beside these, in the treasury, the sacred moneys amounting to two thousand talents, he touched none of these because of piety, and in this respect also he acted in a manner worthy of his virtuous character." See *B.J.* 1.152–53; also Cicero, *Flac.* 67: "But the victorious Gnaeus Pompeius did not touch anything in the Temple after his capture of Jerusalem."

"service," in finances and logistics, which the Jewish authorities in Jerusalem rendered to Gabinius, soon after he restored order in Judea, during his campaign in Egypt.[37] If, on the other hand, we were to imagine that Gabinius did take action to organize taxation in Judea at this time, it would be more likely that such intervention was needed because the revolt led by Aristobulus had made it impossible to continue to impose and to collect the tribute levied by Pompey. Gabinius's action would have been to reimpose it after he had quelled the revolt.

Revolts in Syria and Judea certainly disrupted the collection of tribute the following year (55 B.C.E.), during Gabinius's absence in Egypt, when, according to Dio, the Syrians were "terribly abused by the pirates, and the tax-gatherers, being unable to collect the taxes on account of the marauders, were owing numerous sums" (*Hist.* 39.59).[38] Josephus notes that Gabinius's absence "was the occasion for a general commotion in Syria," and that in Judea Alexander, the son of Aristobulus II, "heading a new Jewish revolt, collected a vast army and proceeded to massacre all Romans in the country" (*B.J.* 1.176).[39]

It appears, then, that although there is no evidence that Gabinius expelled the *publicani* from Judea in 56 B.C.E. or introduced a system of indirect collection, the attempt to collect tribute, through the *publicani,* in the province of Syria and in Judea certainly encountered two problems. First, direct tribute competed with the interests of powerful governors like Gabinius. Second, payment was impeded by the volatile political conditions in the province. It is clear from what Josephus says of the revolt led by Alexander in 55 B.C.E. that the *publicani* became victims of Jewish resistance and revolts. In anticipation of chapter 2, it was not until 47 B.C.E., when Caesar brought some order to the affairs of the Jewish state and levied tribute not on the Jewish population but on the authorities in Jerusalem, that systematic taxation of the territory became possible. With Caesar's organization of taxation in the Jewish state, the activities of the *publicani* in Judea also came to an end.[40]

Appian

Speaking of Pompey's conquest in the East, the second-century historian Appian writes of the Jewish state:

---

37. Braund, "Gabinius," 242–43; see Josephus, *A.J.* 14.98–99; *B.J.* 1.175.

38. See Cicero, *Quint. fratr.* 3.2.2.

39. *A.J.* 14.100 adds that Alexander also closely besieged those Romans who had taken refuge in Mount Gerizim, in Samaria.

40. That it was Julius Caesar who removed the *publicani* from Judaea, see Braund, "Gabinius," 243–44, and the discussion in chapter 2 below.

> The Jewish nation alone still resisted, and Pompey conquered them, sent their king, Aristobulus, to Rome, and destroyed their greatest, and to them the holiest, city, Jerusalem, as Ptolemy, the first king of Egypt, had formerly done. It was afterward rebuilt and Vespasian destroyed it again, and Hadrian did the same in our time. On account of these rebellions the poll-tax imposed upon all Jews is heavier than that imposed upon the surrounding peoples. (*Syr.* 11.8.50)

It is because of F. M. Heichelheim's interpretation of Appian's summary of Jewish history in this text that scholars usually think that it is known what kinds of tribute Pompey imposed on the Jews.[41] His comments are worth citing in full:

> The first Roman organization of taxes in Syria and Palestine was begun by Pompey and elaborated by his successor Gabinius. . . . Syria became a province which had to pay taxes; the Maccabaean kingdom lost all frontier districts and was divided into five συνόδια which were self-governing but had the same capital, Jerusalem; and it seems that a φόρος had to be paid by Jerusalem and its συνόδια. . . . If Appian, Syr., VIII, 50, refers to this early period, Syria paid a land (?) tax of 1 per cent, and Judaea must have paid a poll tax as well as (according to a very probable emendation) a land tax.[42]

Momigliano, much to his credit, refuted Heichelheim's overall thesis,[43] and his objections are still valid. The first problem with Heichelheim's views is the expression ὁ φόρος τῶν σωμάτων βαρύτερος τῆς ἄλλης περιουσίας in Appian's text. The word περιουσίας does not seem to make much sense here. The Loeb edition, following the emendation proposed by Musgrave, gives Appian's last sentence, reflected in the translation cited above, as:

> καὶ δια ταῦτ᾽ ἐστὶν Ἰουδαίοις ἅπασιν ὁ φόρος τῶν σωμάτων βαρύτερος τῆς ἄλλης περιοικίας.

Heichelheim, on the contrary, emended the word περιουσίας to read περὶ οὐσίας and rendered the whole sentence:

> On account of these rebellions (i.e. against Pompey, Vespasian and Hadrian) the poll-tax imposed upon all Jews is heavier than that on landed property (τῆς ἄλλης περὶ οὐσίας). The Syrians and Cilicians are

41. F. M. Heichelheim, "Roman Syria," in *An Economic Survey of Ancient Rome*, vol. 4 (ed. Tenney Frank; Baltimore, Md.: The Johns Hopkins Press, 1938), 231.

42. Ibid.

43. Momigliano, *Ricerche*, 27–30.

> also subject to an annual tax of one-hundredth of the assessed value of the property of each man.[44]

Thus, Pompey imposed on the Jews both a *land tax*, equal to 1 percent of the value of their property, which was a tax paid also by the rest of Syria, and a *poll tax*.

Momigliano argued for and accepted Musgrave's emendation,[45] according to which (as the Loeb edition translates it) "the poll-tax imposed upon all Jews is heavier than that imposed upon the surrounding peoples." The issue of the correct emendation of the text might never be decisively resolved, and it certainly is not sound scholarship to base sweeping theories on either reading. This textual problem is in fact only a minor part of the difficulties that arise if we ask whether or not Appian actually informs us about the taxes imposed on the Jewish state by Pompey.

Appian, writing in about 160 C.E., speaks in fact both retrospectively and vaguely after the second Jewish revolt of 132–135 C.E. His phrase καὶ δὶα ταῦτ' ἐστίν (on account of these) refers comprehensively to the three great Jewish revolts which he lists, that is, against Pompey in 63 B.C.E., against Vespasian in 66–70 C.E., and finally against Hadrian in 132–135 C.E. In Heichelheim's interpretation the poll tax imposed on the Jews would have been cumulative, following each revolt, from Pompey until Hadrian's time, when the poll tax would have surpassed the tribute on landed property. The question remains whether or not Pompey actually imposed a poll tax upon the Jewish state.

A poll tax (*tributum capitis*) without a census (a head count) makes no sense.[46] Some scholars, including Momigliano, doubt that Rome ever levied a poll tax within the Jewish state.[47] Many more scholars are simply confused about the nature of the *tributum capitis* in the Roman Empire. In chapter 5, I shall discuss in detail the topic of the poll tax in Judea, especially in relation to the taxes that resulted from the registration conducted by Quirinius in Syria and in Judea after Archelaus was banished in 6 C.E. Let me observe for the time being, first, that there is nothing to suggest that a census was conducted in Syria and Judea under Pompey. Second, the first clearly attested imposition of a poll tax upon the Jews was the didrachma temple tax, which Vespasian, in 70 C.E., converted into a head tax to be paid to the temple of Jupiter Capitolinus and levied "on all Jews, wheresoever resident."[48] If Pompey had imposed a poll tax upon the

44. Heichelheim, "Roman Syria," 231.
45. Momigliano, *Ricerche*, 27–28.
46. See discussions in chapters 4 and 5 below.
47. Momigliano, *Ricerche*, 28, and chapter 5 below.
48. Josephus, *B.J.* 7.218: "On all Jews, wheresoever resident, he [Vespasian] imposed a

Jews in 63 B.C.E. it would have been upon those Jews living in Palestine, whom he conquered, not on "all Jews," as Appian writes, a phrase reminiscent of Vespasian's levy. Moreover, it does not appear that Hadrian imposed a further poll tax on all Jews in 135 C.E. after the Bar Kokhba revolt. The most obvious conclusion is that the poll tax about which Appian speaks is none other than the one imposed by Vespasian in 70 C.E.[49]

We need to be careful also not to overinterpret Appian's statements about the land tax in Syria and Judea. Josephus reports that, in 70 C.E., Vespasian reserved Jewish Palestine "as his own private property" and gave orders for the land to be leased out (*B.J.* 7.216).[50] Pompey is not known to have treated the Jewish state in the same manner in 63 B.C.E. Appian, here also, could have been speaking from the perspective of what happened in 70 C.E. In sum, although it is likely that Pompey imposed a kind of land tax on the Jews, we do not know, Appian's remarks notwithstanding, the scale of that tax.

Let me add here a note of caution that I shall frequently sound throughout this study. Greco-Roman authors often are notoriously confused on even the most general questions of Jewish history, culture, and religion. Appian is no exception. In the passage under discussion he says that Pompey "destroyed" Jerusalem, "as Ptolemy, the first king of Egypt, had formerly done." Both statements are inaccurate. Elsewhere (*Mithr.* 12.17.117) he maintains that "Aristobulus, the king of the Jews," was among those led in Pompey's victory procession. This is correct.[51] He is, however, not right in asserting that "Aristobulus alone [of the kings taken prisoners] was at once put to death and Tigranes somewhat later." Aristobulus II is actually known to have been exiled in Rome, from where he first escaped in 57 B.C.E. to lead a revolt in Judea. He was defeated and sent back as a prisoner to Rome by Gabinius (Josephus, *A.J.* 14.92–97; *B.J.* 1.171–74). In 49 B.C.E. he was released by Julius Caesar and sent back to Syria with two legions. He met his end, however, before he could set out on his mission, having been poisoned by Pompey's partisans.[52] Appian was not very well informed about the details of Pompey's

---

poll-tax of two drachms, to be paid annually into the Capitol as formerly contributed by them to the temple at Jerusalem." See also Dio, *Hist.* 65.7.2.

49. So also Momigliano, *Ricerche*, 28; and Jean Juster, *Les Juifs dans l'empire romain: leur condition juridique, économique et sociale* (2 vols.; Paris: Librairie Paul Geuthner, 1914), 2:280 and n. 1.

50. Emil Schürer, *The History of the Jewish People in the Age of Jesus Christ, 175 B.C.–A.D. 135* (3 vols. in 4 parts; rev. and ed. Geza Vermes et al.; Edinburgh: T&T Clark, 1973–87), 1:512 and n. 141.

51. See also Plutarch, *Pomp.* 45.4; Pliny, *Nat.* 7.98.26 (does not directly mention Aristobulus).

52. Josephus, *A.J.* 14.123–24; *B.J.* 1.183–84; Dio, *Hist.* 41.18.1.

dealings with the Jewish state, including the taxes Pompey imposed upon it.[53]

Tribute and Exactions

We do not know precisely what tribute Pompey required the Jewish state to pay in 63 B.C.E., although there is no doubt that the Jewish state was made tributary to Rome. I have already suggested that whatever tribute Pompey might have imposed was not effectively collected for two reasons. First, the political and military conditions in the territory hampered collection; and, second, formal taxes conflicted with the powerful financial interests of the governors of Syria. I shall examine both reasons in detail later.

Let me first call further attention to the importance of Josephus's statement that the country and Jerusalem were laid under tribute to the Romans. That "country" was very much reduced by Pompey, who, Josephus says (*B.J.* 1.155; *A.J.* 14.74), "confined the nation within its own boundaries." The Hasmonean kingdom at the time of its conquest included, according to the list in *A.J.* 13.395–97, in the west, every city on the sea coast, except Ascalon, from Rhinocolura as far as Mount Carmel. It extended inland northward as far as the said Valley of Antiochus. Aristobulus I had ventured as far as Iturea.[54] In the south it encompassed Idumea. In the east it included cities from Seleucia in the north to the Moabite city of Zoar southeast of the Dead Sea. Pompey returned the captured territories, except eastern Idumea,[55] to their original inhabitants and joined them to the province of Syria. Josephus specifically mentions the following: in the south, Marisa (and western Idumea); on the coastal plain, Azotus, Jamneia, Arethusa; on the seacoast, Gaza, Joppa, Strato's Tower, and Dora; and in the interland, Gadara, Pella, Hippus, Dium, Scythopolis, and (the city of) Samaria (*A.J.* 14.75–76; *B.J.* 1.155–57). Hyrcanus II had promised to return to the Arabs, as reward for their support of his cause, the territories that they had lost to the Jews—and he probably did (*A.J.* 14.18). It should be assumed also that the district of Samaria received its independence.[56] Consequently, the Jews now held only Judea proper, eastern Idumea, Perea, and Galilee.

53. Appian's erroneous information about Aristobulus is repeated by modern scholars. See, for instance, Robin Seager, *Pompey: A Political Biography* (Berkeley: University of California Press, 1979), 78.

54. According to Josephus, *A.J.* 13.318–19, Aristobulus I annexed part of Iturea to the north of Galilee and forced its inhabitants who wished to remain in the territory to be circumcised.

55. See chapter 4 below.

56. See chapter 4 below.

The city-states that Pompey "liberated" from the Jews, the district of Samaria, as well as what was left of the Jewish state, as we have already noted, became part of the new province of Syria under a Roman governor. Two factors emerge here that are crucial to the discussion of taxation in the Jewish state in the one hundred years that followed: (1) the political status of the Jewish state; and (2) the territory controlled by the Jews. Both changed frequently during this period, depending on the relationship of the Jewish nation to its Roman overlords. The nature of that relationship determined what tribute, if any, the Jews had to pay. The extent of the territory controlled by the Jews determined the kinds and amounts of both the revenue they could raise internally and the tribute they had to pay to the Romans. It will be necessary in this discussion, therefore, to pay attention to both the political status of the Jewish nation and the ramifications of the territorial grants it received from Rome.

One important aspect of Pompey's territorial redistribution was the loss of Joppa to the Jewish state. Joppa served as Judea's opening to the world by sea. The author of 1 Maccabees celebrates its capture and annexation to Judea as the height of Simon's accomplishment: "To crown all his honors he took Joppa for a harbor, and opened a way to the isles of the sea."[57] Joppa's harbors were hazardous, since it had no natural port, its shore being dredged with sand brought up from the sea by the southwest wind. It was further made perilous by dashing waves driven by the northern wind (*A.J.* 15.333; *B.J.* 1.409; 3.419–21). That Joppa could be built, however, and used as a seaport, is illustrated by the event that Josephus recounts about the war in 66 C.E. After Joppa had been destroyed by Cestius's troops—who made an attack on the city "by sea and land"—early in 66 C.E. (*B.J.* 2.507–509), the Jewish rebels rebuilt the city and a fleet. They used its harbors in pirate attacks against ships sailing to the ports of Syria, Phoenicia, and Egypt, until they were blockaded by Vespasian and were exposed to the fury of the wind (*B.J.* 3.414–31).[58] The loss of the city and its harbors in 63 B.C.E. meant that the Jewish state lost both its exit route for trade and the revenues that came from tolls. Both of these elements played important roles in Julius Caesar's decisions regarding the Jewish state.[59]

Whatever tribute Pompey might have imposed on the Jewish state, I observed, could not have been effectively collected because of the political and military conditions present in Palestine. The Romans dealt half-

---

57. 1 Macc 14:5. Josephus in his summary of Simon's reign (*A.J.* 13.215) pays no particular attention to the importance of the seaport. See chapter 2 below.

58. For a discussion of the history of the Jewish population in the territory, see Shimon Applebaum, "The Status of Jaffa in the First Century of the Current Era," *SCI* 89 (1985/1988): 138–44.

59. See chapter 2 below.

heartedly with the problem of pacifying the Jewish state after Pompey's conquest. For the six years following Pompey's defeat of Aristobulus II and the capture of Jerusalem and the temple, the Romans seem to have done nothing about, or at least they were unsuccessful at, subduing the rest of the country and its strongholds. We have already noted that the first three governors, M. Aemilius Scaurus, L. Marcius Philippus, and Cn. Cornelius Lentulus Marcellinus, had neither the political power nor the military means with which to complete the conquest that Pompey had initiated. Moreover, they had their hands full in dealing with the Nabateans. In fact, there is a five-year gap in Josephus's narrative of events in Judea following the capture of Jerusalem in 63 B.C.E. The only action that Josephus records of the Romans before the arrival of Aulus Gabinius as governor in 57 B.C.E. is Scaurus's nearly disastrous campaign against the Arabs (see *A.J.* 14.80–81; *B.J.* 1.159). As Peter Richardson points out, these years must have been filled with historically significant events, especially by the war waged by Alexander, Aristobulus's elder son.[60] From 63 to 51 B.C.E., in fact, Aristobulus II and Alexander staged several revolts in Judea in an attempt to reclaim the throne from Hyrcanus II and his Roman supporters.

Aristobulus II had been ordered by Pompey to surrender the fortresses (Alexandrium, Macherus, and Hyrcania) that he held in Judea, but there is no evidence that the Romans garrisoned them. They were surely not destroyed (see Josephus, *A.J.* 14.52; *B.J.* 1.137). Alexander escaped from captivity before Pompey brought his father and the rest of his family to Rome (*A.J.* 14.79; *B.J.* 1.158). He returned to Palestine and used the fortresses as the bases of his operations, an indication that their control had been repossessed by his father's supporters. During the next five years, from 63 B.C.E. to the beginning of Gabinius's term in 57 B.C.E., Alexander, unimpeded, fortified the strongholds, raised an army, fought a civil war against Hyrcanus and came close to expelling him from Jerusalem. Josephus says that by the time Gabinius was established as governor, Alexander already had overun the country. Alexander had gone to the extent of trying to rebuild the walls of Jerusalem that had been demolished by Pompey. Here the Romans succeeded in preventing his action. That he attempted to rebuild the walls of Jerusalem, however, is a sure indication that Alexander had the country well under his control.[61] "He then went round the country," Josephus writes, "and armed

60. Peter Richardson, *Herod: King of the Jews and Friend of the Romans* (Columbia: University of South Carolina Press, 1996), 101.

61. Peter Richardson (*Herod*, 102) observes, in my view accurately, that Alexander might have replaced Hyrcanus as high priest for a period of time. After defeating Alexander, says Josephus, Gabinius "brought Hyrcanus to Jerusalem, to have charge of the temple" (*A.J.* 14.90; see *B.J.* 1.169).

many of the Jews, and soon collected ten thousand heavy-armed soldiers and fifteen hundred horse" (*A.J.* 14.83). In *B.J.* 1.160 Josephus is even clearer about the course of events during this period:

> Alexander . . . in the course of time mustered a considerable force and caused Hyrcanus serious annoyance by his raids upon Judaea. Having already advanced to Jerusalem and had the audacity to begin rebuilding the wall which Pompey had destroyed, he would in all probability have soon deposed his rival, but for the arrival of Gabinius . . . .[62]

It took Gabinius's forces, under his and Mark Antony's command, together with a Jewish contingent under Peitholaus and Malichus, to defeat Alexander and put down the revolt (Joesphus, *A.J.* 14.84–90; *B.J.* 1.161–70).[63] This means that for the six years following Pompey's conquest of Palestine, the *publicani* could not have collected tribute from the Jews, at least from those in the areas under Alexander, which appears to have been the whole of the Jewish state, except Jerusalem.

We have already seen, in the discussion of the passage from Dio Cassius, that Aristobulus II escaped from Rome with his second son, Antigonus, and led fresh revolts in Judea beginning in 57 B.C.E. Josephus says that "many of the Jews had flocked to Aristobulus, both on account of his former glory and especially because they always welcomed revolutionary movements" (*A.J.* 14.92–93; *B.J.* 1.171). Prominent among the defectors was Peitholaus, who was the "legate" (ὑποστράτηγος) in Jerusalem and had earlier commanded the Jewish troops against Aristobulus's son, Alexander (*A.J.* 14.93; *B.J.* 1.172). Aristobulus was finally besieged and defeated in 56 B.C.E. by the Romans, as he attempted to raise the fortifications at Macherus. He was sent back to Rome for imprison-

62. See Josephus, *A.J.* 14.82: ". . . for Hyrcanus was no longer able to hold out against the strength of Alexander, who was actually attempting to raise again the wall of Jerusalem which Pompey had destroyed."

63. Gabinius at this point took two military and two political steps in the attempt to settle the problem of the Jewish nation: (1) he defeated Alexander and quelled the revolt, although he afterwards merely granted Alexander "pardon for his offences," that is, without removing him from Judaea (*A.J.* 14.89; *B.J.* 1.168); (2) he demolished the fortresses "to prevent their serving as a base of operations for another war" (*B.J.* 1.168; *A.J.* 14.90); (3) he restored order in Judaea and rebuilt the towns and cities that had been ravaged by Alexander and by previous wars (*A.J.* 14.87–88; *B.J.* 1.165–66); and finally (4) he reinstated Hyrancus II as high priest in Jerusalem, a function Hyrcanus had received from Pompey, and thus restored the "traditional" Jewish "aristocracy." He further divided the nation into five districts under five συνέδρια (συνόδους in *B.J.*, see *A.J.* 14.90–91; *B.J.* 1.169–70). Generations of scholars have held that the districts set up by Gabinius were "independent" and that he had by these political measures removed all political power from the hands of Hyrcanus. This cannot be correct in view of what Josephus actually tells us about Jewish "aristocracy." We will come back to the problem of Hyrcanus' political authority in chapter 4.

ment. His children, however, were set free (see *A.J.* 14.94–97; *B.J.* 1.172–74).

In 55 B.C.E., while Gabinius was away on his campaign in Egypt, Alexander again led a revolt in Judea, extending it into Samaria, where he besieged the Romans who took refuge there, and then further extending his campaign into Galilee (Josephus, *B.J.* 1.176–78; *A.J.* 14.100–102).[64] He was again eventually defeated by Gabinius. After this, says Josephus, "Gabinius then proceeded to Jerusalem, where he reorganized the government in accordance with Antipater's wishes" (*B.J.* 1.178; *A.J.* 14.103).[65] As Sherwin-White rightly observes, Gabinius's battles were the first attempt by the Romans at the conquest of the Jewish state and its inhabitants, beyond Pompey's capture of Jerusalem.[66]

M. Licinius Crassus, who succeeded Gabinius as governor of Syria from 54 B.C.E., died in 53 B.C.E. during his campaign against the Parthians. His quaestor, C. Cassius Longinus, arrived in Judea sometime after this to quell a revolt that was led by Peitholaus. He apparently had been at large since he defected from Jerusalem, after having cooperated with the Romans, and joined the revolt led by Aristobulus in 57 B.C.E. Peitholaus was executed by Cassius and, according to Josephus, thirty thousand of his supporters were sold into slavery. In *War,* Josephus adds that Cassius also "bound over Alexander by treaty to keep the peace." Alexander too might have been leading yet another revolt (see *B.J.* 1.180–82; *A.J.* 14.119–21).

To sum up, Roman control of Jewish Palestine from 63 to 51(?) B.C.E. could not have permitted a systematic Roman taxation in the territory. This must certainly be said of the parts of the Jewish state that came under one or the other of the rebelling Hasmonean princes. One may, however, assume that the inhabitants of Jerusalem and the surrounding areas, while they were under Roman control, paid whatever tribute could be raised from them. It is entirely possible that Alexander was faithful to the truce that he had entered into with Cassius in about 51 B.C.E. If so, then it might also be assumed that the Romans had some reprieve for the two years from about 51 B.C.E. until the outbreak of the civil war between Julius Caesar and Pompey in 49 B.C.E. We should bear in mind, however, that Alexander was at large during that entire time, until he was beheaded in Antioch under Pompey's orders "after a trial in which he was accused of the injuries which he had caused to the Romans" (*B.J.*

---

64. See p. 18 above. The battle between his forces and those of Gabinius was fought near Mount Tabor in Lower Galilee.

65. This, in my opinion, was the end of Gabinius's five districts. But this question cannot be argued here.

66. Sherwin-White, "Lucullus, Pompey," 272.

1.185; *A.J.* 14.125–26). By then, in any event, all of Syria was in commotion. When Pompey was killed in 48 B.C.E. after the battle of Pharsalus, the Jewish authorities in Jerusalem transferred their support to Caesar (*A.J.* 14.127–40; *B.J.* 1.187–92).

In *A.J.* 14.77–78, a passage without parallel in *War*, Josephus again summarizes the consequences of the defeat of the Jewish state by Pompey. In place of the earlier statement (*A.J.* 14.74) that Pompey made Jerusalem tributary to Rome, Josephus maintains that "the Romans exacted of us in a short space of time more than ten thousand talents." It would seem at first sight that we have here at last, at least in Josephus's view, the sum paid by the Jewish state in tribute to Rome during the sixteen years from 63 to 47 B.C.E. This, in fact, is not the meaning of Josephus's statement. In the first place, by a "short space of time" Josephus actually means the period from 63 B.C.E. to the accession of the "commoner," Herod, to the throne in 37 B.C.E.[67] Second, for the period between 63 and 47 B.C.E., Josephus records one very significant case of "exaction" by the Romans. M. Licinius Crassus plundered the temple in Jerusalem before his disastrous Parthian campaign. Crassus's exaction is significant because it involved temple funds and was for this reason a particularly sensitive issue for the Jews. It is significant also, for our purposes, because two thousand talents (which Pompey left untouched in the temple treasury) (see *A.J.* 14.72) plus eight thousand talents (the equivalent worth, in Josephus's estimate, of the gold ornaments of the temple) equals ten thousand talents: the amount Josephus says the Romans exacted from the Jews "in a short space of time" (*A.J.* 14.105–9; *B.J.* 1.179). Josephus considers the ten thousand talents removed by Crassus from the temple to be a vast sum of money, so vast that he appeals to the testimony of Strabo's authority in order to convince skeptics that the Jewish temple possessed such wealth. This wealth was lost to the Romans in one single plunder (*A.J.* 14.110–18). This specific loss enables Josephus to put a figure on Jewish losses to the Romans. It is to this exaction that he is pointing when he laments that the Romans exacted more than ten thousand talents from the Jews "in a short space of time."

---

67. The fall of Jerusalem to Herod in 37 B.C.E. and the execution of Aritobulus's last son, Antigonus II, constitute in Josephus's narrative both the second calamity (τὸ πάθος) that befell the city and the finale to Josephus's account of the Hasmonean dynasty. The first calamity was the defeat of Aristobulus II and the capture of Jerusalem by Pompey. The parallelism between the two events is emphasized by Josephus: they both occurred on the same date "as if it [the latter event] were a recurrence of the misfortune which came upon the Jews in the time of Pompey" (*A.J.* 14.487; see *A.J.* 14.66). Herod's occupation of Jerusalem brought the process initiated by the earlier capture of the city to its conclusion. *A.J.* 14.78 and 14.457–91 frame the narrative that lies between them. This narrative unit is also a temporal unit, beginning with the capture of Jerusalem by Pompey and ending with the demise of the Hasmonean household and the triumph of Herod.

Crassus's spoliation, while extreme and memorable, is only a particular instance of Rome's method of irregular taxation. I call it "irregular," first, because it was not at this point positively regulated by any discernible and applicable laws, and, second, because it tended to run parallel to the expectations of "regular" tribute. These "exactions" were tribute, all the same, and consisted of a wide range of demands for payments and services, made upon the state or upon private individuals. Julius Caesar in 47 B.C.E. banned certain kinds of exactions being made from the Jews. I shall discuss these and the general problem in greater detail in the next chapter. At present, it suffices to note that exactions were not payments made to the Roman public treasury, the *aerarium*. Instead, they served the interests of governors and generals. If such interests were sometimes personal, and even private, they were often also military. They, therefore, at least in the view of their subjects, belonged to Rome's overall imperial ends: keeping the Parthians and Nabateans at bay, fighting rival Roman generals, defeating a rival Hasmonean prince in rebellion, and/or maintaining order in the territory and wherever else the governor chose. Becoming "tributary to Rome," meant, along with whatever "regular tribute" Pompey might have imposed on the region, that the Jewish state made contributions in finances, logistics, and personnel to Roman interests in the region.

We have no record of what Pompey demanded in regular tribute. Further, I have shown that this tribute, in any case, could not have been successfully collected. It remains to be emphasized that "tribute" to the Romans by the Jewish state from 63 to 47 B.C.E. consisted principally of the contributions that the Jews made to the interests of the Roman governors and generals who dominated Syria. From this perspective, Crassus's looting of the treasures of the temple in Jerusalem before his Parthian campaign seems to be more than an instance of private greed; and Cicero's bombast against Gabinius, rather than providing details on Gabinius's tax reforms, says much about the conflict of interests among Rome's ruling classes.

We gain an insight from Josephus into what these contributions consisted of, apart from Crassus's plunder. In 65 B.C.E. Scaurus, sent by Pompey into Syria, obtained the promise of money from Aristobulus II (and from Hyrcanus II, according to *A.J.* 14.30). The sum was four hundred talents, according to *A.J.* 14.30, or three hundred talents, according to *B.J.* 1.128. Scaurus accepted the money from Aristobulus and, before he returned to Damascus, with due threats forced Hyrcanus and his Nabatean allies to raise the siege against Aristobulus. Gabinius, apparently (before Scaurus) also took money from Aristobulus; the amount, according to *A.J.* 14.37, was three hundred talents.

Aristobulus II, we are told, sent a "golden vine" to Pompey as he was approaching Coele-Syria. The gift is reported to have been worth five hundred talents.[68] Faced with war, Aristobulus promised to make further payments to Pompey, and to surrender both himself and the city of Jerusalem. The refusal to honor these promises led to Aristobulus and his supporters being besieged in the citadel of the temple, and to his being taken prisoner by Pompey.[69]

From 63 to 47 B.C.E. Hyrcanus II and his supporters in Jerusalem generally kept their Roman overlords happy by giving them money. Josephus (*A.J.* 14.164) says that Antipater, Herod's father and the power behind Hyrcanus's throne, "had formed a friendship with the Roman generals, and after persuading Hyrcanus to send them money, he took this gift and appropriated it for himself, and then sent it as though it came from him and were not a gift from Hyrcanus." They raised troops and provided, both in finances and logistics, for Rome's war efforts. They negotiated with the enemies and even fought in some of the battles themselves. Thus, during Scaurus's campaign against Arabian Petra, the Jews contributed grain and "whatever other provisions he needed" (*A.J.* 14.80; *B.J.* 1.159). Antipater is said to have negotiated terms with Aretas, the Arab king, and to have pledged himself as surety that the Arab would pay three hundred talents to Scaurus.[70] Hyrcanus and Antipater raised auxiliary troops for Gabinius's campaign against Alexander in 57 B.C.E. (*A.J.* 14.83–84; *B.J.* 1.162). For Gabinius's Egyptian campaign to restore Ptolemy Auletes, the Jewish state provided money, arms, grain, and auxiliary troops. Antipater persuaded the Jews of Pelusium to let Gabinius through into Egypt (*A.J.* 14.98–99; *B.J.* 1.175). Finally, during Gabinius's second campaign against Alexander, Antipater negotiated with and won over some of the Jews who had joined Alexander (*A.J.* 14.101–2; *B.J.* 1.177).

Once Pompey was defeated and killed, Hyrcanus and Antipater turned to Caesar's cause in Egypt, apparently in much the same way that they had supported Pompey and his lieutenants in Syria. They contributed auxiliary troops—three thousand "heavy-armed" infantry, according to Josephus;[71] persuaded the Arabian and Syrian princes to join in the war; and convinced the Jews of Egypt "who inhabited the district of Onias" to let Caesar's auxiliary forces pass through. Antipater (and possibly Hyrcanus as well) personally fought in the war (see *A.J.* 14.127–39; *B.J.* 1.187–94).

---

68. Josephus (*A.J.* 14.34–36) cites Strabo as his source here.

69. See Josephus, *A.J.* 14.55–57; *B.J.* 1.139–40; Dio, *Hist.* 37.15.3.

70. *A.J.* 14.81; *B.J.* 1.159: Antipater brought the Arab to consent to paying the said sum.

71. More correctly, perhaps, the number was 1,500, according to Caesar's decree in *A.J.* 14.193.

Conclusion

With the defeat of Aristobulus II and the reorganization of the Jewish state by Pompey, Jewish Palestine became part of the province of Syria and entered into Rome's sphere of influence. The Jewish state became tributary to Rome. Gabinius's conflicts with the *publicani* provide evidence that Pompey in fact imposed a form of direct tribute on the Jews, and that the Senate sold out to the *publicani* the right to collect the tribute. However, we do not know the form and the scale of this tribute. Nevertheless, given that from 63 to 48 B.C.E. Rome's hold on the territory was tenuous, Pompey's tribute (whatever it might have been) could not have been raised in large sections of the Jewish state, except probably during the two years between 51 and 49 B.C.E. In the meantime, tribute to Rome meant mostly exactions in "gifts" and services, that is, various payments and, in general, contributions by the Jewish state to the magistrates who represented Roman interests in the region.

2

Caesar's Favors (47–44 B.C.E.)

One usually should not speak of "favors" where taxes, and in particular colonial taxes, are involved; however, the arrangements that Julius Caesar made with the Jewish state may rightly be called "favors." Josephus, in citing the documents from which our knowledge of these arrangements comes, describes the various grants made by Caesar to the Jewish state, including the taxes, as "honours given our nation" (*A.J.* 14.186). Josephus sets them in the context of the personal privileges and honors that Julius Caesar gave to Hyrcanus II and Antipater, rewards for their services to Caesar in the winter of 47 B.C.E. during his Alexandrian War.[1] As Josephus presents them, the decrees on taxes issued by Julius Caesar were part of the confirmation of the "treaty of friendship and alliance" (*A.J.* 14.185–86) with the Romans, made after the Jews had demonstrated their bravery and, most importantly, their loyalty during Caesar's campaign.

Such grants of favors and privileges by Roman generals to individuals and allied states after a successful campaign are by no means unique. Military assistance and political loyalty were, in fact, the most frequently cited reasons for the grants of privileges and rights by Roman generals. For example, after the Trinovantes of South Britain assisted him in his second expedition against the Cassivellauni, Caesar granted them privileges (Caesar, *Bell. gall.* 5.20–22).[2] I shall return in chapter 4 to the case of Seleucus of Rhosos, who received from Octavian privileges similar to those given by Caesar to Hyrcanus II and Antipater. Seleucus's grants

1. *A.J.* 14.127–36, 193, 211–12; *B.J.* 1.187–92; also *A.J.* 16.52–53, 162–63. See P. J. Sijpesteijn, "Mithradates' March from Pergamum to Alexandria in 48 B.C.," *Latomus* 24 (1965): 122–27; Aryeh Kasher, "New Light on the Jewish Role in the Alexandrian War of Julius Caesar," *World Union of Jewish Studies Newsletter* 14–15 (1979): 15–23; idem, *The Jews in Hellenistic and Roman Egypt: The Struggle for Equal Rights* (Tübingen: Mohr Siebeck, 1985), 13–18.

2. See J. F. Drinkwater, "The Trinovantes: Some Observations on Their Participation in the Events of A.D. 60," *RSA* 5 (1975): 55.

were in gratitude for his participation in naval action, probably in the battle of Philippi in 42 B.C.E.[3] Rhosos, Seleucus's city, might have received grants as well.[4] Likewise, in 78 B.C.E. three naval captains from Greece were granted privileges, including immunity from all liturgies, because at the beginning of the Italian war they "had given valiant and faithful service to our Republic."[5] Furthermore, for their military assistance to Sulla during his war against King Mithridates, the people of Stratonikeia received a vote of privileges from the Senate in 81 B.C.E.[6] In the case of the Jewish state, apart from specific tax regulations, Caesar changed its political status by modifying Judea's relationship with the province of Syria, granting the Jews relative administrative independence.[7]

Caesar did not free the Jewish state from tribute to Rome, but he reorganized and regulated the chaotic regime the Jews had been under since 63 B.C.E. and granted the Jews some concessions. Caesar required that both the tribute for the Jewish state and the fixed tribute for Joppa be raised and paid by the head of the Jewish state in Jerusalem. By so doing, he removed the grounds for the arbitrary exactions that the Jews had thus far endured. He further granted the Jews a series of exemptions, which placed them in an enviable position, and returned significant territories to them from the cities that Pompey had detached from Judea.

It is particularly fortunate that in *A.J.* 14.190–222 Josephus cites a string of decrees that Caesar himself and the Roman Senate issued with regard to the Jewish state. Beyond Josephus's narrative, therefore, we have access to some of the documents that set out the terms of the relationship between Rome and the Jewish nation. The authenticity of the Roman documents quoted by Josephus, especially in *A.J.* 14.190–264, 16.162–73, 19.280–311, however, has been the subject of voluminous and intense scholarly debate. Josephus's reasons for quoting the decrees are overtly apologetic. The documents he cites are fragmentary and out of order; they contain errors ranging from chronological mistakes to textual corruptions. Some scholars, because of these problems, have thought that these documents were forgeries, as Philip S. Alexander puts it, "with an

3. See the discussion in chapter 4 below.

4. Robert K. Sherk, *RDGE:* Senatus Consulta *and* Epistulae *to the Age of Augustus* (Baltimore: Johns Hopkins University Press, 1969), no. 58; Pierre Roussel, "Un Syrien au service de Rome et d'Octave," *Syria* 15 (1934): 33–74; Miriam Pucci Ben Zeev, *Jewish Rights in the Roman World: The Greek and Roman Documents Quoted by Josephus Flavius* (Tübingen: Mohr Siebeck, 1998), 43.

5. Robert K. Sherk, *RGE* (Cambridge: Cambridge University Press, 1984), no. 66 = Sherk, *RDGE*, no. 22. Pucci Ben Zeev, *Jewish Rights*, 47.

6. Sherk, *RGE*, no. 63, lines 71–130 = Sherk, *RDGE*, no. 18. See Pucci Ben Zeev, *Jewish Rights*, 47.

7. I shall argue this in detail in chapter 4.

eye to tangible, political advantage."[8] Moehring, who also thinks that the documents might be forgeries, makes significant points: (1) the authenticity of each document "has to be decided in every single instance," and (2) the documents "must first and foremost be read as part of his [Josephus's] apologetic scheme." Therefore, the documents can be used as historical evidence "only after full allowances have been made for their apologetic character and after their original *Sitz im Leben* has been clearly established."[9] Miriam Pucci Ben Zeev recently produced an excellent comprehensive study of the decrees in light of known Roman official documents of the period.[10] Her study enables us to satisfy Moehring's demand for establishing the "original *Sitz im Leben*" of the documents. I agree with her conclusion that these documents must be considered as authentic *sui generis*, that is, as documents quoted not from their original but from copies or even copies of copies of Greek translations of the Latin original.[11] I also accept Moehring's caution that the historical significance of each decree must be established on the basis of a stringent historical analysis, which, in my view, includes verifying the results against general historical reality. For instance, the authenticity of the decree granting exemption to the Jews from conscription into Roman auxiliary troops would be put in doubt if it could be shown that Roman generals and the *praefecti* of Judea raised auxiliary troops in Judea.

Our focus in this chapter will be mainly on the decrees dealing with taxes, cited in *A.J.* 14.190–95, 200–210. Momigliano provides an earlier detailed study of these decrees.[12] Since generations of scholars have relied on his analyses, which are insightful and often accurate, I shall pay particular attention to them. The principal and immediate problem with the documents is that of establishing a chronological relationship between the fragmentary decrees that Josephus transmits, all together by them-

---

8. P. S. Alexander, "Epistolary Literature," in *Jewish Writings of the Second Temple Period* (ed. M. E. Stone; Philadelphia: Fortress Press, 1984), 588; see also Michel S. Ginsburg, *Rome et la Judée: contribution à l'histoire de leurs relations politiques* (Paris: Jacques Povolozky, 1928), 85–86; Horst R. Moehring, "The *Acta Pro Judaeis* in the *Antiquities* of Flavius Josephus: A Study in Hellenistic and Modern Apologetic Historiography," in *Christianity, Judaism and Other Greco-Roman Cults*, vol. 3 (ed. J. Neusner; Leiden: Brill, 1975), 128, 130, n. 23, 150–52; H. W. Attridge, "Josephus and His Works," in *Jewish Writings of the Second Temple Period* (ed. M. E. Stone; Philadelphia: Fortress Press, 1984), 226.

9. Moehring, "Acta Pro Judaeis," 156–57.

10. Pucci Ben Zeev, *Jewish Rights*; see pp. 1–11 for the debate. On Josephus's historiography, see Shaye J. D. Cohen, *Josephus in Galilee and Rome: His Vita and Development as a Historian* (Columbia Studies in the Classical Tradition 8; Leiden: Brill, 1979).

11. Pucci Ben Zeev, *Jewish Rights*, 357–68.

12. Momigliano, *Ricerche*, 10–36; see in particular pp. 10–27. See also Schalit, *König Herodes*, "Anhang XIII," 777–81. Schalit's discussion includes some account of the previous significant opinions.

selves, and his narrative of the events that occurred from 48 to 44 B.C.E. Since there already exists a good working consensus on this problem in earlier scholarship,[13] my discussion will be brief. Josephus in his narrative registers four accounts of grants and confirmations of grants in the dealings between Hyrcanus II and Julius Caesar.

1. *A.J.* 14.137–148; *B.J.* 1.93–200. When Caesar left Egypt after the Alexandrian War and came to Syria in 47 B.C.E., he confirmed Hyrcanus in the high priesthood. Caesar gave Roman citizenship to Antipater, exempting him from taxation everywhere (*A.J.* 14.137; *B.J.* 1.193–94). On this occasion he also appointed Antipater procurator (ἐπίτροπος) of Judea and granted Hyrcanus permission to restore the walls of the city of Jerusalem.[14] Caesar, Josephus says, sent instructions to the consuls in Rome for the grants to be recorded in the capital (*A.J.* 14.144; *B.J.* 1.200). The decree that Josephus cites in *A.J.* 14.145–48 as being enacted by the Senate to confirm these grants is dated, however, to the time of John Hyrcanus I (135/4–104 B.C.E.).[15]

Caesar arrived in Syria in June of 47 B.C.E. The exact dates of his arrival and departure are matters of controversy.[16] In any event, his presence in Antioch is noted sometime before July 18 by Trebonius (see Cicero, *Att.* 11.20.1).[17] Much like Sulla before him had acted after the Mithridatic war, Caesar, while he was in Syria, received in audience the native rulers who came to pay him homage and gave rewards to all who had been of help to him.[18] It was on this occasion, as Josephus says, that Caesar also honored Hyrcanus II and Antipater, and reorganized the Jewish state with the rest of the East.[19] Caesar's letter to the Sidonians (*A.J.*

---

13. See the summary of the earlier relevant positions in Schürer, *History*, 1:272–74 and nn. 20–24. I shall make specific references, as needed, to Pucci Ben Zeev's discussions.

14. *A.J.* 14.143–44; *B.J.* 1.199–200. In *B.J.* 1.199–200 the permission to rebuild the walls is given to Antipater. It is probable that in various instances Josephus's sources, notably those from Nicolaus of Damascus, put Antipater in the forefront at Hyrcanus's expense. Compare, for instance, *B.J.* 1.194 and *A.J.* 14.137. On this tendency, see *Momigliano, Ricerche*, 10; B. R. Motzo, "Ircano II nella tradizione storica," in *Studi di storia e filologia* (2 vols; Cagliari: R. Università, 1927), 1:1–18; Daniel R. Schwartz, "Josephus on Hyrcanus II," in *Josephus and the History of the Greco-Roman Period: Essays in Memory of Morton Smith* (ed. Fausto Parente and Joseph Sievers; Leiden: Brill, 1994), 211–12.

15. See Momigliano, *Ricerche*, 30–36 and pp. 150–51 and n. 193 below.

16. See Hirtius, *Bell. alex.* 33.6; 66.1–2; T. Rice Holmes, *The Roman Republic and the Founder of the Empire* (3 vols; Oxford: Clarendon, 1923; repr., New York: Russell & Russell, 1967), 3:509–10; Louis E. Lord, "The Date of Julius Caesar's Departure from Alexandria," *JRS* 28 (1938): 25–28, 39–40; Wiseman, "Caesar, Pompey and Rome," 434; Pucci Ben Zeev, *Jewish Rights*, 51.

17. Lord, "Date of Julius Caesar's Departure," 26.

18. Hirtius, *Bell. alex.* 65.4; see Matthias Gelzer, *Caesar: Politician and Statesman* (Cambridge, Mass.: Harvard University Press, 1968), 257–59.

19. For Caesar's reorganization of the East see Hirtius, *Bell. alex.* 65–78; Appian, *Bell.*

14.190–95) belongs to the complex of documents he issued on behalf of Hyrcanus and the Jewish state at this time. The titles that Caesar attributes to himself in the opening of the letter date it to 47 B.C.E. Caesar's second dictatorship ran from October 48 B.C.E. (for a year) until 47 B.C.E.[20]

The letter is accompanied with a copy of the decree that Caesar would have issued to Hyrcanus (*A.J.* 14.192–95).[21] In this decree Caesar appoints Hyrcanus and his sons as ethnarchs and ordains that they "hold the office of high priest of the Jews" (*A.J.* 14.194). Momigliano and Schürer argue that Caesar had previously recognized Hyrcanus's high priestly office in 48 B.C.E., before Hyrcanus's participation in the Alexandrian War. They find evidence for this view in the fragment cited in *A.J.* 14.199, where Hyrcanus and his sons are given the grant to be "high priests and priests." In theory, this early recognition seems plausible and would certainly have marked Caesar's acceptance of Hyrcanus as the legitimate Jewish authority, a reversal of policy in view of Caesar's previous support of Aristobulus (*A.J.* 14.123–24; *B.J.* 1.183–84). The problem, however, is that both Momigliano and Schürer really envision a two-step process in Caesar's conferment of titles on Hyrcanus in order to shore up their view, somewhat circuitously, that Hyrcanus had lost political power under Gabinius. The absence of the title "ethnarch" in *A.J.* 14.199 is the reason why they consider the fragment an earlier recognition of Hyrcanus's status. In their view, then, Caesar in *A.J.* 14.194 would have restored political power to Hyrcanus, having previously recognized his religious function as high priest.[22]

Since this widely held position has some relevance to the question of Caesar's reorganization of the Jewish state and its tribute to Rome, I shall return to it in chapter four. For now it is enough to note, firstly, that in *A.J.* 14.199 Caesar is called "Imperator, Dictator and Consul." He was both dictator and consul four times: in 48, 46, 45, and 44 B.C.E.[23] Without the usual numbers attached to the dictatorship and consulship, it is impossi-

---

civ. 2.91–92; T. Robert S. Broughton, *The Magistrates of the Roman Republic* (3 vols.; New York: American Philological Association, 1951–52; repr., Atlanta, Ga.: Scholars Press, 1984–86), 2:286; Gelzer, *Caesar*, 258–61; Stefan Weinstock, *Divus Julius* (Oxford: Clarendon, 1971), 238; see also Michel Rambaud, "A propos de l'*humanitas* de César," *LEC* 40 (1972): 145–55.

20. See A. E. Raubitschek, "Epigraphical Notes on Julius Caesar," *JRS* 44 (1954): 70; J. A. Crook et al., eds., *CAH*, vol. 9, *The Last Age of the Roman Republic, 146–43 B.C.* (2nd ed.; Cambridge: Cambridge University Press, 1994), 796–98. This year Caesar was not consul (only in 48, 46, 45, and 44). That the decree in *A.J.* 14.190–95 dates from 47 B.C.E. is also accepted by Momigliano, *Ricerche*, 13; Schürer, *History*, 1:271–72 and n. 21; Pucci Ben Zeev, *Jewish Rights*, 51–53.

21. On the complex form of Roman decrees accompanied with letters, see Pucci Ben Zeev, *Jewish Rights*, 44–46, and the various other instances cited there.

22. Momigliano, *Ricerche*, 12–14; Schürer, *History*, 1:271, 274, n. 23.

23. See Crook et al., *CAH* 9:796–98.

ble to decide to which of these years the decree belongs. Second, the decree speaks of Caesar in the third person and is, thus, a *senatus consultum* issued by the Senate to confirm Caesar's grants to Hyrcanus. Whatever its exact date might be, it is a fragment of the *senatus consultum* with which the Senate later confirmed the grants made by Caesar in 47 B.C.E.[24]

2. *A.J.* 14.185. In October, when Caesar arrived in Rome from Syria, and before he set out on his campaign against Scipio and Cato in December of 47 B.C.E., Hyrcanus II sent envoys requesting a confirmation of "the treaty of friendship and alliance with him." Hyrcanus would have known that the highest authority in the Roman Republic was the Senate. Grants made by generals and magistrates stood to be ratified by the Senate, if they were to become law. This was a question of normal procedure. There are numerous instances of similar requests by envoys from foreign states for confirmation of privileges and rights conferred by Roman magistrates. In 46 B.C.E., for instance, the city of Chersonesos sent an envoy to Julius Caesar and the Senate.[25] We also have a letter by Julius Caesar that accompanied a copy of the decree of the Senate confirming the privileges granted by him to the people of Mytilene. This confirmation, issued between the spring of 46 and the winter of 45 B.C.E., was obtained at the request of envoys from Mytilene who asked for "renewed goodwill, friendship and alliance."[26] Earlier, in 81 B.C.E., Sulla wrote to the Dionysiac Artists in Ionia and Hellespont to present to them the decree issued by the Senate in confirmation of his grants of 84 B.C.E. This confirmation was also requested by envoys sent to Rome.[27] A request for ratification by the envoys from Stratonikeia resulted in a *senatus consultum* and an accompanying letter from Sulla. The decree was issued, sometime after Sulla returned to Rome in 83 B.C.E., to confirm the grants that he made in 85 B.C.E. to the people of Stratonikeia for their loyalty to Rome during the Mithridatic War.[28]

As I have already suggested above, the fragment in *A.J.* 14.199 is what remains of the decree issued by the Senate to confirm Caesar's grants of 47 B.C.E., at the request of Hyrcanus's envoys, recorded in *A.J.* 14.194–95. Included with this fragment should be another cited in *A.J.* 14.196–98. Caesar's consulship is also noted in the introduction to this

24. Although Momigliano (*Ricerche*, 11–12) dated the fragment in *A.J.* 14.199 to 48 B.C.E., others have chosen other dates: 49/48, 47, and 44 B.C.E. See Christiane Saulnier, "Lois romaines et les Juifs selon Josèphe," *RB* 88 (1981): 171–72, 196; Schürer, *History*, 1:274, n. 23; Pucci Ben Zeev, *Jewish Rights*, 70–71.

25. See Sherk, *RGE*, no. 82.

26. See Sherk, *RGE*, 83, lines 1–19 = Sherk, *RDGE*, no. 26, col. b, lines 1–19.

27. See Sherk, *RGE*, no. 62A and B = Sherk, *RDGE*, no. 49A and B.

28. Sherk, *RGE*, no. 63 = Sherk, *RDGE*, no. 18. See p. 32 above.

fragment without any specification of the number of times ("Gaius Caesar, Imperator and Consul" [*A.J.* 14.196]). Pucci Ben Zeev has noted, moreover, that the words that follow Caesar's titles in the introduction are not attested in official Roman documents. The lack of a precise date for Caesar's titles in this case, she observes, might be accounted for if the introduction had been a title for a series of documents rather than an introduction to a specific document.[29] In any event, this *senatus consultum* repeats the provisions of Caesar's letter and decree (*A.J.* 14.190–96), with the specification that envoys be sent (to or from) Hyrcanus to discuss "terms of friendship and alliance" (*A.J.* 14.197).[30]

3. *A.J.* 14.221–22. In February of 44 B.C.E. Hyrcanus sent envoys to Caesar to obtain further concessions from him; Caesar, however, died on March 15, 44 B.C.E. The *senatus consultum* issued by the Senate at the envoys' request was dated February 9, 44 B.C.E., but there was no time for the decisions made by Caesar and the Senate in favor of the Jews to be registered before he died.

4. *A.J.* 14.219–21. After his death the Senate confirmed the grants made by Caesar to the Jewish envoys. The document bearing Caesar's decisions in February (3 above) was incorporated into the *senatus consultum* issued on April 11, 44 B.C.E.

The decree quoted in *A.J.* 14.200–201 belongs to these dates. In *A.J.* 14.200 Caesar is said to be "Consul for the fifth time." He became "Consul for the fifth time" in 44 B.C.E. Later that year Caesar was also dictator for the fifth time and for life (*perpetuus*),[31] but the decree makes no mention of this title. Scholars have long noted the problem that arises from the fact that the decree in *A.J.* 14.200–201 grants permission to Hyrcanus to rebuild the walls of Jerusalem, whereas the permission was actually given in 47 B.C.E. (*A.J.* 14.144; *B.J.* 1.199), and the work was already completed by 44 B.C.E.[32] Some have conjectured that πέμπτον ("for the fifth time") in Caesar's title in *A.J.* 14.200 be changed, therefore, either to δεύτερον ("for the second time") or to τρίτον ("for the third time"), in the effort to date the decree either to 47 B.C.E. (Caesar was not consul in this year) or to 46 B.C.E. Such emendations are unnecessary, however, since

29. Pucci Ben Zeev, *Jewish Rights*, 54–55.

30. For a discussion of the problem of the envoys, see Pucci Ben Zeev, *Jewish Rights*, 58–59, and the literature cited there.

31. See Crook et al., *CAH* 9:798; Broughton, *Magistrates*, 2:315, 317–18.

32. *A.J.* 14.156: After seeing Caesar off from Syria, in 47 B.C.E., Antipater "at once raised again the wall which had been demolished by Pompey." *B.J.* 1.201: "his [Antipater's] first act was to rebuild the wall of the capital which had been overthrown by Pompey." See Schürer, *History*, 1:273 and n. 23.

A.J. 14.200–201 is obviously a fragment of a *senatus consultum*. It refers to Caesar in the third person and is formulated in the past tense: Γαίος Καῖσαρ . . . ἔκρινε. The decree must, therefore, be considered a fragment of the *senatus consultum* of 44 B.C.E., incorporating and confirming grants made earlier to the Jews by Caesar.[33] The tax reduction recorded in *A.J.* 14.201 is related to the permission to rebuild the walls, and may have been granted at the completion of the project, sometime after 47 B.C.E.[34]

Caesar's title in *A.J.* 14.202, according to the Greek text, is "Gaius Caesar, Imperator for the second time." The title αὐτοκράτωρ (Imperator) usually appears without the specification of number (e.g., *A.J.* 14.190, 196, 199, 211), since Caesar used it permanently, and had no exclusive significance.[35] "Imperator," therefore, was likely without the specification of number in the original document, while the title "Dictator" was lost from *A.J.* 14.202 just as it was in *A.J.* 14.192, where the Greek text also reads αὐτοκράτωρ τὸ δεύτερον (Imperator for the second time). In the beginning of the letter accompanying the decree, Caesar's title is, correctly: "Gaius Julius Caesar, Imperator and Pontifex Maximus, Dictator for the second time" (*A.J.* 14.190). The Latin text of *A.J.* 14.202 adds "Dictator" from which B. Niese, following Johann Tobias Krebs's suggestion, conjectured the reading αὐτοκράτωρ δικτάτωρ τὸ δεύτερον (Imperator, Dictator for the second time).[36] The document dates, therefore, from 47 B.C.E.

Schürer follows Ludwig Mendelssohn's view that *A.J.* 14.202–4 was a fragment of a decree issued by Caesar in 47 B.C.E., and he considers *A.J.* 14.205–10 to be a fragment of the *senatus consultum* of February 44 B.C.E. According to this view, *A.J.* 14.205–10 would be part of a separate document that seemingly repeats the grant of Joppa (already granted in *A.J.* 14.202). The references to the Senate in §§207, 208, and 209 would confirm it as a fragment of the *senatus consultum* of 44 B.C.E.[37]

---

33. Pucci Ben Zeev, *Jewish Rights*, 75–79.

34. Momigliano (*Ricerche*, 16–19) considers the permission to rebuild the walls of Jerusalem to have been given only in 44 B.C.E. The narrative accounts in *A.J.* 14.144, 156; *B.J.* 1.199–201, he thinks, were part of Nicolaus of Damascus's habitual tendency to emphasize the importance of Antipater. See also Schürer, *History*, 1:273, n. 23.

35. See Ronald Syme, "Imperator Caesar: A Study of Nomenclature," in *Roman Papers*, vol. 1 (ed. E. Badian; Oxford: Oxford University Press, 1979), 367–68; I. Bitto, "La concessione del patronato nella politica di Cesare," *Epigraphica* 31 (1970): 174, n. 20; Elizabeth Rawson, "Caesar: Civil War and Dictatorship," in *CAH*, vol. 9, *The Last Age of the Roman Republic, 146–43 B.C.* (ed. J. A. Crook et al.; 2nd ed.; Cambridge: Cambridge University Press, 1994), 461 and n. 231; Pucci Ben Zeev, *Jewish Rights*, 83–84.

36. See Josephus, *A.J.* 14.202, nn. 7 and f (in Marcus, LCL); Johann Tobias Krebs, *Decreta Romanorum pro Iudaeis facta e Iosepho collecta et commentario historico-critico illustrata* (Lipsis: Sumtibus Caspari Fritsch, 1768), 254–55; Schürer, *History*, 1:273–74, n. 23; Pucci Ben Zeev, *Jewish Rights*, 84.

37. See Schürer, *History*, 1:273–74, nn. 23 and 24. My position in Fabian E. Udoh, "Tribute and Taxes in Early Roman Palestine (63 B.C.E.–70 C.E.): The Evidence from Josephus,"

Actually, *A.J.* 14.202 also refers to Caesar in the third person, as is characteristic of *senatus consulta*, the verb is in the past (aorist) form: Γάιος Καῖσαρ . . . ἔστησε (Gaius Caesar . . . ruled), and the grants that follow are formulated in indirect sentences. For the rest, the technical formulas that the text contains[38] indicate that the provisions of the decree concerning Judea are considered to originate from the Senate. There is no reason to postulate a hiatus between *A.J.* 14.202–4 and *A.J.* 14.205–10.[39] Moreover, the clause "Joppa excluded" in *A.J.* 14.202 does not, in fact, constitute a prior restoration of the city to Jewish control. *A.J.* 14.202–3 deals directly with the tribute due for the city of Jerusalem and with tithes. The clause "Joppa excluded" is best understood as an exception clause, either anticipating the grant of Joppa (in *A.J.* 14.205) or presupposing an earlier grant, the terms of which are set out in *A.J.* 14.205–6.

There are close affinities between the contents of *A.J.* 14.202–10 and the fragments of the letter and decree cited in *A.J.* 14.190–95 and issued by Caesar in 47 B.C.E.: (1) John Hyrcanus II and his sons are recognized as ethnarchs of the Jews (*A.J.* 14.190, 194 = *A.J.* 14.209); (2) they are to be high priests and priests and to receive the rights dictated by Jewish laws (*A.J.* 14.194–95 = *A.J.* 14.203, 208); (3) they are to receive privileges of alliance and friendship with Rome (*A.J.* 14.194–95 = *A.J.* 14.208–9); (4) the Jews are to be free from winter quartering (*A.J.* 14.195 = *A.J.* 14.204); (5) the Jews are to be free from exactions and molestation (*A.J.* 14.195 = *A.J.* 14.204); and (6) the Jewish state is connected with Sidon (*A.J.* 14.190 = A.J. 14.203, 206). The decree in *A.J.* 14.202–10 is distinctive in its content, specifying the terms of the tribute that Hyrcanus was required to pay for the city of Jerusalem (that is, the Jewish state) and for the seaport city of Joppa (*A.J.* 14.202–3, 205–6). However, these are not new additions to Caesar's decree. Hyrcanus's right to rule the Jewish state (in Jerusalem) is recognized in *A.J.* 14.190–95. Although Joppa is not mentioned in this fragment, the grant of the city would have been part of Caesar's decree, which was ratified by the decree of the Senate (*A.J.* 14.205–6), as the exception clause in *A.J.* 14.202 suggests.[40]

(Ph.D. diss., Duke University, 1996), 49–51, followed this view. Momigliano (*Ricerche*, 14–16, 19), on the contrary, considers *A.J.* 14.205–10 to be the earlier document (a *senatus consultum* of December 47 B.C.E.) and *A.J.* 14.202–4 the later document (Caesar's decree of December–April 46 B.C.E.).

38. Such as, *A.J.* 14.205: ἡμῖν ἀρέσκει (it is our pleasure); *A.J.* 14.207: ἀρέσκει τῇ συγκλήτῳ (it is the pleasure of the Senate); and *A.J.* 14.209: ταῦτα δοκιμάζει ἡ σύγκλητος (these the Senate decrees). For similar phrases, see the *senatus consultum* concerning Stratonikeia. Sherk, *RDGE*, no. 18 = Sherk, *RGE*, 63, col. 2, line 88: ἀρέσκειν τῆι συγκλήτωι (it pleases the senate); col. 2, line 130: ἔδοξε (it has been decreed).

39. See also Pucci Ben Zeev, *Jewish Rights*, 93–94.

40. Momigliano (*Ricerche*, 14–15) notes, correctly, that *A.J.* 14.202 presupposed that Joppa had already been incorporated into the Jewish state, since the present passage deals

Schürer is right, then, to reject Mendelssohn's distinction between *A.J.* 14.190–95 and *A.J.* 14.202–4.[41] The decree in *A.J.* 14.190–95 is linked, however, to the whole of *A.J.* 14.202–210. As Pucci Ben Zeev has observed, *A.J.* 14.202–10 repeats and specifies the details of the provisions of Caesar's decree in *A.J.* 14.190–95. This procedure is characteristic of Roman *senatus consulta*.[42] The entire decree is, therefore, a fragment of the *senatus consultum* confirming the grants and provisions made by Julius Caesar in 47 B.C.E. It is the largest fragment of the *senatus consultum* issued between October and December of 47 B.C.E. at the request of Hyrcanus's envoys (*A.J.* 14.185) and belongs together with the other two fragments cited in *A.J.* 14.196–98 and *A.J.* 14.199 (see nos. 1 and 2 above).[43]

In summary:

- *A.J.* 14.190–95 is a copy of the letter sent by Julius Caesar to Sidon (*A.J.* 14.190–91), together with a copy of the decree registering his grants to Hyrcanus and the Jewish state (*A.J.* 14.192–95). Both documents date from the summer of 47 B.C.E.
- *A.J.* 14.196–98 is a fragment of the *senatus consultum* ratifying Caesar's grants and is to be dated between October and December 47 B.C.E.
- *A.J.* 14.199 is another fragment of the same *senatus consultum* of 47 B.C.E.
- *A.J.* 14.200–201 belongs to the *senatus consultum* of April 11, 44 B.C.E., and incorporates earlier decisions made by Caesar about the rebuilding of the walls of Jerusalem and related tax concessions.
- *A.J.* 14.202–10 is another large fragment of the *senatus consultum* of 47 B.C.E. that confirms Caesar's decree in the summer of the same year. It belongs to the complex of documents that Josephus cites in *A.J.* 14.190–91, 192–95, 196–98, and 199.

Scholars have observed in the past that there was no evidence that any Roman magistrate had abolished the taxes imposed on Judea by

---

with its status for taxation. He is, however, misled into considering *A.J.* 14.205–10 to be an earlier document (pp. 15–16, 19), whereas in fact the decision of the Senate in *A.J.* 14.205–6 actually ratifies Caesar's ealier grant of Joppa, which *A.J.* 14.202 presupposes.

41. See Schürer, *History*, 1:274, n. 23. See Mendelssohn, "Senati consulta romana in Iosephi Antiquitatibus," *Acta Societatis Philologicae Lipsiensis* 5 (1875): 193–99. According to Mendelssohn, *A.J.* 14.190–95 would have been issued prior to Antigonus's remonstrations before Caesar. *A.J.* 14.202–4 came after that (see *A.J.* 14.140–42; *B.J.* 1.195–98).

42. Pucci Ben Zeev, *Jewish Rights*, 95–96.

43. See also Pucci Ben Zeev, *Jewish Rights*, 96–97.

Pompey and that Caesar would be expected, in gratitute to Hyrcanus and the Jewish state, to have decreased and not increased those taxes.[44] I have argued in the previous chapter that, whatever tribute Pompey might have imposed on Judea in 63 B.C.E., Rome's tenuous hold on the territory and the concrete financial interests of Roman magistrates in Syria rendered the effective imposition and collection of such tribute impracticable. The outbreak of the civil war in 49 B.C.E. brought further disarray and exactions to Syria at the hands of Pompey and Scipio, who then was the proconsul of Syria (Caesar, *Bell Civ.* 3.3, 31).[45] Josephus's casual remark (*B.J.* 1.87) that after Pompey's death Hyrcanus and Antipater "went over to his opponent and paid court to Caesar" glosses over, first, Pompey's and Scipio's involvement with Judea[46] from 49 to 48 B.C.E. and, second, the continuation by Hyrcanus and Antipater of the *realpolitik* of the previous decade and a half. Judea was not spared the financial exactions imposed by Pompey and Scipio on the other parts of Syria. Consequently, Roman tribute in Judea meant now, as before, exactions in support of the interests of the Roman magistrates who dominated Syria.

If their historical significance is to be understood, Caesar's concessions to the Jewish state in 47 B.C.E. must be placed in this general context. From Caesar's (Rome's) point of view, his ordering of the Jewish state was more than a return to a *status quo ante* that never really existed. Caesar cannot, therefore, be said merely to have "spelled out all the regulations concerning taxation, including those previously established by other magistrates."[47] Caesar's reorganization of taxation in the Jewish state was, at least in part, an effort to establish a rational system for Judea that would be beneficial to the Romans. From the point of view of the Jewish state, a departure from the previous chaos and the arbitrary exactions would be per se favorable. The full implications of Caesar's reorganization—as far as we have knowledge of it—becomes evident, however, when it is seen not only in terms of percentages of produce paid to the Romans, but as a totality of grants and concessions.

Tribute: For the City of Jerusalem, and for the City of Joppa

Gaius Caesar, Imperator for the second time, has ruled that they shall pay a tax [tribute] for the city of Jerusalem, Joppa excluded, every year

44. See, for instance, Krebs, *Decreta*, 257–58.

45. See the passages quoted in chapter 1, p. 15, n. 23.

46. This is evident in the executions of Aristobulus II, sent from Rome by Caesar, and of his son, Alexander, by Scipio (*A.J.* 14.123–25; *B.J.* 1.183–86; Dio, *Hist.* 41.18.1)

47. Pucci Ben Zeev, *Jewish Rights*, 85.

> except in the seventh year, which they call the sabbatical year, because in this time they neither take fruit from the trees nor do they sow. And that in the second year they shall pay the tribute at Sidon, consisting of one fourth of the produce sown, and in addition, they shall also pay tithes to Hyrcanus and his sons, just as they paid to their forefathers. (*A.J.* 14.202–3 [Marcus, LCL]).[48]

> It is also our pleasure that the city of Joppa, which the Jews had held from ancient times when they made a treaty of friendship with the Romans, shall belong to them as at first; and for this city Hyrcanus, son of Alexander, and his sons shall pay tribute, collected from those who inhabit the territory, as a tax [tribute] on the land, the harbour and exports, payable at Sidon in the amount of twenty thousand six hundred and seventy-five *modii* every year except in the seventh year, which they call the sabbatical year, wherein they neither plow nor take fruit from the trees. (*A.J.* 14.205–6 [Marcus, LCL]).[49]

> Gaius Caesar, Consul for the fifth time, has decreed that these men shall receive and fortify the city of Jerusalem, and that Hyrcanus, son of Alexander, the high priest and ethnarch of the Jews, shall occupy it as he himself may choose. And that in the second year of the rent-term one *kor* shall be deducted from the tax [tribute] paid by the Jews, and no one shall make profit out of them, nor shall they pay the same tribute. (*A.J.* 14.200–201 [Marcus, LCL]).[50]

Caesar and the Senate, in the edicts with which they regulated the questions of the tribute to be paid by the Jews, treated the Jewish state as a city-state comprising two principal cities: Jerusalem and Joppa. This view of the Jewish state is evident in the official form of address in Claudius's edict of 45 C.E. (*A.J.* 20.11): "to the rulers, council, and people

---

48. *A.J.* 14.202–3: Γάιος Καῖσαρ αὐτοκράτωρ τὸ δεύτερον ἔστησε κατ' ἐνιαυτὸν ὅπως τελῶσιν ὑπὲρ τῆς Ἰεροσολυμιτῶν πόλεως, Ἰόππης ὑπεξαιρουμένης, χωρὶς τοῦ ἑβδόμου ἔτους, ὃν σαββατικὸν ἐνιαυτὸν προσαγορεύουσιν, ἐπεὶ ἐν αὐτῷ μήτε τὸν ἀπὸ τῶν δένδρων καρπὸν λαμβάνουσι μήτε σπείρουσιν. καὶ ἵνα ἐν Σιδῶνι τῷ δευτέρῳ ἔτει τὸν φόρον ἀποδιδῶσι, τὸ τέταρτον τῶν σπειρομένων πρὸς τούτοις ἔτι καὶ Ὑρκανῷ καὶ τοῖς τέκνοις αὐτου' τὰς δεκάτας τελῶσιν, ἃς ἐτέλουν καὶ τοῖς προγόνοις αὐτῶν.

49. *A.J.* 14.205–6: Ἰόππην τε πόλιν, ἣν ἀπ' ἀρχῆς ἔσχον Ἰουδαῖοι ποιούμενοι τὴν πρὸς Ῥωμαιους φιλίαν, αὐτῶν εἶναι, καθὼς καὶ τὸ πρῶτον, ἡμῖν ἀρέσκει· φόρους τε τελεῖν ὑπὲρ ταύτης τῆς πόλεως Ὑρκανὸν Ἀλεξάνδρου υἱὸν καὶ παῖδας αὐτοῦ παρὰ τῶν τὴν γῆν νεμομένων χώρας λιμένος ἐξαγωγίου κατ' ἐνιαυτὸν ἐν Σιδῶνι μοδίους δισμυρίους ἑξακοσίους ἑβδομήκοντα πέντε ὑπεξαιρουμένου τοῦ ἑβδόμου ἔτους, ὃ σαββατικὸν καλοῦσι, καθ' ὃ οὔτε ἀροῦσιν οὔτε τὸν ἀπὸ τῶν δένδρων καρπὸν λαμβάνουσιν.

50. *A.J.* 14.200–201: Γάιος Καῖσαρ ὕπατος τὸ πέμπτον ἔκρινε τούτους ἔχειν καὶ τειχίσαι τὴν Ἰεροσολυμιτῶν πόλιν, καὶ κατέχειν αὐτὴν Ὑρκανὸν Ἀλεξάνδρου ἀρχιερέα Ἰουδαίων καὶ ἐθνάρχην ὡς ἂν αὐτὸς προαιρῆται. ὅπως τε Ἰουδαίοις ἐν τῷ δευτέρῳ τῆς μισθώσεως ἔτει τῆς προσόδου κόρον ὑπεξέλωνται καὶ μήτε ἐργολαβῶσί τινες μήτε φόρους τοὺς αὐτοὺς τελῶσιν.

of Jerusalem and the whole nation of the Jews . . . ."[51] As Victor Tcherikover has rightly argued, however, Jerusalem was not considered a *polis* in a legal sense.[52] Ruling over the whole nation, Jerusalem stood for "the Jewish nation." Hence, Josephus sometimes uses "Jerusalem" synecdochically to mean "Judea," that is, the Jewish state, as he does in *A.J.* 14.74 when he states that Pompey "made Jerusalem tributary." The two cities, Jerusalem and Joppa, are explicitly granted to Hyrcanus and the Jews in the edicts (*A.J.* 14.200, 205). It is in relation to the grants of the cities that Caesar and the Senate imposed tribute upon Hyrcanus. The "tribute for the city of Jerusalem," therefore, as I shall argue presently, is the tribute imposed on Hyrcanus for the grant of the Jewish state (*A.J.* 14.143–44, 191, 194, 196, 199, 200; *B.J.* 1.199–200). Furthermore, since it was captured and resettled by Simon, Joppa had been an important seaport for the Jewish state and crucial to its economy.[53] Momigliano notes correctly that Caesar, by the gift of the city, understood that the Jewish state could not exist without an opening to the sea.[54] Joppa's importance as a seaport was envisaged by Caesar. This is evident from the fact that the tribute that Caesar demanded for the city was to be paid for its "land, the harbour and exports" (*A.J.* 14.206).[55]

Since several aspects of Momigliano's interpretations of these decrees, adopted by Schalit and popularized in numerous monographs,[56] have become scholarly orthodoxy, I shall begin with a discussion of his position. Momigliano maintains that in *A.J.* 14.202–3 Caesar made three demands. First, everyone, excluding the inhabitants of Joppa, should pay a tax each year, except the sabbatical year, for the city of Jerusalem ("un tributo ὑπὲρ τῆς Ἱεροσολυμιτῶν πόλεως"). This tax would be paid to the Jewish authorities in Jerusalem and would be used to reconstruct and to

---

51. F.-M. Abel (*Géographie de la Palestine* [2 vols.; Paris: J. Gabalda, 1933, 1938], 2:152) and others on the basis of this edict think that Jerusalem was to Judea what the Hellenistic cities were to their surrounding territories. See Victor A. Tcherikover, "Was Jerusalem a Polis?" *IEJ* 14 (1964): 61–63.

52. See Tcherikover, "Jerusalem," 65–78.

53. P. Richardson, *Herod*, 91. See below.

54. Momigliano, *Ricerche*, 14.

55. Thus also the earlier *senatus consultum*, inserted by Josephus in a decree of Pergamum (*A.J.* 14.249–50): "and that it shall be lawful for them to export goods from their harbours and that no king or people exporting goods from the territory of the Jews or from their harbours shall be untaxed except only Ptolemy, king of Alexandria . . . and that the garrison in Joppa shall be expelled, as they have requested." See p. 69 below.

56. See, for instance, Smallwood, *Jews under Roman Rule*, 40–41; Gildas Hamel, *Poverty and Charity in Roman Palestine: First Three Centuries C.E.* (Berkeley: University of California Press, 1990), 144–46; David A. Fiensy, *The Social History of Palestine in the Herodian Period: The Land is Mine* (Lewiston, N.Y.: Edwin Mellen, 1991), 99–100; Jack Pastor, *Land and Economy in Ancient Palestine* (London: Routledge, 1997), 94–96; R. A. Horsley, *Archaeology*, 78.

maintain the city and the temple. It would restore the funds extracted by Crassus from the temple. Second, all should pay an annual tribute consisting of one-quarter of produce to the Romans biannually, that is, one-eighth of the annual produce, to be delivered to the seaport at Sidon. Third, the traditional tithe of 10 percent of the annual produce was to be paid to the priestly class.[57]

Of the inhabitants of Joppa, the *senatus consultum* in *A.J.* 14.206 required that they be exempt from the said tax "for the city of Jerusalem." This exemption derived from their tax payment for their own city, since ὑπὲρ ταύτης τῆς πόλεως in *A.J.* 14.206 corresponds to ὑπὲρ τῆς Ἱεροσολυμιτῶν πόλεως in *A.J.* 14.202.[58] Momigliano considers this tax for the city of Joppa a normal tax ("un φόρος normale") parallel to the tax paid by the inhabitants of the rest of Judea to Hyrcanus "for the city of Jerusalem." This tax for the maintenance and administration of the city of Joppa was raised by Hyrcanus and his sons from the inhabitants of the territory. Moreover, the inhabitants of Joppa paid a special tribute ("un φόρος speciale") derived from the exports (and imports) from Joppa by land or by sea (χώρας καὶ λιμένος ἐξαγωγίου), that is, custom duties ("i dazi"). This tribute was paid to the Romans as compensation for the duties on the goods that entered and left the port at Joppa. These tolls, until then, had gone directly or indirectly to the Romans, ever since the city had been absorbed into the province of Syria by Pompey in 63 B.C.E. Unlike the tribute for Jerusalem, the tribute for Joppa was a fixed amount at 20,675 *modii* (of produce) to be delivered annually to the port at Sidon.[59] According to Momigliano, therefore, the inhabitants of Joppa, exempt from the tax ὑπὲρ τῆς Ἱεροσολυμιτῶν πόλεως ("for the city of Jerusalem"), were, however, exempt neither from the habitual tribute ("abituale φόρος") of the one-eighth of the annual produce nor from the 10 percent tithe.[60]

Hence, concludes Momigliano, the provision of the *senatus consultum* in *A.J.* 14.206 and the terms set by Caesar in the decree of *A.J.* 14.202 were in perfect harmony. In this manner, he thinks, the emendation proposed by Schürer to the Greek text of *A.J.* 14.202, on the basis of the Latin text and according to the interpretation of the passage by both Mommsen and Mendelssohn, is invalidated.[61]

---

57. Momigliano, *Ricerche*, 21.

58. Ibid.

59. Ibid., 21–23.

60. Ibid., 22.

61. The Latin text of the passage in *A.J.* 14.202 reads, ut per singulos annos Ioppenses tributa Hierosolymorum civitati praestent excepto septimo anno ("the inhabitants of Joppa shall pay tribute to the city of Jerusalem except in the seventh year"). Discussing the "local public burdens" borne by those living in the Roman provinces, Theodor Mommsen (*The History of Rome* [trans. William P. Dickson; 5 vols; Glencoe, Ill.: Free Press, 1957], 4:162, n. 1)

Tribute for the City of Joppa

Momigliano certainly is correct to recognize the correlation between ὑπὲρ ταύτης τῆς πόλεως in *A.J.* 14.206 and ὑπὲρ τῆς Ἱεροσολυμιτῶν πόλεως in *A.J.* 14.202. He is, therefore, also justified in rejecting Schürer's reading of *A.J.* 14.202, which seems to require that the inhabitants of Joppa pay taxes to the inhabitants of Jerusalem.[62] In the *senatus consultum* the two cities are parallel to each other: *A.J.* 14.202–3 specifies the tribute "for the city of Jerusalem," distinguishing it from the tribute for the city of Joppa and *A.J.* 14.205–6 lays out the conditions for the grant of the seaport city.[63]

Failing to recognize the consequences of this correlation between the two cities, Momigliano first creates a tax for the maintenance of the city of Jerusalem out of *A.J.* 14.202. The tax "for the city of Jerusalem" is in fact the tribute that the Jews were to deliver at Sidon every two years as the decree stipulates in *A.J.* 14.203. Momigliano is forced, as a result, also to invent a tax for Joppa[64] as a parallel to his so-called "tax for the city of

---

writes, "For example, in Judaea the town of Joppa paid 26,075 [*sic*] *modii* of corn, the other Jews the tenth sheaf to the native princes; to which fell to be added the temple-tribute and the payment to Sidon destined for the Romans." According to Mendelssohn ("Senati Consuta," 199), Caesar decreed ut et ipsa stipendia a Iudaeis inde a Pompeio pendi solita magnopere levaret et partem stipendiorum quae Iopenses a Pompeio Syriae provinciae adiecti . . . Romanis praestabant, Iudaeis concederet. See also p. 201. Emil Schürer (*Geschichte des jüdischen Volkes im Zeitalter Jesu Christi* [2 vols; Leipzig: J. C. Hinrichs, 1901], 1:347, n. 25), therefore, proposes the reading for the Greek text: ὅπως τελῶσιν ὑπὲρ τῆς Ἱεροσολυμιτῶν πόλεως Ἰοπηνοι, ὑπεξαιρουμένου τοῦ ἑβδόμου ἔτους. The editors of the new English edition of Schürer (*History*, 1:274, n. 24) seem to have done away with Schürer's original conjecture, but remain committed to its substance. They comment on the passage: "If it is correct that the commencement of xiv 10, 6 (202–4) belongs to a decree of 47 B.C., part of the taxes of Joppa must already have been ceded to the Jews (i.e. we have to restore from the old Latin text, ἔτους)." There seems to be no reason to restore the word ἔτους in this case, unless it is a (truncated) part of the Greek conjecture from the German edition.

62. See preceding note.

63. Schalit (*König Herodes*, 778–80) proposes the following emendation of *A.J.* 14.202: "das Wort χωρίς gehört vor Ἰόππης, während ὑπεξαιρουμένης, emendiert in ὑπεξαιρουμένου, zu τοῦ ἑβδόμου ἔτους zu setzen ist." This emendation is superfluous, no less because the verb ὑπεξαιρέω has the meanings, among others, "to except" and "to exclude." It does not differ so significantly in meaning from the adverb χωρίς as to warrant the positions of the two words being exchanged as Schalit proposes. Therefore, Ralph Marcus commits no gross contradiction ("krassen Widerspruch"), as Schalit charges, in translating the received Greek text of *A.J.* 14.202 as "Joppa excluded," while he at the same time (correctly) accepts Viereck's emendation in *A.J.* 14.206 of ἔχειν to τελεῖν and translates this passage: "and for this city [i.e., Joppa] Hyrcanus, son of Alexander, and his sons shall pay tribute." See Ralph Marcus, trans., *Josephus: Jewish Antiquities, Books XII-XIV* (ed. and trans. H. St. J. Thackeray et al.; vol. 7 of *Josephus*; LCL; Cambridge, Mass.: Harvard University Press, 1936), 556 and nn. 6, 7.

64. Niese leaves the sentence in *A.J.* 14.206 without a verb. Momigliano (*Ricerche*,

Jerusalem." Nevertheless, again, the only tax for Joppa in the decree, as Momigliano recognizes, is a tribute to be paid to Rome. Thus, when we eliminate these extra taxes, the terms of the tax regulations of the *senatus consultum* in *A.J.* 14.202–3, 205–6 are as follows:

1. Hyrcanus and his sons shall pay tribute for the city of Jerusalem (that is, the Jewish state) previously granted to them (*A.J.* 14.202).
2. This tribute excludes the tribute due for the city of Joppa (*A.J.* 14.202).
3. The tribute for the city of Jerusalem (that is, the Jewish state), in accordance with its own stipulations, shall be delivered at Sidon.
4. The Jews shall receive a grant of the city of Joppa (*A.J.* 14.205).
5. For this city, Hyrcanus and his sons shall pay[65] tribute (*A.J.* 14.206).
6. This tribute for the city of Joppa, in accordance with its own stipulations, shall also be delivered at Sidon (*A.J.* 14.206).
7. The Jews shall pay tithes to the priestly class.[66]

We should note also at this point that the taxable subjects in *A.J.* 14.206 are "Hyrcanus, son of Alexander, and his sons." The terms here are comparable to those imposed by Antiochus Sidetes on John Hyrcanus I for the seaport city (*A.J.* 13.246).[67] Although the fragmentary state of the decree does not permit the identification of the subject referred to as "they" in *A.J.* 14.202–3, it may be assumed that Hyrcanus and his sons are spoken of here as well. Jerusalem (the Jewish state) is granted to Hyrcanus to "occupy it as he himself may choose" (*A.J.* 14.200, 194, 196, 199), although the language of the various grants in the Roman decrees vacillates between Hyrcanus and "the Jews."[68] Moreover, as Momigliano and generations of scholars after him have underscored,[69] it was to Hyrcanus that Caesar and the Senate entrusted the collection and payment of the tribute due to Rome.[70]

21–22), following Mendelssohn's conjecture, reads it with the verb ἔχειν (thus: φόρους τε ὑπὲρ ταύτης τῆς πόλεως Ὑρκανὸν Ἀλεξάνδρου υἱὸν καὶ παῖδας αὐτου <ἔχειν> παρὰ τῶν τὴν γῆν νεμομένων) according to Codex Vaticanus gr. no. 147 and considers this a separate clause from what follows, which is a reference to a tribute to Rome. This reading would involve an extensive emendation of the text and, as A. H. M. Jones points out, would result in a rather curious tax arrangement. See Jones, "Review," 228.

65. I accept the reading τελεῖν in lieu of ἔχειν in *A.J.* 14.206; see n. 63 above.

66. Theodor Mommsen (*History*, 4:162, n. 1), is incorrect in his claim that tithes were to be paid "to the native princes." See n. 61 above.

67. See pp. 68–69 below and Momigliano, *Ricerche*, 22.

68. See n. 77 below.

69. Momigliano, *Ricerche*, 24–27.

70. See pp. 53–57 below.

The *senatus consultum* stipulates that, for Joppa, Hyrcanus should pay 20,670 *modii* (of grain) every year at the neighboring port of Sidon, except in the sabbatical year. This tribute, "on the land, the harbour and exports" (*A.J.* 14.206), is best seen as a compensation to the Romans for the loss of the custom duties (*portoria*) from the seaport at Joppa and the overland trade route,[71] which they had collected since 63 B.C.E., when Joppa was made part of the province of Syria by Pompey.[72] Joppa and the neighboring territories would then have entered into the emerging network of Rome's toll collection posts in Syria, inherited in part from the Seleucid kings.[73] The *senatus consultum* further indicates that the tribute for Joppa was to be raised from those who occupied the territory (παρὰ τῶν τὴν γῆν νεμομένων [*A.J.* 14.206]). Rome usually allowed the cities and the allied states in the provinces to set up their toll stations and collect dues.[74] The best-known example of this policy is the laws on toll collection for the administration of the city of Palmyra.[75] Hyrcanus and the Jewish state would have benefited from this Roman policy.[76] The notice in *A.J.* 14.206

71. See pp. 71–75 below. Similar language occurs in the *senatus consultum* of 73 B.C.E., which resolved the dispute between the *publicani* and the people of Oropos. Sulla is said "to have consecrated of the city and the land and harbors of Oropos all revenues . . ." (καθιερωκέναι τῆς πόλεως καὶ τῆς χώρας λιμένων τε τῶν Ὠρωπίων τὰς προσόδους ἁπάσας . . .)" to the god Amphiaraos. Sherk, *RDGE*, no. 23, lines 45–47 = Sherk, *RGE*, no. 70, lines 45–47.

72. Momigliano, *Ricerche*, 22–23; Schalit, *König Herodes*, 780. Smallwood (*Jews under Roman Rule*, 40) claims that Hyrcanus paid "a tax fixed at 20,675 *modii* of wheat . . . as well as handing over the harbour and export dues charged there." She does not say how she comes to this conclusion, since the text of the edict does not imply it and she, quite rightly, observes that Hyrcanus paid the stipulated tribute "in return for the recovery of an outlet to the sea." Jones had, earlier, proposed an emendation of the text of *A.J.* 14.206 from παρὰ τῶν τὴν γῆν νεμομένων χώρας [καί] λιμένος ἐξαγωγίου to χωρίς λιμένος ἐξαγωγίου and concluded: "Hyrcanus then paid a fixed annual tribute of wheat for Joppa, apart from (i.e. in addition to) the export dues of Joppa; perhaps he drew the import dues himself." See Jones, "Review," 229; and Smallwood, *Jews under Roman Rule*, 41, n. 62.

73. See Siegfried J. de Laet, *Portorium: études sur l'organisation douanière chez les Romains, surtout a l'époque du haut-empire* (Brugge: De Tempel, 1949), 87–88, 339.

74. The *lex Antonia* states for the city of Termessus in Pisidia: "Whatever law for custom duties on (trade by) land and sea the citizens of Termessus Maior in Pisidia have established to be collected within their own borders, that shall be the law for collecting those customs duties, provided that no duty is collected from those who for the public revenues of the Roman People will hold the contracts." Sherk, *RGE*, no. 72, lines 31–35 = Hermannus Dessau, ed., *ILS* (3 vols; Berlin: Weidmanns, 1892–1916), no. 38, lines 31–35. See Livy, 38.44.

75. See J.-B. Chabot, ed. and trans., *CIS* (Paris: Republicae Typographeus, 1926), 2.3, no. 3913; J.-B. Chabot, ed. and trans., *Choix d'inscriptions de Palmyre* (Paris: Imprimerie Nationale, 1922); R. Cagnat, ed., *IGRR* (Paris: Ernest Leroux, 1906; repr., Rome: L'Erma di Bretschneider, 1964), no. 1056; G. A. Cooke, *A Text-Book of North-Semitic Inscriptions* (Oxford: Clarendon, 1903), no. 147; J. F. Matthews, "The Tax Law of Palmyra: Evidence for Economic History in a City of the Roman East," *JRS* 64 (1984): 157–80.

76. The editors of the new English edition of Schürer (*History*, 1:274, n. 24) are, in this

does not reveal, however, how Hyrcanus might have raised the tribute he was required to pay to the Romans. Read together with what follows (παρὰ τῶν τὴν γῆν νεμομένων χώρας λιμένος ἐξαγωγίου [*A.J.* 14.206]), the whole obscure phrase can be taken to suggest nothing more than a close connection between the tribute paid by Hyrcanus and the grant of both the seaport and the surrounding country. Attempts to extract more information from the text, especially by way of emendations, have proven to be futile.

The tribute due each year was set at a fixed amount, in contrast to the variable tribute "for the city of Jerusalem." We can only speculate about the reasons why Caesar and the Senate opted for this system. One such reason might be that, since the Romans previously had some experience collecting tolls from the territory, they could more precisely determine its income in duties. However, since the *senatus consultum* specifies neither how Hyrcanus was to raise the tribute nor how much he was to charge in tolls and direct taxes from the territory, it is unlikely that the fixed sum he paid to the Romans represented the sum total of the duties that could be collected at the port and trade route. We are equally ignorant about the other taxes paid by the inhabitants of Joppa to Hyrcanus. Whatever Hyrcanus raised in excess went to him and the Jewish state.

Tribute for the City of Jerusalem

For the rest of the Jewish state the *senatus consultum* states: "Gaius Caesar . . . ruled that they shall pay tribute for the city of Jerusalem . . . every year except in the seventh year . . . . And that in the second year they shall deliver the tribute at Sidon, consisting of one-fourth of the produce sown . . . ." (my translation).[77] The parallel between this tribute and the one

respect, correct in their claim that "part of the taxes of Joppa must already have been ceded to the Jews" by Caesar in 47 B.C.E. See n. 61 above.

77. Sanders (*Judaism*, 515, n. 52), expressing doubts about *A.J.* 14.203, observed that, first, this text was lacking in the Latin; second, "*kai hina* does not follow grammatically"; and, third, the passage seemed to require a direct payment of the tribute at Sidon by farmers, without the mediation of the Jewish authorities. Josephus's text of the *senatus consultum* in *A.J.* 14.202–10 is certainly too fragmentary and conjectural to permit a valid argument on the basis of its grammatical structure. I suggest, nonetheless, that the three main clauses in *A.J.* 14.202–4 are: ἔστησε . . . ὅπως τελῶσιν . . . (202), καὶ ἵνα . . . ἀποδιδῶσι . . . (203), καὶ ὅπως μηδεὶς . . . ἀνιστῇ (204). The final conjunctions ὅπως and ἵνα are interchangeable, and they are used interchangeably in other successive clauses of the edicts that Josephus cites in *A.J.* 14. For instance, in 14.242 we have: ἵνα. . . ἐξῇ . . ., ὅπως τε μηδεὶς . . . ἐπιτάσσῃ; and in 14.249–50: ἐδογμάτισεν . . . ὅπως μηδὲν ἀδικῇ . . . , ὅπως τε . . . ἀποδωθῇ . . ., ἵνα τε μηδεὶς . . . ᾖ. . . . A similar construction is found, for example, in the *senatus consultum* for Stratonikeia (Sherk, *RDGE*, no. 18, lines 60–63): ὅπως ἡ σ[ύγ]κλ[ητος . . . δῶι, ἵνα φρο[ντίσ]ηι καὶ . . . ποιήσηται, ὅπως . . .

imposed upon Hyrcanus for Joppa is reinforced by the requirement that both be paid at Sidon. The crux of the problem is determining how much Hyrcanus paid in tribute for the Jewish state. The answer lies in the notoriously difficult expression τῷ δευτέρῳ ἔτει in *A.J.* 14.203. Two possible meanings have been proposed for the term: (1) "the year after the sabbatical year,"[78] and (2) "every two years."[79]

It is conceivable that *A.J.* 14.203, continuing to deal with the preceding provisions for the sabbatical year (*A.J.* 14.202), specifies the amount to be paid in the following year. In this event the phrase τῷ δευτέρῳ ἔτει would mean "in the next year," that is, after the sabbatical year, as Schalit argues.[80] Schalit further speculates that the tribute for the year after the sabbatical year was higher than what was paid in the following five years. The rate of one-quarter of the produce in the year following the sabbatical year, in his view, was to compensate for the losses incurred by the exclusion of the sabbatical year. In the other years the Jews paid about a fifth of their produce, which was a relief in comparison to the third demanded by the Seleucids.[81] While I concede that the expression as it stands in *A.J.* 14.203 could be a reference to the year following the sabbatical year, Schalit's argument in favor of this meaning is on the whole somewhat contrived. Schalit does not say why Caesar and the Senate would have insisted on recovering the "losses" incurred by the exclusion of the sabbatical year, when this year was considered exempt from tribute. Besides, the only figures given by the decree are the 25 percent in *A.J.*

φροντισηι. The verb ἵστημι is used in the *senatus consultum* concerning Mytilene (Sherk, *RDGE*, n. 26, col. c, line 23) and in Octavian's letter concerning Seleucus (Sherk, *RDGE*, no. 58, line 68). ἔστησε is the Greek equivalent of the Latin *constituit* (Caesar, *Bell. civ.* 3.1) or *statuit* (*Bell. Alex.* 65.4). See Pucci Ben Zeev, *Jewish Rights*, 84. The decision of the Senate in many *senatus consulta* preserved in Greek are introduced by the conjunction ὅπως. See the instances cited above and others in Pucci Ben Zeev, *Jewish Rights*, 57. There is a noteworthy tension created by an interplay of representation in *A.J.* 14.202–10 as the Senate vacillates between Hyrcanus and "the Jews." This interplay is explicit in 14.205–6: "the city of Joppa, which the Jews had held from ancient times . . . shall belong to them . . .; and for this city Hyrcanus . . . shall pay tribute." Even though Hyrcanus is granted the Jewish state and Joppa, and he is the direct taxable subject, responsible for raising and delivering the tribute, it is still to "the Jews" that the country belongs and they who collectively must pay the tribute.

78. Schalit, *König Herodes*, 780.

79. Momigliano, *Ricerche*, 21.

80. Schalit, *König Herodes*, 780: "δεύτερος hat manchmal die Bedeutung 'der nächste' im Hinblick auf die Zeit."

81. Schalit, *König Herodes*, 780–81; see 1 Macc 10:30. Hamel (*Poverty and Charity*, 146), depending on Schalit's theory, claims that "the expression must simply refer to the year following the sabbatical year." He does not bother to show, however, from where this simple necessity arises. He is also dismissive of Schalit's suggestion that the quota for his year was higher than in the other five years.

14.203. The 20 percent conjectured by Schalit for the other five years of the cycle is unsupported by any evidence. Schalit's conjecture is called for by his theory, because it is extremely unlikely that the Senate would have produced a tax law that specified, and in very vague terms, only the amount to be paid for one year in a seven-year cycle.

The proposal that the Senate's clause τῷ δευτέρῳ ἔτει means "every two years" has in its favor, first, the merit of simplicity and, second, the fact that it offers the best interpretation of the text. Jones, like Momigliano, notes the connection between τῷ δευτέρῳ ἔτει in *A.J.* 14.203 and ἐν τῷ δευτέρῳ τῆς μισθώσεως ἔτει in the fragmentary decree cited in *A.J.* 14.201.[82] Here it is clear that τῷ δευτέρῳ ἔτει means "[in] the second year," not "[in] the next year," and its reference is not a (preceding) sabbatical year, but the years of the tax cycle. Jones, however, rejects the meaning "every two years" for *A.J.* 14.203 on the grounds that this is a "surely impossible" translation of the term [ἐν] τῷ δευτέρῳ ἔτει τῆς μισθώσεως, which, in his view, is how the full expression ought to be understood. Assuming the Roman *lustrum* of a five-year tax cycle, he figures that the Jewish state was to pay tribute at a quota of a twentieth, because "the Jews were at this time a favoured community."[83]

The *lustrum*, connected with the census and taxation in Rome during the Republic, was the five-year term for which the *publicani* were awarded contracts by the censors in Rome to collect the various forms of taxes in the provinces.[84] Jones's 5 percent quota assumes that the Jews were required to pay tribute once, that is, 25 percent in the second year of the five-year cycle. There are insurmountable problems with this proposal, even though it is indeed attractive. First, it is not clear where Jones would fit Caesar's exemption of the sabbatical year into the *lustrum*. Second, it must be noted that the *lustrum* governed contracts awarded to the *societates publicanorum* to raise taxes. Caesar's tax regulation eliminated the mediation of the *publicani* in Judea, as I shall reemphasize below. There is no reason to assume that this regulation operated according to the timetable of those contracts.

Rome's grant of exemption for the sabbatical year establishes a particular tax cycle for the Jewish state consisting of six taxable years and

---

82. Momigliano, *Ricerche*, 24; Jones, "Review," 229. Schalit (*König Herodes*, 780) rejects this connection, declaring that no sense can be made of *A.J.* 14.201.

83. Jones, "Review," 229.

84. See Cicero, *Att.* 6.2; *Fam.* 2.13.4; Theodor Mommsen and Paul Krueger, eds., *The Digest of Justinian* (trans. Alan Watson; 4 vols.; Philadelphia: University of Pennsylvania Press, 1985), no. 49.14.3.6; Lintott, *Imperium Romanum*, 87–90. The tax contract is referred to as τῆς μισθώσεως νόμος in the *senatus consultum* concerning the dispute between the people of Oropos and the *publicani*. Sherk, *RDGE*, no. 23, lines 19, 25, 33, 35, 66 = Sherk, *RGE*, no. 70, lines 19, 25, 33, 35, 66.

recommencing at the end of each sabbatical year. If, as I have argued above, *A.J.* 14.200–201 is a later modification (in 44 B.C.E. or earlier) of the grants ratified in *A.J.* 14.202–10, then the expression ἐν τῷ δευτέρῳ τῆς μισθώσεως ἔτει should be seen as a reference to this cycle, brought into effect by the grants of 47 B.C.E. This would not mean, however, that τῷ δευτέρῳ ἔτει in *A.J.* 14.203 ought to be supplied with τῆς μισθώσεως, as Jones suggests, since *A.J.* 14.202–3 could be a description of the system in action. In support of this view, I observe that the Senate seems to have dealt with the cycle in two segments: (1) annual *payment* (τελῶσιν) of tribute, with the exemption of the sabbatical year (*A.J.* 14.202), and (2) *delivery* (ἀποδιδῶσι) of the tribute at Sidon τῷ δευτέρῳ ἔτει (*A.J.* 4.203).[85] In this event, τῷ δευτέρῳ ἔτει is an indication of how often the Romans expected to receive the tribute from the Jewish state, which does not coincide with the regularity of actual payment. In much the same way, in the *lustrum*, payment was not made to the *publicani* only at the end of the five-year cycle, although it was likely that Rome received from the tax companies the taxes they had collected at the end of the contract cycle.[86]

Thus, it is in my view most likely that Caesar's regulation of 47 B.C.E. stipulated that Hyrcanus deliver to the Romans "every two years," at the port at Sidon, the tribute he had collected from the Jewish state. The timetable ἐν Σιδῶνι τῷ δευτέρῳ ἔτει in *A.J.* 14.203 therefore stands in apposition to κατ᾽ ἐνιαυτὸν ἐν Σιδῶνι in *A.J.* 14.206. Hyrcanus delivered at Sidon "every year" (compensation for) the tolls and dues he raised—every day—at Joppa, whereas "every two years" at Sidon he delivered the tribute he raised in the Jewish state. During the seven-year cycle Hyrcanus would then be expected to render in Sidon one-quarter of the produce of his territory, in the second, fourth, and sixth years.

One final problem remains for which there is no easy solution. If Hyrcanus delivered a tribute consisting of 25 percent of produce at two-year intervals to the Roman authorities in Sidon, it may be assumed that this amount constituted the tribute for the previous and the current years. This would be 12.5 percent of the yearly produce, as Momigliano already surmised.[87] Hyrcanus either collected 25 percent of the produce for the second, fourth, and sixth years of the seven-year cycle (that is, in the years when he made deliveries at Sidon) or he may have demanded that the Jews pay 12.5 percent annually (except the seventh year), as *A.J.* 14.202 seems to suggest. It is impossible to determine which of the two systems he operated.

85. Marcus obscures this difference by translating both verbs as "they shall pay" in the LCL edition of the text.

86. Lintott, *Imperium Romanum*, 89–90.

87. Momigliano, *Ricerche*, 21.

Further Reductions, Collection

The fragment quoted in *A.J.* 14.201 stipulates: "And that in the second year of the rent-term one *kor* shall be deducted from the tax [tribute] paid by the Jews, and no one shall make profit out of them, nor shall they pay the same tribute."

The expression ἐν τῷ δευτέρῳ τῆς μισθώσεως ἔτει ("in the second year of the rent-term") is a reference to the second year in the seven-year cycle, that is, the years Hyrcanus actually was required to make payments to the Romans in Sidon. The fact that the decree grants a reduction in tribute for those years reinforces the possibility that Hyrcanus was expected to collect the stipulated 25 percent in the year of delivery. The point of *what* Hyrcanus actually collected and *when* might be entirely moot, however, since—as I shall note presently—tribute to Rome would have been paid out of Hyrcanus's total income from Judea. Moreover, Caesar and the Senate left it to Hyrcanus to determine what constituted "one-fourth of the produce sown."

The decree itself dates from 44 B.C.E., as I have argued, and is connected with the permission granted in 47 B.C.E. to rebuild the walls of Jerusalem. Momigliano is probably right in linking the reduction in tribute to the cost of the project.[88] In any case, the completion of the task could have served as an occasion for the Jews to ask for further concessions from Caesar, sometime after 47 B.C.E.

The fragmentary state of *A.J.* 14.200–201 does not permit us to know exactly of what amount the reduction in tribute consisted. A reduction of a *kor* (that is, about 360 litres) from the total volume of grain delivered by Hyrcanus to the Romans in Sidon for the Jewish state would have been ridiculously insignificant. The annual tribute for Joppa alone stood at 20,675 *modii* (one *modius* = about 8.75 litres). Either something is missing from the text or the deduction was applied to the individual taxpayer's return, or both. In support of the former possibility, it should be noted that the verb is in the plural (ὅπως . . . τῆς προσόδου κόρον ὑπεξέλωνται). A number may have fallen out before the word κόρον, which is the subject of ὑπεξέλωνται, hence: ". . . *kor* shall be deducted."[89] In the latter case, even the 360 litres would appear to be no less significant than a $550 per capita tax deduction in modern-day America for a family with an annual income of $200,000 (to say nothing of a family with an income of $20,000).

---

88. Ibid., 16, 23.

89. Lowthius suggested the reading κόρους (plural). The meaning of the text is plural, although *kor* might have been used invariably in the Hebrew text of the original request by the Jews. Pucci Ben Zeev, *Jewish Rights*, 77.

Whatever the case may be, we do not know how much Caesar demanded in the end from Judea. The impression, however, is clearly that he tended to demand less, not more.

The claim that Caesar asked for less, rather than more, from the Jewish state is strengthened when we consider that in the case of direct taxation he also did not specify the method of collection. The fixed amount demanded for Joppa assured that the Romans received their cut of the income from custom dues collected in the area. For direct taxes, Caesar demanded a percentage of the annual produce, relative to the yearly harvest. Judea was required, in other words, to pay a *decumae*, the land tax paid in a percentage ("tithe") of the annual produce.

Cicero classified, on the basis of the methods of collection, the direct taxes imposed on the provinces in his time. He divided them into two categories: (1) the *vectigal certum*, which he called *stipendium*, and (2) the *censoria locatio* (*2 Verr.* 3.6.12–15).[90] He gave the taxes in Spain and Africa as instances of the "fixed form" of taxes (*stipendium*). These were more or less regular tributes that originally had been, as he terms them, "a reward for victory and a penalty of defeat" (*2 Verr.* 3.6.12). These taxes were collected through a variety of systems, by the governors, quaestors, or local authorities. C. Gracchus's law of 123 B.C.E. gave the collection of direct tribute in Asia to the *societates publicanorum*, who bid for and bought the right to collect it from the censors in Rome. The province of Asia is the sole example of the *censoria locatio*, that is, of direct taxes contracted out by the censors in Rome. The tribute in Asia, as stated in the speech attributed to Antony cited below, was a *decumae*, a variable percentage of the annual produce. The tribute in Sicily was also a *decumae*; however, its collection was governed by the *Lex Hieronica*. This was a code that probably originated from the Hellenistic rulers of Syracuse and its allied territories, but had been extended by Rome to the rest of Sicily.[91] The right to collect these tithes was sold to private contractors (*decumani*) by the Roman quaestors in Sicily.[92]

---

90. See also chapter 5 below.

91. See Jérôme Carcopino, *La loi de Hiéron et les Romains* (Paris: E. de Boccard, 1914), 77–107; R. T. Pritchard, "Cicero and the *Lex Hieronica*," *Historia* 19 (1970): 352–68; idem, "Gaius Verres and the Sicilian Farmers," *Historia* 20 (1971): 229–38; J. S. Richardson, "The Administration of the Empire," in *CAH*, vol. 9, *The Last Age of the Roman Republic, 146–43 B.C.* (ed. J. A. Crook et al.; 2nd ed.; Cambridge: Cambridge University Press, 1994), 569, 586–87; Lintott, *Imperium Romanum*, 74–76.

92. Except in 75 B.C.E., when only the contracts for grain were awarded in Sicily, while those for other produce were sold in Rome by consuls (there being no censors then). See Cicero *2 Verr.* 3.6.13; 7.18–19; 33.77; 40.90–91. The city also could play a role in collecting the taxes (*2 Verr.* 3.13.34, 29.70–30.71; 36.83); Lintott, *Imperium Romanum*, 75; Jones, *Roman Economy*, 162–63.

Asia and Sicily are the only two available examples of the systems of collection in the provinces during the Republic and early Principate. Asia differed from Sicily in that in Asia the *publicani*, having bought the contract in Rome, were directly responsible for collection through their agents. In contrast, the local contractors collected the taxes from the farmers in Sicily. There actually is little information about how the *censoria locatio* worked in Asia, apart from the fact that the tax companies bid for and bought, in Rome, the contracts to collect the taxes. The *pactiones* mentioned in Cicero's province of Cilicia might be a subcategory of the system in Asia. Local communities negotiated in advance with the *publicani* the amounts to be paid and then farmed out the right of collection to local contractors. Since Cicero speaks of analogous arrangements between cities and the *publicani* (*Att.* 5.14.1; 6.1.16), it is likely, as Lintott suggests, that this would have been the most widely used system of collection for direct taxes in the eastern provinces.[93] The *publicani* would have received a five-year (*lustrum*) contract to collect the lump sums from the cities. Nevertheless, opinion is divided on whether such contracts were let out in Rome or in the provinces by the Roman governors and their quaestors.[94]

Much more is known, thanks to Cicero's prosecution of Verres, about the system of collection in Sicily. Lintott contends that, although this system was unique, some of its elements were analogous to what was done elsewhere in the provinces.[95] Farmers made a declaration (*professio*) on the land sown. The contractors calculated, on the basis of the declarations and the knowledge of the past yields of the various districts, the taxes for the year and made bids for collection (Cicero, *2 Verr.* 3.29.70–30.72).[96] Afterwards, the collectors contracted (in a *pactio*) with the cultivator at the threshing floor for the actual amount due (*2 Verr.* 3.14.35–36). The passages in Cicero indicate that an administrative charge of 10 percent of the

---

93. Lintott, *Imperium Romanum*, 77–78. Lintott points to the general silence about the existence of any other eastern province with a system like the one in Asia during Caesar's dictatorship.

94. Jones, Badian, and Sherwin-White think that the *censoria locatio* in Asia was extended to the other eastern provinces of (Cilicia), Bithynia, and Syria (see below). According to Badian, however, in the provinces other than Asia and Sicily the contracts were between the cities and the *publicani* under the governor's supervision. In Sherwin-White's view, the governor sold the contracts commune by commune. Lintott is, on the whole, undecided. Badian, *Publicans and Sinners*, 79–80; Sherwin-White, "Lucullus, Pompey," 270; Lintott, *Imperium Romanum*, 77.

95. Lintott, *Imperium Romanum*, 75.

96. The bids were made in kind (*2 Verr.* 3.30.72; 32.75–76; 47.113). Lintott (*Imperium Romanum*, 75) points out that the one mention of a bid in cash equivalent (*2 Verr.* 3.39.90) indicates that such valuation would have been necessary if guarantors or security were given for the sum of revenue to be delivered.

assessment (that is, 1 percent of the declared amount) was normally paid to the collectors (*2 Verr.* 3.49.116–50.118).

On account of the strictures in the Gospels against toll collectors (τελῶναι),[97] "tax collectors" are rivaled only by Herod the Great as the villains of the history of Judea in the early Roman period. In fact, all the systems of collection had their problems and were open to abuse. The litany of abuses is already well known;[98] they need not detain us here. It is necessary, however, to reiterate that the problems with the *censoria locatio* in Asia, and wherever else this system might have been used, lay not only with the greed of the *societates publicanorum* and the need for them to fulfill and make profit on their contracts, but also with the provincial governors. By the late Republic, the governors, apart from their own financial interests and greed, could not exercise the strict supervision over the tax companies that was needed without considerable political risks, as Cicero, the *publicani*'s chief champion, observed (*Quint. fratr.* 1.1.32–33).

There is no evidence that tax contracts in Judea, after 63 B.C.E., were sold in Rome.[99] I have argued in chapter 1 that the activities of the *publicani*, whatever their specific role might have been, were frustrated by both the political instability of the region and the demands made by the governors of Syria, such as Gabinius and Scipio. In Appian's text, which constitutes the principal evidence for Caesar's tax reform in Asia, Antony announces to the Greeks of Asia (after the demise of Cassius and Brutus):

97. See Matt 5:46; 9:10–12; 11:18–19; 18:17; 21:31–32; Mark 2:15–17; Luke 3:12–13; 5:29–32; 7:29, 33–34; 15:1–2; 18:9–14; 19:1–10. The coupling "toll collectors and sinners" is particularly significant (see Matt 9:10–11; 11:19; Mark 2:15–16; Luke 5:30; 7:34; and 15:1).

98. Even Cicero was painfully aware of the complaints against the *publicani* (*Quint. fratr.* 1.1.13). According to Livy (45.18.3–4), the Macedonian mines were not leased out, in spite of their immense revenue potential, and the public lands also, because "these could not be farmed without a contractor, and where there was a contractor, there either the ownership by the state lapsed, or no freedom was left to the allied people."

99. Badian argues, on *a priori* grounds, that Pompey must have extended the *censoria locatio* to Syria and the newly organized province of Bithynia-Pontus. Jones includes the province of Cilicia. Sherwin-White contends equally that Pompey established "something similar" in Bithynia-Pontus. In Syria and Cilicia, he claims (citing Cicero, *Prov. cons.* 5.9–10 and *Att.* 5.14.1), tax leases were let by the proconsuls in the provinces to the *publicani*, not in a single block but commune by commune, and the system of *pactiones* "was made universal." Lintott observes, against Badian, that there is no evidence that Caesar abolished the *censoria locatio* in Syria and Bithynia as he did in Asia. Taxation in Syria and Bithynia, he thinks, "took the traditional Seleucid forms, except that now Roman magistrates were the ultimate recipients." It is not clear, he notes, whether Gabinius's dispute with the *publicani* concerned direct rather than indirect taxes. One might point out that in Macedonia the dispute between Piso and the *publicani* was over custom dues (*portoria*; Cicero, *Pis.* 87). Badian, *Roman Imperialism*, 75; idem, *Publicans and Sinners*, 99; Sherwin-White, "Lucullus, Pompey," 270; Lintott, *Imperium Romanum*, 79–80; Jones, *Roman Economy*, 163.

> But when they [tributes] became necessary we did not impose them on you according to a fixed valuation so that we could collect an absolutely certain sum, but we required you to contribute a portion of your yearly harvest in order that we might share with you the vicissitudes of the seasons. When the publicans, who farmed these collections by the authority of the Senate, wronged you by demanding more than was due, Gaius Caesar remitted to you one-third of what you had paid to them and put an end to their outrages: for he turned over to you the collection of the taxes [tributes] from the cultivators of the soil. (Appian, *Bell. civ.* 5.4)[100]

The Asians were not taxed according to a fixed assessment of their landed property (τιμήματα), Cicero's *stipendium*, which would have been easier to collect and more profitable for the Romans but ruinous for the cultivators in the event of a bad harvest. Instead they paid a percentage of their actual harvest. Caesar put an end to the abuses (ὕβρεις) of the *publicani* by turning over to the local authorities the collection of tribute from the farmers. This is assumed to mean that the province paid a lump sum to the governor, rather than to the *publicani*. It is not clear how Caesar expected the local authorities to decide what the total yield for each year would be, and thus how much would be paid to the Roman authorities. Perhaps both parties came to an agreement before the harvest. In any event, Antony clearly saw the entire package to be a favor done to Asia by Caesar.

Caesar was certainly doing the Jewish state a similar favor. His tax regulations in Judea parallel what he is said to have done in Asia. The difference is that in Judea there no longer was a Roman quaestor with whom a deal could be struck on amounts due. Hyrcanus delivered a percentage of the annual produce to the port at Sidon for shipment, which, as we know from Sicily, was the last phase of the collection of tribute (Cicero, *2 Verr.* 3.14.36–17.37).[101] It is entirely possible, as Smallwood seems to assume, that, by analogy with the Sicilian system, Hyrcanus required the cultivator to make a *professio*, such that at harvest he would pay "a fixed proportion of the harvest calculated from the amount of seed sown."[102] We must note, however, that there is no evidence that a cadastre of arable land, following the model of Ptolemiac Egypt, existed for Jewish Palestine during this period.[103] Antipater, whom Caesar appointed "procura-

100. See Dio, *Hist.* 42.6.3; also Caesar, *Bell. civ.* 3.3, 31, 103.

101. R. T. Pritchard, "*Lex Hieronica*," 359; Lintott, *Imperium Romanum*, 75–76.

102. Smallwood, *Jews under Roman Rule*, 40.

103. On the presence of such registers of *profession* in other provinces, see Salvator Riccobono, ed., *Lex agraria*, in *Fontes iuris romani anteJustiniani* (Part 1; ed. Salvator Riccobono; Florence: S. A. Barbèra, 1968), lines 53, 56, 90. Lintott (*Imperium Romanum*, 75 and n. 32) thinks that such declarations probably were used frequently in other provinces as the basis of taxation.

tor of Judea (ἐπίτροπος τῆς Ἰουδαίας)," having granted him Roman citizenship and immunity from taxation (Josephus, *A.J.* 14.137, 143; *B.J.* 1.194, 199),[104] may in some ways have represented Roman financial interests in the Jewish state.[105] Even so, the Romans would have had to be content with what the Jews and their leaders judged to be (and were able to collect as) tribute due to Rome.

Local Taxes

Scholars have long emphasized the fact that Roman taxation in the provinces in the late Republic and the early Principate was not uniform and in general was related to local conditions and traditions.[106] Judea in 47 B.C.E. was no exception to this general observation. Caesar and the Senate were clearly aware of the Jewish local condition when they granted an exemption for the sabbatical year. The tax tradition in Israel in the Second Temple period also included the tithe and the half-shekel temple tax. It is to the tradition of tithing that the Senate referred when it urged that "in addition, they shall also pay tithes to Hyrcanus and his sons, just as they paid to their forefathers" (*A.J.* 14.203). Similar calls for the continuance of the traditional relationship between the Jews and their high priests and priests are found elsewhere in the letter and the *senatus consulta* issued by

104. The term ἐπίτροπος is used very imprecisely by Josephus with regard to the members of the Herodian family. In *A.J.* 14.166 the leading Jews warn Hyrcanus that Antipater, Herod, and his brother Phasael were not Hyrcanus's "stewards in the government" (ἐπίτροποί σου τῶν πραγμάτων). Antony is said later to have entrusted "the administration of the whole of Judea" (πᾶσαν διοικεῖν τὴν Ἰουδαίαν ἐπιτρέπων) to Herod and Phasael, having appointed them tetrarchs (τετράρχας). Antony at the same time recognized Hyrcanus as the legitimate ruler (*B.J.* 1.244). In spite of the exaggeration of Antipater's role in the government of Judea in sections of Josephus's work, it would seem best to define Antipater's functions in relation to Hyrcanus's administration of the country. His role, as Peter Richardson (*Herod*, 105–8) argues, would have been "a combination of military and financial deputy to Hyrcanus, with a broad sphere of influence." It was Hyrcanus who related directly with Rome, not Antipater. See Momigliano, *Ricerche*, 24–27; Richard D. Sullivan, "The Dynasty of Judaea in the First Century," in *ANRW* 2.8:296–354 (1977). For a discussion of Josephus's presentation of Hyrcanus II and Antipater, see D. R. Schwartz, "Hyrcanus II"; and chapter 4 below.

105. So Momigliano, *Ricerche*, 24–27; Smallwood, *Jews under Roman Rule*, 39.

106. M. Rostovtzeff, *The Social and Economic History of the Roman Empire* (Oxford: Clarendon, 1926), 461–62; G. H. Stevenson, "The Provinces and Their Government," in *CAH*, vol. 9, *The Roman Republic, 133–44 B.C.* (ed. S. A. Cook et al.; Cambridge: Cambridge University Press, 1932), 467–71; idem, "The Imperial Administration," in *CAH*, vol. 10, *The Augustan Empire, 44 B.C.–A.D. 70* (ed. S. A. Cook et al.; Cambridge: Cambridge University Press, 1934), 189–93; Jones, *Roman Economy*, 161–68; Badian, *Roman Imperialism*, 18–19; Lintott, *Imperium Romanum*, 74–80; J. S. Richardson, "Administration of the Empire," 585–89; Sanders, *Judaism*, 161–63. See also chapter 4 below.

Julius Caesar and the Senate (*A.J.* 14.194–95, 199, 208). The directive that the Jews should pay tithes to Hyrcanus has proven, nonetheless, to be misleading; it has led some scholars to the false conclusion that Hyrcanus and his Hasmonean ancestors financed the administration of the Jewish state from tithes.[107] The postexilic system of tithing was not designed to meet the secular needs of the state. Its beneficiaries were the temple, its priests, and the Levites.[108] Since the issue of tithes in the Second Temple period is complex, I shall treat it separately in chapter 6.

To the temple and its needs also went the temple tax. I shall discuss this tax in the context of the efforts made by both the Jewish and the Roman authorities to protect—from official seizure and common robbery—the enormous sums that were collected and transported to Jerusalem from the Diaspora.[109] Sanders has already given a sufficient treatment of the problems related to the temple tax as a levy.[110] Moreover, it will be evident in my discussion that the cost of the temple tax on individual Jewish inhabitants of Judea was negligibly small. The real significance of the tax lay in the huge cash flow that it brought from the Diaspora to Jerusalem.[111]

---

107. See, for instance, Schalit, *König Herodes*, 267–70; Aharon Oppenheimer, *The 'Am Ha-Aretz: A Study in the Social History of the Jewish People in the Hellenistic-Roman Period* (trans. I. H. Levine; Leiden: Brill, 1977), 35–36. B. Bar-Kochva and Applebaum reject this thesis, but both see in *A.J.* 14.203 a land tax collected by the Hasmonean state. See B. Bar-Kochva, "Manpower, Economics, and Internal Strife in the Hasmonean State," in *Armée et fiscalité dans le monde antique* (Paris: Éditions du Centre National de la Recherche Scientifique, 1977), 167–96; Shimon Applebaum, *Judaea in Hellenistic and Roman Times: Historical and Archaeological Essays* (Leiden: Brill, 1989), 9–29. In Bar-Kochva's view (pp. 171–73), the Hasmonean tax replaced the Seleucid φόρος imposed on Judea (1 Macc 15:9), and amounted to three hundred talents. Later on in the same article (pp. 185–86) he argues, however, that the Hasmonean tithe replaced "the Hellenistic δεκάτη, which was the main land tax under the Secleucids." Both Bar-Kochva and Applebaum point to the existence of a "secular δεκάτη" in the Greco-Roman world. Applebaum (p. 22) makes reference especially to the distinction between the religious tithe and the state tithe in the Murabbaʿat documents, where the farmer leasing land paid a tithe to the leader of the 135 C.E. revolt (Simon Kosiba) as well as the religious tithe. See P. Benoit et al., *Les grottes de Murabbaʿât* (DJD 2; Oxford: Clarendon, 1961), no. 24C and E. While there is no doubt that the Seleucids and the Romans imposed a form of tithe and the Hasmonean kings probably did the same, the existence of the distinction in documents dating from 135 C.E. of the religious tithe from the state tax is not a proof that Caesar was referring to a Hasmonean state tax. There is no evidence for Hasmonean taxes and their terminology. Besides, the editors of the Murabbaʿat documents and Applebaum himself note that the state tithe in these documents were paid on the lease of "state land." This was not the status of Judea under Julius Caesar. See Benoit et al., *Les grottes de Murabbaʿât*, 123 and 129, n. L. 16; Applebaum, *Judaea in Hellenistic and Roman Times*, 22.

108. See chapter 6 below; also Sanders, *Judaism*, 159–61.

109. See below.

110. Sanders, *Jewish Law*, 49–51, 283–308; idem, *Judaism*, 156.

111. For a discussion of the economic impact of pilgrimage to Jerusalem from the

Even though the Jews had momentarily—between 142 B.C.E. (under Simon the Hasmonean) and the subjection to Rome in 63 B.C.E.—ceased to pay tribute to foreign conquerors, it would be illusory to imagine that the Jews paid no taxes (beyond priestly tithes) under the Hasmoneans. In order to fund their needs, the Hasmoneans must have levied taxes on their Jewish subjects. These taxes supported their personal wealth, the administration of the state that they wrested from the Seleucids, and the maintenance of their army, which had become considerable by the time of Alexander Janneus. Although there is no record of what these taxes were, we do know that the Hasmonean kings maintained a state apparatus for governing the large kingdom they had conquered. They kept—paid and equipped—large forces, including mercenary troops. All this provides evidence that they did indeed impose taxes on their subjects.[112] In 47 B.C.E. John Hyrcanus II no longer possessed his father's large army and extensive territory; nevertheless, he was expected by Caesar to derive a revenue from Judea for the administration of the territory given to him: "That his children shall rule over the Jewish nation and enjoy the revenues of the places given to them" (*A.J.* 14.196; my translation). The Romans also expected the same of other kingdoms and ethnarchies allied to them. This expectation could not have been limited to indirect taxes collected at

---

Diaspora, especially in the Herodian period, see Martin Goodman, "The Pilgrimage Economy of Jerusalem in the Second Temple Period," in *Jerusalem: Its Sanctity and Centrality to Judaism, Christianity, and Islam* (ed. Lee I. Levine; New York: Continuum, 1999), 69–76.

112. In Josephus's view, Hyrcanus I paid for his mercenary troops, in part, from money (three thousand talents) that he stole from David's tomb (*A.J.* 13.249; *B.J.* 1.61). His son Alexander Janneus continued the practice of keeping a mercenary force of up to sixty-two hundred mercenaries (eight thousand in *B.J.* 1.93)—made up of Pisidians and Cilicians (*A.J.* 13.374, 377–78; *B.J.* 1.88–89, 93–95). The Hasmonean state and military expenses listed by Applebaum (*Judaea in Hellenistic and Roman Times*, 17–29) include, apart from pay for troops: construction of garrisons in conquered territories, mobile patrol for these areas, equipment and rations for troops, manufacture and maintenance of artillery and siege equipment, road construction and repair, transportation, remounts and fodder for cavalry, quartering and food for inactive mercenary troops, construction of harbors, building and refitting of ships, and mobilization of crews. He concludes (p. 18) that the imposition of taxes was "clearly necessary," though there is no direct evidence. Applebaum links such taxes to his favorite thesis that the Hasmoneans (and Herod after them) owned extensive "royal lands" and "large estates." Hasmonean taxes, in his view, came from the *cleroi* who cultivated such crown lands. According to Bar-Kochva ("Manpower," 171–73, 185–91), the Hasmoneans imposed a tithe (δεκάτη) equal to the three hundred talents previously paid in φόρος to the Seleucids (see n. 107 above). It was with this tax that the Hasmoneans paid for their mercenary troops. Otherwise the Hasmoneans drew revenue from their private estates, the taxes they collected from the χώρα of the Hellenistic cities they had destroyed, custom dues, tribute from the Arabs of Giladitis and Moabitis, and treasures looted from the Hellenistic cities. See the discussion of the Hasmonean armies in Israel Shatzman, *The Armies of the Hasmoneans and Herod* (Tübingen: Mohr Siebeck, 1991), 11–35.

Joppa. The tribute Hyrcanus paid to the Romans was, therefore, only a percentage of the total revenues that he derived from the territory. There is no record of what his total revenue was, but he received a grant of the territory to "occupy it as he himself may choose" (*A.J.* 14.200).

In summary, it is impossible to determine exact figures for the tribute imposed by Caesar on the Jewish state. Hyrcanus was expected to pay a portion of his total revenue to the Roman quaestor at Sidon. He was, however, at liberty to decide and collect the yearly amounts due. For Joppa he paid a fixed amount in produce, 20,675 *modii* of grain each year in compensation for the custom dues collected at Joppa and the neighboring territory, except the seventh (sabbatical) year in the seven-year cycle. For the Jewish state he paid what he judged to be one-quarter of the produce of the Jewish state every other year, again except in the seventh (sabbatical) year in the seven-year cycle. This tribute was further reduced by amounts that we are unable to calculate.

Thus, at the seaport at Joppa, on overland trade routes and possibly at other toll points, those Jews having business transactions paid custom duties on imports and exports. The inhabitants of Judea paid taxes to Hyrcanus, part of which would be the one-eighth (12.5 percent) annual tribute due to the Romans. Since we cannot determine a figure for the tax paid for the needs of the Jewish state, we are unable to say how much over and above the 12.5 percent Hyrcanus actually levied. In the unlikely hypothesis that the rate of the tax paid to the Jewish administration was the same as was demanded by the Romans, the total annual rate would be twenty-five percent. The Roman tribute was reduced by an unknown amount by 44 B.C.E., however, which renders the attempt to calculate percentages impossible. Tithes also were paid to the priests and Levites.

Territorial Grants: Joppa, "The Villages in the Great Plain," and Lydda

> It is also our pleasure that the city of Joppa, which the Jews had held from ancient times when they made a treaty of friendship with the Romans, shall belong to them as at first . . . . As for the villages in the Great Plain, which Hyrcanus and his forefathers before him possessed, it is the pleasure of the Senate that Hyrcanus and the Jews shall retain them with the same rights as they formerly had, and that the ancient rights which the Jews and their high priests and priests had in relation to each other should continue, and also the privileges which they received by vote of the people and the Senate. And that they be permitted to enjoy these rights at Lydda also. (*A.J.* 14.205, 207–8, Marcus [LCL])[113]

113. Ἰόππην τε πόλιν ἣ ἀπ᾽ ἀρχῆς ἔσχον Ἰουδαῖοι ποιούμενοι τὴν πρὸς Ῥωμαίους φιλίαν,

As part of his regulating the problem of taxes, Caesar restored to the Jewish state some of the territories that Pompey had removed from its control.[114] The restitution of territory that Rome judged to have belonged to a city or a people was part and parcel of normal Roman policy. Numerous inscriptional instances of the practice exist. One of the most pertinent parallels to *A.J.* 14.205, 207–8 is the *senatus consultum* of 81 B.C.E. concerning Stratonikeia:

> [and that Pedasos (?),] Themessos, Keramos and the places, [villages, harbors and the revenues of the] cities which Lucius Corn[elius Sulla, imperator,] *for the sake of* courage and honor [added and assigned to them, that] they should be *permitted* to possess (all of these); . . .(67) about this matter a decree was passed as follows: . . .(93) that their own laws and customs [which] they formerly [enjoyed,] *these* they shall enjoy; [and that whatever laws] and decrees [they themselves] have passed [because of] this [war] against Mithridates, [all these are to be legally binding] *upon them*; and whatever (things) [for the sake of] their courage [and honor,] *according to* the vote of his advisory board, Lucius Sul[la, imperator,] added and assigned to them, (consisting of) [communities (?), revenues,] *lands*, villages and harbors, [these they are to be permitted to keep] . . . .[115]

There is no doubt that in 63 B.C.E. Judea lost Joppa, along with the other cities of the coastal plain: Gaza, Azotus, Jamneia, Dora, and Strato's Tower (*A.J.* 14.75–76; *B.J.* 1.155–57). Since Lydda is not listed by Josephus among these cities, its inclusion in the grants of 47 B.C.E. is puzzling. As for "the villages in the great plain," there now exist two interrelated assumptions that have gained universal scholarly consensus. The first is that "the great plain" referred to in *A.J.* 14.207 is the plain of Esdraelon.[116]

αὐτῶν εἶναι, καθὼς καὶ τὸ πρῶτον, ἡμῖν ἀρέσκει . . . . τάς τε κώμας τας ἐν τῷ μεγάλῳ πεδίῳ, ἃς Ὑρκανὸς καὶ οἱ πρόγονοι πρότερον αὐτοῦ διακατέσχον, ἀρέσκει τῇ συγκλήτῳ ταῦτα Ὑρκανὸν καὶ Ἰουδαίους ἔχειν ἐπὶ τοῖς δικαίοις οἷς καὶ πρότερον εἶχον. μένειν δέ καὶ τὰ ἀπ᾽ ἀρχῆς δίκαια ὅσα πρὸς ἀλλήλους Ἰουδαίοις καὶ τοῖς ἀρχιεροῦσιν καὶ τοῖς ἱερεῦσιν ἦν, τά τε φιλάνθρωπα ὅσα τοῦ τε δήμου ψηφισαμένου καί τῆς συγκλήτου ἐσχον. ἔτι τούτοις τε τοῖς δικαίοις χρῆσθαι αὐτοῖς ἐξεῖναι ἐν Λύδδοις. "Also" (ἔτι) is emended by the translator from ἐπί.

114. I have argued what follows in greater detail in Fabian E. Udoh, "*Jewish Antiquities* XIV. 205, 207–08 and 'the Great Plain,'" *PEQ* 134 (2002): 130–43.

115. Sherk, *RGE*, no. 63, lines 53–99 = Sherk, *RDGE*, no. 18, lines 53–99. See also the *lex Antonia* of 72 or 68 B.C.E. concerning Termessus in Sherk, *RGE*, no. 72, col. 1, lines 12–35 = Dessau, *ILS*, no. 38, lines 31–35; also the *senatus consultum de Aphrodisiensibus*, granted by Antony and Octavian, lines 58–72 in Joyce Reynolds, *Aphrodisias and Rome* (London: Society for the Promotion of Roman Studies, 1982), 59–60, 62.

116. Marcus, in the Loeb edition of the text cited at the beginning of this section, capitalizes the name "the Great Plain," making it a proper name and titular, and in his note (n. a) accompanying the text he comments: "Of Esdraelon, cf. *Ant.* xii.348." Pastor (*Land and Econ-*

The second claims that, on account of the phrase "which Hyrcanus and his forefathers before him possessed" in the *senatus consultum*, the territory that Caesar and the Senate returned to the Jews was a "private royal estate."[117]

"Esdraelon" (Εσδρηλων) is the Greek corruption of the Hebrew name Jezreel. The plain of Esdraelon lies roughly between lower Galilee in the north and Samaria in the south, and between Mount Carmel in the west and Scythopolis in the east. If it was the plain of Jezreel that Caesar

---

omy, 95 and 221, n. 61) claims that, with these remarks, Marcus had "demonstrated that the intention [of *A.J.* 14.207] is the Esdraelon Valley." Schürer (*History*, 1:274) is noncommittal, but cites the text with the titular "the Great Plain." Michael Avi-Yonah, however, is positive. See Michael Avi-Yonah, "Historical Geography of Palestine," in *The Jewish People in the First Century: Historical Geography, Political History, Social, Cultural and Religious Life and Institutions*, vol. 1 (ed. S. Safrai and M. Stern; CRINT 1; Assen: Van Gorcum, 1974), 90; idem, *The Holy Land from the Persian to the Arab Conquests (536 B.C. to A.D. 640): A Historical Geography* (Grand Rapids: Baker Book House, 1977), 80, 82, and 84; Yohanan Aharoni and Michael Avi-Yonah, *The Macmillan Bible Atlas* (rev. 3rd ed.; ed. Anson F. Rainey and Ze'ev Safrai; New York: Macmillan, 1993), 161. Schalit (*König Herodes*, 753–59), accepting Avi-Yonah's thesis, concentrates his discussion on the latter's suggestion that the fertile land of the plain "constituted a royal domain perhaps since the times of the Israelite Kings." See Avi-Yonah, *Holy Land*, 25 and n. 107 (citing 1 Kgs 18:45, 46; 21:1ff.) and 136; also idem, "Historical Geography," 97. For Applebaum ("Economic Life," 635 and nn. 4, 5), *A.J.* 14.207, 208 are proof of the existence of royal lands in Israel, since these texts are "evidence of villages held by Hyrcanus and his successors in the Plain of Esdraelon, and of special rights exercised by the Hasmoneans in the district of Lydda." The references to *A.J.* 14.200 in n. 5 and in p. 634, n. 5 of Applebaum's essay are certainly wrong. In both cases *A.J.* 14.208 is probably intended. Momigliano (*Ricerche*, 14) also accepts Esdraelon; so do Smallwood (*Jews under Roman Rule*, 40), who depends on Schalit's discussion, and Ben-Zion Rosenfeld, "The 'Boundary of Gezer' Inscriptions and the History of Gezer at the End of the Second Temple Period," *IEJ* 38 (1988): 243; also recently, idem, "The Galilean Valleys (*Beqʾaoth*) from the Bible to the Talmud," *RB* 109 (2002): 80 and n. 35.

117. See previous note. This is how Avi-Yonah states the thesis: "The Great Plain, or the Valley of Jezreel, may have been a royal domain from the days of Naboth's vineyard; it must have then passed into the hands of the Assyrians, Babylonians, Persians and the Hellenistic kings, then into the hands of the Hasmoneans and the Herodians. At the time of the Jewish war it belonged to Berenice, sister of Agrippa II, forming a region which was administered from Besara. Previously it must have been administered by Herod Antipas, whose tetrarchy it adjoined." Avi-Yonah, "Historical Geography," 97 and n. 1, citing Josephus, *Vita* 118; also Avi-Yonah, *Holy Land*, 25 and n. 107; 37, 84, and 136. In his view (*Holy Land*, 114), the territory became a Roman imperial domain after 70 C.E. See also Applebaum, *Judaea in Hellenistic and Roman Times*, 25–26. The effort by Rosenfeld ("'Boundary of Gezer.'") to find Hasmonean/Herodian private estates in Gezer was rejected on archaeological grounds by Ronny Reich, "The 'Boundary of Gezer' Inscriptions Again," *IEJ* 40 (1990): 44–46. Joshua J. Schwartz ("Once More on the 'Boundary of Gezer' Inscriptions and the History of Gezer and Lydda at the End of the Second Temple Period," *IEJ* 40 [1990]: 47–57, also refuted claims concerning Gezer on historical grounds, but linked the "private estate" of *A.J.* 14.207 to the grant of Lydda (*A.J.* 14.208), which, he claims, was also a Hasmonean private domain. See below.

restored to the Jewish state, it must be that Pompey had removed the territory from Jewish control in 63 B.C.E. Let me cite the evidence for this apparent loss of the territory as Avi-Yonah presents it: "By order of the conqueror [Pompey. . . t]he Jews lost even Joppa and the estates in the Jezreel Valley." He cites *A.J.* 14.205, 207.[118] He continues on the next page, "[b]esides, Julius Caesar, who was in general friendly to the Jews, repaired some of the worst damages by restoring to Judea in 47 B.C.E. Joppa and the Jezreel Valley." He again cites *A.J.* 14.205, 207.[119] According to Avi-Yonah, we know, therefore, that it was the plain of Esdraelon that was returned to the Jews by Caesar because Pompey took it away from them. And we know that Pompey took it away because, well, Caesar returned it.

While we do know from *A.J.* 14.75–76 (*B.J.* 1.155–57) that Pompey detached the coastal plain and its cities from Jewish control, Josephus nowhere mentions the plain of Esdraelon among the territories excised from the Jewish state by Pompey. It is, moreover, hard to imagine why this territory would have been removed from Jewish control and what would have become of it in the interim. Schalit thinks that it was given back to the Samaritans.[120] According to Aryeh Kasher, this plain would have been given to Scythopolis. In his view, it was subsequently given back to the Jews, "to the detriment of Scythopolis," by Caesar, who did thus "slightly sweeten the bitter pill" of the continued separation of the Jewish population in Galilee from that of Judea.[121] Schalit and Kasher, however, begin by assuming that *A.J.* 14.207 refers to Esdraelon. If Caesar judged it necessary to return portions of a plain to the Jews from among the territories that we actually know had been taken from them, it seems rather that the grant of "Joppa and . . ." calls for the plain of Sharon and not the Valley of Jezreel.

Since scholars who have dealt with *A.J.* 14.207 assume that "the great plain" in Caesar's grant referred to and only to the plain of Esdraelon, it is necessary to ask if the expression τὸ μέγα πεδίον was a title for the plain of Esdraelon in the late Hellenistic and early Roman periods.[122] An examination of the extant literature of the late Hellenistic and early Roman periods, particularly Josephus's terminology, reveals that the designation

118. Avi-Yonah, "Historical Geography," 89 and n. 7.

119. Ibid., 90 and n. 1.

120. Schalit, *König Herodes*, 754.

121. Aryeh Kasher, *Jews and Hellenistic Cities in Eretz-Israel: Relations of the Jews in Eretz-Israel with the Hellenistic Cities During the Second Temple Period, 332 BCE-70 CE* (Tübingen: Mohr Siebeck, 1990), 183.

122. Rosenfeld's article is a study of the terminological development in the designation of plains in the Galilee from the Bible to the Talmud. For the Hellenistic and early Roman periods, see Rosenfeld, "Galilean Valleys," 77–82.

"the great plain" did not in fact refer solely to the plain of Esdraelon. The name was applied also to other plains, including the plain of Sharon. It was the villages of the plain of Sharon, together with the city of Joppa, that Caesar and the Senate restored to Jewish control. Caesar's interest was not in giving back a "private royal estate" to Hyrcanus II. The explanation I propose enables us to account for the hitherto inexplicable mention of Lydda in the *senatus consultum*. The seaport city of Joppa, the plain of Sharon, and Lydda are linked both by the major ancient trade route from Egypt to Syria and Asia, and by the route from Joppa to Jerusalem, the Jewish metropolis.

Table I: The "Great Plain" in Josephus and Probable Locations

Reference in Josephus			Location
B.J.	*A.J.*	*Vita*	
2.188			Esdraelon
2.232	20.118		Esdraelon
2.595		126	Esdraelon
3.39			Esdraelon
3.48			Esdraelon
	8.36		Esdraelon
	15.294		Esdraelon
		115	Esdraelon
		318	Esdraelon
3.59			Asochis
4.54			Asochis
		207	Asochis
4.455			Jordan Valley
	4.100		Jordan Valley
	5.77		Jordan Valley
	7.236		Jordan Valley
	8.381		Jordan Valley
	12.348		Jordan Valley
	5.83		Sharon
	14.207		Sharon
	18.122		Sharon (?)
	5.178		Paneas
	5.276		Paneas
	6.14		Beth-Shemesh
	10.213		Babylon (see Dan 3:1)

It is in Jdt 1:8 that the Valley of Jezreel is first called "the great plain of Esdraelon" (τὸ μέγα πεδίον Εσδρηλων). The plain is said to lie "between Geba and Scythopolis," outside "Israel" as this book delimits it (Jdt 3:9–10).[123] Otherwise, it is called simply "Esdraelon," a designation that in the Bible and the Apocrypha occurs only in this book (Jdt 3:9; 4:6 [refers to the city]; 7:3). The area is also referred to, retrospectively, as "the plain" in Jdt 4:6; 6:11; 7:18; 14:2; and 15:2.[124] It is in 1 Macc 12:49 that this plain is called simply "the great plain" (τὸ πεδίον τὸ μέγα).[125]

This absolute "the great plain" in 1 Macc 12:49 might have led scholars to assume that only Esdraelon was known by this name during the late Hellenistic and early Roman periods.[126] The assumption certainly is reinforced by the fact, as the table above shows, that more often than not it is to Esdraelon that Josephus refers when he speaks of "the great plain," yet he never mentions the region by name. In three of the passages (*B.J.* 3.59; 4.54; and *Vita* 207) the plain of Asochis, which lies northwest of Mount Tabor in the Lower Galilee, is certainly meant.[127]

The Jordan Valley, in spite of the many references to Esdraelon, is in fact "the great plain" par excellence.[128] The territory is called "the great plain before Beth-san" (τὸ πεδίον τὸ μέγα κατὰ πρόσωπον Βαιθσαν) in 1 Macc 5:52.[129] Thus, in his rewriting of 1 Macc 12:49 (relating to Esdraelon) Josephus eliminates the designation "the great plain" from the passage and speaks only of Galilee (*A.J.* 13.192), whereas he makes the reference in 1 Macc 5:52 explicit: "And after crossing the Jordan, they came to the great plain, in front of which lies Beth-sanē, by the Greeks called Scythopolis" (*A.J.* 12.348). Moreover, Josephus in *A.J.* 4.100 writes: "So Moses led his forces down towards the Jordan and encamped on the

---

123. See Aharoni and Avi-Yonah, *Atlas*, 157 and map 212. I assume the dating of the present redaction of Judith to be in the Hasmonean period. See Carey A. Moore, *Judith: A New Translation with Introduction and Commentary* (AB 40B; Garden City, N.Y.: Doubleday, 1985), 67–70.

124. The region is called "the plain of Megiddo" (τὸ πεδίον Μαγεδδαους) in 1 Esd 1:27 [Eng. 1:29] = 2 Chr 35:22.

125. Trypho's troops and cavalry went into Galilee and to "the great plain" in pursuit of Jonathan's soldiers, who were fleeing southward to Judea.

126. Abel (*Géographie*, 1:411) gives the title "LA GRANDE PLAINE" to this territory. He begins his discussion by referring immediately to 1 Macc 12:49.

127. For a discussion of the passages, see Udoh, "Great Plain," 132–3. On Asochis, see Abel, *Géographie*, 1:409–10.

128. The other passages in Josephus relating to the Jordan Valley are discussed in Udoh, "Great Plain," 133–4.

129. This passage describes the routes taken by Judas Maccabeus in his return journey to Zion, following his battles in Gilead, with the Israelites whom he had "rescued." See Aharoni and Avi-Yonah, *Atlas*, 144 and map 190.

great plain over against Jericho; this is a prosperous city, prolific of palm trees and nursery of balsam."[130] Here Josephus echoes the detailed and lengthy description he gave to the region in *B.J.* 4.455–75, including its dimensions, properties, and riches.[131]

The region around Jericho in the Jordan Valley was well known in the ancient world, particularly for its balsam groves and plantations of high-quality date palms.[132] One would have expected, therefore, that if Pompey were to take away "royal estates" from the remnant of the Hasmonean kings, the great plain of the Jordan Valley would have been the most obvious and appropriate area. There is no evidence, however, that the Jews lost this territory to the Romans, that is, before Antony gave it (temporarily) to Cleopatra (*A.J.* 15.93–96, 106–7, 132; *B.J.* 1.361–62).[133] It follows that despite the prominence of the Jordan Valley as the great plain, we cannot conclude that *A.J.* 14.207 refers to it, especially since other plains in Judea were also recognized as "the great plain."

The evidence that the plain of Sharon was also considered "the great plain" comes from Josephus's reading of the biblical account of the early Israelite settlement pattern.[134] His interpretation in *A.J.* 5.80–87 of the biblical account of the distribution of the territory west of the Jordan to the nine and one-half tribes of Israel would fall well within the approximate

---

130. See Num 22:1: "The Israelites set out, and camped in the plains of Moab across the Jordan from Jericho."

131. See Abel, *Géographie*, 1:425–6: "L'usage de désigner la vaste coupure jordanienne sous le nom de *Biqe'âh* est le fait d'une basse époque. A la «Grande Biqe'âh» du Talmud correspond la «Grande Plaine» des hellénisants. Nommé en passant par I Macc. 5, 22, ce μέγα πεδίον est dans Josèphe l'objet d'une description développée qui nous expose la vallée du Jourdain sous son véritable aspect de plaine encaissée, sans en exclure les lacs qu'elle renferme." The reference by Abel to 1 Macc 5:22 is surely an error. 1 Macc 5:52 is intended. See also Rosenfeld, "Galilean Valleys," 79–82.

132. Schürer (*History*, 1:298–300, n. 36) has collected the ancient witnesses; also Avi-Yonah, *Holy Land*, 197–98 and references. Josephus underlines at every occasion that the soil here was at the time the most fertile in Judea (see, for instance, *B.J.* 1.138 [= *A.J.* 14.54]; *A.J.* 4.100; 5.77–78, 82; *B.J.* 1.361 [= *A.J.* 15.96]), such that he thinks that "it would be no misnomer to describe it [the region] as 'divine'" (*B.J.* 4.469). There is ample evidence that the Romans knew of the importance of the region and its potential as a private estate. Pompey invaded Judea through the Jordan Valley and encamped in Jericho before pursuing Aristobulus II to Jerusalem (*A.J.* 14. 48–54; *B.J.* 1.133–39; Aharoni and Avi-Yonah, *Atlas*, 159 and map 215). The region was later carved out of Herod's newly acquired kingdom and given to Cleopatra by Antony, and for it Herod paid a tribute to Cleopatra (*A.J.* 15.93–96, 106–7, 132; *B.J.* 1.361–62), until it was restored to him by Octavian (*A.J.* 15.217; *B.J.* 1.396). Pliny (*Nat.* 12.111–13), noting that the region's balsam groves formerly belonged to the king, comments on their importance to the Romans and on the steps they took to protect the plants during the Jewish revolt of 66 C.E.

133. See chapter 4 below.

134. On *A.J.* 18.120–22, see Udoh, "Great Plain," 133, 134–35.

delimitations into which modern geographers and cartographers have located the original biblical portions as they appear in Josh 14–19.[135] This is true except that in *A.J.* 5.83 Josephus says that "in breadth" (that is, the distance from the southern to the northern boundaries) the territory of the tribe of Ephraim was "from Bethel right up to the great plain." If, as scholars usually assume,[136] the plain of Esdraelon is meant here, then Josephus would have absorbed the territory of Manasseh, whose southern borders were the northern frontiers of Ephraim (Josh 17:7–10), into the land of Ephraim. Actually, Josephus is not guilty of this oversight. Immediately following his delimitation of the northern borders of Ephraim (i.e., the southern border of Manasseh) and after correctly reading Josh 17:11–12, he places the northern boundary of Manasseh in Beth-shean (Scythopolis) and its western extension in Dor on the seacoast.[137]

Both in Josephus's interpretation (*A.J.* 5.82) and (partly) in Josh 18:12–13, Bethel defines the northern boundary of the tribe of Benjamin and the southern boundary of the tribe of Ephraim.[138] In the biblical account, Ephraim's northern boundary runs eastward from Michmethath through Taanath-shiloh to meet the southern border at Jericho and its extension to the Jordan. The "Wadi Qanah" is the landmark for the northern boundary in its westward course from Tappuah to the sea (Josh 16:6b-8a; 17:8–9). The "Wadi Qanah" is either identified (more generally) with the modern Naḥal Qanah (Qanah Brook), which drains into the Yarkon River some 3.5 miles north of Joppa, between Joppa and Apollonia,[139] or with the (hypothetical) river Arsuf lying 1.5 miles north of Apollonia and 11.5 miles north of Joppa.[140] One thing is certain, however, both from the

---

135. See Abel, *Géographie*, 2:44–67 and maps ii-iii; Aharoni and Avi-Yonah, *Atlas*, 60–62 and maps 70–73; James B. Pritchard, ed., *The Times Atlas of the Bible* (London: Times Books, 1987), 64 and map 2.

136. See H. St. J. Thackeray et al., *Josephus* (10 vols.; LCL; Cambridge, Mass.: Harvard University Press, 1926–65), 5:39 and n. f, where the passage is accompanied by the explanatory note "The plain of Esdraelon." Abel (*Géographie*, 1:412 and n. 2) also, assuming that Josephus here speaks of Esdraelon, charges him with incoherence and inexactitude.

137. *A.J.* 5.83–84: "The half-tribe of Manasseh had from the Jordan to the city of Dora and in breadth as far as Bēthēsana, now called Scythopolis." Josh 17:11 reads: "Within Issachar and Asher, Manasseh had Beth-shean and its villages, Ibleam and its villages, the inhabitants of Dor and its villages, the inhabitants of En-dor and its villages, the inhabitants of Taanach and its villages, and the inhabitants of Megiddo and its villages."

138. See also Josh 16:1–7.

139. See Abel, *Géographie*, 2:44–67 and maps ii-iii; Aharoni and Avi-Yonah, *Atlas*, 60–62 and maps 70–73; James B. Pritchard, *Times Atlas*, 64 and map 2; Moshe Kochavi et al., eds., *Aphek-Antipatris 1: Excavations of Areas A and B, the 1972–1976 Seasons* (Tel Aviv: Emery & Claire Yass Publications in Archaeology, 2000), 3, fig. 1.3.

140. Eva Danelius, "The Boundary of Ephraim and Manasseh in the Western Plain," *PEQ* 89 (1957): 55–67; 90 (1958): 32–43, 122–44; Henry O. Thompson, "Kanah," in *ABD* 4:5;

biblical description of the "Wadi Qanah" and from its modern identifications: it flowed into the plain of Sharon.[141] Hence, it is this plain that Josephus calls "the great plain" in *A.J.* 5.83.

The Senate, Joppa, and the Plain of Sharon

The Jordan Valley, the plain of Esdraelon, the plain of Asochis, and the plain of Sharon are all called "the great plain" in Josephus's works, and they were all probably known by this name in the late Hellenistic and early Roman periods. In theory, all four plains are, thus, possible candidates for the territory referred to in *A.J.* 14.207. We must, however, eliminate Asochis, Esdraelon, and the otherwise attractive Jordan Valley as possible options because, as I have noted, there is no evidence that these territories were removed by Pompey from the Jewish state in 63 B.C.E. On the contrary, we do know that the coastal plain, including the plain of Sharon, and its cities were detached from Judea and assigned to the Province of Syria. If Caesar merely returned to the Jews a plain that Pompey had taken away from them, then it was the coastal plain that he gave back to them. This argument *e silentio* is affirmatively supported by Josephus's identification in *A.J.* 5.83 of southern Sharon (from the Yarkon river) as "the great plain." This terminological link enables us conclusively to see why the plain of Sharon must be the territory that Caesar and the Senate granted to the Jews in 47 B.C.E.

Scholars have overlooked two facts that, in my estimation, are crucial to understanding *A.J.* 14.207: (1) the *senatus consultum* returned to the Jews "the villages in the great plain" and not the entirety of a great plain; (2) these villages were given to the Jews in the context of the gift of the seaport city of Joppa. I shall deal first with the second observation.

I have observed already that Caesar and the Senate, in regulating the Jewish state, treated Judea as a city-state comprising two principal cities: Jerusalem and Joppa. Joppa was Judea's hazardous but usable seaport.[142] After it had been captured by Simon and settled with a Jewish population, Joppa became the object of dispute first between Antiochus VII Sidetes and Simon (1 Macc 15:28–16:10; *A.J.* 13.225–27; *B.J.* 1.50–53), and later between John Hyrcanus I, Simon's son and successor, and Sidetes. Sidetes seized Joppa, Gezer, and Pēgae, and besieged Jerusalem in 134–

Edward F. Campbell, "The Boundary Between Ephraim and Manasseh," in *The Answers Lie Below* (ed. Henry O. Thompson; Lanham, Md.: University Press of America, 1984), 67–74.

141. The first part of Danelius's study ("Boundary," 89 [1957]: 55–67, esp. 64) seeks to establish "the fact that the Ephraimites settled the Sharon Plain."

142. *A.J.* 15.333; *B.J.* 1.409; 2.507–9; 3.414–31. See chapter 1.

132 B.C.E. (*A.J.* 13.236–47; *B.J.* 1.61). Hyrcanus sent an embassy to Rome to ask for help (*A.J.* 13.259–66). Michael Avi-Yonah, citing Rome's indecision (see *A.J.* 13.265–66), thinks that Hyrcanus appealed to Rome "in vain." According to Avi-Yonah and a number of other scholars, Hyrcanus sought Rome's recognition of the Jews' right to the territories after Antiochus had lifted the siege of Jerusalem and imposed a tribute for Joppa.[143] Schürer contends, on the contrary, that the threat by Rome was instrumental to Antiochus's otherwise inexplicable restoration of the cities to the Jews, in exchange for the payment of tribute.[144] Josephus actually quotes a *senatus consultum* in relation to this embassy (*A.J.* 13.260–64), which records the request of the Jewish delegation "that Joppa and its harbours and Gazara and Pēgae and whatever other cities and territories Antiochus took from them in war, contrary to the decree of the Senate, be restored to them" (*A.J.* 13.261). It would seem that, although Rome was not prepared to take military action in defense of the rights of the Jewish state, the Senate certainly issued a *senatus consultum.*

Josephus quotes another *senatus consultum* inserted in the decree of Pergamum in *A.J.* 14.248–50, in which the Senate urges that "King Antiochus, son of Antiochus" must return fortresses, harbors, and territory that he had seized from the Jews and expel the garrison at Joppa. Scholars are divided on whether this decree dates from the time of Antiochus Sidetes, as proposed by Mendelssohn (which would require the emendation of "Antiochus son of Antiochus" in *A.J.* 14.249 to "Antiochus son of Demetrius"),[145] or from the period of the campaign of his son Antiochus IX Cyzicenus against Hyrcanus I (*A.J.* 13.270–74, 278). Gérald Finkielsztejn has studied the problem of the chronology of Hyrcanus I's conquests with the help of archaeological finds in the cities that he had conquered. He dates Hyrcanus's first embassy to Rome (*A.J.* 13.259–66) to the period between 127 and 125 B.C.E.[146] The second embassy (*A.J.* 14.248–50) he dates to the period between 107 and 104 B.C.E.[147] On the occasion of this second embassy, the Senate issued verbal but effective threats, which, according to Finkielsztejn, explains the control by Alexander Janneus (Hyrcanus I's second successor) of most of the cities of the coastal plain, including Joppa.[148]

143. Avi-Yonah, *Holy Land*, 59.

144. Schürer, *History*, 1:202–5 and n. 7; also Tessa Rajak, "Roman Intervention in a Seleucid Siege of Jerusalem," *GRBS* 22 (1981): 65–81.

145. See Mendelssohn, "Senati Consuta," 123–58. This hypothesis is accepted by Schürer, *History*, 1:204–6.

146. Gérald Finkielsztejn, "More Evidence on John Hyrcanus I's Conquests: Lead Weights and Rhodian Amphora Stamps," *BAIAS* 16 (1998): 45, 56.

147. Ibid., 49, 51–52, 60.

148. Ibid., 51–52; see *A.J.* 13.324, 395; also discussion in Israel Shatzman, "L'inte-

However one might date the various *senatus consulta* issued by Rome in relation to the dispute over Joppa and which Josephus cites, it is important to realize that the Senate had issued decrees at least twice in the late Hellenistic period recognizing the (ancestral) right of the Jews to Joppa and the surrounding territory between Pēgae and Gezer in the plain of Sharon (*A.J.* 13.261; 14.249–50). The insistence in *A.J.* 14.208 that "the privileges which they [i.e., Hyrcanus and the Jews] received by vote of the people and the Senate" should continue is reminiscent of these earlier votes of the Senate in favor of the Jews. It follows that by granting "the villages in the great plain" to the Jews "with the same rights as they formerly had" (*A.J.* 14.207), the Senate did no more than continue its previous policy of recognizing the ancestral right of the Jews to Joppa and the surrounding territory. It is this ancestral right that the Senate affirmed in stating that the plain was possessed by "Hyrcanus and his forefathers before him" (*A.J.* 14.207), a right already explicitly stated with regard to Joppa itself in *A.J.* 14.205: "the city of Joppa, which the Jews had held from ancient times when they made a treaty of friendship with the Romans, shall belong to them as at first." The repeated insistence on Jewish ancestral right, previously recognized by the Senate, ties the plain and Joppa closely together. Furthermore, that ancestry need not have gone beyond Simon and his alliance with Rome.

The phrase "which Hyrcanus and his forefathers before him possessed" (*A.J.* 14.207) constitutes no evidence, therefore, that "the great plain" that the Senate restored to the Jews was an ancient private crown land belonging to Jewish kings. This "great plain" did not belong to the kings privately any more than did the city of Joppa—or Jerusalem for that matter.[149] Besides, if the Senate's phrase "Hyrcanus and his forefathers" referred to the status of the territory as a private royal estate (and it did not), then by returning it to "Hyrcanus and the Jews" (*A.J.* 14.207, 209) the Senate, in the same stroke, would have annulled that status.[150]

---

grazione della Giudea nell'impero romano," in *Gli Ebrei nell'impero romano* (ed. Ariel Lewin; Florence: La Giuntina, 2001), 30–35.

149. Compare the statements in *A.J.* 14.196, 200, and 205.

150. Schalit (*König Herodes*, 754) contends that the expression "Hyrcanus and the Jews" is a "formula" that points to the individual and collective character of Jewish right to the plain. His distinctions are, however, as subtle as they are futile. Joshua J. Schwartz, *Lod (Lydda), Israel: From Its Origins Through the Byzantine Period, 5600 B.C.E.–640 C.E.* (Oxford: Tempus Reparatum, 1991), 51–52, relying on Schalit's analysis, likewise claims that the Senate "dispossessed the Hasmoneans of their personal possession of these villages and returned them instead to Judea or the Jewish nation in general." See also Joshua J. Schwartz, "Boundary of Gezer," 55–56. Schwartz's opinion makes no sense, since in returning the territories the Senate insists that "the Jews shall retain them with the same rights as they formerly had, and that the ancient rights which the Jews and their high priests and priests had in relation to each other should continue" (*A.J.* 14.207–8). There really is no reason to con-

Joppa, "the Villages in the Great Plain," and Lydda

I return now to my first observation, namely, that it is significant that the Senate returned "villages in the great plain" to the Jews. Much like the Jordan Valley, the plain of Sharon was noted for its fertility. F.-M. Abel observes *à propos* that it was the fertile fields of south Sharon, lying in the Joppa, Lydda, Jamneia triangle, that gave this plain its reputation for fecundity.[151] Archaeological evidence points to the conclusion that, even in the early periods, agricultural settlements in south Sharon were concentrated in these fertile lands.[152] The "villages in the great plain" that Caesar and the Senate conceded to the Jews, together with the city of Joppa and its seaport, were the farmlands that lay in south Sharon from the Yarkon River to Lydda. The territory granted might also have included Gezer and Jamneia, as in the previous Roman decrees, but there is no direct evidence for their inclusion.[153]

The addition of fertile farmland to the Jewish state was not the principal reason dictating Caesar's gift of the "villages" to the Jews, although one cannot overlook the fact that the grant added valuable, arable land to the Jewish state. It is rather the historical, strategic and commercial importance of the territory that makes the grant significant and compelling. In the first place, Caesar's gift of the seaport at Joppa to the Jews

---

strue the villages that the Senate returned to the Jews in *A.J.* 14.207 as Hasmonean "personal possessions." Antony, referring to the territory seized by the Tyrian despot Marion in neighboring Galilee in 43 B.C.E., ordered the Tyrians to return "any places which belonged to Hyrcanus, the ethnarch of the Jews" (*A.J.* 14.317). As far as I know, no scholar has yet suggested that in this instance Hyrcanus's "private estates" had been seized, or that the territories henceforth became a Hasmonean possession. Scholars, on the contrary, romanticize in this case about Jewish peasants having been despoiled of rare farmland. In both cases, in fact, we have at work in the documents an alternation of terminology between the Jews and their representative, John Hyrcanus, a vacillation that I noted above

151. Abel, *Géographie,* 1:415.

152. See R. Gophna and Juval Portugali, "Demographic Processes in Israel's Coastal Plain from the Chalcolithic to the Middle Bronze Age," *BASOR* 269 (1988): 11–28; Harry R. Weeks, "Sharon," in *ABD* 5:1161: "In the S[outh], the alluvial soil suitable for farming stops abruptly just N[orth] of the Yarkon River. Therefore the settlement patterns based on archaeological surveys show clusters of settlements around the Yarkon River and to the S[outh]."

153. U. Rappaport ("La Judée et Rome pendant le règne d'Alexandre Jannée," *REJ* 127 [1968]: 329–31) proposes that *A.J.* 14.208 was based on the earlier *senatus consultum (A.J.* 13.259–64). Rappaport's view is taken over by Rosenfeld ("Boundary of Gezer," 243–44). Rosenfeld wants to believe that the mention of Lydda, and not Gezer, in *A.J.* 14.208 shows that Gezer, on account of its decline, "was attached to the toparchy of Lydda." Joshua J. Schwartz ("Boundary of Gezer," 54–56) insists that Caesar's document "has nothing to do with Gezer."

would have made little or no sense if the Jewish state did not control the outlying territory. The Jews, in this event, could not have controlled, especially at its Joppa/Lydda stretch, the main road that led from Joppa to Jerusalem passing through Lydda: the ancient and notorious Beth-horon route. The route is called a "public road" (δημοσία ἄνοδος) by Josephus in *B.J.* 2.228. In the late Hellenistic and early Roman periods this road was, as Avi-Yonah rightly notes, "the main road between the ancient capital and its port at Jaffa."[154]

In the second place, the strategic and commercial centrality of Lydda for the Jewish state did not lie only in its position as the main axis on the route from Jerusalem to the seaport at Joppa.[155] Lydda was also one of the main axes on the ancient trade and military thoroughfare that linked Egypt to Syria and Asia: the "Way of the Sea." Later, under the Romans, this route became known as the *Via Maris*. It was the principal artery of the Roman coastal route running from Caesarea through Antipatris and Lydda to meet the secondary branch (which went from Caesarea through Joppa) at Jamneia in its southward course to Egypt. Before the Romans, who overcame some of the obstacles, the route avoided the oak forest and swamps of the Yarkon River north of Joppa by taking an eastward turn to Lydda and going north through Aphek (which Herod the Great rebuilt and renamed "Antipatris").[156] The strategic centrality of this route for the region cannot be overstated, as Yehuda Karmon underscores in his important study:

> It may be stressed that this route formed the only possibility for road connection between Egypt and the lands of the Middle East, except Arabia, because any direct movement towards the east met with the obstacles of the Dead Sea or the impassable basalt plateau of Transjordan. Thus, for Egypt, more than for any other country of the Middle East, the

154. Avi-Yonah, *Holy Land*, 185. This route was notorious, particularly its Beth-horon ascent, for the Jewish defeat of great invading Seleucid and Roman armies, who had to take the road to Jerusalem from the plain (see 1 Macc 3:13–24 = *A.J.* 12.288–92; *B.J.* 2.516–21, 546–55). The ascent, along with other places, was fortified by the Seleucid general Bacchides in the apparent attempt to secure the major approaches to Jerusalem (1 Macc 9:50–52 = *A.J.* 13.15–16; see Avi-Yonah, *Holy Land*, 53–54; Aharoni and Avi-Yonah, *Atlas*, 148 and map 198). The road was later turned into a Roman highway. Abel, *Géographie*, 2:220–1 and map x; Avi-Yonah, *Holy Land*, 185 and 187, map 24; Menashe Har-El, "Jerusalem & Judea: Roads and Fortifications," *BA* 44 (1981): 8–19, esp. 14–17; Israel Roll and Etan Ayalon, "Roman Roads in Western Samaria," *PEQ* 118 (1986): 122–23, and 114, fig. 1.

155. Har-El ("Roads and Fortifications," 14, 16) claims that there were, at various historical times, eight routes from Joppa to Jerusalem, four of them passing through Lydda. The road through Beth-horon was the most convenient and the shortest, and it remained of critical importance throughout the history of the region.

156. See Kochavi et al., *Aphek-Antipatris*, 2, 3 and maps.

> Sharon formed part of the main route to other countries, and being much narrower than the southern coastal plain, possessed an even greater strategic significance.[157]

It was the coastal plain together with south Sharon, as George Adam Smith observes,[158] that gave Palestine the reputation of being "the Bridge between Asia and Africa," by reason of its maritime and overland routes.[159] Control over parts of the plain was of critical strategic and commercial importance for the Jewish state. It was this control that the Jews acquired when ownership of Lydda was ceded to them by Antiochus VI (1 Macc 11:34, 57),[160] when Joppa was subsequently captured,[161] and finally when Caesar granted both cities to them in 47 B.C.E.

There is no evidence, however, that the Jews lost control of Lydda and its territory after its ownership had been recognized by Antiochus VI. We must not conclude from its being mentioned in *A.J.* 14.208 that it was excised from the Jewish state by Pompey, as Schalit and others have argued.[162] The text of *A.J.* 14.208 is probably too corrupt to allow us to

---

157. Yehuda Karmon, "Geographical Influences on the Historical Routes in the Sharon Plain," *PEQ* 93 (1961): 52. Karmon's work is the most important study of the location of the route in relation to ancient population distribution and the topography of the plain of Sharon. For the description of the route on the basis of the campaigns in Palestine by the Pharaohs Thutmose III and Seti I, see Abel, *Géographie*, 2:217–19 and map x; also Weeks, "Sharon," 1161–63. Avi-Yonah thinks that the *Via Maris* was the oldest Roman road in Palestine, built during or soon after the revolt of 66–70 C.E. Avi-Yonah, *Holy Land*, 181–82, and 187, map 24; Michael Avi-Yonah, "The Development of the Roman Road System in Palestine," *IEJ* 1 (1950–51): 54–60; see also Shimon Dar and Shimon Applebaum, "The Roman Road from Antipatris to Caesarea," *PEQ* 105 (1973): 91–99; Israel Roll, "The Roman Road System in Judaea," in *The Jerusalem Cathedra*, vol. 3 (ed. Lee I. Levine; Jerusalem: Yad Iẓḥak Ben-Zvi Institute, 1983), 136–61.

158. George Adam Smith, *The Historical Geography of the Holy Land* (25th ed.; New York: Harper & Brothers, 1931), 152.

159. For summaries of the historical significance of the plain, see George Adam Smith, *Historical Geography*, 145–64; Weeks, "Sharon," 1162–63.

160. For previous proposals to grant the territory, see 1 Macc 10:30; 11:28, 34; see also *A.J.* 13.50, 125, 127, 145; Avi-Yonah, *Holy Land*, 55–57; Avi-Yonah, "Historical Geography," 86–87.

161. See Avi-Yonah, *Holy Land*, 57.

162. Schalit, *König Herodes*, 756–59. So also Smallwood, *Jews under Roman Rule*, 28 and n. 26, who depends on Schalit's analysis. She admits, however, that the conclusion that the Jewish state had lost Lydda in 63 B.C.E. is based on *A.J.* 14.208. Joshua J. Schwartz (*Lod (Lydda)*, 52) rejects Schalit's theory and emendations but continues, nonetheless, to argue backwards from *A.J.* 14.208 and to look for reasons why Pompey would have removed Lydda from the Jewish state. See also Joshua J. Schwartz, "Boundary of Gezer," 55–56. Scholars otherwise do not generally assume that Lydda was removed from Jewish control. Abel (*Géographie*, 2:146–48) is circumspect and vague. While Lydda is not among the cities he lists as having been taken away from the Jews in 63 B.C.E., he observes (p. 370) that from

know its exact terms. It is, nonetheless, quite clear that by confirming Jewish control over Lydda, together with the grant of Joppa and the surrounding villages, the Senate restated the historical and strategic connection between the two territories and the villages that lay between them. In so doing, Caesar and the Senate opened a veritable corridor for the Jews from Jerusalem to the seaport through Lydda, granting them control over the coastal trade routes by sea and by land. The Senate could, therefore, justifiably demand that Hyrcanus pay tribute for exports and imports passing through this corridor overland and through the harbor (*A.J.* 14.206). Moreover, it might not be altogether far-fetched to suggest that it is also to adjoining territories in the plain of Sharon that the Senate refers in *A.J.* 14.209 when it states: "the places, lands and farms, the fruits of which the kings of Syria and Phoenicia, as allies of the Romans, were permitted to enjoy by their gift, these the Senate decrees that the ethnarch Hyrcanus and the Jews shall have." Of Schalit's emendations and textual rearrangements of Caesar's edicts, the most plausible and useful is that which, in this text, makes "Hyrcanus and the Jews" allies of the Romans and recipients of the territories, in lieu of the "kings of Syria and Phoenicia."[163] But this solution is purely speculative.

Thus, Caesar's territorial grants of Joppa and the "villages" around this city and Lydda pertain to Caesar's reorganization of Judea's economic realities and its related tax obligations. Those scholars who have long sought to situate the "villages" granted by Caesar in a Hasmonean "private royal estate" have also contended that Rome's management of Judea, beginning with Pompey's territorial redistribution in 63 B.C.E., resulted in an increasing dearth of farmland for Jewish peasants.[164] Caesar's addition of valuable, arable land to the Jewish state would certainly have produced the opposite effect. Moreover, by linking the gift of the seaport city of Joppa to the grant of the villages between Joppa and Lydda, Caesar and the Senate opened a door into Judea for both export and import by sea. The Jewish state now controlled the custom dues at the seaport and on the overland route into Jerusalem. Finally, at Lydda

---

Pompey to Herod the fate of the city depended on the fluctuations of Roman politics. Avi-Yonah (*Holy Land*, 81–82) maintains that Pompey left the four toparchies (Lydda, Haramatha, Apharaema, and Acraba) and the territory of Gezer in the Jewish state. See also Avi-Yonah, "Historical Geography," 89–91; Aharoni and Avi-Yonah, *Atlas*, 161 and map 217; A. H. M. Jones, *The Cities of the Eastern Roman Provinces* (ed. Michael Avi-Yonah et al.; 2nd ed.; Amsterdam: Adolf M. Hakkert, 1983), 257–58, 269; Momigliano (*Ricerche*, 14) merely states that Caesar restituted the territory; and Schürer (*History*, 1:274–75 and n. 24) passes Lydda over in silence.

163. Schalit, *König Herodes*, 754–55; Smallwood, *Jews under Roman Rule*, 40 and n. 61.

164. Pastor (*Land and Economy*, esp. 87–97) attempts to reexamine and move away from this thesis.

the Jewish state had access to and control over the strategic and commercial "Way of the Sea." Later, Herod the Great, recognizing the centrality and potential of the plain of Sharon, would rebuild Aphek into Antipatris and the seaport city of Strato's Tower, on a grand scale, into Caesarea Maritima. In so doing he vastly increased the value of the territory and his control over its resources "on the land, the harbour and exports." He thereby assured the prosperity of the client kingdom over which he ruled, as I shall emphasize in chapter 4.

Grants of Freedom: Billeting, Military Service, and Molestation

The payment of *stipendia* (direct taxes) or, as it later came to be known, *tributa*, whether in the form of a fixed amount or as *decumae* (tithe), did not exhaust the financial demands that Rome made on the provinces in the late Republic and afterwards. I have discussed the *portoria* (custom dues) in relation to Joppa and the overland trade route through Lydda. There is no evidence that, until 70 C.E., Rome considered any part of Judea as *ager publicus* (public land, belonging to the Roman people). There were no mines in Judea either. Therefore, we find no payments of either *vectigal* (rents), for working mines and farming public lands, or *scriptura*, the fee for grazing rights on public lands.

These forms of both direct and indirect taxes are thought to have been, on the whole, considerate. This is certainly the case with what Caesar required from Judea. The discussion of financial demands on provincial communities would, however, be incomplete without the "exactions," corvée, and requisitions that had become part of Rome's provincial administration. The financial burden of billeting troops, furnishing transportation, and compulsorily providing entertainment for traveling Roman officials would have been heavy. Such impositions also were sources of endless aggravation and annoyance.[165] Rome responded to some of the problems raised by the imposition of these demands on provincial communities by granting special immunities to individuals, cities, and allied states, and by a legislative curb on excess and abuse. Caesar's grant of exemptions to Judea was part of the first kind of solution. Since the grant of such privileges was coveted and commonplace, Caesar's concessions to the Jewish state are best understood in the general context of both the development of these demands and Rome's search for redress.

165. See the summaries by Rostovtzeff, *Roman Empire*, 337; Mommsen, *History*, 4:160–66; also J. S. Richardson, "Administration of the Empire," 588–89; and Lintott, *Imperium Romanum*, 92–93.

Billeting

Our knowledge of the practice of demanding winter quarters and compulsory entertainment for Roman troops in the eastern provinces comes from complaints and, primarily, from grants of immunity to select individuals and communities. In Judea we learn of the practice from Caesar's decrees granting freedom to the Jewish state in 47 B.C.E. The exemption is first stated in the decree that accompanied Caesar's letter to Sidon: "Nor do I approve of troops being given winter-quarters among them or of money being demanded of them."[166] The grant is repeated and expanded in the *senatus consultum* (*A.J.* 14.204): "nor shall soldiers be allowed to exact money from them, whether for winter-quarters or on any other pretext, but they shall be free from all molestation."[167]

According to Livy (42.1.7–12), Postumius was unjustifiably angry because the Latin city of Paeneste, located about twenty miles from Rome, had shown him "no mark of respect" when he traveled there as a private citizen. Then, as a consul traveling in 173 B.C.E. to Campania on the Senate's official business, he ordered that the city provide him with quarters, entertainment, and transport animals at public expense. He was the first to make such demands on allies of Rome. Before then, says Livy, Roman commanders were supplied with tents, transport animals, and other military equipment so that they would not demand such supplies or hospitality from allies. Those magistrates who lodged in private homes did so out of their privately developed links of reciprocal hospitality. Postumius set a precedent "of the right of magistrates to make demands of this sort, which grew more burdensome day by day" (42.1.12).

It is probable that Postumius's demands were not absolutely the first break with tradition and that such requisitions were gradually gaining ground by the second century B.C.E.[168] Apart from the burdens that provincial communities would have borne as a result of the simple expectation to give, billeting also became an instrument of coercion in the hands of some Roman governors and generals. Some quartered their troops in order to punish cities,[169] or in order to bribe the Roman soldiers.[170] Billeting, because of the arbitrary damage and distress that it

---

166. *A.J.* 14.195: παραχειμασίαν δὲ ἢ χρήματα πράσσεσθαι οὐ δοκιμάζω.

167. For the textual problems of *A.J.* 14.204, see Krebs, *Decreta*, 267–68; H. St. J. Thackeray et al., *Josephus*, 7:556, nn. 3 and 4.

168. See Lintott, *Imperium Romanum*, 92.

169. Marcus T. Varro on some communities in Spain (Caesar, *Bell. civ.* 2.18).

170. So Scipio in 49 B.C.E. on the "richest cities" of Pergamum (Caesar, *Bell. civ.*3.31). Besieged in Jerusalem in 39/38 B.C.E., Antigonus, in an effort to win over Antony to his side,

caused individuals and whole communities, was a source of endless vexation in the provinces (Plutarch, *Sert.* 6.4). Cicero (*Leg. man.* 13. 38) said he doubted that more enemy cities had been destroyed by Roman arms than had friendly states by the Roman system of quartering. He concluded that the sufferings of the inhabitants of such cities must have been worse than those recently inflicted on Italian subjects (*Pis.* 86, 91).[171]

There were notable exceptions. Cicero himself, while he moved about his province of Cilicia did not receive the traditional provisions that Caesar's *lex Iulia de repetundis* (see below) had made legitimate. He claims that there was not "a single case of billeting" during his adminstration. Before him, the cities of the province that could afford it paid large sums of money to the governor for exemptions from billeting, with the people of Cyprus paying nearly two hundred Attic talents annually. Cicero's entourage, with one exception, likewise did not ask for free hospitality (*Att.* 5.16.3, 21:6–7; 6.2.4). Plutarch (*Luc.* 33.3–4) especially praises Lucullus for never quartering his troops in a friendly Greek city. Cicero claims that Pompey also made his troops sleep under canvas (*Leg. man.* 13.39).[172] Sertorius, too, was loved in Spain because he did not quarter his troops there (Plutarch, *Sert.* 6.4). Like Cicero, C. Memmius, during his governorship of Bithynia in 57 B.C.E., observed the provisions of the *lex Iulia*.[173]

The *lex Porcia*, from about 101–100 B.C.E., set limitations on the demands for provisions and hospitality that a governor could make on Rome's allies. Caesar's own *lex Iulia de repetundis* of 59 B.C.E. further imposed strict limits. It is relevant here to mention the provisions against the requisition of grain, the raising of fleets, and the demand for ship money. The law also enjoined magistrates to respect the privileges that had been given to individual communities (see Cicero, *Pis.* 50, 90; *Flac.* 27; *Prov. cons.* 4.7).

Immunity from billeting was rarely given but much appreciated when it was.[174] A letter, possibly of L. Mummius to the guild of Dionysiac Artists, written sometime after 146 B.C.E., grants the artists, their wives, and their children immunity from billeting, as well as from liturgies, taxes, and war contributions.[175] Sulla's letter of 84 B.C.E. reasserted these

---

apparently induced Silo to quarter part of his troops in Lydda (*A.J.* 14.412; *B.J.* 1.302). Herod gave them quarters in Idumea, Samaria, and Galilee (*A.J.* 14.411; *B.J.* 1.302).

171. See Mommsen, *History*, 5:408; Rostovtzeff, *Roman Empire*, 375; P. A. Brunt, *The Fall of the Roman Republic and Related Essays* (Oxford: Clarendon, 1988), 263.

172. See Brunt, *Fall of the Roman Republic*, 263.

173. Catullus (10.9–13; 28), who probably accompanied Memmius, complains against him.

174. The community would avoid ruinous outrages; see Plutarch, *Sull.* 25.

175. Sherk, *RGE*, no. 37, lines 3–8 = Sherk, *RDGE*, no. 44, lines 3–8. The date and author of the letter are disputed.

grants for the Ionian-Hellespont guild: "[just as formerly, you shall be] *immune* from every liturgy and military service, and you shall not pay [tax or public expenses,] and you shall not [be disturbed by anyone] for supplies [and billeting, and you shall not be forced] to receive any [lodger . . .]."[176] Sometime after 43 B.C.E., Antony confirmed similar grants made earlier to the members of the Association of Victorious Athletes of Asia.[177] It is most likely that immunity from billeting was included in the privileges given to Seleukos and other veterans by Octavian.[178]

The closest parallel to Caesar's grant of immunity from billeting, requisition of food, and compulsory hospitality to the Jewish state remains the privileges granted in 68 B.C.E. by the *lex Antonia* to the city of Termessus Maior in Pisidia:

> No magistrate or promagistrate (or) legate or anyone else shall introduce soldiers into the town of Termessus Maior in Pisidia or into the land of Termessus Maior in Pisidia for the sake of wintering over, nor shall he bring it about that anyone shall introduce soldiers there or that soldiers should winter over there, unless the senate decrees with mention of the (town's) name that soldiers may be brought into winter quarters in Termessus Maior in Pisidia; no magistrate or promagistrate (or) legate or anyone else shall bring it about, or that more should be taken from them than what in accordance with the Porcian Law is or will be required of *them* to give or provide.[179]

The reference in this decree to the *lex Porcia* is an indication that the *lex Iulia* of 59 B.C.E. might have taken over the earlier legislation that specified the legitimate demands for provision and hospitality.[180] A magistrate could demand from provincials no more than the basic requirements such as shelter, beds, salt, firewood, and fodder. He could neither accept gifts nor demand gold crowns (*aurum coronarium*) unless they were voted him in a triumph.[181] One could not expect to receive more than these from the city of Termessus. The prohibition of billeting in the city also is limited by the exception of a specific vote of the Senate. It is not clear whether this was also a provision of the *lex Porcia*.

---

176. Sherk, *RGE*, no. 62B, lines 9–13 = Sherk, *RDGE*, no. 49B, lines 9=13.

177. Sherk, *RGE*, no. 85, lines 14–15 = Sherk, *RDGE*, no. 57, lines 14–15.

178. Sherk, *RDGE*, no. 58, line 35; Sherk, *RGE*, no. 86, n. 9; see Roussel's reading of the fragment of Octavian's letter to veterans: "Invitis eis ne[que] magistr[at]us ceter[os] neque l(e)gatum [n]eque procuratorem [ne]que em[p]torem t[ri]butorum esse [p]lacet neque in domo eorum divertendi <h>iemandique causa (ne)que ab ea quem de(d)uci place<t>" ("Un Syrien," 49).

179. Sherk, *RGE*, no. 72, col. 2, lines 6–17 = Dessau, *ILS*, no. 38, col. 2, 6–17. See also the exemptions in Reynolds, *Aphrodisias and Rome*, no. 8, lines 33–37.

180. Lintott, *Imperium Romanum*, 105.

181. See Cicero, *Att.* 5.10.2, 16.3, 21.5; *Pis.* 90; Pliny, *Ep.* 4.9.6–7.

Compared with the privileges that Caesar and the Senate gave to the Jewish state, the *lex Antonia* is not an absolute prohibition of the requisitioning of food and hospitality, or of winter quartering in Termessus. On the contrary, *A.J.* 14.195 and 204, prohibit both requisitioning and winter quartering in Judea without exceptions. However, Caesar and the Senate did not prohibit the transition of Roman troops through Judea.

There are no reports, in Josephus's narrative or elsewhere, of troop-quartering in Jewish territory in the period from 63–47 B.C.E. The fact that the Jews sought and obtained immunity from the demands, however, indicates that Judea had not been spared the abuses that had become almost universal. After Caesar's death the Senate confirmed the privileges granted to Judea (*A.J.* 14.217–22), and in 41 B.C.E. Antony upheld them (*A.J.* 14.313).[182] Roman legislation and grants of immunity during the Republic presaged the days in the Principate when Roman troops in the provinces would actually build and be quartered in permanent encampments. The reports of troop movements and quartering in Judea, except the cases involving Antigonus and Herod in 39/38 B.C.E. (*A.J.* 14.406–12, 417–18; *B.J.* 4.297–302, 308),[183] leave no reason to doubt that the territory's immunity from billeting was respected.[184]

Military Service

Along with the exemptions that we have just noted, immunities from military obligations granted by magistrates and the Senate included freedom from war contributions and from conscription into the army, legionary (for Roman citizens) or auxiliary (for citizens of provincial cities and allied states).[185] Exemption from war contributions is included in the grants to the Dionysiac Artists,[186] and it also was possibly among the privileges given by Octavian to Seleukos.[187] Exemption from military service was granted in Rome to men who had reached the age of forty-

---

182. See chapter 3.

183. See n. 170 above.

184. A Roman legion was encamped in Jerusalem in 35/34 B.C.E. (*A.J.* 15.72). According to *A.J.* 18.55, Roman (auxiliary) troops under the *praefecti*, normally stationed in Caesarea Maritima, had winter quarters in Jerusalem. These quarters were most probably located in Herod's palace (*B.J.* 2.438–40; compare Mark 15:16), rather than in the Antonia (*B.J.* 5.238–47). During this period the Romans seem also to have garrisoned the fortresses. Masada, Cypros, and Macherus are specifically mentioned (*B.J.* 2.408, 484, 485–86).

185. See in particular D. B. Saddington, *The Development of the Roman Auxiliary Forces from Caesar to Vespasian, 49 B.C.-A.D. 79* (Harare: University of Zimbabwe, 1982).

186. Sherk, *RGE*, no. 37, lines 3–8 = Sherk, *RDGE*, no. 44, lines 3–8.

187. Sherk, *RDGE*, no. 58, col. 2, line 35; see Sherk, *RGE*, no. 86, n. 9.

five, maritime colonists in colonies created after 425 B.C.E., and apparitors of colonial *duumviri*. Also exempt were certain veterans and their children, augurs and their children, and priests.[188] The members of the Association of Victorious Athletes were also exempt,[189] and Sulla confirmed the same right to the Dionysiac Artists of the Ionian and Hellespont guild.[190]

The documents that Josephus quotes do not indicate that Caesar and the Senate granted the Jewish state immunity from war contributions. Nevertheless, Judea did receive exemption from military service: "no one, whether magistrate or pro-magistrate, praetor or legate, shall raise auxiliary troops (συμμαχίαν) in the territories of the Jews" (*A.J.* 14.204). Earlier, the consul Lucius Lentulus[191] granted the Jews who were Roman citizens and resident in Asia Minor exemption from conscription into the Roman army in 49 B.C.E., at the beginning of the civil war between Julius Caesar and Pompey.[192] This exemption was reconfirmed by Dolabella at the request of Hyrcanus II in January 43 B.C.E. at the onset of the civil war following the assassination of Julius Caesar (*A.J.* 14.223–27).[193]

After they came under the Roman sphere of influence, the Jews had fought alongside Roman forces with Gabinius against Alexander (*A.J.* 14.84–85; *B.J.* 1.162–63) and also in Gabinius's campaign in Egypt (*B.J.* 1.175).[194] Caesar himself benefited from the services of Jewish forces during his Alexandrian campaign (*A.J.* 14.127–36, 138–39, 193; *B.J.* 1.187–92). Subsequently, Jewish forces, particularly under the young Herod, contin-

188. See Appian, *Bell. civ.* 2.21, 150; see A. C. Johnson et al., *Ancient Roman Statutes: A Translation* (Corpus of Roman Law 2; Austin: University of Texas Press, 1961), 18, no. 9.

189. Sherk, *RGE*, no. 85, line 14 = Sherk, *RDGE*, no. 57, line 14.

190. Sherk, *RDGE*, no. 49 B, lines 9–10= Sherk, *RGE*, no. 62 B, lines 9–10.

191. Caesar *Bell. civ.* 3.4; Cicero, *Att.* 9.3; Saulnier, "Lois Romaines," 167–69.

192. Lentulus's decree seems to be cited in secondary documents, in two independent versions (*A.J.* 14.228–29, 234, 237 [19]-240). The other decrees are issued by officials of various cities of Asia (*A.J.* 14.230, 231–32, 236–37). Lentulus issued one decree for the Jews who were Roman citizens living in Ephesus, and it was considered to cover all the Jews of Asia. See discussions in Juster, *Les Juifs*, 1:143–44 and n. 8; Giovanni Forni, "Intorno al concilium di L. Cornelio Lentulo console nel 49 a. C.," in *Romanitas-Christianitas: Untersuchungen zur Geschichte und Literatur der römischen Kaizerzeit; Johanes Straub zum 70* (ed. G. Wirth, et al.; Berlin: de Gruyter, 1982), 154–63; Tessa Rajak, "Was There a Roman Charter for the Jews?" *JRS* 74 (1984): 113.

193. Dolabella's edict is also addressed to the city of Ephesus, "the chief city of Asia," but (as might have been the case with Lentulus) he orders that the magistrates of the city "write these instructions to the various cities" (*A.J.* 14.227); see the instructions of the Roman official to the Conventus of Asia in Sherk, *RDGE*, no. 52, lines 42–54 = Sherk, *RGE*, no. 77, lines 42–54. For a discussion of these decrees, see Pucci Ben Zeev, *Jewish Rights*, 139–75.

194. The parallel passage (*A.J.* 14.98–99) does not mention troops in the list of Jewish contributions to the campaign.

ued to take an active part in Roman wars.[195] Caesar and the Senate did not actually prohibit such participation by Jewish armies in Roman campaigns. Rather, they exempted the Jewish state from the obligation, which was imposed by Roman magistrates, to contribute troops to the Roman auxiliary forces.[196]

The grants of immunity from war contributions and military service to groups such as the Dionysiac Artists and the Association of Victorious Athletes, and to individuals such as Seleukos, suggest that these grants were made, as Pucci Ben Zeev observes, to "non-territorial peoples."[197] The inclusion of augurs and priests among those exempt in Rome indicates that religious practices were among the considerations that motivated the grants.[198] The grants to the Dionysiac Artists were made "for the sake of Dionysios *and* [of the other] *gods* and of the way of life which you have preferred."[199] Likewise, Lentulus's decree gave "consideration of their religious scruples" (*A.J.* 14.228) as the reason for exempting the Jews of Asia. These "scruples," are specified in the decree of Dolabella: the Jews "may not bear arms or march on the days of the Sabbath; nor can they obtain the native foods to which they are accustomed" (*A.J.* 14.226).[200]

Considerations for these Jewish religious needs might have, at least in part, induced Caesar to grant the Jews living in Judea immunity from military service. Hyrcanus II, who asked for the exemption,[201] could not

---

195. I list only some of the early instances: In 46 B.C.E. Antipater sent Jewish auxiliary troops (συμμαχίαν) under his sons to fight with Caesar's supporters in the battle of Apamea (*A.J.* 14.268–69; *B.J.* 1.216–17); Cassius and Murcus later put Herod at the head of the auxiliary troops they had raised in Syria; Herod does not seem to have been involved in the conflicts with the *Triumviri* after all (*A.J.* 14.280; *B.J.* 1.225). In 38 B.C.E., however, Herod, interrupting his own wars in Palestine, aided Antony in the siege of Samosata (*A.J.* 14.439–47; *B.J.* 1.321–22).

196. Jews did fight in Roman armies, even if in small numbers. See discussions in Shimon Applebaum, "Jews and Service in the Roman Army," in *Roman Frontier Studies, 1967: The Proceedings of the Seventh International Congress Held at Tel Aviv* (ed. Shimon Applebaum; Tel Aviv: Tel Aviv University, 1971), 181–84; Perlina Varon, "Testimonianze del servizio prestato dagli Ebrei nell'esercito Romano," in *Gli Ebrei nell'impero Romano* (ed. Ariel Lewin; Florence: La Giuntina, 2001), 271–7.

197. Pucci Ben Zeev, *Jewish Rights*, 161–62.

198. See Pucci Ben Zeev, *Jewish Rights*, 546.

199. Sherk, *RGE*, no. 37, lines 3–4 = Sherk, *RDGE*, no. 44, lines 3–4.

200. On the problem of Jews fighting on the Sabbath, see *A.J.* 12.274–77; 1 Macc 2:29–41; *A.J.* 18.318–25, 353–56; *A.J.* 13.251–52; 14.60–65; *B.J.* 1.145–47, 456. The problem of the Roman military diet for Jews was not that they were unaccustomed to foreign foods, as Dolabella seems to suggest, but rather the prohibitions by Jewish dietary laws. One would think that Jews serving in the army would have found their way around eating prohibited foods, as they did in their contacts with Gentiles in other contexts. On food given to Roman soldiers, see R. W. Davies, "The Roman Military Diet," *Britannia* 2 (1971): 122–42.

201. The grants are all made at the request of Jewish authorities. The bulk of adminis-

have been unaware, however, of the economic and human toll that conscription took on a territory. As a result of the exemption, the Jewish state did not bear the economic burden that resulted from the loss of manpower to Roman wars. In addition, the Jews in Palestine were spared the extortion endured elsewhere in the provinces by those who wanted to avoid conscription. Later on, under direct Roman rule, the Jews contributed nothing to the Roman garrisoning of their territory.[202]

Molestation: **Angareia,** *the Temple Tax*

Two important areas remain to be examined in relation to Caesar's and the Senate's grant that soldiers not "be allowed to exact money" from the Jews "on any other pretext, but they shall be free from all molestation" (ἀνεπηρεάστους [*A.J.* 14.204]).[203] The first is the demand for transport (*angareia*) and the second regards the harassments suffered by Jews in connection with the collection, transportation, and storage of the temple tax.

Angareia

As we have already seen, the demand for hospitality (*hospitum*) by traveling Roman soldiers and officials was often paired with the requisition of transport, sometimes known as *angareia*. The Greek substantive ἀγγαρεία, from the Persian loanword ἀγγαρεύω ("to press/force into service," "to requisition"), described the Persian royal postal network.[204] One of the only two instances in which the word ἀγγαρεύω and its cognates occur in Josephus's works is in his paraphrase of the biblical account of Esther's marriage to a Persian king. The king, Josephus says, "sent out messengers called *angaroi* to every nation,[205] inviting them to celebrate the wedding" (*A.J.* 11.203). This information adds to the biblical account; Josephus otherwise follows the *Septuagint* version of the story.[206] The system of req-

---

trative documents from the Roman Empire shows that such actions were not taken by the spontaneous initiative of Roman magistrates. See Fergus Millar, "The Emperor, the Senate, and the Provinces," in *Rome, the Greek World, and the East* (ed. Hannah M. Cotton and Guy M. Rogers; Chapel Hill: University of North Carolina Press, 2002), 156–66.

202. See summary in Schürer, *History*, 1:362–67.

203. Also *A.J.* 14.195: "Nor do I approve . . . of money being demanded of them."

204. Herodotus, *Hist.* 3.126; 8.98; also Xenophon, *Cyr.* 8.6.17–18.

205. διέπεμψε δὲ τοὺς ἀγγάρους λεγομένους εἰς πᾶν ἔθνος (literally, "he sent out the so-called *angaroi* to every nation").

206. The Persian king who weds Esther is Artaxerxes (465–425 B.C.E.) in Josephus. In this he agrees with the Septuagint against the Hebrew text (Esth 1–2; see Ezra 4:6), which

uisitioning transport is attested also in Ptolemaic Egypt.[207] The only reference to requisitioned transport in the Seleucid Empire marks the second occurrence of *angareia* in Josephus's works. Demetrius I is said to have written to Jonathan in 153/152 B.C.E.: "And I command that the Jews' beasts of burden shall not be requisitioned for our army, and that on the Sabbaths and all festivals and the three days preceding a festival the Jews shall be exempt from labour" (*A.J.* 13.52).[208]

The exemption from the requisitioning of beasts of burden is, again, Josephus's addition to the account as it appears in 1 Macc 10:33, where Demetrius is said to have canceled the tribute on livestock, possibly for Jewish returnee captives: "and let all [officials] cancel also the taxes on their livestock."[209] The substitution of the exemption from the requisitioning of Jewish draft animals for Demetrius's cancellation of taxes on livestock is best seen as an instance of Josephus's anachronistic reading of biblical history.[210] Other innovative additions by Josephus to Demetrius's letter are the inclusion of Samaria as a "toparchy" of the Jewish state (*A.J.* 13.50)[211] and the exemption from poll tax (*A.J.* 13.50).[212] Since it appears

names the king as Ahasuerus, identified as Xerxes I (485–465 B.C.E.). Josephus confuses this king with the monarch named in the Septuagint and declares at the beginning of his Esther narrative: "On the death of Xerxes the kingdom passed to his son Asueros, whom the Greeks call Artaxerxes" (*A.J.* 11.184). Moreover, he follows the Septuagint in identifying the month of the wedding as "the twelfth month, called Adar" (*A.J.* 11.202; see LXX Esth 2:16). The Hebrew text speaks of "the tenth month, which is the month of Tebeth" (MT Esth 2:16).

207. P.Teb. 703.70–79, 215–21 (Authur S. Hunt and Gilbart J. Smyly, eds., *The Tebtunis Papyri*, vol. 3 [New York: Oxford University Press, 1933], 1:75, 80).

208. Κελεύω δὲ μηδὲ ἀγγαρεύεσθαι τὰ Ἰουδαίων ὑποζύγια· τὰ δὲ σάββατα καὶ ἑορτὴν ἅπασαν καὶ τρεῖς πρὸ τῆς ἑορτῆς ἡμέρας ἔστωσαν ἀτελεῖς. "For our army" in the translation is Marcus's interpretation of Josephus's ἀγγαρεύεσθαι.

209. Καὶ πάντες ἀφιέτωσαν τοὺς φόρους καὶ τῶν κτηνῶν αὐτῶν. On the difficulties of the passage, see Jonathan A. Goldstein, *1 Maccabees: A New Translation with Introduction and Commentary* (AB 41; Garden City, N.Y.: Doubleday, 1976), 408–9.

210. Goldstein (*1 Maccabees*, 409), who thinks *angareia* might have been at issue in Demetrius's edict, observes that Josephus's paraphrase would have been "a thoroughly plausible interpretation of the text" if he had made the edict say "the Jews and their beasts of burden . . . ," that is, referring to the captured and enslaved Jews.

211. Samaria was not part of the Jewish state under Jonathan. The three districts referred to in 1 Macc 10:30 (alluded to in 1 Macc 10:38; see *A.J.* 13.54) are Lydda, Rathamin, and Aphairema "added to Judaea from Samaria." Grant of the territories is said to have been confirmed by Demetrius II in 144 B.C.E. (1 Macc 11:34; see *A.J.* 13.127). See Aharoni and Avi-Yonah, *Atlas*, 149–50 and map 200. The claim (*C. Ap.* 2.43) that Alexander the Great granted Samaria to the Jews "in recognition of the consideration and loyalty shown to him by the Jews," is baseless. See Adolphe Büchler, "La relation de Josèphe concernant Alexandre le Grand," *REJ* 36 (1898): 20.

212. The only other reference to a poll tax in the Seleucid Empire is Josephus's report of a decree of Antiochus III, granting tax exemptions to "the senate, the priests, the scribes of the temple and the temple-singers" in Judea (*A.J.* 12.142). Elias Bickerman (*Institutions des*

that Josephus revised Demetrius's edict in 1 Macc 10:26–45 from the perspective of the first century C.E., interpolating the realities that were known to him,[213] the reference in *A.J.* 13.52 to requisitioning does not evidence the existence of this practice in the Seleucid Empire.[214] Nonetheless, it is possible that the system of *angareia* entered Roman provincial adminstration through Ptolemaic Egypt, as M. Rostovtzeff has suggested.[215]

According to Seutonius (*Aug.* 49.3), it was Augustus who created the Roman courier system in order to maintain rapid and accurate communication throughout the empire.[216] Claudius's edict of 49/50 C.E. attempted to regulate and mitigate the burden that the *vehiculatio* imposed on Italy and the provinces.[217] It is not clear, however, whether the term *vehiculatio* (later known as the *cursus publicus*)[218] referred only to the Roman imperial postal system or to the general practice of the exaction of services by

---

Séleucides [Paris: Librairie Orientaliste Paul Geuthner, 1938], 111, n. 2) thinks that the poll tax in *A.J.* 13.50 was interpolated by Josephus from Antiochus III's letter. Lintott (*Imperium Romanum*, 79 and n. 51), on the contrary, citing *A.J.* 12.142 and 13.59 [*sic*], claims that the poll tax was "a traditional form of tax in Palestine and almost certainly elsewhere in the Seleucid realms (together with a crown-tax, salt-tax and tax on grain)." Also unfounded is the view by Bar-Kochva ("Manpower," 172–73) that the φόρος in Judea was a tax (in addition to the taxes on produce) equal to three hundred talents. The passages he cites (1 Macc 11:28; 13:15; 2 Macc 4:8; *A.J.* 13.247; and Diodorus, 34–35.1–5) do not support what he claims. M. Rostovtzeff (*The Social and Economic History of the Hellenistic World* [3 vols; Oxford: Clarendon, 1941], 1:466–68) and Bickerman (*Institutions des Séleucides*, 131–32, 179) consider the φόρος in Seleucid Palestine to have been a land tax different from the taxes listed in 1 Macc 10:30. See also A. Mittwoch, "Tribute and Land-Tax in Seleucid Judaea," *Bib* 36 (1955): 352–61.

213. Büchler ("Relation de Josèphe," 19–20) thinks that *A.J.* 13.48–57 reflects Julius Caesar's grants to Judea.

214. According to Lintott, *Imperium Romanum*, 94 and n. 141; and Stephen Mitchell, "Requisitioned Transport in the Roman Empire: A New Inscription from Pisidia," *JRS* 66 (1976): 129, n. 156 (citing also 1 Macc 10:33). M. Rostovtzeff ("Angareia," *Klio* 6 [1906]: 250–51) on the contrary, argues that the prohibition of requisitioning reflects Josephus's own times.

215. Rostovtzeff, *Roman Empire*, 334–36; idem, "Angareia," 251.

216. For evidence for the courier systems in the Republic, see Caesar, *Bell. civ.* 3.101; Suetonius, *Jul.* 57. Cicero sent his mail by the courier system of the *Publicani* (*Att.* 5.16.1, 21.4).

217. Dessau, *ILS*, no. 214 = David C. Braund, *Augustus to Nero: A Sourcebook on Roman History, 31 BC-AD 68* (London: Croom Helm, 1985), no. 582: "Although I have often attempted to relieve not only the colonies and municipalities of Italy but also those of the provinces, likewise the states of each province, from the burdens of transport provision (*oneribus vehiculorum praebendorum*) and although I have thought I had found a sufficient number of remedies, it has nevertheless proved impossible to cope adequately with the evil of men . . . ."

218. See P. A. Brunt, "Addendum I," in *The Roman Economy: Studies in Ancient Economic and Administrative History*, by A. H. M. Jones (Oxford: Blackwell, 1974), 180.

troops and officials on the move. The imperial postal network covered only certain major roads in the empire, and there is no evidence until the third century that an extensive, organized system existed. The postal network, in any event, would not have imposed a significant burden on the communities charged with maintaining it.[219] This postal network must, however, be distinguished from the more general need for transport by Roman military and administrative officials.

Before Postumius's actions in 173 B.C.E., according to Livy (42.1.10), ambassadors who were dispatched in haste were entitled only to single animals. From Cicero's attack on Piso for the indiscriminate distribution of *diplomata* while he was proconsul of Macedonia (*Pis.* 90), it might be inferred that governors and others who held these traveling certificates issued by the Senate were entitled also to requisition transport. Not much is known, however, about the *diplomata* in the late Republic.[220] Furthermore, little evidence exists of requisitioned transport itself during this time. It would seem that there were no universal procedures or comprehensive regulations governing requisitioning, even though transport was certainly needed, not only for the movement of persons but also for military supplies, especially food.[221]

Scholars cite Matt 27:32 and Matt 5:41 as evidence for requisitioning in Palestine during the first century C.E.[222] I need not discuss the problems with the historical reliability of the stories about Simon and the sayings material associated with them. Nevertheless, one need not accept that these passages reflect the actual experience in Palestine.[223] It is sufficient that the authors of these Gospel passages would have known the

---

219. Fergus Millar, *The Roman Empire and Its Neighbours* (2nd ed.; London: Duckworth, 1981), 97; Mitchell, "Requisitioned Transport," 129. Brunt (*Roman Imperial Themes*, 180) observes that the *onera vehiculorum praebendorum* spoken of in Claudius's edict "may from the first have included the provision of transport for supplies as well as for persons, as in the late empire." See Dessau, *ILS*, no. 214; Braund, *Augustus to Nero*, no. 582.

220. See also Cicero, *Att.* 10.17.4; 5.21.7; *Fam.* 7.12.3.

221. See Cicero, *Fam.* 10.18.3; Pliny, *Nat.* 7.135; Mitchell, "Requisitioned Transport," 129, n. 156.

222. Matt 27:32: Τοῦτον [Σίμωνα] ἠγγάρευσαν ἵνα ἄρῃ τὸν σταυρὸν αὐτοῦ ("They compelled this man [Simon] to carry his cross"). See the parallel passage in Mark 15:21: καὶ ἀγγαρεύουσιν παράγοντά τινα Σίμωνα . . . ἵνα ἄρῃ τὸν σταυρὸν αὐτοῦ ("And they compelled a passer-by Simon . . . to carry his cross"). Matt 5:41: Καὶ ὅστις σε ἀγγαρεύσει μίλλον ἕν, ὕπαγε μετ' αὐτοῦ δύο ("And if anyone forces you to go one mile, go also the second mile"). Rostovtzeff, *Roman Empire*, 335; idem, "Angareia," 251; Mitchell, "Requisitioned Transport," 129 and n. 156 (the verb does not occur in Luke 23:26 cited also by Mitchell); Millar, *Roman Empire*, 81, 98.

223. The evidence cited by W. D. Davies and Dale C. Allison, Jr. (*The Gospel According to Saint Matthew* [3 vols; ICC; Edinburgh: T&T Clark, 1988–97], 1:546–47) shows only that the author of Matt 5:41 knew about military requisition of transport, not necessarily in Palestine.

practice of requisitioning by Roman soldiers in the first century C.E. The same may be said of Epictetus (ca. 50–120 C.E.) and his dictum.[224]

There is plenty of documentary evidence of the demand for transport during the later Principate; however, the edict of Sextus Sotidius Strabo (governor of Galatia, ca. 15 C.E.) provides unique insight into the procedures and regulations on the system of requisitioning in the early Principate.[225] In the edict we learn that the inhabitants of Sagalassus were required to set up a service of wagons and draft animals. From this service, imperial procurators and officials on military service (*militantes*), both those with *diplomata* and those passing through from other provinces (senators, *equites*, and centurions), were permitted to requisition a specified amount of transport over a specified distance and at a standard rate that varied with the means of transport requisitioned. The edict, however, prohibited private individuals from using the system. Private persons who required transportation for grain, or for their personal baggage and that of their slaves and freedmen, or those who were entitled to official transportation but required more than what was prescribed, were required to hire it at market rate.

Sotidius's edict ties his transport service to the demand for *hospitum* by requiring that free "shelter and hospitality" (*mansio*, σταθμός) be given to his own staff and to those listed as being entitled to official transportation.[226] All was to be done "in such a way that these do not exact other services without payment from people who are unwilling."[227] It is noteworthy that Sotidius's regulations stemmed from the previous rulings by the Emperors Augustus and Tiberius that sought to prevent the use of transport without payment.[228] Sotidius's regulations indicate that the abuses persisted, nonetheless. Attempts were made by officials to obtain more than was allocated to them, with little or no payment; private persons tried to requisition transport regardless of entitlement. The Gospel material and Epictetus recount these abuses, which were present also in the late Republic. As Mitchell duly emphasizes, however, Sotidius's edict took its place in a long line of imperial regulations that sought to combat the problems of the requisition of hospitality and transport.[229]

---

224. Epictetus, *Diatr.* 4.1.79: "You ought to treat your whole body like a poor loaded-down donkey; as long as it is possible, as long as it is allowed; and if it be commandeered and a soldier lay hold of it (ἂν δ' ἀγγαγεία ᾖ καὶ στρατιώτης ἐπιλάβηται), let it go, do not resist nor grumble. If you do, you will get a beating and lose your donkey all the same." See Rostovtzeff, *Roman Empire*, 592, n. 36; Millar, *Roman Empire*, 98.

225. Text and discussion in Mitchell, "Requisitioned Transport," 107–31; see also Lintott, *Imperium Romanum*, 94–95.

226. Mitchell, "Requisitioned Transport," 107, 108, 127–28.

227. Ibid., 109.

228. Ibid., 107, 109, 114.

229. See list of documents in ibid., 111–12.

To summarize, the connection in Sotidius's edict between his transport service and the demand for *hospitum* suggests that Caesar's grant of immunity from the exactions relating to billeting and *hospitum* would have included the prohibition of the demand for transport. The conditions that prevailed in Judea before 47 B.C.E. would lead us to think that the Jewish state was not immune to the abuses that plagued the rest of the Roman Empire. Moreover, Josephus's reading of 1 Macc 10:33 in *A.J.* 13.52 to mean a prohibition of the requisition of the Jews' pack animals suggests that he was aware of the practice of requisitioning, possibly in Judea. However, Josephus records no instance of requisitioned transport in Jewish Palestine under Roman rule in the late Republic and early Principate. Furthermore, there are no records of complaints from the Jewish state in other sources.

The Temple Tax

I have already noted that the costs of the temple tax on the inhabitants of Judea were negligible and that the significance of this tax lay not in the burden that it imposed on Palestinian Jews but rather in its economic importance for the temple in Jerusalem and the Jewish state. Josephus ends his rendition of Demetrius's edict, discussed above, regarding the grants of freedom from taxes and exactions for the Jews with the summary: "In the same manner do I set free the Jewish inhabitants of my realm and assure them of not being molested."[230] This mirrors the conclusion of the section of Caesar's decree that deals with exactions: "nor shall soldiers be allowed to exact money from them, . . . on any other pretext, but they shall be free from all molestation."[231] Josephus's account of Demetrius's decree, as I have already observed, reflects the problems of Roman rule rather than those of the Seleucid Empire. Josephus characterizes as "molestation" the conflicts between the Jews and both the officials of the Roman provincial administration and, especially, the officials of the Greek cities regarding the rights of the Jews to live according to their laws.[232] It is not at all surprising, therefore, that Josephus also expands on

230. *A.J.* 13.53: Τὸν αὐτὸν τρόπον καὶ τοὺς ἐν τῇ ἐμῇ κατοικοῦντας Ἰουδαίους ἐλευθέρους καὶ ἀνεπηρεάστους ἀφίημι (literally, "in the same way also I permit the Jews who live in my realm to be free and unmolested"). According to 1 Macc 10:35, Demetrius decreed that "no one shall have the authority to exact anything from them or annoy any of them about any matter" (καὶ οὐχ ἕξει ἐξουσίαν οὐδεὶς πράσσειν καὶ παρενοχλεῖν τινα αὐτῶν περὶ παντὸς πράγματος).

231. *A.J.* 14.204: μηδὲ στρατιώταις ἐξῇ χρήματα τούτων εἰσπράττεσθαι . . . ἢ ἄλλῳ τινὶ ὀνόματι, ἀλλ᾽ εἶναι πανταχόθεν ἀνεπηρεάστους.

232. Outside these two decrees and in three other, unrelated, passages (see below), Josephus uses the words ἐπήρεια, ἀνεπηρέαστος, and their cognates, only once in *War* and in

the grant of the right to live in accordance with ancestral laws in Demetrius's decree (*A.J.* 13.54).[233]

Central to Caesar's reorganization of the Jewish state were, first, the confirmation by decree of the freedom of the Jews, as an *ethnos*, to be governed by their own customs. Second, Julius Caesar recognized John Hyrcanus II as ethnarch and "protector" of all Jews, not only those living in Judea but also those living in the Greek Diaspora. The terminology used in the Roman documents cited by Josephus seems to have evolved from the grant to the Jews of the right to live according to their customs to the grant of the right to live according to their laws. It was to cities that Rome gave the freedom to be governed by their own laws. As Pucci Ben Zeev has pointed out, however, the difference between the right to live according to their customs and the freedom to be governed by their laws was insignificant for the Jews, since their customs were codified in the written Law.[234]

It is possible, as we saw, that the demands of the Jewish Law might have motivated Caesar's grant of exemption from military service. This exemption and the requirements that the Jews continue to pay tithes and be exempt from tribute in sabbatical years, however, are the only details of the decrees that are directly related to the Jewish Law. Caesar's decrees and the *senatus consulta* that confirmed them do not identify the specific concessions covered by the freedom to live in accordance with the Jewish customs. The problem, then, is to know if Caesar's general grant of freedom to the Jews to live according to their ancestral customs and the specific grant of immunity from financial exactions and "molestation" might have covered the practice of collecting and exporting money, particularly the temple tax, from the Greek Diaspora to Jerusalem.[235] Since the decrees

---

the sixteenth book of *Antiquities*: *B.J.* 2.286 (the incident of the synagogue in Caesarea, May 66 C.E.); *A.J.* 16.27, 31, 34, 45, 47, 60, 63 (conflicts with the cities of Ionia); 160, 170 (conflicts in Asia and Cyrene). These are the other, unrelated, passages: *A.J.* 15.383 (in his building projects, Herod was more mindful of his own "invulnerability"); *A.J.* 15.23 (Alexandra, Mariamme's mother, felt "insulted" by Herod for appointing someone other than her son as high priest); and *A.J.* 13.382 (the Jews committed countless "insulting and abusive acts" against Alexander Janneus).

233. "I also permit them to live in accordance with their country's laws (τοῖς πατρίοις [πατρῴοις] χρῆσθαι νόμοις) and to observe them, and it is my will that those living in the three districts added to Judea shall be subject to these laws." Compare 1 Macc 10:37–38: "and let them live by their own laws, just as the king has commanded in the land of Judah . . . . As for the three districts . . . let them be annexed to Judaea so that they may be considered to be under no ruler and obey no other authority than the high priest." The reference in 1 Macc 10:37 is to a previous decree by Demetrius that gave the Jews in Judea permission to observe their own laws. That permission is now extended to the soldiers who would be enlisted into Demetrius's army. See Goldstein, *1 Maccabees*, 329–30.

234. See Pucci Ben Zeev, *Jewish Rights*, 416.

235. Magen Broshi ("The Role of the Temple in the Herodian Economy," *JJS* 38 [1987]:

that Josephus cites are fragmentary, it is possible that he left out sections of decrees, or even whole decrees, containing detailed grants by Caesar.[236] On the other hand, Josephus's treatment of the "molestation" of the Jews in Greek cities is so closely linked to the right to collect, store, and transport money to Jerusalem that if there existed such a decree by Caesar, Josephus certainly would have included it among the many others he cites from a later period.

In the early Roman period the regulation for the temple tax found its justification in the biblical tradition of Exod 30:11–16.[237] God commanded Moses that whenever he conducted a census each person twenty years of age and older numbered in the census should pay "half a shekel according to the shekel of the sanctuary (the shekel is twenty gerahs), half a shekel as an offering to the Lord." The money was a ransom for oneself "to the Lord," and was offered "to make atonement" for oneself. Moses was to "appoint it [the money] for the service of the tent of meeting." From all appearances, the payment in Exodus was meant to be made once, but an annual tax of one-third of a shekel emerged after the exile "for the service of the house of our God."[238] There seems to be no link between this levy and the one attested in Exod 30:11–16.[239] Nonetheless, Jews paid a tax of a half-shekel in the early Roman period (*A.J.* 18.312). Although the purpose of this half-shekel tax was similar to that of the regulation in Nehemiah,[240] it does not appear that the levy in Nehemiah continued into the later period.[241] It is likely that the temple tax in its later form was instituted under the Hasmoneans, when there was no monarchy to ensure the sacrifices and upkeep of the temple.[242] This annual tax

34) cites *A.J.* 14.215 in support of his assertion that "one of the most important privileges given to Jews under Julius Caesar and Augustus was the right to transfer money to Jerusalem without hindrance." Similarly, Schürer, *History*, 3.1, 118 and n. 44. We shall see below that this decree is by Octavian; moreover, it is not clear that the money for Jerusalem is the issue here. *A.J.* 14.245, also cited by Schürer, might not deal with money (see below).

236. Pucci Ben Zeev, *Jewish Rights*, 147.

237. See Josephus's account of the passage in *A.J.* 3.194–96; also *m. Šeqal.* 1:4–6. J. Liver, "The Half-Shekel Offering in Biblical and Post-Biblical Literature," *HTR* 56 (1963): 184–85.

238. Neh 10:32–33 [MT vv. 33–34]. The list of the services for which the money could be spent included sacrifices "and all the work of the house of our God."

239. See Liver, "Half-Shekel Offering," 181–84.

240. See *m. Šeqal.* 4:1–4; *A.J.* 3.196. Josephus (*A.J.* 11.174–83) skips the "firm covenant," including the temple levy, in Neh 10.

241. See Liver, "Half-Shekel Offering," 184–90.

242. Broshi, "Role of the Temple," 34. The levy is not directly mentioned in Jewish literature of the Hellenistic period, not even in Tob 1:5–8, which presents the list of the offerings made by the faithful to the temple in Jerusalem. Scholars differ on the time under the Hasmoneans when the tax was instituted. Liver ("Half-Shekel Offering," 190 and n. 47) accepts Bickerman's thesis that the tax was not an established institution until the end of

appears to have been contested by the Qumran sectarians,[243] and the story in Matt 17:24–27 suggests continued opposition to it, this time, however, in some early Christian communities.[244]

The temple tax was paid with the stable Tyrian shekel, equal to four Attic *drachmas* (*tetradrachm*) and four Roman denarii.[245] The Tyrian shekel remained the silver currency of Jewish Palestine in the early Roman period.[246] Half a shekel (*didrachma*), although it is impossible to represent its value in modern terms, was not a large sum. In very general terms, it would be approximately equivalent to the wages for two days of work by a hired laborer, usually considered to be at the bottom of the work force.[247] The sum may also be compared with the one and a half shekels that, according to Josephus (*A.J.* 4.71), were paid to redeem the firstborn male of an unclean animal (cf. Num 18:15–16; Lev 27:27; Exod 13:13; 34:19–20) and the five shekels paid for the redemption of the firstborn son.[248] Philo (*Spec.* 1.139–40) thought that the five-shekel fee in particular was "within the power of even the very poor" and was set "as nearly as possible at a sum within the means of all."

There is no doubt that in the early Roman period most adult Jews in

---

Hasmonean rule or even later. See Elias Bickerman, "La charte Séleucide de Jérusalem," in *Studies in Jewish and Christian History*, vol. 2 (Leiden: Brill, 1980), 75–81; idem, "Héliodore au temple de Jérusalem," in ibid., 167–68. See also A. I. Baumgarten, "Invented Traditions of the Maccabean Era," in *Geschichte-Tradition-Reflexion: Festschrift für Martin Hengel zum 70. Geburtstag*, vol. 1 (ed. Hubert Cancik et al.; Tübingen: Mohr Siebeck, 1996), 201–2. Applebaum (*Judaea in Hellenistic and Roman Times*, 27) though without citing any evidence, suggests that it was John Hyrcanus I and Alexander Janneus who increased the tax from one-third shekel in Nehemiah to a half-shekel.

243. See 4QOrdin I, 6–7: "[*Con*]*cerning* [. . .] money of valuations that a man gives as a ransom for his soul: half a [shekel.] Only once shall he give it during his lifetime—the shekel is twenty gerahs according to [the shekel of the sancturary.]" John M. Allegro, *Qumrân Cave 4.I: 4Q158–4Q186* (DJD 5; Oxford: Clarendon, 1968), 7; Liver, "Half-Shekel Offering," 190–98; Schürer, *History*, 2:271–72 and n. 52.

244. For a discussion of Matt 17:24–27, see David Daube, "Temple Tax," in *Jesus, the Gospels, and the Church: Essays in Honor of William R. Farmer* (ed. E. P. Sanders; Macon, Ga.: Mercer University Press, 1987), 121–34. Citing the discussions in *m. Šeqal.* 1:3 and 1:6, Daube contends that priests in the first century did not pay the tax. He argues that Jesus arrogated priestly prerogatives to himself. For a criticism of his thesis, see Sanders, *Jewish Law*, 50–51; Davies and Allison, *Matthew*, 2:737–49.

245. *A.J.* 3.195; 18.312; *B.J.* 7.218; Matt 17:24–27; *t. Ketub.* 13:3. See Schürer, *History*, 2:272 and n. 54.

246. See chapter 5; *contra* Schürer, *History*, 2:62–66 and 272, n. 54.

247. Modern scholars derive this estimate from Matt 20:2, where the denarius is given as the daily wage for a hired laborer. Tob 5:15 also speaks of a wage of "a drachma a day." See Daniel Sperber, "Costs of Living in Roman Palestine," *JESHO* 8 (1965): 248–71; Sanders, *Jewish Law*, 50; idem, *Judaism*, 156.

248. *A.J.* 4.71; in Num 18:15–16 five shekels is also the redemption price for unclean animals; see Num 3:44–51; Exod 13:13; 22:29; 34:20.

Palestine as well as in the Diaspora paid the tax, whether or not they did so with "utmost zeal," or "cheerfully and gladly," as Philo (*Spec.* 1.77) claims. In the Diaspora the money was collected, stored, and then transported to Jerusalem, probably during one of the pilgrimage festivals,[249] by a convoy of chosen delegates under an escort.[250] The first evidence of money meant for Jerusalem that was being raised in the Diaspora appears in *A.J.* 14.112–13, where Josephus cites Strabo with regard to Mithridates' confiscation (in 88 B.C.E.) of eight hundred talents left in Cos by the Jews. This money, according to Josephus, was "God's" and was deposited there by the Jews of Asia. Pseudo-Aristeas (*Let. Aris.* 40) also mentions a contribution of the "first fruits of offerings for the temple and one hundred talents of silver for sacrifices and the other requirements," sent to Jerusalem from Egypt, possibly as a one-time event.[251] More certain and informative are Cicero's statements in his defense of Flaccus. "Every year," he says (*Flac.* 67), "it was customary to send gold to Jerusalem on the order of the Jews from Italy and from all our provinces (*ex Italia et ex omnibus nostris provinciis*)." He mentions four cities in Asia where Jews in the 60s B.C.E. deposited money meant for the temple in Jerusalem (*Flac.* 68–69): Apamea, Laodicea, Adramyttium, and Pergamum. Philo (*Legat.* 156), implies that the Jewish practice in Rome of collecting money for Jerusalem and the recognition of the right to do so were pre-Augustan.[252]

The temple tax is not directly mentioned in any of these earlier testimonies, nor is it explicitly named in some of the edicts issued by Roman authorities after Julius Caesar confirming the Jewish right to collect and export money to Jerusalem. The letter written (most likely) by Octavian in 42/41 B.C.E.,[253] with the reference there to Julius Caesar's earlier per-

---

249. *A.J.* 17.26; 18.312–13; on the pilgrimages and the large number of pilgrims, see *B.J.* 6.423–25 and Philo, *Spec.* 1.69.

250. *A.J.* 16.172; 18.312–13. Philo, *Spec.* 1.78; *Legat.* 156, 216, 312–13. See Schürer, *History*, 3.1:147–48.

251. See also *Let. Aris.* 33 and 42. The money is depicted as part of a large gift from Ptolemy, not as a levy paid by the Jews. Sanders (*Jewish Law*, 293) conjectures that the author intended Ptolemy's gift to be a precedent permitting the Jews of his own time to send the temple tax to Jerusalem. In Josephus's rendering of the letter, Ptolemy sent "dedicatory offerings as first fruits (ἀπρχάς ἀναθημάτων) for the temple, and one hundred talents of silver for sacrifices and other purposes" (*A.J.* 12.50). The date of the *Letter of Aristeas* is uncertain, probably late second century or early first century B.C.E. See R. J. H. Shutt, trans., "Letter of Aristeas," in *The Old Testament Pseudepigrapha* (2 vols.; ed. James H. Charlesworth; London: Darton, Longman & Todd, 1985), 2:8–9, 15.

252. See E. Mary Smallwood, ed. and trans., *Philonis Alexandrini Legatio Ad Gaium* (Leiden: Brill, 1970), 205, 236.

253. *A.J.* 14.213–16. Some scholars (see Rajak, "Roman Charter," 113; Schürer, *History*, 3.1:118 and n. 44, for instance) consider Julius Caesar to be the author of the decree. This

mission, is the earliest extant Roman official document attesting to the Jewish custom of collecting money. However, no reference is made in this letter to the temple tax or to Jerusalem. Publius Servilius Galba, proconsul of Asia (46–44 B.C.E.),[254] writing to the city of Miletus, confirmed the Jews' right to "handle their produce (τοὺς καρποὺς μεταχειρίζεσθαι) in accordance to their custom" (*A.J.* 14.244–46). The meaning of this right is much disputed. The word καρπός sometimes means "first-fruit" in the Septuagint and other Jewish literature written in Greek. In the later literature "first-fruits" (ἀπαρχαί) often means financial contributions and, specifically, the temple tax.[255] Some scholars have, therefore, equated this right to "handle produce" with the permission to collect "sacred monies."[256] This interpretation reads too much into a text that simply could be a generic confirmation of the Jewish right to deal with their food according to their custom.[257] The letter sent in 43 B.C.E. by Dolabella to Ephesus (Josephus, *A.J.* 14.225–27)[258] grants the Jews of Asia, among others, the right "to follow their native customs and to come together for sacred and holy rites in accordance with their law, and to make offerings for their sacrifices" (*A.J.* 14.227). If the letter is considered to reflect the terms of the petition presented to Dolabella by the envoys sent by Hyrcanus II (*A.J.* 14.225–26), the "offerings for their sacrifices" permitted here may plausibly be for sacrifices in Jerusalem. However, Dolabella could also have confirmed the general right of the Jews to collect "sacred money" without regard to the destination of the sums collected.[259]

It is only in the extant documents from the period under Augustus

---

identification is rendered problematic by the fact that Julius Caesar is cited in the third person in the document (*A.J.* 14.215), as Johnson et al. (*Ancient Roman Statutes*, 91–92 and n. 2) observe. For a discussion of previous views, the identification of Octavian as the author, and date of document, see Pucci Ben Zeev, *Jewish Rights*, 109–10, 114–16.

254. See Schürer, *History*, 3.1:117, n. 37 (2); Pucci Ben Zeev, *Jewish Rights*, 200.

255. See Sanders, *Jewish Law*, 291–99; on Philo, see below. See also Schürer, *History*, 3.1:117, n. 37 (2), and the discussion and literature in Pucci Ben Zeev, *Jewish Rights*, 201–3.

256. Schürer, *History*, 3.1:117, n. 37 (2), "administering their assets according to their usual manner"; Johnson et al., *Ancient Roman Statutes*, 93, n. 2: "apparently revenues destined for transmission to Jerusalem"; John M. G. Barclay (*Jews in the Mediterranean Diaspora from Alexander to Trajan, 323 BCE - 117 CE* [Edinburgh: T&T Clark, 1996], 268), observing that "καρποί could refer to temple dues, funds in general or food supply," translates the phrase "to manage their funds"; Paul R. Trebilco (*Jewish Communities in Asia Minor* [Cambridge: Cambridge University Press, 1991], 199, n. 67) states, "καρπούς . . . could simply refer to Jewish money here."

257. See Dolabella's reference to Jewish "native foods" in his decree (*A.J.* 14.226) discussed above; and the decree of the city of Sardis (*A.J.* 14.259–61), which charges city market officials with the duty of making "suitable food" available for the Jews. See Sanders, *Jewish Law*, 277, 96–97; Pucci Ben Zeev, *Jewish Rights*, 222, 224.

258. See p. 80 above.

259. Pucci Ben Zeev, *Jewish Rights*, 144.

and afterwards that Roman officials speak not only of contributions for the temple in Jerusalem but also explicitly in terms that point to the temple tax. In a speech that he puts in Titus's mouth, Josephus asserts that the Romans had permitted the Jews "to exact tribute for God and to collect offerings, without either admonishing or hindering those who brought them" (*B.J.* 6.335). Augustus's edict of 12 B.C.E. (*A.J.* 16.162–65) is the first extant Roman legal document granting permission to the Jews not only to collect their sacred monies but also to export them to Jerusalem: "their sacred monies shall be inviolable and may be sent up to Jerusalem and delivered to the treasurers in Jerusalem" (*A.J.* 16.163). Augustus imposed stiff penalties on anyone who might steal the monies (*A.J.* 16.164) and against general (official) disregard of the provisions of the edict (*A.J.* 16.165).[260]

Augustus's letter was written after Herod intervened in 14 B.C.E. in favor of the Jews of Ionia (*A.J.* 12.125–27; 16.27–62), who complained to Marcus Vipsanius Agrippa that "they had been deprived of the monies sent as offerings to Jerusalem" (*A.J.* 16.28; see 16.45). Most likely, it is to this period that Augustus's *mandatum*[261] to Gaius Norbanus Flaccus, proconsul of Asia (*A.J.* 16.166) should be dated,[262] which urged that the Jews who "bring sacred monies to send up to Jerusalem, may do this without interference." Norbanus Flaccus himself wrote thereafter to the magistrates and council of Sardis to transmit Augustus's orders (*A.J.* 16.171).[263]

Augustus's permission to the Jews living in Rome is attested by Philo (*Legat.* 156–57): "He [Augustus] knew too that they collect money for sacred purposes from their first-fruits and send them to Jerusalem by persons who would offer the sacrifices,"[264] and Augustus did not prevent this practice. Philo summarizes the contents of Augustus's letter regarding the Jews of Asia. Augustus wrote, Philo says, when he learned that

---

260. For a detailed discussion of the decree, see Pucci Ben Zeev, *Jewish Rights*, 238–56. See also Solomon Zeitlin, "The Edict of Augustus Caesar in Relation to the Judaeans of Asia," *JQR* 55 (1964–65): 160–63.

261. See Fergus Millar, *The Emperor in the Roman World, 31 BC-AD 337* (Ithaca, N.Y.: Cornell University Press, 1977), 157–58, 164; G. P. Burton, "The Issuing of Mandata to Proconsuls and a New Inscription from Cos," *ZPE* 21 (1976): 63–68.

262. This letter is best dated to 12 B.C.E. Millar ("Emperor, the Senate, and the Provinces," 61), Smallwood (*Philonis Alexandrini Legatio Ad Gaium*, 310), and Schürer (*History*, 3.1:118–19 and n. 47) date the letter to sometime soon after 12 B.C.E. Rajak ("Roman Charter," 114, n. 24), critical of Smallwood's chronological argument, proposes a date between 17 and 13 B.C.E. See, however, R. J. Evans, "Norbani Flacci: The Consuls of 38 and 24 B.C," *Historia* 36 (1987): 128, and the discussion by Pucci Ben Zeev, *Jewish Rights*, 259–61.

263. Millar, "Emperor, the Senate, and the Provinces," 161; Schürer, *History*, 3.1:118–19 and n. 47; Pucci Ben Zeev, *Jewish Rights*, 282–83; *contra* Saulnier, "Lois Romaines," 183.

264. See Smallwood, *Philonis Alexandrini Legatio Ad Gaium*, 236–39; Pucci Ben Zeev, *Jewish Rights*, 242.

the Jewish "sacred first-fruits were treated with disrespect." Recognizing that Jews traditionally met to subscribe "the annual first-fruits to pay for the sacrifices which they offer and commissioned sacred envoys to take them to the temple in Jerusalem," Augustus ordered "that no one should hinder the Jews from meeting or subscribing or sending envoys to Jerusalem according to their ancestral practice" (*Legat.* 311–13). The plural "first-fruits" (ἀπαρχαί), as Sanders has shown, is often used by Philo to signify the temple tax.[265] Further, Philo reproduces a copy of the letter from Norbanus Flaccus, this time to the archon of Ephesus, in which Flaccus indirectly cites Augustus's letter to him (*Legat.* 315): "Caesar has written to me that the Jews, wherever they may be, regularly according to their old peculiar custom, make a rule of meeting together and subscribing money which they send to Jerusalem. He does not wish them to be hindered from doing this." It appears, then, that Augustus's grant extended to all the cities of Asia, and that the proconsul wrote to the cities of the province to communicate the emperor's orders.[266]

Together with these documents belong two letters by Marcus Vipsanius Agrippa, one to Ephesus (*A.J.* 16.167–68) with regard to the Jews of Asia, and the other to Cyrene (*A.J.* 16.169–70). There is a general agreement among scholars that both letters, which lack any chronological details, date to the period of Agrippa's second tenure as governor of the eastern provinces (17/16–13 B.C.E.), when he came in close contact with the Jews through his friendship with Herod. The letters are therefore generally dated to 14 B.C.E., the year in which Herod interceded for the Jews of Ionia. Agrippa's letter to Ephesus grants the same right to the Jews as we find in the decree issued by Augustus (*A.J.* 16.163): "that the care and custody of the sacred monies belonging to the account of the temple in Jerusalem shall be given to the Jews in Asia in accordance with their ancestral customs." As in Augustus's decree, those who steal the money are to be treated as temple robbers (*A.J.* 16.168; see *A.J.* 16.164).

The letter to Cyrene confirms the same right: "that the sacred monies may be sent to Jerusalem without interference, as is their ancestral custom." Agrippa refers to a previous letter by Augustus (*A.J.* 16.169), and for the first time we learn from the documents why the Greek cities interfered with the collection and export of the money and sometimes confiscated it. It was alleged in Cyrene that the Jews owed taxes to the city, which, according to Agrippa, they did not owe (*A.J.* 16.170). Scholars dis-

265. Sanders, *Jewish Law*, 294–96; also Smallwood, *Philonis Alexandrini Legatio Ad Gaium*, 237–38; see Philo *Legat.* 156–57, 216, 291, the present passage (*Legat.* 311–16); and *Spec.* 1.77–78. In *Spec.* 1.153–55 and *Mos.* 1.254, ἀπαρχαί may refer to other (dedicatory) contributions from the Diaspora.

266. Schürer, *History*, 3.1:119, n. 47 (3); Smallwood, *Philonis Alexandrini Legatio Ad Gaium*, 310; Pucci Ben Zeev, *Jewish Rights*, 283.

agree about what specific taxes might have been alleged.[267] It is not important that I settle that question here, but it should be noted first that Agrippa agreed with his Jewish suppliants that no taxes were owed. Second, according to Josephus, the Jews of Ionia complained to Agrippa that they were "being forced to participate in military service and civic duties (στρατειῶν καὶ λειτουργιῶν ἀναγκαζόμενοι κοινωνεῖν) and to spend their sacred monies for these things, although they had been exempted from these duties . . ." (*A.J.* 16.28). Nicolaus of Damascus's speech in defense of the Jews framed the problem, however, using the same terms as in Agrippa's letter: "by laying hands on the money which we contribute in the name of God and by openly stealing it from our temple, by imposing taxes upon us . . . " (*A.J.* 16.45; see *A.J.* 16.168, 170).

The Jews seem to have interpreted the permission given them by Rome to live according to their laws as an exemption from civic duties, especially in the form of liturgies, which were essential to the economic life of the cities. It is not at all clear that Agrippa agreed with this interpretation. Exemption from city taxes and liturgies had to be explicitly granted by Rome. There is no evidence that the Jews ever obtained such an exemption. The cities, for their own survival, tried to limit the number of such grants. Mitylene, for instance, received from Caesar the privilege that no one would be exempted from taxes and liturgies in the city.[268] In 6/7 C.E. Augustus intervened on behalf of the city of Cyrene itself ordering that those persons in the province of Cyrenaica who had been honored with Roman citizenship "perform the personal liturgies, nevertheless, in their role as Greeks, with the exception of those to whom in accordance with a law or decree of the senate (or) of my father or of myself, immunity from taxation has been granted. . . ."[269] Jewish failure to participate in the civic and economic life of the cities, especially in economically difficult times, would have made their practice of raising taxes and exporting large amounts of money from the cities to Judea intolerable. In the 60s B.C.E., Flaccus responded to the problem[270] and probably set a precedent by seizing the money. The cities continued periodically to ignore Roman decrees protecting the money and to devise measures meant to prevent its exportation to Judea.

---

267. See discussion in Pucci Ben Zeev, *Jewish Rights*, 271–72, 276–80.

268. On the request by the citizens of Mytilene, Julius Caesar wrote to them: "*nobody* ought *to be* immune (ἀτελῆ) among you according to [your laws and the] privileges which you have had from us . . ." Sherk, *RGE*, no. 83, col. b, lines 26–29 = Sherk, *RDGE*, no. 26, col. b, lines 26–29.

269. Sherk, *RGE*, no. 102, III, lines 57–59. See chapter 4, p. 150 and n. 191 below.

270. On the economic and political circumstances of Flaccus's action, see Marshall, "Flaccus," 148–55; Barclay, *Jews in the Mediterranean*, 266–67; also Pucci Ben Zeev, *Jewish Rights*, 271–72.

It was these grants by Augustus and Agrippa that formed the legal basis for the Jewish right to collect and transport the temple tax to Jerusalem. Hence, Julius Antonius appealed to the decrees and letters by Augustus and Agrippa in confirming the Jewish rights in Asia in his letter of 4 B.C.E.: "Caesar Augustus and Agrippa have permitted them to follow their own laws and customs, and to bring the offerings (ἀπαρχάς),[271] which each of them makes of his own free will and out of piety toward the Deity, travelling together under escort [to Jerusalem] without being impeded in any way" (*A.J.* 16.172). The grants by Agrippa and Augustus are also mentioned together by Philo in a speech given by Jewish elders to Petronius in 40 C.E. (*Legat.* 240).[272]

Before the time of Augustus, as we noted, Jews were already collecting the temple tax in Rome (Philo, *Legat.* 156) and elsewhere in the Roman Empire (*Flac.* 67–69). The export of money was, in general, not illegal in the Roman Empire. Prior to Augustus's and Agrippa's grants, the Jews needed no special permission to send their contributions to Jerusalem. Nevertheless, in the 60s B.C.E. the Senate issued a series of *senatus consulta*, the last one in 63 B.C.E., which explicitly prohibited the export of silver and gold from Rome (Cicero, *Flac.* 67). It was at this time also that Flaccus issued his edict in Asia and proceeded to confiscate Jewish money there. Scholars have usually assumed that the Jews of Rome were formally granted an exemption and that Flaccus's edict had violated that formally granted right.[273] There is no trace of this exemption, however, not even in the works of Philo and Josephus who would have had every interest in citing it. On the other hand, Cicero says that the Jews throughout the empire had continued to send their offerings to Jerusalem during the prohibition (*Flac.* 67–69), and this must be taken to include Rome. Had the Jews in Rome been prevented from forwarding their collection, Cicero would not have failed to seize upon the precedent, which would have made Flaccus's edict and confiscation completely legal.[274] Marshall has argued, therefore, that the Jewish export of the temple tax in the 60s B.C.E., despite the prohibition, was a custom that was allowed to continue *de facto* by the indifference or tolerance of the Roman authorities, and which could be stopped if there was reason to enforce the *senatus consulta* in the particular case. This is precisely what Flaccus did in Asia.[275]

---

271. On ἀπαρχαί, see above.

272. See Smallwood, *Philonis Alexandrini Legatio Ad Gaium*, 278–79; also Jean-Michel Roddaz, *Marcus Agrippa* (Rome: École française de Rome, 1984), 460–62.

273. See Juster, *Les Juifs*, 1:379; Smallwood, *Philonis Alexandrini Legatio Ad Gaium*, 205; eadem, *Jews under Roman Rule*, 126; Alfredo Mordechai Rabello, "The Legal Condition of the Jews in the Roman Empire," in *ANRW* 2.13:711–2, among others.

274. See Pucci Ben Zeev, *Jewish Rights*, 469–70.

275. Marshall, "Flaccus," 145–46; also Pucci Ben Zeev, *Jewish Rights*, 470; Miriam Pucci Ben Zeev, "Did the Jews Enjoy a Privileged Position in the Roman World?" *REJ* 154 (1995): 29–31.

If the right to export the temple tax to Jerusalem existed only as a *de facto* custom in the 60s B.C.E., when a prohibition was in force, it is unlikely that there was need in 47 B.C.E., when there was no interdiction, for Caesar to grant an explicit permission. I have already noted that if such an explicit grant had existed, Josephus certainly would have cited it. Nor does Philo, although referring to the practice, record any explicit grant of the right to collect and export the temple tax before Augustus. Octavian's letter of 42/41 B.C.E. (*A.J.* 14.213–16) states that Caesar, when he banned the *collegia* in Rome (see Suetonius, *Jul.* 42.3), did not forbid the Jews to assemble "or to collect contributions of money or to hold common meals." Consistent with Caesar's grant that the Jews in Judea had the right to live according to their customs, Caesar allowed the practices—which would include the collection of the temple tax—to continue. Octavian's own policy of not banning Jewish assemblies in Rome[276] and his recognition of the same right to Jews elsewhere in the empire were a continuation of that consistency.

Thus, in 12 B.C.E., responding as "Augustus" to the situation in Asia, Octavian referred to the relationship between Caesar and Hyrcanus II. He based his own policy of permitting the Jews to collect and forward the temple tax to Jerusalem on the right, granted by Caesar, whereby the Jews were allowed to "follow their own customs in accordance with the law of their fathers, just as they followed them in the time of Hyrcanus" (*A.J.* 16.162–63). Similarly, although Josephus (through the mouth of Nicolaus) speaks of "many decrees of the Senate and tablets deposited in the Capitol" (*A.J.* 16.48) in support of the Jewish people's "existing right" to observe their customs, he merely cites the one "letter which Caesar wrote to the Senate" in 47 B.C.E. as evidence of Caesar's grant (*A.J.* 16.47–53). That letter appears not to have contained any explicit legislation on the collection and exportation of funds to Jerusalem. It was rather Caesar's relationship with Hyrcanus II (and Antipater) and Caesar's general grant of freedom to the Jews that formed the bases for the request that Agrippa protect the temple tax and other Jewish funds in Asia (*A.J.* 16.52–54). Agrippa's subsequent decision to "confirm their right to continue to observe their own customs" without "molestation" was a conservative one (*A.J.* 16.60).[277] With respect to the collection and exportation of the temple tax, Agrippa must have permitted the continuation of a specific practice, consistent with Caesar's general grant, which existed *de facto* "and did not cause the Roman government any trouble" (*A.J.* 16.60).

In summary, Caesar legalized, in general, the freedom of the Jews to live according to their customs and laws. He permitted, in practice, the

276. On Octavian's ban on *collegia*, see Suetonius, *Aug.* 32.1.

277. In *A.J.* 12.126 Josephus says that Agrippa decided that "it was not lawful for him to make a new rule."

Jews in Rome and elsewhere in the empire to continue their custom of collecting money, including the temple tax. Augustus remained consistent with the policy of maintaining the practice, and in the crisis in Asia regarding the collection and exportation of funds by Jews to Jerusalem, he and Agrippa raised what had existed as a *de facto* custom to the status of an explicit legal right. Caesar's prohibition in 47 B.C.E. of financial exaction and "molestation" in Judea would certainly have included the confiscation by Roman magistrates of Jewish funds in the temple of Jerusalem for "imperial services"; Crassus's plunder in 54 B.C.E. remains the most outstanding example.[278] Josephus, in his redaction of the crisis in Asia, however, applies Caesar's prohibition of "molestation" to the confiscation of Jewish funds in the Diaspora.

Philo opened his discussion of priestly dues, particularly the temple tax, by observing that "the revenues of the temple are derived not only from landed estates but also from other and far greater sources which time will never destroy" (*Spec.* 1.76). The temple tax depended on human capital. Since the Jewish "nation" in "the whole universe" was "very populous," the income from the tax was also "naturally exceedingly abundant." Reliable figures of the Jewish population in the Diaspora are not available. Therefore, we cannot know exactly how much money was contributed each year for the temple. Nevertheless, the fact that the Roman authorities viewed the Jewish temple tax as a major source of income is adequately proven by the fact that Vespasian converted it into a Roman poll tax after 70 C.E.[279] Earlier, as we have seen, the sums were large enough to attract the attention of Flaccus in the 60s B.C.E. City officials in Asia and Cyrenaica afterwards, like Flaccus, considered it a drain on the economies of their cities. Of the gold seized by Flaccus for the *aerarium*, Cicero speaks of "a little less than a hundred pounds" from Apamea, "a little more than twenty pounds" from Laodicea, "a small amount" from Pergamum (*Flacc.* 68), and probably another hundred pounds from Adramyttium.[280] According to M. W. Frederiksen's estimate, the value of gold at this time was about six thousand secterces per pound,[281] a secterce

---

278. See chapter 1. Sabinus, the imperial procurator, is said to have taken four hundred talents from the temple treasury in 4 B.C.E. and Roman soldiers stole some additional amounts (*A.J.* 17.264; in *B.J.* 2.50, four hundred talents is said to be the total amount stolen by both Sabinus and the soldiers). Pilate (26–36 C.E.) used the funds to build an aqueduct to bring water into Jerusalem (*A.J.* 18.60–62; *B.J.* 2.175–77). The last governor of Judea, Florus, took away seventeen talents from the treasury in 66 C.E., "making the requirements of the imperial service his pretext" (*B.J.* 2.293). Each of these cases was followed by popular and bloody revolts. See chapter 5 below.

279. *B.J.* 7.218; Dio, *Hist.* 65.7.2; see Schürer, *History*, 2:272–3; 3.1:54, 58, 122–23.

280. There is a lacuna in the text. See Marshall, "Flaccus," 146 and n. 25.

281. M. W. Frederiksen, "Caesar, Cicero and the Problem of Debt," *JRS* 56 (1966): 132.

being a fourth of a denarius. Marshall judges that the sum for Apamea would be "ca 135,000 denarii/drachmae."[282] The sums might not represent only the temple tax, however, and might include other dedicatory gifts for the temple (*A.J.* 18.312; *B.J.* 5.205).[283] In any event, modern scholars agree that the sums that arrived in Jerusalem each year from the Diaspora were very large.[284]

Rome's grant and defense of the Jewish right to collect and export the temple tax are certainly to be explained partly by the Roman conservative policy of permitting the Jews to perform their religious rites. Equally, John Hyrcanus II must have been motivated by the need to see the Jews perform their religious duty when, soon after Caesar's death, he asked that Dolabella confirm the right of the Jews to observe their ancestral customs (*A.J.* 14.223–27). Hyrcanus would, however, not have missed what seemed so obvious to everyone else, namely, that Caesar had in fact permitted him to raise taxes in territories of the empire outside of Judea.[285] Herod, as he did in the case of Caesar's grant of the plain of Sharon, proved that he did not miss the significance of this right. During the crisis in Asia he used his good offices with Augustus and Agrippa to ensure that the funds were protected.[286] Later, he settled a colony of Babylonian and other immigrant Jews in Batanea, tax free, and created a buffer zone to protect from attack the Jews who came from Babylonia on pilgrimage to Jerusalem, as they brought with them large sums of money (*A.J.* 17.26; 18.310–13).[287]

---

282. Marshall, "Flaccus," 146, n. 27.

283. See Marshall, "Flaccus," 146–47, who also suggests that since Judea was at war and Syria was in anarchy before Pompey's intervention, the Jews of Asia might not have sent their contributions to Jerusalem for some time. The large sums could have been collected and accumulated for several years.

284. See, for instance, Juster, *Les Juifs*, 1:383–85; Sanders, *Jewish Law*, 50; Broshi ("Role of the Temple," 35–36) estimates "some one million drachmas (denarii) annually"; Emilio Gabba, "The Finances of King Herod," in *Greece and Rome in Eretz Israel: Collected Essays* (ed. A. Kasher et al.; Jerusalem: Yad Iẓḥak Ben-Zvi, Israel Exploration Society, 1990), 167.

285. See Saulnier, "Lois Romaines," 187, who sees the grant as a fiscal privilege that was contrary to Roman interests.

286. On his return to Judea, Herod, Josephus says, gave "a general picture of his good fortune and his government of the kingdom, in which, he said, he had not neglected anything that might be to their advantage." He then went on to remit taxes by a quarter (*A.J.* 16.63–64). Broshi ("Role of the Temple," 36) is wrong, however, in considering the temple tax part (10–15 percent) of Herod's income. See chapter 4 below.

287. See chapter 4 below.

3

Cassius and Antony in the East (43–40 B.C.E.)

C. Longinius Cassius's struggle with and eventual success against P. Cornelius Dolabella for control of Syria[1] following the assassination of Julius Caesar in 44 B.C.E. and the outbreak of civil war in 42 B.C.E. brought fresh chaos and exactions to Syria and Judea.[2] Although Hyrcanus took pains to ensure, through Antony and Dolabella, that the favorable policy pursued by Caesar survived Caesar's death (*A.J.* 14.217–27).[3] Cassius, who arrived in Syria at the beginning of 43 B.C.E., did not honor Caesar's tax arrangements for Judea. If Cassius's speech to the Rhodians that Appian provides reflects anything of his attitude, then Cassius was unlikely to have had much respect in general for deals agreed to with Julius Caesar (Appian, *Bell. civ.* 4.70).[4] Further, his financial needs certainly were not such as would have permitted him to abide by the tax concessions granted to the Jewish state by Caesar. Moreover, Hyrcanus, Antipater, and the Jews,"being mindful of the benefits they had received from Caesar" (*A.J.* 14.269), had supported Julius Caesar's cause against that of the Pompeians, since the upheaval in Syria occasioned by the rebellion and assassination of the governor, Sextus Caesar, by Caecilius Bassus in 46 B.C.E. (*A.J.* 14.268–70; *B.J.* 1.216–17).[5] This political alignment at the beginning of the conflicts might also have accounted for the reportedly heavy-handed manner with which Cassius treated the territory.

---

1. Appian, *Bell. civ.* 4.60–62; Dio, *Hist.* 47.28.5–30.7; Elizabeth Rawson, "Cassius and Brutus: The Memory of the Liberators," in *Past Perspectives: Studies in Greek and Roman Historical Writing* (ed. I. S. Moxon et al.; Cambridge: Cambridge University Press, 1986), 111; Schürer, *History*, 1:249–50, 276–77; Alain M. Gowing, *The Triumviral Narratives of Appian and Cassius Dio* (Ann Arbor: University of Michigan Press, 1992), 168–69.

2. The murder of Caesar, according to Josephus (*B.J.* 1.218), "produced a tremendous upheaval" in the region. Rey-Coquais, "Syrie Romaine," 45; Kennedy, "Syria," 709.

3. See chapter 2.

4. Emilio Gabba, *Appiano e la storia delle guerre civili* (Florence: La Nuova Italia, 1956), 183–84; Gowing, *Triumviral Narratives*, 171.

5. See Appian, *Bell. civ.* 3.77; 4.58; Dio, *Hist.* 47.27.

With Cassius's death and the conclusion of the civil war in 42 B.C.E., Judea and the rest of Syria came under Antony's domination. This period for Judea ended with the invasion of Syria by Parthia and the appointment of Herod as king in 40 B.C.E. Josephus's account of the period has to be read together with the other, later narratives of Appian, Dio Cassius, and Plutarch. None of these other authors, however, speaks specifically of the treatment of Judea by Cassius or Antony.

Cassius in Syria (43–42 B.C.E.)

Cassius remained in Syria from the beginning of 43 B.C.E. until he repaired to Asia in the beginning of 42 B.C.E. According to Josephus, Cassius ordered the Jews to pay seven hundred talents of silver.[6] This sum seems to be the tribute exacted by Cassius from the Jewish state, all of which most likely was paid sometime in 43 B.C.E. Hyrcanus and Antipater distributed the charge for raising the tribute to Antipater's sons and to "others," including Antipater's enemy Malichus (*B.J.* 1.220; *A.J.* 14.273). The Jews failed to pay the tribute and Cassius, Josephus says, sold "the officials of the other cities, every last man of them" into slavery[7] and also reduced to servitude the inhabitants of four cities of Judea, namely, Gophna, Emmaus, Lydda, and Thamna.[8] Malichus was saved from execution by the timely intervention of Hyrcanus and/or Antipater, who placated Cassius by sending him one hundred talents (*A.J.* 14.275–76; *B.J.* 1.221–22).[9]

Josephus's account, however, lacks clarity. He asserts that Cassius's treatment of the Jews was "worst of all" (μάλιστα δὲ τὴν Ἰουδαίαν ἐκάκωσεν), an assertion often echoed in modern scholarship.[10] Seen in the general context of Cassius's and Brutus's conduct in the East, however, the

---

6. He speaks of "the Jews" in *B.J.* 1.220, but of "Judaea" in *A.J.* 14.272. Josephus here again uses Judea to refer to the Jewish state. He did so also in the earlier episode involving Cassius; he said that Taricheae, where Cassius killed Peitholaus and sold thirty thousand Jews into slavery, was in "Judea." The city actually was in Galilee (*A.J.* 14.120; *B.J.* 1.180). Money raised by Herod from Galilee must therefore be considered part of the total sum demanded by Cassius from the Jews.

7. *B.J.* 1.221 mentions only "the rest" who were "abused for dilatoriness" by Cassius.

8. *B.J.* 1.222 names Gophna, Emmaus, and "two other places of less importance."

9. In *A.J.* 14.276 it is Hyrcanus (through Antipater) who sent the money to Cassius, whereas in *B.J.* 1.222 Josephus says that it was Antipater who made the payment. See Peter Richardson, *Herod*, 114–15.

10. For instance, Rawson ("Cassius and Brutus," 108) says that Cassius "demanded the huge sum of 700 talents, which the country could not pay." Thus also, Richard A. Horsley, *Galilee*, 114.

Jews were probably not specifically targeted, nor was the amount levied upon them especially exorbitant. The amounts of tribute imposed by Cassius upon the cities of Syria were universally heavy, as Josephus himself observes.[11] Unfortunately we have no figures on what the inhabitants of other parts of Syria, apart from Laodicea, had to pay. Josephus does not compare Judea with other parts of the province, and other authors (Appian, Plutarch, and Dio) say nothing regarding the kinds of levies in Syria of which Josephus speaks.[12] Since Cassius, in Appian's words (*Bell. civ.* 4.58), "raised the standards of a governor" in the province,[13] however, he must have arrogated to himself the right to exact tribute and troops, although Appian associates no auxiliary troops from the province with Cassius's forces, except the "Parthian mounted bowmen" (*Bell. civ.* 4.59, 63, 8).[14] Cassius also demanded ships from Phoenicia, but obtained help only from Sidon.[15]

It is, thus, by comparing Josephus's account of Cassius's treatment of the Jews with his exactions from Laodicea and the cities of Asia that we can gain a useful insight into what Cassius did in Judea.[16] Dio (*Hist.* 47.30.7) observes merely that, after Cassius had defeated Dollabela and taken Laodicea, the inhabitants of the city "suffered no harm apart from a forced contribution of money." No one else was punished. According to

---

11. *A.J.* 14.272: Cassius "imposed heavy tribute" upon the cities of Syria; *B.J.* 1.219: "he went round the towns levying tribute and exacting sums which it was beyond their ability to pay."

12. Dio (*Hist.* 47.28.3) notes of Cassius that "when [he] had secured possession of Syria, he set out for Judea on learning that the followers of Caesar who had been left behind in Egypt were approaching; and without difficulty he won to his cause both them and the Jews." Cassius was otherwise popular in Syria when he arrived there on account of his conduct as quaestor, or rather proquaestor, during the expedition of Crassus (*Hist.* 47.21.2; see 40.28.1–2). Fergus Millar, *A Study of Cassius Dio* (Oxford: Clarendon, 1964), 57–59; Rawson, "Cassius and Brutus," 110–11.

13. According to Appian (*Bell. civ.* 4.57), Cassius had been appointed governor of Syria by Julius Caesar. Following the proscriptions of 43 B.C.E. and after he had left Rome together with Brutus, he was given Crete. The Senate, however, restored Syria to Cassius after it declared Dolabella a public enemy (*Bell. civ.* 4.58; see 3.6–8); compare Dio, *Hist.* 47.21.1; Plutarch, *Brut.* 19.3. Rawson ("Cassius and Brutus," 110) considers the statement that Caesar had given Syria to Cassius (and Macedonia to Brutus) Appian's attempt "to legitimate to some degree their seizure of these provinces (it is probably not true)." See Ronald Syme, *The Roman Revolution* (Oxford: Clarendon, 1956), 107, 115; Elizabeth Rawson, "The Aftermath of the Ides," in *CAH,* vol. 9, *The Last Age of the Roman Republic, 146–43 B.C.* (ed. J. A. Crook et al.; Cambridge: Cambridge University Press, 1994), 475; Gowing, *Triumviral Narratives,* 63 and n. 17.

14. Also Dio, *Hist.* 47.30.3. Appian's explanation of the presence of Parthian horse-archers with Cassius is lame. Rawson, "Cassius and Brutus," 105, 110–11.

15. On troops raised by Cassius from Syria, see Josephus, *B.J.* 1.225; *A.J.* 14.272, 280.

16. Joshua J. Schwartz, *Lod (Lydda),* 54.

Appian, who, like Dio, was favorable to Cassius,[17] he "plundered the temples and the treasury . . ., punished the chief citizens, and exacted very heavy contributions from the rest, so that the city was reduced to the extremest misery" (*Bell. civ.* 4.62).[18] In spite of the apparent similarity between Cassius's treatment of Laodicea and the fate of the Jewish state, Josephus (*B.J.* 1.231; *A.J.* 14.289) does not dwell on the details of Cassius's exactions from this city.

Upon the city of Tarsus, Cassius levied a tribute of fifteen hundred talents (*Bell. civ.* 4.64). There is some similarity between what happened to Tarsus and what happened to some of the cities of Judea as a result of Cassius's actions.[19] According to Appian (*Bell. civ.* 4.64), in Tarsus

> [b]eing unable to find the money, and being pressed for payment with violence by the soldiers, the people sold their public property and after that they coined all the sacred articles used in religious processions and the temple offerings into money. As this was not sufficient, the magistrates sold free persons into bondage, first girls and boys, afterward women and miserable old men, who brought a very small price, and finally young men. Most of these committed suicide. Finally Cassius, on his return from Syria, took pity on their sufferings and released them from the remainder of the contribution.

Appian presents the magistrates of the city, not Cassius, as responsible for the sale of the citizens of Tarsus into slavery. He even manages to turn the incident into an instance of Cassius's benevolence. Dio also excuses Cassius from the extortions in Tarsus. Cassius, he says, "inflicted no severe penalty upon them, except to take away all their money, private and public" (*Hist.* 47.31.3).[20]

We learn, nonetheless, that in both Laodicea and Tarsus Cassius's exactions were heavy and that he had recourse to extreme measures, including the sale of some citizens, against cities that were unable to meet his demands. All of the peoples of Asia, Rhodes aside, paid ten years' worth of tribute to Cassius "within a short space of time" (Appian, *Bell. civ.* 4.74). After he took Rhodes, Cassius executed some citizens, banished others, and seized "all the money that was found, either gold or silver, in the temples and the public treasury" (Appian, *Bell. civ.* 4.73). He also ordered private citizens, those pointedly in possession of gold and silver,

---

17. Gabba, *Appiano*, 178–79; Rawson, "Cassius and Brutus," 110–11; Gowing, *Triumviral Narratives*, 168–73.

18. Laodicea was also devastated by the siege leading up to its capture. Cicero, *Fam.* 12.13.4; Kennedy, "Syria," 709.

19. Joshua J. Schwartz, *Lod (Lydda)*, 53–4.

20. Rawson, "Cassius and Brutus," 111, 115; Gowing, *Triumviral Narratives*, 168–69.

to surrender all their supplies of liquidity. They did so, willy-nilly,[21] delivering a fortune of eighty-five hundred talents, according to Plutarch (*Brut.* 32.2).[22] The plunder of Rhodes was remembered with some bitterness, in spite of the efforts by Appian and Dio to soften its harshness.[23]

Appian (*Bell. civ.* 4.52) concedes that his narrative was limited to the accounts of the capture of the largest cities, particularly to the "celebrated" cases of Laodicea, Tarsus, Rhodes, Patara, and Xanthus. He excludes the "smaller" cities among the many which "suffered the calamity of capture." The four cities, Gophna and Emmaus (*B.J.* 1.222), together with Lydda and Thamna (*A.J.* 14.275), on which Cassius reportedly vented his wrath must be included among the "smaller" cities captured and destroyed by Cassius. These four were the principal cities of four of the eleven divisions/districts (κληρουχίας) into which Judea (region) was divided in the first century C.E. (*B.J.* 3.54–55).[24] Why then were they attacked by Cassius?

For all we know, the Jewish state (unlike Laodicea, Tarsus, and Rhodes) did not take part in the armed resistance against Cassius's dominance. Furthermore, it does not appear that Cassius attacked the Jewish cities in order to subdue the Jewish state because of its strategic importance. Cassius imposed the tribute on the Jewish state as a whole, and he later attacked four toparchies in the region of Judea, a small fraction of

21. Possibly in an effort to show that Cassius was not harsher than Brutus, Appian (*Bell. civ.* 4.81) has Brutus apply the same pressures on the inhabitants of Patara. Gabba, *Appiano*, 183; Rawson, "Cassius and Brutus," 111. Plutarch (*Brut.* 30.2) says that in Rhodes Cassius "managed matters there with undue rigour."

22. Cassius would have made eight thousand talents from gold and silver collected from individuals, and five hundred talents from a fine on the city as a whole. Pursuing his overall theme of comparing Cassius's brutality to Brutus' gentleness (*Brut.* 29.1–2), Plutarch asserts that, on the contrary, Brutus "exacted only a hundred and fifty talents from the Lycians, and, without doing them any other injury." The amount for Lycia is not plausible. Christopher Pelling, "The Triumviral Period," in *CAH*, vol. 10, *The Augustan Empire, 43 B.C.-A.D. 69* (ed. Alan K. Bowman et al.; 2nd ed.; Cambridge: Cambridge University Press, 1996), 7.

23. Dio (*Hist.* 47.33.4) maintains concerning Cassius: "though he did the people no harm, yet he appropriated their ships, money, and public and sacred treasures, with the exception of the chariot of the Sun." See Valerius Maximus 1.5.8; according to Josephus, Herod in 40 B.C.E. found "the city damaged from the war against Cassius" and restored it (*A.J.* 14.378; *B.J.* 1.280); Appian, *Bell. civ.* 4.52, 74. On Appian's defense of Cassius's campaign against Rhodes, see Gabba, *Appiano*, 182–84; Rawson, "Cassius and Brutus," 105, 111; Gowing, *Triumviral Narratives*, 168–71.

24. In this passage Josephus maintains that the ten districts, besides Jerusalem, also coincided with the Roman toparchies. The list of the toparchies and the cities from which they took their names are known from Vespasian's occupation of each of them during the revolt of 66 C.E. (*B.J.* 4.130, 444–52, 486, 550–51). On the toparchies as a whole, especially during Herod's reign, see Abel, *Géographie*, 1:151–53 and map IX; Avi-Yonah, *Holy Land*, 95–96; Schalit, *König Herodes*, 208–11.

the Jewish state. Moreover, unlike Appian's description of the situation in Tarsus, Josephus does not report the extremes to which the Jewish authorities went in the effort to raise the money demanded by Cassius. Specifically, the Jewish authorities did not tamper with their own temple funds and treasures. It seems, therefore, that, however significant and burdensome the tribute might have been,[25] Cassius's attack was not related to the inability of the Jewish state to meet the exaction.

According to Josephus, Cassius was roused to anger by the slowness of the Jews in collecting the tribute (*B.J.* 1.221–22).[26] This is a credible depiction of the situation. The attack could have occurred under two circumstances: (1) Only Galilee, under Herod, and some other sections of the Jewish state met Cassius's deadline; Hyrcanus/Antipater further saved Malichus and the toparchies under his charge. If the rest of the Jewish state failed to pay, Cassius could have attacked the four cities in order to raise funds and to punish the Jewish state. (2) If these four territories, for their own reasons, were particularly dilatory, Cassius's attack on the cities could have been both retaliatory and aimed at raising the funds he needed from them. Josephus's statements in *A.J.* 14.274–75 are both sweeping and misleading: Cassius sold into slavery "the officials of the other cities, every last man of them"; "at that time Cassius reduced to servitude four cities," and he "was moved by anger to the point of doing away with Malichus." It would seem from this account that Cassius attacked more officials than those of the four named cities. The account in *B.J.* 1.221–22 is slightly more precise: "the rest Cassius abused for dilatoriness and then vented his wrath on the cities themselves," reducing them to servitude, and "he was proceeding so far as to put Malichus to death for tardiness in levying the tribute."

Josephus's narrative is misleading, especially in *A.J.* 14.274–75, because he mentions no other overseers between "the first" (that is, Herod) who completed collecting the tribute and "the rest" (including Malichus) whom Cassius attacked. It must be assumed, however, that others whom Josephus does not mention (Herod's brother, Phasael, for instance),[27] successfully made their payments. Those who were abused,

---

25. It is impossible to compare Cassius's demand of seven hundred talents with the tribute paid by Judea under Julius Caesar. Momigliano (*Ricerche*, 48) relates Cassius's exaction to the tribute under Julius Caesar and Herod's income. His theory is unconvincing. Peter Richardson (*Herod*, 115), comparing Cassius's exaction with the tax income of Herod's kingdom, observes: "Cassius's levy of seven hundred talents was equal to the total annual royal income of the larger kingdom in 4 BCE, a substantial sum." See chapter 4 below.

26. Cassius abused the leaders and the cities "for dilatoriness" (εἰς βραδυτῆτα), and he threatened Malichus with death "for tardiness in levying the tribute" (ὅτι μὴ σπεύσας εἰσέπραξεν).

27. Antipater "gave each of his sons a part [of the tribute] to collect" (*A.J.* 14.273; *B.J.* 1.220).

therefore, were the leaders of the cities which Josephus listed. Besides, it is unlikely that Cassius's expedition to Judea was intended to punish the Jewish nation as a whole and extract from it readily available funds. Were this the case, Crassus's former proquaestor, who later himself plundered temples and public treasuries in Laodicea and Rhodes, would have known where to find silver and gold in Judea: the temple in Jerusalem.

Cassius punished those whom he thought were resisting him by their refusal to pay.[28] There were obvious reasons for the Jews to delay payment. In spite of Dio's view that Cassius won the Jews over to his cause and was otherwise popular in Syria (*Hist.* 47.28.3; 47.21.2), Herod's enthusiasm for Cassius and his cause, and Antipater's *realpolitik* were not shared by every member of the Jewish aristocracy and populace. This response was not without reason. The tribute imposed by Cassius did away with the favorable tax concessions granted to the Jews by Julius Caesar. Cassius was in effect returning affairs in Judea to the chaos of the era before Caesar's regulation, when Roman magistrates imposed arbitrary exactions to pay for their wars. Personal resistance to Cassius himself cannot be excluded. For example, Cassius's popularity may have been damaged by memories of Crassus, the Roman magistrate who exacted money from the Jews by robbing the temple (*A.J.* 14.105–9; *B.J.* 1.179).[29] Moreover, following Crassus's disastrous expedition, Cassius

28. Schalit (*König Herodes*, 49 and nn. 174–75) also concludes that Cassius attacked the cities because of dilatoriness. In his view, Malichus intentionally failed to raise his share of the tribute in the hope of hurting Antipater's standing before Cassius. The intrigue misfired. Thus also Joshua J. Schwartz, *Lod (Lydda)*, 54. That Malichus, and the others who failed to pay, may have been trying also to embarrass Antipater and the authorities in Jerusalem is probable, particularly in view of Malichus's subsequent actions. However, Schwartz's proposal, namely, that Malichus governed the four cities and was responsible for collecting Cassius's tribute there is inconsistent with what Josephus actually says in *B.J.* 1.222: "but Antipater saved both his life and the other cities from destruction, by hastily propitiating Cassius with a gift of a hundred talents." Schürer (*History*, 1:277) states that the inhabitants of the four cities were sold by Cassius into slavery because they "did not raise their share" of the tribute. Schürer does not explain why these cities were not as "zealous" for Cassius's cause as Antipater and Herod were. Martin Goodman ("Judaea," in *CAH*, vol. 10, *The Augustan Empire, 43 B.C.-A.D. 69* [ed. Alan K. Bowman et al.; 2nd ed.; Cambridge: Cambridge University Press, 1996], 739) asserts that "some cities in Judaea refused to pay" the levy, which was "dutifully raised" by Herod "first in Galilee and later in Judaea and Syria." As to those who refused to pay, Herod "ruthlessly subjected them to slavery." All this is puzzling. According to Josephus's dubious notice (*B.J.* 1.225), Cassius made Herod "prefect of the whole of Syria (Συρίας ἁπάσης ἐπιμελητήν)" or "governor of Coele-Syria" (στρατηγὸν κοίλης Συρίας) (*A.J.* 14.280). One might infer from this that Herod might have assisted Cassius in his drive for funds in Syria. See Peter Richardson, *Herod*, 116. There is no evidence, however, for Herod's participation in the collection of the tribute imposed upon the Jewish state, beyond his activities in Galilee. It is certainly not the case that Herod sold the inhabitants of the four cities in Judea into slavery.

29. See chapter 1.

had brutally suppressed the Jewish, pro-Hasmonean revolt in Taricheae (*A.J.* 14.119–20; *B.J.* 1.180). Presently, having murdered Caesar, who was overtly sympathetic to the Jews, Cassius was at war with his associates. The Caesarean and Hasmonean[30] elements in the Jewish state would have found Cassius and his tribute odious.

We cannot, unfortunately, determine how significant an annual tax of seven hundred talents of silver would have been for the Jewish state, because we can neither estimate what the total revenue of the territory was nor convincingly compare the sums demanded by Cassius with the amount the Jews paid before and after 43 B.C.E.[31] It is noteworthy, however, that Cassius exacted a cash payment from the Jewish state, as he also demanded from Laodicea, Tarsus, and Rhodes. Cassius desperately needed cash available to pay and bribe the troops whom he had gathered, at the exorbitant rate that had become current, in order to ensure their loyalty.[32] He (and Brutus) had the advantage over their rivals in Rome of the immense wealth of the East, which they could plunder at will.[33] The financial squeeze in Rome brought about, among other exactions, the reimposition of the direct tax on citizens, the *tributum*, which had been abolished in 167 B.C.E.[34] The wealthy citizens resisted the impositions, since it was they who were expected to bear the brunt of them.[35] An emergency levy requiring cash payment, whether or not it is assessed on the value of property, assumes the ready presence of liquidity. Such a tax must be exacted from those in possession of the sums of silver and gold needed, that is, the upper classes.

Similarly, Cassius and Brutus extracted the wealth of the private citi-

---

30. According to Josephus (*B.J.* 1.224), Murcus, when he was governor of Syria, had wanted to execute Malichus "as a revolutionary," who was "stirring up a revolt in Judaea" (*A.J.* 14.279).

31. See chapter 4 below.

32. Helga Botermann, *Die Soldaten und die römische Politik in der Zeit von Caesars Tod bis zur Begründung des zweiten Triumvirats* (Munich: C.H. Beck, 1968), 104–7, 94, for Brutus; Rawson, "Aftermath," 478–88; eadem, "Cassius and Brutus," 105.

33. Pelling, "Triumviral Period," 6.

34. Cicero, *Fam.* 12.30.4; *Ad Brut.*1.18.5; Dio, *Hist.* 46.31.3; see Appian, *Bell. civ.* 3.66. T. Rice Holmes, *The Architect of the Roman Empire* (2 vols; Oxford: Clarendon, 1928), 1:65; Claude Nicolet, *Tributum: recherches sur la fiscalité directe sous la république romaine* (Antiquitas 24; Bonn: Habelt, 1976), 87–91; Rawson, "Aftermath," 488.

35. Appian, *Bell. civ.* 4.34; Cicero, *Ad Brut.* 1.18.5: "Obdurescunt enim magis cottidie boni viri ad vocem tributi." Dio, *Hist.* 47.16.3–4: "Now the reintroduction of the taxes which had been formerly abrogated, or the establishment of new ones, and the institution of the joint contributions, which they levied in large numbers both on the land and on the slaves, caused the people some little distress, it is true; but that those who were in the slightest degree still prosperous, not only senators or knights, but even freedmen, men and women alike, should be listed on the tablets and mulcted of another 'tithe' of their wealth irritated everybody exceedingly."

zens and seized the public treasures of the cities that they reportedly attacked. Cassius did not plunder the Jewish temple, but the burden of his exaction in Judea fell on the upper classes. The incident does not reveal much information on how tax collection was organized in the Jewish state after Julius Caesar's concessions and the departure of the tax companies. It is clear, however, that Antipater's sons, Malichus, and the others who were appointed to raise the levy, would have played a supervisory role. They would have depended on the leading citizens of the toparchies assigned to them for collection of the money. Cassius held them all personally responsible to deliver the sums; if they were unable to collect the full amount, he would have demanded that they make up for the difference using their own resources.[36] Herod's speed at delivering his quota, which merited him Cassius's special favors, may not be explained by his particular efficiency in exacting it from Galilee. Since the Jews were reluctant to pay the levy, it may be assumed that Herod paid parts of it out of his own "private" funds. Likewise, Hyrcanus/Antipater was able to make up for Malichus and the territories under his supervision by sending Cassius one hundred talents "of his own money" (*A.J.* 14.276; *B.J.* 1.222).[37]

Josephus is explicit that Cassius punished officials of the offending Jewish cities.[38] Cassius also sold members of the general population of these cites into slavery. After Philippi, Antony would demand that all who had been sold by Cassius, "whether freemen or slaves," be released (*A.J.* 14.313, 321).[39] It is, however, unlikely that the cities were entirely depopulated or destroyed. Our sources do not say that the cities needed to be rebuilt afterwards. On the contrary, barely four years after Cassius despoiled it, and less than two years after Antony ordered the emancipation of its enslaved citizens, Lydda was again prosperous enough for

---

36. For the collection of tribute by the leading citizens and magistrates of cities in the late Republic and early Principate, see P. A. Brunt, "The Revenues of Rome," *JRS* 71 (1981): 169–70; idem, "Publicans in the Principate," in *Roman Imperial Themes* (Oxford: Clarendon, 1990), 355–57, 388–93, 421–22. See chapter 5 below.

37. On Herod's private wealth during this period, see *A.J.* 14.363–64; *B.J.* 1.268; and chapter 4 below.

38. *A.J.* 14.275: "But the officials of the other cities, every last man of them, were sold as slaves" (ἐπιπράσκοντο δ᾽ αὔτανδροι ὅσοι τῶν ἄλλων πόλεων ἐπιμεληταί); see *B.J.* 1.221. Schalit (*König Herodes*, 48, n. 166) proposed that the word πόλεων in *A.J.* 14.275, which is lacking in the manuscript PE, be excised from the text and that the word ὄχλων be read in lieu of the word ἄλλων. The resulting text (ἐπιπράσκοντο δ᾽ αὔτανδροι οἱ τῶν ὄχλων ἐπιμεληταί κτλ.) would show that the governing class was sold into slavery. Such emendations are, however, unnecessary, since, although the text of *A.J.* 14.275 is indeed corrupt, it is also clear from *B.J.* 1.221 that Cassius did in fact attack the general population of the four cities.

39. See below.

Antigonus to bribe Silo to billet Roman troops in it (*A.J.* 14.412, 418; *B.J.* 1.302).[40]

After Philippi: Antony and the Jewish State (42–31 B.C.E.)

From the point of view of the administration of Jewish Palestine, Mark Antony's possession of the eastern provinces, following the victory of the *Triumviri* over Cassius and Brutus in the autumn of 42 B.C.E. and the accord of Brundisium two years later, must be divided into two distinct periods: (1) from 42 B.C.E. to the Parthian invasion of Syria and the appointment of Herod as king in 40 B.C.E., and (2) from 40 B.C.E. to Antony's defeat in the battle of Actium in 31 B.C.E. Given that this second period coincides with the early part of Herod's reign, we shall be concerned here only with the immediate effects of Antony's organization of the East after Philippi.[41]

This brief period in the history of the Jewish state was marked by two factors. First, there was a significant shift in the internal administrative structure of the territory as increasing powers were given to Antipater's sons Phasael and Herod, culminating in their appointment by Antony as tetrarchs in 41 B.C.E. (*A.J.* 14.326; *B.J* 1.244).[42] Second, there was a determined effort by Hyrcanus and his supporters to undo some of the damage done by Cassius and to secure a reconfirmation of the grants made by Julius Caesar. Herod was a Roman citizen by right of the privilege granted to his father by Julius Caesar. By virtue of this, he already held positions in the Roman administration of the province of Syria, outside of the Jewish state.[43] Herod's and his brother's appointment as tetrarchs of Judea meant, therefore, a more direct Roman presence in the administration of the territory.

---

40. See chapter 2 above. Joshua J. Schwartz (*Lod (Lydda)*, 55) observes: "the fertile lands of the Lod district would have provided ample supplies to feed the Roman forces without causing the local residents undo [*sic*] hardship."

41. Pelling, "Triumviral Period," 9–13.

42. Momigliano, *Ricerche*, 36–39; Goodman, "Judaea," 739; Peter Richardson, *Herod*, 121–24.

43. Notably, his appointment by Sextus Caesar as "governor of Coele-Syria (στρατηγὸν τῆς κοίλης Συρίας)," according to *A.J.* 14.180 (*B.J.* 1.213 adds "and Samaria"). He was later appointed by Cassius either as "governor of Coele-Syria" (στρατηγὸν αὐτὸν κοίλης Συρίας ἐποίησαν), according to *A.J.* 14.280, or as "prefect (or procurator) of the whole of Syria" (αὐτὸν Συρίας ἁπάσης ἐπιμελητὴν καθιστᾶσιν), according to *B.J.* 1.225. In all of these cases the import of the appointments is difficult to determine. Momigliano, *Ricerche*, 36–39; Peter Richardson, *Herod*, 112–13, 116. See above and chapter 4.

In spite of the enthusiasm with which Herod and his father had sought to espouse Cassius's cause, he, his brother, and Hyrcanus seem to have had no difficulty presenting themselves and the Jewish state to Antony as victims of Cassius's abuse.[44] Cassius had mulcted the Jews of seven hundred talents and in the process had attacked and despoiled four recalcitrant cities. When Cassius left Syria in 42 B.C.E., his appointees—Fabius, governor in Damascus, and Marion, the despot of Tyre—had aided Antigonus, the last son of Aristobulus II, in raising the specter of civil war in the Jewish state. It was with their aid that Antigonus made his first bid to return to his father's throne in Jerusalem. Marion had invaded and seized parts of Jewish territory in Galilee (*A.J.* 14.295–99; *B.J.* 1.236–40).[45]

Hyrcanus's embassy to Antony in Ephesus in 41 B.C.E. (Plutarch, *Ant.* 24)[46] obtained redress (*A.J.* 14.304–23). Josephus cites a letter from Antony to Hyrcanus reporting the success of the embassy and the orders he had issued (*A.J.* 14.306–13). Another letter is addressed to the people of Tyre ordering the restoration of captured land (*A.J.* 14.314–18), along with a letter to Tyre addressing the issue of Jewish persons and possessions auctioned by Cassius (*A.J.* 14.319–22). Antony, according to Josephus, also wrote to Sidon, Antioch, and Aradus (*A.J.* 14.323).[47] Putting to work his "notorious Asianic rhetoric,"[48] Antony took on the role of defender of the rights of the Jewish state.[49] Apart from the restoration of territory and property, and the freedom of Jewish slaves, Antony reconfirmed the terms of the grants made to the Jews by Julius Caesar (confirmed by both Antony himself and Dolabella after Caesar's death), including the tax and territorial concessions.[50] Antony assured Hyrcanus and the Jewish

---

44. Schürer, *History*, 1:278; Goodman, "Judaea," 739; Pelling, "Triumviral Period," 11–12.

45. Schürer, *History*, 1:277; 2:129; Peter Richardson, *Herod*, 117–18.

46. Hans Buchheim, *Die Orientpolitik des Triumvirn M. Antonius* (Heidelberg: Carl Winter, 1960), 11–15; Weinstock, *Divus Julius*, 401–2.

47. I consider these documents to be authentic in the same sense in which I consider the other documents cited by Josephus to be authentic. See the discussion in chapter 2; Rawson, "Cassius and Brutus," 108–9; Peter Richardson, *Herod*, 123.

48. Rawson, "Cassius and Brutus," 109.

49. Antony uses the language of friendship between the Jewish state and the Roman people: He is "persuaded" of Hyrcanus's "goodwill" and "friendliest feelings," and considers "your interests as my own" (*A.J.* 14.307–8). He assures Hyrcanus that he wants "to promote the welfare both of you and your nation" and "take care of your interests" (*A.J.* 14.312). The Jewish nation is said to be "our allies" and "friend of the Roman people" (*A.J.* 14.320).

50. *A.J.* 14.313: "And it is my wish that you shall enjoy the privileges granted by me and Dolabella." See *A.J.* 14.217–28 and chapter 2. It would seem that in 41 B.C.E. Hyrcanus shrewdly sent two of the envoys he had previously sent to Antony in 44 B.C.E., and Antony saw this as a renewal of the previous mission sent to him in Rome (*A.J.* 14.222, 307).

state, therefore, that in matters of taxation, there would be a continuity between his policies and those pursued by Julius Caesar on their behalf.[51]

The period of Antony's domination of Syria, according to Schürer, "was one of great oppression for the province." His extravagant lifestyle required vast sums of money, which were supplied by the provinces. Consequently "wherever Antonius went, heavy tribute was exacted; and Palestine had to bear its share."[52] This assessment of the period is based on the report by Appian (*Bell. civ.* 5.7):

> Proceeding onward to Phrygia, Mysia, Galatia, Cappadocia, Cilicia, Coele-Syria, Palestine, Ituraea, and the other provinces of Syria, he imposed heavy contributions on all (ἅπασιν ἐσφορὰς ἐπέβαλλε βαρείας), and acted as arbiter between kings and cities.[53]

Some caution, however, is in order. In the first place, Appian's word ἐσφορά (εἰσφορά) could very well mean "contributions," as opposed to, and paid in lieu of, regular tribute. Appian (*Bell. civ.* 5.6) observes apropos that, apart from demanding that the province of Asia pay nine years' tribute in two years, Antony also "ordered that the kings, princes, and free cities should make additional contributions according to their means." We cannot exclude, obviously, that Antony raised the level of tribute in the province of Syria and imposed special levies on various cities and principalities in the region. We are also made to think, however, of such sums as Herod, for instance, had to pay to Antony in order to extricate himself from Jewish accusations and eventually to secure for himself the Jewish throne.[54]

Antony's need for money extended beyond what was required by "his extravagant lifestyle." He was in need of vast sums to fulfill his promises to the legions after Philippi, as well as to make preparations for future wars.[55] It may be doubted that he succeeded in raising all the money he needed by simply imposing tribute and special contributions.[56]

---

51. Schalit (*König Herodes*, 68) also thinks that the request for the confirmation of the previous rights was one of the favors that the Jewish delegation explicitly asked of Antony in Ephesus. He relates Antony's confirmation, however, only to the rights given to the Jews of the Diaspora, namely, the freedom from military service and the freedom to practice their religion. There is no reason to limit the grants that the Jews obtained from Antony only to these.

52. Schürer, *History*, 1:278.

53. See ibid., 278, n. 45.

54. *A.J.* 14.302–3, 327, 381–82; *B.J.* 1.242; see the discussion of Appian, *Bell. civ.* 5.75 in chapter 5 below.

55. Appian, *Bell. civ.* 5.5–7; Pelling, "Triumviral Period," 10–11.

56. According to Dio (*Hist.* 48.30.2–3), he failed to pay the troops the money he had promised to give them after Philippi. They clamored for it in 40 B.C.E.; see Pelling, "Triumviral Period," 11.

These needs notwithstanding, Antony was also generous in his dispensations and was sensitive especially to the need of the East to recover, as he puts it, "as it were, from a serious illness" (*A.J.* 14.312). Appian's sweeping statement about the heavy imposts levied by Antony comes at the end of a passage (*Bell. civ.* 5.7) in which he narrates the concessions and favors that Antony made to the territories devastated by Cassius. "He gave relief to the cities that had suffered most severely," he writes. Antony is said, therefore, to have returned lost territories to Rhodes. He also freed the Lycians completely from tribute. He converted Laodicea and Tarsus into free cities and released them from all tribute. As he did for the Judeans sold by Cassius, so also "those inhabitants of Tarsus who had been sold into slavery he liberated by an order."[57]

Hyrcanus and his party succeeded in portraying themselves and the Jewish state as victims of Cassius's brutality, a success echoed by Antony's invective against Cassius and the horrors he visited on Judea (*A.J.* 14.308–11, 315–17). Since Antony was eager to portray himself as the champion of their rights, he must have treated the Jewish state with the same sympathy as he treated the other territories abused by Cassius. We may not conclude, from the examples of Lycia, Laodicea, and Tarsus, however, that Antony freed Judea from all tribute. There is no evidence for such a conclusion. He reconfirmed that Judea would continue to pay the same tribute as Caesar demanded from them. That, it appears, was all that Hyrcanus requested.

57. See Pelling, "Triumviral Period," 11.

4

Herodian Taxation (37 B.C.E.–4 B.C.E.)

Herod the Great received the kingship over the Jewish state against his expectations (if we believe Josephus's account).[1] He was a fugitive to Rome from the Parthian forces, which had engulfed Syria and had installed the Hasmonean Antigonus as king in Jerusalem in 40 B.C.E. (Josephus, *A.J.* 14.330–89; *B.J.* 1.248–85). Antigonus's father, Aristobulus II, had resisted Pompey in 63 B.C.E., and until he and Alexander, his first son, were executed by the Pompeians, he and his family had led Judea's resistance against Rome.[2] Antigonus himself, aided by the partisans of Cassius, had previously led a revolt in Judea, in the wake of the confusion that followed Cassius's departure from Syria in 42 B.C.E. (*A.J.* 14.297–99; *B.J.* 1.239–40).[3] Antigonus's career was built on his family's opposition to Roman rule in Judea. He was accordingly declared "an enemy of the Romans," an object of hatred by Roman authorities, especially for becoming an ally of Rome's bitter foes, the Parthians, and accepting the crown from them (*A.J.* 14.382–85; *B.J.* 1.282–84).

Herod's loyalty and, in particular, the loyalty that his father, Antipater, before him had shown to the Romans stood in sharp contrast to Antigonus's—and his family's—"contempt of Rome" (*B.J.* 1.282–84; *A.J.* 14.381–83).[4] Rome had found a faithful ally in Herod. Josephus's account

---

1. According to *A.J.* 14.386–87, Herod had come to Rome "not to claim the kingship for himself, for he did not believe the Romans would offer it to him, since it was their custom to give it to one of the reigning family, but to claim it for his wife's brother [Aristobulus III], who was a grandson of Aristobulus on his father's side and of Hyrcanus on his mother's." Peter Richardson (*Herod*, 129) thinks that Josephus's view "is probably correct."

2. See *A.J.* 14.46–79, 82–97, 100–102, 120, 123–26; *B.J.* 1.131–58, 160–68, 171–74, 176–77, 180–82, 183–86; and chapter 1.

3. See chapter 3.

4. The citation is from *B.J.* 1.284. Both Antony and Octavian, who championed Herod's cause before the Senate, contrasted Antigonus's contempt with what they both recalled of Antipater's "hospitality." Octavian in particular remembered the "hospitality and invariable loyalty" that Antipater gave to his father, Julius Caesar, during his campaign in Egypt. On the parallels between Antigonus's ascent to the throne and Herod's, see, for instance,

of Herod's life and reign is suffused with Herod's sense of obligation—or "friendship"—to Rome, to Antony first and then to Octavian and Agrippa.[5] After Herod's death, Nicolaus of Damascus, Herod's lifelong friend and historian, would reportedly appeal to Augustus's own sense of fidelity in his bid to persuade Augustus to honor Herod's final will: "Caesar," he argued, "would certainly not annul the will of a man who had left everything to his decision, who had been his friend and ally" (*A.J.* 17.246). It is to this personal friendship and patronage between Herod and Antony, and between Herod and Octavian (through his father, Julius Caesar)[6] that Josephus gives much attention in his account of Herod's appointment to the throne. For the Senate, however, granting the crown to Herod was a matter of political and military expedience in the face of a general crisis that had overtaken not only the Jewish state, but the whole of Syria. It was a contrecoup to the Parthian invasion and occupation of Syria, and their installation of Antigonus as king in Jerusalem. "And when the Senate had been aroused by these charges [against Antigonus]," Josephus writes, "Antony came forward and informed them that it was also an advantage in their war with the Parthians that Herod should be king. And as this proposal was acceptable to all, they voted accordingly" (*A.J.* 14.385).[7]

Usually, Rome installed as king in a client state someone from among the members of its ruling family.[8] The Senate, apparently breaking with this foreign policy, appointed Herod to the throne because it saw in him not only the solution to the intractable Hasmonean dynastic problem but

---

Peter Richardson, *Herod*, 126–27. Richardson (p. 128) is correct in speculating that, had Antigonus joined the Caesarians and avoided entanglement with the Parthians, "Judean history might have been very different." The Parthian invasion and Antigonus's subsequent behavior allowed Herod, in A. H. M. Jones's words, "to pose . . . as a champion of Rome who had lost all in defending his dominions against the public enemy" (*The Herods of Judea* [Oxford: Clarendon, 1938], 43).

5. See discussion in Peter Richardson, *Herod*, 226–34.

6. On personal patronage and Rome's imperial administration, see David C. Braund, "Function and Dysfunction: Personal Patronage in Roman Imperialism," in *Patronage in Ancient Society* (ed. Andrew Wallace-Hadrill; London: Routledge, 1989), 137–52.

7. Equally *B.J.* 1.284: "These words stirred the Senate, and when Antony came forward and said that with a view to the war with Parthia it was expedient that Herod should be king, the proposal was carried unanimously." See Peter Richardson, *Herod*, 127–28.

8. This is what Josephus claims (*A.J.* 14.387). See n. 1 above, and Goodman, "Judaea," 740. However, Archelaus I of Cappadocia (the future father-in-law of Herod's son, Alexander), Polemo of Pontus, both of whom also were appointed by Antony, and Juba II of Mauretania (who married Glaphyra after Alexander's death) were not descendants of the native dynasties of their respective kingdoms. See Sullivan, *Near Eastern Royalty*, 161–62, 182–83; Richard D. Sullivan, "The Dynasty of Cappadocia," *ANRW*, 2.7.2:1151–53; David M. Jacobson, "Three Roman Client Kings: Herod of Judaea, Archelaus of Cappadocia and Juba of Mauretania," *PEQ* 133 (2001): 24–25.

also the best means of preserving Judea in Roman control. Herod's immediate task was to return to Judea and to join the Roman effort to rid Syria of the Parthians. The land that Herod was to rule, he had first to conquer through three years of tirelessly campaigning alongside Roman forces.[9] In the long term, Herod's primary duties as "King of the Jews" (*B.J.* 1.282) were his continued personal loyalty and his guarantee of the loyalty on the part of his subjects to Rome. He was also to act as a buffer against Parthian ambitions in Syria.[10]

The discussion of taxation in Judea under Herod and his sons must take place against this background. This is particularly the case with the disputed question of Herod's and his sons' tax obligations to Rome. Does the assessment of their relationship with their Roman overlords allow for the conclusion that Rome imposed an annual tribute on them, separate, that is, from what they needed to do as "friends and allies"? It ought to be clear that the Herods were not free to impose any arbitrary policy—including excessive taxation—on their subjects. Their subjects could be loud in their complaints against what they viewed as tyranny, which Rome in the early Principate did not always disregard. And there was always the fear of unrest and open revolt, which Rome would never tolerate.

Modern scholarship has been ambivalent about the economy of Herod's kingdom and the tax demands that he made on his subjects. On the one hand, more and more scholars now recognize the merits of Herod's financial and administrative abilities and the relative prosperity that his enterprises could have brought to his kingdom.[11] Yet, on the other hand, the view that he spent himself to bankruptcy and taxed his subjects to "helpless poverty" (which has become orthodox) is also widespread and persistent. The following long quotation from Seán Freyne typifies and summarizes this ambivalence:

> It is a fairly widespread assumption that the long reign of Herod the Great was a particularly difficult time financially for the inhabitants of Palestine. Certainly the expenditure was lavish, and we hear of his subjects being in bad financial straits more than once (*Ant.* 15:365; 17:308; *War* 2:85f). Besides, after Caesar's death in 44 B.C.E. Herod had demon-

9. *A.J.* 14.394–439, 448–91; *B.J.* 1.290–320, 323–57.

10. On the "duties" of the vassal kings of the Roman Empire, see especially P. C. Sands, *The Client Princes of the Roman Empire Under the Republic* (Cambridge Historical Essays; Cambridge: Cambridge University Press, 1908; repr., New York: Arno Press, 1975), 49–139; David C. Braund, *Rome and the Friendly King: The Character of the Client Kingship* (London: Croom Helm, 1984), 55–122; Jacobson, "Client Kings," 25–27.

11. I cite only a few of the more recent examples. Broshi, "Role of the Temple," 31–32; Gabba, "Finances," 161–68; Sanders, *Jewish Law*, 161–63; Peter Richardson, *Herod*, 174–318; Pastor, *Land and Economy*, 110–27; Goodman, "Pilgrimage Economy," 69, 71–75.

> strated his ability to raise extra tribute—one hundred talents in Galilee (*Ant.* 14:273; *War* 1:221)—and was rewarded by Cassius with control of financial matters (ἐπιμελήτης) in the whole of Coele-Syria. He himself imposed a heavy fine (one hundred talents also) on the Galilean towns for their insubordination (*Ant.* 14:433; *War* 1:316), and this may have caused further social unrest and unpopularity for Herod with the masses (*Ant.* 14:450) . . . . Despite his self-centered ruthlessness Herod was also a shrewd administrator and businessman. His treatment of the people during the famine of 25 B.C.E.—provision of grain, clothing, etc.—is indicative of his control of the overall financial situation, and his recognition that a prosperous kingdom called for skillful exploitation of its resources. Another example of this far-sightedness is his granting of lands, tax-free, to the Babylonian Jews in Trachonitis and Batanaea. Their presence there as a military colony served the twofold purpose of protecting the kingdom from marauding robbers and of developing the rich agricultural lands of Transjordan (*Ant.* 17:23–31) . . . . Herod's tax system was at least as hard for townspeople, for we hear of sales taxes in Jerusalem about which the people complained to Archelaus (*Ant.* 17:205) and which were subsequently partly removed by Vitellius (*Ant.* 18:90). Taxes on fruits are explicitly mentioned as being remitted, and of course these would have been a greater burden for the poorer townspeople than for their country equals, who could at least produce the necessities of life on their own plots. This sketchy summary of Herod's economic policy as this was likely to have affected Galilean countrypeople is not intended to minimize the real hardships of his reign. Rather it suggests that the picture was not all bleak, and in fact some stabilization of life seems to have come about for those who were prepared to accept Herod and pose no particular threat, real or imagined, to his plans.[12]

Scholars who have espoused the view that this period was a "particularly difficult time financially" for the Jewish state and that this difficulty resulted from Herod's tax policy accept, uncritically, one of the evaluations that Josephus (or one of his sources) gives to Herod's reign.[13] This

---

12. Seán Freyne, *Galilee from Alexander the Great to Hadrian, 323* B.C.E. *to 135* C.E.: *A Study of Second Temple Judaism* (Notre Dame, Ind.: University of Notre Dame Press, 1980), 190–91.

13. Schalit, *König Herodes*, 262–98; Shimon Applebaum, "Herod I," in *EncJud* (Jerusalem: Keter, 1971), 382–5; Applebaum, "Economic Life," 661–67; Shimon Applebaum, "Judaea as a Roman Province: The Countryside as a Political and Economic Factor," *ANRW* (1977): 2.8:375–79; Gerd Theissen, *Sociology of Early Palestinian Christianity* (trans. John Bowden; Philadelphia: Fortress Press, 1978), 39–46; Richard A. Horsley and John S. Hanson, *Bandits, Prophets, and Messiahs: Popular Movements in the Time of Jesus* (Minneapolis: Winston, 1985), 58–63; Richard A. Horsley, *Jesus and the Spiral of Violence: Popular Jewish Resistance in Roman Palestine* (San Francisco: Harper & Row, 1987), 13; Marcus J. Borg, *Conflict, Holiness, and Politics in the Teaching of Jesus* (New York: Edwin Mellen, 1984), 53–54; Oakman, *Jesus and the Economic Questions*, 68–71; Fiensy, *Social History*, 100–105; John Dominic Crossan, *The*

can be seen from the evidence cited by Freyne in support of his general conclusions: *A.J.* 17.308; *B.J.* 2.85ff.[14] Josephus's negative evaluation and the modern theories built on it are, however, contradicted by other positive assessments of the period in Josephus's works. They are opposed especially by the weight of evidence suggesting that Herod's kingdom was prosperous and that he managed it well, that is, to Rome's satisfaction. Antony, and after him Augustus and Agrippa, trusted and rewarded Herod's energy and administrative abilities. His friendship and demonstrated loyalty to Augustus yielded large returns in territorial expansions and revenue. He was entrusted with pacifying and ruling border territories where Rome needed to eliminate unruly elements and extend its influence, and he turned them (for example, Batanea) into stable, prosperous, tax-free Jewish colonies. There seems to be no reason for us to assume that he taxed the rest of his realm to ruination. In any event, the conclusion that he actually did or did not impoverish his kingdom through excessive taxation can be reached not by references to one-sided remarks by Josephus but rather by a comprehensive examination of the evidence at our disposal.

Such a study of the evidence is crucial. Scholars, in particular those who think that Herod's reign was economically oppressive, view the excessive taxes paid by the Jews under Herod as the watershed of the economic problems that led to the Christian movement and to the Jewish revolt of 66 C.E.[15] Under Herod, it is generally claimed, Jewish peasants were crushed by a system of triple taxation: Herod's own excessive taxes were paid on top of tribute to Rome, and temple taxes and tithes.[16]

Historical Jesus: The Life of a Mediterranean Peasant (San Francisco: HarperSanFrancisco, 1991), 218–24.

14. On both passages, see below. The third passage that Freyne cites—*A.J.* 15:365—hardly shows that Herod's subjects were in "bad financial straits," since, on the contrary, it says that Herod remitted a third of the taxes paid by his subjects.

15. For instance, according to Richard A. Horsley (*Spiral of Violence*, 13): "Herod in particular intensified the economic exploitation of the people" in order to support "his elaborate regime and lavish court," his "extensive building projects," and "his astounding munificence to the imperial family and to Hellenistic cultural causes." All of these projects Herod "funded by taxing his people." It was this "intense economic pressure on the peasant producers," continued under the Roman governors after Herod, that produced the economic and social conditions in Judea necessary for the "spiral of violence" that Horsley goes on to describe.

16. Thus Richard A. Horsley, *Archaeology*, 78: "The same tributary political-economic system [i.e., from the Persians to Julius Caesar] was perpetuated, only in a more complicated way, when the Roman Senate installed Herod as their client-king over Judea and the rest of Palestine. The Romans were thus providing an 'income' for their client-kings as well as 'indirect rule' over territories along their eastern frontier. . . . Herod, however, left the Temple and high priesthood intact, still requiring economic support from tithes and offerings despite its reduced political function. This meant that the Galileans had gone from one

The Herods and Roman Tribute

I argued in chapter 3 that, following the defeat of Cassius and Brutus in 42 B.C.E., Antony reconfirmed for the Jewish state the tax concessions that it had received from Julius Caesar. This regime was brought to an end, we have noted, by the Parthian invasion of Syria two years later. The problem is to know to what extent, in fiscal terms, the re-creation of Judea as a kingdom (abolished by Pompey) represented a new reality. Was Herod made "King of the Jews" under the existing, Caesarean, tax terms? Did the Senate, Antony, and Octavian impose new tribute under different terms? In other words, was the Jewish state under Herod and his sons *stipendiaria* as it had been since its conquest by Pompey in 63 B.C.E.? Or was it free from direct annual tribute to Rome?

The discussion of Jewish tax obligations to Rome under the Herods is hampered by the lack of evidence. There is nothing in Josephus's account of Herod's reign to suggest that his subjects paid tribute to Rome. On the contrary, as Schürer correctly observes, it is noteworthy that the Jews who gathered after Herod's death demanded from Archelaus a reduction of both annual and sales taxes (*A.J.* 17.204–5; *B.J.* 2.4). Later, the delegation to Augustus complained of Herodian taxation in an effort to buttress their demand for the abolition of the monarchy (*A.J.* 17.307–8; *B.J.* 2.85–86). There is no mention in either case of Roman tribute. Both Herod and Archelaus, Schürer concludes, acted independently and without restric-

---

to three layers of rulers in the sixty years from the Hasmonean takeover to the imposition of Herod, with three layers of payments due, taxes to Herod and tribute to Rome as well as the tithes and offerings to Temple and priesthood." Further, in *Galilee*, Horsley writes that Rome "reestablished the fundamental tributary political-economic system traditional in the ancient Near East, with Rome now as the ultimate beneficiary" (p. 118). In Judea, "this meant at least a double level of rule and taxation" wherein "Rome claimed its tribute, but taxation also provided a handsome level of revenue for the client-rulers." Thus, "Herod undoubtedly extracted substantial revenues from his subjects," amounting to "900 talents annually." In this work, however, Horsley claims that it "is not completely clear" whether under Herod "the high-priestly regime" continued to receive the tithes granted them by the Romans. He concludes, nonetheless, that "[o]bviously some income remained to sustain the elaborate Temple establishment." Borg (*Conflict, Holiness, and Politics*, 47–49) speaks of Jewish Palestine being subjected to "two systems of taxation" (Roman taxes together with Jewish religious taxes). "The impact," he concludes also, "of the economic crunch was severe, producing signs of social disintegration, such as widespread emigration, a growing number of landless 'hirelings,' and a social class of robbers and beggars." Resistance to Herod, in his view (pp. 53–55), was due to Herod's "reduction of Jewish autonomy on the one hand, and, on the other, his Gentile associations and Romanizing policy." See also literature cited in nn. 3 and 15. On the whole, these views echo Mommsen, *History*, 5:408–9: "In the client-states the forms of taxation were somewhat different, but the burdens themselves were if possible still worse, since in addition to the exactions of the Romans there came those of the native courts."

tion with regard to taxation in Palestine.[17] Momigliano, citing these observations by Schürer, maintains that with Herod the previous system of Roman taxation, which Caesar had established, was terminated. A distinction no longer existed between the tribute to be paid to Rome and the taxes paid to the government in Jerusalem. Now Herod was obliged to pay a fixed annual tribute to Rome from the taxes he collected from his kingdom.[18] Momigliano's view depends on his interpretation of Caesar's decrees,[19] which I showed in chapter 2 to be untenable, given that the decrees regulated only the tribute that the Jews were to pay to the Romans.

Momigliano based the view that Rome continued to raise an annual tribute from Judea on an obscure passage in Appian's *Bell. civ.* 5.75.[20] I shall discuss this text in some detail below. Momigliano's theory that this tribute was taken from Herod's tax revenue is not supported by any evidence. Subsequent scholars, New Testament scholars in particular, have relied directly or indirectly on Momigliano's views on the matter. These scholars speak vaguely either of "Roman taxes" levied upon the people or of Herod being required to pay "a fixed sum" annually to Rome.[21] Such vagueness dissimulates a malaise since, as Schürer points out, "the payment of a lump sum as tribute is quite different from an exaction by the Romans of direct taxes from the individual citizens of the country."[22] Those who imagine that Rome exacted an annual tribute directly from the inhabitants of Herod's kingdom have only their imagination to show for it. Moreover, there is no trace in Josephus's works of lump sums paid by Herod as annual tribute to Rome.

---

17. Schürer, *History*, 1:416.

18. Momigliano, *Ricerche*, 43.

19. See ibid., 43–44.

20. Momigliano, *Ricerche*, 41–42.

21. See Schalit, *König Herodes*, 87 and nn. 105–6, especially pp. 161–62 and nn. 63, 64. Like Momigliano, Schalit depends on Appian, *Bell. civ.* 5.75. He (p. 162, n. 63) also refers to Joachim Marquardt. Far from providing further evidence, however, Marquardt relied on his analysis of Rome's treatment of Judea for his view that client kings paid tribute to Rome. See Joachim Marquardt, *Römische Staatsverwaltung* (ed. Theodor Mommsen and Joachim Marquardt; vol. 4–6 of *Handbuch der römischen Alterthümer*; 2nd ed.; Leipzig: Hirzel, 1881–85; repr., New York: Arno Press, 1975), 1:405–8, 499–500 and n. 7, and the discussion below. Later generations of scholars depend on Momigliano and Schalit including Smallwood, *Jews under Roman Rule*, 85 and nn. 82, 83; and Applebaum, "Economic Life," 661–62 and n. 8. See also Applebaum, "Herod I," cols. 379 and 382; Menahem Stern, "The Reign of Herod and the Herodian Dynasty," in *The Jewish People in the First Century: Historical Geography, Political History, Social, Cultural and Religious Life and Institutions*, vol. 1 (ed. S. Safrai and M. Stern; CRINT 1; Assen: Van Goreum, 1976), 238–9; Harold W. Hoehner, *Herod Antipas* (Cambridge: Cambridge University Press, 1972), 298–300; Freyne, *Galilee*, 191; Hamel, *Poverty and Charity*, 146; see also literature cited in nn. 13, 15, and 16 above.

22. Schürer, *History*, 1:416, n. 85.

In the face of the apparent dearth of direct evidence to support it, the argument from the absence of any mention in Josephus's works of Roman tribute during Herod's rule is an *argumentum e silentio*, and it is applicable most particularly to Herod's reign under Augustus, that is, after 30 B.C.E. The contrary view, namely, that Herod paid tribute to Rome, is for the most part based on a challenge of this *argumentum e silentio*. Momigliano thought that it was beyond any doubt that, after Herod had been appointed king, Judea paid tribute to Rome while Antony dominated Syria (40–30 B.C.E.). The ground for this certitude, apart from Appian's *Bell. civ.* 5.75, is that until the Parthian invasion in 40 B.C.E. the Jewish state was considered *stipendiaria* and continued to pay tribute, as we have noted, consonant with Caesar's legislation. There is no evidence or discernible occasion, Momigliano concludes, that the system would have changed later to Rome's financial disadvantage.[23] In Schalit's view Herod continued to play the role that Caesar had given to his father. He was in this regard no more than a glorified Roman procurator in his own territory.[24]

The next generation of scholars seized upon these ideas and turned the *argumentum e silentio* on its head. Smallwood makes the first explicit move:

> Tribute had been imposed by Pompey in 63 and regulated by Caesar in 47, and the triumvirs had appointed Herod king in 40 on existing tributary terms. There are no references to financial obligations in the context of Octavian's ratification of Herod's position or to the payment of tribute to Rome at any point during his reign, and in the complaints made about taxes immediately after his death not a word was said about Roman exactions. But the *argumentum ex silentio* in this case seems to point to the retention of tribute after 30, not to its abolition. Had it been abolished then or later, the benefaction would hardly have gone unrecorded; and the state of the Roman exchequer in 30 gave little incentive to forego any source of revenue.[25]

Hoehner echoes her:

> In the republican era it was a practice not to impose tribute on client kings, but Pompey had made Palestine tributary and Julius Caesar, although altering some aspects of the tribute, did not abolish it. If there was an abolition of tribute for Palestine, it seems incredible that Jose-

---

23. Momigliano, *Ricerche*, 42.

24. Schalit, *König Herodes*, 162: "so war in Wirklichkeit auch Herodes der Prokurator des Augustus, nur daß dieser Prokurator den Königstitel trug." He again relies on Marquardt, *Römische Staatsverwaltung*, 1:407–8. See below.

25. Smallwood, *Jews under Roman Rule*, 85.

> phus would not have mentioned that fact. There is no evidence for Augustus altering the existing system and the *argumentum ex silentio* in this case is an argument in favour of the continued system of tribute.[26]

The argument, based only on Josephus's silence, against tribute to Rome under Herod, is a weak argument. The reversed *argumentum e silentio* is even weaker, since it appeals to the reader's credulity: if Rome had exempted Herod's kingdom (or better, Herod) from tribute, "it seems incredible" that Josephus did not celebrate it. Since he did not celebrate it, it did not happen! But, why is it "incredible" that Josephus did not celebrate such an exemption? Momigliano did observe, judiciously in my view, that we have even less information on the system of Roman taxation in Herod's kingdom than we have on Judea under Hyrcanus II. This is because Josephus usually furnishes us with such information when he cites the relevant decrees.[27] Although he is aware that they had been issued, Josephus cites no decrees either in relation to Herod's appointment by the Senate in 40 B.C.E. or to his confirmation by Octavian in 30 B.C.E.[28] Thus, Smallwood might be correct that, had Herod been exempted from tribute, "the benefaction would hardly have gone unrecorded."[29] However, the reason why we have no record of such a grant is that the decrees in which the terms of Herod's appointments were recorded are not extant.

New and startling evidence on the question is not forthcoming. Josephus, however, is in fact not as silent on the subject as scholars usually assume him to be. There is more information on Judea under Herod than on any other contemporary client kingdom. In the Republic, as Lintott aptly observes, "the only good evidence for regular taxation of a territory akin to a kingdom concerns Judaea."[30] Not surprisingly, therefore, it is

---

26. Hoehner, *Herod Antipas*, 299; see his n. 5. Thus also Applebaum, "Economic Life," 661: "That Judaea was exempt from tribute under Augustus (as may be understood from Josephus), when it had been imposed by Julius Caesar, is hardly credible." See his n. 8. Freyne (*Galilee*, 191, 206, n. 126) attributes the argument to Hoehner.

27. Momigliano, *Ricerche*, 43.

28. The decree granting kingship to Herod was deposited in the Capitol after the Senate adjourned (*A.J.* 14.388; *B.J.* 1.285). Josephus does not cite its content. A *senatus consultum* probably accompanied Herod's reinstatement by Octavian. This is suggested by *A.J.* 15.196: "Having been granted so favourable a reception and seeing his [Herod's] throne restored to him more firmly than ever beyond his hopes by the gift of Caesar and the decree of the Romans, which Caesar had obtained for him in the interest of his security, he escorted him [Octavian] on his way to Egypt." In the Republic the recognition (*appellatio*) of kings by Rome was, as a rule, granted by the Senate. See Braund, *Rome and the Friendly King*, 23–37; Lintott, *Imperium Romanum*, 32–33, and earlier Jean Gagé, "L'empereur romains et les rois: politique et protocole," *RH* 221 (1959): 245.

29. See Smallwood, *Jews under Roman Rule*, 85.

30. Lintott, *Imperium Romanum*, 35; Andrew Lintott, "What Was the '*Imperium Roma-*

from their interpretations of Rome's dealings with Judea that historians infer what Rome did with the other kingdoms.[31]

Judea, however, is not just "the only good evidence," but, as Braund notes, simply the only evidence there is that Rome might have demanded regular annual tribute from client kings.[32] This "evidence," as it appears in Marquardt, Momigliano, Schalit, and scholars afterwards, depends on two props. The first is that Pompey imposed tribute on Judea under Hyrcanus II, Julius Caesar modified but upheld it, and Antony confirmed it. The second is that the appointment of Herod as king changed nothing in the status quo, since he was appointed under the existing tax terms. The first prop assumes that Judea under John Hyrcanus II was a "client state," that is, according to Lintott, "akin to a kingdom." The second prop assumes this continuum from John Hyrcanus II to Herod and relies explicitly on Appian's *Bell. civ.* 5.75.

Roman Tribute and the Status of Judea

The assumption that Judea was a "client kingdom" from John Hyrcanus II to Herod raises the much discussed question of the articulation of Judea into Rome's imperial structure. Therefore, much as the question of Herod's tax obligations to Rome might be answered with reference to Herod's personal relationship to his suzerains, we must revisit the problem of Judea's status from 63 B.C.E. to 40 B.C.E. Marquardt wrote concerning Judea:

> Tribut hatte Iudaea schon seit Pompeius an die Römer gezahlt und der öfters vorkommende Fall, dass einzelne Landschaften mitten in der Provinz zeitweise einer einheimischen dynastischen Verwaltung übergeben wurden, ist immer so zu denken, dass in den Einkünften des römischen Staates dabei kein Ausfall stattfand. So wie Hyrcanus Tribut zahlte, welchem Caesar deshalb in der Person des Antipater, des Vaters des Herodes, einen ἐπίτροπος beigegeben hatte, so ist auch Herodes selbst fatisch als ein *procurator* des Kaisers mit dem Königstitel zu betrachten.[33]

---

num'?" *Greece & Rome* 28 (1981): 63. Fergus Millar ("Emperors, Kings and Subjects: The Politics of Two-Level Sovereignty," *SCI* 15 [1996]: 162) points out that Josephus's *Antiquities* books 15–17 constitute in effect two hundred pages of "a history of the early Imperial regime."

31. See Badian, *Roman Imperialism*, 78; Lintott, *Imperium Romanum*, 35; Lintott, "What Was the '*Imperium Romanum*'?" 63; and principally Marquardt, *Römische Staatsverwaltung*, 1:405–8.

32. Braund, *Rome and the Friendly King*, 65; see Lintott, *Imperium Romanum*, 35.

33. Marquardt, *Römische Staatsverwaltung*, 1:407–8.

In Marquardt's view, then, Judea after its conquest by Pompey became part of the province of Syria and, consonant with this status, paid tribute to Rome.[34] Its status was demonstrated by the administrative interference by the governor, Gabinius, who divided it into aristocratic boroughs. Further, it contributed troops to the Roman war efforts in the region.[35] Similarly, Herod's kingdom was a "region within the province" of Syria. In other words, from its conquest in 63 B.C.E., and under Herod, the Jewish state was part of the province of Syria, albeit with its own local administration. Thus, Hyrcanus's and Herod's Judea showed that client kingdoms were integral parts of Roman provinces and paid tribute to Rome. Herod, in particular, was (like his father) a Roman procurator with a kingly title.[36]

Momigliano writes dismissively of Marquardt's theory that Judea was inserted into the province of Syria.[37] Pompey, in his view, deprived Hyrcanus of his kingly title but allowed him the title "ethnarch" and considered him a vassal of Rome. From 63 B.C.E. to 6 C.E., therefore, Judea was a vassal kingdom, a formally autonomous state.[38] Since the "client

---

34. Marquardt, *Römische Staatsverwaltung,* 1:405–6: "wurde Iudaea ein Theil der Provinz Syrien, erhielt indess schon damals eine eigene Verwaltung zunächst in Betreff der Steuern, die es seitdem an die Römer zahlte."

35. Ibid., 1:406–7.

36. Ibid., 1:499–500 and n. 7; also Theodor Mommsen, *Römisches Straatsrecht* (ed. Joachim Marquardt and Theodor Mommsen; vol. 1–3 of *Handbuch der römischen Alterthümer;* Leipzig: Hirzel, 1887), 3:683: "Die nicht städtisch geordneten Gemeinden und die abhängigen Fürstenthümer zahlten schon unter der Republik feste Jahrestribute an die römische Regierung." Mommsen (p. 683, n. 3) cites the case of Judea. This view is continued by Badian (*Roman Imperialism,* 78) who holds that "[w]ith Pompey, the client princes become a real part of the empire (*reichsangehörig,* in Mommsen's word), in a sense in which they never had been before." He cites Judea as "the best-known case." He is followed by many scholars. For example, Elizabeth Rawson, "Caesar's Heritage: Hellenistic Kings and and Their Roman Equals," in *Roman Culture and Society: Collected Papers* (Oxford: Clarendon, 1991), 186 and n. 101.

37. Momigliano, *Ricerche,* 6.

38. Momigliano, *Ricerche,* 5–6. According to Schalit (*König Herodes,* 14–15) Pompey's settlement was only the first step toward the establishment of a Roman province in Judea, which came in 70 C.E., after the revolt. In 63 B.C.E. Judea, unlike the surrounding Hellenistic cities, was not included in the province of Syria. Hyrcanus was left with the administration of the territory, as high priest and ethnarch. Momigliano and Schalit are followed by Smallwood (*Jews under Roman Rule,* 27–30), according to whom Pompey set Hyrcanus over a "client kingdom," but with the title "ethnarch." Pompey only prepared Judea "for later incorporation in the empire as a province." The territory, thereafter, "was to remain a client kingdom for nearly seventy years." See Jones, *Cities,* 258: "The total result of Pompey's reorganization of southern Syria was thus as follows. Three native kingdoms or principalities were allowed to survive, the Nabatean, the Iturean, and the Jewish, the last very much reduced." See also Daniela Piattelli, "Ricerche intorno alle relazioni politiche tra Roma e l'ἔθνος τῶν Ἰουδαίων dal 161 A.C. al 4 A.C," *Bullettino dell'istituto di diritto romano* 74 (1972): 293–302; Sullivan, *Near Eastern Royalty,* 217–18; and many others

prince" Hyrcanus paid tribute, it is to be expected that Herod must have continued in the same dependence.

The ambivalent positions held by Schürer best illustrate the difficulty of determining the exact situation of Judea within the Roman imperial structure after 63 B.C.E. He first maintains that "[f]rom 65 B.C. to A.D. 70, Palestine, although not directly annexed to the province of Syria, was nevertheless subject to the supervision of the Roman governor of Syria."[39] He writes further on:

> Because of the scantiness of the sources it is difficult to give an accurate account of the position of Palestine at this time in relation to Rome. This much is certain, however: it was tributary, Jos. *Ant.* xiv 4, 4 (74); *B.J.* i 7, 6 (154), and under the control of the Roman governor of Syria. The question is whether or not it was directly incorporated in the province of Syria. A later observation made by Josephus constitutes an argument for the latter alternative, namely that by the enactment of Gabinius, who divided Palestine into five districts, the land was free from "monarchical government," *B.J.* i 8, 5 (170). Hyrcanus will consequently have stood at the head of the government of the country, and been subject only to the control of the Roman governor.[40]

The problem, it appears, is how to reconcile Hycanus's administrative responsibilities in Judea with the subjection of the territory to the control of the governor of the province of Syria. In order to be "directly annexed" to the province of Syria, need Judea have been without a local administration? Or, in other words, need Judea have been "directly incorporated," that is, without a local government, in order to be considered part of the province of Syria?

More recent discussions of the status of Judea after 63 B.C.E. have paid attention to the complex and much disputed problems of Roman notions of the *provincia* and of the *imperium* of the provincial governors.[41] From

---

39. Schürer, *History*, 1:243; see also Solomon Zeitlin, *The Rise and Fall of the Judaean State: A Political, Social and Religious History of the Second Commonwealth* (Philadelphia: Jewish Publication Society of America, 1962), 1:355, 370.

40. Schürer, *History*, 1:267. Schürer's last statement, meaning that Hyrcanus was at the head of the Jewish state until Gabinius's intervention, is consonant with his later (1:269) assessment of Gabinius's political arrangement: "Gabinius's enactment signified the removal of that remnant of political power which Hyrcanus had still possessed. Pompey had already deprived him of the title of king; now he was stripped of all political authority and restricted to his priestly functions. The country was divided into five districts and 'liberated' from his rule." See below.

41. See, in particular, Shatzman, "L'integrazione della Giudea," 18–25. On *imperium* and *provincia*, see Lintott, "What Was the '*Imperium Romanum*'?"; Lintott, *Imperium Romanum*, 5–42; Andrew Lintott, *The Constitution of the Roman Republic* (Oxford: Clarendon, 1999), 94–102; J. S. Richardson, "*Imperium Romanum*: Empire and the Language of Power," *JRS* 81

the point of view of Rome's increasing sphere of influence and dominion, the Jewish state from the second century B.C.E. had come into the *imperium populi Romani*. Pompey's conquest of the territory, together with the rest of Syria, was in this regard the territorial and administrative realization of that dominion.[42] The Roman Empire in general, once it had become a geographically defined entity, was, in terms of ideology, constitution, and political structure, a complex organization, a large section of which was ruled by kings, dynasts, and tetrarchs.[43] Pompey's Syria was typical.[44] It is worth repeating that the forms of incorporation of various segments of the territory over which Pompey had extended Rome's hegemony developed over time and shifted frequently. With regard to Rome's imperial hegemony in Syria, therefore, Judea under John Hyrcanus II, Herod, and afterwards was in the *provincia* of whoever had the *imperium* (command, power) over the territory.[45]

The problem of Judea's situation within the imperial structure, as Shatzman points out,[46] lies in the administrative tools that Rome used to manage the territory from 63 B.C.E. onward. The confusing multiplicity of titles for Judea's administrative officials is indicative of the attempts made by various Roman imperial authorities to find an acceptable *modus vivendi* between Roman policies and Jewish traditions.[47] Until the creation of the Roman province of Judea, following the First Revolt from 66–74 C.E., when the Jews lost their institutions for self-government, Rome always operated a system of indirect rule in Judea. The difference lay in the people to whom Rome entrusted the direct administration of the territory and the degree of their relative independence from Roman imperial magistrates. Under the *praefecti*, the high priest and the priestly aristocracy were in charge of the daily administration of the territory, including the collection of tribute (*B.J.* 2.405).[48] This two-level system of

(1991): 1–9; J. S. Richardson, "Administration of the Empire," 564–80; Jean-Marie Bertrand, "À propos du mot PROVINCIA: étude sur les modes d'élaboration du langage politique," *Journal des Savants* (July-December 1989): 191–215.

42. See Shatzman, "L'integrazione della Giudea," 38–48.

43. Millar, "Emperors, Kings and Subjects," 161; and the discussion in Martin Goodman, *The Roman World, 44 BC - AD 180* (London: Routledge, 1997), 110–12.

44. See the discussions in Rey-Coquais, "Syrie Romaine," 44–48; Jones, *Cities*, 252–60; Kennedy, "Syria," 703–12.

45. Thus certainly Lintott (*Imperium Romanum*, 25), who compares Judea to Apamea under Dexandros in the first century C.E. See also Shatzman, "L'integrazione della Giudea," 45.

46. Shatzman, "L'integrazione della Giudea," 45.

47. Sullivan, *Near Eastern Royalty*, 217–18.

48. E. P. Sanders, "Jesus' Galilee," in *Fair Play: Diversity and Conflicts in Early Christianity* (ed. Ismo Dunderberg et al.; Leiden: Brill, 2002), 6–9; Sanders, *Judaism*, 170–89, and below.

government was tripled by the influence exercised by a Jewish king, while not directly governing the land.[49]

Josephus writes, in effect, that with the annexation of Judea in 6 C.E., following the death of King Herod and the banishment of "king" Archelaus,[50] "the constitution became an aristocracy, and the high priests were entrusted with the leadership of the nation" (*A.J.* 20.251). "Aristocracy" or "theocracy," that is, the government by priests, which had come into existence in Judea from about the sixth century B.C.E. (*A.J.* 11.111–13),[51] was the internal constitution (πολιτεία) that Josephus considered traditional and preferred.[52] He opposes it to "rule by a king" (βασιλεία), which he rejects.[53] In 6 C.E., according to Josephus, Rome returned Judea to the administrative situation in which Pompey had left it in 63 B.C.E.: direct government by the priestly aristocracy and indirect government by a Roman magistrate. He observes, accordingly, that in 63 B.C.E. this administrative formula was to the delight of "the Jews and their leaders" (presumably priests) who had petitioned Pompey to reinstate the traditional constitution of their country. For them the rule by a king was tantamount to being reduced to "a nation of slaves" (*A.J.* 14.41, 73, 91; *B.J.* 1.153, 169–70). This, notably, was also the view of the Jewish embassy to Augustus after the death of Herod: the "freedom" (*A.J.* 17.227) and the "autonomy of their nation" (*B.J.* 2.80) for which they pleaded would be realized if Augustus would "unite their country to Syria" and "entrust the administration to governors" (*B.J.* 2.80–91; see *A.J.* 17.227). Under Roman rule, the government of Judea by priests was always accompanied by the immediate oversight of a Roman magistrate. Thus, direct government by the

---

49. Agippa I and his son Agrippa II. Millar ("Emperors, Kings and Subjects," 164–65), commenting on Acts 25–26 observes: "In the years leading up to the Jewish Revolt of 66 CE Judea was under a sort of dual local control, both procurator and king being under the adjudication of the Emperor in Rome." The "'High Priests' and leading Jews," however, are also in the picture presented by Millar.

50. In *A.J.* 17.355 Josephus notes that, in 6 C.E., Archelaus's territory "was added to (the province of) Syria," even though a *praefectus* was appointed to administer it. See also *A.J.* 18.1–2. In *B.J.* 2.117 he says that the territory was "reduced to a province." See Theodor Mommsen, *The Provinces of the Roman Empire from Caesar to Diocletian* (2 vols; trans. William P. Dickson; Chicago: Ares Publishers, 1974), 2:185 and n. 1; also chapter 5.

51. Daniel R. Schwartz ("Josephus on the Jewish Constitutions and Community," *SCI* 7 [1983]: 32–34) disputes that both *A.J.* 11.111 and *A.J.* 20.251 need to be interpreted to mean that by "aristocracy" Josephus means government by priests ("hierocracy"). "'Aristocracy,'" he concludes, "denotes not hierocracy but rather government by council," that is, *gerousia*.

52. *A.J.* 4.196–301, esp. 214–18, 223–24; *C. Ap.* 2.145–295, esp. 164–67, 184–89.

53. On βασιλεία see, for instance, *A.J.* 12.360, 389; 13.113, 301; 14.41, 78; 17.273, 280–81; 18.237; 20.241–42. Agrippa I is supposed to have written to Gaius: "It fell to me to have for my grandparents and ancestors kings, most of whom had the title of high priest, who considered their kingship inferior to the priesthood, holding that the office of high priest is as superior in excellence to that of the king as God surpasses men. For the office of one is to worship God, of the other to have charge of men" (Philo, *Legat.* 278).

priestly aristocracy and indirect government by a Roman magistrate were the administrative formula instituted by Rome when Judea—the region—(6–41 C.E.) and the entire Jewish state (44–66 C.E.) were "directly annexed" into Rome's provinces. Such was the case also in the period from 63 to 40 B.C.E.

The correlation between Jewish internal "aristocratic" administration and "direct annexation" is further confirmed by what Josephus says of the period from 63 to 48 B.C.E. Hyrcanus was not a king; Judea was not a client kingdom.[54] Pompey did not give Hyrcanus the title "ethnarch" either. Marquardt maintains that Pompey left Hyrcanus in Judea as high priest and ethnarch.[55] None of the ancient sources he cites as evidence actually supports this view.[56] Momigliano accepts Marquardt's opinion as if it were self-evident.[57] Josephus says actually that Pompey restored the high priesthood to Hyrcanus, and to the Jews their postexilic "theocratic" constitution.

What Josephus says here is the meaning of the two summaries that he gives of Hyrcanus II's reign. In *A.J.* 20.243–45 he first observes that Aristobulus, Hyrcanus's brother and rival, was "both king and high priest of the nation," and then further explains that Pompey restored the high priesthood to Hyrcanus "and permitted him to have the leadership of the nation (τὴν μὲν τοῦ ἔθνους προστασίαν ἐπέτρεψεν), but forbade him to wear a diadem." He writes in *A.J.* 15.180–81:

> After taking the throne on the death of his mother he held it for three months, but was driven from it by his brother Aristobulus. When it was restored to him later by Pompey, he received all his honours back and continued to enjoy them for forty years more.[58] But he was deprived of

54. Sands, *Client Princes*, 121–22, 134, 222–23; Braund, *Rome and the Friendly King*, 65; contra Lintott, "What Was the '*Imperium Romanum*'?" 63.

55. Marquardt, *Römische Staatsverwaltung*, 1:406, text cited above.

56. Marquardt, *Römische Staatsverwaltung*, 1:406 and n. 5: (i) Dio Cassius, *Hist.* 37.16: "The kingdom was given to Hyrcanus, and Aristobulus was carried away" (ἥ τε βασιλεία τῷ Ὑρκανῷ ἐδόθη, καὶ ὁ Ἀριστόβουλος ἀνηνέχθη); (ii) Strabo, *Geogr* 16.2.46 (765): "Now Pompey clipped off some of the territory that had been forcibly appropriated by the Judeans, and appointed Herod to the priesthood" (Πομπήιος μὲν οὖν περικόψας τινὰ τῶν ἐξιδιασθέντων ὑπὸ τῶν Ἰουδαίων κατὰ βίαν ἀπέδειξεν Ἡρώδῃ τὴν ἱερωσύνην); (iii) Josephus, *A.J.* 14.73 (4,4): "[Pompey] restored the high priesthood to Hyrcanus" (τὴν ἀρχιερωσύνην ἀπέδωκεν Ὑρκανῷ). Marquardt's combination, ἀρχιερεὺς καὶ ἐθνάρχης, actually comes from the titles that Caesar gave to Hyrcanus later, as we shall see below.

57. Momigliano, *Ricerche*, 5. Marquardt is followed by a host of other scholars, including Schalit (*König Herodes*, 14 and nn. 50–51) and Smallwood, *Jews under Roman Rule*, 27 and n. 22. Both authors cite *A.J.* 20.244, and Smallwood claims that the title "ethnarch" is implied by the words ἡ προστασία τοῦ ἔθνους in Josephus's passage. More recently, see Saulnier, "Lois Romaines," 174–75; Lintott, *Imperium Romanum*, 25.

58. From 63 to 40 is twenty-three years (or twenty-four years, according to *A.J.* 20.245). That Hyrcanus ruled for forty years is obviously an error.

> them a second time by Antigonus, mutilated in body, and taken prisoner by the Parthians.

That Hyrcanus received back the throne and all his honors and that he was restored to the high priesthood say one and the same thing, with the proviso that Pompey rid Judea of kingly rule.[59] The territory that Pompey granted to Hyrcanus to administer as high priest was under the immediate control of the succession of Roman magistrates from 63 B.C.E. I have already shown in chapter 1 that, although Pompey defeated Aristobulus II and captured Jerusalem in 63 B.C.E., the country was not subdued. From Rome's perspective, Judea belonged to the *provincia* of the magistrate who had the *imperium* to wage the war necessary to conquer and passify it.[60] Hence, after enumerating the cities that Pompey had detached from the Jewish state, Josephus writes (*B.J.* 1.157):

> All these towns he restored to their legitimate inhabitants and annexed to the province of Syria. That province, together with Judea and the whole region extending as far as Egypt and the Euphrates, he entrusted, along with two legions, to the administration of Scaurus; and then he set out in haste across Cilicia for Rome, taking with him his prisoners, Aristobulus and his family.

This passage has often been read as if Josephus meant that Judea was outside of the "the province of Syria" administered by Scaurus. The Loeb translation suggests this understanding. This cannot be the case. In Josephus's second sentence (παραδοὺς δὲ ταύτην τε καὶ τὴν Ἰουδαίαν καὶ τὰ μέχρις Αἰγύπτου καὶ Εὐφράτου, κτλ.), the particles τε καί are epexegetical, detailing in what "this (ταύτην)" consisted, that is, the province of Syria administered by Scaurus and his successors. The province, in other words, is the same as the whole region that lies between Egypt and the

59. Thus also *A.J.* 14.73; *B.J.* 1.153. According to Aharoni and Avi-Yonah (*Atlas*, 161), during this period "Hyrcanus II again became high priest in Jerusalem, but administration was entrusted to Antipater." Thus also Frederic W. Madden, *History of Jewish Coinage and of Money in the Old and New Testament* (London: B. Quaritch, 1864; repr., New York: Ktav, 1967), 75. The view probably goes back to Mommsen (*Provinces*, 174–75). Josephus (*A.J.* 15.177, 182) actually says that it was Hyrcanus who, "when he himself had royal power," because of his mild character, "yielded the greatest part of the administration to Antipater."

60. See generally *A.J.* 14.80–122; *B.J* 1.159–82. In *A.J.* 14.100–102, for instance, Josephus considers the revolts led by Alexander in Judea to be "uprisings and disorder" in Gabinius's "Syria." See also *B.J.* 1.176–77. J. S. Richardson ("Administration of the Empire," 579–80) comments appropriately: "A magistrate or promagistrate in an overseas *provincia* was not orginally or (in the Republican period, at least) primarily administering an area of Roman territory, but commanding Roman forces in a foreign land . . . . Within those very broad boundaries, he had the freedom that was essential to any commander to exercise the power of the Senate and the people of Rome as he saw fit: that indeed was what *imperium* meant."

Euphrates.[61] It includes what remained of Judea, together with the region of Samaria (Samaritis).[62]

To sum up, Marquardt is correct that there is no contradiction between the existence of a local administration in Judea, headed by the high priest, and the territory's annexation into the province of Syria. This was Rome's administrative formula in use when the Jewish state was known to have been "directly annexed." Josephus (*A.J.* 14.77) could rightly, therefore, lament Judea's losses: "For we lost our freedom and became subject to the Romans, and the territory which we had gained by our arms and taken from the Syrians we were compelled to give back to them."[63] Communities like Judea under annexation were commonplace in the provinces of the empire. As Sherwin-White observes in relation to Pompey's organization of Pontus, in principle "a Roman province was an effective system of administration only in areas where local government was established."[64] Administratively, Judea was similar to the Hellenistic cities that Pompey had "liberated" from Jewish rule.[65] Both were "free"; that is, they were not under kingly rule and had relative administrative and financial independence. They used their own laws and were for this reason "autonomous."[66] All were, however, immediately within the *provincia* of the governor of Syria. Although the imposition of tribute is not a direct proof of annexation, territories that were annexed were *stipendiariae*, barring special immunities granted to specific communities.[67] Pompey imposed

61. Appian, *Hist. rom.* 11.8.50: "inland Syria and Coele-Syria, Phoenicia, Palestine, and all the other countries bearing the Syrian name from the Euphrates to Egypt and the sea"; also *Hist. rom.* 12.17.118. Lintott, *Imperium Romanum*, 25: "from the *mons Amanus* at the south-eastern end of Cilicia in the north as far as Egypt in the south."

62. That is, Judea—region, Galilee, Perea, eastern Idumea. Thus, correctly, A. R. C. Leaney, *The Jewish and Christian World 200 BC to AD 200* (Cambridge Commentaries on Writings of the Jewish and Christian World, 200 BC to AD 200; Cambridge: Cambridge University Press, 1984), 95: "The arrangement [by Pompey] returned Judaea, along with other territories, to the position of being part of Syria, now a Roman province under a legate rather than a hellenistic kingdom." Ammianus Marcellinus's report (14.8.12) that Palestine was "formed into a province by Pompey, after he had defeated the Jews and taken Jerusalem, but left [it] to the jurisdiction of a governor" has little value. Even more doubtful are the statements in Appian, *Hist. rom.*11.8.50 and *Hist. rom.* 12.17.118.

63. Sullivan (*Near Eastern Royalty*, 219) claims, wrongly I think, that Josephus's remark about the loss of liberty by the Jewish state "retrojects the conditions of his own day." Sullivan is correct to point out, however, that "in 63 BC much fighting lay ahead before the Jewish state could be termed 'subjected' by Rome."

64. Sherwin-White, *Roman Foreign Policy*, 30.

65. See A. H. M. Jones, "Civitates Liberae et Immunes in the East," in *Anatolian Studies Presented to William Hepburn Buckler* (ed. W. M. Calder and Joseph Kiel; Manchester: Manchester University Press, 1939), 110.

66. See Lintott, *Imperium Romanum*, 154–60.

67. See Jones, "Civitates Liberae"; idem, *Roman Economy*, 6–7, 9; Lintott, *Imperium Romanum*, 38–41.

tribute on Judea as he did on the rest of the province of Syria, and the *publicani* in Syria collected tribute in Judea as well.[68]

Three aspects of the grants made by Julius Caesar to the Jews in 47 B.C.E. effected significant, though hardly radical, administrative changes in Judea. First, Caesar, recognizing the authority that Hyrcanus held in the Jewish theocracy from Pompey's settlement, confirmed Hyrcanus as high priest.[69] He also named him ethnarch, adding that his rule was to be hereditary:

> [I]t is my wish that Hyrcanus, son of Alexander, and his children shall be ethnarchs of the Jews and shall hold the office of high priest of the Jews for all time in accordance with their national customs, and that he and his sons shall be our allies and also be numbered among our particular friends. (*A.J.* 14.194)[70]

It is now a widely held view that by recognizing him as ethnarch Caesar was restoring Hyrcanus to the political power that he had lost when Gabinius organized Judea into *synedria*.[71] This view, however, is without basis. We have already seen that Hyrcanus did not bear the title ethnarch after Pompey's settlement. His administrative authority (προστασία) derived from his high-priestly office. Further, Josephus's narrative of the events of 57 B.C.E. indicates that Hyrcanus had lost control of Jerusalem to Alexander before Gabinius intervened in the civil war.[72] This explains why Josephus says that after the conflicts Gabinius "brought Hyrcanus to Jerusalem" and gave him charge of the temple.[73] There is no

68. See Sherwin-White (*Roman Foreign Policy*, 231), who writes, however: "Pompeius treated the Syrians as a conquered people, though the conquest was not due to himself. Tribute was imposed upon the minor dynasts whom he recognised in southern Syria and Judea. Pompeius thus created a new type of tributary dependency."

69. *A.J.* 14.199; see 14.137, 143; *B.J.* 1.194, 199, and discussion in chapter 2. Before Pompey's death, Judea had been allied with the Pompeians against Caesar in the civil war. Caesar, for his part, had supported Aristobulus's bid to return to power in Judea, a support that Aristobulus's son Antigonus sought to exploit (*A.J.* 14.123–25,140–44; *B.J.* 1.183–86, 195–200).

70. See the decrees cited in 14:192–95, 196–98, 211–12 and the discussions in chapter 2.

71. See, for instance, Momigliano, *Ricerche*, 13–14; Jones, "Review," 228; Schalit, *König Herodes*, 44; Schürer, *History*, 1: 269, 271; Smallwood, *Jews under Roman Rule*, 38–39; Piattelli, "Ricerche," 302–3; Saulnier, "Lois Romaines," 174–76.

72. Hyrcanus "was no longer able to hold out against the strength of Alexander, who was actually attempting to raise again the wall of Jerusalem which Pompey had destroyed" (*A.J.* 14.82). According to *B.J.* 1.160, Alexander "would in all probability have soon deposed his rival, but for the arrival of Gabinius." Alexander's first encounter with Roman forces was in an area near Jerusalem, to which he had withdrawn (*A.J.* 14.85). Peter Richardson (*Herod*, 100) interprets Josephus's statements to mean that "Alexander had a large measure of popular support, especially in Jerusalem, and that Hyrcanus and Antipater were relatively weak." He thinks, however, that "Alexander acquired control of Jerusalem" (p. 101).

73. *A.J.* 14.90; see *B.J.* 1.169. See Peter Richardson, *Herod*, 102; and especially, Sullivan, "Dynasty of Judaea," 2.8:317–18.

indication that Hyrcanus had thereby lost the προστασία in virtue of which he ruled as high priest. Josephus, in his summary of Hyrcanus's reign, does not include 57 B.C.E. and afterwards in his list of the periods during which Hyrcanus was deprived of political power.[74] On the contrary, Josephus says, the overall effect of both Hyrcanus's restoration to Jerusalem and Gabinius's *synedria* was that the people now lived under an "aristocracy" (*A.J.* 14.91). The dynastic rule (δυναστεία) from which the people were thereby relieved (ibid.) was the Hasmonean kingly rule (see *B.J.* 1.19, 37; *A.J.* 14.11; 20.261), which Alexander, in waging the civil war, again was trying to introduce. After he had been restored to Jerusalem, Hyrcanus (and Antipater) continued to act with political authority. They aided the governor in his Egyptian campaign and in his efforts to quell local revolts (*A.J.* 14.98–102).

We do not know how Gabinius's *synedria* actually functioned administratively. The arrangement was, in any event, short-lived.[75] The grant of the title ethnarch to Hyrcanus II belongs to Caesar's recognition of the Jews as an *ethnos*.[76] The *senatus consultum* confirming Caesar's decree grants:

> [t]hat his children shall rule over the Jewish nation (Ἰουδαίων ἔθνους ἄρχῃ) and enjoy the fruits of the places given to them, and that the high priest, being also ethnarch, shall be the proctector of those Jews who are unjustly treated (καὶ ὁ ἀρχιερεὺς αὐτὸς καὶ ἐθνάρχες τῶν Ἰουδαίων προϊστῆται τῶν ἀδικουμένων). (*A.J.* 14.197)[77]

Hyrcanus had the προστασία to act also in the interest of the Jews of the Diaspora.[78] For the Diaspora Jews as well as those in Judea, Caesar's decrees are the first instance of a Roman document permitting them to

---

74. See Peter Richardson, *Herod*, 77–78.

75. The arrangement ended probably in 55 B.C.E., a date generally inferred from *B.J.* 1.178; *A.J.* 14.103. See discussion in Ernest Bammel, "The Organization of Palestine by Gabinius," *JJS* 12 (1961): 159–62.

76. Josephus (*A.J.* 14.117), citing Strabo on the Jews in Alexandria, says the Jews there had "an ethnarch of their own . . . , who governs the people and adjudicates suits and supervises contracts and ordinances, just as if he were the head of a sovereign state"; see also the edict of Claudius cited in *A.J.* 19.283. Piattelli, "Ricerche," 303–5; Pucci Ben Zeev, *Jewish Rights*, 49–51.

77. See chapter 2.

78. Pucci Ben Zeev, *Jewish Rights*, 65–66; also Tessa Rajak, "Jewish Rights in the Greek Cities Under Roman Rule: A New Approach," in *Studies in Judaism and Its Greco-Roman Context* (ed. William Scott Green; Approaches to Ancient Judaism 5; BJS 32; Atlanta: Scholars Press, 1985), 24; Piattelli, "Ricerche," 303–5. Daniel R. Schwartz ("Josephus," 44) notes that "nothing we know about the Hellenistic or Roman empires would lead us to expect that such a position [of a προστάτης] existed, and apart from Josephus, we can find no references to it in sources emanating from Judaea." See also Pucci Ben Zeev, *Jewish Rights*, 57–58.

use their own laws. We noted that, although such permissions were very frequently granted and were an integral part of Rome's imperial administration, Caesar's grant was significant because it changed the *de facto* recognition that the Jews were free to use their laws to a *de iure* right.[79] For those in Judea this was more than the permission to observe their religious customs; it included criminal, civil, and administrative procedures.[80]

Apart from the right to use their laws, the other concessions made to Judea, taken together, indicate that Rome's view of the territory shifted in 47 B.C.E. I have discussed these in detail in chapter 2. The grants of immunity from billeting, military service, and requisition are particularly significant. Important also is the fact that Caesar removed the *publicani* from Judea and entrusted Hyrcanus with the assessment and the collection of tribute.[81]

A second significant aspect of the grants is that Caesar's decree (*A.J.* 14.194) refers to Hyrcanus and his sons as "allies" (συμμάχους) and "friends" (φίλοις). In the *senatus consultum* quoted in *A.J.* 14.197 mention is made of envoys to (or from) Hyrcanus for the purpose of discussing "terms of friendship and alliance" (περὶ φιλίας καὶ συμμαχίας).[82] Josephus observes that after Caesar arrived at Rome from his Egyptian campaign Hyrcanus sent envoys to him "with the request that he should confirm the treaty of friendship and alliance with him" (*A.J.* 14.185).

Otto Roth long ago doubted that Hyrcanus was successful in establishing a συμμαχία, and therefore in obtaining a treaty of alliance (a *foedus*) from the Roman Senate. This would explain why Caesar's decree speaks of Hyrcanus and his sons as allies and friends only at a personal level.[83] More recent discussions on the "vexed question"[84] of the meaning of *socius* and *amicus* have yielded divergent results.[85] "The truth," in Lin-

---

79. See chapter 2 and Miriam Pucci Ben Zeev, "Caesar and the Jewish Law," *RB* 102 (1995): 28–37, especially, against Rajak ("Roman Charter," 112–16), who considers this general permission to be "no more than a fine-sounding verbal gesture" (p. 116). Also Pucci Ben Zeev, *Jewish Rights*, 412–29; and Rajak, "Jewish Rights," 24.

80. See Pucci Ben Zeev, *Jewish Rights*, 430–38.

81. Kasher (*Jews and Hellenistic Cities*, 182–83) suggests that payment at Sidon was meant to emphasize that Judea was not a province and therefore did not pay tribute directly to Roman financial officials. Payment at Sidon is in itself hardly significant for the status of Judea; the absence of Roman financial officials is.

82. "And that envoys be sent to Hyrcanus, son of Alexander, the high priest of the Jews, to discuss terms of friendship and alliance." See chapter 2 and Pucci Ben Zeev, *Jewish Rights*, 58–59.

83. Otto Roth, *Rom und die Hasmonäer* (Leipzig: Hinrichs, 1914), 57–59; see Pucci Ben Zeev, *Jewish Rights*, 64–65.

84. Anthony J. Marshall, "Friends of the Roman People," *AJP* 89 (1968): 39.

85. See especially Sherwin-White, *Roman Foreign Policy*, 58–70. Sherwin-White (pp. 70–79) discusses the early contacts between the Hasmoneans and Rome. The prospect of an

tott's judgment, "almost certainly lies between Sherwin-White's position, that *socius* only designates an ally with a *foedus*, and Gruen's, that the terms 'friendship' and 'alliance', when applied to communities outside Italy, are used for the most part loosely, and that the Romans, even when there were formal relations, were indifferent to their exact terms."[86] Whether or not Hyrcanus obtained a *foedus* designating him *socius* of the Roman people, the terms of the relationship would need to be verified concretely. I noted in chapter 2 that Josephus presented the grants given by Caesar in the context of the "friendship and alliance" between Caesar and Hyrcanus. These grants, confirmed by a *senatus consultum*, constitute the specific terms of the relationship.

Finally, Caesar granted Roman citizenship, with exemption from taxation, to Antipater (*A.J.* 14.137; *B.J.* 1.194) and then named him "procurator" (ἐπίτροπος) of Judea (*A.J.* 14.143; *B.J.* 1.199).[87] Opinions on the administrative significance of Antipater's appointment vary from Marquardt's view that Antipater was Caesar's procurator in Judea to Mommsen's rebuttal, namely, that Caesar did not make Antipater a Roman official.[88] According to Mommsen, Antipater's office was one that was "formally conferred by the Jewish ethnarch," and was no different from the one Antipater had previously held as ὁ τῶν Ἰουδαίων ἐπιμελητής.[89] Smallwood, following Momigliano,[90] assumes that the term ἐπίτροπος is used here of Antipater as it was used later in the imperial period. She concludes that "Antipater's duties are likely to have been confined to the sphere of tax-collection." Antipater, she claims, "was to act as resident representative of Rome, safeguarding Roman financial interests."[91]

---

alliance between Hyrcanus II and Rome is not in view. See Erich S. Gruen, *The Hellenistic World and the Coming of Rome* [2 vols; Berkeley: University of California Press, 1984], esp. 1:13–95; 2:731–51. Gruen (pp. 2:745–51) also treats the topic of the treaty of alliance between Rome and the early Hasmoneans and concludes that evident here also is "[t]he pattern of Roman affirmations on the one hand and lack of implementation on the other." Rome only sent "*pro forma* messages." Earlier, see Louise E. Matthaei, "On the Classification of Roman Allies," *CQ* 1 (1907): 182–204. The relationship between Agrippa I and Claudius involved a treaty (*A.J.* 19.275).

86. Andrew Lintott, *Judicial Reform and Land Reform in the Roman Republic* (Cambridge: Cambridge University Press, 1992), 111; see his own discussion in Lintott, *Imperium Romanum*, 32–34.

87. See chapter 2. On the grants of citizenship and immunity, see A. Gilboa, "L'octroi de la citoyenneté romaine et de l'immunité à Antipater, père d'Hérode," *Revue historique de droit français et étranger* 50 (1972): 609–14.

88. Marquardt, *Römische Staatsverwaltung*, 1:407–8 (see text cited above); Mommsen, *Provinces*, 2:174, n. 1.

89. Mommsen, *Provinces*, 2:174, n. 1; see *A.J.* 14.127, 139 (citing Strabo).

90. Momigliano, *Ricerche*, 26–27.

91. Smallwood, *Jews under Roman Rule*, 39; see also Udoh, "Tribute and Taxes," 188.

Marquardt's opinion (adopted by Momigliano, Schalit,[92] and Smallwood) is attractive and has become pervasive. But Mommsen is surely correct that it is anachronistic to speak of Antipater as an imperial procurator and compare his role in Judea to the positions probably held by Herod under Augustus.[93] Jones established some time ago that "procurator was a term of private law in the later Republic, and it always remained so except when applied to the emperor's procurators."[94] Moreover, even in the early Principate—under Augustus and Tiberius—when various imperial procuratorial posts were established, procurators remained the emperor's private agents.[95] Equally unacceptable is Smallwood's comparison of Antipater with the procurator appointed by Augustus to the "client kingdom" of Cappadocia.[96] The ἐπίτροπος about whom Dio speaks was appointed by Augustus because Archelaus I of Cappadocia was alleged to have been mentally deranged. He was a regent, a governor *pro tempore*, and not Augustus's financial officer in Cappadocia.[97]

There has been a lively discussion on the relationship in Josephus's works between John Hyrcanus II and Antipater.[98] For all that, Antipater's administrative role in Judea is not easy to determine. Neither is Josephus's array of titles for Antipater very helpful.[99] What seems to be clear from both Josephus's narrative and Caesar's decrees that he cites is that effective power resided with Hyrcanus, and Antipater was responsible

92. Schalit, *König Herodes*, 162.

93. See Mommsen, *Provinces*, 2:174–75, n. 1; and Marquardt, *Römische Staatsverwaltung*, 1:407–8 and nn. 1, 2.

94. A. H. M. Jones, "Procurators and Prefects in the Early Principate," in his *Studies in Roman Government and Law* (Oxford: Blackwell, 1960), 117–25.

95. Ibid., 123; also Fergus Millar, "Some Evidence of the Meaning of Tacitus Annals XII.60," *Historia* 13 (1964): 181–87; P. A. Brunt, "Princeps and Equites," *JRS* 73 (1983): 42–75.

96. Smallwood, *Jews under Roman Rule*, 39, n. 60; Dio, *Hist.* 57.17.5.

97. See Sullivan, "Cappadocia," 2.7.2:1159; Braund, *Rome and the Friendly King*, 147; Dio (*Hist.* 57.23.4) uses the word ἐπίτροπος (here meaning "tutor" or "guardian") to describe the person appointed by Tiberius over a Senator in the same condition of mental debility as Dio attributes to Archelaus I. F. E. Romer ("A Case of Client-Kingship," *AJP* 106 [1985]: 83–84) argues that Archelaus was at the time in fact undergoing trial in Rome. After Archelaus died and the kingdom was annexed by Tiberius a governor of equestrian rank (ἱππεῖ ἐπετράπη) was appointed. Dio (*Hist.* 57.17.7) does not give his title. The governor bore the title "procurator" under the emperor Claudius, according to Tacitus (*Ann.* 12.49). See Jones, "Procurators," 118; idem, *Cities*, 181; Sullivan, "Cappadocia," 2.7.2:1159–60.

98. See Daniel R. Schwartz, "Hyrcanus II", and the earlier literature discussed there.

99. Bammel ("Gabinius," 161–62, for instance) suggests that before 47 B.C.E. Antipater's position, as "ἐπιμελητής of the partitioned state of Jerusalem," was "a financial office only." Peter Richardson (*Herod*, 105–6) concludes that "Antipater's role was probably a combination of military and financial deputy to Hyrcanus, with a broad sphere of influence (the most efficient explanation of the varying terms)."

directly to Hyrcanus[100] rather than to Caesar or Roman magistrates in Syria. We have already seen that Caesar entrusted the assessment and collection of tribute to Hyrcanus and the authorities in Jerusalem. I have observed, however, that we know next to nothing about how tax collection was organized in Judea during this period.[101] It is indeed likely that Antipater played a central role in tax collection. Evidence for this view is found in his initiative in organizing the collection of the tribute imposed by Cassius in 43 B.C.E. (*A.J.* 14.271–76; *B.J.* 1.220–22).[102] Whatever Caesar might have intended by appointing Antipater ἐπίτροπος of Judea, and whatever actual administrative roles Antipater might have assumed thereafter, it appears that we need to look also to his enfranchisement in order to appreciate the novelty that Caesar's appointment introduced into the administration of Judea. Antipater might not have been a Roman official, but he certainly was an official who was a Roman. In the late Republic, the privileged status of enfranchised provincials (a relatively rare grant in the Republic) gave them the power to exercise tremendous influence on the politics of their local communities.[103] Antipater's appointment introduced a Roman presence into the direct administration of the territory, a presence continued by Antony's later appointment of Phasael and Herod as tetrarchs in 41 B.C.E. (*A.J.* 14.326; *B.J.* 1.244).[104]

Caesar, we have seen, acted in favor of Judea in the same way as he rewarded other cities and communities that supported him during his military campaign.[105] Caesar's grants to Judea also have been compared to those granted to Termessus in the *lex Antonia*.[106] In all these other cases the favors and immunities amounted to the grant of "freedom," which, as Jones observes, was a question of degree.[107] Similarly, with Caesar's grants Judea attained a new level of freedom. The Jewish state remained, of course, under Rome's hegemony.

There are two favors that Caesar did not grant to Hyrcanus II and Judea. First, Caesar did not make Hyrcanus a king, as he did Mithridates

---

100. The point is argued by Motzo, "Ircano II"; see also Momigliano, *Ricerche*, 26–27; Daniel R. Schwartz, "Hyrcanus II," 210–11; James S. McLaren, *Power and Politics in Palestine: The Jews and the Governing of Their Land 100 BC-AD 70* (Sheffield: Sheffield Academic Press, 1991), 77–78; Peter Richardson, *Herod*, 105–8.

101. See chapters 2 and 3.

102. See chapter 3.

103. A. N. Sherwin-White, *The Roman Citizenship* (2nd ed.; Oxford: Clarendon, 1973), 304; Lintott, *Imperium Romanum*, 161–67.

104. See chapter 3.

105. Amisus (Dio, *Hist.* 42.48.4); Thessaly (Appian, *Bell. civ.* 2.88; Plutarch, *Caes.* 48.1); Cnidus (Plutarch, *Caes.* 48.1); Ilium (Strabo, *Geogr.* 13.1.27); and Pergamum. See Sherk, *RGE*, no. 80; Sherk, *RDGE*, no. 54, and pp. 281–84. See chapter 2.

106. See chapter 2.

107. Jones, "Civitates Liberae," 109.

of Pergamum (Dio, *Hist.* 42.48.4). Although, on account of his enhanced dignity, the Jews might have thought of Hyrcanus as a king,[108] he was, from Rome's point of view, an ethnarch and not a king.[109] The difference between a king and an ethnarch was certainly not lost on the Romans, as is clear from Augustus's treatment of Archelaus after Herod's death: Augustus "appointed Archelaus not king indeed but ethnarch of half the territory that had been subject to Herod, and promised to reward him with the title of king if he really proved able to act in that capacity."[110] Second, Caesar did not grant Judea immunity from tribute, a favor he granted to Ilium (Strabo, *Geogr.* 13.1.27). Judea's "independence," finally, did not imply an exemption from the immediate authority of the governor of Syria.[111] From Caesar's reorganization of Judea until 40 B.C.E. the only recorded action by the governor of Syria in the territory, except the crisis of 43–42 B.C.E.,[112] is Sextus Caesar's intervention to ensure that Herod was not tried and condemned by Hyrcanus (*A.J.* 14.170; *B.J.* 1.211).[113] This absence of interference is better explained by the relative quiet in Judea during the period than by Judea's assumed status as a "client kingdom."[114]

108. See *A.J.* 14.157, 165, 172; *B.J.* 1.202–203, 209, 212.

109. On Roman attitudes toward kings, see Rawson, "Caesar's Heritage"; see also the summary in David C. Braund, "Client Kings," in *The Administration of the Roman Empire, 241 BC-AD 193* (ed. David C. Braund; Exeter: University of Exeter Press, 1988), 93–96.

110. *A.J.* 17.317; *B.J.* 2.94: Caesar "gave half the kingdom to Archelaus, with the title of ethnarch, promising, moreover, to make him king, should he prove his deserts." Nor was the difference lost on Herodias, who, envious that Agrippa I, her brother, was given the title king by Gaius, drove her husband Antipas to ask Gaius for the "higher rank." Gaius countered by banishing Antipas and her (*A.J.* 18. 240–55; *B.J.* 2.181–83).

111. See Jones, "Civitates Liberae," 110. Caesar's grants did not amount to the political autonomy that Schalit (*König Herodes*, 148–55, for instance) envisages. See also Zeitlin, *Rise and Fall*, 1:369–71.

112. See chapter 3.

113. Josephus's accounts of the events surrounding the trial of Herod (*A.J.* 14.168–84; *B.J.* 1.204–15) are convoluted. See McLaren, *Power and Politics*, 67–79. I accept Gilboa's overall argument that the principal reason for Sextus's intervention in Herod's favor was Herod's Roman citizenship and his right not to be tried by a local court. See A. Gilboa, "The Intervention of Sextus Caesar, Governor of Syria, in the Affair of Herod's Trial," *SCI* 5 (1979–80): 185–94; also Sherwin-White, *Roman Citizenship*, 291–306. As McLaren (*Power and Politics*, 71–72) observes, it is actually of little importance whether Sextus ordered Hyrcanus (according to *A.J.* 14.170) or only urged him with threats (according to *B.J.* 1.211). What matters is that he did intervene when Roman interests were at stake.

114. Smallwood (*Jews under Roman Rule*, 45) suggests that Sextus may have acted "*ultra vires*," and he prevented Herod's armed revenge against Hyrcanus because he did not want to have Herod "wreck his powerful kinsman's settlement of Palestine" (p. 46). She is followed by Gilboa ("Intervention," 193), who, following Schalit, also thinks (p. 189) that Caesar had raised Judea's "political and legal position to that of a free state (*civitas libera*)." See also McLaren, *Power and Politics*, 72, 77–78.

Appian's *Bell. civ.* 5.75 and Herod's Appointment

Appian's notice regarding Herod's appointment to the throne of Judea provides, we observed, the only explicit evidence that Herod might have paid tribute to Rome at one period of his reign or the other. For some scholars, Appian supplies the link between the reign of John Hyrcanus II (and Caesar's tax terms) and Herod. Herod, in their view, was appointed by Rome under the same tax provisions established by Julius Caesar, and he continued to pay these taxes throughout his reign.[115] According to others, Antony imposed his own tax terms at Herod's appointment.[116] Hence, Herod either would have paid tribute only during Antony's dominance of the East, ceasing to do so after Actium,[117] or would have continued making payments after Octavian reconfirmed his appointment in 30 B.C.E.[118] Appian in this notice writes:

> After these events Octavian set forth on an expedition to Gaul, which was in a disturbed state, and Antony started for the war against the Parthians. The Senate having voted to ratify all that he had done or should do, Antony again dispatched his lieutenants in all directions and arranged everything as he wished. He set up kings here and there as he pleased, on condition of their paying a prescribed tribute (ἵστη δέ πῃ καὶ βασιλέας, οὓς δοκιμάσειεν, ἐπὶ φόροις ἄρα τεταγμένοις): in Pontus, Darius, the son of Pharnaces and grandson of Mithridates; in Idumea and Samaria, Herod (Ἰδουμαίων δὲ καὶ Σαμαρέων Ἡρῴδην); in Pisidia, Amyntas; in a part of Cilicia, Polemon, and others in other countries.

The principal problem with this text is that, judged by what we know from other sources, especially Josephus, it is fraught with inaccuracies. First, whereas Herod was appointed king in 40 B.C.E. by the Senate, Appian sets Herod's investiture in the context of the actions taken by Antony in 39 B.C.E. before he set out for his campaign against the Parthians. Second, given that Herod was appointed king over the territory that Caesar had given to Hyrcanus, Appian's list omits what ought to have

---

115. Thus Momigliano, *Ricerche*, 42–43; Smallwood, *Jews under Roman Rule*, 85 (see text cited above), and many others.

116. Thus Sherwin-White, *Roman Foreign Policy*, 260: "The new vassal kings were required to pay fixed sums of tribute. Antonius dispensed with the cumbrous and troublesome publican system, based on percentages of farm produce, in favour of direct payment of precise amounts, which the kings raised by their own devices."

117. So, for instance, Mommsen, *Provinces*, 2:175–76, n. 1; Sands, *Client Princes*, 134; Schürer, *History*, 1:317–18, 413.

118. Thus Schalit, *König Herodes*, 161–62, and others. Lintott (*Imperium Romanum*, 25, 35) is vague.

been the core of Herod's kingdom, namely, Judea (and Galilee). Moreover, scholars are divided on the question of the relationship of Idumea and Samaria to the Jewish state after Pompey's terrorial organization in 63 B.C.E. Yet it is over these territories that Appian claims Herod was appointed king.

Appian, it appears, is puddling in *Bell. civ.* 5.75. It is noteworthy that the kings lumped together by Appian actually might have received their kingdoms at different times: Darius in 39 B.C.E. (he reigned until 37 B.C.E.), Polemo in 37 B.C.E. (he died in 8 B.C.E.), and Amyntas in 39 B.C.E. (he died in 25 B.C.E.).[119] Archelaus I of Cappadocia, not named here by Appian,[120] was appointed in 36 B.C.E.[121] Some scholars, however, have sought to bypass the chronological problem by assuming that Appian does not speak of Herod's original grant by the Senate in 40 B.C.E., but rather of a later appointment or "confirmation" by Antony in 39 B.C.E.[122] The discrepancy is otherwise simply ignored.[123] The assumption that Appian's report refers to a later appointment (or confirmation) is a harmonizing maneuver that fails to account for the fact that Appian nowhere narrates the original appointment of the kings. In addition, no occasion can be found in Appian's account for a reappointment of these kings, and especially of Herod only months after his *appellatio* by the Senate.[124] Appian must be writing of the singular fact that Antony was influential in the grant of various kingdoms to some persons,[125] but he is vague, or outright wrong, about the time of their appointments.

---

119. According to Dio (*Hist.* 49.32.3), Amyntas would have been appointed in 36 B.C.E. with Archelaus I of Cappadocia.

120. Appian (*Bell. civ.* 5.7) places the appointment of Archelaus in the context of Antony's tour of the East following Philippi, in 42/41 B.C.E.: "and [Antony] acted as arbiter between kings and cities—in Cappadocia, for example, between Ariarthes and Sisina [Archelaus?], awarding the kingdom to Sisina on account of his mother, Glaphyra, who struck him as a beautiful woman." See Sullivan, "Cappadocia," 2.7.2:1153. Sullivan (*Near Eastern Royalty*, 182) notes that Appian may have confused Sisina, rival of Ariarathes X, with Archelaus.

121. Sullivan, "Cappadocia," 2.7.2:1151–54; Sullivan, *Near Eastern Royalty*, 160–63, 171–72, 182–84; Dio, *Hist.* 49.32.3.

122. Buchheim, *Orientpolitik*, 66–67; and Menahem Stern, ed., *Greek and Latin Authors on Jews and Judaism* (3 vols.; Jerusalem: Israel Academy of Sciences and Humanities, 1974), 2:189.

123. Thus, for instance, Momigliano, *Ricerche*, 41–43; Schalit, *König Herodes*, 162.

124. Dio, *Hist.* 48.34.1 might be read to mean that the *senatus consultum* ratifying Herod's appointment came in 39 B.C.E. See Pelling, "Triumviral Period," 20; Fergus Millar ("Triumvirate and Principate," in *Rome, the Greek World, and the East* [ed. Hannah M. Cotton and Guy M. Rogers; Chapel Hill: University of North Carolina Press, 2002], 248), gives 40 B.C.E. as the date of the ratification, apart from the ratification of "all the official acts of the Triumvirs down to that time," in 39 B.C.E., to which Dio refers.

125. Other ancient authors also stress Antony's role in Herod's appointment: Jose-

There seems to be continuing confusion about the extent of the territory received by Herod in 40 B.C.E.[126] The only relevance of this complex problem to the question of taxation is that some scholars have proposed that Appian's reference is to a later grant of the territories he names (Idumea and Samaria) to Herod and for which Herod paid tribute.[127] The absence of Judea (and Galilee) from Appian's report is otherwise accounted for by emendations to Appian's text. Schalit proposes that the text suffered some corruption, Judea (Ἰουδαίων) being replaced through a copyist's error with Idumea (Ἰδουμαίων).[128] Others suggest that καὶ Ἰουδαίων, which would have stood next to Ἰδουμαίων, was dropped from the text through haplography.[129] Thus, Appian's text "would simply mean that Herod, as king of Judea, Idumea and Samaria, paid tribute."[130]

There is no textual ground for the proposed emendations. They arise merely from the authors' discomfort, from their desire to make Appian's text say what he should have written but most probably did not write. However, it is not at all evident that Appian, writing in the second century C.E., should have known the exact limitation of Herod's kingdom in 40 B.C.E. and that, knowing it, he would have been interested in expressing it with precision.[131] Ancient authors frequently replaced Judea with

---

phus, *A.J.* 14.381–82; *B.J.* 1.282; Strabo, *Geogr.* 16.2.46; Dio, *Hist.* 49.22.6; Tacitus, *Hist.* 5.9. See Peter Richardson, *Herod*, 127–28. That Appian, in the case of Herod, speaks of the events of 40 B.C.E., see also Walter Otto, "Herodes," in *Real-encyclopädie der classischen Altertumswissenschaft*, vol. 2 supplement (ed. A. F. Pauly et al.; Stuttgart: J. B. Metzler, 1913), col. 26; Schürer, *History*, 1:250–51, 281–82 and n. 3; Avi-Yonah, *Holy Land*, 87; Hoehner, *Herod Antipas*, 6 and n. 3; 19 and n. 1.

126. See, for instance, the various statements in Peter Richardson, *Herod*, 70, 131, 155 and n. 7, and map 4.

127. Herod would have paid tribute either for these territories only, according to Mommsen, *Provinces*, 2:175–76, n. 1; or for these territories together with those given to him in 40 B.C.E., according to Momigliano, *Ricerche*, 42; Menahem Stern, *Greek and Latin Authors*, 2:189.

128. Schalit, *König Herodes*, 87 and nn. 105–6, 161–62. The emendation was in fact first proposed by Musgrave in his edition of the Greek text. See Menahem Stern, *Greek and Latin Authors*, 2:189–90.

129. Momigliano (*Ricerche*, 42) rejects this solution. It is accepted as probable by Jones ("Review," 229), who judges Momigliano's arguments to be "on the face of it fantastic." Hoehner (*Herod Antipas*, 298) thinks this is the best explanation of Appian's text.

130. Hoehner, *Herod Antipas*, 298.

131. *Pace* Hahn's confident assertion: "Es wäre unrichtig, diese Nachricht als einfache Flüchtigkeit seitens Appians zu betrachten. Herodes war als König von Iudaia wohl bekannt!" István Hahn, "Herodes als Prokurator," in *Römisches Reich* (ed. Hans-Joachim Diesner et al.; vol. 2 of *Neue Beiträge zur Geschichte der alten Welt*; Berlin: Akademie-Verlag, 1965), 33. Pelling ("Triumviral Period," 22) speculates that "Antony began, rather oddly, by recognizing Herod as 'king of the Idumaeans and Samarians': possibly he acknowledged that Jerusalem was for the moment beyond recovery, and granted him this new title in provisional compensation."

Idumea.[132] There is every reason to accept that Appian wrote Ἰδουμαίων.[133] Appian, as Jones observes,[134] was simply, as he often is, inaccurate.

Greek and Latin authors, to repeat, are often wrong about details of Jewish culture and history.[135] I discussed in chapter 1 the problems that have resulted from Appian's condensing Jewish history from 63 B.C.E. to 135 C.E. in his *Syr.* 11.8.50. Avi-Yonah rightly emphasizes the fact that, were Appian taken at face value, Herod would have had to pay tribute, on the one hand, for territory that he already possessed (Idumea) and, on the other hand, for territory that he had not yet received, (the city of) Samaria.[136] It is indeed possible that Appian's source did mention the extension of the territory over which Herod was appointed king in 40 B.C.E. The added territory would have consisted of western Idumea[137] and the district of Samaria (Samaritis or "the Cuthaean nation").[138]

---

132. Hence, Aelian (*Nat. an.* 6.17), also from the second century (ca. 170–235 C.E.), writing of the enormous serpent that was "enarmoured of a lovely girl," says that the event that he recounts took place "in the country of those known as Judaeans or Edomites [in] the time of Herod the King" (Ἐν τῇ τῶν καλουμένων Ἰουδαιων γῇ ἢ Ἰδουμαίων ᾖδον οἱ ἐπιχώριοι καθ' Ἡρώδην τὸν βασιλέα). Writing earlier (70–19 B.C.E.), the poet Virgil (*Georg.* 3.12) calls the famous date palms of Jericho "the palms of Idumaea" (Primus Idumaeas referam tibi, Mantua, palmas). See Menahem Stern, *Greek and Latin Authors*, 1:317, and for other instances, see 1:316, n. 1.

133. Momigliano (*Ricerche*, 42) thinks such a confusion on Appian's part possible, but he discards this solution. Hoehner (*Herod Antipas*, 298) likewise abandons this suggestion without giving any reason for rejecting it.

134. Jones, "Review," 229.

135. Strabo, distinguished geographer and historian, and Herod's own contemporary, wrote (*Geogr.* 16.2.46): "Now Pompey clipped off some of the territory that had been forcibly appropriated by the Judaeans, and appointed Herod to the priesthood; but later a certain Herod, a descendant of his and a native of the country, who slinked into the priesthood, was so superior to his predecessors, particularly in his intercourse with the Romans and in his administration of affairs of state, that he received the title of king, being given that authority first by Antony and later by Augustus Caesar." Dio writes of Pacorus the Parthian (*Hist.* 48.26.2): "He then invaded Palestine and deposed Hyrcanus, who was at the moment in charge of affairs there, having been appointed by the Romans, and in his stead set up his brother Aristobulus as a ruler because of the enmity existing between them." Compare, however, *Hist.* 48.41.4–5 and 49.22.6, where Aristobulus's son, Antigonus, is correctly identified as the protagonist in 40 B.C.E.

136. Avi-Yonah, *Holy Land*, 86–87.

137. Pompey removed the city of Marisa from the Jewish state (*A.J.* 14.75; *B.J.* 1.156). This is generally accepted to imply the loss of western Idumea. See Avi-Yonah, *Holy Land*, 80. The city was destroyed by the invading Parthian forces (*A.J.* 14.364; *B.J.* 1.269): Idumea was, of course, Herod's native land. That eastern Idumea was part of the Jewish state in 40 B.C.E. is amply attested by *A.J.* 14.353–64, 390–91, 396–400; *B.J.* 1.263–68, 286–87, 292–94.

138. Udoh, "Tribute and Taxes," 167–72. This solution is proposed by Avi-Yonah, *Holy Land*, 86–87; see also Aharoni and Avi-Yonah, *Atlas*, 163–64 and map 221 (Avi-Yonah, however, does not draw any conclusion regarding the topic of taxation) and Peter Richardson, *Herod*, 7.

Momigliano, and Otto before him, confused the city with the district and argued as if Appian's "Samaria" was the same as the territory that Herod received from Octavian in 30 B.C.E.[139]

Even granted that Appian's source contained such information about Herod's kingdom, Appian's text, to borrow Jones's words,[140] would still not bear the weight of the superstruction that scholars have built on it. The text represents an inaccurate, truncated view of the terms under which the Senate conferred the kingship on Herod. At the very best it shows that Appian was aware that Herod was, from the time of his appointment, also king of Idumea and Samaria. We must, therefore, simply concede that Appian's text is too inaccurate to provide trustworthy evidence for the terms under which Herod received his kingdom. It certainly offers no proof that "the triumvirs had appointed Herod king in 40 on existing tributary terms,"[141] especially given that no other ancient author who mentions Herod's appointment alludes to the imposition of tribute.[142]

It is sometimes conjectured that Appian meant that Antony demanded tribute for the additions to Herod's territory.[143] In this fashion the imposition of tribute could be reattached to the probable extension of Herod's territory in 40 B.C.E. Nevertheless, the conjecture does not explain specifically why Herod would have paid for these and not for the territory that

---

139. Momigliano, *Ricerche*, 42–43; Otto, "Herodes," cols. 26 and 49. Momigliano is duly criticized by Jones, "Review," 229; see also Smallwood (*Jews under Roman Rule*, 55 and n. 30) who thinks, however, that Samaritis was "always under Jewish rule." The same confusion is continued by Hahn, "Herodes als Prokurator," 33–34. The confusion of the district of Samaria with the Greek city of Samaria is endemic. It is sometimes impossible to know which is being referred to by Josephus (for instance, compare *A.J.* 14.408 with the parallel passage in *B.J.* 1.299; see *A.J.* 14.412–13, 467; *B.J.* 1.303, 344). The history of the city of Samaria, however, is clear from Josephus: "liberated" by Pompey and rebuilt by Gabinius (*A.J.* 14.75, 88; *B.J.* 4.156, 166), it was in the province of Syria (*A.J.* 14.75–76; *B.J.* 1.156–57) until it was given by Octavian in 30 B.C.E. to Herod, who refounded and named it after his benefactor (*A.J.* 15.217, 292–93, 296–98; *B.J.* 1.396, 403). See Jones, *Cities*, 259, 269, 271; Schürer, *History*, 1:240, 290 and n. 9, 302, 306; 2:160–64. On the contrary, on account of Josephus's silence, the history of the district of Samaria during the period between Pompey's arrangement and Herod's dominion is obscure. Josephus's silence may be taken to mean that Pompey removed Samaria from Jewish rule and added it to the province of Syria. See, for example, the views of Abel, *Géographie*, 2:147; Avi-Yonah, *Holy Land*, 80; Aharoni and Avi-Yonah, *Atlas*, 161 and map 217; Baruch Kanael, "The Partition of Judea by Gabinius," *IEJ* 7 (1957): 99–100 and n. 10; Jones, *Cities*, 258; idem, "Review," 229–30. Josephus (*A.J.* 14.411; *B.J.* 1.302) attests that the district was part of the kingdom that Herod received from Rome. See Avi-Yonah, *Holy Land*, 87.

140. Jones, "Review," 229.

141. Smallwood, *Jews under Roman Rule*, 85.

142. See Strabo, *Geogr.* 16.2.46; Dio, *Hist.* 49.22.6; Tacitus, *Hist.* 5.9.

143. So, for instance, Sands, *Client Princes*, 134; Otto, "Herodes," cols. 26, 48–49; Heichelheim, "Roman Syria," 233; Abel, *Géographie*, 1:361, n. 2.

he inherited from Hyrcanus.[144] On the whole, the insistence that Antony imposed (fixed) annual tribute on Herod and other kings grants to Appian's notice an inherent accuracy that in fact it does not possess. Whether or not it was in his source, Appian's φόρος need not be a reference to an annual tribute. Too much store has been set on the word φόρος, whereas (it should be stressed again) the word is used by classical authors to refer to different kinds of "payments," other than annual tribute.[145]

The other kings who are said to have received kingdoms from Antony are not known to have paid annual tribute to him.[146] The general context of Appian's remarks is Antony's expectation that the kings he appointed would contribute money for his Parthian campaign.[147] More specifically, there is the accusation that Antony was notorious for selling treaties to cities and kingdoms, and crowns to claimants.[148] Of his activities in 41 B.C.E. Dio writes (*Hist.* 48.24.1): "Mark Antony came to the mainland of Asia, where he levied contributions upon the cities and sold the positions of authority; some of the districts he visited in person and to others he sent agents." In Dio's view (*Hist.* 49.32.3–5), Antony's distribution of kingdoms amounted to an "arrogance in dealing with the property of others," for which Romans criticized Antony, though not as much as they censured his allotments to Cleopatra.[149]

In summary, Appian, *Bell. civ.* 5.75 is a garbled account of Herod's appointment. As it stands, the text reflects the probable extension of Herod's kingdom in 40 B.C.E. with the addition of western Idumea and the district of Samaria. The text reflects also the view that Antony

144. Hahn ("Herodes als Prokurator," 33–34) makes the curious suggestion that Herod was only king of Judea and paid rent for (the city of) Samaria, for which he remained procurator until the territory was given to him by Augustus in 30 B.C.E. He confuses, as I noted, the city with the district of Samaria; and he is unable to account for Idumea in Appian's text.

145. Compare, for instance, Appian, *Syr.* 11.7.38 with Polybius, *Hist.* 15.20.7 and 21.43.14. See the discussions in Braund, "Gabinius," 243; Braund, *Rome and the Friendly King*, 63–4.

146. See the studies of the kingdoms by Sullivan, in the literature cited above.

147. Sullivan, *Near Eastern Royalty*, 172; Braund, *Rome and the Friendly King*, 64 and n. 60.

148. See Cicero, *Phil.* 5.4.11 (delivered on 1 January, 43 B.C.E.): "Again, are those monstrous profits to be put up with which the whole household of Marcus Antonius has swallowed? He sold forged decrees, and for a bribe (*in aes accepta pecunia*) commanded that grants of kingdoms, states, and immunities from taxation should be inscribed on brass . . . . There was a lively traffic in every interest of the state in the inner part of the house; his wife, more lucky for herself than for her husbands, was putting up to auction provinces and kingdoms . . . ." See Sands, *Client Princes*, 230.

149. See also Plutarch, *Ant.* 36.2–3, and below.

demanded payment from those whom he supported to the throne. It is noteworthy that whereas Josephus attaches no imposition of tribute to Herod's appointment, he agrees with the general opinion and observes that Antony supported Herod's claim to the throne "because of the money which Herod promised to give to him if he became king, as he had promised once before when he was appointed tetrarch" (*A.J.* 14.381).[150] It seems certain, therefore, that Antony granted the crown to Herod in return for a payment. Josephus notes further that once Herod had defeated his enemies and acceded to the throne in Jerusalem he converted his valuables into money and, according to *Antiquities*, despoiled the rich. "When he had amassed a great sum of silver and gold," Herod transmitted it to Antony (*A.J.* 15.5; *B.J.* 1.358). Whatever the amount that Antony had fixed in 40 B.C.E., the payment that Herod made to him was certainly not an annual tribute.[151]

A King's Accounting

I have shown thus far that between its conquest by Pompey in 63 B.C.E. and the establishment of Herod's kingdom in 40 B.C.E., the status of the Jewish state had undergone some significant changes by virtue of the grants made to it by Roman magistrates, especially Julius Caesar. When Rome gave Herod the crown, the territory that he was to help conquer from Antigonus and liberate from Parthian influence became, for the first time, a Roman client kingdom. I have argued, besides, that there is no evidence that Rome imposed an annual tribute on Herod when he was appointed to the throne. With regard to Roman imperial administration, a scholarly consensus has now emerged that, even though there was no established rule, in practice the client kingdoms in the Republic and early Principate were not subject to annual taxation. No example of a client kingdom that was at the same time tributary has been cited.[152] Herod's

150. For the earlier payments, see *A.J.* 14.326–27; also *A.J.* 14.303; *B.J.* 1.242. Josephus (*A.J.* 14.180) also claims that Sextus Caesar made Herod governor of Syria "in return for money."

151. See also Braund, *Rome and the Friendly King*, 64 and n. 60; Jacobson, "Client Kings," 25.

152. See especially Braund, *Rome and the Friendly King*, 63–73; Braund, "Client Kings," 92; Jacobson, "Client Kings," 25; Pastor, *Land and Economy*, 109–10; Gabba, "Finances," 164; Erich S. Gruen, "The Expansion of the Empire Under Augustus," in *CAH*, vol. 10, *The Augustan Empire, 43 B.C.-A.D. 69* (2nd ed.; ed. Alan K. Bowman et al.; Cambridge: Cambridge University Press, 1996), 156; Schürer, *History*, 1:316–17; Sherwin-White, "Lucullus, Pompey," 269–70; Glen W. Bowersock (*Augustus and the Greek World* [Oxford: Clarendon, 1965], 42–61) maintains that, principally, the kings and dynasts spared the Roman treasury the "further expense" of the "costly and burdensome work of organizing the territory over

realm was neither an exception to this administrative practice nor was it "the best-known case" of the contrary.[153] Herod, like other client kings and as the facts of his reign clearly show, was lord of his realm, with judicial,[154] administrative, military, and financial independence under Rome's hegemony.[155]

The extent of Herod's financial independence from Rome has already been studied in great detail.[156] It is still worth emphasizing, however, that the manner in which Herod actually managed his realm leaves no trace of his kingdom's external tax obligations.[157] He imposed and remitted taxes at will; he stipulated financial and tax obligations for the cities and colonies he founded, all without reference to any supposed debts to Rome. Most revealing in this respect is Herod's gift of Perea and its revenues, with Augustus's permission in 20 B.C.E., to his brother Pheroras. The grant was meant to ensure Pheroras's political and financial independence (*A.J.* 15.362; *B.J.* 1.483).[158] The garrison (φρουρά in *A.J.* 16.292) in Trachonitis, where Herod settled three thousand Idumaeans "and thus restrained the brigands there" (*A.J.* 16.285), was probably free from taxation.[159] In any event, in about 7/6 B.C.E., when he settled Babylonian Jews

---

which they ruled" (p. 42). Gagé, "L'empereur romains"; Francesco de Martino, *Storia della costituzione romana* (7 vols; Napoli: Casa Editrice Dott. Eugenio Jovene, 1958–72), 2:277–81. Earlier studies include Sands, *Client Princes*, 127–39; Oscarus Bohn, "Qua condicione iuris reges socii populi Romani fuerint" (Dissertatio inauguralis historica, Berolini: University of Cincinnati Dissertations, Programmschriften, and Pamphlets in Classical Studies, 1876), 55–64; Karl Johannes Neumann, "Römische Klientelstaaten," *Historische Zeitschrift* 117 (1917): 1–10; Léon Homo, *L'Italie primitive et les débuts de l'impérialisme romain* (Paris: La Renaissance du Livre, 1925), 395–414.

153. Thus Badian, *Roman Imperialism*, 78: "With Pompey, the client princes become a real part of the empire (*reichsangehörig*, in Mommsen's word), in a sense in which they never had been before. They now pay tribute to the Roman people. The best-known case is Judea. How widely the principle applied, we are not told." See also literature cited above.

154. For instance, see *A.J.* 16.1–5. Ernest Bammel, "Die Rechtsstellung des Herodes," *ZDPV* 84 (1968): 73–79; Menahem Stern, "Herod," 240 and n. 2.

155. See Braund, *Rome and the Friendly King*, 105–22; idem, "Client Kings," 89–93; Peter Richardson, *Herod*, 229–30; Jacobson, "Client Kings," 25–33; the discussion of Herod's "four powers" in Schalit, *König Herodes*, 167–298; also F.-M. Abel, *Histoire de la Palestine: depuis la conquête d'Alexandre jusqu'à l'invasion Arabe* (2 vols.; Paris: J. Gabalda, 1952), 1:361–62, who says that Augustus granted Herod the privilege of "exemption totale du tribut."

156. See, for instance, Schalit, *König Herodes*, 256–98.

157. See Schürer, *History*, 1:416; Abel, *Histoire*, 1:362.

158. The account in *War* has it that, apart from the gift of the territory, Herod asked Caesar for permission to appoint Pheroras tetrarch. In *Antiquities* Josephus says that Herod "asked of Caesar a tetrarchy for his brother Pheroras." Herod appointed governors for the provinces of his realm, such as Costobarus in Idumea, without any reference to the emperor. He, however, could not create quasi-independent territories and appoint tetrarchs to govern them. See Peter Richardson, *Herod*, 234.

159. In 11/10 B.C.E. Peter Richardson (*Herod*, 280–81) observes that the settlers were "no doubt veterans who were owed land grants."

in neighboring Batanea, he "promised that this land should be free of taxes and that they should be exempt from all the customary forms of tribute [εἰσφορῶν, that is, "taxes"], for he would permit them to settle on the land without obligation" (*A.J.* 17.25 §23). A large number of Jews, Josephus says, from all parts settled there, attracted by the territory's "immunity from all taxation" (*A.J.* 17.27).[160]

The history of taxation in this territory, as Josephus traces it, is noteworthy. After Herod's death, his son Philip, who acquired the territory, imposed small taxes but only for a short period of time. Agrippa I and his son "did indeed grind them down"—with taxes—although the two kings "were unwilling to take their freedom away." After the Herods, the Romans, although they continued to preserve their independence, completely crushed them "by the imposition of tribute" (*A.J.* 17.27–28). In a word, the settlers in Batanea did not pay tribute to Rome until they ceased to be governed by Herod and his successors.[161]

To this category of evidence belong the lessons that can be learned from Antony's grant, soon after 37 B.C.E., of parts of Herod's realm to Cleopatra.[162] The incident is important for the question of taxation because it is the only instance in which Herod is reported to have paid tribute for some parts of the territory he ruled. The territories that Antony could have given to Cleopatra fell into three categories: (1) the coastal cities of Phoenicia and Palestine, which, since Pompey, had become part of the Roman province of Syria; (2) those coastal cities that were free, namely, Tyre, Sidon, and Ascalon; and (3) client territories, namely, the domain of Lysanias, Herod's kingdom, and Malchus's kingdom of Arabia.[163] Cleopatra's long-term goal, as it is has been noted, may have been to regain control of what had once been Ptolemaic Palestine.[164] This goal, however, was frustrated by Antony's reticence. It appears that she was content, at least in the short term, to receive the revenues that accrued to her from the territories that Antony gave to her, which were now tributary. The city-states she received, while they probably retained their

160. See Peter Richardson, *Herod*, 281.

161. See Millar, *Roman Near East*, 51–52.

162. *A.J.* 15.79, 88–95; *B.J.* 1.361; Plutarch, *Ant.* 36.2; Dio, *Hist.* 49.32.4–5. The gifts were probably made in 36 B.C.E., as they are in Plutarch and Dio, although the chronology of Josephus's account seems to suggest 34 B.C.E. Sherk, *RGE*, no. 88, implies that the grant of Chalcis was in 37/36 B.C.E.; see Schürer, *History*, 1:288–89 and n. 5, 298–300; Peter Richardson, *Herod*, 164–65.

163. Antony gave her "the cities between the Eleutherus river and Egypt" (*A.J.* 15.95; *B.J.* 1.361); "Phoenicia, Coele Syria, Cyprus, and a large part of Cilicia; and still further, the balsam-producing part of Judea, and all that part of Arabia Nabataea which slopes toward the outer sea" (Plutarch, *Ant.* 36.2). See Kennedy, "Syria," 709.

164. Thus, for instance Jones, *Herods*, 49: "The first stage of her [Cleopatra's] programme was to restore the empire of the Ptolemies to its ancient limits, as they had stood in the days of her great forebear Arsinoe Philadelphus."

administrative independence, transferred their tribute from the province of Syria to her.[165]

Matters were different for the free states. Tyre and Sidon were not given to Cleopatra because, as Josephus underscores, Antony knew these cities "to have been free from the time of their ancestors" (*A.J.* 15.95; see *B.J.* 1.361). They were free allies of the Roman people, and Antony could not make them tributary without further ado, and without prejudice to their acknowledged status.[166] Likewise, if the three client states: Lysanias's domain, Herod's Judea, and Malchus's Arabia had been tributary to Rome, it would have been enough for Antony to order that they transfer their revenues to Cleopatra. Instead, Antony was under pressure to find a pretext for executing Lysanias in order to give his domain to Cleopatra. He would have had to deal in a similar manner with both Herod and Malchus if Cleopatra were to have their kingdoms as well.[167] In other words, for them to become Cleopatra's possessions, the client territories needed first to lose their relative financial sovereignty.[168]

Antony was unwilling—and also unable in the case of Malchus—to depose either king.[169] He deprived them of portions of their realms and gave these to Cleopatra. She rented out Lysanias's domain to Zenodorus.[170] Herod surrendered those parts of the coastal plain that were in

---

165. Plutarch and Dio include portions of Crete, Cyrene, and Cyprus among the territories she received. All three had become Roman provinces in 68/67 B.C.E., 74 B.C.E., and 58 B.C.E. (Cyprus was annexed to the province of Cilicia) respectively.

166. See Jones, *Herods*, 57. Tyre had probably been granted independence by Ptolemy II Philadelphus in 274 B.C.E. Both Tyre and Sidon regained their autonomy from the weakened Seleucid kingdom in 126/125 B.C.E. and 111 B.C.E. respectively. Ascalon was free in 104 B.C.E. See Schürer, *History*, 2:88 and n. 8, 90–91; Abel, *Géographie*, 2:136. Pompey and the Romans, at least until Augustus, recognized and respected the freedom of Tyre and Sidon. Tyre enjoyed this relationship with Rome under a treaty (it is thus called *foederata* and αὐτόνομος; see references in Schürer, *History*, 2:93, n. 28). Ascalon was never taken by the Hasmoneans, and it is singled out among the coastal towns of Palestine by Pliny (*Nat.* 5.68) as an *oppidum liberum*. See Millar, *Roman Near East*, 287–88; Kasher, *Jews and Hellenistic Cities*, 182–83; Schürer, *History*, 2:94, 105–8; Jones, *Cities*, 258–59.

167. *A.J.* 15.92: Lysanias was accused of "bringing in the Parthians against the interests of the (Roman) government"; see *B.J.* 1.360. He was allied to Antigonus and the Parthians in 40 B.C.E. (*A.J.* 14.330–33; *B.J.* 1.248–49; Dio, *Hist.* 49.32.5).

168. The speech that Josephus puts into Herod's mouth in *A.J.* 15.131 underscores this risk: "I need only ask who (but we) freed them [the Arabs] from fear when they were in danger of losing their autonomy and becoming slaves of Cleopatra" (τῆς οἰκείας ἀρχῆς ἐκπεσεῖν καὶ δουλεύειν Κλεοπάτρᾳ).

169. Josephus's statement (*B.J.* 1.440) that Cleopatra "brought both King Lysanias and the Arab Malchus to their end" is erroneous. See Peter Richardson, *Herod*, 165 and n. 62.

170. In *A.J.* 15.344 Josephus says that Zenodorus "had leased the domain of Lysanias" (see also *B.J.* 1.398). Parts of the territory, Iturea, were added to Herod's domain by Augustus in 23 B.C.E. and finally, at Zenodorus's death, in 20 B.C.E. (*A.J.* 15.343–60; *B.J.* 1.398–400;

his domain. The most noteworthy of these cities was Joppa.[171] Rather than lose control of the region of Jericho, however, he consented to retain it and to pay tribute to Cleopatra in return. He also acted as surety that Malchus would likewise pay tribute for the parts of his territory that had gone to Cleopatra.[172] Herod clearly could not afford to lose the revenues from the palm and balsam groves of Jericho[173] and certainly would have continued to net an annual profit after he had paid off the two hundred talents that he reportedly owed Cleopatra in tribute.[174]

Malchus eventually refused to honor the tax agreement with Cleopatra.[175] Herod, unlike Malchus, depended on Antony's goodwill for his hold on his kingdom.[176] He nevertheless sorely resented that he had to pay tribute for a portion of his realm. In his view, as Josephus has him

---

see below). See discussion in Peter Richardson, *Herod*, 68–72; also Jones, *Cities*, 269–70; Schürer, *History*, 1:565–66.

171. The territory probably included Jamneia (see chapter 2). Joppa, already returned to the Jewish state by Julius Ceasar, was in Herod's domain in 39 B.C.E. (see chapter 2 and *A.J.* 14.396; *B.J.* 1.292–93). Joppa is named among the (coastal) cities "which had been taken from him by her [Cleopatra]," but restored to Herod by Octavian in 30 B.C.E. (*A.J.* 15.217; *B.J.* 1.396–97). *Contra* Momigliano, *Ricerche*, 42–43; see Jones, "Review," 229; and Peter Richardson, *Herod*, 91–92.

172. *A.J.* 15.96: "Herod met her and leased from her those parts of Arabia that had been given to her and also the revenues of the region about Jericho." According to *B.J.* 1.362 Herod leased his own territory back for the sum of two hundred talents. *A.J.* 15.107 and 132 specify that Herod acted as surety for a further two hundred talents for the Arabian territory. See Jones, *Herods*, 50. Peter Richardson (*Herod*, 165–67 and nn. 68 and 74) reads these various statements to mean that Herod leased "(unspecified) parts of Arabia that were a part of Antony's gift to Cleopatra" and "then sublet the Arabian territory back to Malichus." This can hardly be correct.

173. Josephus (*A.J.* 15.96) notes in passing the economic significance of the territory. See chapter 2 and Peter Richardson, *Herod*, 166–67. Jones (*Herods*, 50) finds a political reason for Herod's decision to pay tribute for the territory: "The last thing which Herod wanted was the establishment of an Egyptian administration and an Egyptian army in his kingdom, or in the neighbouring parts of the Nabatean kingdom—Cleopatra's concession from Malchus would seem to have been the districts east of the Dead Sea."

174. Peter Richardson (*Herod*, 166–67, n. 70) conjectures that the two hundred talents "equalled half Herod's total income in 4 BCE from all of Judea, Samaritis, and Idumaea, or the total income of Galilee and Paraea." Herod, he suggests, might have gotten Jericho for nothing. He (pp. 166–67, n. 74) dismisses as "unlikely" the interpretation by Jones (*Herods*, 50) that Herod leased Jericho for two hundred talents and that he was surety for a further two hundred talents from Malchus. Herod would have had to pay four hundred talents in the years when Malchus was in default. This amount, Richardson observes, "is so large (the equal of the total income of Judea, Samaritis, and Idumea) that Herod would quickly have gone broke." That assumes, however, that Herod did pay the sum owed by Malchus and ignores the fact that Herod went to war instead against the Arab.

175. For this "disloyalty" (ἀπιστίαν) Antony permitted Herod to go to war against Malchus (*A.J.* 15.110; *B.J.* 1.365).

176. Josephus (*A.J.* 15.106) observes that "Herod fulfilled his contract (δίκαιος), since he thought it would be unsafe to give her any reason to hate him."

state, "no one had a right to expect the Jews to pay tribute for their possessions to anyone or to give up a portion of their land."[177] Whether or not one accepts that Herod made this statement, it nonetheless speaks of the attitude of Josephus's sources and probably of Josephus himself to the matter of tribute to Rome. In 30 B.C.E. Octavian returned the region to its original status in Herod's kingdom, that is, free from tribute (*A.J.* 15.217; *B.J.* 1.396–97).[178]

Herod's realm per se may, thus, be said to have been free from Roman tribute. Its revenues would also have been immune by virtue of their being the income of Herod, Roman citizen and "friend and ally of the Roman people."[179] I revisit here the financial implications for the Herodian family of the grant of citizen together with immunity to Antipater by Julius Caesar in 47 B.C.E. As I noted above, one of the outcomes of the lively debate on the meaning of the status of *socius et amicus populi Romani* is that the privileges attached to this status must be verified in each individual case. Immunity from taxation, although granted in the one extant document in which this status is given to individuals during the Republic, seems to be a special privilege not implied by the status itself.[180] Herod's personal status as "friend and ally of the Roman people" may not, therefore, per se be taken to include the privilege of immunity from Roman taxation.

That Antipater's family and their descendants were Roman citizens by virtue of Caesar's grants to Antipater is universally accepted, in spite of Josephus's silence on the issue, and is evident in the titles borne by Herod and his descendants.[181] We noted that the grant of citizenship to

---

177. Καίτοι γε ἄξιον ἦν μηδενὶ τῶν ὄντων Ἰουδαίους φόρον ἢ τῆς χώρας ἀπόμοιραν τελεῖν (*A.J.* 15.133, see from §132). Hoehner (*Herod Antipas*, 300) misconstrues the significance of the episode and claims: "The practice of paying tribute as a client king existed even during Antony's rule, for Herod had to pay tribute on the districts assigned to Cleopatra."

178. The grants were in addition to other territorial gifts, namely, Strato's Tower, Joppa, Anthedon, Gaza, Gadara, Hippus, and (the city of) Samaria (see n. 139 above).

179. *A.J.* 17.246: φίλος καὶ συμμάχος = *(rex) sociusque et amicus*. For Herod as Φιλορωμαῖος = *amicus populi romani*, see A.J. 15.387; W. Dittenberger, ed., *OGIS* (2 vols.; Leipzig: Hirzel, 1903–5), no. 414; as Φιλοκαίσαρα = *amicus Caesaris*, see *B.J.* 1.400; Dittenberger, *OGIS*, no. 427. See Braund, *Rome and the Friendly King*, 23–25, 105–7; Braund, "Client Kings," 80–81, 94–95; Jacobson, "Client Kings," 25–26; Peter Richardson, *Herod*, 204–8.

180. The *senatus consultum de Asclepiade Clazomenio sociisque* of 78 B.C.E., was given in favor of three Greek naval officers who had served under Sulla. The three officers, notably, did not receive citizenship. Sherk, *RDGE*, no. 22 = Sherk, *RGE*, no. 66. For discussions, see Sherk, *RDGE*, 128–32; Marshall, "Friends," 39–55.

181. See, in general, Sullivan, "Dynasty of Judaea," 2.8:296–354, who observes that "[a]ll descendants of Herod can be properly termed Julii" (p. 305); they "could properly bear the *nomen* Julius, in that Herod's father Antipater had obtained Roman citizenship from Julius Caesar" (p. 313). That Herod bore the *tria nomina* appears in the statue base from Kos, which honors "King Gaius Julius Herodes." See David M. Jacobson, "King Herod,

Antipater brought a Roman presence into the direct administration of Judea by the appointments, first, of Antipater as ἐπίτροπος and, later, of Phasael and Herod as tetrarchs.[182] Roman franchise permitted Herod also to serve in the Roman administration of the province of Syria.[183] He was appointed governor (στρατηγός) of Coele-Syria (and [the city of] [see *B.J.* 1.229; *A.J.* 14.284] Samaria according to *B.J.* 1.213) by Sextus Caesar in 47/46 B.C.E. (*A.J.* 14.180).[184] In 43/42 Cassius made him governor of Coele-Syria, probably continuing the earlier appointment.[185] The view that he was at this time "procurator of all Syria,"[186] as Josephus says in *B.J.* 1.225, needs some corrective.[187] Augustus also gave Herod, as king, some procuratorial responsibilities in Syria, though the extent of his involvement is impossible to determine.[188] The view, however, that Herod

---

Roman Citizen and Benefactor of Kos," *BAIAS* 13 (1993/94): 31–35; and Kerstin Höghammar, *Sculpture and Society: A Study of the Connection Between the Free-Standing Sculpture and Society on Kos in the Hellenistic and Augustan Periods* (Uppsala: University of Uppsala Press, 1993), 43 and 123, cat. no. 13. Agrippa I bore the *tria nomina,* as is attested in the Athenian inscription honoring his daughter, Julia Berenice. Agrippa is called "King Julius Agrippa" (Ἰουλίου Ἀγρίππα Βασιλέως). Dittenberger, *OGIS,* no. 428. Braund (*Rome and the Friendly King,* 44) suggests that Agrippa's *praenomen* was likely Gaius. His son's *praenomen* was Marcus. See also Peter Richardson, *Herod,* 106; Schürer, *History,* 1:316–17; especially pp. 451–52 and nn. 41–42. On kings and Roman citizenship see Braund, *Rome and the Friendly King,* 39–53; Braund, "Client Kings," 82–83; Jacobson, "Client Kings," 26.

182. See chapter 2 and above. For the role that the grant of citizenship played in the later royal appointments of Herod's descendants, see Braund, *Rome and the Friendly King,* 44–45.

183. On Roman citizenship as a prerequisite for the provincial élite who aspired to administrative posts in the empire, see Nicolet, *World of the Citizen,* 20–21. Lintott (*Imperium Romanum,* 167) observes that enfranchisement of provincials permitted them to form "channels of communication with the allies for emperors and other Roman authorities. As such, they were an important part of the system of patronage that created and sustained the ruling class throughout the empire, making it manageable and useful in the service of the emperor." See also Brunt, *Roman Imperial Themes,* 273–74.

184. On Coele-Syria, see Millar, *Roman Near East,* 423–24; on Herod's appointment, see Peter Richardson, *Herod,* 112.

185. *A.J.* 14.280: στρατογὸν αὐτὸν κοίλης Συρίας ἐποίησαν.

186. Συρίας ἁπάσης ἐπιμελητὴν καθιστᾶσιν; or "prefect of the whole of Syria," according to *LCL*; see *B.J.* 1.399.

187. See Hahn, "Herodes als Prokurator," 25–33. Appian (*Bell. civ.* 4.63) writes that "Cassius left his nephew in Syria with one legion." Peter Richardson (*Herod,* 116 and n. 84) thinks that this notice entails "no necessary contradiction with Herod's role" in the region under Cassius. In his view, "either a maximalist or minimalist reading" of Herod's role must be avoided, and Herod must be said to have had "some role in the region of southern Lebanon, southern Syria, and northern Jordan (in today's terms). . . ."

188. According to *B.J.* 1.399, Augustus in 20 B.C.E. made Herod "procurator of all Syria (Συρίας ὅλης ἐπίτροπον)," subjecting other procurators to his authority. In *A.J.* 15.360, Augustus "associated him with the procurators of Syria (ἐγκαταμίγνυσι δ' αὐτὸν τοῖς ἐπιτροπεύουσιν τῆς Συρίας)," with the requirement that they seek his consent on all their decisions. These claims are exaggerated. Both passages are embedded in Josephus's narratives of Augustus's grants to Herod of Trachonitis, Batanea, Auranitis, and the territory of

was an imperial procurator in the territory that he governed is, as I have argued, baseless.[189]

The implications of the grant of immunity to Antipater have received no attention, however. The terms of Octavian's edict (issued about 41 B.C.E.) granting Roman citizenship to Seleucus of Rhosos suggest that already during the Triumvirate Rome also had begun to separate the privilege of immunity from the grant of citizenship to individuals in the provinces.[190] Augustus's edict of 7–6 B.C.E. concerning the inhabitants of Cyrene makes this distinction explicit: "If any people from the Cyrenaican province have been honored with (Roman) citizenship, I order them to perform the personal (?) liturgies, nevertheless, in their role as Greeks, with the exception of those to whom in accordance with a law or decree of the senate (or) decree of my father or myself, immunity from taxation has been granted along with the citizenship."[191] Josephus himself received Roman citizenship from the emperor Vespasian after he arrived in Rome in 70 C.E. (*Vita* 423). It was only much later that Domitian (81–96 C.E.) "added to [his] honours" and exempted his domains in Judea from taxation (*Vita* 429).[192] This later separation of the two privileges explains why Josephus, writing probably in retrospect, specifically states that, together with Roman citizenship, Caesar also gave Antipater "exemption from taxation everywhere (ἀτέλειαν πανταχοῦ)" (*A.J.* 14.137; see *B.J.* 1.194).[193]

Zenodorus (Panea). This might indicate, as Peter Richardson suggests (*Herod*, 234), that Herod's procuratorial duties were "confined to border regions" of Syria. So also Braund, *Rome and the Friendly King*, 84–85. In any event, as Schürer suggests (*History*, 1:319 and n. 122) it cannot be a question of a formal subordination of Syria's procurators to Herod. Josephus's statements must be received with the appropriate dose of skepticism.

189. As Braund (*Rome and the Friendly King*, 84–85) shows, although a person could conceivably pass from being king to being a Roman official, and vice versa, there is no instance of a king who, while still ruling, was at the same time a Roman official.

190. Sherwin-White, *Roman Citizenship*, 245, 296–300. Sherwin-White (p. 245 and n. 3) refers to Pierre Roussel, who writes: "Dès lors, même à l'époque républicaine, un πολίτης ῥωμαῖος ἀνείσφορος apparaîtrait comme un privilégié par rapport à un simple citoyen romain. Tout au moins peut-on dire, en reprenant une expression de J. Lesquier, qu'il obtient «le maximum des immunités dont peut jouir un *civis*»" (Roussel, "Un Syrien," 54). According to Marshall ("Friends," 46–47 and n. 17), the privileges granted to Seleucus "constitute distinct grants which are hereditary in their own right, since they do not derive from the recipients' single hereditary status as new Roman citizens."

191. Sherk, *RGE*, no. 102, lines 56–59; J. G. C. Anderson, "Augustan Edicts from Cyrene," *JRS* 17 (1927): 35–36; III, lines 56–59 (lines 58–59: ἐκτὸς τ[ο]ύτ<ι>ων οἷς . . . ἀνεισφορία ὁμοῦ σὺν τῆι πολειτήαι δέδοται); Sherwin-White, *Roman Citizenship*, 271–72, 304; Lintott, *Imperium Romanum*, 163–64; Fergus Millar, "Empire and City, Augustus to Julian: Obligations, Excuses, and Status," *JRS* 73 (1983): 84–85.

192. Josephus adds that the exemption was "a mark of the highest honour to the privileged individual."

193. That Caesar and the Senate issued decrees confirming Antipater's grants is sug-

Since, as we noted in chapter 2, Octavian's grants to Seleucus are similar to those made by Caesar to Antipater, Octavian's decree should enable us to clarify the terms and the implications of Antipater's privileges.[194] Antipater's citizenship and immunity were a reward *virtutis causa* for his distinguished military service during Caesar's Alexandrian campaign in 47 B.C.E.[195] Likewise, Seleucus, together with others, received privileges for his distinguished service to Octavian in 42 B.C.E., during the war against Julius Caesar's assassins.[196] Seleucus's tax exemption, like Antipater's, had the largest application: total immunity, together with exemption from military and local public services.[197] The tax exemptions are enumerated and without exceptions: (1) immunity from Roman as well as local taxation;[198] and (2) immunity from tolls in all

---

gested by *A.J.* 16.53. This decree is not extant. Josephus, who is aware that such a decree existed, cites (on the instance of John Hyrcanus II) a decree that dates from an earlier period (*A.J.* 14.144–48). See Pucci Ben Zeev, *Jewish Rights*, 22.

194. Octavian's documents in favor of Seleucus are divided into the decree itself (col. II), accompanied by three letters (cols. I, III, IV). See Greek texts in Roussel, "Un Syrien," 34–36; Victor Ehrenberg and A. H. M. Jones, eds., *Documents Illustrating the Reigns of Augustus and Tiberius* (Oxford: Clarendon, 1949), 123–26, no. 301; Sherk, *RDGE*, no. 58 = Sherk, *RGE*, no. 86. On the comparison between Caesar's grants to Antipater and those made by Octavian to Seleucus, see especially Gilboa, "L'Octroi," 610–14. Roussel ("Un Syrien," 57) also draws a parallel between Seleucus and Antipater.

195. See chapter 2.

196. Seleucus served under Octavian (col. II, lines 10–15; col. IV, lines 88–89) as a naval officer. Octavian calls him ναύαρχος ἐμός in col. III, line 76 and in col. IV, line 88. That there were others honored for the same reason by Octavius is stated in col. IV, lines 89–91. There exists also a fragment of Octavian's generic edict on veterans, granting them immunity (*immunitas*). See Latin text, Sherk, *RDGE*, 303; Roussel, "Un Syrien," 48–49. The earliest known instance of the practice of granting citizenship to veterans for distinguished service is the *Decretum Cn. Pompeii Strabonis*, which in 89 B.C.E. granted citizenship to a group of Spanish calvarymen. Roussel, "Un Syrien," 45–46; Sherwin-White, *Roman Citizenship*, 245–46.

197. Col. II, lines 20–23: πολειτείαν καὶ ἀνεισφορίαν τῶν ὑπαρχόν[των δίδ]ομεν οὕτω[ς οἵτινες τῶ]ι ἀρίστωι νόμωι ἀρίστωι τε δικαίωι πολεῖται [ἀνείσφο]ρο[ί εἰσιν, καὶ στρατείας λει]του[ργία]ς τε δημοσίας ἁπάσης πάρε[σις ἔστω]. Sherk, *RGE*, no. 86, lines 20–23: "*we give* (Roman) citizenship and tax-exemption for his present proper | ty in the same way as [those] (Roman) citizens [who are] tax-exempt by the best law and the best legal right, | and [they are to have] *immunity* [from military service] and from every public | *liturgy*." See col. II, lines 10–11 where Seleucus is granted πολειτείαν καὶ ἀνεισφορίαν πάντων τῶν [ὑπαρχόν]των. The immunity granted to Seleucus corresponds to the *immunitas omnium rerum* granted by Octavian to veterans in the generic decree (lines 9–11). Sherk, *RDGE*, 303–5; Roussel, "Un Syrien," 51–52; Sherwin-White, *Roman Citizenship*, 304.

198. Col. II, lines 20–22: "ἀνεισφορία and ἀλειτουργία refer to Roman and local taxes. Lines 51–52 are fragmentary: . . .] τούτων τῶν πραγμάτων τέλος οὔτε πολειτείαν οὔ[τε δημοσι]ώνην παρ' αὐτ[οῦ εἰσπράττειν]. Sherk, *RGE*, no. 86, col. II, line 52: "no government or | *publican* [shall levy on him] a tax for these things." See Roussel, "Un Syrien," 57 and n. 9. Thus also the *senatus consultum* of 78 B.C.E., Sherk, *RDGE*, no. 22, line 12: τὴν σύνκλητον κρίνειν, ὅπως οὗτοι τέκνα ἔκγονοί τε αὐτῶν ἐν ταῖς ἑαυτῶν πατρίσιν ἀλειτούργητοι πάντων τῶν πραγμάτων καὶ ἀνείσφοροι ὦσι (the Senate decides that they, their children, and descendants

free cities and regions of a province through which he might import or export goods.[199] Antipater, Seleucus, and the other beneficiaries of these immunities were, as Sherwin-White notes, "*cives Romani optimo iure immunes*," that is, "they are equated with Roman citizens of Italy, the true 'Romans by origin', who were *immunes* simply because they had been exempt from tribute since its abolition in Italy in 167 B.C."[200]

Seleucus's immunity, like his citizenship, was hereditary, extending to "his parents, his children, his descendants, his wife who hereafter will be his."[201] The same extension of privileges to parents, children and descendants, and wife is attested in Octavian's decree on veterans.[202] Similarly, the grant of immunity given to the sailors in the *senatus consultum* of 78 B.C.E. was received also by their children and descendants.[203] At a later time, possibly after Domitian (81–96 C.E.),[204] the grants of citizenship and other privileges to veterans were no longer extended to their parents.[205] In the first century B.C.E. and after, however, grants of citizenship and immunity applied to the recipient's children and descendants. Thus, if Antipater's immunity may be said to have been "personal" it is because, like his citizenship, this immunity was not part of a general grant made to a region and it applied to him and his family no matter where they resided.[206] At the time when the inhabitants of Judea, under Hyrcanus II, paid tribute to Rome, Antipater and his children were exempt.

---

are to be immune in their own cities from all liturgies and from the tribute). See Marshall, "Friends," 48–49 and n. 21; Roussel, "Un Syrien," 52–53.

199. Col. II, lines 50–52. Exemptions from import duties are restricted to goods destined for personal consumption. See Roussel, "Un Syrien," 57–58.

200. Sherwin-White, *Roman Citizenship*, 304.

201. Roussel, "Un Syrien," 34, col. II, lines 19–21: [Αὐτῶι καὶ γ]ονεῦσι, τέκνοις ἐκγόνοις τε αὐτοῦ γυναικί τε τούτου ἥτις με[τὰ τούτου] ἔστ[αι. . . .] πολειτείαν καὶ ἀνεισφορίαν τῶν ὑπαρχόν[των δίδ]ομεν. Sherk (*RGE*, no. 86, col. II, line 19 and n. 6) admits that he "accidentally omitted" the word ἐκγόνοις from the Greek text in *RDGE*, 295, col. II, line 19. See, however, col. II, line 23.

202. See Sherk, *RDGE*, 303, lines 8–9: "Ipṣis parentibu[s lib]erisque eorum e[t uxo]ribus qui sec[um]que erunt im[mu]nitatem omnium rerum d[a]re . . . ."

203. Sherk, *RDGE*, no. 22, line 12: ὅπως οὗτοι τέκνα ἔκγονοί τε αὐτῶν ἐν ταῖς ἑαυτῶν πατρίσιν ἀλειτούργηται πάντων τῶν πραγμάτων καὶ ἀνείσφοροι ὦσιν.

204. Domitian's decree granting immunity to veterans included parents: "liberati immunes esse debent ipsi, coniuges liberique eorum parentes . . . ." See Roussel, "Un Syrien," 58.

205. See Roussel, "Un Syrien," 51–52.

206. Roussel ("Un Syrien," 57) observes concerning Seleucus's privileges: "Ces exonérations sont valables, quel que soit le lieu où Séleukos établira son domicile. De même César avait accordé à Antipatros de Judée πολιτείαν ἐν Ρώμῃ καὶ ἀτέλειαν πανταχοῦ." See also the inscription from Celeia, Noricum: "C. Iulius Vepo donatus civitate Romana viritim et immunitate ab divo Aug. vivos fecit sibi et Boniatae Antoni fil. coniugi et suis." Ehrenberg and Jones, *Documents*, no. 360; Braund, *Augustus to Nero*, no. 787.

Subsequently, Pheroras would not have paid tribute to Rome for the revenue that he raised in taxes from Perea.[207] The same was true of Herod and his descendants: they paid no tribute to Rome for the income that accrued to them from the territories they governed.

The evidence that this conclusion is correct for Herod's descendants is circumstantial. First, in Josephus's account of the partition of Herod's kingdom and its revenues, Augustus is said neither to have imposed nor taken account of Roman tribute (*A.J.* 17.317–21; *B.J.* 2.93–98).[208] This is an *argumentum e silentio*. The weight of the evidence is so great, nonetheless, that Hoehner, for example, is forced to circumvent it by claiming with regard to Antipas:

> Augustus allowed him to receive 200 talents for Galilee and Perea. It is probable that the money for running the government, for his building programme, and for Roman tribute was collected in a form of taxation over and above the 200 talents he was allowed to receive.[209]

This is most improbable. Hoehner's "form of taxation over and above" Antipas's two hundred talents is Hoehner's own invention, which permits him to integrate tribute to Rome into Augustus's allocation of territories and revenues. Josephus actually says that Antipas's revenue was the expected annual taxes from Perea and Galilee (φορά τε ἦν τάλαντα διακόσια τὸ ἐπ' ἔτος) (*A.J.* 17.318).[210]

There is no mention of tribute in the subsequent narratives about Archelaus, Antipas, and Agrippa. Some positive indications of Rome's financial relationship to Herod's children come from Augustus's dealing with Archelaus and Tiberius's later treatment of Philip, most of whose tetrarchy lay outside of the Jewish state. Philip's case is somewhat less controversial, so I shall examine it first. Philip died in 33/34 C.E. Josephus writes of the end of his reign: "Since he had died childless, Tiberius took over his territory and annexed it to the province of Syria. Nevertheless, he

---

207. See above.

208. See discussion below. Schürer (*History*, 1.417) observes, correctly, that in Augustus's settlement, "it is throughout a question of the revenues of the native princes, Archelaus, Antipas and Philip, and the very absence of any reference at this juncture to a Roman tax speaks for its non-existence."

209. Hoehner, *Herod Antipas*, 74–75. See Freyne, "Herodian Economics," 32: "The exact amount of tribute in land and poll tax that Antipas had to pay to Rome is not known, even though Josephus does inform us that he was allowed 200 talents in personal income from his combined territories." See also Richard A. Horsley, *Galilee*, 175.

210. Peter Richardson, *Herod*, 24: "The sum of these figures approximated Herod's tax base and the relative wealth of each area." Hoehner leaves unexplained what would be the purpose of the tax revenues from Galilee and Perea if not for Antipas's administration of the territory. He does not explain either how his new "form of taxation" would figure in his overall assessment of Antipas's system of taxation. See Hoehner, *Herod Antipas*, 75–79.

ordered that the tribute which was collected in his tetrarchy should be held on deposit" (*A.J.* 18.108).[211]

The annexation of a client territory where the ruler died and left no successor was Rome's standard administrative procedure. What is startling and at the same time revealing is Tiberius's treatment of the taxes that were raised from the tetrarchy that Philip left behind. With annexation, the taxes from the territory would ordinarily have been assumed by the provincial authorities who now collected them. Tiberius, however,[212] ordered that what was collected be put in a deposit. Tiberius evidently considered the taxes to belong to the deceased tetrarch's legacy, and if he had left a successor, both the territory *and the taxes* would have gone to his heir, with nothing left for Rome. Tiberius's order was an extraordinary double act of benevolence. First, not intending to annex the territory permanently, Tiberius waited to appoint a (Herodian) successor to Philip.[213] Second, in the meantime, the territory was to be administered by the Romans without the benefit of the revenues that were derived from it.[214] Three years later, Gaius gave the territory and its revenues (together with the arrears) to his protégé, Agrippa I (*B.J.* 2.181; *A.J.* 18.237).[215] No portion of the revenues of Philip's tetrarch went to the Romans who administered it after his death; certainly none of it went to them while Philip lived and ruled the territory.[216]

---

211. *A.J.* 18.108: Τὴν δ' ἀρχήν, οὐ γὰρ κατελίπετο παῖδας, Τιβέριος παραλαβὼν προσθήκην ἐπαρχίας ποιεῖται τῆς Σύρων, τοὺς μέντοι φόρους ἐκέλευσε συλλεγομένους ἐν τῇ τετραρχίᾳ τῇ ἐκείνου γενομένῃ κατατίθεσθαι. Josephus's φόρους should be translated as "taxes" rather than "tribute." It is clearly a question of the taxes that were paid to Philip before he died.

212. Josephus's particle μέντοι ("yet," "nevertheless") is significant.

213. Nikos Kokkinos (*The Herodian Dynasty: Origins, Role in Society and Eclipse* [Sheffield: Sheffield Academic Press, 1998], 268–69) argues plausibly that Tiberius intended to add Philip's tetrarchy to the domain of Antipas, who was in Tiberius's good favors. Tiberius died in March 37 C.E. before he could effect the transfer. See also Smallwood, *Jews under Roman Rule*, 182; and Hoehner, *Herod Antipas*, 251. On Antipas's friendship with Tiberius, see *A.J.*18.36.

214. Jones (*Herods*, 175) notes this point. His view of Tiberius's interim arrangements for the territory, however, is baffling. He writes that Philip "died without issue and on his death Tiberius annexed his tetrarchy. He did not, however, consider it ripe for direct Roman rule, and he therefore ordered that the local administration should be provisionally maintained and the revenues kept separate from those of Syria till he should appoint a successor." See also Smallwood (*Jews under Roman Rule*, 182), who says that Tiberius put the territory temporarily "under the administration of the legate of Syria." Momigliano (*Ricerche*, 75) merely observes that Philip's tetrarchy during these three years had a particular financial administration.

215. Two years later, not only did Gaius add Antipas's territory to Agrippa's kingdom, after he had banished the tetrarch, he also gave him Antipas's and his wife's property (*A.J.* 18.252–55). According to Suetonius (*Cal.* 16.3), when Gaius appointed Antiochus IV king of Comagene in 37 C.E., he reimbursed the new king for the revenues that had been paid to the treasury during the twenty years from its annexation in 17 C.E. (see Tacitus, *Ann.* 2.42).

216. See also Schürer, *History*, 1:419: "If no taxes flowed from his tetrarchy into the

One sees the difference between Tiberius's treatment of Philip's estate and the manner in which Augustus earlier disposed of Archelaus's territory. Augustus, after he banished Archelaus, confiscated his property into the imperial treasury (*A.J.* 17.344; *B.J.* 2.111), annexed his ethnarchy into a province and assessed it for the sake of taxation, and appointed a *praefectus* to govern it. Josephus says that it was at this time, that is, in 6/7 C.E.,[217] that Quirinius, who had been appointed governor of Syria, was instructed to conduct an assessment of property in the province (καὶ τιμητὴς τῶν οὐσιῶν γενησόμενος) and also came to Judea "in order to make an assessment of the property of the Jews" (ἀποτιμησόμενός τε αὐτῶν τὰς οὐσίας) (*A.J.* 18.1–2; 17.355).[218] The many attempts to date Quirinius's census to the time of Herod the Great on the basis of Luke 2:1–7 have been futile.[219] If, as is traditionally assumed, the "King Herod of Judea" in Luke 1:5 is Herod the Great and Luke's narrative is read in conjunction with the chronology provided by Matt 2:1–23, then the author of Luke's

---

Roman treasury even after Philip's death, much less would this have been the case during his lifetime." Millar, *Roman Near East*, 52: "There seems to be a clear implication both that these revenues would otherwise have been shipped out elsewhere and that a rough equivalence between Roman and dynastic tribute revenues could be assumed."

217. According to *A.J.* 17.342, Archelaus was deposed in his "tenth year" (see *Vita* 5), that is (according to *A.J.* 18.26), "in the thirty-seventh year after Caesar's [Augustus's] defeat of Antony at Actium." The battle of Actium was fought in 31 B.C.E. In *B.J.* 2.111, however, Josephus writes that Archelaus was banished "in the ninth year of his rule." The discrepancy between these accounts of the length of Archelaus's reign might be due to the difference between the beginning of Archelaus's rule in 4 B.C.E., following Herod's death, and the official recognition of his claim to the throne by Augustus a few months later. According to Dio (*Hist.* 55.27.6), Archelaus, "who was accused by his brothers of some wrongdoing or other, was banished beyond the Alps and his portion of the domain was confiscated to the state." This occurred "in the consulship of Aemilius Lepidus and Lucius Arruntius," that is, in 6 C.E. (*Hist.* 55.25.1). See Schürer, *History*, 1:356 and n. 13.

218. See discussion in chapter 5.

219. There are numerous debates on the topic. See, for instance, Harold W. Hoehner, *Chronological Aspects of the Life of Christ* (Grand Rapids: Zondervan, 1977), 13–23; and the extensive discussions principally in Horst R. Moehring, "The Census in Luke as an Apologetic Device," in *Studies in New Testament and Early Christian Literature: Essays in Honor of Allen P. Wikgren* (ed. David Edward Aune; Leiden: Brill, 1972), 144–60; Schürer, *History*, 1:399–427; Joseph A. Fitzmyer, *The Gospel According to Luke: Introduction, Translation, and Notes* (2 vols; 2nd ed.; AB 28, 28A; Garden City, N.Y.: Doubleday, 1986), 1:392–407; Raymond E. Brown, *The Birth of the Messiah: A Commentary on the Infancy Narratives in Matthew and Luke* (Garden City, N.Y.: Doubleday, Image Books, 1977), 412–18. 547–56 ; John P. Meier, *A Marginal Jew: Rethinking the Historical Jesus* (3 vols.; New York: Doubleday, 1991–2001), 1:212–14; Brook W. R. Pearson, "The Lucan Censuses, Revisited," *CBQ* 61 (1999): 262–82. Although Pearson (p. 264) promises to offer "fresh evidence" on the topic, his article rehashes old assumptions and arguments about the existence of "a Roman-style process of census and taxation in Herod's kingdom." Mark D. Smith, "Of Jesus and Quirinius," *CBQ* 62 (2000): 278–93; also E. P. Sanders, *The Historical Figure of Jesus* (London: Penguin, 1993), 52–54; Millar, *Roman Near East*, 46; Peter Richardson, *Herod*, 300–301.

Gospel was either too theologically enmeshed to notice, or he was simply ill-informed, as he indeed was in Acts 5:36–37, about the date of the census.[220] It is also possible, as Smith argues, that the author of Luke actually thought that Jesus was born in 6 C.E. at the time of the census.[221]

Whether the author of Luke was wrong about the time of the census or correctly placed Jesus' birth in 6 C.E., the introduction of a Roman census and tribute into Judea (the region) coincided with the deposition of Archelaus and the consequent annexation of Judea in 6 C.E. Augustus apparently had no reason to be particularly benevolent toward the incompetent Archelaus. More importantly, he foresaw no Herodian successor to Archelaus. Augustus, therefore, destined the revenues, now to be assessed by Rome, from the new procuratorial province to the imperial coffers.[222] The annexation marked the end of Archelaus's tribute-free administration of the territory. The fact that Rome was to raise tribute in Palestine was, as Schürer notes, *novum et inauditum*.[223] Josephus's account suggests that the events surrounding Archelaus's misrule of his ethnarchy, his deposition and banishment, the annexation of the territory, Quirinius's census and the imposition of tribute were all cataclysmic. They led to a national rebellion: "a Galilaean, named Judas, incited his countrymen to revolt, upbraiding them as cowards for consenting to pay tribute to the Romans and tolerating mortal masters, after having God for their lord" (*B.J.* 2.118). According to Josephus's narrative, these events had lasting effects, eventually giving rise to the Zealot movement.[224]

---

220. Brown, *Birth of the Messiah*, 554; Millar, *Roman Near East*, 46–47. Meier (*Marginal Jew*, 1:213) sums up this general view: "Attempts to reconcile Luke 2:1 with the facts of ancient history are hopelessly contrived." Mark D. Smith ("Jesus and Quirinius," 282 and n. 20) cites and rejects this general view, which he terms "a relatively new but nonetheless constraining orthodoxy." T. P. Wiseman ("'There Went Out a Decree from Caesar Augustus . . . ,'" *NTS* 33 [1987]: 479–80) speculates that Luke might have been referring to a partial edict that Augustus might have sent out to provincial governors in 6/7 C.E. This edict would have required that the governors provide up-to-date lists of all Roman citizens for the purpose of the inheritance tax imposed upon all citizens by Augustus in 6 C.E. Luke's fault, in Wiseman's view, would be in failing to distinguish this census (of Roman citizens) from the provincial census carried out by Quirinius in Judea and Syria.

221. Mark D. Smith, "Jesus and Quirinius," 285–93.

222. Josephus (*A.J.* 17.355) states this very clearly: "Now the territory subject to Archelaus was added to (the province of) Syria, and Quirinius, a man of consular rank, was sent by Caesar to take a census of property in Syria and to sell the estate of Archelaus." *A.J.* 18.2: "Quirinius also visited Judaea, which had been annexed to Syria, in order to make an assessment of the property of the Jews and to liquidate the estate of Archelaus."

223. Schürer, *History*, 1:419.

224. *A.J.* 18.3–4 relates the revolt more to the census that preceded the introduction of the Roman tribute: "Although the Jews were first shocked to hear of the registration of property, they gradually condescended, yielding to the arguments of the high priest Joazar, the son of Boethus, to go no further in opposition. . . . But a certain Judas, a Gaulanite from a

This transition may be contrasted with the change from Antipas to Agrippa I following Antipas's deposition and banishment in 39 C.E. (*A.J.* 18.252–55; *B.J.* 2.183). There were no revolts in Galilee and Perea, and the reason must be that Antipas's banishment was not followed by annexation and the imposition of Roman tribute. In 40 C.E. Agrippa, as Philo reports, would write to Gaius: "[I]n view of the multitude of benefits with which you have enriched me I might perhaps have had the courage to beg myself that my homeland should obtain if not Roman citizenship at least freedom and remission of tribute . . ." (*Legat.* 287).[225] Judea (Jerusalem in particular), the "homeland" about which Agrippa speaks,[226] had been under direct Roman rule and tributary since 6 C.E. "Freedom" and "remission of tribute" would have meant the removal of Jerusalem (and the rest of Judea) from direct Roman administration together with the grant of immunity.[227] These honors, which Agrippa would not dare to ask from Gaius, came shortly afterwards, when Claudius added Judea to

---

city named Gamala, who had enlisted the aid of Saddok, a Pharisee, threw himself into the cause of rebellion. They said that the assessment carried with it a status amounting to downright slavery, no less, and appealed to the nation to make a bid for independence." Menahem, the Zealot leader of the revolt in 66 C.E. was the "son of Judas surnamed the Galilaean—that redoubtable doctor who in old days, under Quirinius, had upbraided the Jews for recognizing the Romans as masters when they already had God . . ." (*B.J.* 2.433). Similarly, Eleazar, head of the Sicarii at Masada was "a descendant of the Judas who . . . induced multitudes of Jews to refuse to enroll themselves, when Quirinius was sent as censor to Judaea. For in those days the Sicarii clubbed together against those who consented to submit to Rome and in every way treated them as enemies, plundering their property, rounding up their cattle, and setting fire to their habitations; protesting that such persons were no other than aliens, who so ignobly sacrificed the hard-won liberty of the Jews and admitted their preference for the Roman yoke" (*B.J.* 7.253). See Schürer, *History*, 1:419; Peter Richardson, *Herod*, 29; Mark D. Smith, "Jesus and Quirinius," 282.

225. Philo, *Legat.* 287: θαρρήσας ἂν ἴσως αἰτήσασθαι τῇ πατρίδι καὶ αὐτός, εἰ καὶ μὴ τὴν Ῥωμαϊκὴν πολιτείαν, ἐλευθερίαν γοῦν ἢ φόρων ἄφεσιν, κτλ. See Smallwood, *Philonis Alexandrini Legatio ad Gaium*, 124–27; eadem, *Jews under Roman Rule*, 178–79. On the question of the authorship of the letter, see Daniel R. Schwartz, *Agrippa I: The Last King of Judaea* (Tubingen: Mohr Siebeck, 1990), 200–202.

226. Agrippa speaks of Jerusalem. Philo, *Legat.* 278: "My native city is Jerusalem (ἔστι δέ μοι Ἱεροσόλυμα πατρίς) in which is situated the sacred shrine of the most high God." And *Legat.* 281: "As for the holy city, I must say what befits me to say. While she, as I have said, is my native city (ἐμὴ μέν ἐστι πατρίς) she is also the mother city not of one country Judea but of most of the others in virtue of the colonies sent out at divers times to the neighbouring lands . . . ." For Jerusalem as synecdoche for Judea, see Josephus, *A.J.* 14.74 and chapter 2.

227. ἐλευθερίαν γοῦν ἢ φόρων ἄφεσιν: On "freedom" (*libertas* or *autonomia*) and "immunity" from direct Roman taxation (*immunitas*, also the Greek term ἀτέλεια) for Judea, see discussions above. Smallwood (*Philonis Alexandrini Legatio ad Gaium*, 296, n. on *Legat.* 287) observes accurately that the two grants combined were "the highest privilege then available to provincial communities." She, however, goes on to assert that Jerusalem "enjoyed no position of privilege in the empire until its re-foundation by Hadrian as the pagan colony of Aelia Capitolina after the Jewish revolt of 132–5."

Agrippa's kingdom in 41 C.E. (*A.J.* 19.274–75; *B.J.* 2.215–16).[228] As soon as he arrived in Jerusalem, Agrippa demonstrated his financial and administrative independence by remitting "the tax on every house" which had been levied by the Romans on the inhabitants of the city (*A.J.* 19.299).[229]

Augustus's banishment of Archelaus serves as an example of the interest this emperor took in the internal administration of client kingdoms.[230] Earlier, during the interregnum between Herod's death and Archelaus's accession, Augustus had intervened to reduce by a quarter the tax paid by the inhabitants of the region of Samaria, as a reward for their not joining in the revolts that followed Herod's death (*A.J.* 17.319; *B.J.* 2.96). Tiberius intervened to regulate Philip's estate after Philip died. Gaius deposed Antipas and installed Agrippa I. These and the other known interventions by Rome in the affairs of the territories under Herod and his descendants are entirely in keeping with Rome's imperial relationship with her client kings. On the whole, however, Rome's attitude toward Herod's rulership, and that of his successors, is expressed in the statement that Josephus attributes to Antony: "it was improper to demand an accounting of his reign from a king, since in that case he would not be a king at all, and those who had given a man this office and conferred authority upon him should permit him to exercise it" (*A.J.* 15.76).[231]

Rather than demanding from the Herods an account in the form of an annual tribute, the emperors asked for friendship, loyalty, and a compe-

---

228. Kokkinos (*Herodian Dynasty*, 289) notes appropriately that with Claudius's grants, Agrippa obtained "all that he had ever wished for."

229. Kokkinos (*Herodian Dynasty*, 292) sees some evidence of Agrippa's reorganization of the Judean economy in "a new issue of coins and especially in the new standard weights for the local market." See below.

230. The banishment also serves as evidence of Rome's impatience with the maladministration of client territories. Archelaus was removed at the urging of a delegation from Judea and Samaria which brought charges to Augustus of Archelaus's "cruelty and tyranny" (*A.J.* 17.342; *B.J.* 2.111). On Augustus's interest in the administration of client kingdoms, see Suetonius, *Aug.* 48: "He also united the kings with whom he was in alliance by mutual ties, and was ready to propose or favour intermarriages or friendships among them. He never failed to treat them all with consideration as integral parts of the empire, regularly appointing a guardian for such as were too young to rule or whose minds were affected, until they grew up or recovered; and he brought up the children of many of them and educated them with his own." Sands, *Client Princes*, 119; Bowersock, *Augustus and the Greek World*, 52–61; Braund, "Client Kings," 76–78; Peter Richardson, *Herod*, 227–29; Jacobson, "Client Kings," 22, 25–27.

231. Antony was reportedly responding to Cleopatra, who had induced him to summon Herod to account for the execution of the young Aristobulus III. Rome, of course, intervened when Roman interests were at stake. Claudius, fearing a revolt, ordered Agrippa I to discontinue the work of extending and fortifying the walls of Jerusalem (*A.J.* 19.326–27). Marsus the governor of Syria broke up a gathering of the kings brought together by the same Agrippa (*A.J.* 19.338–42).

tent administration of their domains. In the case of Herod, at least, friendship and loyalty were demonstrated by military support and the exchange of gifts.[232]

Herod's Taxes

The task of appraising the kinds and levels of taxes that Herod and his successors imposed on their subjects suffers desperately from the absence of sufficient evidence. Concrete information on Herod's revenue is almost nonexistent with the result that we know almost nothing about the total, the form, and the extent of the income of Herod's kingdom.[233] It is thus impossible to identify accurately the types of taxes that the Herods imposed and to describe them in more than general terms. In spite (or perhaps because) of this lack of sources, Schalit and numerous scholars after him established a theoretical framework that permitted them to attribute various forms of taxes to Herod and his sons. Herod's kingdom, they maintain, in addition to mirroring Roman imperial administration, was an extension of the Hellenistic kingdoms, both Ptolemaic and Seleucid.[234] Hence, Herod can be said to have imposed on the Jews all the forms of taxes that might be discerned from Ptolemaic Egypt, Seleucid Syria, and anywhere in the Roman Empire.

According to Schalit, therefore, Herod must have levied the following taxes:[235]

1. Poll tax (*tributum capitis*)
2. Income and property tax (*tributum soli*)
3. Salt tax
4. Crown tax
5. Sales and occupational tax
6. House tax
7. Custom duties
8. Sundry payments

Hoehner in turn proposes that the following taxes were imposed by Herod Antipas, as his father Herod the Great had done:[236]

---

232. *A.J.* 15.194–201; *B.J.* 1.393–97; *A.J.*16.128; Peter Richardson, *Herod*, 226–34; on Rome's relationship also with other client kings, see Braund, *Rome and the Friendly King*, 55–103; Jacobson, "Client Kings," 26–27.

233. See, for example, Schalit, *König Herodes*, 262–63.

234. Ibid., 264–65, 298.

235. Ibid., 265–98.

236. Hoehner, *Herod Antipas*, 75–77.

1. Land tax (on produce)
2. Poll tax
3. Fishing tolls
4. Custom duties
5. Purchase and sales taxes (on slaves, oil, clothes, hides, furs, and other valuable commodities)
6. Professional tax (on leather workshops, butchery, prostitution, the use of water, pasturing)
7. Religious dues

Hoehner's land tax is from "Syrian times" and "the time of Caesar." The poll tax is conjectured out of the Jewish accusations against Herod (*A.J.* 17.308). The fishing tolls are from "Roman times," while evidence for custom duties comes from Strabo (*Geogr.* 16.1.27), Pliny (*Nat.* 12.63–65), and the Gospels (Mt 9:9; Mk 2:14; Lk 5:27). Purchase and sales taxes are derived from Josephus (*A.J.* 17.205; *B.J.* 2.4), but the list of specific items taxed and items on the list of taxable professions come from a Palmyra inscription, dated to 137 C.E.[237]

This procedure, which allows each scholar the convenience of attributing to Herod any number of taxes that the scholar might choose from Ptolemaic, Seleucid, and Roman systems of taxation, is obviously arbitrary. It cannot establish with any certainty what taxes were actually paid within Herod's kingdom. In addition, the view of Herod's kingdom that the procedure assumes is particularly problematic. Ptolemaic and Roman Egypt were in many respects unique. The territorial unity of the region, its peculiar agriculture, dependent on the Nile, and the existence of a well-organized civil service, allowed for such administrative structures and institutions as could not be transferred elsewhere.[238] About Attalid taxation virtually nothing is known. Information on Seleucid revenues is sparse, and much of what is known comes from the Seleucid relationship with Judea.[239] To what degree did Seleucid demands on the Jews constitute a Seleucid tax "system"? As I pointed out in chapter 1, the general view that the Romans and Herod afterwards inherited the Seleucid system of taxation from the Hasmonean kings runs into two problems. First,

237. Ibid., 75–76 and n. 1.

238. See Claire Préaux, *L'économie royale des Lagides* (Brussels: Éditions de la Fondation Égyptologique Reine Élisabeth, 1939). Jones (*Roman Economy*, 175, n. 118) observed long ago that "Egypt is exceptional not only in its tax system but also in the wealth of evidence it supplies." See also especially Brunt, "Revenues of Rome," 162–63; and Lutz Neesen, *Untersuchungen zu den direkten Staatsabgaben der römischen Kaiserzeit, 27 v. Chr.-284 n. Chr.* (Antiquitas 32; Bonn: Habelt, 1980), 25–102, 117–30.

239. See Bickerman, *Institutions des Séleucides*, 106–32; Rostovtzeff, *Hellenistic World*, 1:464–72; Mittwoch, "Tribute and Land-Tax."

the Hasmoneans were supposed to have liberated the Jewish state from Seleucid (tax) oppression. We cannot, therefore, expect them to have continued to maintain and operate this same Seleucid tax regime. Second, we actually know nothing about Hasmonean taxation, as Schalit concedes.[240] Herod's kingdom was a "Hellenistic kingdom," no doubt, but the "Hellenistic" character of its institutions must be established and verified in each specific case, not merely assumed.[241]

Under the Republic and early Principate, forms of taxes and tax rates were not uniformly applied, even in Egypt.[242] This certainly follows from the accepted view that, in general, Rome took over the tax regimes already in existence in conquered territories, adapting them to specific circumstances and to her own needs. The result was that different provinces, city-states, groups, and individuals within provinces and city-states developed an infinite variety of tax obligations and exemptions with their Roman suzerains.[243] The Jews were subject to different rules at different periods in their relationship with Rome. We have seen above that, following Herod's death in 4 C.E., Augustus intervened to reduce by 25 percent the tax paid by the Samaritans. The Samaritans, consequently, must have been taxed by Archelaus at a different rate than was demanded from the rest of his ethnarchy. It is not inconceivable, as we shall see below, that under Herod the Samaritans and other segments of his kingdom were subject to a variety of taxes and rates. The inhabitants of Batanea, we saw, did not pay any taxes.[244]

The evidence available suggests that Herod's kingdom mirrored cer-

---

240. *Schalit, König Herodes*, 265.

241. For the Hellenistic character of the client kingdoms, see Braund, *Rome and the Friendly King*, 75–90; Jacobson, "Client Kings," 30–33. From the point of view of Herod's building projects and architecture, see the essays in Klaus Fittschen and Gideon Foerster, eds., *Judaea and the Greco-Roman World in the Time of Herod in the Light of Archaeological Evidence* (Gottingen: Vandenhoeck & Ruprecht, 1996).

242. See Brunt, "Revenues of Rome," 161–63.

243. See P. A. Brunt, "Addendum II," in *The Roman Economy: Studies in Ancient Economic and Administrative History*, by A. H. M. Jones (Oxford: Blackwell, 1974), 183, correcting Jones's theory: "However it is clear, and important, that the Roman government never sought to impose uniformity in taxation on all provinces. Rome normally took over the existing tax-system, and though changes were occasionally introduced, diversity persisted even after Diocletian. In census regulations of his time (first century, C.E.) the classification of lands in Asia, the Greek islands and Egypt differed, and yet another system, perhaps of the same period, is attested in Syria, while the unit of tax-assessment was not the same in Africa or in Italy as in the eastern provinces." See also Brunt, "Revenues of Rome," 161–62; Ramsay MacMullen, *Roman Government's Response to Crisis* (New Haven: Yale University Press, 1976), 131–35; and Elio Lo Cascio, "La struttura fiscale dell'impero Romano," in *L'impero Romano e le strutture economiche e sociali delle province* (ed. Michael H. Crawford; Como: Editioni New Press, 1986), 29–59.

244. See pp. 144–45 above.

tain specific patterns of taxation notable elsewhere in the Roman Empire. That pattern was, however, marked by adaptability and variety. Given the financial freedom that he enjoyed, Herod would have imposed such taxes as were suited to his economic needs and political agenda, the full details of which we do not know. It is, for instance, impossible to know if he adjusted and maintained some of the taxes that Caesar (and Antony) had imposed on the Jews, as Momigliano speculates,[245] or if, as is more likely, he devised his own system to which he added and remitted new forms of taxes as the need arose. Some aspects of his taxation can be discerned from the extant sources.

Land and Property Taxes

Josephus often links direct taxation under Herod with agricultural produce. In *A.J.* 15.109 Josephus says that Herod found the necessary revenues and resources to send help to Antony at the beginning of the battle of Actium. Herod was able to assist Antony because Herod had brought stability to his kingdom "and the countryside had been furnishing him much good pasture already for some time" (καὶ τῆς χώρας εὐβοτουμένης αὐτῷ πολὺν ἤδη χρόνον).[246] On this occasion Herod probably sent cash together with grain to Antony (*A.J.* 15.189); however, Josephus only specifically mentions the "many thousand measures of corn" that Herod sent (*B.J.* 1.388). Shortly afterwards, when Octavian passed through Syria on the way to his campaign against Antony and Cleopatra in Egypt, Herod received and entertained Octavian and the soldiers in Ptolemais. Herod furnished the troops with provisions for the journey across the desert. Water and wine are specifically mentioned (*A.J.* 15.198–200).[247] The account in *Antiquities* intimates that it was especially the cash gift of eight hundred talents, which Herod made to Octavian, that left the impression that Herod had done more than his restricted kingdom could afford (*A.J.* 15.200).[248]

---

245. Momigliano, *Ricerche*, 49. In Momigliano's view, Herod adopted, with hardly any modifications, the taxes imposed on the Jewish state by Julius Caesar. See below.

246. My translation. The LCL edition renders it: "Herod, whose country had been yielding him rich crops for a long time . . . ." See *B.J.* 1.171: "for he was now rid of disturbances in Judaea and had captured the fortress of Hyrcania, hitherto held by the sister of Antigonus."

247. See *B.J.* 1.394–95. Here Josephus does not mention the wine.

248. The money is not mentioned in the parallel account in *B.J.* 1.395. Here Josephus observes that "[t]he thought could not but occur both to Caesar himself and to his soldiers that Herod's realm was far too restricted, in comparison with the services which he had rendered them."

Earlier in his reign, when he needed to transmit large sums of money to Antony, Herod despoiled the rich (*A.J.* 15.5–7; *B.J.* 1.358).[249] Six to seven years afterwards, although probably not as short of cash as he was originally, Herod's economic and tax basis clearly remained in agriculture. This was because his kingdom was landlocked and limited to Galilee, Samaria, Judea and Idumea. He derived his revenues mostly from direct taxation on landed property.[250] Octavian responded to Herod's predicament and "generous spirit" by extending his territory to include Jericho, Gadara, Hippus, and Samaria, in the interior; and Gaza, Anthedon, Joppa, and Strato's Tower, on the Mediterranean coast (*A.J.* 15.217; *B.J.* 1.396).

That Herod taxed landed property is confirmed by what Josephus says about the drought and famine of 27/26 B.C.E. Even Herod was in want "for he was deprived of the revenue [taxes] which he received from the (products of the) earth" (τῶν τε φόρων οὓς ἐλάμβανεν ἀπὸ τῆς γῆς ἀφῃρημένῳ). Josephus distinguishes these taxes from Herod's "money" (χρήματα), which he says the king had spent "in the lavish reconstruction of cities" (*A.J.* 15.303, 305). In order to raise the cash he needed to import grain from Egypt, Herod "cut up into coinage all the ornaments of gold and silver in his palace" (*A.J.* 15.306).[251] Some five or seven years later, when Herod is said to have remitted a third of the taxes paid by the Jews, Josephus observes that it was "under the pretext of letting them recover from a period of lack of crops" (πρόφασιν μὲν ὡς ἀναλάβοιεν ἐκ τῆς ἀφορίας) (*A.J.* 15.365).[252]

The extension of Herod's territory in 30 B.C.E. by Octavian meant, of course, greater revenues from direct taxes. I shall, however, emphasize shortly that the economic significance of many of these cities lay in the fact that Herod derived considerable (cash) revenues through indirect taxes from them.[253] Jericho, on account of its balsam and date plantations, was an essential source of income (from export of these products) for Herod, such that, rather than lose the territory, he was prepared to pay an annual

---

249. See above and also *A.J.* 15.264.

250. See also Pastor, *Land and Economy*, 105–6. Later on, in about 9 B.C.E., Herod was said again to be in want of cash because he "had spent large sums of money both on external needs and on those of the realm." Interestingly, on this occasion Herod is not reported to have tried to raise the cash he needed by taxing the people. Instead he went at night to rob David's tomb, believing that what was left after John Hyrcanus I had robbed it "was sufficient to pay for all his lavish gifts." He found no money but carried away "many ornaments of gold and other valuable deposits" (*A.J.* 16.179–83; also *A.J.* 7.394, where Josephus says that Herod "took away a large sum of money").

251. See Peter Richardson, *Herod*, 222–23; Pastor, *Land and Economy*, 115–27. As Richardson points out (p. 223, n. 18), Herod probably used the metal to produce bullion for trade rather than mint coins, as Josephus suggests.

252. See Peter Richardson, *Herod*, 236.

253. See also Pastor, *Land and Economy*, 106–7.

tribute of two hundred talents to Cleopatra. Gaza, Joppa, and Strato's Tower gave Herod access to major overland trade routes. Gaza, Anthedon, and Joppa were also seaports.[254] Josephus's statements about Herod's income tend to distinguish the revenues that Herod received from direct taxes from those that he derived, in cash, from indirect taxes and other sources. Direct taxes were land taxes and furnished Herod with produce.

Unfortunately, we do not know much more about Herod's taxes on landed property (*tributum soli*). We do not know if the taxes applied to landed property as such or to produce. Did Herod's subjects pay taxes according to the size of their arable land, or did they pay a percentage of the harvest? Although wheat was certainly taxed, we do not know which additional produce was taxed and at what initial rate, that is, before Herod undertook to reduce taxes.

On the basis of the extant evidence, it cannot be said whether or not Herod levied taxes on other kinds of property than land.[255] The possibility must therefore be left open that Herod might have imposed some taxes, other than tolls and duties, that required cash payments. This notwithstanding, Richard Duncan-Jones's conclusions regarding the question of taxes paid with money in the Roman Empire must hold true also for Herod's kingdom:

> Where there is any evidence, the land-tax visibly remained a tax in kind in a number of the provinces. This apparently recognised the limited extent to which money could be extracted from an agricultural population in which ownership of money was sporadic. Cicero's comments on attempts to exact money from the Sicilian farmer are worth recalling: he says that for a farmer to hand over something which he could not grow would mean selling off his equipment ('Nummos vero ut det arator, quos non exarat, quos non aratro ac manu quaerit, boves et aratrum ipsum atque omne instrumentum vendat necesse est').[256]

The "Head Tax"

Fergus Millar points out that, although we should assume that both a land tax (*tributum soli*) and a head tax (*tributum capitis*) were paid in the

254. See Peter Richardson, *Herod*, 177–79, 189. Herod restored Anthedon and named it Agrippias (*B.J.* 1.87; *A.J.*13.357) or Agrippeion (Ἀγρίππειον; *B.J.* 1.416) after his benefactor M. Vipsanius Agrippa. Its restoration might have been completed by the second round of Agrippa's sojourn in Asia (17/16–13 B.C.E.). See Duane W. Roller, *The Building Program of Herod the Great* (Berkeley: University of California Press, 1998), 128–29, who thinks Anthedon was built after 12 B.C.E.

255. On the "house tax," see below.

256. Richard Duncan-Jones, *Structure and Scale in the Roman Economy* (Cambridge: Cambridge University Press, 1990), 198, see from p. 187; Cicero, *Verr.* 2.3.199. See also Millar, *Roman Near East*, 49–50; Brunt, *Roman Imperial Themes*, 531–32.

provinces of the Roman Empire, we do not know how the taxation of property was related to the taxation of individuals in the empire generally, and in Syria in particular.[257] The *tributum capitis* was not introduced in the various provinces of the empire until the necessary census had been conducted in them. The first recorded census was the one taken by Augustus in Gaul, and probably Spain, in 27 B.C.E.[258] Provincial census was a new phenomenon. It was put into effect, as has been noted, gradually and over a period of many years. Rome seems to have used it particularly when assessing newly acquired territories. The evidence suggests that in the early Principate censuses were not widespread, even in the provinces of the empire.[259]

Jones thinks it "probable" that Herod imposed a poll tax on his subjects. He considers the census conducted by Quirinius in 6 C.E. to be "the first census properly so called that had ever been held in Judaea." As for the poll tax exacted by Herod, Jones postulates that "its assessment had no doubt been based as in Ptolemaic Egypt on annual returns of population by the village clerks."[260] In his view, Herod's "financial machinery" was "modelled on that of Egypt."[261] Schalit also has recourse to Ptolemaic Egypt. Herod, he argues, carried out a census in his kingdom, from 20 B.C.E., on a six-yearly basis.[262] According to Hoehner, it was Augustus, rather than Herod, who conducted the census (mentioned in Luke 2:1–5)

---

257. Millar, *Roman Near East*, 110.

258. Dio, *Hist*. 53.22.5: "He [Augustus] took a census of the inhabitants [of Gaul] and regulated their life and government. From Gaul he proceeded into Spain, and established order there also." This information seems fortuitous. Dio does not say if Augustus took a census elsewhere before or after the one in Gaul. See the discussion in chapter 5.

259. See, for instance, Dominic W. Rathbone, "The Imperial Finances," in *CAH*, vol. 10, *The Augustan Empire, 43 B.C.-A.D. 69* (ed. Alan K. Bowman et al.; Cambridge: Cambridge University Press, 1996), 309–23. Rathbone writes (p. 312): "But, starting in Egypt, Augustus introduced an annual poll-tax in cash, Roman-style census arrangements gradually spread through the eastern provinces, and Roman fiscality—and, with it, monetization—was brusquely introduced to the northern and central European provinces." And (p. 322), "[t]he evidence suggests that, outside Egypt, censuses were not regular and neutral operations but occasional delibrate attempts to increase the tribute assessments of individual provinces. . . ." See also Rathbone, "Egypt, Augustus and Roman Taxation," 94–99; and Brunt, "Revenues of Rome," 163–66, 171–72. Brunt (p. 166) concludes here that "general considerations make it probable that in some form they [censuses] were universal and regular in the Principate." He later modifies this view, however, writing in Brunt, *Roman Imperial Themes*, 533: "I now feel less sure that censuses were taken in the Principate as often and as systematically as they should have been for fair and efficient distribution of the tax load." See also Neesen, *Staatsabgaben*, 39–44; J. A. Crook, "Augustus: Power, Authority, Achievement," in *CAH*, vol 10, *The Augustan Empire, 43 B.C.-A.D. 69* (ed. Alan K. Bowman et al.; Cambridge: Cambridge University Press, 1996), 130. See chapter 5.

260. Jones, *Herods*, 168.

261. Jones, *Herods*, 86.

262. Schalit, *König Herodes*, 272–78.

in Herod's kingdom at a time when Herod had fallen into disfavor with the emperor. Hoehner does not say on what basis both Herod and Antipas levied poll taxes, as he claims, on their subjects.[263]

Brook W. R. Pearson has more recently revived Schalit's thesis that Herod maintained (what Pearson terms) "a Roman-style system of census and taxation" in his kingdom, and he too looks to Egypt to support his view.[264] Since his arguments are symptomatic of the attempts to make generalizations regarding Herod's kingdom on the basis of what is known about Egypt, I shall examine these arguments here in some detail. Pearson states that "Herod was emphatically *not* an independent king. He was totally dependent on Rome for his power, influence, kingdom, and freedom (not to mention that he was a Roman citizen)."[265] It is this view and the conclusion that follows it, namely, that "while Herod's administrative system was not a provincial one, it still drew from the Roman model,"[266] that constitute Pearson's "clear evidence both that Herod must have had a well-organized system of taxation and that he needed to, and did, exercise strict social control over his people."[267] Thus, Pearson claims, "it is most likely that Herod implemented the extremely effective process of census and taxation that the Romans had used throughout their empire both to fill their coffers and to control the various peoples and groups whom they ruled."[268] Given the complexity and variety of systems of taxation in the Republic and early Principate, however, Pearson's basic presumption that everywhere in the provinces of the Roman Empire there was "an extremely effective process of census and taxation,"

---

263. See also Seán Freyne, "The Geography, Politics, and Economics of Galilee and Quest for the Historical Jesus," in *Studying the Historical Jesus: Evaluations of the State of Current Research* (ed. Bruce Chilton and Craig A. Evans; Leiden: Brill, 1994), 87. According to Freyne, Antipas's "200 talents in personal income" was presumably "collected on the basis of *tributum soli* or land tax and *tributum capitis* or poll tax, as was general practice throughout the Roman world." Freyne does not say, however, how Antipas assessed the "poll tax" he is said to have collected.

264. Pearson, "Lucan Censuses," 265–77.

265. Ibid., 267; emphasis in original.

266. Ibid., 271–72.

267. Ibid., 268–69. For the idea that Roman censuses were conducted for the sake of social control, Pearson (p. 266) relies on R. S. Bagnall and B. W. Frier, *The Demography of Roman Egypt* (Cambridge Studies in Population, Economy, and Society in Past Time 23; Cambridge: Cambridge University Press, 1994), 29–30. Bagnall and Frier write concerning the census in Egypt: "It is entirely possible that both taxation and control of the population were among the government's motives from the beginning of the periodic census. . . . It is also possible that the symbolic value of the poll tax, representing subjection to Roman power, extended to the census itself—that the census itself was a means of demonstrating Roman control of the world."

268. Pearson, "Lucan Censuses," 268.

is unwarranted.[269] The assumption, therefore, that Herod "must have" duplicated this process in his kingdom is gratuitous.[270]

As evidence that the Roman-style census was conducted elsewhere in client kingdoms, he cites the case, narrated by Tacitus, of the principality of Archelaus II. The inhabitants (the Cietae) revolted because they were "pressed to conform with the Roman usage by making a return of their property and submitting to a tribute. . . ."[271] Possibly on account of Tacitus's calling the prince "Archelaus of Cappadocia (Cappadoci Archelao)," Pearson seems to be confused about the territory over which Archelaus ruled. Thus, against Raymond E. Brown, who points out that Cappadocia had been annexed into a Roman province in 17 C.E. by Tiberius following the death of Archelaus I,[272] Pearson asks, "but why, then, is it Archelaus's son, Archelaus the Younger, who is imposing this census on his people?" In his view Archelaus II ruled over his father's territory, Cappadocia, and the situation which Tacitus reports proves beyond any doubt that Cappadocia, like Herod's Judea, was "a little of both," that is, "a client kingdom, responsible for its own affairs" and "a dependent territory, directly ruled by the Romans."[273] Thus, Pearson concludes, "especially in this phase of the relationship between Cappadocia and Rome, . . . the census was a Roman imposition carried out by the king." All this proves that "the Roman census process was something

269. Ibid. Pearson (p. 273 and nn. 31, 32) appeals to Rathbone's work to justify his claim that the tax practices in Egypt "reflected standard Roman administrative practice." See Rathbone, "Ancient Economy"; idem, "Egypt, Augustus and Roman Taxation," 81–82. Rathbone's work does not seek to establish a monolithic Roman administrative practice, but rather to look for ways in which data from Egypt might clarify processes and phenomena observed elsewhere in the Roman Empire. Thus, Rathbone, "Ancient Economy," 161: "My starting assumptions are that there was great regional diversity in the society and economy of the classical world in general, rather than a peculiar chasm between Egypt and the rest of that world, but that behind this general diversity there were also similar and at times even identical economic developments for which the Egyptian evidence provides a keyhole on a much wider panorama."

270. Although Pearson considers his description of the relationship of Herod's kingdom to the Roman Empire as "clear evidence" (p. 268), he admits immediately thereafter (p. 269) that his argument only "goes a long way towards establishing a circumstantial case for the existence of a system of census and taxation in Herod's kingdom."

271. Tacitus, *Ann.* 6.41: "Cietarum natio Cappadoci Archelao subiecta, quia nostrum in modum deferre census, pati tributa adigebatur . . . ."

272. Brown, *Birth of the Messiah*, 552, n. 15; Dio, *Hist.* 57.17.7; Tacitus, *Ann.* 2.42. Brown himself is uncertain about the limits and status of the territory of Archelaus II. He writes in the main text of his work that the Cietae "were his [Archelaus's] subjects in the Cilician section of Cappadocia" and in the accompanying note he observes that, following annexation, "the Cappadocian kingdom was under a more direct Roman tax control than was the kingdom of Herod the Great."

273. Pearson, "Lucan Censuses," 272, n. 28.

which extended to *all* of Rome's territories, whether they were administered by client 'kings' or by Roman governors."[274]

For all we know, the Cietae were among the inhabitants of the mountainous regions of Cilicia known as ("The Rough Cilicia") Cilicia Tracheia. The region, according to Strabo, "was naturally well adapted to the business of piracy both by land and by sea . . . with all this in view, I say, the Romans thought that it was better for the region to be ruled by kings than to be under the Roman prefects sent to administer justice, who were not likely always to be present or have armed forces with them" (*Geogr.* 14.5.6).[275] Archelaus I (father-in-law of Herod's son, Alexander) received the region, possibly at the same time as the coastal plains of Cilicia, from Augustus in 20 B.C.E. as an extension of Archelaus's kingdom of Cappadocia.[276] After the annexation of Cappadocia in 17 C.E. Tiberius gave Cilicia Tracheia to Archelaus's son, Archelaus II, probably already in 19 C.E.,[277] in much the same way as Augustus, Gaius, and later Claudius gave various regions of Herod's kingdom to Herod's descendants while other parts were annexed. The younger Archelaus certainly was not king of Cappadocia at the time when this part of his father's former kingdom was under direct Roman rule, as Pearson imagines.

This means that Tacitus's passage shows the opposite of what Pearson seeks to prove: In 36 C.E., that is, about sixty-three years after Augustus conducted the census in Gaul and forty years after Herod's death, a client king attempted to conduct a census and exact taxes in accordance with "Roman usage" (*nostrum in modum deferre census*).[278] The imposition provoked a revolt that the dynast proved incapable of putting down. It required the action of the governor of Syria to quell the unrest.[279] The

274. Ibid., 273; emphasis in original.

275. Sullivan, "Cappadocia," II.7.2:1156; Jones, *Cities*, 202–8. Jones (p. 208), echoing Strabo, says the region was "a country of unruly tribes and robber chiefs which needed more constant and more intimate supervision than a Roman governor could give." See, however, Braund, *Rome and the Friendly King*, 91–92.

276. Strabo, *Geogr.* 12.1.4.535; 12.2.11.540; 14.5.6.671; Dio, *Hist.* 54.9.2; Sullivan, "Cappadocia," II.7.2:1155–56; Jones, *Cities*, 208; Gruen, "Expansion of the Empire Under Augustus," 153.

277. Sullivan, "Cappadocia," II.7.2:1167; Sullivan, *Near Eastern Royalty*, 182–87; Jones, *Cities*, 208; Millar, "Emperors, Kings and Subjects," 166.

278. Both A. N. Sherwin-White (*Roman Society and Law in the New Testament* [Oxford: Clarendon, 1963], 163, n. 4) and Brown (*Birth of the Messiah*, 552) are correct in maintaining that the census in Cilicia was undertaken by Archelaus II. It was not a Roman imposition. *Pace* Pearson, "Lucan Censuses," 172–73.

279. Tacitus, *Ann.* 6.42. For Pearson ("Lucan Censuses," 273), the presence of Roman troops in Archelaus's territory is further proof "that Rome had a much larger part to play in this 'kingdom' than is often assumed." The fact that Rome would act to quell revolts in a client kingdom, it is usually assumed, fell within the limits of the "freedom" enjoyed by client kings. See Braund, *Rome and the Friendly King*, 94–95.

similarities between this incident and what occurred in Judea in 6 C.E. are obvious. Archelaus's census in Cilicia, like Quirinius's in Judea, was the first conducted in the region. The "Roman-style" census and taxation were no more acceptable among the Cietae in 36 C.E. than they were among the Jews in 6 C.E. In either case, if a similar process had been introduced before, we would have heard of it. Yet, between about 19 C.E. when he acquired the territory and 36 C.E. when he conducted the ill-fated census, Archelaus must have raised taxes. He would have done so in ways similar to what his father Archelaus I and Herod had done, that is, through ways other than "Roman-style" census and taxation.[280]

It is to be doubted also that the word κωμογραμματεῖς in *A.J.* 16.203 (κωμῶν γραμματεῖς in *B.J.* 1.479) provides, as Pearson argues, "direct evidence" that "goes a long way to prove" that Herod conducted Roman censuses in his kingdom.[281] Pearson is certainly correct that the word is used in the papyri from Egypt to designate the clerk connected with census registrations. The connection that Pearson seeks to establish between this function, as testified in Egypt, and the word as Josephus uses it, however, is very tenuous. Pearson contends, first, that Josephus, being a Roman citizen, "would have been aware of both the office and its function"; second, that Josephus "assumes that his readers will know exactly what the office entails"; and, third, that "[it] is difficult to believe that this office . . . was drastically different in Herod's kingdom" from what it was in Egypt.[282]

In the first place, Pearson seems to be unaware of the fact that Josephus uses titles of Greco-Roman officials (ἐπίτροπος, ἐπιμελητής, στρατηγός, etc.) very imprecisely, so that even where similar titles can be found elsewhere, the specific functions of the officials in Judea must be verified in each individual case.[283] In general, the direct connection between a title in Josephus and a specific function cannot be assumed. Second, the term κωμογραμματεῖς, which occurs in Josephus's works only in *A.J.* 16.203 (and its parallel in *B.J.* 1.479), comes in an indirect speech reporting what Salome's daughter told her mother of what Herod's sons Alexander and Aristobulus purportedly said. There is very little that can be historical in what Josephus is saying here. At the very best, he may be said to narrate

280. Archelaus was probably imitating the Roman census just instituted in the recently annexed Cappadocia. See also the remarks on Tacitus's text by Millar, "Emperors, Kings and Subjects," 166–67: "Such passing reports, though suggestive, are hardly satisfactory. This last one, however, does indicate clearly that a census of a type imitated from the (quite recently instituted) Roman provincial census could be applied within the bounds of a dependent kingdom. But it remains a mere illusion."

281. Pearson, "Lucan Censuses," 270–71.

282. Pearson, "Lucan Censuses," 271.

283. See p. 207, n. 1; also Schürer, *History*, 1:270–72 and n. 13.

the incidents in Herod's court in terms that he hopes his readers can understand. Therefore, even if Josephus and his readers knew of the office of a κωμογραμματεύς, we cannot assume that such an office existed in Judea or that its functions must be the same as in Egypt.

The crux of the problem with Pearson's evidence is, thus, that he does not show that the word κωμογραμματεῖς was recognizably the term for census officials throughout the Roman Empire, outside of Egypt. Actually, this function seems to have been fulfilled by officials known by a wide variety of titles; κωμογραμματεῖς was probably not among them.[284] The γραμματεῖς ("clerks," "scribes," "secretaries," "recorders," etc.) are ubiquitous in Josephus's works, as they are in the Synoptic Gospels and Acts; Josephus often adds the term to his rewriting of biblical passages.[285] They fulfill a wide range of functions: secretaries to kings, scribes of the temple and of the Sanhedrin, readers of the sacred text, judges of the people, and so on. If Josephus knew that κωμογραμματεῖς were indeed the officers specifically responsible for taking censuses in Judea, one would have expected him to use the term in *A.J.* 7.319, where he narrates David's eventful census of 2 Sam 24:1–9 (1 Chr 21:1–6). Josephus writes instead: "Joab, therefore, taking along the chiefs of the tribes and scribes,[286] went through the Israelite country and noted down the extent of the population." This is particularly remarkable since the γραμματεῖς are Josephus's addition to the biblical passage. These γραμματεῖς are recorders, like Susa in *A.J.* 7.293, who, notably, was not in charge of tribute, since this charge fell on Adoramus.

Josephus's κωμογραμματεῖς seem, then, to be no more than scribes whose particular distinction is to be found in the fact that their education and skills (so, in fact, *A.J.* 16.203 and *B.J.* 1.479) permit them to serve only the needs of villagers. They are humble village clerks (*B.J.* 1.479: κωμῶν γραμματεῖς), different, that is, from the exalted and skilled secretaries of kings, like Diophantus in *A.J.* 16.319 (*B.J.* 1.529), or the scribes who served in the temple (*A.J.* 11.128; 12.142; ἱερογραμματεῖς in *B.J.* 6.291) and the Sanhedrin (Aristeus, in *B.J.* 5.532). It is in this peculiarity that the purported taunt by Herod's sons lies.

---

284. Brunt, "Revenues of Rome," 165–66. Brunt (p. 166) observes that there are only two known cases of slave clerks who dealt with censuses "at a lower level." He thinks that census records were generally kept by provincial procurators, and it was "magistrates or *leitourgoi* of the *civitates*" who conducted the registrations. In the cities of the Roman type, they were probably done by *quinquennales*. In general, it is impossible to tell what titles the local census officials bore.

285. See, for instance, *A.J.* 6.120; 7.319; 11.128. On the contrary, βασιλικοὶ γραμματεῖς καὶ κωμογρμματεῖς και τοπογραμμτεῖς are terms used technically in Egypt to denote functions solely within the Egyptian financial system. See Dittenberger, *OGIS*, no. 664.

286. Ἰώαβος δὲ τοὺς ἄρχοντας τῶν φυλῶν παραλαβὼν καὶ γραμματεῖς.

Pearson has neither successfully shown that Rome conducted censuses in client kingdoms, nor has he discovered a Roman census official in Herod's Judea. There is indeed nothing to suggest that Herod conducted censuses in his kingdom, on the basis of which he levied a "head tax" on his subjects.[287]

Tolls and Duties on Goods in Transit

Everything points to the conclusion that Herod's tax revenues must have come primarily from indirect taxes collected in the form of tolls and duties (*portaria*). Tolls and duties were ubiquitous and constituted important sources of revenue for provinces and city-states of the empire during this period.[288] Tolls and duties were easy to impose and to collect. As we noted in chapter 2, Rome permitted dependent states to collect their tolls.[289] The nature of the territory that Herod controlled and his own enterprises point to the prominence of these sources of revenue in his kingdom. The kingdom included various semi-autonomous cities, namely, Gaza, Gadara, Hippus, Azotus, and Jamneia. He refounded and rebuilt a number of others, notably, Samaria-Sebaste, Strato's Tower (Caesarea), Anthedon (Agrippias), Pegae (Antipatris), Geba, and Esbus. Trade between and within these cities, and transit trade through them, would normally have attracted tolls and duties.[290]

Of even greater importance is the control of the long-distance trade routes that Herod obtained with the expansion of his kingdom. I empha-

287. A different question might be raised, namely, how Herod assessed his kingdom for the purposes of the land tax (*tributum soli*). The answer to this question is that we do not know. See the speculative attempts to find an answer in Nikos Kokkinos, "The Relative Chronology of the Nativity in Tertullian," in *Chronos, Kairos, Christos II: Chronological, Nativity and Religious Studies in Memory of Ray Summers* (ed. Jerry E. Vardaman; Macon, Ga.: Mercer University Press, 1998), 128–31.

288. For tolls and duties in the Roman Empire, see R. Cagnat, *Étude historique sur les impôts indirects chez les Romains jusqu'aux invasions des Barbares, d'après les documents litéraires et épigraphiques* (Paris: Imprimerie Nationale, 1882); de Laet, *Portorium*; Peter Ørsted, *Roman Imperial Economy and Romanization: A Study in Roman Imperial Administration and the Public Lease System in the Danubian Provinces from the First to the Third Century A.D.* (Copenhagen: Museum Tusculanum, 1985), 251–58; Lintott, *Imperium Romanum*, 83–35.

289. See the *lex antonia* about Termessus, Sherk, *RGE*, no. 72, lines 31–35; Livy, *Hist.* 38.44; Lintott, *Imperium Romanum*, 83–84; and chapter 2.

290. For the commercial significance of Herod's projects, see Peter Richardson, *Herod*, 188–91; for a discussion of trade in Israel mostly in the later Roman period, see Ze'ev Safrai, *The Economy of Roman Palestine* (London: Routledge, 1994), 222–321; David Adan-Bayewitz and Isadore Perlman, "The Local Trade of Sepphoris in the Roman Period," *IEJ* 40 (1990): 154–72; for tolls and duties in Judea, see de Laet, *Portorium*, 333–44; Schürer, *History*, 1:373–76.

sized in chapter 2 that Joppa and the Great Plain, which Julius Caesar restituted in 47 B.C.E. to Judea, were crucial to the Jewish state. Apart from opening the Jewish state to sea trade through the port at Joppa, acquisition of the territory gave the Jews some control over the *via maris* running north into Syria and beyond, and south into Egypt. The Romans considered the revenues from the region so significant that Julius Caesar imposed a special tribute on Hyrcanus II to compensate for the loss of the tolls and duties that Rome had collected there.[291] Herod reinforced and extended his control and vastly increased the revenues, by rebuilding old Pegae into Antipatris and Strato's Tower into Caesarea. Josephus says that Herod built Caesarea in order to remedy the insufficiencies of the seaport at Joppa (*A.J.* 16.331–34). At its completion in 10 B.C.E., Caesarea was the largest harbor in the Mediterranean. By virtue of its location and facilities, the city along with its harbor remained for centuries to come one of the principal sea-port entries into Palestine and Syria, controlling and rearranging the patterns of trade in the region.[292] Tolls remained an important source of income in Caesarea long after Herod. John the toll collector (τελώνης) was singled out in 66 C.E. by Josephus as one of the prinicipal citizens (δυνατοί) of the city (*B.J.* 2.287). To Joppa and Caesarea, Herod added Anthedon (Agrippias).

Anthedon stood between Gaza and Ascalon, where Herod had a palace (*A.J.* 17.321; *B.J.* 11.98). Gaza was an important commercial center. It was the coastal outlet for the overland southern trade routes from Arabia. Gaza was also a meeting point between these overland routes and the coastal route, the *via maris*.[293] The southern routes brought frankincense

---

291. Ze'ev Safrai (*Economy of Roman Palestine*, 223) notes that "the Romans levied on Hyrcanus a yearly land tax and harbor tax for Joppa to the amount of 20,665 *modia* (*Ant.* 14.206) or approximately 135.5 tons of wheat. Joppa was the major Jewish port, and a tax of 135.5 tons of wheat was ridiculously low, proving that there was only a minimal amount of export from the city." I noted in chapter 2 that it was difficult to say what the relationship might have been between the amount Hyrcanus paid in tribute for the territory and the actual amount raised in tolls and duties at Joppa. What is essential for our point is that the region was significant enough in Roman estimation to attract a special tribute.

292. Kenneth Holum and Robert Hohlfelder, eds., *King Herod's Dream: Caesarea on the Sea* (New York: W. W. Norton, 1988), 72–105; Avner Raban, "Caesarea," in *NEAEHL* (4 vols.; ed. Ephraim Stern et al.; Jerusalem: Israel Exploration Society & Carta, 1993), 1:270–91; Roller, *Building Program*, 133–44; Peter Richardson, *Herod*, 178–79; also de Laet, *Portorium*, 339–41.

293. See Jones, *Cities*, 290; Peter Richardson, *Herod*, 57, 64. On the centrality of Gaza for the southern trade routes during the Hellenistic period, particularly from the evidence of the Zenon papyri, and during the Roman period, see Victor A. Tcherikover, "Palestine Under the Ptolemies: A Contribution to the Study of the Zenon Papyri," *Mizraïm* 4–5 (1937): 24–30; Préaux, *L'économie royale*, 362–63; A. Negev, "The Date of the Petra-Gaza Road," *PEQ* 98 (1966): 89–98; Daniel T. Potts, "Trans-Arabian Routes of the Pre-Islamic Period," in *Itinéraires et voisinages* (ed. Jean-François Salles; vol. 1 of *L'Arabie et ses mers bor-*

and myrrh, pepper and other spices, cotton, and probably silk from southern Arabia, eastern Africa, India, and as far east as China through Arabia and the Mediterranean coasts to Palestine, Syria, Egypt, Rome, and the West. Spices and incense were very expensive items, but were consumed in enormous quantities because they had become essential to life in the Roman world. They were necessary ingredients in food, medicines, and cosmetics, and particularly in cultic life.[294] Large amounts of incense were needed for temple services in Jerusalem, for example. The exorbitant costs that these items commanded in the Roman world were mostly due to the tolls, dues, and the costs of transportation and protection, which were paid in transit.[295]

The southern trade routes were controlled by the Nabateans, and Idumea connected Nabatean Arabia to Gaza.[296] The rise of the Idumean

---

dieres; Lyon: G. S. Maison de l'Orient, 1988), 133–35; Schürer, *History*, 2:100–101; Aryeh Kasher, *Jews, Idumaeans and Ancient Arabs* (Tubingen: Mohr Siebeck, 1988), 89; Aryeh Kasher, "Gaza During the Greco-Roman Era," in *The Jerusalem Cathedra: Studies in the History, Archaeology, Geography and Ethnography of the Land of Israel*, vol. 2 (ed. Lee I. Levine; Jerusalem: Yad Iẓḥak Ben-Zvi Institute, 1982), 63–78; Glen W. Bowersock, *Roman Arabia* (Cambridge, Mass.: Harvard University Press, 1983), 2, 15–27.

294. For instance, in the New Testament: Matt 2:11; Mark 16:1; Luke 1:8–12; 23:56–24:1; John 19:39. See Nigel Groom, *Frankincense and Myrrh: A Study of the Arabian Incense Trade* (London: Longman, 1981), 1–21.

295. On frankincense and myrrh, see Pliny, *Nat.* 12.51–71; on the route through Gaza in the first century and the duties incurred he writes (63–65): "[Frankincense] can only be exported through the country of the Gebbanitae, and accordingly a tax is paid on it to the king of that people as well. Their capital is Thomma, which is 1487½ miles distant from the town of Gaza in Judea on the Mediterranean coast; the journey is divided into 65 stages with halts for camels. Fixed portions of the frankincense are also given to the priests and the king's secretaries, but beside these the guards and their attendants and the gate-keepers and servants also have their pickings: indeed all along the route they keep on paying, at one place for water, at another for fodder, or the charges for lodging at the halts, and the various octrois; so that expenses mount up to 688 denarii per camel before the Mediterranean coast is reached; and then again payment is made to the customs officers of our empire. Consequently the price of the best frankincense is 6, of the second best 5, and the third best 3 denarii a pound." Strabo (*Geogr.* 16.4.24), writing earlier in the first century, traces the overland route to Rhinocolura south of Gaza: "Now the loads of aromatics are conveyed from Leucê Comê to Petra, and thence to Rhinocolura, which is in Phoenicia near Aegypt, and thence to the other peoples." See in general, Gus W. Van Beek, "Frankincense and Myrrh," *BA* 23 (1960): 70–95; J. Innes Miller, *The Spice Trade of the Roman Empire: 29 B.C. to A.D. 641* (Oxford: Clarendon, 1969); Manfred G. Raschke, "New Studies in Roman Commerce with the East," *ANRW* 2.9.2:604–1361. Raschke's work provides helpful correctives to Miller's views. Groom, *Frankincense and Myrrh*; Millar, *Roman Near East*, 515–16; Broshi, "Role of the Temple," 33–35.

296. On the economic connections between Gaza and the Nabateans, see de Laet, *Portorium*, 333–34; Ya'akov Meshorer, *Nabataean Coins* (Qedem 3; Jerusalem: Hebrew University of Jerusalem, 1975), 3, 9–11; Bowersock, *Roman Arabia*, 22–23; Groom, *Frankincense and Myrrh*, 199–213; Philip C. Hammond, *The Nabataeans: Their History, Culture and Archaeology* (Gothenburg: Paul Äströms Förlag, 1973), 65–68; also Kasher, *Jews, Idumaeans and Ancient Arabs*, 88–89.

Herod as king was closely linked with the city of Gaza and Nabatean trade. According to Josephus (*A.J.* 14.10), Herod's Idumean grandfather, Antipas, was appointed "the governor of the whole of Idumaea" by Alexander Janneus and his successor wife, Alexandra. It was reported that Antipas "made friends of the neighbouring Arabs and Gazaeans and Ascalonites, and completely won them over by many large gifts." It was important for the Jewish state and its control of the trade routes that the governor of Idumea be Idumean, and thus able to build the bridge between the Arabs and the Gazaeans. This privileged position enabled Antipas to amass the wealth and influence that permitted his son, Antipater, and grandson, Herod, later to supplant the weakened Hasmoneans in Judea (*A.J.* 14.8; *B.J.* 1.123).[297] Antipater, Herod's father, confirmed the connection between Idumea and Arabia by marrying into the Arabian aristocracy (*B.J.* 1.181; see *A.J.* 14.121–22).[298]

Herod himself showed no less political astuteness in appointing the Idumean Costobarus "governor of Idumaea and Gaza." Herod bound Costobarus further to his family by marrying his sister Salome to him (*A.J.* 15.254). Much like Herod's own grandfather and father, Costobarus "set no limit to his hopes," and had in view to become sole ruler of Idumea "and achieve greater things." He had "good reason for this," says Josephus, "both in his lineage and in the wealth which he had acquired through continual and shameless profit-seeking" (*A.J.* 15.257). Antony, however, refused to accept Costobarus's offer to give Idumea to Cleopatra.[299] Until 30 B.C.E., therefore, Herod continued to exercise as much control over the trade routes as the Hasmoneans before him had gained in

---

297. See discussion in Kasher, *Jews, Idumaeans and Ancient Arabs*, 89–90, 109; Peter Richardson, *Herod*, 62–64, 78–79. Richardson (p. 78 and n. 105) intimates, erroneously, that it was Antipater, rather than his father, Antipas, who had been the governor of Idumea. Josephus makes frequent references to Antipater's "clout" with the Arabs: Antipater used his influence with Aretas III, with whom he was "a very good friend," to persuade the Arab king to receive Hyrcanus II and then to invade Judea in the attempt to install Hyrcanus as king in Jerusalem (*A.J.* 14.14–18; *B.J.* 1.123–26). In 62 B.C.E. Scaurus, who was marching against Petra, sent Antipater as his envoy to Aretas "because of their friendly relations." Antipater's diplomacy stemmed the arm of war, as the Arab agreed to pay three hundred talents, for which Antipater himself was surety (*A.J.* 14.80–81; *B.J.* 1.159). Antipater left sums of money in deposit with the Arabs and Herod himself passed on money to Aretas's successor, Malchus. When Herod fled from the Parthians in 40 B.C.E., however, Malchus was "unduly forgetful of the ties of friendship with his [Herod's] father" and refused to give him any help (see *A.J.* 14.370–73; *B.J.* 1.274–76).

298. See Sullivan, *Near Eastern Royalty*, 215, who suggests that Cypros might have been the daughter of Aretas III; also the discussion in Peter Richardson, *Herod*, 62–63.

299. Pardoned for this treachery, Costobarus continued in his post until about 27 B.C.E., when, now divorced from Salome, he was executed by Herod for hiding Herod's enemies and Antigonus's allies (the sons of Baba) since 37 B.C.E. (*A.J.* 15.258–66). See Peter Richardson, *Herod*, 221–22.

Idumea. When Octavian added Gaza to Herod's kingdom in 30 B.C.E.,[300] he handed Herod complete control of the territory and the trade routes, along with the immense income that came from them. The income from Gaza reverted to the Romans, as we learn from Pliny (*Nat.* 12.65), when Gaza was reattached to the province of Syria after Herod's death.[301] Augustus, by later extending Herod's kingdom to include Auranitis, Batanea, and Trachonitis, also gave Herod a hold on the trade route going north across Transjordania to Damascus.

Unfortunately, again, our sources do not permit us to determine directly for which items and at what rate, generally, tolls and duties were paid. It is impossible to estimate how much money poured into Herod's coffers from indirect taxes. It is clear, however, first, that Herod's wealth derived in large part from his family's involvement with the Nabatean trade and other business interests in Idumea, Gaza, and Ascalon. Second, Herod himself continued to reap vast profits from these trade routes and from the new ones that his greatly expanded kingdom made available to him.[302]

Sales Taxes

Evidence that Herod imposed duties on sales in his kingdom comes from demands made after Herod's death that Archelaus remove "the taxes that had been levied upon public purchases and sales and had been ruthlessly exacted" (*A.J.* 17.205).[303] Our information is, again, very limited. As a result, we do not know exactly what kinds of sales and which parts of the kingdom were affected by the tax, and what rates were assessed. In about 37 C.E. Vitellius, the governor of Syria, is said to have "remitted to the inhabitants of the city all taxes on the sale of agricultural produce," on the occasion of his visit to Jerusalem.[304] About forty-one years lay between

---

300. It is generally recognized that Gaza was not in Herod's kingdom before this grant, contra Jones, *Cities*, 269 and 460–61, n. 57, who, on the basis of *A.J.* 15.254, holds that Antony in 40 B.C.E. gave the city to Herod. Josephus's statement in this passage that Costobarus was appointed "governor of Idumea and Gaza" soon after 37 B.C.E. results from Josephus's retrojecting Costobarus' title after 30 B.C.E. into the earlier period.

301. See de Laet, *Portorium*, 333–34 and the passage cited in n. 295 above.

302. See Peter Richardson, *Herod*, 56 and 64. Applebaum ("Economic Life," 665) concedes that "[t]he customs and excise of his [Herod's] ports and inland duties must have yielded no mean revenue."

303. *A.J.* 17.205: ἄρσεις τῶν τελῶν ἃ ἐπὶ πράσεσιν ἢ ὠναῖς δημοσίαις ἐπεβάλλετο πρασσόμενα πικρῶς ᾐτοῦντο; in the parallel passage in *B.J.* 2.4 the protesters demanded "the abolition of the duties" (ἀναιρεῖν τὰ τέλη).

304. *A.J.* 18.90: Οὐιτέλλιος τὰ τέλη τῶν ὠνουμένων καρπῶν ἀνίησιν εἰς τὸ πᾶν τοῖς ταύτῃ κατοικοῦσιν.

Herod's death and Vitellius's visit to Jerusalem. Judea had meanwhile been under direct Roman rule since 6 C.E. Nonetheless, scholars usually equate the taxes remitted by Vitellius with the dues that Herod is said to have imposed on sales. F. M. Heichelheim, whose view is often repeated, writes therefore: "We also know of a market duty in Jerusalem from the time of the Jewish kings to the first procurators, which Vitellius abolished in 36 A.D."[305]

The obstacle to postulating a continuity of sales taxes from Herod to Vitellius is that Josephus's accounts of the events after Herod's death clearly indicate that Archelaus consented to remove the duties.[306] We are not told, however, whether he actually removed them once he returned from Rome. If, as is likely, Archelaus did remove the taxes, the duties that were later abolished by Vitellius would have been imposed by the Roman *praefecti* after Archelaus had been banished. It is noteworthy that, whereas Herod's sales taxes appear to have affected the whole of Judea, the later taxes only affected the city of Jerusalem.[307] Moreover, these duties were imposed only on produce and food items, probably brought into the city for sale (τὰ τέλη τῶν ὠνουμένων καρπῶν). This might explain why the taxes were so onerous. On the contrary, Josephus's vague statement that Herod levied duties on "public purchases and sales" (ἐπὶ πράσεσιν ἢ ὠναῖς δημοσίαις) could mean that Herod's taxes were paid on a variety of items sold in the public forum—the marketplace. Schalit would be correct, in this event, in estimating that the tolls levied by Herod were collected in the marketplaces in Jerusalem. He overdraws the meaning of Josephus's

---

305. Heichelheim, "Roman Syria," 238. See, among other authors, Schürer, *History*, 1:374 and n. 100: "In addition to import and export duties, in Judaea as elsewhere indirect duties of another sort had to be paid: for instance, a market toll in Jerusalem, introduced by Herod but abolished by Vitellius in A.D. 36." He cites *A.J.* 17.205 and 18.90. Freyne, *Galilee*, 190–91: "Herod's tax system was at least as hard for townspeople, for we hear of sales taxes in Jerusalem about which the people complained to Archelaus (*Ant.* 17:205) and which were subsequently partly removed by Vitellius (*Ant.* 18:90). Taxes on fruits are explicitly mentioned as being remitted. . . ." Smallwood (*Jews under Roman Rule*, 172) notes that Vitellius "remitted the taxes previously levied on the sale of agricultural produce in the city." She does not say when the duties were imposed. She observes (p. 105), however, that all that Archelaus could promise regarding the demand that Herodian sales taxes be abolished was "to indicate his willingness to meet their requests when the supreme power was legally his."

306. According to Josephus, Archelaus "made no opposition" to the demand that the taxes be removed (*A.J.* 17.205). *B.J.* 2.4: "To all these requests, in his desire to ingratiate himself with the people, he readily assented."

307. Josephus says that taxes were "remitted to the inhabitants of the city." His concluding remark that Vitellius, by his actions in Jerusalem, had "bestowed these benefits upon the nation" bears especially on the issue of the vestments of the high priest and its ornaments, although this also would have been of immediate concern to the inhabitants of the city (*A.J.* 18.90–95; see *A.J.* 15.405).

passage, however, when he speculates that it implies that Herod registered all sales in his kingdom and kept records of them in Jerusalem.[308]

House Tax

Josephus writes that Agrippa I, when he arrived at Jerusalem after receiving Archelaus's former ethnarchy from Claudius in 41 C.E., "recompensed the inhabitants of Jerusalem for their goodwill to him by remitting to them the tax on every house, holding it right to repay the affection of his subjects with a corresponding fatherly love" (*A.J.* 19.299). On the strength of this statement, Heichelheim comments: "In Jerusalem under the Roman administration there was a house tax, which probably went back to the time of Herod, until Agrippa I came to the throne."[309] In the note following his observation Heichelheim points to the following evidence:

> M. Baba Bathra I 4/5 speaks of a contribution of the citizens of a town towards the building and the restoration of the walls. In the second century A.D., i.e. at the date of the passage, the contribution was levied in proportion to property; but there is a tradition in the Mishna (loc. cit.) that an earlier regulation imposed a levy on each house, which might have been the house-tax of Josephus.[310]

The region that Agrippa received in 41 C.E., it must be recalled, had been under direct Roman rule since 6 C.E. Here again, however, Heichelheim's view that the said "house tax" is to be traced back to Herod has been a staple among scholars.[311]

The "earlier regulation" about which Heichelcheim speaks is the passage in the Mishnah that states:

> One [who dwells in a town] is compelled [to contribute towards the cost of] a wall for the town [and towards the cost of] double doors and a bolt. Rabban Simon ben Gamaliel says, Not all cities need a wall. How long must one be in a town to be deemed as of the citizens of the town?—

---

308. See Schalit, *König Herodes*, 286–88.

309. Heichelheim, "Roman Syria," 236.

310. Ibid., 236, n. 33.

311. For instance, Schalit, *König Herodes*, 290 and n. 504, who cites Heichelheim and writes in turn: "Es ist sehr wahrscheinlich, daß die Einrichtung der Haussteuer in Judäa erstmalig das Werk des Herodes war." Smallwood (*Jews under Roman Rule*, 197) observes that one of Agrippa's "earliest actions in 41 was to remit the house tax in Jerusalem (a tax normally paid by all householders in walled towns for the building and upkeep of the walls)—a blatant bid for popularity."

> Twelve months. If one bought a dwelling-house therein, he is straightway considered as of the citizens of the town. (*m. B. Bat.* 1:5)[312]

Of significance here is the phrase "if one bought a dwelling-house therein."[313] The plain meaning of the whole passage is to establish the legal grounds on which a person could be considered a resident of a town, and therefore liable to contribute to the building of the walls of the town. Correctly speaking, the tax under consideration should be termed a "wall tax." Those who lived in a town for twelve months were also liable, whether or not they owned a house. Ownership of real estate only meant that one was instantly qualified as a resident and was subject to paying the tax, no more. The discussion in *b. B. Bat.* 7a and 8a indicates that wherever and whenever this tax might have been levied, it was either paid "according to means" (that is, in proportion to one's assessed income rather than as a flat, head tax) or according to the "proximity of his house to the wall." The passage in the Mishnah does not tell us *how* the contribution was assessed. There is nothing either in the Mishnah or in the discussion in the Talmud to suggest, as Heichelheim assumes, that the contribution for the building of a city wall was assessed and referred to as a "house tax."

Moreover, Heichelheim's reference to the mishnaic passage as an "earlier regulation" fudges the issue of the date when the practice of imposing taxes for the building and upkeep of city walls began. Rabban Simon ben Gamaliel, to whom the tradition in the Mishnah refers, is most likely Simeon ben Gamaliel II. He flourished under the emperors Hadrian and Antonius Pius (ca. 117–160).[314] The tradition therefore dates to the period after 70 C.E. Even if one were to give the tradition the most

---

312. Cited by Heichelheim, "Roman Syria," 236, n. 33. See also Smallwood in n. 311 above.

313. Heichelheim ("Roman Syria," 236, n. 33) juxtaposes this passage with the discussions in *b. B. Bat.* 7a and 8a, which he quotes: "R. Eleazar (c. 130–160 A.D., Palestine) inquired of R. Johanan: 'Is the impost (for the wall) levied as a poll-tax or according to means?' He replied: 'It is levied according to means, and do you, Eleazar my son, fix this ruling firmly in your mind.' According to another version R. Eleazar asked R. Johanan whether the impost was levied in proportion to the proximity of the resident's house to the wall or to his means. He replied: 'In proportion to the proximity of his house to the wall.'. . . Rabbi (c. 135–210 A.D., Sepphoris) levied the impost for the wall on the Rabbis. . . . Rabbi has explained that (in Ezra, VII, 24) *minda* means the king's tax, *belo* the poll tax and *halach* denotes *annona*."

314. See Schürer, *History*, 2:372–73 and 368, n. 51: "In the Mishnah, the much-mentioned Rabban Simeon ben Gamaliel is as a rule to be understood as the son of Gamaliel II, especially in mAb. 1:18. Besides mAb. 1:17, only mKer. 1:7 relates perhaps to Simeon son of Gamaliel I." See also George Foot Moore, *Judaism in the First Centuries of the Christian Era: The Age of the Tannaim* (2 vols.; Cambridge, Mass.: Harvard University Press, 1927–30), 1:86–89.

generous interpretation and assume that Simeon ben Gamaliel I is meant, the practice it implies would still belong to the period of direct Roman rule in Judea. Simeon ben Gamaliel I was prominent at the time of the revolt in 66 C.E. (see *B.J.* 4.159; *Vita* 190–98). The conclusion would be that the Romans, from an unspecified time, required the inhabitants of walled cities in Palestine to pay for the walls of their city. The discussion in *b. B. Bat.* 7a and 8a, in comparing this requirement to the Roman poll tax, supports this conclusion. Josephus's "house tax," therefore, should not be confused with the rabbinic "wall tax."

The meaning of Josephus's phrase "the tax on every house" (τὰ ὑπὲρ ἑκάστης οἰκίας) cannot be established with certainty. The closest examples of such a tax are Roman.[315] Lucullus, according to Appian, imposed "taxes on slaves and house property" (τέλη δ' ἐπὶ τοῖς θεράπουσι καὶ ταῖς οἰκίας) on the province of Asia in 71/70 B.C.E., in order to raise money to pay for the debt that the province still owed on a fine imposed on them by Sulla (*Hist. rom.* 12.83).[316] Similarly, Appius Claudius imposed a house tax on the province of Cilicia (Cicero, *Fam.* 3.8.3–5; also *Att.* 5.16.2),[317] and at the outbreak of the civil war in 49 B.C.E. Scipio, Pompey's general, exacted extraordinary contributions including a house tax on the inhabitants of Asia.[318] The Roman taxes come in an assortment of names: *exactio ostiorum*, *ostiarium* (a doortax), and *columnarium* (a pillartax).[319]

315. Schalit (*König Herodes*, 290, n. 504) notes that the "house tax" existed in the Greco-Roman world. For evidence he cites, besides Heichelheim, Rostovtzeff, *Hellenistic World*, 316, 954, 962, 994. In his survey of Egypt under the early Ptolemies Rostovtzeff (*Hellenistic World*, 1:316) writes: "On the other hand, there were elaborate taxes on property, for example, on houses and on slaves . . . ." Rostovtzeff offers neither evidence nor description of the taxes on houses about which he speaks. As Préaux (*L'économie royale*, 387–92) describes it, the Ptolemaic tax on houses, the σταθμός, was the obligation to give lodging in one's house to soldiers, cleruchs, and visiting administrative officials. It was a requisition in use when necessary, especially in times of war and military maneuvers, but which, because of the scarcity of inhabitable space in Egypt, became a constant levy. There are no house or other property taxes known from Seleucid Syria. Bickerman (*Institutions des Séleucides*, 118) writes apropos: "Dans notre relevé des taxes séleucides on cherche vainement plusieurs impôts sur la propriété, sur le capital ou sur le revenu, par exemple sur les successions, sur le bétail, etc., que nous retrouvons si nombreux dans l'Egypte ptolémaïque."

316. See Rostovtzeff, *Hellenistic World*, 2:954.

317. See Rostovtzeff, *Hellenistic World*, 2:962; Lintott, *Imperium Romanum*, 77–78.

318. That is, according to Caesar's accusations (Caesar, *Bell. civ.* 3.32): "In capita singula servorum ac liberorum tributum imponebatur; columnaria, ostiaria, frumentum, milites, arma, remiges, tormenta, vecturae imperabantur; cuius modo rei nomen reperiri poterat, hoc satis esse ad cogendas pecunias videbatur." See Rostovtzeff, *Hellenistic World*, 2:994; Lintott, *Imperium Romanum*, 78.

319. A "pillar tax" was probably in force in Rome in about 45 B.C.E. Cicero (*Att.* 13.6.1) bids Atticus: "Make sure whether I owe any pillar-tax at all (Columnarium vide ne nullum debeamus)."

Therefore, the house tax referred to by Josephus appears to have been a tax on real estate. As Josephus presents it, the tax was levied only on the inhabitants of Jerusalem.[320] House taxes, like other capitation taxes in the late Republic, were levied by Roman magistrates as extraordinary, emergency exactions.[321] "The tax on every house" that Agrippa remitted might have been imposed on the inhabitants of Jerusalem by one of the Roman *praefecti* at an unknown time as a punishment for one of the many confrontations with the Romans (under Pilate for instance), or in an emergency about which we have no documentation.[322] It is thus unlikely that Herod had imposed it.

Epilogue

If the house tax in *A.J.* 19.299 could be shown to be Herodian, it would have constituted our only evidence that Herod levied taxes on property other than land. Since this is not the case, the tax structure for Herod's kingdom may be said with certainty to have included: (1) a land tax assessed either on the value of property or a percentage of yield; (2) tolls and duties; and (3) a tax on sales, most likely levied in the marketplace.

The economic conditions of Judea under Herod have become the battleground for the fierce ideological battles fought by scholars with regard to the causes of the Jewish revolt of 66 C.E. and the rise of early Christianity. The economic despair brought about by Herodian and Roman taxes, it is alleged, drove Judean "peasants" to the protest movement now called Christianity and to open revolt in 66 C.E. Rome, I have argued, derived no direct taxes from Herod's kingdom, or portions of it, while the territory was governed by Herod and his descendants. In support of the view that Herod's own taxes were excessive, scholars commonly cite three factors: (1) Herod's "total annual royal income," which is thought to have come from taxes and to have been very large; (2) the magnitude of Herod's building projects; (3) Josephus's negative evaluations of Herod's reign.

There is now a growing body of literature, to which I shall refer below, that suggests that traditional interpretations both of the economic significance of Herod's building program and of Josephus's negative assessment of Herod's economic achievements should be revised. Such revisions would require a full study of the Herodian economy, which is

320. The Mishnah's tax for city walls was levied on the residents of all walled cities.

321. This point is repeatedly made by Rostovtzeff, *Hellenistic World*, 3:1563, n. 28; 1566, n. 41. See also Lintott, *Imperium Romanum*, 78; Rathbone, "Egypt, Augustus and Roman Taxation," 94–95.

322. See Brunt, "Revenues of Rome," 168; contra Neesen, *Staatsabgaben*, 59.

now long overdue.[323] The scope of the present study requires that we pay detailed attention only to the matter of taxation in Herod's kingdom.

According to Josephus's account of the events following Herod's death, when Sabinus, Augustus's procurator for the province of Syria, arrived in Jerusalem, he demanded the account of Herod's estate from Herod's treasury officials (διοικηταὶ τῶν πραγμάτων) (*A.J.* 17.223; *B.J.* 2.18). Later on, Sabinus and the governor of Syria, Varus, sent a report to Augustus "concerning the amount of the property and the size of the annual revenue" from Herod's kingdom (*A.J.* 17.229; see *B.J.* 2.25). These statements suggest that at the time of Herod's death Roman authorities had concrete information about the revenues that accrued to Herod from the territories subjected to him. Josephus, in his narrative of the division of Herod's kingdom by Augustus, attaches to each territory the amount of revenue allotted to its recipient. Scholars assume in general, therefore, that the revenues reported by Josephus add up to the annual revenue of the whole of Herod's kingdom. Momigliano was the last person who tried to demonstrate that this was indeed the case, and it is to the figures he put forward that scholars usually appeal when dealing with Herod's tax income.[324]

Josephus's account of the financial implications of Augustus's partition of Herod's kingdom may be summarized as follows:

1. Galilee and Perea: annual revenues for both amounted to two hundred talents (paid in taxes to Antipas).[325]
2. Batanea, Trachonitis, Aurinitis, Gaulanitis with Paneas: annual tax income of one hundred talents (paid to Philip).[326]
3. Judea, the province of Samaria, Idumea, the seaport cities of Caesarea and Joppa, together with Samaria-Sebaste (and Jerusalem): produced annual income of six hundred talents, according to *A.J.* 17.319–20, or four hundred talents, according to *B.J.* 2.96–99 (paid to Archelaus).

---

323. Peter Richardson (*Herod*, 28) provides a summary of his views but otherwise desists from a full treatment of the question. For Antipas's Galilee, see Freyne, "Geography, Politics, and Economics," 104–21; and idem, "Herodian Economics."

324. Momigliano, *Ricerche*, 45–50; see the speculations in Applebaum, "Judaea as a Roman Province," 2.8:374–77.

325. *A.J.* 17.318: καὶ τούτῳ μὲν ἥ τε Περαία καὶ τὸ Γαλιλαῖον ὑπετέλουν, φορά τε ἦν τάλαντα διακόσια τὸ ἐπ᾽ ἔτος. *B.J.* 2.95: ἐγένετο δὲ ὑπὸ τούτῳ μὲν ἥ τε Περαία καὶ Γαλιλαία, πρόσοδος διακοσίων ταλάντων.

326. *A.J.* 17.319: Βαταναία δὲ σὺν Τραχωνίτιδι καὶ Αὐρανῖτις σύν τινι μέρει οἴκου τοῦ Ζηνοδώρου λεγομένου Φιλίππῳ τάλαντα ἑκατὸν προσέφερεν. *B.J.* 2.95: Βατανέα δὲ καὶ Τράχων Αὐρανῖτίς τε καὶ μέρη τινὰ τοῦ Ζήνωνος οἴκου τὰ περὶ Πανιάδα, πρόσοδον ἔχοντα ταλάντων ἑκατόν, ὑπὸ Φιλίππῳ τέτακτο.

4. Jamneia and Azotus, the palm groves of Phaselis, and the king's palace in Ascalon together with five hundred thousand pieces of coined silver, that is, fifty talents:[327] for a total annual revenue of sixty talents (allotted to Salome, Herod's sister) (*A.J.* 17.321; *B.J.* 2.98).[328]
5. Samaria (the region) had one fourth of the taxes it had previously paid to Herod remitted by Augustus (*A.J.* 17.319; *B.J.* 2.96).[329]
6. The revenues from Gaza, Gadara, Hippus (*A.J.* 17.320; *B.J.* 2.97) (possibly also Esobonitis and Anthedon)[330] were also lost, since these cities were reattached to the province of Syria.

Thus:

Archelaus	=	600 (*Antiquities*) or 400 (*War*) talents
Antipas	=	200 talents
Philip	=	100 talents
Salome	=	60 talents

This gives a total of 960 talents (*Antiquities*) or 760 talents (*War*).

The fact that Momigliano undertook to demonstrate how Josephus's sums add up to the tax revenue of Herod's kingdom should alert us to the difficulties in Josephus's report.[331] The first of these difficulties is the discrepancy between *Antiquities* and *War* in the figures given for Archelaus's annual income. The difference of two hundred talents is not negligible; it is the sum that Josephus gives for the annual revenue from Galilee. This is probably why it was central to Momigliano's calculation that he show that Archelaus's annual revenue was six hundred talents as in *Antiquities* rather than four hundred talents as in *War*.[332]

327. *A.J.* 17.321. Herod left ten million pieces of coined silver in his legacy to Augustus (*A.J.* 17.190). In Herod's previous will this sum is given as one thousand talents (*A.J.* 17.146; *B.J.* 1.646). Similarly the legacy bequeathed to the empress (and the children, friends, and freedmen of the emperor) is five million pieces of silver in *A.J.* 17.190, and five hundred talents in *A.J.* 17.146; *BJ* 1.646. One talent is equivalent, therefore, to ten thousand pieces of silver. This conclusion is supported by the analysis of Josephus's talent by Friedrich Hultsch, "Das hebräische Talent bei Josephus," *Klio* 2 (1902): 70–72.

328. Her territories were to remain under Archelaus's jurisdiction (*A.J.* 17.322; *B.J.* 2.98).

329. Momigliano (*Ricerche*, 46) is correct that, in spite of the ambiguities in the texts, Augustus's tax reduction could not have applied to all of Archelaus's ethnarchy since it was a reward for not revolting. The region of Samaria alone merited the concession (*A.J.*17.289; *B.J.* 2.69).

330. The two cities are not explicitly mentioned in Josephus's list. Both cities were attacked by the Jewish rebels in 66 C.E. (*B.J.* 2.458, 460). See Schürer, *History*, 1:104, 166.

331. Momigliano (*Ricerche*, 45) admits that his demonstration is complicated by the fact that the figures transmitted by Josephus raise "molti problemi preliminari."

332. See Momigliano, *Ricerche*, 47–49.

In order to go from Julius Caesar to Herod, Momigliano passes, first, through Herod's gift of Perea to his brother Pheroras. Josephus alludes to the financial objectives of the grant in two difficult and apparently conflicting passages. He writes in *War* (1.483) that Pheroras "had a private income of a hundred talents, exclusive of the revenue derived from the whole of the transJordanic region."[333] In *Antiquities* (15.362) he writes, however, that "Herod asked of Caesar a tetrarchy for his brother Pheroras, and alloted to him from his own kingdom a revenue of a hundred talents."[334] According to Momigliano, the passage in *Antiquities* means that the one hundred talents came from the revenues from Perea, whereas a literal reading of the passage in *War* would give the meaning that Pheroras had a personal patrimony of one hundred talents, quite separate from Herod's gifts. Thus, he concludes, Josephus must be interpreted to say that the income from Perea was one hundred talents, since Josephus summarizes better in *Antiquities* the clumsy passage in *War*.[335]

Momigliano's second set of figures is taken from the seven hundred talents exacted by Cassius in 43 B.C.E.[336] The Jews paid to Cassius, he argues, the tribute that they had paid through normal channels since 47 B.C.E. Seven hundred talents also was Herod's revenue from Idumea, Judea, Perea, and Galilee: that is, one hundred talents each for Galilee and for Perea plus five hundred talents for Idumea and Judea. To this sum should be added the one hundred talents that Momigliano arbitrarily assigns to Samaria.[337] Thus, Archaleus's territory (Idumea, Judea, and Samaria) should be said to have yielded six hundred talents.

Momigliano, however, does not consider the possibility that, with regard to Perea, the passage in *Antiquities* could mean that, apart from the gift of the tetrarchy, Herod also made a grant of one hundred talents to his brother. Josephus (*A.J.* 15.362) goes on, in fact, to state that Herod's gift (of one hundred talents) was to secure Pheroras's hold on the tetrarchy so that, in the event of Herod's death, Herod's sons "might not seize possession" of the tetrarchy.[338] The προσόδους δὲ ἰδίας in *B.J.* 1.483 would, in this case, be the patrimony set up for him by Herod with the grant of one hundred talents. In other words, the sum of one hundred talents is

333. *B.J.* 1.483: προσόδους δὲ ἰδίας εἶχεν ἑκατὸν τάλαντα, τὴν δὲ πέραν Ἰορδάνου πᾶσαν ἐκαρποῦντο χώραν.

334. *A.J.* 15.362: . . . αὐτὸς ἀπονείμας ἐκ τῆς βασιλείας πρόσοδον ἑκατὸν ταλάντων.

335. Momigliano, *Ricerche*, 47–48.

336. See chapter 3.

337. Momigliano, *Ricerche*, 46–48.

338. For the view that the income of one hundred talents was in addition to the revenues of Perea, see, for instance, Peter Richardson, *Herod*, 234: "[Pheroras] was made financially secure with a grant of one hundred talents per year plus the income of Peraea."

separate from the revenue derived by Pheroras from Perea;[339] we have no information about the income yielded to him by Perea.

On the whole, Momigliano's theory depends on his interpretation of Caesar's decree in *A.J.* 14.202–6. In his view Caesar demanded that the Jews pay taxes to the Jewish authorities for the administration of Jerusalem and Joppa, as well as tribute to Rome. The sums that Momigliano computes for Herod's revenue represent these various taxes taken together,[340] and from which Herod paid tribute to Rome.[341] We have already seen that Momigliano's interpretation of Caesar's decree was erroneous.[342] Since Caesar regulated only the tribute paid to Rome by the Jewish state, the decree tells us nothing about the total tax revenue of the Jewish state. The comparison that Momigliano draws between Judea's putative revenue under Julius Caesar and Herod's income is, therefore, baseless.

As for his appeal to Cassius's levy, Momigliano's arguments have already been rejected by Jones.[343] First, if Cassius's tribute was not arbitrarily determined (to meet his needs), it was based not on the total internal revenue of the Jewish state, but on its tribute to Rome. Second, it cannot be assumed that the seven hundred talents represented Judea's tribute for one year, since Cassius, as we noted, demanded as much as ten years' tribute from Asia. Finally, the tribute paid by the Jews to Rome under Caesar was in kind. Cassius's levy and the revenues of Herod's heirs are given in talents. If, as Momigliano theorizes, the level of taxation remained the same under Herod as it was set by Caesar (and exacted by Cassius), the price of wheat would need to have remained unchanged for the forty three years, that is, from 47 B.C.E. to 4 B.C.E. This is not possible.[344]

In short, the very significant inconsistency between the sums that Josephus gives in *Antiquities* and in *War* cannot be explained away. There are other notable inconsistencies in the amounts of money reported by Josephus in relation to Herod's estate. For instance, Josephus first states (*A.J.* 17.146; *B.J.* 1.646) that Herod left a bequest of one thousand talents to the emperor. He afterwards says that Augustus gave fifty talents (from

---

339. Momigliano (*Ricerche*, 47) thinks that only *B.J.* 1.483 would support this conclusion.

340. Momigliano, *Ricerche*, 49: "basterà che noi rendiamo esplicito un elemento implicito della dimostrazione ora fatta perchè sia assicurato un importantissimo elemento della politica tributaria di Erode: *egli non modificò o modificò solo lievemente il gettito delle imposte quale era fissato in Giudea alla morte di Cesare*" (emphasis in original).

341. Momigliano, *Ricerche*, 43.

342. See the discussion in chapter 2.

343. Jones, "Review," 230.

344. On the price of wheat, see Duncan-Jones, *Structure and Scale*, 143–55.

his own legacy) to Herod's two unmarried daughters.[345] Yet he goes on to say that Augustus "further distributed" his legacy of one thousand talents to Herod's other children, that is, excluding the dowries for Herod's two daughters (according to *B.J.* 2.99–100). In *A.J.* 17.322–23 Josephus writes that, besides the fifty talents given as dowries,[346] the emperor also distributed to Herod's children fifteen hundred talents "out of the amount left to him." How much, then, did Herod give to Augustus? One thousand talents? One thousand and fifty talents? Fifteen hundred talents? Fifteen hundred and fifty talents, or even more?

My point is that, even if we were to assume that Augustus received precise information about Herod's annual revenue, Josephus's figures do not appear to represent a faithful transmission of that information. The sums reported by Josephus are best received as approximations, by Josephus himself or by his various sources, of the values of Herod's bequests to the members of his family.[347] We cannot, therefore, with the sources now available, determine accurately how much income Herod derived from his kingdom.

Further still, Josephus's language consistently suggests that the incomes he allocates to Herod's sons were tax revenues to be derived from the respective territorial allotments. He, however, does not say which taxes. Herod, we have seen, must have collected vast sums from indirect taxes, particularly from duties and tolls. Josephus does not indicate what fraction of his allocations came from such taxes. We are left with two possibilities: If the sums represent overall tax revenues from the respective regions, then they must include indirect taxes. In this event, it would be impossible to know how much Herod and his heirs received in direct taxes and how much they collected in indirect taxes. Further, we would be unable to account for the revenues that were lost when Herod's important sources of indirect taxes, namely, Gaza (and probably Anthedon) were removed from Archelaus's territory. If, on the other hand, indirect taxes are not included in Josephus's figures, then we would have left out of the tally of Herod's income an essential source of his tax revenues.

Momigliano, probably aware of these problems, makes no reference to indirect taxes in his assessment of Herod's income, even though he ear-

345. That is, 250,000 pieces of coined silver each. Augustus is said to have given these sums to the daughters "in addition" to "the legacy" left to them by Herod in his will. See K. C. Hanson, "The Herodians and Mediterranean Kinship," *BTB* 20 (1990): 13; and Peter Richardson, *Herod*, 39.

346. A.J. 17.322: "To each of his two unmarried daughters, beside what their father left them, Caesar made an additional gift of two hundred and fifty thousand pieces of coined silver."

347. Peter Richardson, *Herod*, 24: "The sum of these figures approximated Herod's tax base and the relative wealth of each area."

lier recognized the importance, under Julius Caesar, of the tolls and duties paid at Joppa.[348] Caesarea and Anthedon, he claims, paid a minimum of taxes during Herod's lifetime, barely ten talents in all.[349] In his view, the revenues from Gaza, Gadara, and Hippus together would hardly have surpassed the sixty talents that Salome received from Azotus, Jamneia, and Phaselis.[350] Both of these views are unacceptable. It is indeed possible that the direct taxes paid to Herod by the inhabitants of these cities were small. The income from tolls and duties, however, would have been very significant. Anthedon probably was in operation soon after 23 B.C.E.[351] Although formally inaugurated in 10 B.C.E. (*A.J.* 16.136–41; *B.J.* 1.415), both the city of Caesarea and its harbor were in use already in 15 B.C.E.[352] Archelaus received Caesarea with its harbor in full operation. The Romans (our sources explicitly state) benefited from the tolls and duties collected at Gaza, following the city's annexation.[353]

In spite of Momigliano's conjectures, we know nothing actually about the taxes that Herod received from Samaria,[354] or from Gadara, Hippus, and Esbonitis. Consequently, we do not know how Archelaus's revenues differed from Herod's as a result of both the 25-percent reduction granted to Samaria and the removal of the three cities from Archelaus's domain. The revenues that Josephus attributes to Salome also raise some problems. Phaselis was not only a settlement; it was part of Herod's development of the palm groves in the Jordan valley.[355] We do not know how much of Salome's income came from the exploitation of the palm groves and how much she received in the forms of indirect and direct taxes. Besides, we cannot tell whether the palace in Ascalon, added to her estate by Augustus, was only a royal residence[356] or Herod's means

---

348. Momigliano, *Ricerche*, 14–15, 21–23. See the discussion in chapter 2.

349. *Momigliano, Ricerche*, 48–49.

350. Ibid., 46.

351. Roller (*Building Program*, 129) speculates that Herod's construction in the city might have consisted of minor repairs and might have been undertaken "probably after Marcus Agrippa's death in 12 B.C."

352. Josephus (*A.J.* 16.13) says that Herod received and entertained Agrippa and his Roman entourage at Caesarea, "at the harbour which had been constructed by him." A year later Herod, returning from Agrippa's Pontic campaign, "landed at Caesarea" (*A.J.* 16.62). Peter Richardson (*Herod*, 264) thinks that Herod departed from Caesarea in a newly constituted navy.

353. See above.

354. See Momigliano, *Ricerche*, 47.

355. Peter Richardson, *Herod*, 178: "Herod prized his huge royal estates in the Jericho area, from which he derived a substantial income. A new city to the north of Jericho, extensively irrigated, would have stimulated new agricultural developments to complement Jericho's riches and encourage new trade. It [Phaselis] was on an important north-south transportation route, easily accessible to Jerusalem."

356. So Momigliano claims (*Ricerche*, 46–47, n. 7): "ma si trattava di una abitazione

of maintaining a hold on family business interests in the city.[357] Salome also received a one-time cash legacy of fifty talents. Josephus's summary of her revenues is ambiguous. In *B.J.* 2.98 he writes that "her revenue from all sources amounting to sixty talents" (συνήγετο δ' ἐκ πάντων ἑξήκοντα προσόδου τάλαντα). According to *A.J.* 17.321, however: "Altogether, then, she had a revenue of sixty talents yearly" (ἦν δὲ καὶ ταύτῃ πρόσοδος ἐκ πάντων τάλαντα ἑξήκοντα ἐπ' ἔτος). The comment in *Antiquities* implies that Salome's "revenue of sixty talents yearly" was apart from her legacy of fifty talents.[358] Josephus does not say if Salome's revenue was derived from taxes.

In other words, even assuming the optimistic hypothesis that Josephus's numbers represent approximations of the value of Herod's bequests to his successors at the time of his death, we are ignorant of the relationship between these legacies and Herod's income. Moreover, it is impossible to determine what portions of the revenues were raised through direct taxes, and what parts accrued to their beneficiaries from indirect taxes and other sources.

Momigliano tried to show that the tax revenue of Herod's kingdom remained static from 47 B.C.E. to 4 B.C.E. Other scholars often transfer the same notion of a fixed income to the territories inherited by Herod's children. Hence, Schürer writes, "Archelaus was to derive from his territories an income of 600 talents, Antipas 200 talents, and Philip 100 talents."[359] According to Jones, Archelaus was faced with the following quandary:

> though his principality was the largest and by far the wealthiest—his revenue was 600 talents as against Antipas' 200 and Philip's 100—he had the unhappy distinction of possessing the capital of a much diminished kingdom. He was thus faced with the equally unpopular alternatives of either overburdening his principality with taxation in order to maintain the same scale of expenditure as his father or drastically reducing his establishment, thus causing wide-spread unemployment.[360]

If we assume that Archelaus's ethnarchy yielded a tax revenue of six hundred talents annually, Archelaus can be thought of as "overburdening his

---

regale (*Ant.*, XVII, 321: τὴν ἐν Ἀσκάλωνι βασίλειον οἴκησιν) e quindi il reddito doveva essere minimo."

357. Nothing is otherwise known of this property. For Herod's family connections with the "Arabs and Gazaeans and Ascalonites," see *A.J.* 14.10 and the discussion above.

358. See Peter Richardson, *Herod*, 40: "[Salome] was made ruler (*despotēs*) of three important cities (Jamnia/Yavneh, Azotus, Phaselis), was given a one-time gift and an annual revenue, and inherited the royal palace in Ashkelon." Momigliano, *Ricerche*, 46: "50 talenti delle tre città—Azotos, Iamnia e Phasaelis—cui redditi andavano a Salome."

359. Schürer, *History*, 1:333; Hoehner, *Herod Antipas*, 74–75: "As far as Antipas was concerned, Augustus allowed him to receive 200 talents for Galilee and Peraea."

360. Jones, *Herods*, 166.

principality with taxation" in one of two ways: either (1) the sum of six hundred talents constitutes an excessive tax burden for his territory, as it would have been under Herod; or (2) Archelaus needed to raise new tax revenues, over and above the designated six hundred talents. Jones does not say which of the two he has in mind. He is, therefore, also vague about what Archelaus's alternative tax policy could have been. By "drastically reducing his establishment," Archelaus could be said either to cut taxes and, thus, collect less than six hundred talents annually or to refuse to impose higher levels of taxation.

Jones's vagueness results from the fact that Archelaus's six hundred talents and the other amounts given by Josephus are phantom sums: Herod's actual tax revenues could have been more or they could have been less.[361] This is evident from what Josephus says of Agrippa I: he "derived as much revenue as possible from these territories, amounting to twelve million drachmas" (*A.J.* 19.352),[362] that is, twelve hundred talents, and apparently more than Herod's income. Forty-five years separated Agrippa's rule from his grandfather's. During this time Herod's successors had added their improvements to Herod's projects, which would have increased their tax bases and their overall revenues. Particular mention is made of Archelaus's village and estate in the Jordan valley; the cities of Tiberias and Sepphoris in Galilee (*A.J.* 18.27, 36–38; *B.J.* 2.168), Julia in Perea, all founded by Antipas; Caesarea in Paneas and Julias-Bethsaida in the lower Gaulanitis, both founded by Philip (*A.J.* 18.28; *B.J.* 2.168). Besides, Philip and Agrippa are said to have imposed taxes on the inhabitants of Batanea, who had been immune under Herod (*A.J.* 17.27–28).[363] Agrippa also had additional territory, Abila, northwest of Lebanon, which was given to him by Claudius.[364]

Six hundred, two hundred, one hundred, twelve hundred talents may very well represent Josephus's approximations of the annual incomes of Herod's successors at some point in their reigns.[365] It should

---

361. According to Jones (*Herods*, 166), Archelaus chose the course of "drastically reducing his establishment." Hoehner (*Herod Antipas*, 75 and n. 5) speculates that "[h]igh taxes may have been also a part of Archelaus' unbearable tyranny," but warns that this point "should not be pressed, for his deposition is adequately explained by the fact that he was a bad ruler." Smallwood (*Jews under Roman Rule*, 116), on the contrary and in line with Jones's views, thinks that Archelaus's reign was marked by "a personal lack of initiative, and economic stagnation in his ethnarchy may have contributed to the discontent which grew among his subjects through his reign."

362. *A.J.* 19.352: προσωδεύσατο δ' ὅτι πλείστας αὐτῶν προσφορὰς διακοσίας ἐπὶ χιλίαις μυριάδας.

363. See above.

364. *A.J.* 19.275: "But he [Claudius] also added Abila, which had been ruled by Lysanias, and all the land in the mountainous region of Lebanon as a gift out of his own territory."

365. Daniel R. Schwartz (*Agrippa I*, 112–13 and n. 22) argues that Agrippa's income

be evident, however, that these were not fixed incomes. Moreover, as with Herod and his sons, we cannot determine what percentage of Agrippa's revenue was derived from the Jewish portions of his extensive kingdom. Neither can we apportion his revenue according to his sources of income. The result is that in Agrippa's case, as in the cases of his predecessors, we do not know what Josephus means when he says that a territory "produced a revenue of . . . talents."

Since it is not known how much was paid by the Jews to Herod in taxes,[366] the attempts to evaluate, for the most part negatively, the impact of his tax policies on Jewish Palestine are at best impressionistic and fictional.[367] Hoehner gives a simple formulation of the first ground for the assessments: "Herod's building programme was so immense that taxes must have been heavy."[368] There is, in other words, a direct correlation between Herod's expenditure, if a value could be put on it, and the levels of direct taxation that Herod imposed on his Jewish subjects.[369] This connection is belied, however, by two considerations to which only brief attention needs to be paid in this study. (1) Herod had available to him a wide range of resources, apart from direct and indirect taxes.[370] (2) Herod's enterprises were not mere white elephants, and there exists an observable relationship between the expansion of his kingdom and the largesse of his undertakings.

(two thousand talents, according to his conversion of the drachma) is given for Agrippa's whole reign (see also pp. 150–51). In any event, the sum "simply indicates Josephus' calculations concerning Agrippa's potential income" (p. 151).

366. *Pace* the mostly fantastic speculations by Oakman, *Jesus and the Economic Questions*, 68–72.

367. Peter Richardson (*Herod*, 12–13) makes the same point about the many assessments of Herod's "personality." On scholarly debates about evaluating Herod's reign, see Daniel R. Schwartz, "On Abraham Schalit, Herod, Josephus, the Holocaust, Horst R. Moehring, and the Study of Ancient Jewish History," *Jewish History* 2 (1987): 9–13.

368. Hoehner, *Herod Antipas*, 75. See, among many other authors, Richard A. Horsley, *Galilee*, 218: "Herod's expenditures were obviously enormous. . . . Herod engaged in extensive building projects. . . . He made numerous gifts on a grand scale both to imperial figures and to Hellenistic cities. Some of the resources he needed to meet these huge expenses were derived from the extensive royal estates, including the highly profitable balsam plantation near Jericho. But most of his revenues were derived from the 'rich crops of the *chōra*' (*Ant* 15.109, 303). Herod's 'income' from all his territories amounted to over 900 talents annually toward the time of his death (*Ant.* 17.317–21)."

369. Richard A. Horsley (*Galilee*, 218–19) writes of Herod Antipas: "Such heavy taxation by a client-ruler continued under Antipas, whose revenue from Galilee and Perea was 200 talents a year. The rebuilding of one city and the foundation of a completely new one were ambitious projects for a ruler with such a limited revenue base. . . . The first part of his reign would have had a severely draining effect on the producers in villages and towns of Galilee and Perea, whose 'surplus' product was virtually his only economic base."

370. See especially Momigliano, *Ricerche*, 51–52; Jones, *Herods*, 91–92; Schalit, *König Herodes*, 257–62; Abel, *Histoire*, 1:382; Broshi, "Role of the Temple," 32–33; Gabba, "Finances," 160–69; Menahem Stern, "Herod," 260–61; Pastor, *Land and Economy*, 108–9.

The immensity of Herod's enterprises points not to crushing tax burdens, but rather to the prosperity of his realm and to his personal wealth. If, to take one critical example, the temple could have been rebuilt on the Herodian scale at the cost of taxing Jewish peasants, one would wonder why it had not been rebuilt by the pious Hasmoneans who ruled Judea for more than a 125 years.[371] The temple and many of Herod's other enterprises were paid for with funds from his personal resources, which included the following:

1. Family and personal wealth, to which, at the deaths of his brothers Phasael and Joseph,[372] Herod came into sole possession.[373] Herod's early involvement in the Roman administration of the province of Syria, within and beyond the confines of the Jewish state, gave him ample opportunity to be individually wealthy before coming to the throne. He was governor of Galilee and of Coele-Syria (and Samaria) under Julius Caesar, governor of Coele-Syria under Cassius, and tetrarch of the Jewish state under Antony.[374] As king, Herod, in an exchange of gifts, received from Augustus "half the revenue from the copper mines of Cyprus." Augustus also "entrusted him with the management of the other half" (*A.J.* 16.128).[375]

---

371. Goodman ("Pilgrimage Economy," 69) rightly points out that the basis for Jerusalem's evidently "exceptionally prosperous society . . . can hardly have been the exploitation of the agrarian hinterland in the Judean hills which, despite the panegyrical remarks of Josephus (*War* 3, 49–50), was too poor and too far from the coast for the encouragement of cash crops for interregional trade." Broshi ("Role of the Temple," 36) maintains that "the half-shekel due must have accounted for 10–15% of Herod's income" and therefore enabled him "to finance his grand designs." This is not credible. The temple tax was paid not to Herod but to the temple. If Herod, like some of the subsequent *praefecti* of Judea, had tried to appropriate the temple treasury for financing "state service," it would have been listed among his crimes. Herod, according to Josephus (*A.J.* 17.162), in the last days of his life lamented Jewish ingratitude for the fact that he himself had built the temple at great expense and adorned it with noteworthy dedicatory gifts, "whereas the Hasmoneans had been unable to do anything so great for the honour of God in the hundred and twenty-five years of their reign." As Peter Richardson (*Herod*, 185; also p. 247) points out, Herod's contribution to the rebuilding of the temple needs a complete work of its own.

372. Phasael died during the Parthian invasion in 40 B.C.E. (*A.J.* 14.367–68; *B.J.* 1.271–72). Joseph died in 38 B.C.E. in a battle against Antigonus (*A.J.* 14.448–50; *B.J.* 1.323–25). Herod was left with his last brother, Pheroras.

373. He removed a portion of his wealth to the safety of Idumea before his flight from the Parthians in 40 B.C.E. (*A.J.* 14.364; *B.J.* 1.268).

374. See above.

375. That was in 12 B.C.E. Herod is said to have presented Augustus with three hundred talents. Gabba ("Finances," 163 and n. 15, following Marquardt and T. R. S. Broughton) sees a business transaction in this exchange. Herod's three hundred talents would, in their view, have been a payment *una tantum* for the right to exploit the mines. According also to Schalit (*König Herodes*, 261), Herod obtained half of the copper mines "für die Summe von dreihundert Talenten." Josephus, however, places Herod's gift to Augustus in the context of the spectacles and doles that the emperor was giving to the

Herod probably received and managed other, less significant, imperial domains to his own profit.

2. The estate of the extinct Hasmonean dynasty, which Herod acquired, in cash,[376] treasures, land, and palaces. To these should be added the property confiscated from the members of the Jewish aristocracy who had been sympathetic to the Hasmoneans or were in other ways opposed to Herod (see *A.J.* 15.5–6; 17.307; *B.J.* 1.358–59; 2.84). He is likely also to have obtained the estate of the dynasts—Zenodorus, for instance, whose territories were added by Augustus to his domain.

3. Revenues from landed estates and other natural resources that Herod exploited. The issue of "private estates" in Jewish Palestine has remained contentious.[377] There can be no doubt, in any case, that Herod exploited sections of his kingdom, within and outside of Jewish Palestine, for his own profit. Best known are the balsam and palm estates in Jericho and Phaselis.[378] Herod appears to have owned and exploited landed properties in or near Arabia, part of which was rented as grazing land by the Arabs.[379] Proceeds from the royal exploitation of domains, mines, quarries and other natural resources within Herod's kingdom were for the king's revenues. When Josephus distinguishes between "public funds" and the king's "private" revenues, he means by the former only the temple treasury.[380] State revenues were one and the same as the king's wealth.

---

inhabitants of Rome. It is better to see here another example of the exchange of "gifts" that was an essential part of the "friendship" that bound Herod as a "client king" to the people of Rome and personally to the emperor. In Herod's case, the emperor always rewarded his "generosity" handsomely. See Marquardt, *Römische Staatsverwaltung*, 2:261, n. 1; T. Robert. S. Broughton, "Roman Asia Minor," in *An Economic Survey of Ancient Rome*, vol. 4 (ed. Tenney Frank; Baltimore, Md.: Johns Hopkins University Press, 1938), 651–52; see also Peter Richardson, *Herod*, 226–34, 278; Jacobson, "Client Kings," 25–27; Braund, *Rome and the Friendly King*, 183.

376. For instance, money (χρήματα), about three hundred talents, was left untouched in Jerusalem by the Parthians in 40 B.C.E. (*A.J.* 14.363; *B.J.* 1.268).

377. See Applebaum, "Judaea as a Roman Province," 2.8:355–95; Fiensy, *Social History*; Pastor, *Land and Economy*; Freyne, "Herodian Economics," 32–35. See also the literature cited in chapter 2.

378. With this foundation, Josephus says, Herod "made the surrounding region, formerly a wilderness, more productive through the industry of its inhabitants" (*A.J.* 16.145; 18.31; see *B.J.* 1.418; 2.167). Josephus calls it "the palm-groves of Phasaelis" (*B.J.* 2.167). Other indications by Josephus of royal land under Herod are vague. Herod is said to have left, in his penultimate will, "large tracts of territory" to his relatives (*B.J.* 1.646; see *A.J.* 17.147). He is supposed otherwise to have "dedicated groves and meadow-land" to communities, while "[m]any cities, as though they had been associated with his realm, received from him grants of land" (*B.J.* 1.422–23).

379. They withheld payment of rent when Herod was humiliated by Augustus for attacking them (*A.J.* 16.291).

380. See *A.J.* 14.113: "Now there is no public money among us except that which is God's" (ἡμῖν δὲ δημόσια χρήματα οὐκ ἔστιν ἢ μόνα τὰ τοῦ θεοῦ). Hence, Agrippa I initiated

4. That Herod earned revenues from money-lending ventures is known especially from his dealings with the Arabs. According to *A.J.* 16.343, he lent five hundred talents to the Arab viceroy Syllaeus.[381] In *A.J.* 16.279 Herod is said to have given sixty talents in loan to the Arab king Obadas through Syllaeus.[382] The terms of the loans were that when time for payment expired Herod "should have the right to recover the amount of the loan from all of Syllaeus' country" (*A.J.* 16.343).[383] Herod probably also lent money to other needy dignitaries and to cities. There is no direct evidence for this, however, except the numerous debts and taxes that Herod is said to have discharged. "[I]t was thus, for instance," Josephus writes, "that he lightened the burden of their annual taxes for the inhabitants of Phaselis, Balanea and various minor towns in Cilicia" (*B.J.* 1.428).[384] Gabba suggests that this passage "must be understood in the context of Herod's having had a concession from the Roman state to collect either the domain income (*vectigalia*) and/or the direct (*stipendium*) and indirect (*vectigalia*) taxes in these areas, and of his being able to afford the generosity of renouncing part of the proceeds."[385] This is not tenable.[386] Josephus's statement that Herod relieved communities of their "debts and taxes" most probably means that he paid off the money that they owed, as he did for the inhabitants of Chios in Asia.[387] Some of the

---

the rebuilding of the walls of Jerusalem "at the public expense," that is, with funds from the temple treasury (*A.J.* 19.326–27; see *B.J.* 2.218–19; 5.147–52; see Tacitus, *Hist.* 5.12).

381. Josephus uses the term ἐπίτροπος in *B.J.* 1.487. Strabo (*Geogr.* 16.4.23) also refers to him by this title. On Syllaeus, see *A.J.* 16.220–25; *B.J.* 1.487; Strabo (*Geogr.* 16.4.23–24); Bowersock, *Roman Arabia*, 46–53.

382. It is not clear from Josephus's account whether the same loan is meant.

383. Mediation by the governors of Syria, Saturninus and Volumnius, failed to persuade the Arabs to repay the loan. This default on the loan is given as a reason why Herod invaded Arab territory in about 9 B.C.E. (*A.J.* 16.280–85, 343–55; see *B.J.* 1.574–77). Jones (*Herods*, 91–92) thinks that Herod "had reduced the Nabatean kingdom to economic vassalage." This seems to be an exaggeration. See Peter Richardson, *Herod*, 279–81; Kasher, *Jews, Idumaeans and Ancient Arabs*, 156–73.

384. *B.J.* 1.428: καθάπερ Φασηλίταις καὶ Βαλανεώταις καὶ τοῖς περὶ τὴν Κιλικίαν πολιχνίοις τὰς ἐτησίους εἰσφορὰς ἐπεξεκούφισεν.

385. Gabba, "Finances," 163.

386. Gabba links the concession to collect taxes to Josephus's notice that Herod had been associated by Augustus with the procurators of Syria (*A.J.* 15.360; *B.J.* 1.399). He cites Momigliano (*Ricerche*, 54), in whose view this function might imply that Herod was involved with the collection of taxes in Syria. As we observed above, this is an improbable reading of Josephus's passage. As for Gabba's argument from Josephus's terminology, it suffices to reiterate that terminological precision, in Josephus or in other ancient authors, is a poor guide in the effort to define specific kinds of payment. In fact, in *B.J.* 1.428, Josephus uses the Greek words φόρος and εἰσφορά interchangeably; he writes in the first part: "The enumeration of the debts and taxes discharged by himself would be endless" (ἀνήνυτον ἂν εἴη χρεῶν διαλύσεις ἢ φόρων ἐπεξιέναι).

387. Εἰσφορά is Josephus's term for tax in this passage (A.J.16.26): διέλυσε δὲ Χίοις τὰ πρὸς τοὺς Καίσαρος ἐπιτρόπους χρήματα καὶ τῶν εἰσφορῶν ἀπήλλαξε. See Otto, "Herodes," col.

debts he forgave, however, might have been from money that he himself had lent.

There now exists a sizable body of scholarly debate about the "strategy and rationale" for Herod's very complex and daunting program of foundations and munificences. Josephus introduces his list of Herod's enterprises with the statement: "Thenceforth he advanced to the utmost prosperity; his noble spirit rose to greater heights, and his lofty ambition was mainly directed to works of piety" (*B.J.* 1.400).[388] He then goes on to list the projects according to various kinds of "piety" that motivated Herod: piety toward Judaism and its temple; piety toward his imperial patrons (Antony, Augustus, and Agrippa), piety toward the members of his family; and piety toward his own self (*B.J.* 1.401–21).[389] Following Josephus's lead, at least in part, scholars have often viewed Herod's enterprises as "memorials" (see μνήμης in *B.J.* 1.419), "unproductive monuments,"[390] undertaken out of paranoia and megalomania. More recent and detailed studies of these projects have shown that Josephus's categorizations of Herod's motives, and the negative scholarly evaluations that depend on them, are all too simplistic.

In addition to the dynamics of Hellenistic kingship and the demands on client kings to participate in imperial, international politics,[391] economic needs and interests were at the heart of many of Herod's foundations within and without his kingdom. Most significant among those within his realm are the facilities in Caesarea, Sebaste, Agrippias, Antipatris, and Phaselis. As Peter Richardson suggests, these projects and numerous others that Herod undertook in the 20s and afterwards fell within an overall strategy of stimulating the economy of Judea, especially by opening up the territory to trade and by providing employment.[392] To this list must be added the temple, one of the greatest adornments of its time and certainly one of the reasons why Pliny thought that Jerusalem in the first century was "by far the most famous city of the East and not of Judea only" (*Nat.* 5.70).[393]

73; Schalit, *König Herodes*, 417; and Roller, *Building Program*, 127–28 and n. 15. Gabba ("Finances," 163, n. 16) rejects this understanding of the text. See also Peter Richardson, *Herod*, 272–73 and n. 46.

388. *B.J.* 1.400: ἔνθεν ἐπὶ πλεῖστον μὲν εὐδαιμονίας προύκοψεν, εἰς μεῖζον δ᾽ ἐξήρθη φρόνημα καὶ τὸ πλέον τῆς μεγαλονοίας ἐπέτεινεν εἰς εὐσέβειαν.

389. Josephus (*B.J.* 1.422–28) then goes on to catalogue Herod's gifts "to the whole world." See Peter Richardson, *Herod*, 191; also Roller, *Building Program*, 260. Roller points out that Josephus's list—probably originating from Nicholaus of Damascus—"shows the type of philosophical cataloguing in which Hellenistic historians delighted."

390. Applebaum, "Economic Life," 666.

391. Braund, *Rome and the Friendly King*, 75–80; Jacobson, "Client Kings," 31–33; Roller, *Building Program*, 259.

392. Peter Richardson, *Herod*, 188–91, 193–94.

393. Pliny, *Nat.* 5.70: "Hierosolyma longe clarissima urbium Orientis non Iudaeae

It is in connection with his projects on the Temple Mount that we have Herod's only comments on his motivations for his building enterprises (*A.J.* 15.382–87). He reportedly told his Jewish subjects that his projects had brought benefits (including security) not only to himself, but also to all of them. He had been mindful of their needs. The buildings in Judea and beyond had been a "most beautiful adornment" that has "embellished our nation." His projects on the Temple Mount, he said, would be "the most pious and beautiful of our time." He was now able to undertake this enterprise because he had "brought the Jewish nation to such a state of prosperity as it has never known before," since it had enjoyed "a long period of peace and an abundance of wealth and great revenues."[394]

Security, adornment, piety, and the expression of prestige and prosperity; none of these motivations should be isolated from the others or from the economic objectives of his enterprises.[395] Reportedly undertaken in order to rectify his and his predecessors' long neglect of "pious duty" (*A.J.* 15.386–87), Herod's buildings on the Temple Mount were a beautiful tribute to world Judaism, a place of worship, and a vast economic enterprise. At its construction and for more than eighty years afterwards work on the temple provided employment for thousands of Jewish builders and artisans. In about 64 C.E., when it appeared that all

---

modo . . . ." Josephus himself comments that the three towers built by Herod into the walls of Jerusalem were "for magnitude, beauty and strength without their equal in the world." Herod had built them because of "his innate magnanimity and his pride in the city" (*B.J.* 5.161–62). In the speech announcing the project to rebuild the temple, Herod points at "the various buildings which we have erected in our country and in the cities of our land and in those of acquired territories," as self-evident proof of the prosperity of the nation (*A.J.* 15.384). Recent archaeological excavations have revealed the extent and splendor of Herod's architectural undertakings on the Temple Mount, elsewhere in Jerusalem, and in Palestine generally. A complete listing of the extensive publications in this field cannot be given here. On Jerusalem and the temple, see, among others, Kathleen M. Kenyon, "Some Aspects of the Impact of Rome on Palestine," *JRAS* 2 (1970): 181–91; Benjamin Mazar, *The Mountain of the Lord* (Garden City, N.Y.: Doubleday, 1975); idem, "Herodian Jerusalem in the Light of the Excavations South and South-West of the Temple Mount," *IEJ* 28 (1978): 230–37; Meir Ben-Dov, *In the Shadow of the Temple: The Discovery of Ancient Jerusalem* (trans. Ina Friedman; Jerusalem: Keter, 1982; repr., New York: Harper & Row, 1985); N. Avigad, *Archaeological Discoveries in the Jewish Quarter of Jerusalem: Second Temple Period* (Jerusalem: Israel Exploration Society & the Israel Museum, 1976); Peter Richardson, *Herod*, 185–86, 195; Roller, *Building Program*, 176–78; also Ephraim Stern et al., eds. *NEAEHL* (4 vols.; Jerusalem: Israel Exploration Society & Carta, 1993), 2:719–47.

394. On the speech, see Roller, *Building Program*, 260–61; also Peter Richardson, *Herod*, 247–48.

395. For some classifications of the motives for Herod's buildings, see Peter Richardson, *Herod*, 191–96; see Ehud Netzer, "Herod's Building Projects: State Necessity or Personal Need?" in *The Jerusalem Cathedra*, vol. 1 (ed. Lee I. Levine; Jerusalem: Yad Izḥak Ben-Zvi Institute, 1981), 55–60.

work on the temple had been completed, Josephus says that Agrippa II consented that the eighteen thousand workers who were thus about to lose their employment (*A.J.* 20.219–22)[396] be paid out of temple funds to pave the streets of Jerusalem with white stones.[397] Herod made provisions for commercial activities in the temple complex.[398] The most important economic value of the huge expansion of the temple complex remains, however, that its prestige drew hundreds of thousands of Jews each year from Palestine and the Diaspora to Jerusalem on pilgrimage. The pilgrims from the Diaspora brought to Jerusalem large sums of money, collected abroad, in temple taxes and votive gifts. Everyone spent money in Jerusalem and the surrounding territory for lodging, food, and on whatever else was needed for themselves, and for sacrifices and worship.[399] Herod's temple was a national treasury, an employer of tens of thousands of Jewish builders, tradesmen, and craftsmen and an incentive to national and international trade. It became, for these reasons, one of the most important factors in the economy of Jerusalem and the Jewish state.[400]

The view that Herod's buildings and munificences were not paid for principally by the direct taxes he imposed upon Jewish peasants is borne out by the clear correlation that exists between the chronology of his most extensive projects and the dates of the expansion of his kingdom. Between 37 B.C.E. and 30 B.C.E. Herod's territory was limited to Judea, Galilee, Samaria, Idumea, and Perea. Besides, sometime after 37 B.C.E. Herod lost Joppa and complete control over the lucrative Jericho estates. During this period, his principal projects were the following:

1. The fortress Alexandrium was restored by Herod in 39/38 B.C.E. while he was still reconquering his kingdom (*A.J.* 14.419; *B.J.* 1.308).[401]

---

396. Work on the temple continued after Herod's death. In *A.J.* 15.391 Josephus mentions that the foundation of the temple had to be raised "in the time of Nero." According to *B.J.* 5.36, before the revolt of 66 C.E., "the people and the chief priests" decided to underpin the temple and raise it. Agrippa II "at immense labour and expense, brought down from Mount Libanus the materials for that purpose, beams that for straightness and size were a sight to see." See also John 2:20.

397. Agrippa refused the request to raise the height of the east portico.

398. See Peter Richardson, *Herod*, 188.

399. See Goodman, "Pilgrimage Economy"; Lee I. Levine, "Second Temple Jerusalem: A Jewish City in the Greco-Roman Orbit," in *Jerusalem: Its Sanctity and Centrality to Judaism, Christianity, and Islam* (ed. Lee I. Levine; New York: Continuum, 1999), 60–66.

400. See the discussion of the temple in Sanders, *Judaism*, 47–102, in particular pp. 83–92.

401. Work on the fortress was actually done by Herod's brother Pheroras. See Roller, *Building Program*, 87, 129–31; Peter Richardson, *Herod*, 198.

2. Antonia, the Hasmonean fortress *Bari*, was rebuilt by Herod, soon after 37 B.C.E., into a fortress/palace, which Herod named after his patron, Antony (*A.J.* 15.409).[402]

3. The fortress Hyrcania had been the refuge for Antigonus's sister, and Herod did not capture it until sometime before 31 B.C.E. It is possible that at about this time Herod began the work (which would last for the next fifteen years) of embellishing it (*B.J.* 1.364).[403]

4. Masada, although it was certainly refortified by Herod early, its embellishment belongs to the later and more opulent period of Herod's reign.[404]

5. Macherus, leveled by Gabinius, might have been refortified during the early years of Herod's reign but, like Masada, it was adorned much later.[405]

6. Cypros (*A.J.* 16.143; *B.J.* 1.407, 417) and the Hasmonean palace in Jericho were refortified by Herod probably before 30 B.C.E. The palace was the scene of the murder (by drowning) of Herod's brother-in-law Aristobulus III in about 35 B.C.E. (*A.J.* 15.53–56; *B.J.* 1.437).[406]

---

402. See *A.J.* 18.92; *B.J.* 1.401; 5.238–46. *A.J.* 15.292 and *B.J.* 1.401 imply that the fortress was Herod's palace until he built a new palace some time later. See L.-H. Vincent, "L'Antonia, palais primitif d'Hérode," *RB* 61 (1954): 87–107; Roller, *Building Program*, 87, 175–6; Peter Richardson, *Herod*, 197.

403. See Roller, *Building Program*, 170–71; Peter Richardson, *Herod*, 198; contra Jones (*Herods*, 75), who thinks that this fortress had already been restored by 35/34 B.C.E. when Herod was summoned by Antony to Laodicea.

404. On Herodian Masada, see *B.J.* 7.285–303. Josephus is clear that Masada was refurbished and furnished with weapons and food "as a refuge for himself" against Jewish opposition and, especially, against Cleopatra's ambition. Work on the fortress, therefore, goes back to the period before 31 B.C.E., probably as a matter of first priority, given that Herod had found secure refuge there for his family in 40 B.C.E. In 30 B.C.E. he left his family there again when he went to meet Octavian and an uncertain future (*A.J.* 14.361–62, 390–91, 397–98; 15.184). Yigael Yadin (*Masada: Herod's Fortress and the Zealots' Last Stand* [New York: Random House, 1966], 11) dates its refortification to the period between 36 and 30 B.C.E. See Roller, *Building Program*, 187–90; Peter Richardson, *Herod*, 198; also Louis H. Feldman, "Masada: A Critique of Recent Scholarship," in *Christianity, Judaism and Other Greco-Roman Cults: Studies for Morton Smith at Sixty* (ed. Jacob Neusner; Leiden: Brill, 1975), 3:219–48.

405. According to *B.J.* 7.172–77, Herod built Macherus as a fortification against Arabia. Abel (*Géographie*, 2:371) dates its reconstruction to the period between 25 and 13 B.C.E. Peter Richardson (*Herod*, 198) also postulates a date in the 20s B.C.E. See, however, Roller, *Building Program*, 184–85.

406. Peter Richardson (*Herod*, 198, 199) dates the fortress Cypros to the 30s B.C.E. and the reconstruction of the palace to sometime between 37 and 35 B.C.E. Roller (*Building Program*, 171, 182–83) thinks that Herodian projects in Jericho might not have begun until after 30 B.C.E., when Herod received back full ownership of the territory. He (p. 88), however, considers Cypros and "Herodeion, in Peraia" to date probably from the early period.

Herod's building program, as it has been noted, began slowly.[407] In the seven years between 37 and 30 B.C.E. Herod rebuilt some existing fortresses in his kingdom and refurbished some palaces. He founded no city, nor did he build any civil structure in his kingdom or any building outside his realm. During this period he was clearly preoccupied with security from both internal and external opposition. It is from his activities during these years that the charge of paranoia as a motivation for his building program comes. This charge is exaggerated, given that Herod did not afterwards continue to fortify his territory.[408] In comparison with his later enterprises, Herod's early projects betray the economic constraints under which he worked.[409] Securing his kingdom, a frontier of the Roman Empire, was all he had the resources to achieve.

The major phase of Herod's building program began in 27 B.C.E. with the foundation of Samaria/Sebaste and accelerated in the late 20s and early 10s to dazzling speed and proportions. Work on Sebaste and the other foundations was initiated at least three years after Octavian had greatly expanded Herod's kingdom in 30 B.C.E. (and again in 23 B.C.E.). With these new territories, Herod had available to him the revenues derived not only from a tax base that extended beyond Judea, but especially from the estates and from tolls and duties collected in the cities and trade routes that he now controlled.[410]

The second ground for the negative evaluations of Herod's tax poli-

407. See Roller, *Building Program*, 87–8.

408. The accusation derives to a large degree from the interpretation that Josephus gives to Herod's building projects that he gathers together in *A.J.* 15.292–98. The passage begins with a long list of fortresses. He writes with regard to the building of Samaria-Sebaste (*A.J.* 15.296–98): "And at this time, being eager to fortify Samaria, he arranged to have settled in it many of those who had fought as his allies in war . . . . This he did because of his ambition to erect it as a new (city) . . . and even more because he made his ambitious scheme a source of security to himself . . . . He surrounded the city with a strong wall . . . and seeing the necessity of security, he made it a first-class fortress by strengthening its outer walls." Caesarea, he says (*A.J.* 15.293), was built by Herod as "a fortress for the entire nation." Kasher (*Jews and Hellenistic Cities*, 200–201) commenting on these passages, postulates that Herod built the two cities "on the basis of an obvious geo-strategic concept. According to that concept, control of the Sebaste-Caesarea axis and the Samaria region would gain Herod greater internal security. . . ." It is very doubtful, however, that Herod's urban projects in both cities and elsewhere, Josephus notwithstanding, had military or security purposes. See Peter Richardson, *Herod*, 225.

409. Roller (*Building Program*, 87–88) finds an explanation in the political instability in Herod's kingdom and the insecurity resulting from the intrigues of Antony and Cleopatra.

410. In the general context of Herod's "ambitious" projects and the "generosity" of his benefactions, Josephus claims, "Caesar himself and Agrippa often remarked that the extent of Herod's realm was not equal to his magnanimity, for he deserved to be king of all Syria and of Egypt" (*A.J.* 16.141). There is a clear connection between the extent of one's territory and the resources one commands.

cies is formulated (also simply) by Menahem Stern: "we hear of grave complaints concerning the heavy taxes which weighed upon the people in Herod's reign. They were undoubtedly heavy. . . ."[411] The "complaints" against Herod's taxes are contained in three segments of Josephus's works and are mostly related to the end of Herod's life. The first set of complaints is in the demands made by the Jews to Archelaus after Herod died (*A.J.* 17.204–5; *B.J.* 2.4). The second set is in the speech by the Jewish embassy to Augustus (*A.J.* 17.306–8; *B.J.* 2.85–86). The third is in Josephus's summaries of Herod's legacy (*A.J.* 16.154–56; 17.191; 19.329).

A detailed analysis of these various negative assessments must be undertaken within a study of their contexts and of Josephus's sources.[412] Such an investigation is well beyond the scope of our present study. Nevertheless, it is clear that what Josephus writes about Herodian taxation is part of Josephus's and his sources' polemics against Herod. The charges of economic mismanagement stand in stark contrast to Josephus's narrative of events, and to many other passages in which Josephus celebrates the prosperity and benefits of Herod's rule.[413] Hence, Josephus sums up Herod's life by writing (*A.J.* 17.191) that "[h]e was a man who was cruel to all alike and one who easily gave in to anger and was contemptuous of justice. And yet he was as greatly favoured by fortune as any man has ever been . . . ." This image of Herod contrasts sharply with that of the man who, Josephus says in *B.J.* 1.400, "advanced to the utmost prosperity; his noble spirit rose to greater heights, and his lofty ambition (μεγαλονοίας, or "noble generosity") was mainly directed to works of piety." This is the Herod, Josephus says (*B.J.* 1. 428–30), whose "noble generosity (μεγαλονοίας) was thwarted by the fear of exciting either jealousy or the suspicion of entertaining some higher ambition," whose "genius was matched by his physical constitution."[414]

Josephus's personal explanation (*A.J.* 16.150–59) of what he sees as Herod's conflicting character offers some insight into the causes of the polemics against Herod and the charges of maladministration. While there might be some truth to the view that Herod was in conflict with his Jewish subjects because they failed to indulge his craving to be honored,[415] Josephus's objection to Herod's economic policy is that:

---

411. Menahem Stern, "Herod," 259 and n. 3. He cites *A.J.* 17.308 and *B.J.* 2.85–86.

412. See comments, for instance, in Cohen, *Josephus in Galilee and Rome,* 48–66; Lee I. Levine, *Jerusalem: Portrait of the City in the Second Temple Period, 538 B.C.E.–70 C.E.* (Philadelphia: Jewish Publication Society, 2002), 182–83.

413. See *A.J.* 15.109, 189, 311–12, 317–18, 383, 387; *B.J.* 1.387–88, 400.

414. See Peter Richardson, *Herod,* 191 and n. 59.

415. Herod expected the Jewish upper classes to make gifts to the distinguished guests who visited Judea (see, for instance, *B.J.* 1.512 and the accusation in *A.J.* 17.308). Josephus thinks that Herod expected his Jewish subjects to give him "the very same attentions which

> since he [Herod] was involved in expenses greater than his means, he was compelled to be harsh toward his subjects, for the great number of things on which he spent money as gifts to some caused him to be the source of harm to those from whom he took this money. And though he was aware of being hated because of the wrongs that he had done his subjects, he decided that it would not be easy to mend his evil ways—that would have been unprofitable in respect of revenue—, and, instead, countered their opposition by seizing upon their ill-will as an opportunity for satisfying his wants. (*A.J.* 16.154–55)

Herod, in other words, despoiled his (Jewish) subjects for the sake of his expenditure in "gifts" to individuals and communities outside of Judea. He operated a "tax-and-spend" economic policy for the benefit of "foreigners and those who were unattached to him."[416]

This, in essence, is also the charge against Herod that the Jewish embassy brings to Augustus:

> For he had tortured not only the persons of his subjects, but also their cities; and while he crippled the towns in his own dominion, he embellished those of other nations, lavishing the life-blood of Judea on foreign communities. In place of their ancient prosperity and ancestral laws, he had sunk the nation to poverty and the last degree of iniquity. (*B.J.* 2.85–86)

Further:

> To be precise, he had not ceased to adorn neighbouring cities that were inhabited by foreigners although this led to the ruin and disappearance of cities located in his own kingdom. He had indeed reduced the entire nation to helpless poverty after taking it over in as flourishing a condition as few ever know. (A.J. 17.307)[417]

---

he showed to his superiors" by offering him the same gifts as he himself gave to others. However, Josephus says, the Jews "found it impossible to flatter the king's ambition with statues or temples or such tokens" because "the Jewish nation is by law opposed to all such things and is accustomed to admire righteousness rather than glory" (*A.J.* 16.157–58). On the conflict that might have resulted from Jewish rejection of wealth as a status indicator, and of "evergetism" as a means of earning political and social prestige, see Goodman, *Ruling Class of Judaea*, 124–33; and idem, "Origins," 39–53. For the role of evergetism in the Greco-Roman world, see Paul Veyne, *Le pain et le cirque: sociologie historique d'un pluralisme politique* (Paris: Éditions du Seuil, 1976).

416. See *A.J.* 16.159. Josephus's reflection comes at the end of his list of the benefactions that Herod "conferred on the cities in Syria and throughout Greece and on whatever places he may have happened to visit" (*A.J.* 16.146–49).

417. Josephus reports that Herod's son, Alexander, hoped to escape condemnation for killing his father by bringing similar charges against Herod before Augustus. According to the speech attributed to Alexander by Eurycles, "he would first proclaim to the world the

There is plenty of archaeological and literary evidence, including Josephus's own works, which shows that Herod adorned cities outside of his realm as well as cities within his kingdom that his observant Jewish subjects would have considered foreign cities. There is, therefore, much basic truth to the complaint. The connection that is made, however, between Herod's projects in "foreign cities" and his impoverishment of Judea is invidious. First, the Judea over which Herod became king in 40 B.C.E. was not "in as flourishing a condition as few ever know"; the conditions in the country at the end of Herod's life cannot be compared, therefore, with nostalgia for the territory's "ancient prosperity."

Second, it is certainly false that Herod built and adorned foreign cities, whereas he abandoned the cities within his kingdom to "ruin and disappearance." Josephus expresses this view in the last of his summaries of Herod's reign (*A.J.* 19.329):

> It was generally admitted that he was on more friendly terms with Greeks than with Jews. For instance, he adorned the cities of foreigners by giving them money, building baths and theatres, erecting temples in some and porticoes in others, whereas there was not a single city of the Jews on which he deigned to bestow even minor restoration or a gift worth mentioning.

The accusation is as curious as it is false, seeing that Josephus himself refutes it. Most of Herod's enterprises, and all of his most significant projects, were situated in Judea and in the adjacent territories that formed part of his kingdom.[418] If Herod took something of "the life-blood of Judaea" in taxes, he also spent enormous sums of money in the territory, much more than he is known to have spent in foreign nations. His expenditures outside of his domain were often in areas with large communities of Diaspora Jews. These benefactions could not have been the cause of Judea being reduced to "helpless poverty."[419]

The constant element in these charges of maladministration is the perception that Herod visited a twofold woe on the Jewish people: he overthrew their "ancestral laws," replacing them with "the last degree of iniquity," and he "lavished the life-blood of Judaea on foreign communi-

---

sufferings of his nation, bled to death by taxation, and then go on to describe the luxury and malpractices on which the money obtained by its blood was lavished, the characters of the men who had grown rich at his and his brother's expense, and the motives which had led to the favouritism shown to particular cities" (*B.J.* 1.524).

418. See Roller, *Building Program*, 128–213; Peter Richardson, *Herod*, 176–91, 197–201.

419. Peter Richardson, *Herod*, 31–32. Richardson (pp. 174–77, 201–2, 264–73) has shown that Herod's benefactions to Greek cities were directed mostly toward cities with large Jewish Diaspora populations. These benefactions were part of a calculated strategy of advancing Jewish interests in the Mediterranean world.

ties." Some of his Jewish subjects objected to Herod's benefactions, especially where these were seen to contravene Jewish law. This objection is turned into the accusation that he "crippled" his own kingdom through excessive taxation in order to enrich foreign nations. Josephus writes in the same vein about Herod's great grandson, Agrippa II, and his benefactions to Berytus: "He thus transferred to that place well-nigh all the ornaments of the kingdom. The hatred of his subjects for him consequently increased because he stripped them of their possessions to adorn a foreign city" (*A.J.* 20.211–12).[420]

What Josephus says of Herod and Agrippa II may be compared with what he says about Agrippa I, the latter's father. Agrippa I probably raised much more revenue than Herod did from the kingdom (*A.J.* 19.352).[421] He imposed taxes on territories that had been immune from taxation under Herod (*A.J.* 17.28).[422] We learn also that Agrippa was more spendthrift and extravagant than his grandfather. Both were equally φιλότιμος and equally rejoiced in εὐφημία.[423] Both spent profligately on their Roman patrons.[424] Agrippa indulged in the same kinds of objectionable activities in the Greek cities as Herod did, and in very significant ways he went even further from Jewish custom than Herod had gone.[425] His

420. This passage comes in the midst of Josephus's description of Agrippa II's actions in Judea under Albinus (governor from 62 to 64 C.E.). Although Agrippa was not king of Judea, the cities Tiberias and Traricheae (in Galilee), and Julia (in Perea) were given to him by Nero (*A.J.* 20.159; *B.J.* 2.252). The subjects of Agrippa's "kingdom," are very likely Jews. See Daniel R. Schwartz, *Agrippa I*, 157 and n. 41. In *Vita* 52, Josephus reports the rumor that Agrippa would be put to death by Nero "on the indictment of the Jews." See Braund, *Rome and the Friendly King*, 66–67.

421. See the discussion above.

422. See above. It is noteworthy that in spite of the reportedly heavy taxes that Agrippa and his son imposed on them, the inhabitants of Batanea apparently remained tenaciously faithful to the two kings, as may be seen by the events during the revolt of 66 C.E. (*A.J.* 17.29–31; *B.J.* 2.421, 481–83, 556; *Vita* 46–61, 177–84, 407–9).

423. Agrippa I was hailed as a god in Caesarea. He died soon after (*A.J.* 19.344–50; see Acts 12:20–23).

424. See Josephus's lengthy description of Agrippa's extravagance in *A.J.* 18.147–237.

425. On Agrippa's iconic coins, see Madden, *Jewish Coinage*, 103–11; J. Meyshan, "The Coinage of Agrippa the First," *IEJ* 4 (1954): 186–200; Ya'akov Meshorer, *Jewish Coins of the Second Temple Period* (trans. I. H. Levine; Tel-Aviv: Am Hassefer & Masada, 1967), 70–80, 138–41; Schürer, *History*, 1:451 and n. 40. Agrippa placed his own head on coins, the first of the Herods (and any Jewish ruler) to do so. A coin figuring himself/Tyche holding palm branch and rudder has also been found in Meiron. See Joyce Raynor and Ya'akov Meshorer. *The Coins of Ancient Meiron* (Meiron Excavation Project; Winona Lake, Ind.: ASOR/Eisenbrauns, 1988), 24, 127. On Herod's coins see Peter Richardson, *Herod*, 211–15; Donald T. Ariel, "The Jerusalem Mint of Herod the Great: A Relative Chronology," *INJ* 14 (2000–2002): 99–124. Agrippa I erected statues of members of his family, and possibly of himself, outside the Jewish territory under his rule. At his death the statues of his daughters were desecrated in Caesarea and Samaria-Sebaste (*A.J.* 19.356–57). See Daniel R. Schwartz, *Agrippa I*, 130–34.

only recorded building activity in Judea, the fortification and extension of the walls of Jerusalem, was undertaken with the use of public (temple) funds. The project remained unfinished by the order of Emperor Claudius.[426] Agrippa managed his estate worse than Herod had done.[427]

Yet Josephus contrasts Agrippa I with Herod:

> Now King Agrippa was by nature generous in his gifts and made it a point of honour to be high-minded towards gentiles; and by expending massive sums he raised himself to high fame. He took pleasure in conferring favours and rejoiced in popularity, thus being in no way similar in character to Herod, who was king before him. The latter had an evil nature, relentless in punishment and unsparing in action against the objects of his hatred. (*A.J.* 19.328)

Whereas Herod was seen to have lavished his resources on foreign nations and done nothing for the Jews that was worth mentioning, "Agrippa, on the contrary, had a gentle disposition and he was a benefactor to all alike. He was benevolent to those of other nations and exhibited his generosity to them also; but to his compatriots he was proportionately more generous and more compassionate" (*A.J.* 19.330).

The public perceptions of the two kings by some of their Jewish subjects stood at opposite ends of the spectrum. The reason for the perception was not the respective tax policies of the two rulers and their contributions to the economy of the Jewish state. On the contrary, the policies and contributions were evaluated in light of the perceptions. Agrippa, in Josephus's view, could do nothing wrong.[428] The only Jewish protest that Josephus records against him, by a certain Simon who questioned the

---

426. *A.J.* 19.326–27; *B.J.* 2.218–19; 5.147–52; see above. Tacitus (*Hist.* 5.12) writes, however: "Moreover, profiting by the greed displayed during the reign of Claudius, they had bought the privilege of fortifying their city, and in time of peace had built walls as if for war." See Daniel R. Schwartz, *Agrippa I*, 140–44.

427. Herod, when he died, left behind thousands of talents in cash and treasures. Agrippa left behind a trail of debts. Josephus is laconic on the issue: "he borrowed much, for, owing to his generosity, his expenditures were extravagant beyond his income, and his ambition knew no bounds of expense" (*A.J.* 19.352). "From so extensive a realm wealth soon flowed in to Agrippa, nor was he long in expending his riches" (*B.J.* 2.218). Momigliano (*Ricerche*, 80) sees in Agrippa's maladministration the reason why his kingdom was absorbed into the province of Syria after his death in 44 C.E. See Jones, *Herods*, 213; Daniel R. Schwartz, *Agrippa I*, 149–53.

428. See Jones, *Herods*, 212: "Agrippa could do with approbation what for Herod was wicked impiety." Jones argues that between the reign of Herod and the reign of Agrippa the Jewish "public sentiment" had changed and that, consequently, at least some Jews "were now prepared to allow that a man might be a good Jew and yet conform, at any rate outside Judaea, with the ways of the world."

king's religious credentials, is offered by Josephus as an example of Agrippa's reconciliatory character (*A.J.* 19.332–34). Josephus sees nothing contrary to the law about Agrippa's building of a theater and other structures in Berytus or in Agrippa's attendance at theaters there and elsewhere (*A.J.* 19.335–37).[429] In Josephus's view, Agrippa's provision of fourteen hundred gladiators, for fights in the amphitheater in Berytus, was an illustration of the king's "noble generosity." Such gladiatorial combats were not reprehensible, since they led to the annihilation of criminals "so that while they were receiving their punishment, the feats of war might be a source of entertainment in peace-time" (*A.J.* 19.337).[430]

Agrippa's reign, therefore, is viewed as a period of prosperity for the Jews, while Herod is said to have taxed the Jews into misery.[431] When Agrippa died, there were apparently neither demands for tax reductions nor Jewish delegations to Claudius decrying Agrippa's excesses.[432]

Agrippa was not perceived as a Jewish king who disregarded Jewish law; Herod was. The complaint against Herod was that he spent Jewish resources outside Judea on projects that were not sanctioned by the Law. Josephus actually never says that Herod's taxes were per se "heavy," in the same way that he says that Cassius's exactions in 43 B.C.E. were beyond the people's ability to pay.[433] The Jewish envoys to Augustus

---

429. Agrippa I continued the games instituted by Herod in Caesarea, and he attended them (*A.J.* 19.343–45). Herod, on the contrary, was said to have introduced "practices not in accord with their custom, by which their way of life would be totally altered, and [for] his behaving in appearance as the king but in reality as the enemy of the whole nation" (*A.J.* 15.281). An assassination plot was hatched against him because of the images on the trophies in the theater that Herod is said to have built in Jerusalem (see *A.J.* 15.276–91).

430. Josephus writes concerning Herod's provision of gladiatorial combats: "When the practice began of involving them [exotic animals] in combat with one another or setting condemned men to fight against them . . . to the natives it meant an open break with the customs held in honour by them. For it seemed glaring impiety to throw men to wild beasts for the pleasure of other men as spectators, and it seemed a further impiety to change their established ways for foreign practices" (*A.J.* 15.274–75).

431. Thus, Aharoni and Avi-Yonah, *Atlas*, 185: "his reign was regarded as the last peak in the Second Temple period, before disaster overcame the nation." Menahem Stern ("Herod," 259–60) suggests that the increase in revenue under Agrippa "can be partly explained by the development of additional agricultural areas of the kingdom." Under Herod, he adds, the "Jewish peasantry bore the main weight of taxation." Stern offers no evidence either for the agricultural plots developed by Agrippa or for any tax reform inaugurated by Agrippa that would have redistributed the tax burden "equally among all parts of the population."

432. The inhabitants of Caesarea and Samaria-Sebaste reveled at his death. Josephus (*A.J.* 19.356–59) thinks that this reaction was unjust; both cities, he says, had forgotten the king's benefactions. It is probable, however, that the Greek inhabitants of Agrippa's kingdom, unlike some of his Jewish subjects, paid attention to the consequences of his administration of their territory and reacted to his death with celebrations.

433. See chapter 3.

reportedly accused Herod's tax officials of extortion.[434] Likewise, the sales taxes in Jerusalem were said to have been "ruthlessly exacted." Those who clamored to have these taxes removed by Archelaus also wanted him to "lighten" their annual taxes (*A.J.* 17.204–5; *B.J.* 2.4). However, this demand in itself is not an indication of the level of taxation. Augustus, as we noted, reduced the taxes of the region of Samaria by a quarter. This reduction was to reward the region's loyalty; the reduction is not evidence that the region's taxes were proportionately too heavy.

In the ancient world, no less than in our times, taxes were always an irksome nuisance to be avoided if possible. Colonial taxes, "exactions" paid to a government of occupation, the impositions of tyrannical and unpopular rulers, are by their very nature oppressive. Complaints about excessive taxation and economic maladministration are sometimes political, not economic, statements.[435] Herod was very unpopular with some Jews, whose views we read in Josephus's negative assessments of Herod's reign; they experienced the taxes they paid to him as an oppressive burden, regardless of the actual levels of taxation. Herod appears, nonetheless, not to have been insensitive to the economic needs of his kingdom and to the political implications, among his Jewish subjects, of his external expenditures. He had some grasp of the economics and politics of tax cuts.

Thus, Herod received no tax revenues for the year 28/27 B.C.E. Josephus says that on account of the drought and subsequent famine that afflicted Herod's kingdom that year, Herod was "deprived of the revenue [taxes] which he received from the (products of the) earth" (*A.J.* 15.303).[436] Instead, he undertook a national relief and economic recovery program

434. *A.J.* 17.308: "In addition to the collecting of the tribute [taxes] that was imposed on everyone each year, lavish extra contributions had to be made to him and his household and friends and those of his slaves who were sent out to collect the tribute [taxes] because there was no immunity at all from outrage unless bribes were paid." The parallel in *B.J.* 2.84–86 does not have these charges.

435. The Jewish embassy to Augustus had the political aim of abolishing the Herodian monarchy. They needed to bring such charges against Herod as would impress the emperor and secure their objective (*A.J.* 17.304; *B.J.* 2.80). Likewise, the inhabitants of Gadara, in search of autonomy (which meant the removal of their city from Herod's kingdom), accused Herod of "violence and pillage and the overthrowing of temples" (*A.J.* 15.357). See Peter Richardson, *Herod*, 23–32, 233–34. The Jewish and Samaritan embassy against Archelaus apparently accused him of "cruelty and tyranny." Augustus took the charges seriously and banished Archelaus (*A.J.* 17.342–44; *B.J.* 2.111–13; Dio, *Hist.* 55.27.6). Subjects could bring complaints against a king for the political end of deposing him. The nature of the charges they presented to the emperor seems to depend on what would achieve their political goal. Braund, *Rome and the Friendly King*, 66–67. On complaints by provincials against governors and Roman magistrates, see Millar, *Emperor in the Roman World*, 443–44; P. A. Brunt, "Charges of Provincial Maladministration Under the Early Principate," in *Roman Imperial Themes* (Oxford: Clarendon, 1990), 53–95.

436. See above. For the dating of the famine, see Peter Richardson, *Herod*, 222 and n. 17; and Schürer, *History*, 290–91 and n. 9.

(*A.J.* 15.303–16).[437] In 20 B.C.E., at the height of his building projects, he reduced by one third the taxes paid by the Jews (*A.J.* 15.365).[438] He reduced them again by a quarter in 14 B.C.E.[439]

The political context of this last reduction is particularly significant. Herod had just returned from Asia, where, after his campaign with Marcus Agrippa, he had devoted his resources to the needs of some of the cities there, especially those cities with large Jewish populations. He had won also a more direct victory for the Diaspora Jews, and for the temple in Jerusalem, by securing the right of the Ionian Jews to collect the temple tax and send it to Jerusalem. He could confidently declare, therefore, to his Jewish subjects in Jerusalem that "thanks to him they [the Jews of Asia] would be unmolested in future" (*A.J.* 16.63).[440] He was also aware that his expenditures on the Greek cities would draw sharp criticism from his opponents at home. By remitting the taxes on his Jewish subjects, he sought to do something that would be to the "advantage" of the Jews within his kingdom. In addition, he wanted to reassure them that his benefactions abroad were not economically ruinous for his kingdom, that they did not spell more taxes for his subjects. The "general picture of his good fortune and his government of the kingdom" that he presented to them was indeed real.

Josephus reports that the tax reduction of 14 B.C.E. favorably impressed Herod's Jewish subjects, who "went away with the greatest joy, wishing the king all sorts of good things" (*A.J.* 16.65). Herod sought to avert the very charge that was later brought against him, namely, that he despoiled

---

437. In his summaries of the effects of Herod's actions, Josephus speaks of how Herod's "solicitude," "goodwill and protective attitude" (εὔνοια καὶ προστασία), "munificence and zeal," "solicitude and the timeliness of his generosity" brought about a reversal of attitude toward Herod in Judea, even among his most hostile critics, improved relations with his neighbors in Syria, and earned him an international reputation (*A.J.* 15.308, 311, 315–16). On Herod's εὔνοια, see, for instance, Dittenberger, *OGIS*, no. 414. For an analysis of Josephus's double portrait of Herod in the 20s, see Peter Richardson, *Herod*, 222–26.

438. Josephus's "at this time" refers back to *A.J.* 15.354, and Augustus's visit to Syria. Herod has just received the grant of the territory of Zenodorus (*A.J.* 15.360) and also ceded Perea to his brother Pheroras (*A.J.* 15.362). According to *A.J.* 15.365, Herod remitted the taxes "to the people of his kingdom" (τοῖς ἐν τῇ βασιλείᾳ). Since, however, Josephus says that this was done in order to win the goodwill of those who had been disaffected because of "the dissolution of their religion and the disappearance of their customs" (*A.J.* 15.365), it must be that the reduction affected mostly the Jewish sections of Herod's kingdom. Josephus says that Herod reduced the taxes "under the pretext of letting them recover from a period of lack of crops" (*A.J.* 15.365). It is not clear what, in Josephus's view, was the religious and political disaffection that Herod was aiming to counter. Peter Richardson (*Herod*, 236–37) argues that the tax reduction was related to the Sabbatical Year.

439. "After giving a general picture of his good fortune and his government of the kingdom, in which, he said, he had not neglected anything that might be to their advantage, in a cheerful mood he remitted to them a fourth of their taxes for the past year."

440. See chapter 2.

the Jews to enrich Greek cities. He obviously failed. The odium and sense of oppression that persisted among some of his Jewish subjects, nonetheless, cannot be expressed in percentages of produce.[441] This means that, in spite of the "complaints" against Herod, the question of his oppression of his Jewish subjects must be separated from the assessment of the actual scale of Herodian taxation. If the reductions in 14 B.C.E. did not apply only to the taxes for that year,[442] then Herod would have reduced the taxes he received from the Jewish parts of his realm by about 50 percent (33 percent and again 25 percent of the new rate) in the six-year period from 20–14 B.C.E. These reductions indicate that the Jews paid less, rather than more, taxes as Herod's reign progressed. They probably paid considerably less than the taxes paid by the other inhabitants of Herod's dominion.

441. See also Pastor, *Land and Economy*, 110–15.

442. *A.J.* 16.64: "he remitted to them a fourth of their taxes for the past year" (τὸ τέταρτον τῶν φόρων ἀφίησιν αὐτοῖς τοῦ παρεληλυθότος ἔτους).

5

Taxation of Judea under the Governors

If our conclusion in the previous chapter is correct, namely, that the Jewish state paid no tribute to Rome under Herod and his successors, Judea (the region) began to pay tribute again, for the first time since 40 B.C.E., after the deposition of Archelaus and the consequent annexation of Judea in 6 C.E.[1] This period ended when the territory was granted to Agrippa I in 41 C.E. At Agrippa's death in 44 C.E., the whole of Jewish Palestine again was annexed into a province. The territory of Herod Antipas, which had been given to Agrippa I by Gaius in 39 C.E., therefore came under direct Roman rule and became tributary in 44 C.E.

Josephus says that after Archelaus was deposed and banished, that is, in 6/7 C.E., Quirinius was appointed governor of Syria and was instructed to conduct an assessment of property in the province (καὶ τιμητὴς τῶν οὐσιῶν γενησόμενος). Quirinius also came to Judea "in order to make an assessment of the property of the Jews (ἀποτιμησόμενός τε αὐτῶν τὰς οὐσίας) (*A.J.* 18.1–2; 17.355). Thus, the annexation of Judea in 6 C.E. was followed by a provincial census. The central questions concerning provincial

1. *A.J.* 18.2: "Coponius, a man of equestrian rank, was sent along with him [Quirinius] to rule over (ἡγησόμενος) the Jews with full authority." *B.J.* 2. 117: "The territory of Archelaus was now reduced to a province (εἰς ἐπαρχίαν), and Coponius, a Roman of the equestrian order, was sent out as procurator (ἐπίτροπος), entrusted by Augustus with full powers, including the infliction of capital punishment." In *A.J.* 17.355 Josephus says that "the territory subject to Archelaus was added to (the province of) Syria." In spite of Josephus's terminology in *B.J.* 2.117, the governor of Judea bore the title *praefectus* (ἔπαρχος) during the reigns of Augustus and Tiberius, as did the governor of Egypt, who also was of equestrian rank. Despite *A.J.* 17.355, Judea belonged to Strabo's (*Geogr.* 17.3.25) third category of imperial provinces: "to some of these he sends as curators men of consular rank, and to others men of praetorian rank, and to others men of the rank of knights." Although Judea was a province in its own right, its governor was to some degree subordinate to the imperial legate (*legatus Augusti pro praetore*) in Syria. See Jones, "Procurators," 119–23; and, generally, Millar, "Emperor, the Senate, and the Provinces"; also Goodman, "Judaea," 750–52; Schürer, *History*, 1:357–61.

taxation in Jewish Palestine relate to how one evaluates the nature and the consequences of Quirinius's census. The inadequacies of the extant sources limit how detailed our knowledge of the census of 6 C.E. can be and, consequently, the characteristics of Roman taxation in Judea during the period. As they have done with regard to other periods of Roman rule, scholars have tended to fill the gaps also in this case with information from other provinces of the empire, particularly from Egypt. What is known of the census in other provinces should certainly help us to understand the process in Judea. However, it appears that there was more than one kind of provincial census in the Roman Empire. Moreover, since the amount of information on the census in Judea exceeds what is available from other provinces, apart from Egypt, this census should give us some insights into the nature of some of the provincial censuses and the taxes that resulted from them.

Judea and the Provincial Census

It is by chance that we know that Augustus conducted a census in Gaul, and possibly also in Spain, in 27 B.C.E.[2] Dio provides no information about other censuses conducted by Augustus before and after those in Gaul (and Spain). Livy's *Periochae* 134[3] confirms the notice by Dio. Augustus conducted a census in Gaul again in about 12 B.C.E. through Nero Claudius Drusus.[4] Another census followed in 14–15 C.E., conducted by Germanicus.[5] Under Nero a census is said to have been taken

---

2. Dio, *Hist.* 53.22.5: "He [Augustus] took a census of the inhabitants [of Gaul] and regulated their life and government. From Gaul he proceeded into Spain, and established order there also." See chapter 4 and n. 258.

3. "When Gaius Caesar had brought about a peaceful settlement and had arranged a definite organization for all the provinces, he was also given the title of Augustus . . . . When he held assizes at Narbo, a census was conducted of the three Gauls (census a tribus Galliis . . . actus), which his father Caesar had conquered."

4. Livy, *Per.* 138: "Drusus conducted the census." See Braund, *Augustus to Nero,* no. 570: "They [the inhabitants of Gallia Comata] were the ones who gave my father Drusus the benefit of safe, internal peace and a secure rear when he was conquering Germany, although he was called to war while conducting a census, a practice then new and strange to the Gauls (et quidem cum [a] census novo tum opere et inadsueto Gallis ad bellum advocatus esset)" = Dessau, *ILS*, no. 212, col. 2, lines 35–38.

5. Tacitus, *Ann.* 1.31: "The supreme command rested with Germanicus, then engaged in assessing the tribute of the Gaulish provinces (agendo Galliarum censui tum intentum); *Ann.* 1.33: "In the meantime, Germanicus . . . was traversing the Gallic provinces and assessing their tribute (census accipienti), when the message came that Augustus was no more." Tacitus, *Ann.* 2.6: "Publius Vitellius and Gaius Anitius were sent to assess the Gallic tribute (missis ad census Galliarum)."

in Gaul in 61 C.E.[6] According to Dio, Nero had the census lists of the Gallic provinces at his disposition in Rome.[7]

An inscription credits Augustus with having sent a magistrate to conduct a census in Lusitania.[8] Tiberius took a census in the province of Narbonensis.[9] Both Jones and Brunt assume that the revolt of the Cietae in 36 C.E. against the census conducted there by Archelaus II[10] implies that a census had been taken in Cappadocia when Archelaus I's kingdom was annexed in 17 C.E.[11] This might have been the case, even though neither Dio (*Hist.* 57.17.7) nor Tacitus himself (Tacitus, *Ann.* 2.42)[12] mentions a census in Cappadocia in 17 C.E.[13] Brunt cites other epigraphic evidence for census officials; he also considers that where there is evidence for a levy of the *tributum capitis* a census must also have been conducted. This is the case with Britain under Nero.[14] The information he gathers, however, belongs to the later Principate.[15]

The scarcity of evidence on provincial censuses in the early Principate has left open the question whether the census was taken in all the provinces and at regular intervals. Jones thought that, beginning with Augustus and for the next two and a half centuries, "[r]egular censuses were required in all provinces both to register property and to count the population."[16] The evidence does not support this generalization.[17] Brunt

6. Tacitus, *Ann.* 14.46: "In the Gallic provinces, an assessment was held by Quintus Volusius, Sextius Africanus, and Trebellius Maximus." Jean Gagé et al., *L'année épigraphique* (Paris: Presses Universitaires de France, 1973), no. 175: "Q(uinto) Volusio . . . legato] | Caesaris at census accipiendos | prouinciae Belgicae." Mention is made also of a census in 83 C.E. See Brunt, "Revenues of Rome," 171.

7. Dio, *Hist.* 59.22.3: "At another time he [Nero] was playing at dice, and finding that he had no money, he called for the census lists of the Gauls (τὰς τῶν Γαλατῶν ἀπογραφάς) and ordered the wealthiest of them to be put to death . . . ."

8. Theodor Mommsen, ed., *CIL* (Berlin: Apud Georgium Reimerum, 1883), vol. 10, no. 680; Pliny (*Nat.* 3.28) gives some population figures for the region.

9. Dessau, *ILS*, no. 950: "memoriae | Torquati Novelli P. f. . . . [*leg.* a]d cens. accip. et dilect. et | [*proco*]s. provinciae Narbon. . . ." On Novellius Torquatus, see Pliny, *Nat.* 14.22.144–46.

10. Tacitus, *Ann.* 6.41: "Cietarum natio Cappadoci Archelao subiecta, quia nostrum in modum deferre census, pati tributa adigebatur . . . ." See chapter 4.

11. Jones, *Roman Economy*, 165, n. 81; Brunt, "Revenues of Rome," 164, 172.

12. See also Suetonius, *Tib.* 37.4; Sullivan, "Cappadocia," 2.7.2:1159–61.

13. Tacitus (*Ann.* 2.42) adds that the income from Archelaus's kingdom (fructibusque eius) was sufficient to allow Tiberius to reduce the Roman 1-percent sales tax to one-half of a percent.

14. Dio, *Hist.* 62.3.3 (κεφαλὰς ὑποτελεῖς περιφέρειν); possibly also Tacitus, *Ann.* 12.34 (tributis intemerata coniugum et liberorum corpora retinerent).

15. Brunt, "Revenues of Rome," 164, 171–72; also Jones, *Roman Economy*, 173–74, n. 114.

16. Jones, *Roman Economy*, 165.

17. Neesen (*Staatsabgaben*, 39–42) rejects this conclusion for the imperial provinces; his view is contested by Brunt ("Revenues of Rome," 163–64).

proposes a more nuanced position, namely, that "some kind of census" was taken in every province of the empire. The provincial census in this sense would have been "universal" in the early Principate.[18] Yet it is odd that a "universal" practice of such administrative importance should be so sparcely attested that we have evidence of it only by "mere chance."[19] The frequency of the census in Gaul might have been related to the importance of the province to the war in Germany, which entailed the need repeatedly to assess revenues.[20] Censuses were conducted in Judea, (possibly) Cappadocia, and (later) Dacia at the point of their annexation.[21] Quirinius conducted the census in Syria (and Judea) in 6 C.E. as a special mission from the emperor; there is no evidence that a census had been taken in Syria before 6 C.E.[22] The annexation of Judea appears to have been the occasion for this census, which covered the whole of Syria.[23]

In the early Principate, the census in the provinces appears to have been haphazardly conducted. It was used especially when new territories were annexed or when there was need to assess a province's revenues.[24] It was the case of Judea that shook Brunt's earlier faith in the universality and regularity of provincial censuses:

> Given the disturbance that Quirinius' census provoked in Judaea, we may think it strange that Josephus mentions no later registration, not even to remark on the absence of protests. I now feel less sure that censuses should have been taken in the Principate as often and as systematically as they should have been for fair and efficient distribution of the tax load.[25]

---

18. Brunt, "Revenues of Rome," 163–64.

19. Ibid., 164.

20. Brunt (*Roman Imperial Themes*, 533) puzzles over the case of Gaul: "The proliferation of testimony to censuses in Gaul is puzzling. Granted that elsewhere governors usually took the census without recording it in career inscriptions, it remains hard to see why in Gaul consular commissioners should so often have been appointed specially for the purpose. . . . It looks as if for reasons that elude us the government adopted a special policy for Gallic censuses; alternatively, we might after all conclude that a census was held in Gaul more often than in other regions, where it may have been much less frequent than I argued."

21. Under Trajan (Lactantius, *Mort.* 23.5). See Jones, *Roman Economy*, 165, n. 81; Brunt, "Revenues of Rome," 164, 171.

22. See Schürer, *History*, 1:406. Josephus's statements show that Quirinius's census in Syria "was not based on a fixed cycle." For attempts to argue for several censuses in Syria and Judea by taking the word πρώτη in Luke 2:2 to mean "prior to," "before," "the first of them," or "earlier than," see Pearson, "Lucan Censuses," 278–82 and the literature he cites.

23. See Schürer, *History*, 1:259, 405.

24. See chapter 4 and n. 259.

25. Brunt, *Roman Imperial Themes*, 533; see chapter 4 and n. 259.

The silence of our sources confutes any attempt to postulate a system of regular Roman censuses in Judea before 66 C.E.[26] A census would have been expected when Agrippa's kingdom was annexed and when Antipas's former tetrarchy was annexed for the first time in 44 C.E. There is, however, no trace of a census being conducted at this point. Menahem Stern speculates that the experience of the rebellion that accompanied the census of 6 C.E. might have caused the Roman authorities "not to be over-hasty in instituting a new census after a given period, but to use other means of bringing their statistics up to date."[27] Josephus (*B.J.* 6.422–25) narrates the story of how Cestius Gallus, the governor of Syria, before the beginning of the revolt in 66 C.E.,[28] asked the chief priests "by any means possible" to conduct a census of the population of Jerusalem. This census was not for the purpose of taxation. According to Josephus, it was intended instead to convince the emperor Nero of the strength of the city. The chief priests did not count people; they counted the victims of the Passover sacrifice.

Josephus's story might be legendary.[29] It implies, however, that Josephus did not think that either Nero or the governor of Syria had up-to-date census cadastres for Judea,[30] as Nero was reported to have had for Gaul.[31] There is simply no evidence and it is very doubtful that

26. The "indirect evidence" for regular censuses in Judea that Kokkinos believes he has found in Josephus's works and elsewhere comprises random pieces of information that cannot stand up to scrutiny. See Nikos Kokkinos, "Crucifixion in A.D. 36: The Keystone for Dating the Birth of Jesus," in *Chronos, Kairos, Christos: Nativity and Chronological Studies Presented to Jack Finegan* (ed. Jerry Vardaman and Edwin M. Yamauchi; Winona Lake, Ind.: Eisenbrauns, 1989), 139–41.

27. Menahem Stern, "The Province of Judaea," in *The Jewish People in the First Century: Historical Geography, Political History, Social, Cultural and Religious Life and Institutions*, vol. 1 (ed. S. Safrai and M. Stern; CRINT 1; Assen: Van Gorcum, 1974), 331. Stern emphasizes, correctly, that "outside Egypt we have no certain knowledge of any province in which censuses were conducted at fixed intervals."

28. Cestius probably went to Jerusalem during the Passover in 66 C.E. (*B.J.* 2.280).

29. See Menahem Stern, "Province of Judaea," 331 and n. 2.

30. Edward Dąbrowa (*The Governors of Roman Syria from Augustus to Septimius Severus* [Bonn: Habelt, 1998], 57 and n. 531) thinks that Cestius Gallus visited Judea in order to carry out "a periodic population census, the term of which just happened to fall in that year, and was not at the governor's own initiative as the historian [Josephus] implied." If a population census was Gallus's motive, his method was certainly bizarre. Dąbrowa actually assumes without any justification that there were "periodic population" censuses in Judea.

31. 2 Sam 24:1–25 and 1 Chr 21:1–27 suggest that a census was a contentious issue in Israel. Josephus, in his rewriting of the biblical passages (*A.J.* 7.318–34), locates David's "sin" not in the census itself but in the fact that the king "forgot the injunctions of Moses who had prescribed that, when the populace was numbered, half a shekel should be paid to God for every person" (*A.J.* 7.318). The suggestion by Brunt (*Roman Imperial Themes*, 520) that the census in 6 C.E. might have been "seen as a violation of divine commands" is rejected by Kokkinos, "Relative Chronology," 131 and n. 35. However, Kokkinos's con-

other censuses were conducted in the province with any regularity after 6 C.E.[32]

Scholars do not agree on the format of the provincial census. The practice, we noted, has been to fill out the gaps in our knowledge with information from Egypt. Thus, Jones writes in passing that "[i]n Egypt the population census was taken at intervals of 14 years, because the lower age for the poll tax was 14; children down to newly born infants were counted, and brought into the poll tax lists, as they came of age. Deaths were reported by relatives." He, however, thinks the land surveys and the "house-to-house census in Egypt . . . hardly provided models applicable elsewhere."[33] Scholars, nevertheless, have long pointed to the census in Egypt as the model for provincial censuses elsewhere, including Judea.[34] Departing from this view, Brunt responds to Lutz Neesen's objections by proposing, first, that "[c]ertainly there was no uniform type of census,"[35] and second he hints that the provincial census might have been modeled after the "old census of Roman citizens," rather than the Egyptian house-to-house registrations (κατ' οἰκίαν ἀπογραφαί). The format of the Roman census of citizens, Brunt observes, is reflected in the *forma censualis* described by the third-century jurist Ulpian:[36]

> [I]n the old Roman census the imperial government had a model for the registration of property which could have been applied in the provinces and which would have permitted assessment and taxation of all capital: Roman citizens had been obliged to declare not only Italian land and the equipment for farming it, but also cash, debts due to or from others, clothing, jewels, slaves of all sorts . . . and *aedificia* . . . and to estimate the

---

tention that "the Jews of the Second Temple period were in effect regularly numbered by means of levying the half-shekel tax" is puzzling.

32. Rathbone ("Egypt, Augustus and Roman Taxation," 98) concludes from the data from Gaul that "Egypt was unique in having a regular cycle of seven- and then fourteen-yearly censuses."

33. Jones, *Roman Economy*, 165 and nn. 81 and 82.

34. See, typically, Schürer, *History*, 1:403–4. Schürer first states that the provincial census "was conducted in the same manner as the census of Roman citizens." He then writes (p. 403), however, that "[a] clear idea of this can only be gained in the case of Egypt," and he goes on to describe the systems of κατ' οἰκίαν ἀπογραφαί and ἀπογραφαί there. Rathbone ("Egypt, Augustus and Roman Taxation," 86–99) argues that Augustus introduced the "Roman-style system of registration" into Egypt, probably in 10/9 B.C.E.

35. Brunt, "Revenues of Rome," 163; see also p. 167: "It must be premised that as the census must have taken different forms in different provinces . . . the compilers of the *Digest* (L. 15. 4) would have misled us, if we were to think that Ulpian was describing a procedure followed in all parts."

36. Brunt, "Revenues of Rome," 163: the "form of the old Roman census . . . corresponds more closely than the Egyptian to that 'forma censualis' which Ulpian describes." See Ulpian, *Cens.* 3; Mommsen and Krueger, *Digest*, 4: L.15.4.

> value of their property apparently in accordance with formulae laid down by the censors . . . . Provincials too had to make such estimates for the property they returned (*infra*, cf. Jos. AJ XVIII, 3), no doubt again in accordance with formulae.[37]

Hence, Rathbone confidently declares that "[t]he normal provincial census seems to have registered all private property, including farmland, as well as the population, and therefore seems to have been modelled on the Republican census of Roman citizens."[38]

Josephus, in his accounts, refers twice to Quirinius's census simply as a "registration" (ἀπογραφή)."[39] Josephus's terminology in these passages might convey the impression that he is referring to a census similar to the Egyptian κατ' οἰκίαν ἀπογραφαί, that is, a registration of persons (together with property). However, this is not the case. Apart from these two passages (*A.J.* 18.3; *B.J.* 7.253), Josephus does not use the word ἀπογραφή elsewhere in his works.[40] The phrase ποιεῖσθαι τὰς ἀπογραφάς in *B.J.* 7.253 actually is equivalent to the verb ἀπογράφειν, meaning, in this case, "to register as one's own property" or "to declare as liable to taxation."[41] This interpretation of the phrase in *B.J.* 7.253 is confirmed by the fact that Josephus in this passage refers ("as we have previously stated") to his earlier accounts of the events surrounding Quirinius's census in Judea.[42]

Moreover, the statement in *A.J.* 18.3 that the Jews were shocked at first to hear of the registration (τὸ κατ' ἀρχὰς ἐν δεινῷ φεροντες τὴν ἐπὶ ταῖς ἀπογραφαῖς ἀκρόασιν) is sandwiched between other descriptions of the census. In the description following the statement about the Jews' initial shock, Josephus says that those who were persuaded by the high priest Joazar went ahead, nevertheless, and "declared . . . the value of their property" (ἀπετίμων τὰ χρήματα). This mirrors Josephus's statements preceding *A.J.* 18.3, namely, that Quirinius arrived in Judea "in order to make an assessment of the property of the Jews" (ἀποτιμησόμενός τε αὐτῶν τὰς οὐσίας), since he was sent by Augustus as "censor," that is, an assessor of

37. Brunt, "Revenues of Rome," 166–67.

38. Rathbone, "Egypt, Augustus and Roman Taxation," 98.

39. *A.J.* 18.3: "[T]he Jews were at first shocked to hear of the registration of property (ἐπὶ ταῖς ἀπογραφαῖς)." *B.J.* 7.253: Judas "induced multitudes of Jews to refuse to enroll themselves (μὴ ποιεῖσθαι τὰς ἀπογραφάς), when Quirinius was sent as censor to Judaea."

40. The word ἀπογραφάς is restored in *A.J.* 12.31 (LCL) from *Let. Aris.* 24.9, and it occurs in the context of the decree issued by Ptolemy Philadelphus.

41. See Henry George Liddell et al., *Greek-English Lexicon* (9th ed with revised supplement; Oxford: Clarendon, 1996), 194, s.v. ἀπογραφεύς, ἀπογραφή, κτλ. Cf. ἀπογραφὰς ἐποιήσατο in Dio, *Hist.* 53.22.5.

42. See *B.J.* 2.118 and 433. In both passages Josephus does not mention the census per se but rather emphasizes the point that the rebels viewed the payment of Roman tribute as "tolerating mortal masters, after having God for their lord" (*B.J.* 2.118).

property (τιμητὴς τῶν οὐσιῶν γενησόμενος) to the province (*A.J.* 18.2 and 18.1).

Louis Feldman in the LCL edition is, therefore, justified in translating the phrase τὴν ἐπὶ ταῖς ἀπογραφαῖς in *A.J.* 18.3 as "the registration of property."[43] In all the other accounts of the census, Josephus speaks of it as an assessment, a valuation of property.[44] Josephus uses the verb ἀποτιμάω and its cognate substantive ἀποτίμησις only in the context of Quirinius's census in Syria and Judea. This is true but for one exception, that is, in *A.J.* 5.76. In this passage about Joshua, Josephus gives a description, lacking in his statements about the census, of what Quirinius's "assessment" might have entailed:

> Joshua sent out men to measure the country, attaching to them certain expert surveyors, from whom by reason of their skill the truth would not be hid, instructions being given them to assess separately the extent of the favoured land and of that which was less fertile (ἐντολὰς δοὺς ἀποτιμήσασθαι τῆς τε εὐδαίμονος ἰδίᾳ τὸ μέτρον γῆς καὶ τῆς ἧσσον ἀγαθῆς).[45]

Quirinius's assessment was not a population census.[46] It might instead have been a land survey of the kind that Caracalla is said to have ordered

---

43. H. St. J. Thackeray's "to enroll themselves" for μὴ ποιεῖσθαι τὰς ἀπογραφάς in *B.J.* 7.253 is misleading.

44. *A.J.* 17.355: "Now the territory subject to Archelaus was added to (the province of) Syria, and Quirinius, a man of consular rank, was sent by Caesar to take a census of property in Syria (ἀποτιμησόμενος τὰ ἐν Συρίᾳ) . . . ." *A.J.* 18.4: "They [the rebels, Judas and Saddok] said that the assessment (τήν τε ἀποτίμησιν) carried with it a status amounting to downright slavery . . . ." *A.J.* 18.26: "Quirinius had now liquidated the estate of Archelaus; and by this time the registrations of property that took place (ἤδη καὶ τῶν ἀποτιμήσεων πέρας ἐχουσῶν) in the thirty-seventh year after Caesar's defeat of Antony at Actium were complete."

45. See Josephus's further statements about Palestine in *A.J.* 5.77–79. Josephus is rewriting Josh 18:8: "Joshua charged those who went to write the description of the land, saying, 'Go throughout the land and write a description of it, and come back to me . . . .'"

46. A population census appears to be implied by the use of the word ἀπογραπή in Luke 2:2 and the subsequent narrative. See Millar, *Roman Near East*, 46: "It is important to stress that the taking of a census of this type, the counting of a provincial population and the assessment of their property for the purpose of the payment of tribute, was not a long-standing feature of Roman government, but an innovation by Augustus." Millar points out that Luke is "wholly misleading and unhistorical" in implying that a "Roman census was imposed in Galilee," which in 6/7 C.E. was under Antipas. Luke is also misleading and unhistorical if the census he envisions in Judea is "the counting of a provincial population." Mark D. Smith ("Jesus and Quirinius," 288–90) evades this problem (probably inadvertently), first, by recognizing that "a census would require people to register where they lived and worked and owned property, for the objective of a Roman census was to ascertain the resources of a region so the government could provide suitable infrastructure and, of course, determine the potential for tax revenue and auxiliary troop recruitment" (p. 289).

of the territory of Pessinus in Anatolia in 216 C.E.[47] The Jews who participated in the census would have appeared on the lists (ἀπογραφαί) only insofar as they owned (landed) property. It is also probable that, following the initial survey, the state depended on individual proprietors to update the lists by declarations to local officials, especially in the event of a change of ownership, and that the records, as Brunt observes, were generally "defective and antiquated."[48]

We find a format similar to the census in Judea—as presented by Josephus—in the later census returns of 127 C.E. from the neighboring province of Arabia, which was formed in 106 C.E. A well-preserved return is found in the Babatha archive.[49] A fragment of a second return by another individual ("—os son of Simon") from the same village was published by Lewis, and it might have come from the same cave as the Babatha archive.[50] Babatha (Babtha) lived in the village of Maoza, south of the Dead Sea, in the district of Zaora. The document (P.Yadin 16) begins by attesting that it is a verified copy of the "document of registration" (ἀπογραφῆς) that is posted in the basilica at Rabbath-Moab, where the declaration was made before the magistrate. The declaration follows:[51]

> In the reign of Imperator Caesar divi Traiani Parthici filius divi Nervae nepos Traianus Hadrianus Augustus pontifex maximus tribuniciae potestatis XII consul III, in the consulship of Marcus Gavius Gallicanus and Titus Atilius Rufus Titianus four days before the nones of December, and according to the compute of the new province of Arabia year twenty-second month Apellaios the sixteenth, in the city of Rabbath-Moab. As a census of Arabia is being conducted by Titus Aninius Sextius Florentinus, legatus Augusti pro praetore,[52] I, Babtha daughter of Simon, of Maoza in the Zoarene [district] of the Petra administrative region, domiciled in my own private property in the said Maoza, regis-

---

He then argues that "Joseph continued to own property" in Bethlehem and "needed to go to Bethlehem to maintain proper title to his property and to pay his taxes" (p. 290).

47. J. Devreker, "Une inscription inédite de Caracalla à Pessinonte," *Latomus* 30 (1971): 353–62. Devreker (p. 355) points out that nothing similar to Caracalla's survey is known to have been undertaken by any other emperor, except Diocletian's (285–306 C.E.) cadastral operation in Syria. See Jones, *Roman Economy*, 165, n. 81; Brunt, *Roman Imperial Themes*, 533.

48. Brunt, *Roman Imperial Themes*, 533.

49. Naphtali Lewis et al., *The Documents from the Bar Kokhba Period in the Cave of Letters: Greek Papyri* (JDS 2; Jerusalem: Israel Exploration Society, the Hebrew University of Jerusalem, & the Shrine of the Book, 1989), no. 16.

50. Naphtali Lewis, "A Jewish Landowner in the Province of Arabia," *SCI* 8–9 (1985–88): 132–37.

51. Ibid., 133–35.

52. P.Yadin 16, lines.11–13: ἀποτιμήσεως Ἀραβίας ἀγομένης ὑπὸ Τίτου Ἀνεινίου Σεξστίου Φλωρεντείνου πρεσβευτοῦ Σεβαστοῦ ἀντιστρατήγου, κτλ.

> ter what I possess[53] (present with me as my guardian being Judanes son of Elazar, of the village of En-gedi in the district of Jericho in Judaea, domiciled in his own private property in the said Maoza), viz. within the boundaries of Maoza a date orchard called Algiphiamma, the area of sowing one saton three kaboi of barley, paying as tax, in dates, Syrian and mixed fifteen sata, "splits" ten sata, and for crown tax one "black" and thirty sixtieths, abutters a road and the Sea; within the boundaries of Maoza a date orchard called Algiphiamma, the area of sowing one kabos of barley, paying as tax a half share of the crops produced each year, abutters *moschantic* estate of our lord Caesar and the Sea; within the boundaries of Maoza a date orchard called Bagalgala, the area of sowing three sata of barely, paying as tax, in dates, Syrian and Noaran(?) one koros, "splits" one koros, and for crown tax three "blacks" and thirty sixtieths, abutters heirs of Thesaios son of Sabakas and Iamit son(?) of Manthanthes; within the boundaries of Maoza a date orchard called Bethphaaraia, the area of sowing twenty sata of barley, paying as tax, in dates, Syrian and Noaran (?) three Kaboi, "splits" two koroi, and for crown tax eight "blacks" and forty-five sixtieths, abutters Tamar daughter of Thamous and a road.
>
> Translation of subscription: I, Babtha daughter of Simon, swear by the *genius* of our lord Caesar that I have in good faith registered as has been written above. I, Judanes son of Elazar, acted as guardian and wrote for her. [2nd hand] Translation of subscription of the prefect: I, Priscus, prefect of cavalry, received [this] on the day before the nones of December in the consulship of Gallicanus and Titianus.

The returns contain no information about previous censuses in the province. In P.Yadin 24.5, Besas, guardian of the children of Babatha's second husband (Judah) by his first wife, files a counterclaim to unidentified date orchards. In his deposition Besas maintains that "Judah son of Eleazar Khthousion, your late husband, registered date orchards in Maoza in your name in the census" (ἐν τῇ ἀπογραφῇ).[54] It is not clear if the deposition is referring to the census of 127 C.E. or to an earlier one. Millar speculates that if a census had been taken first in the province in 107 C.E. after its annexation, "there may have been a ten-year cycle, with an intervening one in about 117."[55] Ulpian's *forma censualis* (*Cens.* 3) assumes a

53. P.Yadin 16.15: ἀπογράφομαι ἃ κέκτημαι.

54. Against Lewis's suggestion that the word ἀπογραφή here might refer "to a registration upon transfer of ownership," Martin Goodman ("Babatha's Story," review of *Y. Yadin, The Documents from the Bar Kokhba Period in the Cave of Letters: Greek Papyri, JRS* 81 [1991]: 171) insists that the word refers "to registration in the census, such as was carried out for these or other date orchards in *P. Yadin* 16." See Naphtali Lewis et al., *Documents*, 107, who also wonders whether the word might be "a reference to the census of AD 127."

55. Millar, *Roman Near East*, 97.

ten-year interval,[56] although his specifications for Syria (*Cens.* 2) assume a fourteen-year cycle,[57] as was used in Egypt.

It is noteworthy that, like Josephus's description of the census of Judea under Quirinius, the census of Arabia by Florentinus is called ἀποτιμήσις Ἀραβίας,[58] that is, a registration of property. Babatha registered four date orchards.[59] "—os son of Simon" in the fragment registered, probably among other pieces of property, "a yearly half share" of a barley field and "a half share of a date orchard."[60] The "formula" of both declarations is similar to the first part of Ulpian's *forma censualis* for the registration of landed property, indicating for each property the kind, location, name, size of property, and two boundary plots.[61] It lacks other details, however, the most outstanding of which is the fact that Babatha does not give the value of her property.[62]

Martin Goodman observes that P.Yadin 16 shows that "census registration was not unduly complicated."[63] Babatha's census declaration is surprisingly simple, in comparison with the items that, according to Ulpian[64] and Brunt's "old Roman census" of Roman citizens, ought to be listed as liable to taxation. She listed only her date orchards, even though the documents in the archive show her to have been a wealthy woman. Brunt retreated from his earlier generalization: "Again I now doubt if all personal estate was registered everywhere . . . . The difficulty of ascertaining and estimating personal possessions in general was clearly great."[65]

Babatha's return is especially notable for the absence of personal

---

56. Mommsen and Krueger, *Digest*, 4: L.15.4; Brunt, "Revenues of Rome," 165.

57. Mommsen and Krueger, *Digest*, 4: L.15.3; Brunt, "Revenues of Rome," 164–65.

58. P.Yadin 16.11–12; see text in n. 52 above. Naphtali Lewis, "Jewish Landowner," 133, line 10: ἀποτιμήσεως Ἀραβίας.

59. The expression ἀπογράφομαι ἃ κέκτημαι in P.Yadin 16.15 is thus equivalent to Josephus's ποιεῖσθαι τὰς ἀπογραφάς in *B.J.* 7.253. See Naphtali Lewis, "Jewish Landowner," 134, lines 13–14: . . . ἀπογράφομαι ἐμαυτὸν ἐτῶν τριάκοντα . . . [. .] . . νιον. Lewis conjectures: "I . . . register myself, thirty years old, [as owner of?] . . . ."

60. Naphtali Lewis, "Jewish Landowner," 134, lines 14–19.

61. Ulpian, *Cens.* 3; Mommsen and Krueger, *Digest*, 4: L.15.4: "It is laid down in the list of rules for the census (forma censuali) that land must be entered in the census in this way: the name of each property, the community, and the *pagus* to which it belongs, its nearest two neighbors; then, how many *jugera* of land have been sown for the last ten years, how many vines vineyards have, how many *jugera* are olive-plantations and with how many trees, and how many *jugera* of land have been used for hay for the last ten years, how many *jugera* of pasture there are, likewise of wood for felling. The man who declares anything must value it."

62. Naphtali Lewis ("Jewish Landowner," 134, lines 14–15) also gives no valuation of the property.

63. Goodman, "Babatha's Story," 171.

64. Ulpian, *Cens.* 3; Mommsen and Krueger, *Digest*, 4: L.15.4.

65. Brunt, *Roman Imperial Themes*, 533.

information, contrary to Ulpian's prescript: "[i]t is necessary to indicate age in compiling censuses, because age confers on some people nonpayment of tax . . . . The relevant age is that at the time of the census."[66] The fragment does provide, however, the age of "—os son of Simon" (ἐτῶν τριάκοντα).[67] Lewis's caution on this passage is, however, worth recalling:

> ἐμαυτὸν ἐτῶν τριάκοντα, which has no parallel in *P. Yadin* 16, is probably no more than a stylistic variation in the declaration formula. Otherwise, if the phrase is taken to constitute the declarant's registration for a census of persons, it becomes necessary to assume that such a personal declaration was not required of Babatha because she was a woman. With these two documents as the sole evidence, that assumption must be regarded as at best speculative.[68]

In the regulation just cited on the need to indicate age on census lists, Ulpian uses as his example "the provinces of Syria," where, he says, "men are bound to pay poll-tax from fourteen, women from twelve, in both cases up to sixty-five."[69] But we cannot accept his testimony as evidence for a population census in the region[70] and, at the same time, assume that women were not numbered in 127 C.E.[71] Moreover, both Babatha and "—os son of Simon" appear on their respective census returns as paying tribute only in relation to the pieces of landed property that they declare. The assessment in 127 C.E., like the one in 6 C.E., was thus not a population census.[72]

---

66. Ulpian, *Cens.* 2; Mommsen and Krueger, *Digest*, 4: L.15.3.

67. Naphtali Lewis, "Jewish Landowner," 134, line 13; see n. 59 above

68. Ibid., 136.

69. Ulpian, *Cens.* 2; Mommsen and Krueger, *Digest*, 4: L.15.3. Ulpian is echoed by Heichelheim, "Roman Syria," 237: "All men from 14 to 65 years of age and all women from 12 to 65 years were obliged to pay a *tributum capitis* in the Syrian province"; and by Jones, *Roman Economy*, 164–65: "*Tributum capitis* was a poll tax, levied at a flat rate on adults, from the age of 12 or 14 to 65, sometimes on males only, as in Egypt, sometimes on both sexes, as in Syria." This is repeated in numerous forms by scholars. See below.

70. Ulpian is the only evidence we have, outside of Egypt, for the age of liability. See Rathbone, "Egypt, Augustus and Roman Taxation," 97, who speculates that "variations between provinces may be suspected, though possibly there was a tendency towards standardisation."

71. Menahem Stern ("Province of Judaea," 331 and n. 4) is probably not trying to avoid this problem when he writes, "We know from a later legal source that the *tributum capitis*, which involved a wider conception than the poll-tax, was imposed throughout Syria on males between the ages of fourteen and sixty-five." He cites Ulpian but excludes Ulpian's reference to women.

72. Millar (*Roman Near East*, 110) acknowledging the incongruity between Ulpian and Babatha's census return, sounded a note of caution: "In other words the realities of the process by which the Roman state lived off its subjects, in this as in other areas, escape us."

Judea and Provincial Taxes

The issue of the format of provincial censuses is important because the format of a census determined the kinds of taxes that resulted from it.[73] It is worth emphasizing that if it is true that there was no uniform provincial census in the early Principate, it follows that taxes also were not uniformly levied in all the provinces.[74] Babatha registered only her four date orchards, and all of her taxes, thus, are related to these pieces of property. The comments by W. D. Davies and Dale C. Allison, Jr., on the word κῆνσος in Matt 22:17 illustrate the confusion that persists among New Testament scholars on the subject of Roman provincial taxation:

> The word [κῆνσος] refers to the Roman *census*, a tax upon agricultural yield (*tributum soli*) and personal property (*tributum capitis*). The *tributum capitis* was collected through census, or registration (Lk 2.1–5; Acts 5.37), and probably amounted to one denarius a year.[75]

---

73. The topic of Roman provincial taxation still needs a thorough reinvestigation. See Rathbone, "Ancient Economy," 94. Neesen's *Staatsabgaben* is already dated; Lintott (*Imperium Romanum*, 70–96) deals with the late Republic.

74. See, again, Brunt, "Addendum II," 183: "the form each provincial census took may have varied with local conditions; the Egyptian land surveys and house-to-house returns were not the model, any more than the diversification of taxes in Egypt was adopted elsewhere; by the same token we cannot argue from the tax system of any province to any other." MacMullen (*Response to Crisis*, 129–52, esp. pp 131–32): "The list that we call as a whole 'Roman taxation' was indeed very confused, even casual. The cause lay in a philosophy of government prevailing among the conquerors: 'get the most for the least.' So, in the course of expansion as little as possible was added to the bother and business of rule . . . . The structure that grew up, then, combined long-established diversity, alternating strictness and relaxation, demand pressing upon resistance, and makeshifts responsive to temporary needs . . . . What the entire structure of taxation lacked, of course, was logic." Lo Cascio ("La Stuttura Fiscale," 29–35) concedes that there was an initial lack of uniformity in the Roman system of taxation: "l'iniziale variabilità nei tipi d'imposta e nei tipi d'imposizione . . . e la stessa differente incidenza quantitativa del tributo nelle varie aree potrebbero non essere soltanto, e anche all'inizio, il portato di un'irrazionale e indiscriminata politica di spoliazione . . . " (p. 35). Following Brunt's earlier view that provincial censuses were universally and regularly conducted (p. 38), however, Lo Cascio attempts to argue, against MacMullen, that there was a progressive rationalization and standardization of the Roman system of taxation.

75. Davies and Allison, *Matthew*, 3:214. They depend on (see their n. 30) Schürer (*History*, 1:401–2), who writes that there were two kinds of direct taxes for the provinces: "The first [i.e. *tributum soli*] was paid partly in kind, partly in money. The second (*tributum capitis*) included various kinds of personal taxes, namely, a property tax which varied according to a person's capital valuation, as well as a poll-tax proper at a flat rate for all *capita*. In Syria, in for example Appian's time, a personal tax was levied amounting to 1% of the property valuation." See also Menahem Stern, "Province of Judaea," 331.

For the sake of terminological clarity, I shall try again to categorize, at the great risk of oversimplification, the known forms of direct provincial taxes, outside of Egypt,[76] in the early Principate. The *tributum soli* was the tax on landed property. Cicero, we have seen, classified provincial tribute, the *tributum soli*, as being either a *vectigal certum* (*stipendium*) or a *censoria locatio* (*decumae*, "tithe"). Whereas the *stipendium* was a fixed amount, the *decumae* was a variable amount, a percentage of the annual produce (2 *Verr.* 3.6.12–15).[77] Ulpian's *Cens.* 3 and Appian's *Syr.* 11.8.50 imply that, following a provincial census, tribute would be assessed as a percentage of the total valuation of landed property. The *tributum soli* thus assessed would have been a fixed amount, like Cicero's *stipendium*. The *tributum soli* could also be assessed as a (variable) percentage of the annual yield, like Cicero's *decumae*. Contrary to the notion that the provincial census eliminated the need for the *decumae*,[78] Babatha paid (for different fields) both a fixed amount and a percentage of her yield.[79]

The Roman *tributum capitis*, or capitation tax (ἐπικεφάλαιον), is a more complicated topic. The term ἐπικεφάλαιον was applied to various capitation charges imposed upon individuals, *per caput* and in general paid in cash. We noted in chapter 4 that in the late Republic capitation taxes were local ad hoc exactions. Instances are the taxes imposed by Appius Claudius on the inhabitants of the province of Cilicia,[80] and by Scipio on the inhabitants of Asia.[81] These taxes from the Republic are distinct from the poll tax, the *tributum capitis*,[82] or φόρος τῶν σωμάτων[83] (known in Egypt as the λαογραφία), which made its appearance in the Principate. The later *tributum capitis* properly so called was a head tax

76. For Egypt, see Sherman LeRoy Wallace, *Taxation in Egypt: From Augustus to Diocletian* (Princeton: Princeton University Press, 1938), 11–95, 116–213; Neesen, *Staatsabgaben*, 84–92, 99–102, 125–30; Naphtali Lewis, *Life in Egypt Under Roman Rule* (Oxford: Clarendon, 1983), 159–76; Rathbone, "Egypt, Augustus and Roman Taxation," 82–93.

77. See chapter 2.

78. Jones, *Roman Economy*, 164: Augustus, with the census, "introduced the uniform and more rational system of taxation which is attested later in the empire." The land tax was now "a percentage of the assessed value." Jones's view is rejected by Brunt, "Addendum II," 182; idem, "Publicans," 355–57, 360–93.

79. A fixed amount for orchards nos. 1, 3, and 4 (P.Yadin 16.17–21, 24–38); "a half share of the crops produced each year" for orchard no. 2 (P.Yadin 16.21–24).

80. Cicero, *Fam.* 3.8.3–5; also *Att.* 5.16.2; Lintott, *Imperium Romanum*, 77–78; Rathbone, "Egypt, Augustus and Roman Taxation," 95. See chapter 4.

81. Caesar, *Bell. civ.* 3.32; Lintott, *Imperium Romanum*, 78; Rathbone, "Egypt, Augustus and Roman Taxation," 95; Neesen, *Staatsabgaben*, 9, 12, 62, 118. See chapter 4.

82. Ulpian, *Cens.* 2; Mommsen and Krueger, *Digest*, 4: L.15.3; Paul, *Cens.* 2; Mommsen and Krueger, *Digest*, 4: L.15.8.

83. Dio, *Hist.* 62.3.3 (Britain): τῶν σωμάτων αὐτῶν δασμὸν ἐτήσιον φέρομεν. Probably Appian, *Syr.* 11.8.50: ὁ φόρος τῶν σωμάτων (imposed on "all Jews"); see chapter 1 and below.

assessed through a census at a flat rate on qualifying members of the population.[84] Since the terms (ἐπικέφαλαιον, *tributum capitis*, and φόρος τῶν σωμάτων) overlap,[85] however, it is often easy to confuse this tribute with the more general capitation taxes, and it is equally difficult to determine how the two kinds of capitation taxes overlap with and might relate to the *tributum soli*.[86]

Tributum Soli

Since the census of 6 C.E. was, as Josephus describes it, a valuation of property, direct provincial tribute in Judea came in the form of *tributum soli*, a tax on landed property. This conclusion is supported by the two census returns from the region which, though they are from a later period, closely parallel Josephus's depiction of the census in Judea. There is other, although it is little and indirect, evidence that suggests that Rome continued to levy in Judea a *tributum soli* similar to that decreed by Julius Caesar and the Senate in 47 B.C.E. (*A.J.* 14.201–10).[87] During the crisis (in 39–41 C.E.) that resulted from the emperor Gaius's attempt to have his statue erected in the Jerusalem temple, Jewish leaders asked the legate of Syria, Petronius, to caution Gaius that the Jews were sitting down in protest, and that "since the land was unsown, there would be a harvest of banditry, because the requirement of tribute could not be met" (*A.J.* 18.273–75).[88] Josephus mentions stores of "imperial corn" (Καίσαρος σῖτον) that existed in the villages of Upper Galilee in 66 C.E. (*Vita* 71).[89] At a later time

84. See the use of the terms by Rathbone, "Egypt, Augustus and Roman Taxation," 86–97.

85. Dio (*Hist.* 62.3.3) also refers to the tribute as κεφαλὰς ὑποτελεῖς; see n. 14 above. Appian (*Bell. pun.* 8.20.135) says that at the end of the Punic Wars in 146 B.C.E. the Romans imposed τοῖς δὲ λοιποῖς φόρον ὥρισαν ἐπὶ τῇ γῇ καὶ ἐπὶ τοῖς σώμασιν, ἀνδρὶ καὶ γυναικὶ ὁμοίως. Rathbone ("Egypt, Augustus and Roman Taxation," 95, n. 43) thinks that Appian's tribute ἐπὶ τοῖς σώμασιν is "an erroneous retrojection of the imperial situation." Rathbone (p. 97) also considers that "the lumping in of fixed capitation charges, such as trade-taxes (*cheironaxia*) and, after A.D. 70, the Jewish tax, with the poll-tax proper as part of the *tributum capitis*, which is well-attested in Egypt, was probably common practice."

86. See Brunt, "Revenues of Rome," 166–68; and Neesen, *Staatsabgaben*, 117–20. Brunt (p. 168), writing against Neesen, observes quizzically: "Moveables (if we except the *instrumentum fundi*) cannot be brought under *tributum soli*. We must then infer that *tributum capitis* had a wider connotation than N. admits, and that *caput* must have meant something like 'personality'; for analogies we may think of its sense as 'civic status' or of its use in the late empire as a unit of taxable wealth, equivalent to *iugum*." See also Brunt, *Roman Imperial Themes*, 349–50; Duncan-Jones, *Structure and Scale*, 196–97.

87. See chapter 2.

88. See *B.J.* 2.200; also Schürer, *History*, 1:394–97.

89. See below.

Domitian exempted Josephus's property in Judea from taxation (*Vita* 429; see also 422, 425). It should be borne in mind, however, that by this time all Jewish territory was imperial property and subject to tribute (or, possibly, rent) (*B.J.* 7.216–17).[90]

Extant sources do not provide details about the organization of the provincial *tributum soli* in Judea. We do not know if the tribute touched landed property itself or the annual produce. Julius Caesar asked for a percentage of the annual produce, and this system could have continued under the *praefecti* after Quirinius's assessment. Appian (*Syr.* 11.8.50) reports, in the middle of the second century C.E., that the "Syrians and Cilicians also are subject to an annual tax of one hundredth of the assessed value of the property of each man."[91] It is often assumed that the inhabitants of Judea also, being part of Syria, paid a tribute of 1 percent of the total value of their assessed property.[92] As Millar points out, however, Appian's report "manages to combine sweeping assertions with a lack of concrete details." Moreover, Babatha's census return shows nothing of the system that Appian describes. There is no valuation of her total landed property. Instead, she pays taxes at a rate assessed on each individual piece of property.[93] Thus, Appian's system of valuation and rate of taxation may not have applied to Judea in the first century.[94]

When assessed on the value of property, the *tributum soli* in the provinces may have been levied not only on the landed property itself, but also on its appurtenances (*instrumentum fundi*), that is, on whatever was needed for the exploitation of the property: slaves, animals, equipment used for cultivation and processing of crops, wagons, boats, farm buildings and storage facilities, and so on.[95] There is no hint of similar valuations in Judea and especially in Babatha's census return. I share

---

90. The legal and financial consequences of Vespasian's treatment of the territory are not clear. See Schürer, *History*, 1:512 and n. 141.

91. ἔστι δὲ καὶ Σύροις και Κίλιξιν ἐτήσιος, ἑκατοστὴ τοῦ τιμήματος ἑκάστῳ. See Jones, *Roman Economy*, 164.

92. See Heichelheim, "Roman Syria," 231, and many other authors who depend on his work.

93. See Millar, *Roman Near East*, 110.

94. Menahem Stern ("Province of Judaea," 331, for example) thinks that "the scale of taxation did not alter much in the period of direct Roman rule" from what Julius Caesar had imposed on the Jews. P. A. Brunt, "Addendum III," in *The Roman Economy: Studies in Ancient Economic and Administrative History*, by A. H. M. Jones (Oxford: Blackwell, 1974), 183: "The 1 percent capital levy in Syria is attested only for a time after Vespasian."

95. For instance, Tacitus, *Ann.* 13.51: "In the provinces over sea [under Nero], the transport of grain was made less expensive, and it was laid down that cargo-boats were not to be included in the assessment of a merchant's property nor treated as taxable." Neesen, *Staatsabgaben*, 57–61; Brunt, "Revenues of Rome," 166. Brunt (p. 164) rejects Neesen's (p. 59) treatment of the cargo boats in this passage as an *instrumentum fundi*.

Brunt's later doubt that, for Judea, an attempt was made in the provincial census to assess all capital.[96]

Tributum Capitis

A population census—a registration of persons in a household (κατ' οἰκίαν ἀπογραφή)—is necessary for the imposition of a poll tax. The format of the census in 6 C.E. and Babatha's census return constitute *prima facie* rebuttals of the view that the inhabitants of Judea paid a *tributum capitis*—the poll tax—before 70 C.E. However, several pieces of evidence have been cited that seem to indicate the contrary, particularly: (1) Appian's statement in *Syr.* 11.8.50; (2) the "tribute to Caesar" episode in the Gospels; and (3) the passage by the jurist Ulpian on the census registration and the notice by the jurist Paul concerning the foundation of the Roman colony in Caesarea.

Appian's statement that "the poll-tax imposed upon all Jews is heavier than that imposed upon the surrounding peoples," as I showed in chapter 1, is a retrospective explanation of the condition of the Jews in the second century C.E.[97] The "poll tax" about which Appian speaks is the temple tax converted by Vespasian into a head tax imposed on all Jews in the empire after the fall of Jerusalem in 70 C.E. (*B.J.* 7.218).[98]

"At the time of Tiberius," Heichelheim writes, "Judaea paid a poll tax of one denarius, which had been introduced after the dethronement of Archelaos and the confiscation of his kingdom."[99] For evidence, Heichelheim cites Mark 12:13–17 and its parallels in Matt 22:15–22 and Luke 20:20–26, and a page of an article by Martin Rist.[100] This view, namely, that the Gospel passages provide evidence that "under Tiberius" the Jews paid "a poll tax," which had been introduced in Judea through the census of 6 C.E. has become an orthodoxy among ancient historians and New

---

96. Brunt, *Roman Imperial Themes*, 533; see above.

97. Jones (*Roman Economy*, 173, n. 114) attributes Appian's taxes to "Syria from 63 B.C." According to Schürer (*History*, 1:402), however, the taxes in *Syr.* 11.8.50 belong to "Appian's time."

98. Dio, *Hist.*, 65.7.2; See chapter 1. Rathbone ("Egypt, Augustus and Roman Taxation," 97, n. 48) thinks that Appian is "talking about extra charges (such as the 'Jewish tax') rolled in with the poll-tax proper." See also Neesen, *Staatsabgaben*, 119–20. Heichelheim ("Roman Syria," 237) writes erroneously that "Vespasian introduced the *fiscus Judaicus*, a poll tax which amounted to two denarii yearly, to take the place of the tithes which had been spent upon the temple before its destruction . . . ." Vespasian's poll tax replaced the temple tax, not "tithes."

99. Heichelheim, "Roman Syria," 237.

100. Heichelheim, "Roman Syria," 237, n. 36; see Martin Rist, "Caesar or God (Mark 12:13–17)? A Study in Formgeschichte," *JR* 16 (1936): 317–31.

Testament scholars alike. The passages are, therefore, worth discussing in detail.

Mark 12:13–17 is the well-known pericope about the payment of "tribute to Caesar." Jesus was reportedly asked in Jerusalem (v. 14): "Is it lawful to pay taxes to the emperor, or not?" The text translated here by the NRSV actually reads in Greek: ἔξεστιν δοῦναι κῆνσον Καίσαρι ἢ οὔ; Jesus, in response, asked for a denarius (v. 15). After the coin was brought to him, he asked his interlocutors, "Whose head is this, and whose title?" They answered, "The emperor's" (v. 16). Jesus then said, "Give to the emperor the things that are the emperor's, and to God the things that are God's."[101]

Many New Testament scholars, going back to the views of Rudolf Bultmann, accept on form-critical grounds that the Gospel passage, in particular the saying in Mark 12:17//Matt 20:22//Luke 20:25, is an authentic Jesus tradition.[102] Davies and Allison summarize this consensus: "Scholars have generally refrained from composing hypothetical tradition-histories for Mark 12.13–17 par. Apart from v. 13 there are few signs of Mark's hand, and most have found in the stylized scene authentic reminiscence."[103] Wolfang Weiss rejects this consensus, as does John Meier, who writes on Mark 12:13: "Hence Mark 3:6 and 12:13, as they stand in Mark's text, tell us nothing reliable about particular incidents in the life of the historical Jesus."[104]

The question whether or not the saying in Mark 12:17//Matt 20:22//Luke 20:25 is historically realible does not need to be argued here. Nor must we determine whether Jesus might have been questioned at some point in his life about the payment of tribute to Rome. It is important to emphasize, however, that the story as it now stands is part of Mark's Gospel narrative, and the same is true of the parallels in Matthew and in Luke. In the narrative structure of the Gospels, the incident takes place in Jerusalem.[105] Apart from this (indirect) piece of information,

---

101. Mark 12:17: Τὰ Καίσαρος ἀπόδοτε Καίσαρι καὶ τὰ τοῦ θεοῦ τῷ θεῷ.

102. Rudolf Bultmann, *The History of the Synoptic Tradition* (trans. John Marsh; Oxford: Blackwell, 1963), 26: "It is hardly possible that the saying of Jesus in v. 17 ever circulated independently. It is much more likely that we have an apophthegm here which was conceived as an unity and excellently constructed. Only in v. 13 can we discern any of Mark's editorial work. There is no reason, in my view, for supposing that this is a community product."

103. Davies and Allison, *Matthew*, 3:211. See, among other authors, Vincent Taylor, *Formation of the Gospel Tradition* (London: Macmillan, 1949), 64–65; idem, *The Gospel According to St. Mark* (2nd ed.; London: Macmillan, 1966), 477–78; John Dominic Crossan, *Four Other Gospels: Shadows on the Contours of Canon* (Minneapolis: Winston, 1985), 85–86; Crossan, *Historical Jesus*, 352, 438.

104. Meier, *Marginal Jew*, 3:565; Wolfgang Weiss, *"Eine neue Lehre in Vollmacht": die Streit- und Schulgespräche des Markus-Evangeliums* (Berlin: Walter de Gruyter, 1989), 202–34.

105. See Millar, *Roman Near East*, 48.

however, the narrative part of the pericope has no statement of time or place, and the only indication of what is at stake in the dialogue is that Jesus' interlocutors were sent in order "to trap him in what he said" (Mark 12:13).[106] This means, consequently, that scholars have to reconstruct the narrative context of the incident.

Rist, whom Heichelheim cites,[107] thinks that "an earlier gospel tradition dealing with the problem of the payment of taxes by the Jews to their Roman conquerors has been adapted to the Gentile-Christian situation in which emperor worship, not the payment of tribute to a foreign power, had become a pressing issue." The dialogue about the denarius, in Rist's view, did not belong to the original story. Thus, whereas "it may be reasonably assumed that Jesus was questioned not once but several times concerning the advisability of paying taxes to Rome; for this was a burning issue among the Jews of his day," with the introduction of the coin bearing the image of Caesar into the narrative, "the emphasis of the pericope shifts from the Jewish problem of paying tribute to Caesar to the Christian dilemma of worshipping him as a god."[108] Rist departs from the more prevalent view that the narrative context (*Sitz im Leben*) of the story *as it now stands* is the question of payment of tribute to Rome.

Rist's work is significant because it investigates the historical plausibility of the assumptions of the pericope's (reconstructed) narrative context. This is also Meier's approach. He raises questions about the historicity of Jesus' interlocutors ("some Pharisees and some Herodians") in Mark 12:13.[109] Other scholars usually assume that the pericope's narrative context contains authentic, that is, historical "reminiscence." The precise question (to use Meier's formulation[110]) is whether Mark 12:13–17 and its parallels supply us with any specific historical information about taxation in Judea during Jesus' time.[111] The answer to this question lies in two

106. Matt 22:15: "[T]he Pharisees went and plotted to entrap him in what he said." Luke 20:20: "[T]hey [the chief priests, the scribes, and the elders, see v. 1] watched him and sent spies who pretended to be honest, in order to trap him by what he said."

107. We should note that neither on p. 317 nor anywhere else in his article does Rist assert what Heichelheim attributes to him, namely, that Mark 12:13–17 is evidence of the historical fact that the Jews paid a poll tax amounting to one denarius.

108. Rist, "Caesar or God," 319, 325, 326.

109. Meier, *Marginal Jew*, 3:560–65; also idem, "The Historical Jesus and the Historical Herodians," *JBL* 119 (2000): 740–46.

110. See Meier, *Marginal Jew*, 3:565.

111. In answer to this question, it is interesting to note that historians of Roman imperial administration cite the New Testament passages as evidence for conditions in Judea. See, for example, Heichelheim, "Roman Syria," 237, cited above; Jones (*Roman Economy*, 173–74, n. 114) cites Mark 12:14 and observes: "I know no other specific evidence, outside of Judaea, for Augustus' responsibility [for capitation taxes] . . . ." Brunt, "Revenues of Rome," 164: "The intimate connection between census and direct taxation in the minds of provincials in

references in the passages: first, the phrase "to pay a *census*" in the question put to Jesus, ἔξεστιν δοῦναι κῆνσον Καίσαρι ἢ οὔ; (Mark 12:14; Matt 22:17) and, second, Jesus' call for a denarius, φέρετέ μοι δηνάριον, in Mark 12:15 (see Matt 22:19; Luke 20:24). In the New Testament, the word κῆνσος occurs only in Mark 12:14; Matt 22:17, 19; and Matt 17:25, where Jesus, commenting on the demand for the temple tax (*didrachma*), asks Simon, "from whom do kings of the earth take toll or tribute" (οἱ βασιλεῖς τῆς γῆς ἀπὸ τίνων λαμβάνουσιν τέλη ἢ κῆσον)? The view that Judea paid a poll tax during Jesus' lifetime is derived from the word κῆνσος in these passages. "It means 'poll-tax,'" write Davies and Allison on the expression τέλη ἢ κῆνσον in Matt 17:25, "[t]ogether the two words cover indirect and direct taxes, that is, taxes of every kind (cf. Rom 13.7, where φόρος and τέλος perform this function)."[112]

Judaea appears from the fact that *kensos* can be used as eqivalent to *phoros* (Matt. 22, 17 and Mark 12, 14 with Luke 20, 22), just as in Egypt *laographia* meant poll-tax." Rathbone, "Egypt, Augustus and Roman Taxation," 88: "the close Judaean parallel of the use of *kensos* (*census*) in Matthew and Mark to denote the Roman poll-tax based on the census is a strong indication that the new extended use of the term *laographia* in Egypt reflected the introduction of a Roman-style poll-tax." New Testament scholars appeal to the conditions in Judea as they are reconstructed by historians of imperial administration. Typically, see Davies and Allison, *Matthew*, 3:214: "The word [κῆνσος] refers to the Roman *census*, a tax upon agricultural yield (*tributum soli*) and personal property (*tributum capitis*). The *tributum capitis* was collected through census, or registration (Lk. 2.1–5; Acts 5.37), and probably amounted to one denarius a year." They cite (n. 30) Schürer, *History*, 1:399–427, who discusses the census under Quirinius without mentioning Mark 12:13–17 and parallels. F. F. Bruce, "Render to Caesar," in *Jesus and the Politics of His Day* (ed. Ernst Bammel and C. F. D. Moule; Cambridge: Cambridge University Press, 1984), 253: "a census was held under the supervision of the legate of Syria, P. Sulpicius Quirinius, to assess the annual amount which the new province could reasonably be expected to raise. Under the principate the tribute consisted mainly of a tax on landed property (*tributum agri* or *tributum soli*), calculated on the estimated annual yield in crops and cattle, together with a tax on personal property of other kinds (*tributum capitis*)." To justify this view, Bruce (n. 30) cites Ulpian, in *Digest*, L.15.4 and Paul, in *Digest*, L.15.8. Jewish historians appeal to both. Thus, Menahem Stern, "Province of Judaea," 331–32: "A conjecture has been made on the basis of the New Testament that the poll-tax imposed on Judea at the end of the Second Temple period was at the rate of one denarius. It might also be possible to conclude from the New Testament that the poll-tax in Roman Palestine was called, at least among the populace, and perhaps in the official terminology, by the Latin name of *census*, like the population survey which formed the basis of the tax, just as in Egypt the Greek equivalent for *census*, λαογραφία, also meant 'population census.'" He cites (p. 331, n. 5) the Gospel passages and Heichelheim, "Roman Syria," 237. Schalit (*König Herodes*, 272 and n. 427) likewise, cites the Gospel passages, Heichelheim (p. 237), and Rist (p. 317).

112. Davies and Allison, *Matthew*, 2:744. Matt 22:17, see above. Taylor, *Mark*, 479: "The word κῆνσος, Mt. xvii.25, xxii. 17, 19, is a transliteration of the Latin *census*, 'poll-tax'. . . . The tax in question was paid directly into the Imperial *fiscus* and was especially hateful to Jews as a sign of subjection and because the coinage (δηνάριον) bore the name and image of Caesar." Bruce, "Render to Caesar," 257–8: "The word rendered 'tribute' is κῆνσος, a loanword from Latin *census* ('assessment', 'tax'). . . ." See literature cited in the previous note.

Luke 20:22 renders the parallel to Mark 12:14 as ἔξεστιν ἡμᾶς Καίσαρι φόρον δοῦναι ἢ οὔ.[113] This strengthens the view, as we see in Davies and Allison, that the words κῆνσος and φόρος are interchangeable and that, therefore, κῆνσος means "tax." Since the *tributum* was abolished in 167 B.C.E., the census of Roman citizens ceased to be used for tax purposes.[114] The Latin word *census* could not have been synonymous with the word *tributum* in the first century C.E.[115] The Greek word κῆνσος does not occur in Josephus's works. G. H. R. Horsley has gathered the available occurrences of the word in inscriptions and papyri.[116] There is no case cited in which the word can be taken to mean "tax," rather than "census" or "registration."[117] The earliest attestation of the word is in the inscription from the first century B.C.E. (Bizye, Black Sea Region): βασιλέα Κό[τυ](ν) βασιλέως Ῥησκουπορέως υἱ[ὸν] Ῥωμαῖοι οἱ πρώ(τ)ως κατακληθέντες εἰς κῆνσον ἑατῶν (sic) θεόν. Horsley notes that this is "clearly a reference to the Roman census and therefore relevant for the NT occurrences at Mt. 17.25; 22.17,19; Mk. 12.14." The meaning of the word here also is clearly "census" or "assessment" rather than "tax." Other attestations of the word are from the second century C.E. and later. There is, in any case, no instance in which the Greek word is used to mean "tax" or "tribute."[118]

The view that the word κῆνσος in Mark 12:14, Matt 22:17,19 and 17:25 means "tax" is, therefore, surmised from the supposition that Roman provincial censuses since Augustus were an assessment *for the purpose of taxation*. The terms κῆνσος and φόρος in the Gospel passages contain no further information beyond this supposition. They are only vague recollections of the fact that there once had been a census in Judea, leading to Roman taxation.[119] These terms and the "reminiscence" from which they

113. Translated by the NRSV as "Is it lawful for us to pay taxes to the emperor, or not?"

114. See discussions in T. P. Wiseman, "The Census in the First Century B.C," *JRS* 68 (1958): 59–75; Nicolet, *World of the Citizen*, 49–88.

115. "Tax" is not one of the meanings given for *census* in Lewis and Short, *Latin Dictionary*, 315.

116. G. H. R. Horsley, ed., *A Review of the Greek Inscriptions and Papyri Published in 1978* (vol. 3 of *NewDocs*; North Ryde: Macquarie University Press, 1983), 70–71 no. 44.

117. G. H. R. Horsley (*Greek Inscriptions and Papyri Published in 1978*, 71) points out correctly, that "κῆνσος never occurs in census returns, where the standard word is the common ἀπογραφή."

118. The 1968 (repr. of the 9th edition [1940]) edition of *LSJ*, (s.v κῆνσος) gives to this word the meaning "I. Lat. *census*," and cites Matt 22:19. For the meaning, "II. *poll-tax*," it cites Matt 17:25. The "Revised Supplement" to the 1968 reprint, however, has the following entry for κῆνσος: "after '*Ev.Matt.*' insert '17.25' and delete section II." In the "Revised Supplement" to the 1996 reprint, the entry reads: "for '= Lat. *census*' read '*assessment* (for tax purposes)'; after '*Ev.Matt.*' insert '17.25' II, delete the section." See Liddell et al., *LSJ*, "Supplement," 176. In other words, the compilers of the lexicon have come to the conclusion that there is no evidence to corroborate the meaning "tax," "poll-tax," and the like.

119. Luke 2:1–5, together with the fact that Acts 5:36–37 places Theudas (who was

arise tell us nothing specific about Roman taxation in Jewish Palestine in the second and third decades of the first century C.E. The Gospel writers do not tell us if the census resulted in a poll tax, a *tributum capitis*, a *tributum soli*, direct taxes, indirect taxes, or any other form of tribute. To postulate otherwise is simply to indulge in a circular argument.[120]

The second significant issue, we noted, is Jesus' call in the Gospel passages for a denarius. The formulation of Jesus' demand in Mark (12:15c: φέρετέ μοι δηνάριον ἵνα ἴδω) and Luke's rendering of it (20:24a: δείξατέ μοι δηνάριον) do not directly imply that there exists a relationship between the denarius and the tax due to Caesar. This relationship is established by Matthew's version of both Jesus' demand and the response of his audience (22:19): ἐπιδείξατέ μοι τὸ νόμισμα τοῦ κήνσου. οἱ δὲ προσήνεγκαν αὐτῷ δηνάριον, "'Show me the coin used for the tax.' And they brought him a denarius." The denarius is, thus, the "coin of the κῆνσος." If the connection that is made here between Roman taxation in Jewish Palestine and the denarius is a true reminiscence of the conditions in Judea under the *praefecti*, Matthew's passage would constitute the only direct evidence we have that Rome levied taxes *in coins* from the territory, and in denarii precisely. Whether or not taxes were levied and collected in denarii, all three Gospel passages suggest (or so scholars claim) that the Roman denomination was current in Judea at the time when Jesus lived.

The evidence available does not allow us to settle decisively the question whether or not the *tributum soli* was paid only in kind. For the Roman Empire in general, the issue of the modes of payment for direct taxes, in kind or in cash, raises complex problems.[121] Jones's view that Augustan provincial censuses introduced pro rata land taxes paid in cash is not supported by the evidence.[122] It is impossible to know how much of the tax revenue that Rome raised in its provinces was collected in coins, and what impact this would have had on the empire.[123] Although the

---

active in about 45 C.E. [see *A.J.* 20.97–99]) before the revolts that accompanied the census of 6 C.E., indicates that the Gospel writers' recollection of the census and its consequences was imprecise.

120. Κῆνσος in Matt 17:25 is not an independent attestation of the word, since it is taken over by the author of Matthew's Gospel from Matt 22:15 = Mark 12:14. The expression τέλη ἢ κῆνσος in Matt 17:25 might not represent a conscious attempt to distinguish between indirect and direct taxes.

121. See chapter 4 and n. 256; Keith Hopkins, "Taxes and Trade in the Roman Empire, 200 B.C.-A.D. 400," *JRS* 70 (1980): 101–25; Brunt, "Revenues of Rome," 161–62; Duncan-Jones, *Structure and Scale*, 187–98; Millar, *Roman Near East*, 49–50.

122. A. H. M. Jones, "Rome and the Provincial Cities," *Revue de l'histoire du droit* 39 (1971): 528 and 540; idem, *Roman Economy*, 164–65.

123. See the discussions in Kenneth W. Harl, *Coinage in the Roman Economy, 300 B.C. to A.D. 700* (Baltimore, Md.: Johns Hopkins University Press, 1996), 231–49.

Roman Empire was to some extent monetized, its economic basis remained for the most part agricultural.

Babatha paid part of her tax in produce (measures of dates) (*P. Yadin* 16.19–32). She also paid a "crown tax" (στεφανικόν) (16.20, 27, 32) calculated in relation to her landed property, in cash. For her second property she paid half of her produce and no cash payment for the "crown tax" (16.21–24). "—os son of Simon," on the contrary, seems to have paid his tax only in cash.[124] The "crown tax" is not explicitly mentioned in his return. A comparison of the amount of his cash payment with the amounts recorded in Babatha's census return suggests that "—os son of Simon" paid the equivalent amount to Babatha's "crown tax." We do not know what portion of the *tributum soli* was paid as a "crown tax," or why. It is possible that "crown tax" is a term used in the Babatha census return to refer to the equivalent payment in cash for taxes that also could have been paid in produce.

Josephus's only account of the actual collection of tribute in the province of Judea seems to suggest that cash payment might have been involved. What he says, however, is ambiguous. After Agrippa II had harangued the rebellious Jews in 66 C.E. for not paying their tribute to Caesar,[125] he advised them: "If you wish to clear yourselves of the charge of insurrection, re-establish the porticoes and pay the tax [tribute] (καὶ τελέσετε τὴν εἰσφοράν); for assuredly the fortress does not belong to Florus, and it is not Florus to whom your money will go" (*B.J.* 2.404). Leading Jews then went into the villages around Jerusalem and levied the tribute (*B.J.* 2.405).[126] Josephus says that it was "rapidly (ταχέως) collected," and he gives the amounts due in arrears as forty talents (*B.J.* 2.405). The apparent speed with which the tribute was collected and the fact that Josephus presents the figures in talents might imply that the payment was made in cash. The situation that Josephus describes was that of an emergency, and the Jewish leaders might have exacted cash contributions. It need not necessarily have been the case, however, that the Jewish leaders collected cash, since payments that were made in produce could very well have been assessed in cash.[127]

The conclusion that, in general, payment was made in kind may be drawn from the presence of stores of "imperial corn" (Καίσαρος σῖτον) in

---

124. Naphtali Lewis, "Jewish Landowner," 134, lines 15–16.

125. *B.J.* 2.403: οὔτε γὰρ Καίσαρι δεδώκατε τὸν φόρον.

126. Agrippa subsequently sent a delegation to Florus in Caesarea "in order that he might appoint some of their number to collect the tribute in the country" (*B.J.* 2.407).

127. According to Suetonius (*Jul.* 25), Caesar assessed the tribute he imposed on Gaul in cash, even though payment would have been made in kind. See Brunt, "Revenues of Rome," 161–62. Josephus provides cash values for the revenues of Herod's kingdom. See the discussion in chapter 4.

the villages of Upper Galilee. Tribute thus collected in produce could, if necessary, be converted into needed cash, as is illustrated by Josephus's charge that his rival, John of Gischala, wanted to seize this stock of grain in order to use the proceeds from it to repair the walls of his hometown (*Vita* 70–73).[128]

The New Testament scholars who maintain that Rome assessed and collected taxes in denarii cite the bilingual (Palmyrene/Greek) inscription from Palmyra. According to F. F. Bruce:

> Jesus's reply, 'Bring me a *denarius*; let me see it', suggests that the Roman tribute was to be paid in Roman money. That this was indeed so is indicated on a Greek inscription from Palmyra (dated A.D. 136/7) which lays down that various dues are to be paid in *denarii* (εἰς δηνάριον) and cites as evidence a rescript of Germanicus Caesar (who exercised a *maius imperium* in the eastern provinces from A.D. 17 to 19) to Statilius (perhaps financial procurator of Syria), directing that all state taxes (τέλη) are to be collected in asses (εἰς ἀσσάριον), i.e. in Roman coinage (the *as* being then one-sixteenth of a *denarius* in value).[129]

Bruce refers to the inscription (lines 153–56) as it is presented in *OGIS* 629:[130]

> Τὸ τοῦ σφάκτρου τέλος εἰς δηνάριον ὀφείλει λο[γεύεσθαι,]
> καὶ Γερμανικοῦ Καίσαρος διὰ τῆς πρὸς Στατείλι[ον
> ἐπισ]||τολῆς διασαφήσαντος ὅτι δεῖ πρὸς ἀσσάριον
> πά[ντα] τὰ τέλη λογεύεσθαι· τὸ δὲ ἐντὸς δηναρίου τέλο[ς
> τῇ] συνηθείᾳ ὁ τελώνης πρὸς κέρμα πράξει. τῶ[ν δὲ]
> διὰ τὸ νεκριμαῖα εἶναι ῥειπτουμένων τὸ τέλ[ος οὐκ ὀφείλεται]

Dittenberger's text is, unfortunately, inaccurate.[131] For instance, he restores the word πάντα in line 156, that is, in the reference to the letter from Ger-

128. See above.

129. Bruce, "Render to Caesar," 258. Similarly, Henry St. John Hart, "The Coin of 'Render Unto Caesar . . .': A Note on Some Aspects of Mark 12:13–17; Matt. 22:15–22; Luke 20:20–26," in *Jesus and the Politics of His Day* (ed. Ernst Bammel and C. F. D. Moule; Cambridge: Cambridge University Press, 1984), 241: "The δηνάριον is the kind of coin in which the tribute is calculated and in which, by implication, it is to be paid." Bruce's and Hart's views are adopted by others, for example, Davies and Allison, *Matthew*, 3:215 and n. 42.

130. Bruce, "Render to Caesar," 258, n. 59; see Hart, "Coin," 241, n. 2. Hart refers also to R. Cagnat, *IGRR*, 3:1056. Davies and Allison, *Matthew*, 3:215, n. 42.

131. Matthews, "Tax Law," 157: "The standard publication of the Greek text alone in W. Dittenberger's *Orientis Graeci Inscriptiones Selectae* (OGIS) II (1905), no. 629, is unsatisfactory from many points of view. It makes insufficient use of the Palmyrene text for establishing points of detail in the Greek text where this is incomplete, contains misunderstandings and in its omissions and unclear presentation makes no sense of the structure of the text."

manicus. This misled Bruce to assert that Germanicus directed that *all* taxes were to be paid in *asses*. This passage has been restored more correctly in other editions of the decree, as in *CIS* (2.3, no. 3913, lines 182–84):[132]

> 182 καὶ Γερμανικοῦ Καίσαρος διὰ τῆς πρὸς Στατείλι[ον ἐπισ-]
> 183 τολῆς διασαφήσαντος ὅτι δεῖ πρὸς ἀσσάριον ἰτα[λικόν]
> 184 τέλη λογεύεσθαι·

This agrees with Chabot's Latin translation of the Palmyrene text:

> quemadmodum etiam Germanicus Caesar | in epistola, scripta ad Statilium, explicuit | debere vectigalia ad italicum assem | exigi.[133]

J. F. Matthews renders the whole passage as follows:

> 181 The tax on animals for slaughter should be reckoned in denarii, as Germanicus Caesar also made clear in his letter to Statilius, to the effect that taxes should be reckoned in Italian asses. Any tax of less than a denarius the tax collector will exact according to custom in small coin. In the case of animals rejected on account of natural death the tax is not due.[134]

Manifestly, Germanicus did not write that *all* state taxes should be collected in *asses* or in denarii, but that tolls be reckoned in Italian *asses*. That other denominations were acceptable can be seen in the cases in which the tolls to be paid were less than a denarius. The local Palmyrene coin is said explicitly in these cases to be acceptable. The necessity for reckoning the tolls in Italian *asses* is completely comprehensible, since in this fashion a standard value could be established in a market in which merchandise might arrive from every part of the empire, and from Parthia and India. Babatha and "—son of Simon" did not pay their taxes in denarii. Their taxes were reckoned in the local currency, in "blacks" (μελαίνας) and their fractions (of sixty units of *lepta*).[135]

---

132. Chabot, *CIS*, no. 3913. See also Cooke, *Text-Book*, no. 147. Chabot provides a Latin translation of the Palmyrene text to accompany the incomplete text in R. Cagnat, *IGRR*, 3:1056.

133. R. Cagnat, *IGRR*, 3:1056; see also Chabot, *Choix d'inscriptions*, 35: "comme l'a exposé Germanicus César dans la lettre qu'il écrivit à Statilius: 'Il est de règle que les impôts soient perçus à la valeur de l'as italique.'"

134. Matthews, "Tax Law," 179. Before Matthews's translation, that of Heichelheim was the fullest English text available; see Heichelheim, "Roman Syria," 250–54. He rendered the passage (p. 253): "as Caesar Germanicus made clear in a letter to Statilius, in which he stated that the dues must be reckoned in the Italian as."

135. P.Yadin 16.20–21, 27–28, 32; Naphtali Lewis, "Jewish Landowner," 134, lines 16–17; see also p. 137. The coinage used in these documents has not been identified. See Naphtali Lewis et al., *Documents*, 16.

Moreover, it should be emphasized that the Palmyra inscription is not about Roman tribute but about tolls and duties (τέλη, *portoria*) paid on a variety of goods listed on the inscription. Further, these tolls, as Matthews underlines, following the works by H. Seyrig and J.-P. Rey-Coquais, were not those imposed on the goods passing through Palmyra by the caravan trade that gave the city its remarkable prosperity.[136] The inscription comes from the decree of the *boulē* of the city, regulating tolls on the goods destined for the local economy of the city and its territory. The taxes in the inscription, therefore, were not Roman ("state") taxes, but tolls that the city of Palmyra levied and collected for its internal administration. Nor is it known who Statilius was, to whom Germanicus addressed his letter. That he was a procurator of Syria is one conjecture. Another idea is that he was an "appointed official at Palmyra," like the person mentioned in lines 129–30 of the tax laws (in Matthews's translation). At the very most, Germanicus's rescript might have sought, unsuccessfully, to regulate also the collection of tolls on the caravan trade, in which the Romans had a stronger hand.[137]

For a very long time scholars have thought that Jesus was shown a coin from the second series of Tiberius's denarii issued starting from about 15 C.E., which is thought to have been minted in Lugdunum (Gaul).[138] This, again, is an opinion derived from common sense: since Tiberius (14–37 C.E.) was the emperor at the time at which the incident supposedly occurred, the coin must have been that of Tiberius. Hart, who reevaluated this so-called problem of "identification," concluded, however:

> It remains highly probable that the coin shown to Jesus was one of the huge second series of *denarii* of Tiberius according to the standard "identification." To determine between this and his earlier series, or some earlier *denarius* of Caesar Augustus himself, also bearing the εἰκών and ἐπιγραφή of Caesar, is not now in our power, nor is it probable that it ever will be.[139]

---

136. Matthews, "Tax Law," 158, 172–73; H. Seyrig, "Le statut de Palmyre," *Syria* 22 (1941): 155–74, esp. p. 161; Rey-Coquais, "Syrie Romaine," 55, n. 151.

137. Matthews, "Tax Law," 161: "The tax law of 137 cites pronouncements by Germanicus Caesar (A.D. 18) and subsequent governors of Syria including Domitius Corbulo (60–63) and Licinius Mucianus (67–69), either issued for the specific use of Palmyra or at least applied to it by analogy with other cities in Syria."

138. The identification goes back to Madden, and probably earlier. See Madden, *Jewish Coinage*, 247 and n. 3: "It is excessively probable that the coin here engraved is a representation of the actual type that was shown to our Lord. This was the tribute money payable by the Jews to the Roman Emperor." He cites Matt 22:17, 19 and parallels, noting that "[t]he κηνσὸς was a poll-tax, and the φόρος [in Luke 20:24] a payment for state purposes"! On the location of minting, see Harold Mattingly, *Coins of the Roman Empire in the British Museum* (1923; repr., London: Trustees of the British Museum, 1965), 1:125–27, nos. 34–38, 42–45, 48–60, plates 22 and 23; also Hart, "Coin," 243, 246–47.

139. Hart, "Coin," 248.

The identification of the coin in the Gospel passages with an issue of Tiberius's coins argues from the conclusion; it assumes what the passages are supposed to prove, namely, that the imperial denarius was current in Jewish Palestine and was required for Roman taxation. As Leo Kadman put it: "These questions and answers were only possible when Jesus could assume that the silver pieces found in the purse of the man in the street were Roman or Roman imperial coins, with the image and legend of the emperor."[140] In 1945, Spencer Kennard challenged this assumption. He concluded that the hoards of coins in Syria at that time seemed "to indicate when taken in connection with the extensive finds of bronze coinage that the denarius can have had very little place in the lives of Jesus' Jewish contemporaries."[141]

Madden and Kadman relied excessively on literary sources (the Hebrew Bible, the New Testament, classical, rabbinic, and Christian literatures) in their study of coin currency in Jewish Palestine. The mention of the denarius in the Gospel, therefore, provides them with proof that the denarius was the silver coin in Jewish pockets in the second and third decades of the first century C.E. Thus, Kadman judges that Tyrian coins "were not in regular currency in Palestine, where the silver coins in circulation were almost exclusively Roman or Roman Imperial. Both the Gospels and Josephus refer to the use of this coinage only."[142]

Donald Ariel departs from this methodology and draws historical conclusions about currency only when the numismatic evidence warrants them.[143] His study provides the "systematic recording of the detail and locality of finds" of imperial denarii, the absence of which, according to Hart, prevented Kennard's argument from being cogent.[144] Counting surface, excavation, and hoard finds in Jerusalem, Ariel identified seven Roman coins dated before 67/68 C.E.[145] Of the seven coins, one (no. 54) is a silver denarius of Augustus (dated 2 B.C.E.–11 C.E.), one (no. 61) is a gold *Aureus* of Tiberius (dated 14–37 C.E.), and only one (no. 60) is a silver denarius of Tiberius (dated 14–37 C.E.). This coin was minted in Rome. Two other facts emerge from Ariel's study. First, Roman silver tetra-

---

140. Leo Kadman, "Temple Dues and Currency in Ancient Palestine in the Light of Recent Discovered Coin-Hoards," in *Atti del congresso internazionale di numismatica, Roma, 1961*, vol. 2 (Rome: Istituto Italiano di Numismatica, 1965), 70. Kadman is cited with approval by Hart, "Coin," 241, n. 2.

141. Spencer J. Kennard, Jr., "Syrian Coin Hoards and the Tribute Question," *AThR* 27 (1945): 248–52; quotation from p. 252.

142. Leo Kadman, "Temple Dues and Currency in Ancient Palestine in the Light of Recent Discovered Coin-Hoards," *Israel Numismatic Bulletin* 1 (1962): 10.

143. Donald T. Ariel, "A Survey of Coin Finds in Jerusalem (Until the End of Byzantine Period)," *LASBF* 32 (1982): 273–326.

144. Hart, "Coin," 245.

145. Ariel, "Survey," 312–14, table 3.

drachms and denarii were found in Jerusalem in significant numbers only after 69 C.E., especially after the reign of Vespasian. Second, in the period before 69 C.E., there was, on the contrary, a continued preponderance of Tyrian silver coins.

This picture is confirmed by finds of silver coins in Qumran and its surrounding areas. In the excavation of the site in 1955 three hoards with probably a total of 561 coins were found in Stratum II. Six of these were reportedly Roman denarii dating from 85/84 B.C.E.–41 B.C.E., and thirty-three of the coins were Seleucid tetradrachms and didrachms (minted in Tyre). The rest were Tyrian *sheqels* and half-*sheqels*.[146] These coins and other coin finds were part of Roland de Vaux's argument about the history of the site.[147] The final report on the excavations, with de Vaux's notes, records three hoards totaling 561 Tyrian coins in site 120.[148] The earliest Roman coins in this report are of Vespasian, from 69–70 C.E. in site 35,[149] and from 73 C.E. in site 29.[150] De Vaux noted earlier that Roman coins began to appear in the area in 67/68 C.E.[151]

Hart admitted that "hitherto early imperial denarii (i.e. those of Augustus and of Tiberius) have been rather few in authentic finds in Palestine." He, however, took the *Isfiya* Hoard find to be "evidence beginning to corroborate the picture afforded by the literary evidence of the New Testament and Josephus, certainly adding to the scanty evidence of earlier authenticated finds, that the Roman *denarius* played its part in the monetary system of Palestine in the time of the Gospels."[152] Hart's optimism is hardly justified, however. The *Isfiya* Hoard has not been published properly. According to Kadman, the hoard of about 4,500 coins contained 3,400 Tyrian shekels, 1,000 Tyrian half-shekels and "160 Roman Denarii of Augustus."[153] Yaᶜakov Meshorer apparently remarked regarding the hoard: "This hoard includes 3,400 Tyrian shekels, and 1,000 half-shekels dated from 40 B.C. to 53 A.D., and also 160 Roman denars.

146. M. Sharabani, "Monnaies de Qumrân au Musée Rockefeller de Jérusalem," *RB* 85 (1980): 274–84; see esp. p. 275.

147. Roland de Vaux, *Archaeology and the Dead Sea Scrolls* (London: British Academy, 1973), 34–41.

148. J.-B. Humbert and A. Chambon, *Fouilles de Khirbet Qumrân et de Aïn Feshkha* (Gottingen: Vandenhoeck & Ruprecht, 1994), 329–30; J.-B. Humbert and A. Chambon, *The Excavations of Khirbet Qumran and Ain Feshkha: Synthesis of Roland de Vaux's Field Notes* (trans. Stephen J. Pfann; Göttingen: Vandenhoeck & Ruprecht, 2003), 52.

149. Humbert and Chambon, *Fouilles de Qumrân*, 304; Humbert and Chambon, *Excavations of Khirbet Qumran*, 25.

150. Humbert and Chambon, *Fouilles de Qumrân*, 302; Humbert and Chambon, *Excavations of Khirbet Qumran*, 23.

151. De Vaux, *Archaeology*, 37–38, 41, 123, n. 1.

152. Hart, "Coin," 244–45.

153. See Kadman, "Temple Dues and Currency," 9–10.

Although Kadman wrote that all the denars are of Augustus, I can say for sure that at least 30 of them are of the Tiberius type." Meshorer also observed that "these Tiberius denars are quite rare in this part of the world," and he called the *Isfiya* Hoard "the only good example of a find including such coins."[154]

Hoards, by themselves, do not reflect actual currency, since conditions under which hoards are made include the times of crisis, when wealth usually is converted into the highest value and stowed away.[155] A quantitative analysis that also takes into account excavation and surface finds, such as Ariel provides, is necessary for determining actual currency. Moreover, the Tyrian coins in the *Isfiya* Hoard, as Meshorer notes, date from 40 B.C.E. to 53 C.E.[156] The *terminus post quem* for their hiding is, therefore, 53 C.E.,[157] that is, at least twenty-four years after Jesus. This date also is close enough to 66/70 C.E. to suggest that the coins were left hidden away during the First Revolt, or even at a later date.[158]

Whenever it was (in the second half of the first century C.E., or afterwards) that the coins in the *Isfiya* Hoard might have been hidden away, the proportion of the Roman denarii to Tyrian coins in the hoard is significant. It contained about 4,400 Tyrian coins to 160 Roman denarii, of which about 30 were of Tiberius. The finds from Qumran reveal a similar proportion. Tyrian coins also represent the largest percentage of all the coins found in the Upper Galilee (Khirbet Shemaᶜ, Gush Ḥalav, and Meiron)[159] and in Sepphoris.[160] Ariel concludes from his analysis of the coinage in Jerusalem that the Roman denarius did not become current in

---

154. In a private correspondence, published in Hart, "Coin," 248.

155. See discussions, for instance, in Harl, *Coinage*, 1–20; Patrick Bruun, "Site Finds and Hoarding Behaviour," in *Scripta Nummaria Romana: Essays Presented to Humphrey Sutherland* (ed. R. A. G. Carson and Colin M. Kraay; London: Spink, 1978), 114–23; M. H. Crawford, "Coin Hoards and the Pattern of Violence in the Late Republic," *PBSR* 37 (1969): 76–81; Donald T. Ariel, "The Coins from the Surveys and Excavations of Caves in the Northern Judean Desert," *ᶜAtiqot* 41, no. 2 (2002): 285–86.

156. See also Kadman, "Temple Dues and Currency," 9.

157. So also, ibid., 10.

158. Kadman ("Temple Dues and Currency," 10–11) thinks that the coins in the hoard, intended for payment of the temple tax, were concealed by a convoy of Jews traveling from Phoenicia to Jerusalem in May 67 C.E. For other interpretations of the hoard, see Arye Ben-David, *Jerusalem und Tyros: Ein Beitrag zur palästinensischen Münz- und Wirtschaftsgeschichte* (Basel: Kyklos-Verlag, 1969), 33–39.

159. Richard S. Hanson, *Tyrian Influence in the Upper Galilee* (Cambridge, Mass: American Schools of Oriental Research, 1980), 51–54. Hanson (pp. 51–52) observes that "[e]xcept for a goodly number of *antoniani* from the last half of the 3rd century C.E., Roman imperial coins are relatively sparse from the time of Roman conquest to the reign of Valerian, and most of the supply for that era came from local mints."

160. See Raynor and Meshorer, *Coins of Ancient Meiron*, 83–85; also Freyne, "Geography, Politics, and Economics," 115.

Jerusalem until after 70 C.E., although some Roman coins did circulate in the region. The silver currency of the region was Tyrian shekels.[161] Tyrian shekels and half-shekels formed the basis of the silver currency of the entire region throughout the period before the Jewish Revolt in 66 C.E.[162]

To summarize, some taxes, particularly tolls and duties, would have been paid in cash. However, the imperial denarii were not required for Roman taxation, and they did not form the basis of the silver currency of the region. The connection that is made in the Gospels, especially in Matt 22:19, between Roman taxation in Judea and the denarius does not offer any specific historical information about taxation in Jewish Palestine during Jesus' lifetime.

The other significant references to the *tributum capitis* in Syria, possibly including Judea,[163] are, first, Paul's report concerning Caesarea and, second, Ulpian's passage on the census registration (in Syria). According to Paul "[t]he deified Vespasian made Caesarea a colony without adding that they should possess *jus Italicum*, but he remitted the poll-tax there; and the deified Titus then interpreted the ruling to mean that their territory had also been made immune. The Capitolienses seem to be in the same position" (*Cens.* 2).[164] Paul's is a retrospective account, in the third century, of the formation of Caesarea into a Roman colony by the emperor Vespasian (69–79 C.E.). Caesarea, from its foundation by Herod the Great, remained part of the Jewish state until 70 C.E., after which it was settled with colonists by Vespasian.[165] If the *tributum capitis* from which Vespasian exempted the colonists was already in force in the region at the time of the exemption, then it was levied also in the rest of

161. Ariel, "Survey," 284–85, 300–301.

162. See also Dan Barag, "Tyrian Currency in Galilee," *INJ* 6–7 (1982–83): 12: "Tyrian silver shekels were undoubtedly in predominance during the first century B.C. and until the cessation of Tyre's silver issues in the mid 60's of the first century A.D. Josephus refers to Tyrian silver speaking of John Gishala who invested in oil, paying Tyrian tetradrachms: Τυρίου νομίσματος, ὃ τέσσαρας Ἀττικὰς δύναται. This predominance was, however, fairly general in Palestine, at least in the Jewish areas. After the cessation of the autonomous Tyrian silver issues the silver in circulation in Galilee was normal Roman Provincial silver struck at Antioch." See *B.J.* 2.592.

163. See Brunt, "Revenues of Rome," 172.

164. Paul, *Cens.* 2: "Diuus Uespasianus Caesarienses colonos fecit non adiecto, ut et iuris Italici essent, sed tributum his remisit capitis: sed diuus Titus etiam solum immune factum interpretatus est. similes his Capitulenses esse uidentur." Mommsen and Krueger, *Digest*, 4: L.15.8.7. For the formation of Caesarea into a colony by Vespasian, see also Pliny, *Nat.* 5.14.69. Jones, *Cities*, 277; Schürer, *History*, 2:117–18; Fergus Millar, "The Roman *Coloniae* of the Near East: A Study of Cultural Relations," in *Roman Eastern Policy and Other Studies in Roman History: Proceedings of a Colloquium at Tvärminne 2–3 October 1987* (ed. Heikki Solin and Mika Kajava; Helsinki: Finnish Society of Sciences and Letters, 1990), 26–27.

165. See the discussion in Schürer, *History*, 2:115–18.

Judea. We do not know, however, that such a tax was levied before 70 C.E. The Babatha census returns make it necessary to extend that doubt to the period afterwards.[166] In any event, Paul is assuming the situation in Palestine after 70 C.E., when the Decapolis had been refounded into *Capitolias* (before 98 C.E.)[167] and Jerusalem had been established as *Aelia Capitolina* by Hadrian (117–138 C.E.).[168] We have noted already that it is not clear what were the legal and fiscal implications of the fact that, in 70 C.E., Vespasian converted the whole of Judea into his private property and farmed out the land (*B.J.* 7.216–17).[169] Vespasian, apparently, was notorious, according to Suetonius, for "his love of money." He imposed new taxes on the provinces and increased and even doubled existing ones.[170]

Paul's notice has other problems. He might be making distinctions that existed in the third century. Moreover, his statement that Titus interpreted Vespasian's exemption from *tributum capitis* "to mean that their territory had also been made immune" from *tributum soli* (solum) indicates that Vespasian's *tributum capitis* was more than the head tax. Brunt thinks that the possibility "that *tributum capitis* had a wider connotation" than a tax levied on persons and real estate "might perhaps explain why Titus *construed* immunity from *tributum capitis* as comprising immunity from *tributum soli* (Dig. L. 15. 8. 7), and why *caput* acquired its later sense in the tax system."[171] In other words, if Ulpian is to be believed in his assertion that "in the provinces of Syria men are bound to pay poll-tax from fourteen, women from twelve, in both cases up to sixty-five" (*Cens.* 2),[172] scholars have yet to determine what *tributum capitis* means for both Paul and Ulpian and at what time, before the third century, this tax was introduced into different parts of Syria.

Josephus is aware of per capita taxes. Expanding 2 Sam 8:14, he claims that David collected, in Idumea, "tribute both from the country (as a whole) and from the separate individuals therein" (φόρους ὑπέρ τε τῆς

---

166. See above, and Millar, *Roman Near East*, 110.

167. See Schürer, *History*, 1:182–83, 2:521.

168. See Dio, *Hist.* 69.12.1; Millar, "Roman *Coloniae*," 28–30.

169. See above.

170. Suetonius, *Vesp.* 16.1: "For not content with reviving the imposts which had been repealed under Galba, he added new and heavy burdens, increasing the amount of tribute paid by the provinces, in some cases actually doubling it . . . ." See Brunt, "Addendum II," 183.

171. Brunt, "Revenues of Rome," 168, author's emphases; see n. 86 above.

172. Mommsen and Krueger, *Digest*, 4: L.15.3. See above. Brunt ("Revenues of Rome," 165) thinks that "the evidence for *tributum capitis* is so chancy and scattered that it is hard to believe that it was not universal, though not of course uniform in incidence." Millar (*Roman Near East*, 110), citing the same evidence, thinks that in Syria "[w]e have to assume that both a land tax (*tributum soli*) and a 'head-tax' were payable." Both authors, of course, attach the provisos already noted.

χώρας καὶ τῆς ἑκάστου κεφαλῆς παρ' αὐτῶν ἐδέχετο) (*A.J.* 109).[173] He mentions a head tax in the letter of Antiochus III (*A.J.* 12.142) and in the letter of Demetrius II (*A.J.* 13.50).[174] In the long catalog of provinces and their subjection to Roman power that King Agrippa II recounts in his speech to the Jewish rebels (*B.J.* 2.380–87), Africa is said to "pay tribute of all kinds" (ἔξωθεν παντοίως φορολογοῦνται) besides "their annual produce (χωρὶς δὲ τῶν ἐτησίων καρπῶν), which feeds for eight months of the year the populace of Rome" (*B.J.* 2.383). It is only to Egypt, however, that Agrippa explicitly attributes both a poll tax (καθ' ἑκάστην κεφαλὴν εἰσφορᾶς) paid in cash and a land tax: "besides money she sends corn to feed Rome for four months" (*B.J.* 2.385–86). The first mention of a *per capita* tribute paid by the Jews in Judea in the early Roman period is the temple tax,[175] converted by Vespasian into a head tax imposed upon all Jews after the fall of Jerusalem in 70 C.E.[176]

Other Taxes and the System of Collection

The most important form of provincial indirect taxes was tolls and duties. Rome inherited the system of indirect taxes developed by Herod and his successors, discussed in chapter 4. It is possible that the governors adapted these systems to fit their own needs. Albinus (who was governor from 62 to 64 C.E.), according to Josephus's complaint, did, "in his official capacity, steal and plunder private property and burden the whole nation with extraordinary taxes" (*B.J.* 2.272–73).[177] Albinius probably was not alone among the governors to have done so. I argued in chapter 4 that the "house tax" remitted by Agrippa I in 41 C.E. had been levied by one of the governors whom he succeeded (*A.J.* 19.299). Likewise, I suggested that the duties imposed on agricultural produce, probably brought into Jerusalem for sale (τὰ τέλη τῶν ὠνουμένων καρπῶν), which Vitellius remitted to the inhabitants of Jerusalem in 37 C.E., were imposed by the governors (*A.J.* 18.90).[178]

---

173. Bruce ("Render to Caesar," 253–54, n. 30) suggests that in this passage "Josephus probably transfers the situation of his day into an earlier period." It is, however, far from clear that Josephus here is making a distinction between a *tributum soli* and a *tributum capitis*, as Bruce implies.

174. On both passages see chapter 2 and n. 212.

175. See *A.J.* 3.194: εἰσφορὰν αὐτῷ προσέταξεν εἰσφέριεν σίκλου τὸ ἥμισυ καθ' ἕκαστον. *A.J.* 7.318: ὑπὲρ ἑκάστης κεφαλῆς αὐτοῦ τῷ θεῷ τελεῖν ἡμίσικλον.

176. See above. *B.J.* 7.218; Dio, *Hist.* 65.7.2. The temple-tax episode in Matt 17:24–27, which links that tax to τέλη ἢ κῆνσον, that is, (Roman) "taxes," belongs to the period after 70 C.E.

177. *B.J.* 2.272–73: τὸ πᾶν ἔθνος ἐβάρει ταῖς εἰσφοραῖς.

178. See chapter 4.

The system of tax collection in provincial Judea has remained elusive. John R. Donahue's now classic (at least among New Testament scholars) study of tax collectors in the New Testament is based on the notion that "direct taxes, at this time, were under the supervision of the central authority," whereas "indirect taxes, the tolls and other imposts, were farmed out to individual lessees."[179] In his view, therefore, "[d]uring the rule of the prefects and procurators the direct taxes, the poll tax and the land tax were not farmed out. The officials in charge of collecting these were in direct employ of the Romans."[180] He does not discuss the primary sources. Donahue is certainly correct that Julius Caesar abolished the Roman *publicani* from Judea and, consequently, "the classical system of publicans ceases to exist in Palestine."[181] His principal contribution to the question of tax collection in Judea is the recognition that the τελῶναι in the New Testament are not tax collectors, "those who collect the direct taxes," but toll collectors, that is, "functionaries or employees at the toll center (*telōnion*) as well as the rich man who buys the right to collect the tolls."[182]

Brunt argues that in the provinces of the empire the individual taxpayer was "liable to his city, the city to the Roman government. Collection within city territories was normally in the hands of local magistrates or liturgical officials."[183] This system would have existed "in every province from the time that the use of publicans was discarded."[184] Goodman observes, against Brunt, that in Babatha's census return there is no "sign of a role for the magistrates of the *polis* as is customarily reckoned normal."[185] In the one report of tax collection by Josephus (*B.J.* 2.405, 407), the arrears of tribute were collected in the villages around Jerusalem by "the magistrates and the members of the council" (ἄρχοντες καὶ βουλευταί [*B.J.* 2.405]).[186] It appears from this that the priestly aristocracy and the Sanhedrin were responsible for the collection of tribute, which they delivered afterwards to the Roman governor.

Josephus seems to suggest that the magistrates and members of the Sanhedrin personally collected the tribute. Even in the crisis of 66 C.E.

---

179. John R. Donahue, "Tax Collectors and Sinners: An Attempt at Identification," *CBQ* 33 (1971): 48–49. After Julius Caesar abolished "the publican system totally," he says (p. 44), "the system in Palestine would again resemble the Egyptian system; the collection of direct taxes firmly under control of the central government and the leasing out, by means of small contracts, of indirect taxes."

180. Ibid., 45.

181. Ibid., 44; see Brunt, "Addendum II," 181; and chapter 2.

182. Ibid., 54, 59.

183. Brunt, "Revenues of Rome," 168; see Jones, *Roman Economy*, 165.

184. Brunt, "Revenues of Rome," 169.

185. Goodman, "Babatha's Story," 172; see Brunt, "Revenues of Rome," 166; idem, *Roman Imperial Themes*, 334–35, 534–35.

186. See above.

described by Josephus, and certainly under normal conditions, they probably played a supervisory role, using agents who actually collected the tribute from the farmer. Herod levied taxes through his agents, described in *A.J.* 17.308 as "his slaves who were sent out to collect the tribute." Similarly, the high priestly aristocracy had their own "slaves" (δοῦλοι) and "servants" (οἰκέται), whom, Josephus says, they used for collecting tithes (*A.J.* 20.181, 206–7).[187] These might have been their agents for collecting taxes as well. If the authorities in Jerusalem were, thus, responsible for collecting tribute, King Agrippa's appeal (through the same "magistrates and principal citizens"[188]) to the governor, Florus, to "appoint some of their number to collect the tribute in the country [i.e., apart from the environs of Jerusalem]" would be an admission that the revolt of 66 C.E. had rendered the normal system of collection ineffective.[189]

Philo (*Legat.* 199–203) accuses C. Herennius Capito of fomenting in Jamneia the events that led to Gaius ordering his statue to be erected in the Jerusalem temple. Capito, Philo writes (*Legat.* 199), "cherishes a spite against the population. When he came there he was a poor man but by his rapacity and peculation he has amassed much wealth in various forms." According to Josephus, in 35/36 C.E., Capito had sent troops after Agrippa I in order to recover money that Agrippa "owed the Imperial treasury at Rome" (*A. J.* 18.158).[190] Josephus calls him "the procurator of Jamnia" (Ἰαμνείας ἐπίτροπος). Capito was the imperial procurator who managed the imperial estate bequeathed by Salome, Herod's sister, at her death to Julia, the wife of Augustus. Julia passed the estate on to the imperial family (*A.J.* 18.31; *B.J.* 2.167). The estate consisted of the cities Jamneia and Azotus, the palm groves of Phaselis, and the king's palace in Ascalon (*A. J.* 17.189, 321; *B.J.* 2.98); to these Augustus added Archelais after Archelaus had been banished (*A.J.* 17.340; 18.31). Capito is listed on an inscription as procurator for Julia (PROC. IVLIAE. AVGVSTAE), Tiberius (PROC. TI. CAESARIS. AVG.), and Gaius (PROC. C. CAESARIS. AVG. GERMANICI).[191] Philo, therefore, is misleading when he calls Capito "the tax-collector for Judaea" (*Legat.* 199).[192]

---

187. See chapter 6 below.

188. *B.J.* 2.407: ἄρχοντας αὐτῶν ἅμα τοῖς δυνατοῖς.

189. Agrippa II sent the delegation after he realized "that the passions of the revolutionaries were now beyond control, and indignant at the insults which he had received." He left Jerusalem for his domain (*B.J.* 2.407).

190. See Fergus Millar, "The Fiscus in the First Two Centuries," *JRS* 53 (1963): 33.

191. Alf. Merlin, ed., *L'année épigraphique, 1941* (Paris: Presses Universitaires de France, 1942), no. 105. See also idem, ed., *L'année épigraphique, 1947* (Paris: Presses Universitaires de France, 1948), 39. Tiberius Julius Mellon, mentioned on a fragment of a sarcophagus discovered near Jamneia, was probably the procurator, appointed by Julia, before Capito. See Alf. Merlin, ed., *L'année épigraphique, 1948* (Paris: Presses Universitaires de France, 1949), no. 141: IVLIA. GRATA TI. IVLII. AVG. L. MELLONTIS. PROC.

192. Philo, *Legat.* 199: φόρων ἐκλογεὺς ὁ Καπίτων ἐστὶ τῶν τῆς Ἰουδαίας. See Millar, "Fis-

There were, it would seem, no Roman tax collectors in the Jewish parts of the province of Judea. Tribute was collected by Jewish agents.[193] We do not know, however, how the amount of direct tribute for each year was fixed or if the collection of tolls and duties was farmed out to lessees by the governor.[194] Such a system of tax farming for duties and tolls would have resembled systems noted elsewhere in the empire.[195] The two toll collectors known by name in the Gospels are Jewish: Levi/Matthew (Mark 2:17 // Luke 5:27–32; Matt 9:9–13); and Zacchaeus, the ἀρχιτελώνης in Luke 19:1–10. John, the toll collector (Ἰωάννης ὁ τελώνης), was one of the leading Jews (οἱ δυνατοί) of Caesarea (*B J.* 2.287, 292).[196] If toll collection was leased to contractors in Judea, it appears that both the contractors and their agents were Jews.

Conclusions

All the evidence points to the conclusion that direct tribute in the province of Judea was *tributum soli*, paid mostly (though perhaps not exclusively) in kind. I have argued that the Roman denarius was not required for the payment of tribute in the province. The same evidence excludes the possibility that the *tributum capitis*, resulting from a census of persons, was levied in the province before 70 C.E. Tolls and duties continued to be an essential component of taxation, as they had been under Herod and his successors. The governors also imposed occasional levies.[197] The extraordinary exactions, particularly when they took the form of a diversion of temple funds, seem to have been especially onerous.[198] There can be no certain conclusions about the manner in which Rome collected

cus," 33 and n. 56; Smallwood, *Philonis Alexandrini Legatio Ad Gaium*, 261; Schürer (*History*, 1:394 and n. 169) suggests that "Ἰαμνείας be read also in the text of Philo instead of Ἰουδαίας."

193. See Schürer, *History*, 1:372; contra Donahue, "Tax Collectors and Sinners," 45, who makes the curious statement that "[t]hough Roman citizenship was not required for the office of tax collector, it was often granted and many of the tax collectors *de facto* were Jews."

194. So, for instance, Schürer, *History*, 1:374–76. Pliny (*Nat.* 12.32.64–65) says that custom duties for frankincense were paid to "the customs officers of our empire" (iterumque imperii nostri publicanis penditur) at Gaza. See chapter 4. Although Pliny in this passage calls the city "the town of Gaza in Judaea on the Mediterranean coast," Gaza, after Herod's death, had become part of the province of Syria (*A.J.* 17.320; *B.J.* 2.97).

195. See Brunt, "Publicans," 406–20.

196. Brunt ("Publicans," 409) cautions that these collectors might not have collected tolls for Rome. John might have been an agent of the city of Caesarea, and a collector in Galilee under Antipas (as Levi/Matthew might have been) did not collect Roman taxes.

197. For the empire, see, e.g., Suetonius, *Nero* 38. Brunt, "Revenues of Rome," 170.

198. See chapters 1 and 2. Sabinus, the imperial procurator, in 4 B.C.E. (*A.J.* 17.264;

direct and indirect taxes in the region, although in general it might be said that the Jewish aristocracy was responsible for collecting (direct) tribute.

Tacitus reports (*Ann.* 2.42) that in about 17 C.E. "[t]he provinces, too, of Syria and Judea, exhausted by their burdens, were pressing for a diminution of the tribute."[199] Scholars have accepted this statement as evidence that Roman taxes in the province were "oppressive."[200] Tacitus's passing allusion does not tell us whether or not the situation received redress.[201] From what is said of Tiberius elsewhere, one might imagine that he lowered the taxes.[202] Tacitus (*Ann.* 1.76) records that in 15 C.E. "Achaia and Macedonia protested against the heavy taxation." Tiberius responded by turning them into imperial provinces. Similarly, Tacitus says that Tiberius settled "the commotion in the East" by dispatching Germanicus there "with powers overriding, in all regions he might visit, those of the local governors holding office by allotment or imperial nomination" (Tacitus, *Ann.* 2.43). In 17 C.E. Tiberius also came to the relief of the cities of Asia that had been ravished by an earthquake. He remitted their taxes for five years.[203] Other provinces benefited from imperial largesse in the form of relief from tribute. For instance, the young Nero pleaded the cause of various cities and they received grants; Apamea, which had been struck by an earthquake, had its tribute remitted for five years (Tacitus, *Ann.* 12.58). In 53 C.E. the inhabitants of Byzantium were "under stress of their financial burdens, they applied for exemption or an abatement." They received relief "for the next five years" from Claudius (Tacitus, *Ann.* 12.62–63).[204]

B.J. 2.50); Pilate between 26 and 36 C.E.(*A.J.* 18.60–62; *B.J.* 2.175–77); Florus, in 66 C.E. (*B.J.* 2.293). In each of these instances, as we have already noted, popular and bloody revolts ensued.

199. Tacitus, *Ann.* 2.42: et provinciae Suria atque Iudaea, fessae oneribus, deminutionem tributi orabant.

200. Among numerous other authors, see Schürer, *History*, 1:372–73 and n. 92; Menahem Stern ("Province of Judaea," 332 and n. 6) says that "the taxes were felt to be a sore burden" and adds that "[t]he situation probably became worse under an emperor like Nero." According to Millar (*Roman Near East*, 48), Tacitus's report shows that "the impact of taxation was felt in both provinces" of Syria and Judea.

201. See Millar, *Roman Near East*, 48.

202. See Ramsay MacMullen, "Tax-Pressure in the Roman Empire," *Latomus* 46 (1987): 737.

203. Tacitus, *Ann.* 2.47; a cash grant also of ten million secterces was given to the Sardanians. See Dio, *Hist.* 57.17.7: "large sums of money were remitted from their taxes and large sums were also given them by Tiberius." Dio (*Hist.* 57.17.8) adds that Tiberius refrained "scrupulously from the possessions of others." Tiberius also remitted for three years the tribute of the cities of Achaia that had been destroyed by earthquake (Tacitus, *Ann.* 4.13).

204. See MacMullen, "Tax-Pressure," 737 and nn. 2, 3.

It is probable that the first one hundred years of the Roman Empire, as MacMullen suggests, was a "sort of tug of war going between two contrary impulses in government," that is, on the one hand, the need to "take its subjects' property away from them" and, on the other hand, "to be popular at the same time."[205] The emperors certainly were sensitive to the problems of fiscal pressures in the provinces.[206] They were sensitive to the prospect of revolts. However, as Brunt notes, the causes of tax-related revolts were not always limited to the rate of taxation itself: ". . . we cannot tell how far it was resented as a mark of subjection, or because assessment or exaction was unjust and brutal . . . rather than because it was intrinsically onerous."[207] The revolt in 6 C.E. led by Judas the Galilean was, according to Josephus, because the rebels thought that paying tribute to the Romans was "tolerating mortal masters, after having God for their lord" (*B.J.* 2.118).[208] The issue was not the rate of taxation, which as yet had not been imposed, but the fact itself of Roman taxation.

Scholarly opinion is divided about whether provincial taxes were heavy in the Principate. Our sources do not permit us to form a complete picture of taxation in the province of Judea before 70 C.E. We do not know how it related to taxation in the rest of the empire, and what impact it had on the lives of individuals.[209] Therefore, one cannot speak with dogmatic certitude about the role that the levels of taxation played in the Jewish revolt of 66 C.E.

---

205. Ibid., 738.

206. According to Dio (*Hist.* 57.10.5), when the overzealous governor of Egypt, Aemilius Rectus, sent Tiberius more money than was stipulated, he sent back the message: "I want my sheep shorn, not shaven." See Tacitus, *Ann.* 4.6: "He [Tiberius] saw to it that the provinces were not disturbed by fresh impositions and that the incidence of the old was not aggravated by magisterial avarice or cruelty. . . ."

207. Brunt ("Revenues of Rome," 170) sees here also causes for the various tax revolts reported during the early Principate.

208. See *B.J.* 2.433; *A.J.* 18.4: the census and taxation "carried with it a status amounting to downright slavery, no less, and [Judas] appealed to the nation to make a bid for independence."

209. See Brunt, "Revenues of Rome," 170–71; Millar, *Roman Near East*, 48–49.

6

Tithes in the Second Temple Period

> Gaius Caesar, Imperator for the second time, has ruled that . . . in addition, they shall also pay tithes to Hyrcanus and his sons, just as they paid to their forefathers.[1]

The fact that Caesar and the Roman Senate included the payment of tithes in their decree on taxation for Judea emphasizes the importance of tithing to the Jewish state. As it has often been noted, Jews paid tithes on top of other religious dues[2] and state taxes.[3] In order to clarify the Senate's decree and its practical application, I shall discuss in some detail three main problems that have often been raised in relation to tithing in the Second Temple period, that is, from about 538 B.C.E. to 70 C.E.: (1) the beneficiaries of the so-called Levitical tithes (priests or Levites); (2) centralized collection; and (3) the tithe of livestock. It is necessary to discuss this period as a whole in order to clarify the question of the actual practice of tithing in the early Roman period.

Priests in the sanctuaries of Israel, according to earlier traditions, lived from the sacrifices offered by pilgrims. This is evident from the stories of the priests of Shiloh and of Nob (1 Sam 2:12–17; 21:1 [MT 2]-7). Such sacrifices, it appears, included "tithes."[4] Besides, the close relationship between

1. *A.J.* 14.202, 203: πρὸς τούτοις ἔτι καὶ Ὑρκανῷ καὶ τοῖς τέκνοις αὐτοῦ τὰς δεκατας τελῶσιν, ἃς ἐτέλουν καὶ τοῖς προγόνοις αὐτῶν. See chapter 2.

2. In particular the temple tax. See chapter 2.

3. See the literature cited particularly in chapter 4.

4. Apart from the Deuteronomic legislation, there are three undisputed references to "tithes" in early biblical literature: (1) Amos's contemptuous satire of Israel's religious rites at Jeroboam's sanctuary in Bethel (Amos 4:4–5); (2) Jacob's promise at Bethel "to tithe a tithe" to God (עַשֵּׂר אֲעַשְּׂרֶנּוּ לָךְ) of all that God would give to him (Gen 28:22); and (3) Abraham apparently giving to Melchizedek, the priest-king of Salem, "a tithe of everything" (Gen 14:20: וַיִּתֶּן־לוֹ מַעֲשֵׂר מִכֹּל). 1 Sam 8:15–17 is not direct evidence for the existence of tithes during the monarchy. Samuel's threat in this passage that the king whom Israel demanded would take one-tenth of their grain and vineyards and one-tenth of their flock to give to his officers is not verified in the subsequent narrative.

the Israelite kings and the "royal" cult sites (Jerusalem, Bethel, and Dan) would suggest that cult officials in these centers benefited from royal patronage (and state taxation), and that the king supervised their resources. Nonetheless, there is still much truth in Julius Wellhausen's idea that the organization of tithes as it appears in the Priestly sources and in the extant postexilic literature belongs to the period after the exile.[5] Of the later, rabbinic literature I shall deal in particular with the Mishnah. Without assuming that any specific mishnaic tradition dates to the period before 70 C.E., I shall, nonetheless, accept the view that the general assumptions that underlie rabbinic discussions on tithes in the Mishnah would have been shared also by pre-70 C.E. Pharisees.[6]

Tithes: For Priests or for Levites?

Biblical Laws and Postexilic Harmonizations

Laws and practices of tithing in postexilic Israel were marked by attempts to reconcile three conflicting sets of biblical laws accepted to be equally binding. These laws are in Deuteronomy, Leviticus, and Numbers.

Deuteronomy 14:22–29; 12:5–7, 11–12, 17–19; 26:12–15. According to Deut 14:22–26, every year the farmer sets aside a tithe of grain, wine, and oil. He should consume his tithe (as well as the firstlings of the flock and herd) in the presence of God "in the place that he will choose as a dwelling for his name" (14:22), not in the high places or in the towns (see 12:5–7, 17–19). If the distance to the "place" is too long to allow the transportation of the tithe and the firstling, they should be turned into money and the money should be spent "for whatever you wish—oxen, sheep, wine, strong drink, or whatever you desire" (14:24–26). The pilgrim should consume these items there together with his household (and the Levite) in joyful celebration (see 12:11–12, 18–19).

5. Julius Wellhausen, *Prolegomena to the History of Ancient Israel* (New York: Meridian Books, 1957), 156–67. Wellhausen's thesis that the tithe was "eaten by those who bring it in sacred banquets" certainly needs to be modified, since it is not evident that tithes did not exist (also) as offerings from which cult officials benefited. This does not detract from the point that the laws and the institutions that appear in Leviticus and Numbers and in the literature of the Second Temple period cannot, in their present form, be taken to have been in use during the period before the exile.

6. I am indebted for what follows to Sanders's insightful discussions of various aspects of tithing in the Second Temple period. See Sanders, *Jewish Law*, 43–48, 236–38, 283–308; idem, *Judaism*, 146–69, 428–31.

However, every third year (presumably in the seven-year cycle), that is, in the third and in the sixth years of the cycle, "the full tithe of your produce for that year" is not to be consumed in Jerusalem but should be brought into storage within the towns and given to "the Levites . . . the resident aliens, the orphans, and the widows" who live in them (14:27–29). This injunction is reiterated and confirmed in liturgical form in 26:12–15, which further requires that the farmer should on this third year, "the year of the tithe," make an avowal.

Leviticus 27:30–33

> All tithes from the land, whether the seed from the ground or the fruit from the tree, are the Lord's; they are holy to the Lord. If persons wish to redeem any of their tithes, they must add one-fifth to them. All tithes of herd and flock, every tenth one that passes under the shepherd's staff, shall be holy to the Lord. Let no one inquire whether it is good or bad, or make substitution for it; if one makes substitution for it, then both it and the substitute shall be holy and cannot be redeemed.

Numbers 18:21–32. Every tithe in Israel is given to the Levites, who, like the priests, have no allotment of landed property (vv. 23–24), in return for the service they perform. It is to be eaten by the Levites and their households anywhere, as they would eat produce from their own fields (v. 27; see v. 30). From the tithe that they receive they make their offerings and sacrifices, including the payment of tithes: they must set aside "an offering from it to the Lord, a tithe of the tithe" (v. 26), which they present to the "priest Aaron" (vv. 28–29).

The Deuteronomic legislation, according to which all tithes were consumed in a ritual banquet (in Jerusalem) each year, except years 3 and 6 in the seven-year cycle, was probably never implemented in its integrity after the exile. The importance of this legislation is to be sought, therefore, in the transition from pre- to postexilic institutions. It is otherwise well known that Second Temple legislation harmonized the three sets of biblical laws into "first tithe," "second tithe," and "poor tithe."[7]

The earliest attempt at harmonization is found in Tob 1:6–8. The work is dated to the third or second century B.C.E. and is represented by three major Greek recensions. According to the Siniaticus tradition of texts (**S**), Tobit, assuming the seven-year cycle, offered six tithes to the Levites (years 1 to 6 = Num 18); he spent six other tithes in Jerusalem (years 1 to 6 = Deut 14:22–26); and two for the poor (years 3 and 6 = Deut 14:27–29). This means that in years 3 and 6 he offered three tithes. He offered no

7. See Sanders, *Jewish Law*, 43–44; idem, *Judaism*, 146–49.

tithe in the seventh year, this being the sabbatical year. Thus, in the six years he offered tithes according to what Sanders calls "the fourteen tithe system."[8] According to the Alexandrinus and Vaticanus textual traditions (**BA**), Tobit accepted an eighteen tithe system: in each of the six years he provided for three sets of tithes, namely, to the Levites, for expenditure in Jerusalem, and to the poor.[9]

Jubilees 32:1–15 (see also 13:25–27)[10] explicitly mentions "a second tithe" offered by Jacob (v. 9) and draws a general conclusion from it: "And therefore it is decreed in the heavenly tablets as a law to tithe the tithe again in order to eat it before the Lord from year to year in the place where it is determined that his name shall dwell . . ." (vv. 10 and 11).[11] This passage and the entire narrative imply a "first tithe" to be given to the descendants of Levi (also 13:25–27). The author, however, says nothing about any tithes for the needs of the poor.[12] *Jubilees*, therefore, presents a "twelve tithe system": two in each of the six years (one for the priests, and one for celebrating in Jerusalem).[13]

Josephus, writing at the end of the first century C.E., says that Moses commanded the people to offer two tithes (one to the Levites and/or priests and one for expenditure in Jerusalem) in each of the six years, and

8. See *Sanders, Judaism*, 148–49.

9. Ibid.; idem, *Jewish Law*, 44.

10. *Jubilees* was written in the second century B.C.E.

11. The legislation in *Jubilees* is almost identical to that of the *Temple Scroll* (11QT). The *Temple Scroll* (11QT LXIII) also imposes an annual "second tithe." The tithe is to be brought each year to the temple. "And those who dwell at a distance of three-days' journey from the temple shall bring whatever they can bring. And if they cannot carry it, let them sell it for money and bring the money and buy with it grain, wine and oil and cattle and sheep . . ." (11QT LXIII, 12–15). The tithe is to be eaten only on "holy days," that is, "on the days of the feast" and not "on working days in their sorrows, for it is holy" (11QT LXIII, 15–17). It is to be eaten for one year, that is, from the corresponding Feast of First Fruits to the next. Thereafter, "all that remains of their feasts shall be consecrated and burnt . . ." (11QT LXIII, 4–12). See Yigael Yadin, *The Temple Scroll* (3 vols; Jerusalem: Israel Exploration Society, 1977–83), 2:181–84; and the discussion in Yadin, *Temple Scroll*, 1:114–16.

12. Sanders (*Judaism*, 149) thinks that in *Jubilees* "there was a first tithe, given to the Levites, and that in at least some years a third tithe was given to the poor." That first tithes in *Jubilees* would go to the Levites (as in Num 18) is controversial. It is improbable, in view of the overwhelming emphasis on the priesthood of Levi and his sons in the present passage. It is also directly contradicted by *Jub* 13:25–27, where the author comments on the encounter between Abraham and Melchizedek and, apparently referring to Lev 27:30–33, says that God gave tithes to the priests (see below). A tithe for the poor seems to be excluded by the fact that second tithes are to be eaten "from year to year." If the tithe for the poor is assumed, then *Jubilees* would present either a fourteen- or an eighteen-tithe system.

13. *Jubilees* 32:1–15 by itself would imply that the "first tithe" offered to the priests was only "the whole tithe of oxen and sheep" ordered in v. 15. But this is contradicted by the mention of "grain and wine and oil" in 13:26.

an additional tithe in years 3 and 6 for "widowed women and orphan children." This gives a total of fourteen tithes, as in Tobit (**S**) (*A.J.* 4.68, 205, 240).[14]

The rabbis also harmonized Num 18, Deut 14, and Deut 26 (reading Lev 27 in light of these other passages) into a twelve-tithe system, but with a different combination. For each of the six tithe years, "first tithes" are to be paid (to the Levites), after "the heave-offering of tithe"—that is, a tenth of the tenth—is removed and given to the priests (Num 18). In the first, second, fourth, and fifth years, "second tithes" are to be spent in Jerusalem (Deut 14). Finally, the "poor tithe" replaces the second tithe in the third and sixth years (Deut 14 and 26). Thus, the farmer offers two tithes in every one of the six years.[15]

Clearly, there was no single system to which everyone agreed. In actual practice individuals would have chosen the system that corresponded to their piety, group affiliation, and economic capabilities.[16]

"First Tithes" to Priests and to Levites

The dramatic increase of priestly powers and income in the Second Temple period, many scholars claim, meant that priests gradually replaced Levites as the recipients of tithes. As a result, it is said, by the first century C.E. tithes were no longer paid to Levites but to priests.[17] Surprisingly,

---

14. See Sanders, *Judaism*, 149.

15. See the summaries in Herbert Danby, ed. and trans., *The Mishnah: Translated from the Hebrew with Introduction and Brief Explanatory Notes* (New York: Oxford University Press, 1933), 20, n. 9; 73, n. 6; also the discussions especially in the tractates *Pe'ah, Demai, Maʿaserot, Maʿaser Sheni* and *Yadaim* 4.3. See the listing in *Maʿaser Sheni* 5.6. See also Sanders, *Judaism*, 149.

16. Sanders, *Jewish Law*, 45; he suggests (*Judaism*, 149) that Josephus's fourteen-tithe system represents priestly views as against those of the Pharisees, reproduced in the Mishnaic twelve-tithe system. This view would receive further support if *Jubilees* is seen to present a fourteen-tithe system as well.

17. See, among other authors, Wellhausen, *Prolegomena*, 165–67; Moshe Weinfeld, "Tithe," in *EncJud*, vol. 15 (Jerusalem: Keter, 1972), cols. 1161–62; Jacob Milgrom, *Numbers* במדבר*: The Traditional Hebrew Text with the New JPS Translation and Commentary* (JPS Torah Commentary; Philadelphia: Jewish Publication Society, 1990), "Excursus 46," 432–36, esp. 435–36. Apart from a few (minor) additions and modifications, Milgrom's "Excursus" reproduces Weinfeld's encyclopedia article *verbatim*. Jacob Milgrom, "Studies in the Temple Scroll," *JBL* 97 (1978): 502–4; S. Safrai, "Religion in Everyday Life," in *The Jewish People in the First Century: Historical Geography, Political History, Social, Cultural and Religious Life and Institutions*, vol. 2 (ed. S. Safrai and M. Stern; CRINT 1; Philadelphia: Fortress Press, 1976), 822–3; Menahem Stern, "Aspects of Jewish Society: The Priesthood and Other Classes," in ibid., 584–86, 596; Marcello Del Verme, "La 'prima decima' nel Giudaismo del secondo tempio," *Hen* 9 (1987): 5–38; idem, "Les dîmes hébraïques dans l'œuvre de Josèphe et dans le nouveau testament," in *Rashi 1040–1990: Hommage à Ephraïm E. Urbach* (ed. Gabrielle Sed-Rajna; Paris: Cerf, 1993), 122–29, 135–36.

this theory is held even by those scholars who think that the legislation found in the Priestly Code (Lev and Num) was in force during the monarchy. These scholars, however, fail to account for the contradictory requirements in the code itself.[18]

The disagreement in the sources about the "types" of tithes should make us wary of suggestions that any particular legislation "reflects" the totality of actual practice.[19] Extant postexilic literature manifests the same level of disagreement about the recipients of the so-called Levitical tithes as the biblical laws on which they depend. Neither the theory of priestly appropriation of Levitical right nor the suggestion that in postexilic Israel tithes were paid only to Levites in accordance with Num 18 (reproduced by later rabbinic halakah)[20] completely accounts for that conflicting evidence. This is why Baumgarten, after noting the "fluidity of terminology" in the use of the Greek δεκάτη in some of the extant sources, called for "a re-examination of some of the sources scholars have taken to reflect the arrogation by the Second Temple priests of the levitical tithe," in order to determine if any such change did actually occur.[21]

---

18. Weinfeld ("Tithe," col. 1159, for instance) argues that "holy to the Lord" in Lev 27:30–33 means that tithes were allocated to the priests and their household (see Lev 23:20; Num 5:8; 18:12–14). In his overall theory (cols. 1159–60), however, he maintains that, during the monarchy, tithes were given to the Levites for their private consumption and for the maintenance of royal temple cities—only one tenth of the tithe went to priests of the central shrine in Jerusalem. In other words, in his view, only the legislation in Num 18 was implemented. This choice seems arbitrary. With regard to the period of the Second Temple, he expresses doubt (col. 1161) that the priestly law of Num 18 was "implemented at all after the disruption of the monarchy," since "Israelite law codes . . . were formulated in an idealistic way and therefore cannot be judged against a realistic and pure historical background." Yet he cites Nehemiah (and 2 Chronicles), which reflects the provisions of Num 18, as evidence for the organization of tithes after the exile.

19. Weinfeld ("Tithe," col. 1161) rightly points out that "from Ezra's time the whole pentateuchal literature was considered a total unity (the Law of Moses) and the people had to comply with the Torah as a whole."

20. Schürer (*History*, 2:257–60, esp. 259) implies in his discussion that during the Second Temple period Levites received tithes in accordance with Num 18. Though Sanders says that "Levites and priests collected the tithe in person," and cites instances where the recipients of tithes were clearly priests, he holds that Levites received first tithes and gave priests the tithe of tithe. See Sanders, *Judaism*, 149–50; idem, *Jewish Law*, 46–48, 292, and 366, n. 30. So also Joseph M. Baumgarten, who rejects the theory of priests' usurpation of Levitical rights to tithes (see Baumgarten, "On the Non-Literal Use of Maʿăśēr/Dekatē," *JBL* 103 [1984]: 246–49; idem, "The First and Second Tithes in the Temple Scroll," in *Biblical and Related Studies Presented to Samuel Iwry* (ed. Ann Kort and Scott Morschauser; Winona Lake, Ind.: Eisenbrauns, 1985), 6–10. Gedalyahu Alon (*Jews, Judaism and the Classical World: Studies in Jewish History in the Times of the Second Temple and Talmud* [trans. Israel Abrahams; Jerusalem: Magnes Press, 1977], 91) thinks that until the time of Hyrcanus II tithes were distributed in Jerusalem "to priests (and Levites) *pro rata*." Tithes went to priests and Levites until John Hyrcanus I, in Oppenheimer's view (*'Am Ha-Aretz*, 30–42), and to priests thereafter.

21. Joseph M. Baumgarten, "On the Non-Literal Use," 247, 249, n. 24.

Baumgarten's study shows that several texts that are often cited to demonstrate priestly usurpation of tithes are inconclusive as evidence. In many of the passages the word "tithe" refers to offerings (and taxes) other than the "Levitical tithe." These and other similar texts, examined below, should not be used as evidence in support of the view that priests had taken over as the recipients of the "Levitical tithes."

Nehemiah 13:4–13 [12:44]. These passages deal with the appointment of priests and Levites to supervise the storehouses set up by Nehemiah and to distribute the tithes stored there. This does not prove that priests took over a Levitical prerogative.[22]

Tobit 1:6–8. According to the short recension (**BA**), Tobit brought to Jerusalem: (1) Firstfruits and tithes [of produce] (τὰς ἀπαρχὰς καὶ τὰς δεκάτας τῶν γενημάτων) together with the first of fleece. These he gave to the priests (τοῖς ἱερεῦσιν τοῖς υἱοῖς Ααρων) (v. 6). (2) A tithe of all his produce (πάντων τῶν γενημάτων τὴν δεκάτην). This he gave to the Levites (τοῖς υἱοῖς Λευι) who served in Jerusalem (v. 7). In the long text (**S**) he brought: (1) Firstfruits, firstlings, tithes of his livestock (τὰς ἀπαρχὰς καὶ τὰ πρωτογενήματα καὶ τὰς δεκάτας τῶν κτηνῶν), and the first of fleece. He gave all these to the priests, the sons of Aaron (vv. 6b-7a). (2) The tithe (τὴν δεκάτην) of grain, wine, olive oil, pomegranates, figs, and other fruits. These he gave to the Levites who ministered in Jerusalem (v. 7b).

It is impossible to establish which one of the texts of Tobit is original; nor can we decide, *pace* Del Verme, which of them reproduces actual contemporary practice and which merely repeats biblical legislation. If the short text (**BA**) reflects contemporary reality, then it must be that tithes were thought to be due *both* to priests and to Levites. Further, the long text (**S**), which supposedly only rehashes the legislation in Num 18, does not say that the priests in Jerusalem received a tenth from the tithe that Tobit offered to the Levites.

Moreover, it is not certain that the τὰς δεκάτας τῶν γενημάτων that Tobit (**BA**) is said to have offered to the priests were tithes of produce. The Hellenistic word γένημα, "product," "fruit," "yield," "increase," generally used in the LXX to translate various Hebrew words, in particular תְּבוּאָה, refers in most instances to agricultural produce. The word does appear sometimes, however, in place of the classical Greek word γέννημα and in these cases means "offspring" of animals (for instance in Lev 25:7),

22. *Pace* S. Safrai ("Religion in Everyday Life," 821), who thinks that these passages show "that priests usually got the actual tithe" even in Nehemiah. Similarly Del Verme ("La 'Prima Decima,'" 8), who sees here "un ulteriore indizio del processo di crescente potere dei sacerdoti sull'istituto della 'prima decima.'"

and of humans (as in 1 Macc 1:38; 3:45).[23] In the text under consideration, τὰ πρωτογενήματα in (**S**) 1:6b must be rendered "firstlings" (of livestock), against Thackeray's view. By the same token τὰς δεκάτας τῶν γενημάτων in (**BA**) 1:6 could mean "the tithes of livestock," particularly since these are listed together with firstfruits and the first of fleece. This would fill, in this recension, the lack of the truly priestly offerings: firstlings and tithes of livestock.[24]

Judith 11:13,[25] and Hecataeus of Abdera cited by Josephus in C. Ap. 1.188.[26] Jdt 11:13 is part of a speech made to a (mythical) Gentile audience and in *Apion* 1.188 Josephus cites a Gentile author. In neither case would we expect subtle distinctions between priests and Levites. Aharon Oppenheimer rightly points out, in the case of Judith, that in this and in other such passages the word "priests" is imprecise and may include Levites.[27] The passage from Judith contains other confusing generalizations. If it mirrored contemporary practice, we would need to conclude that in the author's time (2nd century B.C.E.) firstfruits were offered only of grain, and tithes were of wine and oil, and that tithes could not be touched except by priests. All this is unlikely. Baumgarten suggests that "the most cogent explanation is that *dekatai* refers not to the levitical tithes but to the *tĕrûmâ*, restricted to the priesthood."[28]

1 Maccabees 10:31;[29] 11:35.[30] Both texts are parts of the tax concessions

23. Unfortunately, in our critical editions of the LXX, we cannot verify Thackeray's opinion that in the Septuagint γένημα (with πρωτογένημα) "is carefully distinguished from γέννημα" and is "always being used of the fruits of the ground except in I Macc (i.38, iii.45)." See H. St. J. Thackeray, *A Grammar of the Old Testament in Greek According to the Septuagint* (Hildesheim, N.Y.: Georg Olms, 1987), 118.

24. Baumgarten thinks δεκάτη is used here "first in the extended sense of a priestly donation such as the *tĕrûmâ* and then literally for the levitical tithe" ("On the Non-literal Use of Maʿăśēr/Dekatē," 247); see Del Verme, "La 'prima decima,'" 10–11; also Sanders, *Jewish Law*, 291.

25. "They have decided to consume the first fruits of the grain and the tithes of the wine and oil, which they had consecrated and set aside for the priests who minister in the presence of our God in Jerusalem—things it is not lawful for any of the people even to touch with their hands."

26. "[T]he total number of Jewish priests who receive a tithe of the revenue (οἱ τὴν δεκάτην τῶν γινομένων λαμβάνοντες) and administer public affairs is about fifteen hundred."

27. Oppenheimer, *'Am Ha-Aretz*, 40 and n. 50, citing Zech 3:7; Ps 135:2; and esp. Deut 18:7.

28. Joseph M. Baumgarten, "On the Non-Literal Use," 247–48; Del Verme, "La 'prima decima,'" 18–19. The use of narrative hyperbole cannot be excluded.

29. Καὶ Ιερουσαλημ ἔστω ἁγία καὶ ἀφειμένη καὶ τὰ ὅρια αὐτῆς, αἱ δεκάται καὶ τὰ τέλη, "Jerusalem and its environs, its tithes and its revenues, shall be holy and free from tax."

30. Καὶ τὰ ἄλλα τὰ ἀνήκοντα ἡμῖν ἀπὸ τοῦ νῦν τῶν δεκατῶν καὶ τῶν τελῶν τῶν ἀνηκόντων ἡμῖν καὶ τὰς τοῦ ἁλὸς λίμνας καὶ τοὺς ἀνήκοντας ἡμῖν στεφάνους, πάντα ἐπαρκέσομεν αὐτοῖς,

first made to Jonathan by the Seleucid king Demetrius I in 152 B.C.E. and confirmed, following Jonathan's request, by his son Demetrius II in 145 (see from v. 28). A host of arguments could be brought against the suggestion that in these passages the Seleucid kings were releasing the Jews from the tithes that the Law required them to pay. I shall not rehearse them all here. 1 Macc 10:31 is already rendered incomprehensible, probably through translations from Greek to Hebrew and back again. Josephus appears to have understood the intent of the text, which he rewrote as: "And it is my wish that the city of Jerusalem shall be sacred and inviolable and be free to its borders from the tithe and tolls."[31] Demetrius proposed, according to Josephus, to make Jerusalem and its borders free from the taxes and tolls paid to the crown. Josephus clearly did not think that Demetrius had freed the inhabitants of Jerusalem and its surrounding territories from paying tithes as required by the Law.

We therefore must adopt the interpretation proposed by Bickerman: The tenths and tolls (αἱ δεκάται καὶ τὰ τέλη) are the value-added tax and transit tolls imposed on goods entering Jerusalem. The "tenth" in question is neither the Jewish tithe nor an exact percentage of merchandise paid as tax, but merely its fiscal designation.[32] These indirect tolls paid in Jerusalem, from which Demetrius I grants the Jews freedom, are mentioned again in the subsequent letter of the exiled Demetrius II.[33] Del Verme's attempt to make this the moment when the Seleucids handed the collection of tithes to the Hasmoneans is futile.[34] The kings did not grant Jonathan the "tithes"; they released the people from all such payments.[35]

Philo, Virt. *95.*[36] It was already noted long ago that Philo uses δεκάτη

"And the other payments henceforth due to us of the tithes, and the taxes due to us, and the salt pits and the crown taxes due to us—from all these we shall grant them release."

31. *A.J.* 13.51: καὶ τὴν Ἱεροσολυμιτῶν πόλιν ἱερὰν καὶ ἄσυλον εἶναι βούλομαι καὶ ἐλευθέραν ἕως τῶν ὅρων αὐτῆς ἀπὸ τῆς δεκάτης καὶ τῶν τελῶν.

32. Bickerman, *Institutions des Séleucides*, 116–17; see also Goldstein, *1 Maccabees*, 408.

33. 1 Macc 13:39b: καὶ εἴ τι ἄλλο ἐτελωνεῖτο ἐν Ιερουσαλημ, μηκέτι τελωνείσθω, "and whatever other tax has been collected in Jerusalem shall be collected no longer."

34. Del Verme, "La 'prima decima,'" 20–24.

35. Josephus (*A.J.* 13.49), interpreting 1 Macc 10:29, says that Demetrius I remitted to Jonathan the collection of the third part of grain and half of the fruits that previously went to the crown. Josephus does not mention the grant of tithes to Jonathan.

36. "The laws bid us give as first fruits to the officiating priests tithes of corn and wine and oil and domestic animals and wool and bring from the autumn produce of the fields and the other tree fruits offerings proportional to their gains in full baskets with hymns composed in honour of God. These hymns are preserved in written records in the sacred books" (Κελεύουσιν οἱ νόμοι δεκάτας μὲν ἀπό τε σίτου καὶ οἴνου καὶ ἐλαίου καὶ θρεμμάτων ἡμέρων καὶ ἐρίων ἀπάρχεσθαι τοῖς ἱερωμένοις, ἀπὸ δὲ τῆς κατ' ἀγροὺς ὀπώρας καὶ τῶν ἄλλων ἀκροδρύων κατὰ τὸ ἀνάλογον τῆς κτήσεως ἐν ταλάροις πλήρεσι κομίζειν σὺν ᾠδαῖς εἰς τὸν θεὸν πεποιημέναις, ἃς ἀναγράπτους στηλιτεύουσιν αἱ ἱερώταται βίβλοι). The evidence of *Virt.* 95 is

here in a broad sense to mean offerings to the priests.[37] This is readily confirmed by the mention of domestic animals and wool. A tithe of livestock is not among the priests' sources of income detailed by Philo in *Spec.* 1.132–52. The first of fleece, not a tithe, is commanded in Deut 18:4 as an offering to the priests. Everywhere else in Philo's works tithes belong to the Levites, and in accordance with the legislation of Num 18:21–32 (*Spec.* 1.156–57; *Mut.* 2, 191–92). But Philo uses the Greek word ἀπαρχή and the cognate verb so loosely that he frequently speaks of ἀπαρχή when he means "tithe."[38] The reverse usage is the case in *Virt.* 95.

Other passages more clearly, and undeniably, speak of priests as the rightful recipients of tithes:

1. Testament of Levi *9.3–4,*[39] *and* Jub. *13:25–27,*[40] *32:1–15.*[41] There is a clear polemical tone to all three of these passages. The intimate connec-

---

cited by Menahem Stern, "Aspects of Jewish Society," 585, n. 8. S. Safrai ("Religion in Everyday Life," 822) notes that the text is obscure; so also Del Verme, "La 'prima decima,'" 26–27.

37. Bernhard Ritter, *Philo und die Halacha* (Leipzig: Hinrichs, 1879), 117, cited in Joseph M. Baumgarten, "On the Non-Literal Use," 246, n. 9.

38. As a parallel to the expression δεκάτας . . . ἀπάρξασθαι in *Virt.* 95, see δεκάτας . . . ἀπάρξασθαι in *Spec.* 1.157, with which Philo describes the offering of the "tithe of tithe" by the Levites to the priests. In fact, Philo calls this offering simply ἀπαρχή in *Mut.* 2, and in §191 he calls it ἀπαρχῆς ἀπαρχή. Finally, interpreting Lev 25:32–34, Philo says that Levites (τοῖς νεωκόροις) "were not allotted a section of land by the law, which considered that they were sufficiently provided for by the first-fruits (τὰς ἀπαρχάς). . . ." See *Spec.* 2.120, also 1.156–58. On Philo's use of ἀπαρχή, see chapter 2, and Sanders, *Jewish Law*, 290–96.

39. "When we came to Bethel my father, Jacob, saw a vision concerning me that I should be in the priesthood. He arose early and paid tithes for all to the Lord, through me." Text as in H. C. Kee, trans., "Testament of the Twelve Patriarchs: Testament of Levi," in *The Old Testament Pseudepigrapha*, vol. 1 (ed. James H. Charlesworth; London: Darton, Longman & Todd, 1983), 791.

40. "And the Lord ordained it (as) an ordinance forever that they should give it to the priests, to those who minister before him so that they might possess it forever. And there is no limit of days for this law because he ordained it for eternal generations so that they might give one tenth of everything to the Lord: grain and wine and oil and oxen and sheep. And he gave (it) to his priests to eat and drink with rejoicing before him." Text as in O. S. Wintermute, trans., "Jubilees," in *The Old Testament Pseudepigrapha*, vol. 2 (ed. James H. Charlesworth; London: Darton, Longman & Todd, 1985), 84. Caquot has reconstructed the lacuna in v. 25. He translates it as: "Il arma des gens de sa maison . . . . Abraham [remit] auprès de lui (*id est*, Melkisedeq) et de sa descendance la dîme première pour le Seigneur." See André Caquot, "Le livre des Jubilés, Melkisedeq et les dîmes," *JJS* 33 (1982): 257–64, esp. p. 261.

41. Jacob at Bethel "put garments of the priesthood upon him [Levi] and he filled his hands" with sacrifices and tithes of clean animals in payment of his vow (see 27.27); Wintermute, "Jubilees," 116–17 and 109. The emphasis here is on the "second tithe" (see above) and on the tithe of livestock (Lev 27:32, see below).

tion of both the *Testament of Levi* and *Jubilees* to the Qumran documents links these texts to the priestly ideology and debates prevalent in the Qumran documents. The claim by priests to tithes in the *Testament of Levi* and *Jubilees* might represent a polemic within the priesthood or between some priests and other groups.[42] This will be important in understanding the claim also made in *Jubilees* to the tithe of livestock. Meanwhile, it is intriguing that the *Temple Scroll,* which has very close affinities with *Jubilees*, proposes a view diametrically opposed to it. The traces of the underlying polemic are, nonetheless, unmistakable 11QT LX, 6–7:

6 וללויים מעשר הדגן והתירוש והיצהר אשר
7 הקדישו לי לראישונה

6 And to the Levites, one tenth of the grain and the wine and the oil which
7 they dedicated to me at first . . .[43]

Tithes belong then to Levites, according to the *Temple Scroll.* The document recognizes, however, that it previously had been consecrated to the Lord, a reference to Lev 27:30, and therefore to priests. We do not know to what time in the historical past the author's "at first" refers. It must be to a time when priests, in the author's view, could still lay claim to tithes.[44] The *Scroll* grants a higher status to the Levites than was actu-

42. Del Verme ("La 'prima decima,'" 13–15) considers *Jubilees* to be from the Qumran environment. He, however, still thinks its claims represent the normal practice of the Second Temple period. Baumgarten thinks that *Jub.* 32.1–8 "gives prominence to Levi as the ancestor of both priests and Levites and the recipient of tithes." See Joseph M. Baumgarten, "On the Non-Literal Use," 248, n. 16; Joseph M. Baumgarten, "First and Second Tithes," 7. It is not clear, however, that *Jub.* 30:18 ("And the seed of Levi was chosen for the priesthood and levitical [orders] to minister before the Lord always just as we [angels] do") actually speaks of priests and Levites.

43. Yadin, *Temple Scroll*, 2:272; see Joseph M. Baumgarten, "On the Non-Literal Use," 250. Sir 35:8b (LXX) bids the worshiper: "dedicate your tithe with gladness" (καὶ ἐν εὐφροσύνῃ ἁγίασον δεκάτην). Del Verme ("Les dîmes hébraïques," 16–18) is unconvincing in his attempt to equate the tithe in this passage with an offering to priests, on the basis of the Hebrew fragments of Sir 7:31 found in the Cairo Genizah. The text in question speaks of תרומת קדש, correctly rendered ἀπαρχὴν ἁγίων by the Septuagint.

44. This is how Joseph M. Baumgarten ("First and Second Tithes," 7) sets the time frame: Originally tithes were consecrated to the Lord and were therefore assigned to the priesthood. When the Levites were chosen to minister in God's presence, they became the exclusive recipients of the Levitical tithe. In his view, therefore, 11QT (also *Jubilees*) sees the allocation of tithes to the priesthood as having taken place *before* the Levites came on the scene. Yadin (*Temple Scroll*, 1:161–62) wonders "whether there is any connection between the tithing laws of the scroll . . . and the mishnaic text on the abrogation of the avowal concerning tithes by Yoḥanan the high priest."

ally likely in the Second Temple period and gives them prerogatives that recognizably belonged to the priests.[45] The *Scroll*'s innovations are polemical.[46]

2. The inscription מעשר כוהן was found by Yadin among the vessels from Masada. Baumgarten suggests that it is "likely to have designated the priestly portion of the levitic tithe"; but this is far from certain.[47]

3. Josephus offers us the largest range of possibilities. We begin with those passages in which the priests' right to tithes is clearly attested.

(i) *A.J.* 1.181 (see from §179). Abraham offered Melchizedek the tithe of the spoil, and he accepted the gift (see Gen 14:20). Unlike the author of *Jubilees*, Josephus does not draw a general rule out of his interpretation of the encounter. It was, however, as a priest officiating in Jerusalem that Melchizedek received the tithe from Abraham.[48]

(ii) *A.J.* 20.181, 206–7.[49] In both texts Josephus says that the high priests, through their slaves, took possession, at the threshing floors, of the tithes "that were due to the priests" (τὰς τοῖς ἱερεῦσιν ὀφειλομένας

---

45. The text cited above goes on to give "the shoulder from those who offer sacrifice" to the Levites (11QT LX, 6–7). Yadin, *Temple Scroll*, 2:272. Milgrom ("Temple Scroll," 502) comments on this passage: "The most radical innovation, however, is the assignment of the shoulder of the well-being offering to the Levites. Neither is the shoulder ever considered a sacred portion nor are the Levites ever awarded sacrificial flesh. The sect's ruling can be shown to be based on its interpretation of Deut 18:1–3." Milgrom also discusses the other innovative prerogatives.

46. Milgrom ("Temple Scroll," 503) sees in the polemic the demand that Levitical tithes usurped by the priests be restored to them. Joseph M. Baumgarten ("On the Non-Literal Use," 247–48, n. 16) links the polemic to innovations purportedly introduced by the Hasmoneans, who centralized the collection of tithes and asserted "their priestly prerogatives at the expense of the Levites." However, if this is right and its result was that "priests were now recognized as legitimate recipients under the aegis of the 'treasury,'" as Joseph M. Baumgarten ("First and Second Tithes," 9) suggests, then the polemic must relate to priestly claims to tithes in the author's own time. On the Hasmoneans and tithes, see below. Yadin (*Temple Scroll*, 1:161) also thinks that the intention of the *Temple Scroll* is "unmistakably polemical." In his view (1:162) the "stress on Levitical tithes and the enumeration of the tribute . . . are, like the obligation to give the shoulder to the Levites, characteristic of the tendency of our scroll, and of the scrolls in general, to emphasize the special status of the Levites . . . ."

47. Yadin, *Masada*, 96; Joseph M. Baumgarten, "On the Non-Literal Use," 251, n. 32.

48. According to *A.J.* 1.180, Abraham was received by "the king of Solyma, Melchisedek; this name means 'righteous king,' and such was he by common consent, insomuch that for this reason he was moreover made priest of God; Solyma was in fact the place afterwards called Hierosolyma." In *B.J.* 6.438 Josephus writes of Jerusalem: "Its original founder was a Canaanite chief, called in the native tongue 'Righteous King'; for such indeed he was. In virtue thereof he was the first to officiate as priest of God and, being the first to build the temple, gave the city, previously called Solyma, the name of Jerusalem."

49. See below for a fuller discussion of both texts.

δεκάτας [§181]; τὰς τῶν ἱερέων δεκάτας [§206]). The result was that the poorer priests, who previously were fed from the tithes, starved to death.

(iii) *Vita* 63.[50] The priests Joazar and Judas,[51] Josephus's fellow commanders sent to Galilee in 66 C.E., made a fortune "from the tithes which they accepted as their priestly due" (ἐκ τῶν διδομένων αὐτοῖς δεκατῶν, ἃς ὄντες ἱερεῖς ὀφειλομένας ἀπελάμβανον).

(iv) *Vita* 80. Josephus himself renounced that right:

> I scorned all presents offered to me as having no use of them; I even declined to accept from those who brought them the tithes which were due to me as a priest (ἀλλ' οὐδὲ τὰς ὀφειλομένας μοι ὡς ἱερεῖ δεκάτας ἀπελάμβανον παρὰ τῶν κομιζόντων).

Josephus's language in these four sets of passages is unambiguous. While it is possible that what was due to priests in these texts included more than tithes, the problem that the passages present cannot be solved by assuming that he meant offerings other than tithes.[52]

In his summaries of biblical laws, Josephus is ambiguous, saying that tithes are to be paid:

(v) to "the Levites along with the priests" (*A.J.* 4.68)[53]

(vi) to "the priests and Levites" (*A.J.* 4.205).[54] Likewise, tithes are given to both "priests and Levites" in his summaries of 2 Chr 31:4–19 (*A.J.* 9.273–74), and of Neh 7–13 (*A.J.* 11.182).

(vii) to Levites (*A.J.* 4.240, 242)[55]

Continuing the interpretation of the Torah, Josephus actually says that Levites had to deduct a tithe for the priests from the tithes that they received annually from the people (*A.J.* 4.69).[56] It is unlikely that in the

---

50. See the discussion below.

51. See *Vita* 29.

52. Joseph M. Baumgarten ("On the Non-Literal Use," 248–49) suggests that by "tithes" Josephus might have meant "priestly dues, including *tĕrûmâ*."

53. "Furthermore he ordained that the people should pay a tithe of the annual produce of the ground to the Levites along with the priests" (πρὸς τούτοις δὲ καὶ τὸν λαὸν διέταξε τῶν ἐπετείων καρπῶν δεκάτην αὐτοῖς τε τοῖς Λευίταις καὶ ἱερεῦσι τελεῖν).

54. "Let a tithe of the fruits be set apart by you, beside that which I appointed to be given to the priests and Levites" (χωρὶς ἧς διέταξα τοῖς ἱερεῦσι καὶ Λευίταις δεδόσθαι).

55. "In addition to the two tithes which I have already directed you to pay each year, the one for the Levites and the other for the banquets . . . . And when any man, . . . having offered tithes of all, along with those for the Levites and for the banquets, is about to depart for his own home, let him stand right opposite the sacred precincts and render thanks to God for having delivered his race from the insolence of the Egyptians and given them a good land and spacious to enjoy the fruits thereof; then, after attesting that he has paid the tithes in accordance with the laws of Moses . . . ."

56. Some scholars hold that wherever Josephus says that tithes were paid to priests and Levites he means that it was paid to Levites who gave a tithe of it to the priests. This

summaries (our numbers v-vii) Josephus is merely repeating biblical legislation and narrative, whereas in the other passages (our numbers i-iv) he is reflecting actual practice.[57] His summary of Neh 7–13, for instance, is not faithful to the legislation on tithes in that book. Josephus admits that the "constitution" that Moses left was "in a scattered condition," which needed some classification.[58] The laws that he reports in *A.J.* 4.67–75, 196–306 are drawn from every section of the Torah, harmonized, and on many occasions modified. The harmonization that produced his version of "types of tithes" is evident since his sources are as clear as they are contradictory.

That Josephus has harmonized Lev 27:30–33 with the legislation in Numbers is readily accepted.[59] He has eliminated—not forgotten—the tithe of livestock.[60] He also omitted the 20 percent added value for the redemption of tithes (Lev 27:31). It is impossible to know, in this instance, whether he thought that this due should not be paid. In any case, if, alongside the legislation in Numbers, Josephus also thought that priests were entitled to tithes as Leviticus implies, he would have said creatively that tithes were to be given "to priests and to Levites."

Josephus thought that priests also were entitled to tithes, not just the 10 percent from Levitical tithes. In actual narrative he never mentions Levites receiving tithes. Yet there were Levites in his time who accepted the same conflicting biblical legislations. They performed their duties in the temple[61] and sometimes held positions of responsibility in the community.[62] They also were capable of demanding what they saw to be their

view appears to be an attempt to harmonize Josephus's statements and bring them in line with rabbinic halakah. See Del Verme ("La 'prima decima,'" 28 and n. 66), who cites with approval Hanoch Albeck's introduction to the tractate Mishnah *Maʿaśerot*; see also Sanders, *Jewish Law*, 44 (not citing Albeck), 292, and 366, n. 30. This view is rejected by Oppenheimer, *'Am Ha-Aretz*, 39–40 and n. 47. It is contradicted by the facts that Josephus relates (our numbers ii-iv).

57. This is the view of Del Verme, "La 'prima decima,'" 27–34.

58. Josephus's "innovation" consists in such "classification" (*A.J.* 4.196–97). Josephus's retelling of biblical history (and law) may be said to point to his own contemporary thought (and practice) in at least two instances: first, in his harmonizations and, second, when his departure from the biblical text cannot be accounted for in other ways. This is persuasive especially when both his departure and the results of his harmonizations can be confirmed from other sources.

59. Sanders (*Jewish Law*, 44) argues that Josephus read Leviticus in light of Numbers and Nehemiah. "Its one-tenth 'to the Lord' is understood to mean 'to the Levites, who themselves give some to the priests.'"

60. See below.

61. Oppenheimer (*'Am Ha-Aretz*, 40) observes apropos: "Nor from the practical aspect can it be assumed that the Levites, who did all the hard work in the Temple, would have continued to do it without some compensation."

62. "As rulers let each city have seven men long exercised in virtue and in the pursuit

right (*A.J.* 20.216–17).[63] Mishnaic legislation, presumably representing pre-70 Pharisaic opinion, consistently states that tithes are to be given to the Levites.[64] And so does Philo.[65] The author of the *Temple Scroll*, we saw above, concedes them this right. It is reasonable to think that they must have claimed it.

Numbers 18:21–32; Leviticus 27:30–33 in Ezra/Nehemiah's Restoration

The evidence of 2 Chronicles and Nehemiah does not permit us to think that there existed a time, back in the pristine days of the Second Temple period, when only Levites were entitled to and did receive tithes.

One of the most remarkable aspects of the history of the priesthood in Israel is the emergence of the Levites as temple officials subordinate to the "sons of Aaron," the priests. The origin and the process of this stratification of the priesthood are very controverted and have remained obscure.[66] By the close of the preexilic period, in any event, there existed a body of impoverished and disfranchised priests whose right to officiate in the temple in Jerusalem was not guaranteed and who eventually

---

of justice; and to each magistracy let there be assigned two subordinate officers of the tribe of Levi" (*A.J.* 20.214; see §287 and *B.J.* 2.571). Both the specification of the number of magistrates and the assignment of Levitical assistants are Josephus's additions to biblical legislation (compare Deut 16:18; 17:8–13; 21:5).

63. See below.

64. See, among other passages, *m. Maʿaś. Š.* 5:9–10; *m. Yebam.* 9:4–6; 10:1; *Mishnah Peʾah* 8:2; 1:6. *m. Peʾah* 1.6 deals, apparently, with a situation in which a priest or a Levite might keep or pay tithes for grain which he has bought. Menahem Stern ("Aspects of Jewish Society," 585) thinks that a "literal reading" of the passage shows that "the tithes are to be shared in equal measure between priests and Levites." I cannot see how the passage should be interpreted in this way.

65. See passages discussed above.

66. Several events in the history of Israel may have started the process: (1) the exclusion and banishment of Abiathar (and his family) by Solomon and the elevation of Zadok (and his family) to the Jerusalem priesthood; (2) the revolution led by Jeroboam I, who probably appointed non-Levitical priests to his sanctuaries; (3) the fall of the northern kingdom and the consequent displacement of cult personnel to the south; (4) Hezekiah's and, particularly, Josiah's (Deuteronomic) reforms, which centralized the cult in Jerusalem and destroyed local cult centers in Judah and in Israel. See Wellhausen, *Prolegomena*, 121–67; Schürer, *History*, 2:250–56 and the literature cited there; Menahem Haran, *Temples and Temple-Service in Ancient Israel: An Inquiry Into the Character of Cult Phenomena and the Historical Setting of the Priestly School* (Oxford: Clarendon, 1978), 58–148; Baruch A. Levine, "Levites," in *ER*, vol. 8 (ed. Mircea Eliade; New York: Macmillan, 1987), 523–31; idem, *Numbers 1–20: A New Translation with Introduction and Commentary* (AB 4A; New York: Doubleday, 1993), 279–90 (commentary on Num 8); Merlin D. Rehm, "Levites and Priests," in *ABD*, vol. 4 (ed. David Noel Freedman et al.; New York: Doubleday, 1992), 297–310.

assumed the role of "Levites." By the time of the Chronicler and of the compiler of Ezra and Nehemiah, the process of disfranchisement seems to have ended and that of reintegration to have been well under way.[67] Hence, the phrase "the priests and the Levites," with its variants, had become standardized; and the existence of the two distinct groups could be said to be "written in the book of Moses" (Ezra 6:18).[68]

It is, therefore, not at all surprising that it is in the Priestly document, in which the stratification of the priesthood is expressed for the first time, that we also find the law according to which tithes are to be given to Levites. Deuteronomy's legislation on tithes is understandable in the social context in which the impoverished country "Levitical priest"—unable to officiate in Jerusalem and to share in the prerogatives of the priesthood, but retaining a right to it (Deut 18:6–8)—needed to be supported by part of the tithes. The farmer consumed some of these, henceforth, in Jerusalem (Deut 12:11–12, 17–19; 14:22–27; see 15:11), and some he gave to the "Levitical priest" *in toto* every three years (Deut 14:28–29; 26:12–16). The legislation in Num 18:21–32, on the contrary, stands in a context in which the semantic field of the designation "Levites" had changed radically. The Levites are no longer priests estranged from the central sanctuary and its privileges, but have been integrated into it. They, however, share neither in the priestly office nor in the priests' sources of income (18:1–20). Their service of maintenance is rewarded with the gift of every tithe in Israel. Frank Crüsemann notes rightly that the formulation in Num 18:21–32 could not have preceded the legislation in Deuteronomy.[69] If the stratification of the priesthood as represented by Numbers is the culmination of the long process of which Deuteronomy retains some traces, the grant of all tithes to the temple-attendant Levites must be seen as a parallel development in that process. Tithes that in the Deuteronomic code were designed to assuage the *conditio misera* of the dispossessed priests in the "towns" of Israel have in Numbers become the reward for the services rendered in Jerusalem by the priests—turned Levites.[70]

The idea that tithes were for priests and/or for the officiating temple

---

67. More than two hundred years lie between Josiah's reform (ca. 628 B.C.E.) and the crystallization of postexilic institutions at the end of Nehemiah's governorship (ca. 410 B.C.E.).

68. Neh 12:45–46, like Chronicles, attributes the formation of the two distinct orders to David (and Solomon); see 1 Chr 23–26 and 2 Chr 8:14.

69. Frank Crüsemann, "Der Zehnte in der israelitischen Königszeit," *WD* 18 (1985): 46.

70. Weinfeld is correct in observing that the allocation of tithes to Levites in Deuteronomy is the result of the destruction of the provincial sanctuaries and the consequent impoverishment of the provincial cult officials. However, he thinks that the abolition of the sanctuaries meant that tithes were no longer needed and that the legislation in Deuteronomy amounts to a "novelty," a "liberalization," and a "secularization" of the institution with respect to the previous practice in which tithes were given to cult officials (Levites) in

personnel was also alive in the early postexilic period. This is crucial for the transition into the restoration after the exile. At the level of legislation we must recall, first, that Deuteronomy's country Levites had a claim to the priesthood. Second, Lev 27:30–33 testifies to the tradition that tithes were for the central sanctuary, for priests.[71] Leviticus as a whole lacks the notion of a division within the ranks of the priesthood.[72]

It is not probable, concretely, that all non-Jerusalem priests gave up their claim to the priesthood without a fight. It is improbable also that they all adhered to the stratification described by Numbers. Numbers is too strident in its ideological and legislative purity to reflect actual social reality, which was bound to be much more murky and ambivalent. The priestly redaction of the Korah incident in Num 16–17 shows clearly that the exclusive election of the Jerusalem priesthood (the Aaronic priesthood, according to Numbers) and the consequent subordination of the "Levites" were stiffly contested and needed an etiological narrative to legitimize them.[73] Subsequently, the history of the priesthood continued

---

the Levitical cities. It is very doubtful that the so-called "Levitical cities" ever existed; it is even more doubtful that they would have been the cult centers that Weinfeld's theory supposes them to have been. If the Levites were "cult officials" of the provincial sanctuaries, they would have been priests, as Ezekiel (44:10–14) and the Deuteronomic Code say they were. The destruction of the sanctuaries, one would have thought, should have led to the progressive centralization of the economic basis of the cult, as we witness in Numbers and in the subsequent Second Temple literature, rather than render tithes obsolete as Weinfeld proposes. In any event, Weinfeld's position does not take account of the fact that the Levites of Numbers are not cult officials of provincial sanctuaries but rather temple attendants of the central sanctuary, and it is as such that they receive tithes. On the contrary, although the Levites of Deuteronomy are *personae miserabiles*, a fact that Weinfield finds it difficult to fit into his theory, they are also priests. See Weinfeld, "Tithe," cols. 1160–61; idem, *Deuteronomy 1–11: A New Translation with Introduction and Commentary* (AB 5; New York: Doubleday, 1991), 34–44.

71. Lev 27:30–33 is an appendix to the Holiness Code and dates from the final redaction of Leviticus, but the tradition which it represents could be much older.

72. Lev 25:32–34, the only reference to Levites, does not specify their cultic functions.

73. Num 17 is completely of priestly composition. The account in Num 16 is generally thought to introduce the story of Korah—and the theme of the legitimation of the Aaronide priesthood—into an earlier (JE) narrative (Num 16:1b-2, 12–14, 23–34; see Deut 11:6). For Num 16–17, see Baruch A. Levine, *Numbers 1–20*, 428–32. On Deut 11:6, see Weinfeld, *Deuteronomy 1–11*, 443–44. Josephus's and Philo's lengthy redactions of the stories in Num 16–17 leave no doubt as to what, in their opinions, was at stake—the "undisputed possession of the priesthood" by Aaron and his sons against the claims of the Levites (see *A.J.* 4.14–66; Philo, *Mos.* 2.174–86, 275–87). Ezek 44:10–14 (probably a postexilic interpolation) offers a different rationalization. Hanson sees in 1 Chr 15–16 some evidence of "instability among various Levitical families, and the efforts of such families to secure their positions within the temple cult" in the early Second Temple period. Paul D. Hanson, "1 Chronicles 15–16 and the Chronicler's Views on the Levites," in *"Sha'arei Talmon": Studies in the Bible, Qumran, and the Ancient Near East Presented to Shemaryahu Talmon* (ed. Michael Fishbane and Emmanuel Tov; Winona Lake, Ind.: Eisenbrauns, 1992), 69–77.

to be marked by divisive turbulence until the close of the early Roman period. Josephus (*A.J.* 20.216–17) reports with indignation that in the waning days of the Judean state (about 64 C.E.) those Levites who were temple singers demanded and obtained from King Agrippa II and the Sanhedrin the right to wear linen robes "on equal terms with the priests." Levites never gave up completely the struggle to regain full priestly dignity.

The distribution of tithes in 2 Chronicles and in Nehemiah reflects complex ideological and social realities within which the restoration of cultic life in Israel was accomplished after the Babylonian exile. According to 2 Chr 31:4–19,[74] after Hezekiah had reestablished the orders of priests and of Levites and had restored temple sacrifice, the king commanded the dwellers of Jerusalem "to give the portion due to the priests and the Levites, so that they might devote themselves to the law of the Lord" (v. 4). Not only the inhabitants of Jerusalem but also the people of Israel[75] "gave in abundance the firstfruits (רֵאשִׁית) of grain, wine, oil, honey, and of all the produce of the field; and they brought in abundantly the tithe of everything" (v. 5). From the cities of Judah were brought (by the people of Israel and Judah who lived there) "tithe of cattle and sheep, and the tithe of dedicated things that had been consecrated to the Lord their God" (v. 6).[76] Since the abundance of supplies exceeded the needs of the moment, the king ordered that storehouses be prepared in the temple and appointed officers to be in charge of distribution (vv. 11–21).

The tithes, firstfruits, and dedicated things together constituted "the portion due to the priests and the Levites." Although the Levites were

74. I take the narrative to represent realities (or the author's ideal of the realities) of the Chronicler's time, that is, between 400 and 200 B.C.E. The in-gathering of tithes during the time of Hezekiah is probably to be read in the context of the Chronicler's attempt to reattach the structures that he attributes to Hezekiah's reform (2 Chr 29:1–31:21) to those structures which, according to the author, David had instituted. Nevertheless, not even the Chronicler's reevaluation of David's cultic organization includes the institution of tithes. As we shall note below, the earliest he could push the practice is to the reign of Hezekiah.

75. The naming of Israel, that is, the inhabitants of the northern kingdom, as contributors of first fruits and tithes is for the most part visionary. Josephus (*A J.* 9.264–66), rejecting this idealization, claims that the Israelites treated Hezekiah's invitation with scorn and killed the prophets who exhorted them to comply.

76. "Tithes of dedicated things" (מַעְשַׂר קָדָשִׁים) is problematic, and one might accept the RSV's reading of the passage: "tithe of cattle and sheep, and the dedicated things . . . ." This would agree with v. 12, which lists three categories of offerings brought into the store-chambers: contributions (תְּרוּמָה), referring apparently to the first fruits; tithes (מַעֲשֵׂר); and dedicated things (קֳדָשִׁים). On the basis of Num 18:24, where תְּרוּמָה appears as synonym for מַעְשַׂר בְּנֵי־יִשְׂרָאֵל, and of Mal 3:8, 10, which interchange כָּל־הַמַּעֲשֵׂר for הַמַּעֲשֵׂר וְהַתְּרוּמָה, Baumgarten suggests the reading "the tribute of dedicated things" in 2 Chr 31:6. He points out that "*maʿăśēr* is capable of being used in the generalized sense of any hieratical gift" ("On the Non-Literal Use," 246).

responsible for the storage and distribution of the tithes and offerings to the priests and Levites, the portion for the priests was not a tithe of the tithe given to the Levites (2 Chr 31:11–19). Tithes belonged, without distinction, to *both priests and Levites*. Both seem to have received portions of the tithes, firstfruits, and even the most holy things (v. 14).

The organization of tithes in 2 Chr 31:4–19 corresponds to the Priestly tradition of Lev 27:30–33. The Chronicler appears to be responsible for the interpretive designation of "priests and Levites" as the beneficiaries of tithes.

In Nehemiah, on the contrary, tithes are organized and distributed according to the Priestly legislation in Num 18:21–32: the people give tithes to the Levites, who in turn give a tithe of the tithe (מַעֲשַׂר הַמַּעֲשֵׂר, Neh 10:39 [Eng. v. 38]; see 12:47)[77] to the priests. Nehemiah, unlike 2 Chronicles, otherwise maintains a terminological distinction between the portions in the storehouse of the temple that went to priests and what was given to Levites—always tithes (from which the priests' portion had been removed).[78]

Vestiges in Nehemiah of priestly claim to tithes might be found in the provision that priests, "the descendants of Aaron," be with Levites when the Levites receive tithes from the farmer (Neh 10:39a [Eng. v. 38a]).[79]

All the available evidence, therefore, points to the conclusion that Josephus's expression "to priests and to Levites" represents the variety in contemporary opinion and practice. The farmer would have given his

---

77. See Num 18:26–28; v. 26 = מַעֲשֵׂר מִן־הַמַּעֲשֵׂר. Whereas the people themselves bring the firstfruits, the firstlings, and other priestly portions, to the storehouse of the temple, they give the tithes to the Levites, who bring the tithe of tithe to the priests in the temple (Neh 10:36–38a, 38b-40 [Eng. vv. 35–37a, 37b-39]). The legislation in Num 18 does not provide for a centralized collection and distribution of tithes, a feature prominent in 2 Chronicles and Nehemiah. The pledge to offer tithes in Neh 10:36–40 [Eng. vv. 35–39] might appear as part of a commitment to return to preexilic practices. In fact, some of the practices are clearly innovations, for example, the one-third shekel temple tax (vv. 33–34 [Eng. vv. 32–33]), only alluded to in Exod 30:13, and the wood offering (v. 35 [Eng. v. 34], see 13:31), which Lev 6:12–13 would make necessary but does not impose.

78. See Neh 10:36–38a, 38b-40 [Eng. vv. 35–37a, 37b-39]. In Nehemiah it would seem that only the tithe of tithe and the other priestly offerings (תְּרוּמָה) are brought to the storehouses of the temple. The term תְּרוּמָה appears to refer to a separate offering alongside first fruits and firstlings in 10:38a [Eng. v. 37a] and in 12:44. In 2 Chr 31:10 it apparently means "offerings," including tithes, but in 2 Chr 31:12; Neh 10:40 [Eng. v. 39]; 13:5 only the priestly portions are meant. See Sanders, *Jewish Law*, 290 and 365, n. 19. The distinction between the two kinds of portions—for the priests and for the Levites—is observed as the offerings are gathered into the storehouses (Neh 12:44; 13:5, see vv. 10–13). In the distribution, the Levites receive their portion (of tithes), from which they set aside the priests' portion (Neh 12:47).

79. The organization of tithes is said to be according to what is written in the Law (Neh 10:37 [Eng. v. 36]; 12:44; 13:5), meaning only Num 18. Tithing of animals is not mentioned, and the legislation in Deuteronomy is ignored.

tithe either to the one whom his ideological allegiance dictated or to the person (priest or Levite) who was there to collect it. The legislation that the Levites were to deduct a tithe for the priests from the tithes that they received (*A.J.* 4.69) might only mean that Levites also were bound to pay tithes to priests, even from the tithes that they themselves received.

Centralized Collection

It is conceivable that Josiah's centralization of the cult resulted also in the centralization of "offerings" for the clergy. With regard to tithes, Deuteronomy's demand that they be consumed only in Jerusalem, except during the third year, seems to point toward such centralization. By reason, most probably, of the absence of a monarchy upon which the centralized temple service would have depended, tithes were crucial to the maintenance of temple worship in the period of restoration after the exile. This is clear from the refrain that the storage of food in the temple kept the Levites (and priests) at their posts and devoted to their ministry.[80] Tithes provided "the daily portions" for the officiating priests and Levites (Neh 12:47; see 2 Chr 31:10) while they ministered in the temple. Malachi's challenge to the people clearly states this purpose (Mal 3:10):

> Bring the full tithe into the storehouse, so that there may be food in my house, and thus put me to the test, says the Lord of hosts; see if I will not open the windows of heaven for you and pour down for you an overflowing blessing.

Failure to do so caused the Levites to abandon their temple service and return to the cultivation of their fields.[81] The house of God was therefore robbed and neglected (Mal 3:8–9; Neh 10:40 [Eng. v. 39]; 13:10–14). In Nehemiah, as in 2 Chronicles, the rationale for levying tithes and for collecting them into storage in Jerusalem is not to provide dispossessed priests with a means of livelihood. The reason is, instead, the need to feed officiating Levites (and priests) and, in this manner, to guarantee that temple service would continue uninterrupted.

Scholars have often stated that in the Second Temple period tithes were brought by pilgrims to Jerusalem, where they were then collected in

80. See 2 Chr 31:4 and Josephus's interpretation: "The king [Hezekiah] . . . ordained that the tithes and first-fruits should be given by the people to the priests and Levites in order that they might always apply themselves to their divine office and be uninterrupted in their service of God" (*A.J.* 9.273; also Neh 11:44; 13:4–14).

81. In Nehemiah Levites (and priests) have fields (שָׂדֶה, 13:10) and landed property (אֲחֻזָּה, 11:3), which are considered their inheritance (נַחֲלָה, 11:20) within the cities of Judah.

the temple. They are surprised that Josephus's companions in Galilee should have collected tithes individually in 66 C.E. and that, according to the rabbis, tithes could be given anywhere in Israel.[82] Actually, the offering of tithes during festival pilgrimages is clearly attested only in Tob 1:6–8. However, Tobit's offering of tithes in Jerusalem is necessitated by the historical context within which his narrative is cast: the apostate Israel of Jeroboam I. Tobit's action, according to the author of this work, testifies to his outstanding piety and fidelity to the true cult, "as it is prescribed for all Israel by an everlasting decree," in the midst of Israel's apostasy. It was he alone who paid his tithes, not in the shrines of Israel but in the designated place of worship—Jerusalem—in accordance with the Deuteronomic ideal. This can hardly be considered clear evidence for general practice in postexilic times.

Philo's *Spec.* 1.152 also is cited as evidence for a centralized collection, storage, and distribution of tithes in the temple.[83] This passage deals not with tithes but with priests' offerings, firstfruits,[84] which in the subsequent passage Philo clearly distinguishes from tithes (allotted to the Levites).[85] Philo's point here, strictly speaking, is not centralized collection but rather the ethical convenience deriving from the fact that firstfruits are gifts offered to God, from whom, as it were, the priests then receive them. This idea implies the practical need for a system of storage and distribution. Nevertheless, the idea itself could be derived without any reference to such a system from the fact that, according to the Law, the gifts were primarily offered to God in the temple and only secondarily to the priests (see Num 18:8–20).

Judith 11:13[86] appears to be more relevant, even though this text raises more questions than it actually answers. The phrase "the priests

82. See the discussion below.

83. See Oppenheimer, *ʿAm Ha-Aretz*, 31–32. According to S. Safrai, tithes were offered in Jerusalem "from the exile down to Hasmonean times." This was an "ancient custom" which Philo knew but which had disappeared in his day. Safrai cites *Spec.* 1.132–50, which says nothing on the subject ("Religion in Everyday Life," 823 and n. 5).

84. "But that none of the donors should taunt the recipients, it [the Law] ordered the first-fruits to be first brought into the temple (κελεύει τὰς ἀπαρχὰς εἰς τὸ ἱερὸν κομίζεσθαι πρότερον) and then taken thence by the priests. It was the proper course that the first-fruits (ἀπαρχάς) should be brought as a thank-offering to God by those whose life in all its aspects is blessed by His beneficence, and then by Him, since He needs nothing at all, freely bestowed with all dignity and honour on those who serve and minister in the temple. For if the gift is felt to come not from men but from the Benefactor of all, its acceptance carries with it no sense of shame." See above and Sanders, *Jewish Law*, 291–97.

85. Philo, *Spec.* 1.156–57. Sanders (*Judaism*, 150) also cites *Spec.* 1.152, but he speaks generally of central storage and distribution of priestly offerings. He therefore stays close to Philo's meaning. See also Alon, *Jews*, 89–90.

86. See the discussion above.

who minister in the presence of our God in Jerusalem" seems to indicate that tithes were collected for consumption by officiating priests (and Levites) in Jerusalem. There is, however, no indication that pilgrims would bring the offerings there. Quite to the contrary, the people could not even touch them! Tithes and the temple are linked also in 1 Macc 3:49. Faced with the impending devastation of Jerusalem ordered by Antiochus IV in 165 B.C.E., Judas and his brothers, as they lamented, displayed the vestment of the priesthood, the firstfruits, and tithes, and they stirred up the Nazirites. This passage is a clear illustration of the importance that tithes had assumed for the temple cult by the second century. The passage does not prove, however, that the only way Jews could have offered "first tithes" was to bring them to the temple.[87] The author does not say whether Judas displayed the "first tithes" or the "second tithes."

The addition in the Septuagint to the Hebrew text of 1 Sam 1:21 is also often cited as evidence. In addition to offering sacrifices, Elkanah, according to the Greek text, brought "all the tithes of his land" to Shiloh.[88] Josephus reproduces this same addition in *A.J.* 5.346: "They [Samuel's parents] came therefore again to offer sacrifices for the birth of the child and brought their tithes also [to Shiloh]."[89] Both the translator of the Septuagint and Josephus, insofar as he is not merely repeating the tradition, were anxious to have Elkanah fulfill all his obligations, including the payment of tithes. If we accept Josephus's (and the Septuagint's) addition here to reflect actual practice, we need to reckon also with Josephus's claim in the same passage that Elkanah was "a Levite of the middle classes, of the tribe of Ephraim" who offered tithes of the produce of his land.[90]

To sum up, neither Nehemiah nor 2 Chronicles supports the theory that in the beginning of the Second Temple period "Levitical tithes" were brought to Jerusalem by the farmers during the festivals. Instead, it appears that Levites (and priests), under the supervision of appointed

87. See Oppenheimer, *ʿAm Ha-Aretz*, 31: "Even as it was obligatory to bring to the Temple the first fruits, the priests' garments, and the sacrifices of the Nazirite, so the taking of the tithes to the Temple and their distribution there constituted the only way of observing the commandment of the tithe." See also Alon, *Jews*, 91.

88. 1 Sam 1:21 (LXX): Καὶ ἀνέβη ὁ ἄνθρωπος Ελκανα καὶ πᾶς ὁ οἶκος αὐτοῦ θῦσαι ἐν Σηλωμ τὴν θυσίαν τῶν ἡμερῶν καὶ τὰς εὐχὰς αὐτοῦ καὶ πάσας τὰς δεκάτας τῆς γῆς αὐτοῦ.

89. See 1 Sam 1:24(-28). Josephus does not mention tithes among Elkanah's offerings in *A.J.* 5.343, which is the parallel passage to 1 Sam 1:21.

90. Ἀλκάνης Λευίτης ἀνὴρ τῶν ἐν μέσῳ πολιτῶν τῆς Ἐφράμου κληρουχίας, κτλ. (*A.J.* 5.342). 1 Sam 1:1 says that Elkanah was an Ephraimite. Levites were, supposedly, from the tribe of Levi. 1 Chr 6:22–28, 33–38 counts Elkanah and Samuel among the Levites and traces their genealogy forward and backward to Levi through Levi's second son Izhar. Further, Levites were supposedly without landed property—for agricultural purposes—for which reason they received tithes.

temple officials, collected tithes from the countryside[91] for storage and distribution in the temple.

What is confirmed by both texts, and by the other passages that I have discussed, is that strenuous and repeated efforts were made by responsible authorities to collect and store food for officiating priests and Levites.[92] This does not exclude in any way the probability that some, especially those in the neighborhood of Jerusalem, would have found it convenient (and probably pious) to bring their "Levitical tithes" to Jerusalem during a pilgrimage. The system of centralized collection seems to have had a difficult start, as can be seen in Nehemiah's repeated attempts and failures to organize it. Malachi's rebuke and plea also suggest a wholesale refusal to pay (see Neh 12:44–47; 13:4–13; Mal 3:8–12). It would be reasonable to expect, nonetheless, that by the early Hellenistic period, the centralized system, like the temple state itself, was fully established. The practice seems to have continued under the supervision of the high priests until the last decade of the existence of the Jewish state.

The number of priests and Levites must have increased in the late Hellenistic and early Roman periods.[93] A sizable number of these traveled to and remained in Jerusalem while their courses performed temple services, and they needed to be fed. Therefore, the system of centralized

---

91. Neh 10:38 [Eng. v. 37]: "in all our rural towns" (בְּכֹל עָרֵי עֲבֹדָתֵנוּ); see 12:44. This is not contradicted by Neh 12:47; 13:12; Mal 3:10; and 2 Chr 31:4–7, which speak of tithes being brought to the storehouses (by the people). These passages either deal with initial and emergency situations (2 Chr 31:4–7; Neh 13:12) or simply mean that the people made the necessary contributions. See also Weinfeld, "Tithe," col. 1161.

92. This is an innovation attributed in 2 Chr 31:11–20 to Hezekiah. David, according to 1 Chr 26:20–28, had treasuries and dedicated gifts in the temple, over which he appointed Levites. It is very doubtful that "Levites" existed as subordinate temple officials during David's reign. In any event, David's treasuries contained dedicatory offerings, "for the maintenance of the house of the Lord," which rulers of Israel from Samuel to David and their officers made to the sanctuary, and the spoils of war (vv. 26–28). David is not portrayed as having organized tithes. Oppenheimer (*'Am Ha-Aretz*, 32) thinks this practice was initiated by Ezra and Nehemiah. This is plausible, although he ignores the fact that in Nehemiah tithes are not brought to Jerusalem by the farmers.

93. According to Ezra 2:36–42//Neh 7:39–45, the priests and Levites who returned at the time of Zerubbabel and Joshua were 4,630 (Neh = 4,649). Of these there were 4,289 priests, 74 Levites, 128 singers (Neh = 148), 139 doorkeepers (Neh = 138). In Jerusalem, at the time of Nehemiah, there lived 1,192 priests and 284 Levites, according to Neh 11:10–18. An even larger number must have lived in the towns and villages (see Neh 11:3). At a (probably) later time there were 3,700 priests and 4,600 Levites (1 Chr 12:26; these numbers are projected into David's reign). Pseudo-Aristeas (*Let. Arist.* 95 [ca. 170 B.C.E.]) speaks of over 700 priests (and probably Levites) officiating at one time in the temple, bringing the number in the twenty-four courses to about 16,800. Josephus (*C. Ap.* 2.108) says that (in his days) there were 20,000 priests (and probably Levites) belonging to four "tribes." All these numbers are most probably exaggerated. For discussions of the numbers of priests and Levites, see Jeremias, *Jerusalem*, 198–205; and Schürer, *History*, 2:254–56.

collection continued to work for the purpose for which it had been established.

This is the overall context in which Julius Caesar stipulated that, in addition to other taxes, the Jews "shall also pay tithes to Hyrcanus and his sons, just as they paid to their forefathers" (*A.J.* 14.203).[94] It is often assumed that Caesar was in his decree recognizing for John Hyrcanus II the same right that his grandfathers had claimed over tithes. The Hasmoneans, from John Hyrcanus on, it is said, had taken control of tithes and used them not for the needs of the temple but for the "secular" administration of the Jewish state.[95]

The basis for this view is the explanations in the Talmud of an obscure passage in the Mishnah: "Johanan the High Priest did away with the Avowal concerning the Tithe . . . . And in his days none needed to inquire concerning *demai*-produce" (*m. Maʿaś. Š.* 5:15, repeated in *m. Soṭah* 9:10). Neither the Mishnah nor the Talmud actually identifies the high priest in question, but scholars have speculated that either John Hyrcanus I (135/4–104 B.C.E.)[96] or John Hyrcanus II (63–40 B.C.E.),[97] his grandson, is meant.

Obviously, the talmudic explanations are late. One should therefore be wary of hearing in them "echoes" of momentous historical changes about which we have no trace in contemporary literature. Their value as historical evidence is further undermined by the fact that the explanations are contradictory. This is clear if we ask what the high priest in question actually did and what the consequences of his action were. According to the Jerusalem Talmud (*y. Maʿaś. Š.* 5:5; *y. Soṭah* 9:11), the high priest abolished the confession because: (1) some people were suspected of giving their tithes to the priests, and he sought to discourage this; (2) he sent inspectors into the villages who found that all the people properly separated heave offering, whereas only some separated first and second tithes;

---

94. See text at the beginning of this chapter.

95. See chapter 2 and n. 107. The idea that Caesar decreed that tithes be paid to the Hasmoneans seems to have originated from Mommsen, *History*, 4:162, n. 1. The view that the Hasmoneans took control of tithes is articulated by Schalit, *König Herodes*, 262–71, esp. 267–70. Schalit is followed by many others. See, for instance, Oppenheimer, *ʿAm Ha-Aretz*, 29–42; Alon, *Jews*, 96–102; Joseph M. Baumgarten, "On the Non-Literal Use," 247–48, n. 16; idem, "First and Second Tithes," 9; S. Safrai, "Religion in Everyday Life," 822; idem, "Relations Between the Diaspora and the Land of Israel," in *The Jewish People in the First Century: Historical Geography, Political History, Social, Cultural and Religious Life and Institutions*, vol. 1 (ed. S. Safrai and M. Stern; CRINT 1; Assen: Van Gorcum, 1974), 201 (here he says that the "later Hasmonean kings and the high priests were engaged in a fierce struggle with the circles who favoured the direct distribution of the dues among the ordinary priests in the towns and villages"); Del Verme, "La 'prima decima,'" 20–24.

96. According to Schalit and others.

97. According to Alon and Safrai.

(3) he, therefore, ordered that each one should designate heave offering and the heave offering of tithe (and give them directly to the priest), that the second tithe should be "deconsecrated" with money to be spent in Jerusalem, and that the poor person's tithe should be left unharvested and should be claimed by anyone who showed proof of poverty; (4) he abolished the confession (Deut 26:13–15, the part "I have given it to the Levites") in order to save Israel from perjury and guilt and so to preserve Israel's praiseworthiness; (5) Eleazar b. Paḥhora and Judah b. Petora took tithes by force. Although the high priest could have stopped them he did not, but instead he abolished the confession. This was to his discredit.

Moreover, it was unnecessary to ask about *demai*-produce because the high priest set up "pairs" (זוגות). Both tractates maintain that "at first" the farmer divided his tithe into three parts: for (the friends of) priests and Levites, and for the treasury, for the poor and the "associates" in Jerusalem. Legal fees were paid from the treasury for the plaintiff who traveled to Jerusalem (*y. Maᶜaś. Š.* 5:5). This was to the high priest's credit.

According to the Babylonian Talmud (*b. Soṭah* 47b-48a), the high priest abolished the confession (and it was unnecessary to ask about *demai*-produce) because: (1) "people were not presenting it according to the regulation; for the All Merciful said that they should give it to the Levites whereas we present it to the priests"; (2) the high priest's inspectors found that the people separated the great *tĕrûmâ,* and not the first and second tithes; (3) the high priest, therefore, decreed that anyone who bought food from the *ᶜam ha-aretz* must himself separate from it the heave offering of tithe and give it to a priest, that they must set aside and eat the second tithe in Jerusalem, and that the Levite and poor person who demanded their respective tithes must prove that these had not already been given to them.

The various conclusions that scholars have drawn from the (selective) use of these explanations are even more contradictory. Should we assume that the high priest's ruling was the consequence of tithes being given to priests (rather than to Levites), or contrarily that his ruling brought about the practice of giving tithes to priests? It cannot be true both that the high priest took control of tithes for his own—secular—purposes and that through his action priests gained control of tithes, to the detriment of the Levites. The "pairs," it is said, against the plain sense of the texts, were the collectors of tithes, which had now become a state-enforced tax. The complete efficiency with which this state tax was collected made it unnecessary to inquire about *demai*-produce. If this is the case, it cannot also be true that in the Hasmonean period the payment of tithes had declined and that Caesar's decree was needed to reinforce it.

There can be little doubt that the Hasmonean high priests/kings took steps to reorganize the collection of tithes after they restored the temple cult and gained control of the Jewish state. Exactly what they did, however, is lost to us and cannot be recovered from late talmudic discussions.

Two other observations should be made against the view that the Hasmoneans had appropriated tithes. First, if priests and Levites officiating in the temple had lost their means of livelihood to the Hasmonean "state," there would have been unmistakable echoes in the extant literature. We would then have seen the defiance of hungry priests (and Levites) and the disruption of temple worship instead of "halakic" arguments by Pharisees.

Second, the view assumes, and it is sometimes stated, that it was with the 10 percent of produce that the Hasmoneans collected from the Jewish farmers that they paid for the administration of their (later) extensive territory, their equally extensive and costly wars, and their diplomatic initiatives and accumulated their personal wealth. Hence, according to Applebaum, before the Roman period, Jewish peasants "had been virtually free of fiscal exactions since the liberation of Judaea by Simeon, and certainly never, even under Jannaeus, had borne taxation equivalent to that of the Seleucids."[98] This is simply impossible.[99] The fact that Caesar's edict called for tithes to be paid to Hyrcanus II does not imply that tithes should be Hyrcanus's source of income for the administration of the territory that Caesar gave to him.

In chapter 2 I emphasized that Caesar (and the Senate), when dealing with the complete tax obligations that they placed on the Jewish state,[100] took into account Judea's local conditions, for example, the sabbatical year and local taxation, of which tithes were an important element. Cae-

---

98. Applebaum, "Economic Life," 661. For Applebaum's views about Hasmonean taxation, see chapter 2 and n. 112. It is Grant (*Economic Background*, 92–93) who explicitly articulates the idea that, in the Roman period, tithing and other religious dues added to Israel's multiple levels of oppressive taxation. In Israel's theocracy, Grant contends, religious dues stood for what elsewhere was civil tax; they were of the extent "to support the Government, to equip and pay armies and build navies." Like Applebaum, Grant (pp. 91–92, n. 3) considers the tithe in Caesar's decree to be different from and in addition to the religious tithe. He therefore maintains that "civil taxes, both the Roman and before them the later Maccabaean and Herodian, were *over and above*" all the crushing religious dues that were "designed to be the *sole* tribute of the holy people consecrated to Yahweh" (p. 100; emphases in original).

99. See the discussion in Sanders, *Judaism*, 157–60: Biblical legislation on tithing up to Nehemiah does not envisage a Jewish national army, and no such army existed at the time when the tithe system came into effect under Persia; if the Hasmoneans had robbed the priests and Levites of their dues, we would have to explain why priests and Levites did not starve, why the Levites continued to serve in the temple rather than flee to their fields, and why the pietist literature of the period contains no criticisms of the Hasmoneans for robbing the Levites.

100. Tribute was imposed on the temple state centered in Jerusalem (ὑπὲρ τῆς Ἱεροσολυμιτῶν πόλεως [*A.J.* 14.202–3]), with Joppa as its seaport city (*A.J.* 14.205–6). See chapter 2.

sar's edict confirms Hyrcanus's supervisory responsibility, as the high priest and head of the temple state,[101] for the organization of the system upon which the running of the temple had come to depend. This confirmation does not mean that Hyrcanus II, "his sons" (he had none), and "their forefathers" had appropriated tithes. Tithes were an important source of income for the upkeep of temple personnel. Like the temple tax, they needed to be explicitly protected by the Romans.[102]

A further indication that tithes were collected for the care of temple personnel up to the time when the temple was destroyed comes from Josephus's accounts of the failure of the system. Summarizing the conditions that prevailed in Jerusalem from about 59 C.E. until the outbreak of the war with Rome in 66 C.E., Josephus writes (*A.J.* 20.180):

> There now was enkindled mutual enmity and class warfare between the high priests, on the one hand, and the priests and the leaders of the populace of Jerusalem, on the other hand. Each of the factions formed and collected for itself a band of the most reckless revolutionaries and acted as their leader . . . . No, it was as if there was no one in charge of the city, so that they acted as they did with full licence.

The epitome of this complete breakdown of law and order in the city was the conduct of the high priestly aristocracy (*A.J.* 20.181):

> Such was the shamelessness and effrontery which possessed the high priests that they actually were so brazen as to send slaves to the threshing floors to receive the tithes that were due to the priests, with the result that the poorer priests starved to death.[103]

The situation was such that (*A.J.* 20.206–7):

> [the high priest] Ananias had servants who were utter rascals and who, combining operations with the most reckless men, would go to the threshing floors and take by force the tithes for the priests; nor did they refrain from beating those who refused to give. The high priests were guilty of the same practices as his slaves, and no one could stop them. So

---

101. See *A.J.* 14.194, 196–99, 200; and the discussion in chapter 2. Sanders, *Judaism*, 514, n. 24: "The statement that the Jews should pay Hyrcanus and his sons a tithe was simply Caesar's confirmation that the high priest could continue to collect the tithe; the context is assurance that Hyrcanus' previous rights will be respected."

102. The allusion to tithes must have come at the request of the Jewish authorities. See chapter 2.

103. καὶ συνέβαινεν τοὺς ἀπορουμένους τῶν ἱερέων ὑπ᾽ ἐνδείας τελευτᾶν. He concludes the account by noting, "Thus did the violence of the contending factions suppress all justice."

> it happened that time that those of the priests who in olden days were maintained by the tithes now starved to death.[104]

The two incidents that, according to Josephus, resulted in the deaths of priests relate to the same continuous atmosphere of civil strife in Jerusalem and its neighborhood, prior to the outbreak of general revolt, when the chaos had not yet spread to the other cities of Palestine.[105] Ananias, the officiating high priest, was specifically guilty of gross misconduct, and so were members of the priestly aristocracy, "the high priests."

Some deaths among priests most probably did occur, as Josephus maintains, as a result of the breakdown of order in Jerusalem, although we must be careful not to exaggerate their numbers. The problem is to understand why these priests should have starved to death from a shortage of food. Sanders has twice, in his words, "puzzled" over this problem.[106] At first, he suggested that the deaths came about because "some priests took to an extreme the biblical laws that they should live on the proceeds of the temple and eat holy food." These priests would have taken it upon themselves to eat *only* priestly offerings and dues.[107] It is possible that there existed in the first century C.E. a group of extremist priests who lived off of offerings and dues only. This may be conjectured from the conduct of some priests in other circumstances.[108] The proposal, however, still fails to be entirely convincing for two reasons. First, there is nothing in Josephus's account to suggest that extremism was the cause of the priests' deaths. Second, in the event that the priests were "food extremists," there would have been other food than tithes to live on, as Sanders himself points out.[109] Lately, persuaded apparently by Hyam

---

104. καὶ τῶν ἱερέων τοὺς πάλαι ταῖς δεκάταις τρεφομένους τότε συνέβαινε θνήσκειν τροφῆς ἀπορίᾳ.

105. Josephus's reports span the period between the end of Felix's procuratorship (and the beginning of Festus's) and the end of Festus's rule (and the arrival of Albinus), that is, from 59/60 C.E. to 62 C.E.

106. See *Sanders, Jewish Law*, 24–26; idem, *Judaism*, 149, 324, 512, n. 3.

107. *Sanders, Jewish Law*, 26; see from p. 25; idem, *Judaism*, 512, n. 3.

108. Josephus relates two instances, both of which took place during the same period (59–61 C.E.), in which priests took food restrictions to an extreme: (1) Priests refused to eat leavened bread during Passover even though there was a drought in the country and this was the only bread available in Jerusalem (*A.J.* 3.320–21). The consumption of leavened bread during Passover is against biblical law, and Josephus offers the priests' behavior as a (praiseworthy) instance of Jewish obedience of Mosaic laws even under duress. (2) Priests (Josephus's own acquaintances) who were sent to Rome by the *praefectus* Felix and were imprisoned there lived on figs and nuts only. Here again Josephus commends their conduct. They were "very excellent men" who "even in affliction . . . had not forgotten the pious practices of religion" (*Vita* 13–14). See Sanders, *Jewish Law*, 24–25.

109. Sanders, *Jewish Law*, 25–26.

Maccoby, Sanders speculates that the priests in question were destitute and were forced to rely entirely on temple dues. He remains puzzled, however, admitting that "the populace would have given more food to keep priests from starving."[110]

Sanders's second proposal takes into account an essential element in Josephus's two stories: that those affected were among the priests who were impoverished (τοὺς ἀπορουμένους τῶν ἱερέων) and who were supported (fed) from tithes. We know from Neh 13:10; 11:3, 20[111] that priests (and Levites) owned landed property, and some were even rich enough to refuse tithes. Josephus himself serves as an example of such priests.[112] Poorer priests would have depended to a greater extent on the offerings. Sanders correctly points out also that Josephus's stories "assume that the only food available to the priests was stored in a central place," and that "all the temple's food stores were stolen and that the priests could not collect food."[113] As I shall argue shortly, besides what was collected for the storehouses of the temple, tithes were offered to and were collected by individual priests (and Levites) in the towns and villages of Israel. Josephus himself testifies to the fact that even in the midst of the crisis and impending war, the priests who were able to organize collection could, away from Jerusalem, make a fortune from tithes (*Vita* 63). Thus, the priests in Jerusalem would not have died if only they could have left Jerusalem. They were instead among those poor priests who depended upon the organized system of centralized collection, storage, and distribution in Jerusalem. It is not too difficult to identify this category of persons: the old and sickly priests (who were unable to leave Jerusalem).

The existing civil strife in Jerusalem decidedly would have rendered unfeasible the "good organization,"[114] by virtue of which the temple treasuries were supplied, from the times of Zerubbabel and Nehemiah, and those who relied upon them were assured of food. Josephus's stories reveal that the administrative structures of Jerusalem, and of the temple, had collapsed in 59/60 C.E. The priestly aristocracy (presided over by the

---

110. Sanders, *Judaism*, 512, n. 3.

111. See n. 81 above.

112. *Vita* 422 and 80, and above.

113. *Sanders, Jewish Law*, 25.

114. Sanders reasons that if the food stores of the temple had been depleted and the priests could not collect food, there were still sacrifices being offered. These could not have fed all the priests (all eighteen thousand or so of them) every day "but with good organization and appeals for more sacrifices to be brought, and for freewill offerings to be made, one would think that starvation could have been avoided." Sanders, *Jewish Law*, 25–26; and Sanders, *Judaism*, 512, n. 3: "The stories are still puzzling, since (as I observed before) one would expect that the populace would have given more food to keep the priests from starving."

high priest in office) thus not only failed to provide for the needs of the temple and its dependents but also actively diverted its resources to their own personal advantage. Although we do not know exactly what happened, Josephus's stories portend what certainly would have occurred if Hyrcanus II, or earlier Hasmoneans, had appropriated tithes and had used them for ends other than the needs of the temple.

Offered Also to Individual Priests and Levites

The actual practice of tithing throughout postexilic Israel was certainly much more complex than would permit us to speak of a unilateral "custom" in any of its aspects. The high priest and temple officials endeavored to raise what was needed by officiating personnel and other dependents of the temple. At the same time, from the restoration to the destruction of the temple in 70 C.E., tithes continued to be collected also by individual priests and Levites. We must insist here that this is not a practice that replaced the collection of tithes for the temple treasuries by temple officials. Of the latter part of the period we have firm evidence from Josephus's account of his own life. While his companions, the priests Joazar and Judas, amassed large sums of money for themselves from tithes in Galilee (*Vita* 63, 29),[115] Josephus himself refused the same offerings, although he had the right to receive them (*Vita* 80).[116]

In mishnaic legislation, "Levitical tithes" and the 1 percent due to the priests (the "heave-offering of tithes") should be offered after the produce has been "stacked" at the granary (*m. Pe*ʾ*ah 1:6)*.[117] They could be given to the Levites and priests anywhere in the land of Israel.[118] Rabbinic discussion in general does not assume that first tithes were offered by the farmers in Jerusalem. It is surprising that the rabbis expect that the 1 percent due to the priests should be given to them by the farmers themselves, and not by the Levites.[119] This does not agree with the literal meaning of Num

115. See above.

116. See above. No abuses are involved here, unlike what Josephus reports of the actions of the high priests in Jerusalem. He says that the priests Joazar and Judas were "men of excellent character" (*Vita* 29). In *Vita* 80 Josephus trumpets his own righteousness on the basis that it was his right as a priest, as it was the right of his companions, to collect tithes.

117. On other produce and generally, see *m. Ma*ʿ*aś.* 1:2ff.

118. See *m. Ma*ʿ*aś. Š.* 5:9. The discussion in *m. Bik.* 2:2 excludes that first tithes, unlike second tithes (and firstfruits), must be brought to Jerusalem by the farmers. *m. Beṣ (= Yom Ṭob)* 1:6 (cited by S. Safrai, "Religion in Everyday Life," 822 and n. 10) does not mention tithes.

119. See *m. Ma*ʿ*aś. Š.* 5:6, 9, and 10. This is a general assumption in the discussions on

18. The Mishnah makes no mention of the collection of tithes for the needs of the temple. This does not prove, however, that tithes were not collected for this purpose before the temple was destroyed. From the Mishnah we only learn that, according to the rabbis, the farmer did not have to bring his first tithe to Jerusalem, since it could be offered anywhere. The absence in mishnaic discussions of tithes collected for the sake of temple personnel might be due to the fact that the temple had long been destroyed and the rabbis were concerned with providing a means of livelihood for the priests and Levites scattered throughout Israel. It is noteworthy that later rabbinic tradition recalled the practice of gathering tithes into "treasuries" for distribution rather as something that had taken place in times past (בראשונה).[120]

The authors from the earlier period (of restoration) deal almost exclusively with the system of collection for the temple.[121] They assume that the beneficiaries of tithes were the priests and Levites who officiated at the temple and who (at least for the time when they performed their duties) resided in the city.[122] Away from the temple, priests and Levites, according to Nehemiah, lived off of their land (Neh 11:3; 13:10).

Nevertheless, the conclusion that throughout the Second Temple period priests and Levites received offerings of tithes in their towns of residence can also be drawn from matters of practical consideration. Only a fraction of priests and Levites actually resided in Jerusalem and only one of twenty-four courses officiated in any one week. Centralized collection and distribution could have benefited only those who resided and/or officiated in Jerusalem. And the others? According to 2 Chr 31:15–19 distributors were appointed for the priests and Levites in "the cities of the priests," and also in "the fields of common land belonging to their towns, town by town." It would be absurd to imagine that tithes of grain, fruits, and other (perishable) food items were first collected from the towns and villages of Israel, hauled to Jerusalem, and then hauled back to the towns and villages to the numerous priests and Levites who lived there. It

---

demai; see in particular *m. Ma'aś. Š.* 4:4; 6:1.

120. *Y. Ma'aś. Š.* 5:56d; *y. Soṭah* 9:24a, discussed above.

121. Neh 10:38–40 [Eng. vv. 37–39]; 12:44, 47; 13:4–13; see 2 Chr 31:4–14.

122. See Josephus' summary of Neh 7–13 (*A.J.* 11.181–82): "But, Nehemiah, seeing that the city had a small population, urged the priests and Levites to leave the countryside and move to the city and remain there, for he had prepared houses for them at his own expense; and he also told the people who cultivated the land to bring tithes of their produce to Jerusalem in order that the priests and Levites, having a perpetual source of livelihood, might not abandon the temple service. And so, as they gladly obeyed Nehemiah's ordinance, the city of Jerusalem came to have a larger population in this way." His assertion (against Neh 10:38–39 [Eng. vv. 37–38]) that the people brought tithes to Jerusalem results from the exaggerated statement (against Neh 11:1–3, 20) that all the priests and Levites left

would be even less feasible for all priests and Levites, young and old (2 Chr 31:15), to travel to Jerusalem in order to receive their portions.[123] 2 Chr 31:15–19, apart from being ideal, is quite obscure and leaves open the possibility that the produce distributed in the cities and towns was collected and stored there.

Tithes of Livestock

Leviticus 27:32–33 imposes a tithe on domestic animals. The tithe, we observed, is mentioned neither in Josephus's nor in Philo's detailed lists of priestly dues. It is lacking in Nehemiah's account of tithes, as also in Judith's. The payment of this tithe is, however, implied by 2 Chr 31:6 and Tob (**S**) 1:6. *Jub.* 13:26–27 derives it from the interpretation of Abraham's tithe to Melchizedek, and it is explicitly imposed in *Jub.* 32:15:

> And the whole tithe of oxen and sheep is holy to the Lord and it will belong to the priests who will eat it before him year after year because it is so ordered and engraved on the heavenly tablets concerning the tithe.

None of the texts that require the tithe of livestock specify whether one-tenth of one's holdings is meant (as Lev 27:32 and *Jub.* 32:15 seem to stipulate) or a tenth of the annual increase. The former option would have constituted an extreme and crippling tax on capital. Mishnaic legislation, moreover, treats the tithe as a "second tithe": the owner sacrificed and consumed it in Jerusalem; it could be offered also as peace or as thanksgiving offerings. Priests had no part in it. Moreover, it could be left until it contracted a blemish; then it could be consumed as common food.[124] There is, consequently, widespread doubt that in the Second Temple period this tithe was ever observed in the form in which it appears in Lev 27:32–33.[125]

---

their towns and dwelt in Jerusalem.

123. Weinfeld ("Tithe," cols. 1158–59) says, correctly, that Mal 3:10; Neh 10:38–39; 12:44; 13:5; 12–13; and 2 Chr 31:4ff show that tithes were collected and stored in the temple by temple personnel, who also provided transportation. He, however, points to Neh 13:13, which deals with distribution to officiating priests and Levites only, as evidence of how tithes were distributed in general. He ignores the larger problem of distribution outside Jerusalem.

124. *M. Maʿaś. Š.* 1:1; *m. Bek.* 9:1–8; *m. Zebaḥ.* 5:8 (see 1:2; 10:3); *m. Ḥag.* 1:4; *m. Menaḥ.* 7:5–6. See Sanders, *Jewish Law*, 336–37, n. 5; also p. 45; idem, *Judaism*, 150.

125. Among other scholars, see Sanders, *Jewish Law*, 45, 336–37, n. 5. Schürer (*History*, 2:259) thinks that even in the Chronicler's time the tithe of animals might not have been more than an ideal. S. Safrai ("Religion in Everyday Life," 825) passes the tithe over in silence. He observes that the practice of tithing everything, though wide-spread, was "con-

The occurrence of the tithe in *Jubilees* suggests that the subject continued to be alive and controverted. This appears to be confirmed by the fragmentary evidence from the *Temple Scroll*. In 11QT XXXVII, 10, the list of priestly portions to be consumed within the inner temple court includes the phrase ולמעשׂרות ("and for the tithes"). Jacob Milgrom, noting the plural form, suggests that this included both the tithe of animals and the (Levitical) tithe. Baumgarten, who observes that the list is of animal sacrifices, limits it only to the tithes of livestock.[126] In addition, in 11QT LX, 2–3, where all the priestly entitlements are listed, the expression וכל] [לבהמתמה is found. In Milgrom's estimation, the restoration of מעשׂר here is incontestable.[127]

Clear and conclusive evidence can be found in the programmatic and polemical letter of the Qumran community, the so-called *Miqṣat Maʿaśe Ha-Torah* (4QMMT). The relevant passage reads (4QMMT B 63–64):[128]

ומעשר הבקר והצון לכוהנים הוא

And (likewise) the tithe of the herd and of the flock should be given to the priests.

This demand is one of the twenty or so halakic points of contention raised by the group and for which they had separated themselves from the majority of the people and from the temple cult.[129] The controversial legislation in this document makes it certain that in the early Hasmonean period[130] the view that Lev 27:32–33 imposed a tithe of livestock to be given to the priests was contested. Those who supported the imposition did not prevail. Their view was the opinion of a (priestly) minority, which

---

fined to those who were particularly strict." According to Baruch A. Levine (*Numbers 1–20*, 451), tithing animals was a known practice at the time Numbers was written (in the late postexilic period), although the tithe is not covered by its legislation. Levine does not say if the legislation was enforced.

126. Milgrom, "Temple Scroll," 519–20; Joseph M. Baumgarten, "On the Non-Literal Use," 251, n. 32. See Yadin, *Temple Scroll*, 2:159.

127. See Milgrom, "Temple Scroll," 520. Yadin (*Temple Scroll*, 2:271) comments, however, that the "sentence resists satisfactory restoration."

128. Elisha Qimron and John Strugnell, eds., *Qumran Cave 4, V: Miqṣat Maʿaśe ha-Torah* (DJD 10; Oxford: Clarendon, 1994), 54–55. See Elisha Qimron and John Strugnell, "An Unpublished Halakhic Letter from Qumran," in *Biblical Archaeology Today: Proceedings of the International Congress on Biblical Archaeology, Jerusalem, April 1984* (ed. Joseph Aviram and Avraham Biran; Jerusalem: Israel Exploration Society, 1985), 400–407.

129. "[And you know that] we have separated ourselves from the multitude of the people [and from all their impurity] and from being involved with these matters and from participating with [them] in these things" (4 QMMT C 7–8). This is part of the exhortation that concludes the document.

130. 4QMMT is dated to the period between 159 and 152 B.C.E. See Qimron and

betook itself to the desert.[131] Whether or not the mishnaic/Pharisaic view prevailed, the conclusion is that tithes of livestock were not given to priests by the majority.

Summary and Conclusion

I assume that most Jews in the early Roman period made some effort to observe biblical law. Biblical legislation on tithing, we have seen, was complex and in some respects contradictory. Some of its requirements were controvertible even in the later Second Temple period. Therefore, it is not possible to speak of a single, uniform tradition in any of the questions that we have examined. Individual Jews must have harmonized the various requirements according to their ideological affiliation and economic abilities.

In the early Roman period, therefore, Jews would have given a "first tithe," some people to priests and others to Levites, during six years of the seven-year cycle. However, the existence of the category "*demai*-produce" ("doubtful-if-tithed") and also rabbinic discussions show that some people were reluctant to give (either to Levites or to priests) the most substantial part of the first tithe, that is, the 9/100 part of their produce. They did, however, more willingly offer the "tithe of tithe," that is, the 1 percent that was to be given exclusively to the priest.[132] In addition, Jews would have made a "second tithe" available for entertainment and festivities during a pilgrimage to Jerusalem. It should be noted, however, that this was not a tax—just as expenditures for the celebration of Thanksgiving are not a tax in contemporary America.[133] Some people would

---

Strugnell, *Miqṣat Maʿaśe ha-Torah*, 109–21.

131. "Our halakha," Qimron writes, "then, represents the prevailing view in the Second Temple period, and is based on the literal interpretation at that time of the expression 'holy unto the Lord'" (Qimron and Strugnell, *Miqṣat Maʿaśe ha-Torah*, 166). This can hardly be the case. Qimron himself concludes from his analysis of the evidence that this document is "a systematic exposition of the reasons why a group of Zadokites separated from another group (possibly also Zadokite in origin) and who followed what would later be called Pharisaic law, and then from the 'majority of Israel' who also followed that group's teaching" (p. 121). The preceding passage (4QMMT B 62–63) demands that "[fruits of] trees with edible fruit planted in the Land of Israel" be given, like firstfruits, to the priests. This could be a reference to tithes of produce (Lev 27:30–31). Qimron thinks that the "Fruits of the Fourth Year" are meant. It is significant that Josephus says that the "Fruits of the Fourth Year" are also to be treated as second tithes, that is, eaten by the owner in Jerusalem (*A.J.* 4.226–227; so Lev 19:23–25). Qimron and Strugnell (*Miqṣat Maʿaśe ha-Torah*, 164–65) consider the Qumranic view (that the fruits ought to be given to the priests) also to have been widely, though not unanimously, held.

132. See *m. Demai*; also Sanders, *Jewish Law*, 47–48, 237–38.

have given a tithe for the needs of the poor in lieu of this tithe in the third and the sixth years, according to the system we find in the Mishnah. Others would have set aside a tithe for celebrations in Jerusalem even during these years, as Josephus says. It must be mentioned also that some people, at least sometimes, did not care for the needs of the poor. The tithe of livestock, which would have been very expensive, was treated generally as a second tithe: it was part of the sacrifices and festivities in Jerusalem.

Two systems of collection existed side by side from the beginning of the Second Temple period to the destruction of the temple in 70 C.E. First, individual priests and Levites collected the "first tithes" in the villages of Israel and, second, the high priests supervised the collection and storage of tithes for the needs of temple personnel in Jerusalem.

Tithes were instituted in the postexilic Jewish temple state in order to provide food for temple personnel, especially when they were officiating, and in this manner to ensure that temple services would continue uninterrupted. Second tithes, when they were harmonized out of biblical laws, guaranteed that the pilgrim had the means to celebrate in Jerusalem. It also helped the economy of Jerusalem, since it was required that money from the tithe be spent in the city. Tithes were never intended to serve the needs of the state. Jews gave tithes while they were under Persian domination. Tithes coexisted with the tribute that the Jews paid to the Ptolemaic and Seleucid kings. They also coexisted with the taxes imposed by the Hasmoneans. For a very long time, then, the Jews in Judea were accustomed to the tradition of "dual taxation."[134] Tithes, therefore, did not constitute a hitherto unknown and extraordinary burden in the early Roman period. Further, if it is true that in the early Roman period there was "no offsetting tax credit for religious taxes paid,"[135] it is also clear that, as religious dues, tithes were largely voluntary contributions. There existed enough "loopholes" in the system that those who were unable (or unwilling) to contribute could have evaded at least the most expensive demands.

133. Sanders (*Jewish Law*, 45–46) observes correctly that the expenditure of the second tithe in Jerusalem "was an entertaining and highly enjoyable thing to do," and it was "doubtless a command which was usually cheerfully obeyed." The rabbis trusted that the ordinary people were faithful in separating this tithe (Sanders, *Jewish Law*, 238).

134. See Sanders, *Judaism*, 157–61.

135. See Peter Richardson, *Herod*, 28.

Epilogue

At the end of this study, the reader might want an explicit answer to the question that has dominated the discussion of the economic conditions of Jewish Palestine during the early Roman period: namely, whether or not taxation in Roman Palestine was "oppressive." This question may be traced back at least to the work of Gerald D. Heuver, who wrote in 1903: "The background of Jesus' teaching is one of business depression, panic, and poverty." In his view, "[n]otwithstanding all the advantages which Palestine had in Jesus' time, advantages of soil, climate, location, commerce, and immigrants, the people were very poor."[1] The evidence for Heuver's assessment of the economic conditions of early Roman Palestine came from the Gospel material, including: the "debtors going to prison"; the "creditors discounting bills"; the "man trying to build a tower which he was not able to complete for lack of funds"; the "woman whose living was only two mites"; and Jesus expecting every woman to behave like the one who, "having lost a drachma, and on recovering it, [invited] all her friends and neighbors to share in her joy." In sum: "In one of Jesus' parables, everybody except the king is bankrupt; the steward is in debt to the king, the servant to the steward." Everywhere in Palestine, including even the "prosperous Galilee," the question of "what to eat and to wear created anxiety."[2]

Those responsible for this state of affairs in Palestine were "the Romans, the Herods, and the rich—though some blamed their own sin for it." Heuver writes: "Herod was one of the worst men that ever lived. . . . [He] was a fiend." Given that Herod's wars and extravagant building projects were very expensive, it is to be expected that "[t]he taxes imposed by Herod were enormously heavy." Likewise, after Herod died, Archelaus was "fond of building" and Antipas was also "a builder." In order to raise the money they needed for their extravagant projects and for "what

1. Gerald D. Heuver, *The Teachings of Jesus Concerning Wealth* (Chicago: Flemming H. Revell, 1903), 27.

2. Ibid., 27–28; Heuver explicitly cites Matt 18:23–35 and Luke 12:22; 15:8–10.

the Roman government demanded," the Herods imposed taxes on nearly everything: produce of land, "one-tenth for grain and one-fifth for wine and fruit"; persons, "one denarius on every person, exempting only aged people over sixty-five years, and girls and boys under the age of twelve and fourteen respectively"; income, at the rate of "one per cent"; trades, "such as that of hosier, weaver, furrier, and goldsmith"; movable property, "such as horses, oxen, asses, ships, and slaves"; homes, "at least the city homes"; and "what was publicly bought and sold." Besides, there was "bridge money and road money to be paid" and, of course, duties on imported goods which "varied from two and one-half to twelve per cent."[3]

Over and above these Herodian and Roman taxes, "every city had its local administration and raised money to pay its officials, maintain and build synagogues, elementary schools, public baths, and roads, the city walls, gates, and other general requirements."[4] Heuver does not list tithes and other religious dues among the oppressive taxes imposed on the Jews of Jesus' time because tithes, he says, "had the approval of Jesus."[5] Nonetheless, the modern view that the Jews were burdened by three levels of taxation is quite evident in Heuver's discussion. To these three levels of financial burden Heuver adds the "very poor" fiscal arrangements in the Roman Empire by which the collection of taxes was "farmed out to the highest bidders, who in turn would farm them out again." All these levels of tax-farming added a "very large" percentage to the already extortionate taxes.[6]

Heuver concedes, "[h]ow large the [Herodian] taxes were will probably never be known." Similarly, he admits that "[h]ow much the Roman government collected cannot be ascertained" and that "we cannot know" how large the "income" added to the taxes by tax-farmers was. These lacunae notwithstanding, Heuver is certain that "[a] richer country than Palestine would have been drained by such extravagances" as the Herods indulged in. In Palestine, therefore, under "these unfortunate economic

---

3. Heuver, *Teachings of Jesus*, 28–33.

4. Ibid., 33.

5. Ibid., 151. Heuver (pp. 151–52) clearly has an eye to the need for the practice of tithing and for other contributions in the Christian churches. In his view, although Jesus would have been opposed to "the erection of the command to tithe into an absolute rule," he was "unalterably loyal" to "the principle upon which the command to tithe rested," namely, that "God is the owner of all, and we must recognize it by stated contributions." It is, in fact, through such contributions and the recognition of "God's right to our goods" that will come "the awakening to righteousness," for which the church has long hoped and prayed, and the Christian world will shake itself "free from the deadly avarice which paralyzes its progress."

6. See Heuver, *Teachings of Jesus*, 33–34.

conditions—anarchy, war, extravagance, and taxation—the people grew poorer and poorer. Business became more and more interrupted, and want, in growing frequency, showed its emaciated features." The rich exacerbated these conditions by dealing relentlessly with those who had fallen into debt: "Rich men who remitted to their debtors were rare, the unmerciful creditors with the bailiff at hand were frequent."[7]

Scholars writing after Heuver in general do not refer to his work. This, surprisingly, is true even of Frederick C. Grant, whose work, like Heuver's, was written under the influence of the pragmatist Chicago school of theology.[8] Scholars hardly have departed from Heuver's project, his conclusions, and the evidence he cited. Regarding the project of the Chicago school of theology, Case, speaking of what he termed "the 'new' New Testament study," proposed to reread "the history [of Christianity] in the light of contemporary social experience," that is, by paying particular attention to "the environments, attitudes, and activities in real life of those persons and groups who, from generation to generation, constituted the membership of the new movement."[9] Heuver, and Grant after him, applied Case's social-historical methodology to the Jesus movement in Palestine during Jesus' lifetime. They both focused on the economic conditions of Jewish Palestine as the background of Jesus' ministry. It was their view, as Grant noted, that "the study of the economic background of Jesus' teaching throws into clearer relief the principles which He set forth, and sheds light upon more than one problem in the history of the beginnings of Christianity."[10] The project and methodology proposed by Case, Heuver, and Grant blossomed into the social-scientific study of both the New Testament and early Christianity, marked in the 1970s by the appearance of such works as Gerd Theissen's *Soziologie der Jesusbewegung*.[11]

---

7. Ibid., 31, 33, 34, 36–37.

8. Heuver's work was originally a doctoral dissertation presented at the department of New Testament Literature and Interpretation in the University of Chicago's Graduate Divinity School. Grant's original dissertation was submitted at the Western Theological Seminary in Chicago. Both authors acknowledge their indebtedness to two of the foremost members of the faculty of the Chicago school of theology, namely, Shirley Jackson Case (Grant) and Shailer Mathews (Heuver).

9. Shirley Jackson Case, *The Social Origins of Christianity* (Chicago: University of Chicago Press, 1923); see the title of his chapter 1, and pp. 36–37.

10. Grant, *Economic Background*, 14. Thus, Heuver also interprets Jesus' ministry in the light of Jesus' "attitude . . . to his country's unhappy condition and his plan for its social redemption, if he had such a plan . . ." (see Heuver, *Teachings of Jesus*, 91 *et passim*).

11. See Gerd Theissen, *Soziologie der Jesusbewegung: ein Beitrag zur Entstehungsgeschichte des Urchristentums* (Munich: Kaiser, 1977; Eng., Theissen, *Sociology*). Bengt Holmberg (*Sociology and the New Testament: An Appraisal* [Minneapolis: Fortress Press, 1990], 1) does not include Case and Heuver among the scholars who, in the early decades of the twentieth

I ought to note one further characteristic of the social-historical project established by Heuver and Grant: their theses are theological. Heuver wants to answer the question: "Did Christ teach anything concerning social, economic, and property questions that can be used, and that should be used, to make God's kingdom come now and here, in the midst of the business and the pleasure of this work-a-day world, as well as hereafter in the glories and activities of the life of heaven?"[12] If Heuver explores "the attitude of Jesus to his country's unhappy condition and his plan for its social redemption," it is so that he can demonstrate that Jesus, the "great friend of the unfortunate and the fallen," was indeed "tremendously interested in people's economic conditions. Consequently no man is a true follower of Jesus who is indifferent to the subjects that relate to people's material possessions." Jesus was not a revolutionist or a reformer; he had neither an economic plan nor an economic system. Rather, he "sought to better the people's material conditions by making the people themselves better." He "planned to make men better through the agency of the church. He worked to that end in connection with the Jewish church as long as its leaders would let him, and when they cast him out, he organized a church of his own." Hence, "the future of society rests with the Christian church." For human society the church is the "agency for its redemption" and the church will apostatize if, like "the Jewish church" and unlike Jesus, it fails to "be efficient in improving people's economic conditions" by "saving man from sin."[13]

The study of the economic conditions of early Roman Palestine was a means for Heuver to establish his theological thesis.[14] Heuver finds the connection between these conditions, Jesus' teachings, and Heuver's own world in the simple observation that Jesus' world was not "utterly different from what ours is." For, in fact, Jesus "met with a civilization and conditions not very different from our own; a mixed, progressive people in touch with the whole world, and he spent most of his time amid the

century, "analysed and described early Christianity as connected in a thousand ways with the social reality of its own world." He (p. vii) is aware, however, that "most of the activity [of New Testament Sociology] takes place in North America" and "regrets" the "'European' character" of his bibliography. Richard A. Horsley (*Sociology and the Jesus Movement* [New York: Crossroad, 1989], 2), recognizes the role of the Chicago school, especially Case and Mathews, as the precursors of the sociological studies of the New Testament.

12. Heuver, *Teachings of Jesus*, 6.

13. Heuver, *Teachings of Jesus*, 91, 171, 200 (*et passim*), 38–39 (and pp. 5–7), 201–2.

14. Heuver's thesis of economic depravity is paralleled by a thesis of religious and social depravity, which resulted from "the failure of the Jewish church of Jesus' day" (*Teachings of Jesus*, 57). He writes: "The period of Jesus' life fell in a dark age of Judaism . . . . Religious life was at a low ebb. There were places in which people were hired to attend the synagogue, that the worship of God might continue." See ibid., 57–73.

busiest and most progressive portion of them, the Galileans, those who most felt the quickening influences of the foreign immigrants."[15]

Likewise, Grant's analysis of the economic conditions of Palestine in the Hellenistic and early Roman periods was undertaken in order to highlight "facts of economic significance."[16] These facts were meant to support his thesis that "pre-Christian Jewish Messianism was nurtured and sustained by the disappointed hopes of a buoyantly optimistic nation" where "[t]he peasants, the agricultural labourers of Palestine, the overcrowded industrial populace of the Jewish cities, the commercial classes overburdened by oppressive taxation, eagerly shared this dream," that is, the dream of a future promise of "national autonomy following liberation from the hated yoke of foreign sovereignty." Jewish Messianism, therefore, was "a hope deriving its vitality from the conflict of religious faith with intolerable economic and political conditions."[17]

Jesus, appearing "at a time when the Jewish nation was confronted with the severest crisis in its long history," did not act as a "social revolutionary." Instead, he "'spiritualized' the hope of the Kingdom, purged it of its nationalistic limitations, and made it a purely religious concept." He made it "a gospel of freedom, spiritual as well as economic, religious as well as social: first spiritual and then economic and social." Rather than promulgating a program for social and economic revolution, Jesus "launched a revolutionary spiritual and ethical movement, whose full and final fruits must certainly include political, economic, social reformation, but which in itself involves vastly more than this."[18]

Long after Heuver and Grant, sweeping generalizations about the economic conditions, and especially about taxation, in Palestine during the early Roman period have continued to prelude theological constructs.[19] The Christian movement certainly had roots in the political, religious, social, and economic factors in early Roman Palestine. Moreover, I think that it is a sound theological principle to assume that the revelation of God is the revelation of the concrete human person at the same time. The "contexts," therefore, in which scripture is produced and received must include the concrete social, political, and economic conditions in which scripture came into existence and is read. I must admit, however, that sound theology, while not opposed to history, is not sound history. In

15. Ibid., 22.

16. Grant, *Economic Background*, 15.

17. Ibid., 9–10, 138.

18. Ibid., 139, 140–41.

19. A long list of authors is not required. See, for instance, Borg, *Conflict, Holiness, and Politics*, 43–87, and the rest of this work; Oakman, *Jesus and the Economic Questions*, esp. 1–10, 95–220; K. C. Hanson and Douglas E. Oakman, *Palestine in the Time of Jesus* (Minneapolis: Fortress Press, 1998), 99–130.

general, those scholars who have sought to derive the Jesus movement from the economic conditions prevalent in Palestine in the third decade of the first century C.E. are guilty of arguing from theological conclusions. The gravity of the historical "crisis" in Palestine which they describe is dictated by the scope of the theological "solution" that Jesus is thought to have brought to the social and economic problems of his day (and of the modern author's day).

Apart from this risk of theologizing history, the scholars who appeal to "social-scientific" descriptions of the economic conditions of early Roman Palestine need to resolve the methodological problems that arise from the attempt to apply sociological or anthropological models to the Gospel material. I do not need to enter into this debate.[20] Let me note, however, that the verisimilitude of the results of this methodological procedure depends on the plausibility of each author's exegetical assumptions and on the accuracy of the historical descriptions that serve as data. My discussion of Mark 12:13–17 and the parallel passages in Matt 22:15–22 and Luke 20:20–26 brings to light the problems inherent in the general and naive assumption that certain Gospel passages, particularly the sayings material, "reflect" the historical, that is, the social and economic conditions of Palestine in the first century C.E. Unless one were to accept a priori that such passages come from authentic Palestinian sources (which is hardly the case), the details they contain can only "reflect," if at all, the social and economic realities familiar to their authors and the communities to which they belonged. These details, consequently, may not collectively provide us with an accurate "picture" of the economic and social life in first-century Palestine.[21] This is to say that, although such a history must critically take into account the Gospel material, the Gospels themselves cannot serve as the primary source for the historical description of the specific economic patterns and behaviors that were at work in Palestine during the early Roman period.[22] Mark 12:13–17 and similar Gospel

---

20. See Cyril S. Rodd, "On Applying a Sociological Theory to Biblical Studies," *JSOT* 19 (1981): 95–106; and the discussion in Holmberg, *Sociology*, 6–17.

21. Richard A. Horsley (*Sociology*, 5) observes that "we must simply cease speaking of early Christianity generally, as if there ever was such a historical entity." He continues: "Our evidence is sufficiently clear to indicate that the early Christian movement was diverse geographically and culturally. Sociological analysis must therefore concentrate on particular communities in particular situations insofar as possible." The Gospels are, in fact, part of the evidence for the diversity of early Christianity and for its diverse social and economic locations. The view that the sayings material, especially the parables, in the synoptic Gospels comes from Jesus and, therefore, provides an authentic picture of life in first-century Palestine belongs especially to the works of C. H. Dodd and Joachim Jeremias. See C. H. Dodd, *The Parables of the Kingdom* (rev. ed.; New York: Charles Scribner's Sons, 1961); Joachim Jeremias, *The Parables of Jesus* (London: SCM, 1954; repr., 1985).

22. Oakman (*Jesus and the Economic Questions*, 6) admits that in order to "insure sound

passages do not enable us to reconstruct a system of taxation in force in Palestine during Jesus' time.

In my earlier study, I observed that the scarcity of evidence makes it impossible to estimate in actual figures the costs of taxation and its economic impact on the Jews. Therefore, the usual generalizations which claim that taxation in early Roman Palestine was excessive and oppressive assert more than we can actually know.[23] We still are not able, with reference to verifiable figures, to estimate what percentages of their income the Jews in Palestine paid in tribute and taxes during the various periods of Roman rule. Nonetheless, in light of the present study, I restate my previous observation more definitely: the general view that excessive taxation of the Jewish state in the early Roman period was the cause of observable economic depravity in the first century C.E. is not supported by the evidence.

Scholarly opinion, as I have already noted, is divided on whether or not provincial taxes were heavy during the early Principate. I have noted further that it is not possible, on account of the lack of evidence, to provide a full picture of taxation in Palestine during the early Roman period and to assess fully its effects on the lives of individuals at various economic levels. The arguments used to build an impression of continuous tax oppression and economic depravity in Palestine do not stand up to scrutiny. Palestine was not continually "oppressed" by three levels of ruinous taxes from 63 B.C.E. until the Revolt of 66 C.E.

From 63 B.C.E. to 49 B.C.E. Roman tribute was not a significant economic factor in the Jewish state, since the tribute could not have been collected. Caesar's grants to the Jewish state in 47 B.C.E. were entirely consistent with those that he and other Roman magistrates made to favored provincial cities and communities. Some of the grants were in response to specific Jewish needs, such as the exemption from taxation during the sabbatical year and the right to collect and transport the temple tax to Jerusalem. The restitution of Joppa and the surrounding "great

---

methodology," and avoid the obvious problem of circularity, the description of "the general features and problems of the economy of first-century Palestine" must rely on "the use of non-biblical evidence." Unable to avoid the problem, however, he contends that "the historical task only progresses through such a circular or dialectical process" (p. 105).

23. See Udoh, "Tribute and Taxes," 334. Hanson and Oakman (*Palestine*, 114) reject this conclusion on the grounds that I did not "incorporate comparative or social systems perspectives into such a judgment." I can only answer that the tax "situation" that they describe (and, ironically, ascribe to me) is wishful. "Herod the Great," they surmise for instance (p. 114), "claimed 25–33 percent of Palestinian grain within his realm and 50 percent of the fruit from trees. Direct taxation also included poll (head) taxes in money . . . ." They are under no pressure to offer any evidence and instead cite (p. 115) *A.J.* 17.306–8 as "a powerful indictment of economic pressure put upon the whole land." No amount of "comparative or social systems perspectives," I am afraid, can make up for pseudo-historiography.

plain" of Sharon to the Jewish state along with the reductions in taxes requested for and obtained by Hyrcanus II are further indications that Caesar and the Senate paid attention to the particular economic needs of the Jewish state (including their local tax needs). The Jews considered Caesar's grants and tax arrangements to be "honors." When they are evaluated in the light of Rome's general imperial policies, the grants certainly placed the Jewish state among the privileged provincial communities, although they did not constitute special Jewish privileges per se.

I have argued that, under Herod and his successors, the Jewish "client state" paid no direct annual tribute to Rome. Herod's kingdom was prosperous. His extensive building and other projects are evidence of that prosperity. Herod did not rely, and could not have relied, on direct annual taxes on farm produce levied on Jewish peasants in order to pay for his many projects. On the contrary, the evidence suggests that Herod seemed to have used the leverage of his tax policies in order to deflect Jewish criticisms and resentments of his rule. The result is that as Herod's reign advanced and his realm expanded, the Jews paid progressively less in direct annual tribute. In spite of the sums that Josephus provides as the annual income of Herod Antipas and of Agrippa I, we cannot determine how they raised their revenues and how the Jews in Galilee (for Antipas) and in both Galilee and Judea (for Agrippa I) were affected by the taxes they imposed. It is noteworthy that, despite his tax policies and excesses, Agrippa I was held in high esteem by the Jews.

Most significant for the discussion of Roman tax policies in the Jewish state under the governors is the conclusion that, following the census of 6 C.E., the province of Judea paid a direct tribute consisting only of a *tributum soli*, collected mostly in kind. It is reasonable to suppose that the Jews, although no longer paying taxes to the Herodian client princes, paid taxes for the local administration of the state. These would have been similar to the levies paid by the Jews under John Hyrcanus II (and by the citizens of the surrounding city-states), although we do not know the amount paid.

I do not mean by these remarks to discount the fact that at least some Jews perceived Roman tribute, when it was paid, and taxes paid to the Herods as "oppressive." In discussing Herodian taxes I argued that this perception and the resulting complaints against Herod must be separated from the question of the actual levels of Herodian taxes. The complaints against Herod serve as an illustration of the fact that such complaints and eventual tax-related revolts were not always caused by "excessive" tax rates. I doubt that Herod could have reduced taxes enough to satisfy the Jews whose voices we hear in the complaints against him. Similarly, whatever the actual levels of tribute and taxes paid under the governors might have been, the problem as it is expressed by the authors of the revolt of 6 C.E. (and by the Gospel passage in Mark 12:14–15) was Rome's right to impose tribute upon the Jews, not the amount imposed. This right seems to have been contested and debated in Palestine probably late into the first and second centuries. Thus, the question of the oppressiveness of taxes during the early Roman period ceases to be merely an economic question. It belongs rather to the complex problem of Jewish response to Roman imperialism.

Bibliography

Abel, F.-M. *Géographie de la Palestine*. 2 vols. Paris: J. Gabalda, 1933–38.

———. *Histoire de la Palestine: depuis la conquête d'Alexandre jusqu'à l'invasion Arabe*. 2 vols. Paris: J. Gabalda, 1952.

Adan-Bayewitz, David, and Isadore Perlman. "The Local Trade of Sepphoris in the Roman Period." *Israel Exploration Journal* 40 (1990): 154–72.

Aharoni, Yohanan, and Michael Avi-Yonah. *The Macmillan Bible Atlas*. Rev. 3rd ed. Edited by Anson F. Rainey and Ze'ev Safrai. New York: Macmillan, 1993.

Alexander, P. S. "Epistolary Literature." Pp. 579–96 in *Jewish Writings of the Second Temple Period*. Edited by M. E. Stone. Philadelphia: Fortress Press, 1984.

Allegro, John M. *Qumrân Cave 4, I: 4Q158–4Q186*. Discoveries in the Judaean Desert of Jordan 5. Oxford: Clarendon, 1968.

Alon, Gedalyahu. *Jews, Judaism and the Classical World: Studies in Jewish History in the Times of the Second Temple and Talmud*. Translated by Israel Abrahams. Jerusalem: Magnes Press, 1977.

Anderson, J. G. C. "Augustan Edicts from Cyrene." *Journal of Roman Studies* 17 (1927): 33–48.

Applebaum, Shimon. "Economic Life in Palestine." Pp. 631–700 in *The Jewish People in the First Century: Historical Geography, Political History, Social, Cultural and Religious Life and Institutions*, vol. 2. Edited by S. Safrai and M. Stern. Compendia Rerum Iudaicarum Ad Novum Testamentum 1. Philadelphia: Fortress Press, 1976.

———. "Herod I." Pp. 375–85 in *Encyclopaedia Judaica*. Jerusalem: Keter, 1971.

———. "Jews and Service in the Roman Army." Pp. 181–84 in *Roman Frontier Studies, 1967: The Proceedings of the Seventh International Congress Held at Tel Aviv*. Edited by Shimon Applebaum. Tel Aviv: Tel Aviv University, 1971.

———. "Judaea as a Roman Province: The Countryside as a Political and Economic Factor." Pp. 355–96 in *Aufstieg und Niedergang der römischen Welt* Part 2, *Principat*, 8. Edited by Hildegard Temporini and Wolfgang Haase. New York: de Gruyter, 1977.

———. *Judaea in Hellenistic and Roman Times: Historical and Archaeological Essays*. Leiden: Brill, 1989.

———. "The Status of Jaffa in the First Century of the Current Era." *Scripta classica Israelica* 89 (1985/1988): 138–44.

———. "The Zealots: The Case for Revaluation." *Journal of Roman Studies* 61 (1971): 155–70.

Ariel, Donald T. "The Coins from the Surveys and Excavations of Caves in the Northern Judean Desert." *ʿAtiqot* 41, no. 2 (2002): 281–304.

———. "The Jerusalem Mint of Herod the Great: A Relative Chronology." *Israel Numismatic Journal* 14 (2000–2002): 99–124.

———. "A Survey of Coin Finds in Jerusalem (Until the End of Byzantine Period)." *Liber Annuus Studii Biblici Franciscani* 32 (1982): 273–326.

Arnold, W. T. *The Roman System of Provincial Administration to the Accession of Constantine the Great*. 3rd ed. Revised by E. S. Bouchier. Oxford: Blackwell, 1914.

Attridge, H. W. "Josephus and His Works." Pp. 185–232 in *Jewish Writings of the Second Temple Period*. Edited by M. E. Stone. Philadelphia: Fortress Press, 1984.

Avigad, N. *Archaeological Discoveries in the Jewish Quarter of Jerusalem: Second Temple Period*. Jerusalem: Israel Exploration Society & the Israel Museum, 1976.

Avi-Yonah, Michael. "The Development of the Roman Road System in Palestine." *Israel Exploration Journal* 1 (1950–51): 54–60.

———. "Historical Geography of Palestine." Pp. 78–116 in *The Jewish People in the First Century: Historical Geography, Political History, Social, Cultural and Religious Life and Institutions*, vol. 1. Edited by S. Safrai and M. Stern. Compendia Rerum Iudaicarum Ad Novum Testamentum 1. Assen: Van Gorcum, 1974.

———. *The Holy Land from the Persian to the Arab Conquests (536 B.C. to A.D. 640): A Historical Geography*. Grand Rapids: Baker Book House, 1977.

Badian, E. *Publicans and Sinners: Private Enterprise in the Service of the Roman Republic*. Ithaca, N.Y.: Cornell University Press, 1972.

———. *Roman Imperialism in the Late Republic*. Ithaca, N.Y.: Cornell University Press, 1968.

Bagnall, R. S., and B. W. Frier. *The Demography of Roman Egypt*. Cambridge Studies in Population, Economy, and Society in Past Time 23. Cambridge: Cambridge University Press, 1994.

Bammel, Ernest. "The Organization of Palestine by Gabinius." *Journal of Jewish Studies* 12 (1961): 159–62.

———. "Die Rechtsstellung des Herodes." *Zeitschrift des deutschen Palästina-Vereins* 84 (1968): 73–79.

Barag, Dan. "Tyrian Currency in Galilee." *Israel Numismatic Journal* 6–7 (1982–83): 7–13.

Barclay, John M. G. *Jews in the Mediterranean Diaspora from Alexander to Trajan, 323 BCE–117 CE*. Edinburgh: T&T Clark, 1996.

Bar-Kochva, B. "Manpower, Economics, and Internal Strife in the Hasmonean State." Pp. 167–96 in *Armée et fiscalité dans le monde antique*. Paris: Éditions du Centre National de la Recherche Scientifique, 1977.

Baumgarten, A. I. "Invented Traditions of the Maccabean Era." Pp. 197–210 in *Geschichte-Tradition-Reflexion: Festschrift für Martin Hengel zum 70. Geburtstag*, vol. 1. Edited by Hubert Cancik, Hermann Lichtenberger, and Peter Schäfer. Tübingen: Mohr Siebeck, 1996.

Baumgarten, Joseph M. "The First and Second Tithes in the Temple Scroll." Pp. 5–15 in *Biblical and Related Studies Presented to Samuel Iwry*. Edited by Ann Kort and Scott Morschauser. Winona Lake, Ind.: Eisenbrauns, 1985.

———. "On the Non-Literal Use of Maʿăśēr/Dekatē." *Journal of Biblical Literature* 103 (1984): 245–61.

Ben-David, Arye. *Jerusalem und Tyros: Ein Beitrag zur palästinensischen Münz- und Wirtschaftsgeschichte*. Basel: Kyklos-Verlag, 1969.

Ben-Dov, Meir. *In the Shadow of the Temple: The Discovery of Ancient Jerusalem*. Translated by Ina Friedman. Jerusalem: Keter, 1982. Repr., New York: Harper & Row, 1985.

Benoit, P., J. T. Milik, and Roland de Vaux, eds. *Les grottes de Murabbaʿât*. Discoveries in the Judaean Desert 2. Oxford: Clarendon, 1961.

Bertrand, Jean-Marie. "À propos du mot PROVINCIA: étude sur les modes d'élaboration du langage politique." *Journal des Savants* (July–December 1989): 191–215.

Bickerman, Elias. "La charte Séleucide de Jérusalem." Pp. 44–85 in *Studies in Jewish and Christian History*, vol. 2. Leiden: Brill, 1980.

———. "Héliodore au temple de Jérusalem." Pp. 159–91 in *Studies in Jewish and Christian History*, vol. 2. Leiden: Brill, 1980.

———. *Institutions des Séleucides*. Paris: Librairie Orientaliste Paul Geuthner, 1938.

Bitto, I. "La concessione del patronato nella politica di Cesare." *Epigraphica* 31 (1970): 79–83.

Bohn, Oscarus. "Qua condicione iuris reges socii populi Romani fuerint." Dissertatio inauguralis historica. Berolini: University of Cincinnati Dissertations, Programmschriften, and Pamphlets in Classical Studies, 1876.

Borg, Marcus J. *Conflict, Holiness, and Politics in the Teaching of Jesus*. New York: Edwin Mellen, 1984.

Botermann, Helga. *Die Soldaten und die römische Politik in der Zeit von Caesars Tod bis zur Begründung des zweiten Triumvirats*. Munich: C. H. Beck, 1968.

Bowersock, Glen W. *Augustus and the Greek World.* Oxford: Clarendon, 1965.

———. *Roman Arabia.* Cambridge, Mass.: Harvard University Press, 1983.

———. "Social and Economic History of Syria under the Roman Empire." Pp. 63–80 in *La Syrie de l'époque achéménide à l'avènement de l'Islam.* Vol. 2 of *Archéologie et histoire de la Syrie.* Edited by Jean-Marie Dentzer and Winfried Orthmann. Saarbrücken: Saarbrücker Druckerei und Verlag, 1989.

Braund, David C. *Augustus to Nero: A Sourcebook on Roman History, 31 BC-AD 68.* London: Croom Helm, 1985.

———. "Client Kings." Pp. 69–96 in *The Administration of the Roman Empire, 241 BC–AD 193.* Edited by David C. Braund. Exeter: University of Exeter Press, 1988.

———. "Function and Dysfunction: Personal Patronage in Roman Imperialism." Pp. 137–52 in *Patronage in Ancient Society.* Edited by Andrew Wallace-Hadrill. London: Routledge, 1989.

———. "Gabinius, Caesar, and the *Publicani* of Judaea." *Klio* 65 (1983): 241–44.

———. *Rome and the Friendly King: The Character of the Client Kingship.* London: Croom Helm, 1984.

Broshi, Magen. "The Role of the Temple in the Herodian Economy." *Journal of Jewish Studies* 38 (1987): 31–37.

Broughton, T. Robert S. "Roman Asia Minor." Pp. 499–950 in *An Economic Survey of Ancient Rome,* vol. 4. Edited by Tenney Frank. Baltimore: Johns Hopkins University Press, 1938.

———. *The Magistrates of the Roman Republic.* 3 vols. New York: American Philological Association, 1951–52. Repr., Atlanta, Ga.: Scholars Press, 1984–86.

Brown, Raymond E. *The Birth of the Messiah: A Commentary on the Infancy Narratives in Matthew and Luke.* Garden City, N.Y.: Doubleday, Image Books, 1977.

Bruce, F. F. "Render to Caesar." Pp. 243–49 in *Jesus and the Politics of His Day.* Edited by Ernst Bammel and C. F. D. Moule. Cambridge: Cambridge University Press, 1984.

Brunt, P. A. "Addendum I." Pp. 179–80 in *The Roman Economy: Studies in Ancient Economic and Administrative History,* by A. H. M. Jones. Oxford: Blackwell, 1974.

———. "Addendum II." Pp. 180–83 in *The Roman Economy: Studies in Ancient Economic and Administrative History,* by A. H. M. Jones. Oxford: Blackwell, 1974.

———. "Addendum III." Pp. 183–85 in *The Roman Economy: Studies in Ancient Economic and Administrative History,* by A. H. M. Jones. Oxford: Blackwell, 1974.

———. "Charges of Provincial Maladministration under the Early Principate." Pp. 53–95 in *Roman Imperial Themes*. Oxford: Clarendon, 1990.
———. *The Fall of the Roman Republic and Related Essays*. Oxford: Clarendon, 1988.
———. "Princeps and Equites." *Journal of Roman Studies* 73 (1983): 42–75.
———. "Publicans in the Principate." Pp. 354–432 in *Roman Imperial Themes*. Oxford: Clarendon, 1990.
———. "The Revenues of Rome." *Journal of Roman Studies* 71 (1981): 161–72.
———. *Roman Imperial Themes*. Oxford: Clarendon, 1990.
Bruun, Patrick. "Site Finds and Hoarding Behaviour." Pp. 114–23 in *Scripta Nummaria Romana: Essays Presented to Humphrey Sutherland*. Edited by R. A. G. Carson and Colin M. Kraay. London: Spink, 1978.
Buchheim, Hans. *Die Orientpolitik des Triumvirn M. Antonius*. Heidelberg: Carl Winter, 1960.
Büchler, Adolphe. "La relation de Josèphe concernant Alexandre le Grand." *Revue des études juives* 36 (1898): 1–26.
Bultmann, Rudolf. *The History of the Synoptic Tradition*. Translated by John Marsh. Oxford: Blackwell, 1963.
Burton, G. P. "The Issuing of Mandata to Proconsuls and a New Inscription from Cos." *Zeitschrift für Papyrologie und Epigraphik* 21 (1976): 63–68.
Cagnat, R. *Étude historique sur les impôts indirects chez les Romains jusqu'aux invasions des Barbares, d'après les documents litéraires et épigraphiques*. Paris: Imprimerie Nationale, 1882.
———, ed. *Inscriptiones graecae ad res romanas pertinentes*. Paris: Ernest Leroux, 1906. Repr., Rome: L'Erma di Bretschneider, 1964.
Campbell, Edward F. "The Boundary Between Ephraim and Manasseh." Pp. 67–74 in *The Answers Lie Below*. Edited by Henry O. Thompson. Lanham, Md.: University Press of America, 1984.
Caquot, André. "Le livre des Jubilés, Melkisedeq et les dîmes." *Journal of Jewish Studies* 33 (1982): 257–64.
Carcopino, Jérôme. *La loi de Hiéron et les Romains*. Paris: E. de Boccard, 1914.
Case, Shirley Jackson. *The Social Origins of Christianity*. Chicago: University of Chicago Press, 1923.
Chabot, J.-B., ed. and trans. *Choix d'inscriptions de Palmyre*. Paris: Imprimerie Nationale, 1922.
———, ed. and trans. *Corpus inscriptionum semiticarum*. Paris: Republicae Typographeus, 1926.
Cohen, Shaye J. D. *Josephus in Galilee and Rome: His Vita and Development as a Historian*. Columbia Studies in the Classical Tradition 8. Leiden: Brill, 1979.

Cooke, G. A. *A Text-Book of North-Semitic Inscriptions*. Oxford: Clarendon, 1903.

Crawford, M. H. "Coin Hoards and the Pattern of Violence in the Late Republic." *Papers of the British School at Rome* 37 (1969): 76–81.

Crook, J. A. "Augustus: Power, Authority, Achievement." Pp. 113–46 in *The Augustan Empire, 43 B.C.–A.D. 69*. Vol. 10 of *The Cambridge Ancient History*, 2nd ed. Edited by Alan K. Bowman, Edward Champlin, and Andrew Lintott. Cambridge: Cambridge University Press, 1996.

Crook, J. A., Andrew Lintott, and Elizabeth Rawson, eds. *The Last Age of the Roman Republic, 146–43 B.C.* Vol. 9 of *The Cambridge Ancient History*. 2nd ed. Cambridge: Cambridge University Press, 1994.

Crossan, John Dominic. *Four Other Gospels: Shadows on the Contours of Canon*. Minneapolis: Winston, 1985.

———. *The Historical Jesus: The Life of a Mediterranean Peasant*. San Francisco: HarperSanFrancisco, 1991.

Crüsemann, Frank. "Der Zehnte in der israelitischen Königszeit." *Wort und Dienst* 18 (1985): 21–47.

Dąbrowa, Edward. *The Governors of Roman Syria from Augustus to Septimius Severus*. Bonn: Habelt, 1998.

Danby, Herbert, ed. and trans. *The Mishnah: Translated from the Hebrew with Introduction and Brief Explanatory Notes*. New York: Oxford University Press, 1933.

Danelius, Eva. "The Boundary of Ephraim and Manasseh in the Western Plain." *Palestine Exploration Quarterly* 89 (1957) 55–67; 90 (1958): 32–43, 122–44.

Dar, Shimon, and Shimon Applebaum. "The Roman Road from Antipatris to Caesarea." *Palestine Exploration Quarterly* 105 (1973): 91–99.

Daube, David. "Temple Tax." Pp. 121–34 in *Jesus, the Gospels, and the Church: Essays in Honor of William R. Farmer*. Edited by E. P. Sanders. Macon, Ga.: Mercer University Press, 1987.

Davies, R. W. "The Roman Military Diet." *Britannia* 2 (1971): 122–42.

Davies, W. D., and Dale C. Allison, Jr. *The Gospel According to Saint Matthew*. 3 vols. International Critical Commentary. Edinburgh: T&T Clark, 1988–97.

de Laet, Siegfried J. *Portorium: études sur l'organisation douanière chez les Romains, surtout a l'époque du haut-empire*. Brugge: De Tempel, 1949.

Del Verme, Marcello. "Les dîmes hébraïques dans l'œuvre de Josèphe et dans le nouveau testament." Pp. 121–37 in *Rashi 1040–1990: Hommage à Ephraïm E. Urbach*. Edited by Gabrielle Sed-Rajna. Paris: Cerf, 1993.

———. "La 'prima decima' nel Giudaismo del secondo tempio." *Henoch* 9 (1987): 5–38.

de Martino, Francesco. *Storia della costituzione romana*. 7 vols. Napoli: Casa Editrice Dott. Eugenio Jovene, 1958–72.

de Vaux, Roland. *Archaeology and the Dead Sea Scrolls*. London: British Academy, 1973.

Dessau, Hermannus, ed. *Inscriptiones latinae selectae*. 3 vols. Berlin: Weidmann, 1892–1916.

Devreker, J. "Une inscription inédite de Caracalla à Pessinonte." *Latomus* 30 (1971): 353–62.

Dittenberger, W., ed. *Orientis graeci inscriptiones selectae*. 2 vols. Leipzig: Hirzel, 1903–5.

Dodd, C. H. *The Parables of the Kingdom*. Rev. ed. New York: Charles Scribner's Sons, 1961.

Donahue, John R. "Tax Collectors and Sinners: An Attempt at Identification." *Catholic Biblical Quarterly* 33 (1971): 39–61.

Drinkwater, J. F. "The Trinovantes: Some Observations on Their Participation in the Events of A.D. 60." *Rivista storica dell'antichità* 5 (1975): 53–57.

Duncan-Jones, Richard. *Structure and Scale in the Roman Economy*. Cambridge: Cambridge University Press, 1990.

Ehrenberg, Victor, and A. H. M. Jones, eds. *Documents Illustrating the Reigns of Augustus and Tiberius*. Oxford: Clarendon, 1949.

Elliott, John H. "Social-Scientific Criticism of the New Testament: More on Methods and Models." *Semeia* 35 (1986): 1–33.

Evans, R. J. "Norbani Flacci: The Consuls of 38 and 24 B.C." *Historia* 36 (1987): 121–28.

Feldman, Louis H. "Masada: A Critique of Recent Scholarship." Volume 3, pp. 219–48 in *Christianity, Judaism and Other Greco-Roman Cults: Studies for Morton Smith at Sixty*. 4 vols. Edited by Jacob Neusner. Leiden: Brill, 1975.

Fiensy, David A. *The Social History of Palestine in the Herodian Period: The Land is Mine*. Lewiston, N.Y.: Edwin Mellen, 1991.

Finkielsztejn, Gérald. "More Evidence on John Hyrcanus I's Conquests: Lead Weights and Rhodian Amphora Stamps." *Bulletin of the Anglo-Israel Archaeological Society* 16 (1998): 33–63.

Fittschen, Klaus, and Gideon Foerster, eds. *Judaea and the Greco-Roman World in the Time of Herod in the Light of Archaeological Evidence*. Göttingen: Vandenhoeck & Ruprecht, 1996.

Fitzmyer, Joseph A. *The Gospel According to Luke: Introduction, Translation, and Notes*. 2 vols. Anchor Bible 28, 28A. Garden City, N.Y.: Doubleday, 1986.

Forni, Giovanni. "Intorno al concilium di L. Cornelio Lentulo console nel 49 a. C." Pp. 154–63 in *Romanitas-Christianitas: Untersuchungen zur Geschichte und Literatur der römischen Kaizerzeit. Johannes Straub zum 70*. Edited by G. Wirth, K. H. Schwarte, and J. Heinrichs. Berlin: de Gruyter, 1982.

Frederiksen, M. W. "Caesar, Cicero and the Problem of Debt." *Journal of Roman Studies* 56 (1966): 128–32.

Freyne, Seán. *Galilee from Alexander the Great to Hadrian, 323 B.C.E. to 135 C.E.: A Study of Second Temple Judaism*. Notre Dame, Ind.: University of Notre Dame Press, 1980.

———. "The Geography, Politics, and Economics of Galilee and Quest for the Historical Jesus." Pp. 75–121 in *Studying the Historical Jesus: Evaluations of the State of Current Research*. Edited by Bruce Chilton and Craig A. Evans. Leiden: Brill, 1994.

———. "Herodian Economics in Galilee: Searching for a Suitable Model." Pp. 23–46 in *Modelling Early Christianity: Social Scientific Studies of the New Testament in Its Context*. Edited by Philip F. Esler. New York: Routledge, 1995.

Gabba, Emilio. *Appiano e la storia delle guerre civili*. Florence: La Nuova Italia, 1956.

———. "The Finances of King Herod." Pp. 160–68 in *Greece and Rome in Eretz Israel: Collected Essays*. Edited by A. Kasher, U. Rappaport, and G. Fuks. Jerusalem: Yad Iẓḥak Ben-Zvi, Israel Exploration Society, 1990.

Gagé, Jean. "L'empereur romains et les rois: politique et protocole." *Revue historique* 221 (1959): 221–60.

Gagé, Jean, Marcel LeGlay, H.-G Pflaum, and Pierre Wuilleumier, eds. *L'année épigraphique*. Paris: Presses Universitaires de France, 1973.

Gelzer, Matthias. *Caesar: Politician and Statesman*. Cambridge, Mass.: Harvard University Press, 1968.

Gilboa, A. "The Intervention of Sextus Caesar, Governor of Syria, in the Affair of Herod's Trial." *Scripta classica Israelica* 5 (1979–80): 185–94.

———. "L'octroi de la citoyenneté romaine et de l'immunité à Antipater, père d'Hérode." *Revue historique de droit français et étranger* 50 (1972): 609–14.

Ginsburg, Michel S. *Rome et la Judée: contribution à l'histoire de leurs relations politiques*. Paris: Jacques Povolozky, 1928.

Goldstein, Jonathan A. *1 Maccabees: A New Translation with Introduction and Commentary*. Anchor Bible 41. Garden City, N.Y.: Doubleday, 1976.

Goodman, Martin. "Babatha's Story." Review of Y. Yadin, *The Documents from the Bar Kokhba Period in the Cave of Letters: Greek Papyri*. *Journal of Roman Studies* 81 (1991): 169–75.

———. "Judaea." Pp. 737–81 in *The Augustan Empire, 43 B.C.–A.D. 69*. Vol. 10 of *The Cambgridge Ancient History*. 2nd ed. Edited by Alan K. Bowman, Edward Champlin, and Andrew Lintott. Cambridge: Cambridge University Press, 1996.

———. "The Origins of the Great Revolt: A Conflict of Status Criteria." Pp. 39–53 in *Greece and Rome in Eretz Israel: Collected Essays*. Edited by

A. Kasher, U. Rappaport, and G. Fuks. Jerusalem: Yad Izḥak Ben-Zvi, Israel Exploration Society, 1990.

———. "The Pilgrimage Economy of Jerusalem in the Second Temple Period." Pp. 69–76 in *Jerusalem: Its Sanctity and Centrality to Judaism, Christianity, and Islam*. Edited by Lee I. Levine. New York: Continuum, 1999.

———. *The Roman World, 44 BC—AD 180*. London: Routledge, 1997.

———. *The Ruling Class of Judaea: The Origins of the Jewish Revolt Against Rome, A. D. 66–70*. Cambridge: Cambridge University Press, 1987.

Gophna, R., and Juval Portugali. "Demographic Processes in Israel's Coastal Plain from the Chalcolithic to the Middle Bronze Age." *Bulletin of the American Schools of Oriental Research* 269 (1988): 11–28.

Gowing, Alain M. *The Triumviral Narratives of Appian and Cassius Dio*. Ann Arbor: University of Michigan Press, 1992.

Grant, Frederick C. *The Economic Background of the Gospels*. Oxford: Oxford University Press, 1926.

Groom, Nigel. *Frankincense and Myrrh: A Study of the Arabian Incense Trade*. London: Longman, 1981.

Gruen, Erich S. "The Expansion of the Empire under Augustus." Pp. 147–97 in *The Augustan Empire, 43 B.C.–A.D. 69*. Vol. 10 of *The Cambridge Ancient History*, 2nd ed. Edited by Alan K. Bowman, Edward Champlin, and Andrew Lintott. Cambridge: Cambridge University Press, 1996.

———. *The Hellenistic World and the Coming of Rome*. 2 vols. Berkeley: University of California Press, 1984.

Hahn, István. "Herodes als Prokurator." Pp. 25–43 in *Römisches Reich*. Vol. 2 of *Neue Beiträge zur Geschichte der alten Welt*. Edited by Hans-Joachim Diesner, Rigobert Günther, Johannes Mathwich, and Gerhard Schrot. Berlin: Akademie-Verlag, 1965.

Hamel, Gildas. *Poverty and Charity in Roman Palestine: First Three Centuries C.E.* Berkeley: University of California Press, 1990.

Hammond, Philip C. *The Nabataeans: Their History, Culture and Archaeology*. Gothenburg: Paul Åströms Förlag, 1973.

Hanson, K. C. "The Herodians and Mediterranean Kinship." *Biblical Theology Bulletin* 19 (1989): 75–84, 142–51; 20 (1990): 10–21.

Hanson, K. C., and Douglas E. Oakman. *Palestine in the Time of Jesus*. Minneapolis: Fortress Press, 1998.

Hanson, Paul D. "1 Chronicles 15–16 and the Chronicler's Views on the Levites." Pp. 69–77 in *"Sha'arei Talmon": Studies in the Bible, Qumran, and the Ancient Near East Presented to Shemaryahu Talmon*. Edited by Michael Fishbane and Emanuel Tov. Winona Lake, Ind.: Eisenbrauns, 1992.

Hanson, Richard S. *Tyrian Influence in the Upper Galilee*. Cambridge, Mass: American Schools of Oriental Research, 1980.

Haran, Menahem. *Temples and Temple-Service in Ancient Israel: An Inquiry Into the Character of Cult Phenomena and the Historical Setting of the Priestly School*. Oxford: Clarendon, 1978.

Har-El, Menashe. "Jerusalem & Judea: Roads and Fortifications." *Biblical Archaeologist* 44 (1981): 8–19.

Harl, Kenneth W. *Coinage in the Roman Economy, 300 B.C. to A.D. 700*. Baltimore: Johns Hopkins University Press, 1996.

Harland, Philip A. "The Economy of First-Century Palestine: State of the Scholarly Discussion." Pp. 511–27 in *Handbook of Early Christianity: Social Science Approaches*. Edited by Anthony J. Blasi, Jean Duhaime, and Paul-Andre Turcotte. Walnut Creek, Calif.: AltaMira Press, 2002.

Hart, Henry St. John. "The Coin of 'Render Unto Caesar . . .': A Note on Some Aspects of Mark 12:13–17; Matt. 22:15–22; Luke 20:20–26." Pp. 241–48 in *Jesus and the Politics of His Day*. Edited by Ernst Bammel and C. F. D. Moule. Cambridge: Cambridge University Press, 1984.

Heichelheim, F. M. "Roman Syria." Pp. 121–257 in *An Economic Survey of Ancient Rome*, vol. 4. Edited by Tenney Frank. Baltimore: Johns Hopkins University Press, 1938.

Heuver, Gerald D. *The Teachings of Jesus Concerning Wealth*. Chicago: Flemming H. Revell, 1903.

Hoehner, Harold W. *Chronological Aspects of the Life of Christ*. Grand Rapids: Zondervan, 1977.

———. *Herod Antipas*. Cambridge: Cambridge University Press, 1972.

Holmberg, Bengt. *Sociology and the New Testament: An Appraisal*. Minneapolis: Fortress Press, 1990.

Holmes, T. Rice. *The Architect of the Roman Empire*. 2 vols. Oxford: Clarendon, 1928.

———. *The Roman Republic and the Founder of the Empire*. 3 vols. Oxford: Clarendon, 1923. Repr., New York: Russell & Russell, 1967.

Holum, Kenneth, and Robert Hohlfelder, eds. *King Herod's Dream: Caesarea on the Sea*. New York: W. W. Norton, 1988.

Homo, Léon. *L'Italie primitive et les débuts de l'impérialisme romain*. Paris: La Renaissance du Livre, 1925.

Hopkins, Keith. "Taxes and Trade in the Roman Empire, 200 B.C.–A.D. 400." *Journal of Roman Studies* 70 (1980): 101–25.

Horsley, G. H. R., ed. *A Review of the Greek Inscriptions and Papyri Published in 1978*. Vol. 3 of *New Documents Illustrating Early Christianity*. North Ryde: Macquarie University Press, 1983.

Horsley, Richard A. *Archaeology, History, and Society in Galilee: The Social Context of Jesus and the Rabbis*. Valley Forge, Pa.: Trinity Press, 1996.

———. *Galilee: History, Politics, People*. Valley Forge, Pa.: Trinity Press, 1995.

———. *Jesus and the Spiral of Violence: Popular Jewish Resistance in Roman Palestine*. San Francisco: Harper & Row, 1987.

———. *Sociology and the Jesus Movement*. New York: Crossroad, 1989.

Horsley, Richard A., and John S. Hanson. *Bandits, Prophets, and Messiahs: Popular Movements in the Time of Jesus*. Minneapolis: Winston, 1985.

Höghammar, Kerstin. *Sculpture and Society: A Study of the Connection Between the Free-Standing Sculpture and Society on Kos in the Hellenistic and Augustan Periods*. Uppsala: University of Uppsala Press, 1993.

Hultsch, Friedrich. "Das hebräische Talent bei Josephus." *Klio* 2 (1902): 70–72.

Humbert, J.-B., and A. Chambon. *The Excavations of Khirbet Qumran and Ain Feshkha: Synthesis of Roland de Vaux's Field Notes*. Translated by Stephen J. Pfann. Göttingen: Vandenhoeck & Ruprecht, 2003.

———. *Fouilles de Khirbet Qumrân et de Aïn Feshkha*. Göttingen: Vandenhoeck & Ruprecht, 1994.

Hunt, Authur S., and Gilbart J. Smyly, eds. *The Tebtunis Papyri*. Vol. 3. New York: Oxford University Press, 1933.

Jacobson, David M. "King Herod, Roman Citizen and Benefactor of Kos." *Bulletin of the Anglo-Israel Archaeological Society* 13 (1993/94): 31–35.

———. "Three Roman Client Kings: Herod of Judaea, Archelaus of Cappadocia and Juba of Mauretania." *Palestine Exploration Quarterly* 133 (2001): 22–38.

Jeremias, Joachim. *Jerusalem in the Time of Jesus: An Investigation Into Economic and Social Conditions during the New Testament Period*. Translated by F. H. Cave and C. H. Cave. Philadelphia: Fortress Press, 1969.

———. *The Parables of Jesus*. London: SCM, 1954. Repr., 1985.

Johnson, A. C., P. R. Coleman, and E. Card Bourne, eds. and transs. *Ancient Roman Statutes: A Translation*. Corpus of Roman Law 2. Austin: University of Texas Press, 1961.

Jones, A. H. M. *The Cities of the Eastern Roman Provinces*. Edited by Michael Avi-Yonah, George Dean, Henri Seyrig, Michael Gough, and Joyce Reynolds. 2nd ed. Amsterdam: Adolf M. Hakkert, 1983.

———. "Civitates Liberae et Immunes in the East." Pp. 103–17 in *Anatolian Studies Presented to William Hepburn Buckler*. Edited by W. M. Calder and Joseph Kiel. Manchester: Manchester University Press, 1939.

———. *The Herods of Judaea*. Oxford: Clarendon, 1938.

———. "Procurators and Prefects in the Early Principate." Pp. 117–25 in his *Studies in Roman Government and Law*. Oxford: Blackwell, 1960.

———. "Review and Discussion." Review of Arnaldo Momigliano, *Ricerche sull' organizzazione della Guidea sotto il dominio romano*. *Journal of Roman Studies* 25 (1935): 228–31.

———. *The Roman Economy: Studies in Ancient Economic and Administrative History*. Edited by P. A. Brunt. Oxford: Blackwell, 1974.

———. "Rome and the Provincial Cities." *Revue de l'histoire du droit* 39 (1971): 513–51.

Juster, Jean. *Les Juifs dans l'empire romain: leur condition juridique, économique et sociale*. 2 vols. Paris: Librairie Paul Geuthner, 1914.

Kadman, Leo. "Temple Dues and Currency in Ancient Palestine in the Light of Recent Discovered Coin-Hoards." *Israel Numismatic Bulletin* 1 (1962): 9–11.

———. "Temple Dues and Currency in Ancient Palestine in the Light of Recent Discovered Coin-Hoards." Pp. 69–76 in *Atti del congresso internazionale di numismatica, Roma, 1961*, vol. 2. Rome: Istituto Italiano di Numismatica, 1965.

Kanael, Baruch. "The Partition of Judea by Gabinius." *Israel Exploration Journal* 7 (1957): 98–106.

Karmon, Yehuda. "Geographical Influences on the Historical Routes in the Sharon Plain." *Palestine Exploration Quarterly* 93 (1961): 43–60.

Kasher, Aryeh. "Gaza During the Greco-Roman Era." Pp. 63–78 in *The Jerusalem Cathedra: Studies in the History, Archaeology, Geography and Ethnography of the Land of Israel*, vol. 2. Edited by Lee I Levine. Jerusalem: Yad Izḥak Ben-Zvi Institute, 1982.

———. *Jews and Hellenistic Cities in Eretz-Israel: Relations of the Jews in Eretz-Israel with the Hellenistic Cities During the Second Temple Period, 332 BCE–70 CE*. Tübingen: Mohr Siebeck, 1990.

———. *Jews, Idumaeans and Ancient Arabs*. Tübingen: Mohr Siebeck, 1988.

———. *The Jews in Hellenistic and Roman Egypt: The Struggle for Equal Rights*. Tübingen: Mohr Siebeck, 1985.

———. "New Light on the Jewish Role in the Alexandrian War of Julius Caesar." *World Union of Jewish Studies Newsletter* 14–15 (1979): 15–23.

Kee, H. C., trans. "Testament of the Twelve Patriarchs: Testament of Levi." Pp. 788–95 in *The Old Testament Pseudepigrapha*, vol. 1. Edited by James H. Charlesworth. London: Darton, Longman & Todd, 1983.

Kennard, Spencer J., Jr. "Syrian Coin Hoards and the Tribute Question." *Anglican Theological Review* 27 (1945): 248–52.

Kennedy, David. "Syria." Pp. 703–36 in *The Augustan Empire, 43 B.C.–A.D. 69*. Vol. 10 of *The Cambridge Ancient History*. 2nd ed. Edited by Alan K. Bowman, Edward Champlin, and Andrew Lintott. Cambridge: Cambridge University Press, 1996.

Kenyon, Kathleen M. "Some Aspects of the Impact of Rome on Palestine." *Journal of the Royal Asiatic Society* 2 (1970): 181–91.

Klausner, J. "The Economy of Judea in the Period of the Second Temple." Pp. 179–205 in *Herodian Period*. Edited by Michael Avi-Yonah. World

History of the Jewish People: First Series, Ancient Times 7. 1930. Jerusalem: Massada, 1975.

Kochavi, Moshe, Pirhiyah Beck, and Esther Yadin, eds. *Aphek-Antipatris 1: Excavations of Areas A and B, the 1972–1976 Seasons*. Tel Aviv: Emery & Claire Yass Publications in Archaeology, 2000.

Kokkinos, Nikos. "Crucifixion in A.D. 36: The Keystone for Dating the Birth of Jesus." Pp. 133–63 in *Chronos, Kairos, Christos: Nativity and Chronological Studies Presented to Jack Finegan*. Edited by Jerry Vardaman and Edwin M. Yamauchi. Winona Lake, Ind.: Eisenbrauns, 1989.

———. *The Herodian Dynasty: Origins, Role in Society and Eclipse*. Sheffield: Sheffield Academic Press, 1998.

———. "The Relative Chronology of the Nativity in Tertullian." Pp. 119–31 in *Chronos, Kairos, Christos II: Chronological, Nativity and Religious Studies in Memory of Ray Summers*. Edited by Jerry E. Vardaman. Macon, Ga.: Mercer University Press, 1998.

Krebs, Johann Tobias. *Decreta Romanorum pro Iudaeis facta e Iosepho collecta et commentario historico-critico illustrata*. Lipsiae: Sumtibus Caspari Fritsch, 1768.

Kreissig, Heinz. "Die landwirtschaftliche Situation in Palästina vor dem judäischen Krieg." *Acta Antiqua Academiae Scientiarum Hungaricae* 17 (1969): 223–54.

———. *Die sozialen Zusammenhänge des judäischen Krieges: Klassen und Klassenkampf in Palästina des 1. Jahrhunderts v. u. Z.* Berlin: Akademie-Verlag, 1970.

Leaney, A. R. C. *The Jewish and Christian World 200 BC to AD 200*. Cambridge Commentaries on Writings of the Jewish and Christian World, 200 BC to AD 200. Cambridge: Cambridge University Press, 1984.

Levine, Baruch A. "Levites." Pp. 523–31 in *Encyclopedia of Religion*, vol. 8. Edited by Mircea Eliade. New York: Macmillan, 1987.

———. *Numbers 1–20: A New Translation with Introduction and Commentary*. Anchor Bible 4A. New York: Doubleday, 1993.

Levine, Lee I. *Jerusalem: Portrait of the City in the Second Temple Period, 538 B.C.E.–70 C.E.* Philadelphia: Jewish Publication Society, 2002.

———. "Second Temple Jerusalem: A Jewish City in the Greco-Roman Orbit." Pp. 53–68 in *Jerusalem: Its Sanctity and Centrality to Judaism, Christianity, and Islam*. Edited by Lee I. Levine. New York: Continuum, 1999.

Lewis, Charlton T., and Charles Short. *A Latin Dictionary*. Rev. and enl. ed. Oxford: Clarendon, 1984.

Lewis, Naphtali. "A Jewish Landowner in the Province of Arabia." *Scripta classica Israelica* 8–9 (1985–88): 132–37.

———. *Life in Egypt Under Roman Rule*. Oxford: Clarendon, 1983.

Lewis, Naphtali, Yigael Yadin, and Jonas C. Greenfield, eds. *The Documents from the Bar Kokhba Period in the Cave of Letters: Greek Papyri.* Judean Desert Studies 2. Jerusalem: Israel Exploration Society, the Hebrew University of Jerusalem, & the Shrine of the Book, 1989.

Liddell, Henry George, Robert Scott, and Stuart Henry Jones. *Greek-English Lexicon*. 9th ed. with revised supplement. Oxford: Clarendon, 1996.

Lintott, Andrew. *The Constitution of the Roman Republic*. Oxford: Clarendon, 1999.

———. *Imperium Romanum: Politics and Administration*. London: Routledge, 1993.

———. *Judicial Reform and Land Reform in the Roman Republic*. Cambridge: Cambridge University Press, 1992.

———. "What Was the 'Imperium Romanum'?" *Greece & Rome* 28 (1981): 53–67.

Liver, J. "The Half-Shekel Offering in Biblical and Post-Biblical Literature." *Harvard Theological Review* 56 (1963): 173–98.

Lo Cascio, Elio. "La struttura fiscale dell'impero Romano." Pp. 29–59 in *L'impero Romano e le strutture economiche e sociali delle province*. Edited by Michael H. Crawford. Como: Editioni New Press, 1986.

Lord, Louis E. "The Date of Julius Caesar's Departure from Alexandria." *Journal of Roman Studies* 28 (1938): 14–40.

MacMullen, Ramsay. *Roman Government's Response to Crisis*. New Haven: Yale University Press, 1976.

———. "Tax-Pressure in the Roman Empire." *Latomus* 46 (1987): 737–54.

Madden, Frederic W. *History of Jewish Coinage and of Money in the Old and New Testament*. London: B. Quaritch, 1864. Repr., New York: Ktav, 1967.

Marcus, Ralph, trans. *Josephus: Jewish Antiquities, Books XII-XIV*. Vol. 7 of *Josephus*. Edited and translated by H. St. J. Thackeray, Marcus Ralph, L. H. Feldman, and Allen Wilgren. Loeb Classical Library. Cambridge, Mass.: Harvard University Press, 1936.

Marquardt, Joachim. *Römische Staatsverwaltung*. Vol. 4–6 of *Handbuch der römischen Alterthümer*. 2nd ed. Edited by Theodor Mommsen and Joachim Marquardt. Leipzig: Hirzel, 1881–85. Repr., New York: Arno Press, 1975.

Marshall, Anthony J. "Flaccus and the Jews of Asia (Cicero *Pro Flacco* 28.67–69)." *Phoenix* 29 (1975): 139–54.

———. "Friends of the Roman People." *American Journal of Philology* 89 (1968): 39–55.

Matthaei, Louise E. "On the Classification of Roman Allies." *Classical Quarterly* 1 (1907): 182–204.

Matthews, J. F. "The Tax Law of Palmyra: Evidence for Economic History in a City of the Roman East." *Journal of Roman Studies* 64 (1984): 157–80.

Mattingly, Harold. *Coins of the Roman Empire in the British Museum*. 1923. Repr., London: Trustees of the British Museum, 1965.

Mazar, Benjamin. "Herodian Jerusalem in the Light of the Excavations South and South-West of the Temple Mount." *Israel Exploration Journal* 28 (1978): 230–37.

———. *The Mountain of the Lord*. Garden City, N.Y.: Doubleday, 1975.

McLaren, James S. *Power and Politics in Palestine: The Jews and the Governing of Their Land 100 BC-AD 70*. Sheffield: Sheffield Academic Press, 1991.

Meier, John P. "The Historical Jesus and the Historical Herodians." *Journal of Biblical Literature* 119 (2000): 740–46.

———. *A Marginal Jew: Rethinking the Historical Jesus*. 3 vols. New York: Doubleday, 1991–2001.

Mendelssohn. "Senati consulta romana in Iosephi Antiquitatibus." *Acta Societatis Philologicae Lipsiensis* 5 (1875): 87–288.

Merlin, Alf., ed. *L'année épigraphique, 1941*. Paris: Presses Universitaires de France, 1942.

———, ed. *L'année épigraphique, 1947*. Paris: Presses Universitaires de France, 1948.

———, ed. *L'année épigraphique, 1948*. Paris: Presses Universitaires de France, 1949.

Meshorer, Yaʿakov. *Jewish Coins of the Second Temple Period*. Translated by I. H. Levine. Tel-Aviv: Am Hassefer & Masada, 1967.

———. *Nabataean Coins*. Qedem 3. Jerusalem: Hebrew University of Jerusalem, 1975.

Meyshan, J. "The Coinage of Agrippa the First." *Israel Exploration Journal* 4 (1954): 186–200.

Milgrom, Jacob. *Numbers* במדבר: *The Traditional Hebrew Text with the New JPS Translation and Commentary*. JPS Torah Commentary. Philadelphia: Jewish Publication Society, 1990.

———. "Studies in the Temple Scroll." *Journal of Biblical Literature* 97 (1978): 501–23.

Millar, Fergus. *The Emperor in the Roman World, 31 BC–AD 337*. Ithaca, N.Y.: Cornell University Press, 1977.

———. "Emperors, Kings and Subjects: The Politics of Two-Level Sovereignty." *Scripta classica Israelica* 15 (1996): 159–73.

———. "The Emperor, the Senate, and the Provinces." Pp. 271–91 in *Rome, the Greek World, and the East*. Edited by Hannah M. Cotton and Guy M. Rogers. Chapel Hill: University of North Carolina Press, 2002.

———. "Empire and City, Augustus to Julian: Obligations, Excuses, and Status." *Journal of Roman Studies* 73 (1983): 76–96.

———. "The Fiscus in the First Two Centuries." *Journal of Roman Studies* 53 (1963): 29–42.

———. "The Roman *Coloniae* of the Near East: A Study of Cultural Relations." Pp. 7–58 in *Roman Eastern Policy and Other Studies in Roman History: Proceedings of a Colloquium at Tvärminne 2–3 October 1987.* Edited by Heikki Solin and Mika Kajava. Helsinki: Finnish Society of Sciences and Letters, 1990.

———. *The Roman Empire and Its Neighbours*. 2nd ed. London: Duckworth, 1981.

———. *The Roman Near East: 31 BC–AD 337*. Cambridge, Mass.: Harvard University Press, 1993.

———. "Some Evidence of the Meaning of Tacitus Annals XII.60." *Historia* 13 (1964): 181–87.

———. *A Study of Cassius Dio*. Oxford: Clarendon, 1964.

———. "Triumvirate and Principate." Pp. 241–70 in *Rome, the Greek World, and the East*. Edited by Hannah M. Cotton and Guy M. Rogers. Chapel Hill: University of North Carolina Press, 2002.

Miller, J. Innes. *The Spice Trade of the Roman Empire: 29 B.C. to A.D. 641*. Oxford: Clarendon, 1969.

Mitchell, Stephen. "Requisitioned Transport in the Roman Empire: A New Inscription from Pisidia." *Journal of Roman Studies* 66 (1976): 106–31.

Mittwoch, A. "Tribute and Land-Tax in Seleucid Judaea." *Biblica* 36 (1955): 352–61.

Moehring, Horst R. "The *Acta Pro Judaeis* in the *Antiquities* of Flavius Josephus: A Study in Hellenistic and Modern Apologetic Historiography." Pp. 124–58 in *Christianity, Judaism and Other Greco-Roman Cults*, vol. 3. Edited by J. Neusner. Leiden: Brill, 1975.

———. "The Census in Luke as an Apologetic Device." Pp. 144–60 in *Studies in New Testament and Early Christian Literature: Essays in Honor of Allen P. Wikgren*. Edited by David Edward Aune. Leiden: Brill, 1972.

Momigliano, Arnaldo. *Ricerche sull'organizzazione della Giudea sotto il dominio romano, 63 a. C.-70 d. C.* Bologna: Annali della R. Scuola Normale Superiore di Pisa, 1934. Repr., Amsterdam: Adolf M. Hakkert, 1967.

Mommsen, Theodor, ed. *Corpus inscriptionum latinarum*. Berlin: Apud Georgium Reimerum, 1883.

———. *The History of Rome*. Translated by William P. Dickson. 5 vols. Glencoe, Ill.: Free Press, 1957.

———. *The Provinces of the Roman Empire from Caesar to Diocletian*. Translated by William P. Dickson. 2 vols. Chicago: Ares Publishers, 1974.

———. *Römisches Straatsrecht*. Vol. 1–3 of *Handbuch der römischen Alterthümer*. Edited by Joachim Marquardt and Theodor Mommsen. Leipzig: Hirzel, 1887.

Mommsen, Theodor, and Paul Krueger, eds. *The Digest of Justinian*. Translated by Alan Watson. 4 vols. Philadelphia: University of Pennsylvania Press, 1985.

Moore, Carey A. *Judith: A New Translation with Introduction and Commentary*. Anchor Bible 40B. Garden City, N.Y.: Doubleday, 1985.

Moore, George Foot. *Judaism in the First Centuries of the Christian Era: The Age of the Tannaim*. 2 vols. Cambridge, Mass.: Harvard University Press, 1927–30.

Motzo, B. R. "Ircano II nella tradizione storica." Vol. 1, pp. 1–18 in *Studi di storia e filologia*. 2 vols. Cagliari: R. Università, 1927.

Neesen, Lutz. *Untersuchungen zu den direkten Staatsabgaben der römischen Kaiserzeit, 27 v. Chr.-284 n. Chr.* Antiquitas 32. Bonn: Habelt, 1980.

Negev, A. "The Date of the Petra-Gaza Road." *Palestine Exploration Quarterly* 98 (1966): 89–98.

Netzer, Ehud. "Herod's Building Projects: State Necessity or Personal Need?" Pp. 48–61 in *The Jerusalem Cathedra*, vol. 1. Edited by Lee I. Levine. Jerusalem: Yad Iẓḥak Ben-Zvi Institute, 1981.

Neumann, Karl Johannes. "Römische Klientelstaaten." *Historische Zeitschrift* 117 (1917): 1–10.

Nicolet, Claude. *Tributum: recherches sur la fiscalité directe sous la république romaine*. Antiquitas 24. Bonn: Habelt, 1976.

———. *The World of the Citizen in Republican Rome*. Translated by P. S. Falla. Berkeley: University of California Press, 1980.

Oakman, Douglas E. *Jesus and the Economic Questions of His Day*. Lewiston, N.Y.: Edwin Mellen, 1986.

Oppenheimer, Aharon. *The ʿAm Ha-Aretz: A Study in the Social History of the Jewish People in the Hellenistic-Roman Period*. Translated by I. H. Levine. Leiden: Brill, 1977.

Ørsted, Peter. *Roman Imperial Economy and Romanization. A Study in Roman Imperial Administration and the Public Lease System in the Danubian Provinces from the First to the Third Century A.D.* Copenhagen: Museum Tusculanum, 1985.

Otto, Walter. "Herodes." Pp. 1–200 in *Real-encyclopädie der classischen Altertumswissenschaft*, vol. 2 supplement. Edited by A. F. Pauly George Wissowa, and Wilhelm Kroll. Stuttgart: J. B. Metzler, 1913.

Pastor, Jack. *Land and Economy in Ancient Palestine*. London: Routledge, 1997.

Pearson, Brook W. R. "The Lucan Censuses, Revisited." *Catholic Biblical Quarterly* 61 (1999): 262–82.

Pelling, Christopher. "The Triumviral Period." Pp. 1–69 in *The Augustan*

Empire, 43 B.C.–A.D. 69. Vol. 10 of *The Cambridge Ancient History*. 2nd ed. Edited by Alan K. Bowman, Edward Champlin, and Andrew Lintott. Cambridge: Cambridge University Press, 1996.

Piattelli, Daniela. "Ricerche intorno alle relazioni politiche tra Roma e l' ἔθνος τῶν Ἰουδαίων dal 161 A.C. al 4 A.C." *Bullettino dell'istituto di diritto romano* 74 (1972): 219–340.

Potts, Daniel T. "Trans-Arabian Routes of the Pre-Islamic Period." Pp. 127–62 in *Itinéraires et voisinages*. Vol. 1 of *L'Arabie et ses mers bordieres*. Edited by Jean-François Salles. Lyon: G. S. Maison de l'Orient, 1988.

Préaux, Claire. *L'économie royale des Lagides*. Brussels: Éditions de la Fondation Égyptologique Reine Élisabeth, 1939.

Pritchard, James B., ed. *The Times Atlas of the Bible*. London: Times Books, 1987.

Pritchard, R. T. "Cicero and the *Lex Hieronica*." *Historia* 19 (1970): 352–68.

———. "Gaius Verres and the Sicilian Farmers." *Historia* 20 (1971): 229–38.

Pucci Ben Zeev, Miriam. "Caesar and the Jewish Law." *Revue biblique* 102 (1995): 28–37.

———. "Did the Jews Enjoy a Privileged Position in the Roman World?" *Revue des études juives* 154 (1995): 23–42.

———. *Jewish Rights in the Roman World: The Greek and Roman Documents Quoted by Josephus Flavius*. Tübingen: Mohr Siebeck, 1998.

Qimron, Elisha, and John Strugnell, eds. *Qumran Cave 4, V: Miqṣat Maʿaśe ha-Torah*. Discoveries in the Judaean Desert 10. Oxford: Clarendon, 1994.

———. "An Unpublished Halakhic Letter from Qumran." Pp. 400–407 in *Biblical Archaeology Today: Proceedings of the International Congress on Biblical Archaeology, Jerusalem, April 1984*. Edited by Joseph Aviram and Avraham Biran. Jerusalem: Israel Exploration Society, 1985.

Raban, Avner. "Caesarea." Pp. 270–91 in *The New Encylopedia of Archaeological Excavations in the Holy Land*. 4 vols. Edited by Ephraim Stern, Lewinson-Gilboa, and Aviram Joseph. Jerusalem: Israel Exploration Society & Carta, 1993.

Rabello, Alfredo Mordechai. "The Legal Condition of the Jews in the Roman Empire." Pp. 662–762 in *Aufstieg und Niedergang der römischen Welt* Part 2, *Principat*, 13. Edited by Hildegard Temporini and Wolfgang Haase. New York: de Gruyter, 1980.

Rajak, Tessa. "Jewish Rights in the Greek Cities Under Roman Rule: A New Approach." Pp. 19–35 in *Studies in Judaism and Its Greco-Roman Context*. Vol. 5 of *Approaches to Ancient Judaism*. Edited by William Scott Green. Brown Judaic Studies. Atlanta: Scholars Press, 1985.

———. "Roman Intervention in a Seleucid Siege of Jerusalem." *Greek, Roman and Byzantine Studies* 22 (1981): 65–81.

———. "Was There a Roman Charter for the Jews?" *Journal of Roman Studies* 74 (1984): 107–23.

Rambaud, Michel. "A propos de l'*humanitas* de César." *Les études classiques* 40 (1972).

Rappaport, U. "La Judée et Rome pendant le règne d'Alexandre Jannée." *Revue des études juives* 127 (1968): 329–31.

Raschke, Manfred G. "New Studies in Roman Commerce with the East." Pp. 604–1378 in *Aufstieg und Niedergang der römischen Welt* 9.2, Part 2, *Principat.* Edited by Hildegard Temporini and Wolfgang Haase. New York: de Gruyter, 1980.

Rathbone, Dominic W. "The Ancient Economy and Graeco-Roman Egypt." Pp. 159–76 in *Egitto e storia antica dell'Ellenismo all'età Araba.* Edited by Lucia Criscuolo and Giovanni Geraci. Bologna: Cooperativa Libraria Universitaria Editrice, 1989.

———. "Egypt, Augustus and Roman Taxation." *Cahiers du centre Gustave Glotz* 4 (1993): 81–112.

———. "The Imperial Finances." Pp. 309–23 in *The Augustan Empire, 43 B.C.–A.D. 69.* Vol. 10 of *The Cambridge Ancient History.* 2nd ed. Edited by Alan K. Bowman, Edward Champlin, and Andrew Lintott. Cambridge: Cambridge University Press, 1996.

Raubitschek, A. E. "Epigraphical Notes on Julius Caesar." *Journal of Roman Studies* 44 (1954): 65–75.

Rawson, Elizabeth. "The Aftermath of the Ides." Pp. 468–90 in *The Last Age of the Roman Republic, 146–43 B.C.* Vol. 9 of *The Cambridge Ancient History.* 2nd ed. Edited by J. A. Crook, Andrew Lintott, and Elizabeth Rawson. Cambridge: Cambridge University Press, 1994.

———. "Caesar: Civil War and Dictatorship." Pp. 424–67 in *The Last Age of the Roman Republic, 146–43 B.C.* Vol. 9 of *The Cambridge Ancient History.* 2nd ed. Edited by J. A. Crook, Andrew Lintott, and Elizabeth Rawson. Cambridge: Cambridge University Press, 1994.

———. "Caesar's Heritage: Hellenistic Kings and and Their Roman Equals." Pp. 169–88 in *Roman Culture and Society: Collected Papers.* Oxford: Clarendon, 1991.

———. "Cassius and Brutus: The Memory of the Liberators." Pp. 101–19 in *Past Perspectives: Studies in Greek and Roman Historical Writing.* Edited by I. S. Moxon, J. D. Smart, and A. J. Woodman. Cambridge: Cambridge University Press, 1986.

Raynor, Joyce, and Ya'akov Meshorer. *The Coins of Ancient Meiron.* Meiron Excavation Project. Winona Lake, Ind.: ASOR/Eisenbrauns, 1988.

Rehm, Merlin D. "Levites and Priests." Pp. 297–310 in *The Anchor Bible Dictionary,* vol. 4. Edited by David Noel Freedman, Gary A. Herion, David F. Graf, John David Pleins, and Astrid B. Beck. New York: Doubleday, 1992.

Reich, Ronny. "The 'Boundary of Gezer' Inscriptions Again." *Israel Exploration Journal* 40 (1990): 44–46.

Rey-Coquais, J.-P. "Syrie romaine, de Pompée à Dioclétien." *Journal of Roman Studies* 68 (1978): 44–73.

Reynolds, Joyce. *Aphrodisias and Rome*. London: Society for the Promotion of Roman Studies, 1982.

Riccobono, Salvator, ed. *Lex agraria*. In *Fontes iuris romani anteJustiniani*. Part 1. Edited by Salvator Riccobono. Florence: S. A. Barbèra, 1968.

Richardson, J. S. "The Administration of the Empire." Pp. 564–98 in *The Last Age of the Roman Republic, 146–43 B.C.* Vol. 9 of *The Cambridge Ancient History*. 2nd ed. Edited by J. A. Crook, Andrew Lintott, and Elizabeth Rawson. Cambridge: Cambridge University Press, 1994.

———. "*Imperium Romanum*: Empire and the Language of Power." *Journal of Roman Studies* 81 (1991): 1–9.

———. *Roman Provincial Administration, 227 BC to AD 117*. Basingstoke: Macmillan, 1976.

Richardson, Peter. *Herod: King of the Jews and Friend of the Romans*. Columbia: University of South Carolina Press, 1996.

Rist, Martin. "Caesar or God (Mark 12:13–17)? A Study in Formgeschichte." *Journal of Religion* 16 (1936): 317–31.

Ritter, Bernhard. *Philo und die Halacha*. Leipzig: Hinrichs, 1879.

Rodd, Cyril S. "On Applying a Sociological Theory to Biblical Studies." *Journal for the Study of the Old Testament* 19 (1981): 95–106.

Roddaz, Jean-Michel. *Marcus Agrippa*. Rome: École française de Rome, 1984.

Roll, Israel. "The Roman Road System in Judaea." Pp. 136–61 in *The Jerusalem Cathedra*, vol. 3. Edited by Lee I. Levine. Jerusalem: Yad Iẓḥak Ben-Zvi Institute, 1983.

Roll, Israel, and Etan Ayalon. "Roman Roads in Western Samaria." *Palestine Exploration Quarterly* 118 (1986): 113–34.

Roller, Duane W. *The Building Program of Herod the Great*. Berkeley: University of California Press, 1998.

Romer, F. E. "A Case of Client-Kingship." *American Journal of Philology* 106 (1985): 75–100.

Rosenfeld, Ben-Zion. "The 'Boundary of Gezer' Inscriptions and the History of Gezer at the End of the Second Temple Period." *Israel Exploration Journal* 38 (1988): 235–45.

———. "The Galilean Valleys (*Beqʾaoth*) from the Bible to the Talmud." *Revue biblique* 109 (2002): 66–100.

Rostovtzeff, M. "Angareia." *Klio* 6 (1906): 249–58.

———. *The Social and Economic History of the Hellenistic World*. 3 vols. Oxford: Clarendon, 1941.

———. *The Social and Economic History of the Roman Empire*. Oxford: Clarendon, 1926.

Roth, Otto. *Rom und die Hasmonäer*. Leipzig: Hinrichs, 1914.

Roussel, Pierre. "Un Syrien au service de Rome et d'Octave." *Syria* 15 (1934): 33–74.

Saddington, D. B. *The Development of the Roman Auxiliary Forces from Caesar to Vespasian, 49 B.C.–A.D. 79*. Harare: University of Zimbabwe, 1982.

Safrai, S. "Relations Between the Diaspora and the Land of Israel." Pp. 184–215 in *The Jewish People in the First Century: Historical Geography, Political History, Social, Cultural and Religious Life and Institutions*, vol. 1. Edited by S. Safrai and M. Stern. Compendia Rerum Iudaicarum Ad Novum Testamentum 1. Assen: Van Gorcum, 1974.

———. "Religion in Everyday Life." Pp. 793–833 in *The Jewish People in the First Century: Historical Geography, Political History, Social, Cultural and Religious Life and Institutions*, vol. 2. Edited by S. Safrai and M. Stern. Compendia Rerum Iudaicarum Ad Novum Testamentum 1. Philadelphia: Fortress Press, 1976.

Safrai, Ze'ev. *The Economy of Roman Palestine*. London: Routledge, 1994.

Sanders, E. P. *The Historical Figure of Jesus*. London: Penguin, 1993.

———. "Jesus' Galilee." Pp. 3–41 in *Fair Play: Diversity and Conflicts in Early Christianity*. Edited by Ismo Dunderberg, Christopher Tuckett, and Kari Syreeni. Leiden: Brill, 2002.

———. *Jewish Law from Jesus to the Mishnah: Five Studies*. London: SCM Press, 1990.

———. *Judaism: Practice and Belief, 63 BCE–66 BCE*. London: SCM Press, 1992.

Sands, P. C. *The Client Princes of the Roman Empire Under the Republic*. Cambridge Historical Essays. Cambridge: Cambridge University Press, 1908. Repr., New York: Arno Press, 1975.

Saulnier, Christiane. "Lois romaines et les Juifs selon Josèphe." *Revue biblique* 88 (1981): 161–98.

Schalit, Abraham. *König Herodes: Der Mann und sein Werk*. Berlin: Walter de Gruyter, 1969.

Schürer, Emil. *Geschichte des jüdischen Volkes im Zeitalter Jesu Christi*. 2 vols. Leipzig: J. C. Hinrichs, 1901.

———. *The History of the Jewish People in the Age of Jesus Christ, 175 B.C.–A.D. 135*. 3 vols. in 4 parts. Revised and edited by Geza Vermes, Fergus Millar, Martin Goodman, and Matthew Black. Edinburgh: T&T Clark, 1973–87.

Schwartz, Daniel R. *Agrippa I: The Last King of Judaea*. Tübingen: Mohr Siebeck, 1990.

———. "Josephus on Hyrcanus II." Pp. 210–32 in *Josephus and the History of the Greco-Roman Period: Essays in Memory of Morton Smith*. Edited by Fausto Parente and Joseph Sievers. Leiden: Brill, 1994.

———. "Josephus on the Jewish Constitutions and Community." *Scripta classica Israelica* 7 (1983): 30–52.

———. "On Abraham Schalit, Herod, Josephus, the Holocaust, Horst R. Moehring, and the Study of Ancient Jewish History." *Jewish History* 2 (1987): 157–71.

Schwartz, Joshua J. *Lod (Lydda), Israel: From Its Origins Through the Byzantine Period, 5600 B.C.E.-640 C.E.* Oxford: Tempus Reparatum, 1991.

———. "Once More on the 'Boundary of Gezer' Inscriptions and the History of Gezer and Lydda at the End of the Second Temple Period." *Israel Exploration Journal* 40 (1990): 47–57.

Seager, Robin. *Pompey: A Political Biography*. Berkeley: University of California Press, 1979.

Seyrig, H. "Le statut de Palmyre." *Syria* 22 (1941): 155–74.

Sharabani, M. "Monnaies de Qumrân au Musée Rockefeller de Jérusalem." *Revue biblique* 85 (1980): 274–84.

Shatzman, Israel. *The Armies of the Hasmoneans and Herod*. Tübingen: Mohr Siebeck, 1991.

———. "L'integrazione della Giudea nell'impero romano." Pp. 17–46 in *Gli Ebrei nell'impero romano*. Edited by Ariel Lewin. Florence: La Giuntina, 2001.

Sherk, Robert K. *Roman Documents from the Greek East:* Senatus Consulta *and* Epistulae *to the Age of Augustus*. Baltimore: Johns Hopkins University Press, 1969.

———. *Rome and the Greek East to the Death of Augustus*. Cambridge: Cambridge University Press, 1984.

Sherwin-White, A. N. "Lucullus, Pompey and the East." Pp. 229–73 in *The Last Age of the Roman Republic, 146–43 B.C.* Vol. 9 of *The Cambridge Ancient History*. 2nd ed. Edited by J. A. Crook, Andrew Lintott, and Elizabeth Rawson. Cambridge: Cambridge University Press, 1994.

———. *The Roman Citizenship*. 2nd ed. Oxford: Clarendon, 1973.

———. *Roman Foreign Policy in the East, 168 B.C. to A.D. 1*. Norman: University of Oklahoma Press, 1984.

———. *Roman Society and Law in the New Testament*. Oxford: Clarendon, 1963.

Shutt, R. J. H., trans. "Letter of Aristeas." Pp. 7–34 in *The Old Testament Pseudepigrapha*, vol. 2. Edited by James H. Charlesworth. London: Darton, Longman & Todd, 1985.

Sijpesteijn, P. J. "Mithradates' March from Pergamum to Alexandria in 48 B. C." *Latomus* 24 (1965): 122–27.

Smallwood, E. Mary, ed. and trans. *Philonis Alexandrini Legatio Ad Gaium*. Leiden: Brill, 1970.

———. *The Jews under Roman Rule: From Pompey to Diocletian*. 2nd ed. Leiden: Brill, 2001.

Smith, George Adam. *The Historical Geography of the Holy Land*. 25th ed. New York: Harper & Brothers, 1931.

Smith, Mark D. "Of Jesus and Quirinius." *Catholic Biblical Quarterly* 62 (2000): 278–93.

Sperber, Daniel. "Costs of Living in Roman Palestine." *Journal of the Economic and Social History of the Orient* 8 (1965): 248–71.

Stern, Ephraim, Ayelet Lewinson-Gilboa, and Joseph Aviram, eds. *The New Encyclopedia of Archaeological Excavations in the Holy Land*. 4 vols. Jerusalem: Israel Exploration Society & Carta, 1993.

Stern, Menahem. "Aspects of Jewish Society: The Priesthood and Other Classes." Pp. 561–630 in *The Jewish People in the First Century: Historical Geography, Political History, Social, Cultural and Religious Life and Institutions*, vol. 2. Edited by S. Safrai and M. Stern. Compendia Rerum Iudaicarum Ad Novum Testamentum 1. Assen: Van Gorcum, 1976.

———. "The Province of Judaea." Pp. 308–76 in *The Jewish People in the First Century: Historical Geography, Political History, Social, Cultural and Religious Life and Institutions*, vol. 1. Edited by S. Safrai and M. Stern. Compendia Rerum Iudaicarum Ad Novum Testamentum 1. Assen: Van Gorcum, 1976.

———. "The Reign of Herod and the Herodian Dynasty." Pp. 216–397 in *The Jewish People in the First Century: Historical Geography, Political History, Social, Cultural and Religious Life and Institutions*, vol. 1. Edited by S. Safrai and M. Stern. Compendia Rerum Iudaicarum Ad Novum Testamentum 1. Assen: Van Gorcum, 1976.

———, ed. *Greek and Latin Authors on Jews and Judaism*. 3 vols. Jerusalem: Israel Academy of Sciences and Humanities, 1974.

Stevenson, G. H. "The Imperial Administration." Pp. 182–217 in *The Augustan Empire, 44 B.C.–A.D. 70*. Vol. 10 of *The Cambridge Ancient History*. Edited by S. A. Cook, F. E. Adcock, and M. P. Charlesworth. Cambridge: Cambridge University Press, 1934.

———. "The Provinces and Their Government." Pp. 437–74 in *The Roman Republic, 133–44 B.C.* Vol. 9 of *The Cambridge Ancient History*. Edited by S. A. Cook, F. E. Adcock, and M. P. Charlesworth. Cambridge: Cambridge University Press, 1932.

Sullivan, Richard D. "The Dynasty of Cappadocia." Pp. 1125–68 in *Aufstieg und Niedergang der römischen Welt* 7.2. Part 2, *Principat*. Edited by Hildegard Temporini and Wolfgang Haase. New York: de Gruyter, 1980.

———. "The Dynasty of Judaea in the First Century." Pp. 296–354 in *Aufstieg und Niedergang der römischen Welt* 8, Part 2, *Principat*. Edited by

Hildegard Temporini and Wolfgang Haase. New York: de Gruyter, 1977.

———. *Near Eastern Royalty and Rome: 100–30 BC*. Toronto: University of Toronto Press, 1990.

Syme, Ronald. "Imperator Caesar: A Study of Nomenclature." Pp. 360–77 in *Roman Papers*, vol. 1. Edited by E. Badian. Oxford: Oxford University Press, 1979.

———. *The Roman Revolution*. Oxford: Clarendon, 1956.

Taylor, Vincent. *Formation of the Gospel Tradition*. London: Macmillan, 1949.

———. *The Gospel According to St. Mark*. 2nd ed. London: Macmillan, 1966.

Tcherikover, Victor A. "Palestine Under the Ptolemies: A Contribution to the Study of the Zenon Papyri." *Mizraïm* 4–5 (1937): 1–82.

———. "Was Jerusalem a Polis?" *Israel Exploration Journal* 14 (1964): 61–78.

Thackeray, H. St. J. *A Grammar of the Old Testament in Greek According to the Septuagint*. Hildesheim/New York: Georg Olms, 1987.

Thackeray, H. St. J., Marcus Ralph, L. H. Feldman, and Allen Wilgren, eds. and transs. *Josephus*. 10 vols. Loeb Classical Library. Cambridge, Mass.: Harvard University Press, 1926–65.

Theissen, Gerd. *Sociology of Early Palestinian Christianity*. Translated by John Bowden. Philadelphia: Fortress Press, 1978.

———. *Soziologie der Jesusbewegung: Ein Beitrag zur Entstehungsgeschichte des Urchristentums*. Munich: Kaiser, 1977.

Thompson, Henry O. "Kanah." P. 5 in *The Anchor Bible Dictionary*. 6 vols. Edited by David Noel Freedman et al. New York: Doubleday, 1992.

Trebilco, Paul R. *Jewish Communities in Asia Minor*. Cambridge: Cambridge University Press, 1991.

Udoh, Fabian E. "*Jewish Antiquities* XIV. 205, 207–08 and 'the Great Plain.'" *Palestine Exploration Quarterly* 134 (2002): 130–43.

———. "Tribute and Taxes in Early Roman Palestine (63 B.C.E.–70 C.E): The Evidence from Josephus." Ph.D. diss., Duke University, Durham, N.C., 1996.

Van Beek, Gus W. "Frankincense and Myrrh." *Biblical Archaeologist* 23 (1960): 70–95.

Varon, di Perlina. "Testimonianze del servizio prestato dagli Ebrei nell'esercito Romano." Pp. 271–77 in *Gli Ebrei nell'impero Romano*. Edited by Ariel Lewin. Florence: La Giuntina, 2001.

Veyne, Paul. *Le pain et le cirque: sociologie historique d'un pluralisme politique*. Paris: Éditions du Seuil, 1976.

Vincent, L.-H. "L'Antonia, palais primitif d'Hérode." *Revue biblique* 61 (1954): 87–107.

Wallace, Sherman LeRoy. *Taxation in Egypt: From Augustus to Diocletian.* Princeton: Princeton University Press, 1938.

Weeks, Harry R. "Sharon." Pp. 1161–63 in *The Anchor Bible Dictionary.* 6 vols. Edited by David Noel Freedman et al. New York: Doubleday, 1992.

Weinfeld, Moshe. *Deuteronomy 1–11: A New Translation with Introduction and Commentary.* Anchor Bible 5. New York: Doubleday, 1991.

———. "Tithe." Pp. 1156–62 in *Encyclopaedia Judaica,* vol. 15. Jerusalem: Keter, 1972.

Weinstock, Stefan. *Divus Julius.* Oxford: Clarendon, 1971.

Weiss, Wolfgang. *"Eine neue Lehre in Vollmacht": Die Streit- und Schulgespräche des Markus-Evangeliums.* Berlin: Walter de Gruyter, 1989.

Wellhausen, Julius. *Prolegomena to the History of Ancient Israel.* New York: Meridian Books, 1957.

Wintermute, O. S., trans. "Jubilees." Pp. 36–142 in *The Old Testament Pseudepigrapha,* vol. 2. Edited by James H. Charlesworth. London: Darton, Longman & Todd, 1985.

Wiseman, T. P. "Caesar, Pompey and Rome, 59–50 B. C." Pp. 368–423 in *The Last Age of the Roman Republic, 146–43 B.C.* Vol. 9 of *The Cambridge Ancient History.* 2nd ed. Edited by J. A. Crook, Andrew Lintott, and Elizabeth Rawson. Cambridge: Cambridge University Press, 1994.

———. "The Census in the First Century B.C." *Journal of Roman Studies* 68 (1958): 59–75.

———. "'There Went Out a Decree from Caesar Augustus . . . .'" *New Testament Studies* 33 (1987): 479–80.

Yadin, Yigael. *Masada: Herod's Fortress and the Zealots' Last Stand.* New York: Random House, 1966.

———. *The Temple Scroll.* 3 vols. Jerusalem: Israel Exploration Society, 1977–83.

Zeitlin, Solomon. "The Edict of Augustus Caesar in Relation to the Judaeans of Asia." *Jewish Quarterly Review* 55 (1964–65): 160–63.

———. *The Rise and Fall of the Judaean State: A Political, Social and Religious History of the Second Commonwealth.* Philadelphia: Jewish Publication Society of America, 1962.

Index of Passages

OTHER JEWISH TEXTS

Josephus

Against Apion

(Contra Apionem)

Jewish Antiquities

(Antiquitates judaicae)

Index of Modern Authors

Index of Subjects